MATERNAL AND CHILD HEALTH NURSING

MATERNAL and CHILD HEALTH NURSING

A. JOY INGALLS, R.N., M.S.

Instructor, Maternal and Child Health Nursing,
Grossmont Vocational Nursing School,
La Mesa, California

M. CONSTANCE SALERNO, R.N., M.S.

Associate Professor of Pediatric Nursing,
San Diego State College,
San Diego, California

With 520 illustrations

SECOND EDITION

The C. V. Mosby Company

SAINT LOUIS   1971

DEDICATED TO THE BEDSIDE NURSE—WHATEVER HER TITLE

PREFACE

In the relatively brief span of four years much has changed in the world we formerly knew. Knowledge has expanded, techniques have been perfected, perspectives and priorities have undergone reevaluation, and attitudes have been modified. However, change in itself should not be held suspect—only the motivation and consequences of differences are legitimately questioned.

In preparing the revision of this text, the problem of content appeared particularly difficult. Authors wish for a specially clear crystal ball to visualize the needs of students during this fast moving period. We have tried to be responsive to some needs expressed by nursing students working in maternal and child health areas who have used the text by incorporating certain suggestions in this writing. Some decisions, as always, were made on the basis of feasibility and the annoying limitations of space and time.

Although the basic structure of the text remains much the same, certain chapter divisions have been reorganized, considerable material has been added, and a significant amount has been rewritten in an effort to update the contents. Major additions are an introductory discussion of the methods and implications of population increase and control and a section treating basic understanding of fluid and electrolyte balance. Effort has been made to expand the discussion of obstetrical complications and to include current pediatric concepts.

This edition happily welcomes as co-author Constance Salerno, Associate Professor of Pediatric Nursing, San Diego State College. Mrs. Salerno contributed generously to the first edition and has enriched the present offering with many ideas and insights, particularly in the sections devoted to pediatrics. Her varied experience in nursing education qualifies her exceptionally well to contribute to this text.

As before, many doctors, nurses, and therapists have aided in helping to shape and evaluate the contents. Particular thanks should be given for the suggestions of Trude Seligman, R.P.T., Coordinator of Physical and Occupational Therapies, Children's Health Center, San Diego. Sincere appreciation continues to be merited by Karla Barber and Dean Jones, photographers, and my helpful artist-sister, Mary Fritchoff. Probably the one who deserves the most credit for seeing that the mechanics of the revision were finally completed is Mrs. Anne Blythe, whose typographical assistance was invaluable. Appreciation should also be expressed to my director, Ellen M. Abbott, who graciously offered both encouragement and assistance.

Those associated with the writing of the first edition of this text have been gratified by its general reception. Although primarily prepared for use by practical or vocational nursing students, its use by several levels of nursing students has been noted with interest. It is hoped that much of the contents of the book will prove beneficial to nurses of varying backgrounds, for its perspective is that of the nurse at the bedside.

A. JOY INGALLS

CONTENTS

UNIT XI
COMMON PEDIATRIC PROBLEMS AND THEIR NURSING CARE

UNIT I

PERSPECTIVES AND BASIC PRINCIPLES

1

Perspectives in maternal and child health

Nurses working in hospital maternity and pediatric departments and clinics need to know about the development of these specialties and the current goals of these services not only locally but also from a national perspective. This brief introductory chapter contains some definitions and important statistics and a short historical review designed to increase the student's appreciation of the progress that has been made and the problems that still remain.

Today most nurses would agree that, comparatively speaking, the obstetrical department is probably the happiest area of the hospital. Here the gift of life is manifest in a dramatic and meaningful way, which should enrich our appreciation and understanding of its mystery and value. Here success rather than failure is the general rule. However, success has not always been associated with maternity, and in the not too distant past what was meant to be most creative was often the prelude to death or invalidism. Obstetrics, now defined as the art and science of maternal and newborn infant care, has not always been scientific or artful.

Statistical proof of progress

To help you understand the tremendous progress that has been made in the field of maternal and child health during recent years it will be necessary to introduce some statistics; however, they need not be complicated or lengthy to tell an important story. Among health statistics we often encounter the term "mortality rate," which means the number of persons per given population who died in a given period of time.

Maternal mortality

Maternal mortality now refers to the number of mothers who die per 100,000 live births.

Significant changes. In 1915 maternal mortality equaled 608/100,000. It was conservatively estimated by the late Mary Breckinridge, former director of the Frontier Nursing Service, that more women died in childbirth during the years 1846 to 1942 than United States soldiers were lost in the Mexican, Civil, Spanish-American, and First World Wars. Maternal mortality for the United States in 1967 was 28.0/100,000, five less than that cited in the first edition of this text.*

---

*U. S. Department of Health, Education, and Welfare, Public Health Service Vital Statistics of the United States, 1967, vol. 11, Mortality, pp. 1-40; Monthly Vital Statistics Report, vol. 17, Aug. 15, 1969.

Although this figure represents a splendid reduction in the maternal death rate, it should be much lower. The national statistics for 1967 continue to demonstrate the great difference between the maternal death rate among nonwhite mothers (69.5/100,-000) and white mothers (19.5/100,000), reflecting a significant inequality in the availability or use of maternity services. Shifting centers of population, lack of education, and strained, understaffed public facilities all help contribute to a higher maternal death rate than should be recorded by the United States.

Leading causes. Statistically, as of 1967 the most common causes of maternal death (when abortions with various complications were computed separately) were the toxemias, about 19%; hemorrhage, about 14%; infection, about 13%; and reported abortion of all types, about 16%.* Hemorrhage is by far the most important complication of pregnancy and childbirth. It should be appreciated that many times hemorrhage may predispose a mother to fall victim to other difficulties such as infection. Hemorrhage is the most common major obstetrical complication.

The toxemias of pregnancy include several associated signs and symptoms such as elevated blood pressure (hypertension), albumin in the urine (albuminuria), and an abnormal amount of fluid in the tissues (edema). Edema reveals itself by swelling and rapid weight gain, headache, and, in extreme cases, even convulsions. The basic cause of such signs and symptoms is unknown. The greatest progress in the reduction of maternal mortality has been in the prevention of infection.

Fetal mortality

Another type of statistic that is often cited is fetal mortality, a combination of words that may mean different things to different people. The usual definition is the number of fetuses of 20 weeks' gestational development or more that die before birth. However, in 1950 the World Health Organization (WHO) recommended that the definition be based on death of a fetus before its complete removal from its mother regardless of age. We have no accurate way to determine the extent of fetal death as defined by WHO, but we know that the waste of life is very significant. The loss of a pregnancy before the fetus is *viable* (sufficiently developed to live independently outside his mother), regardless of the cause, is termed an abortion by professional personnel. However, the nurse is cautioned in the use of this term because some lay persons may associate the word abortion only with the illegal termination of pregnancy.

Infant mortality

Infant mortality statistics concern the number of children per 1,000 live births who die before their first birthday. In 1900 the average rate in those states reporting was 200/1,000; in 1967 the rate had dropped to 22.4/1,000.* But lest we become too self-congratulatory, we should be aware that this figure ranks approximately thirteenth among the nations recording such statistics (Fig. 1-1). Reduced to more shocking proportions, our infant mortality statistics mean that one out of every 44 babies born dies before his first birthday. Our national lag in lowering infant mortality is related to the reasons cited for the rate of maternal mortality. It is no doubt caused by the many different economic, cultural, and educational backgrounds and levels found in the United States and our failure to meet the needs of these diversified groups. Our international standing may also be influenced slightly by the different ways statistics are formulated in various countries, despite attempts at standardization. However, the fact remains that, comparatively speaking, our performance leaves much to be desired.

---

*U. S. Department of Health, Education, and Welfare, Public Health Service Vital Statistics of the United States, 1967, vol. 11, Mortality, pp. 1-40. In Monthly Vital Statistics Report, vol. 19, March 4, 1971, infant mortality for 1968 was 21.7.

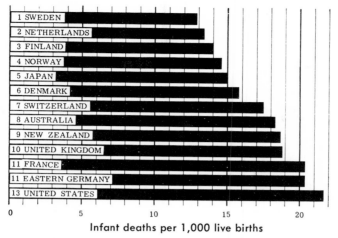

FIG. 1-1. Infant mortality in comparable nations as reported to the United Nations in 1968. (From Faulkner, F.: Children, May-June, 1970, with permission from the U. S. Department of Health, Education, and Welfare, Office of Child Development, Children's Bureau.)

About 70% of infant deaths occur in the first 28 days of life, the *neonatal* period. The leading causes of infant death are immaturity, asphyxiation (improper ventilation), congenital malformations, influenza and pneumonia, and birth injury. Prematurity is the leading cause of neonatal death. It will readily be seen that any methods decreasing the incidence of prematurity or improving medical-nursing management of premature infants would profoundly affect infant mortality statistics. The most commonly used definition of prematurity is a birth weight of less than 5½ pounds, although it is recognized that not all infants of low birth weight are born before term.

Another statistical category that is gaining prominence is *perinatal mortality*. This figure includes recorded fetal deaths of more than 20 weeks' gestation added to the neonatal mortality.

Progress in obstetrics

Although we have a great deal of room for improvement in our maternity care, it is also clear that conditions have changed radically for the better in the last fifty years. It would be worthwhile for us to discuss the major reasons for this great progress.

Acceptance of the germ theory

First, the acceptance of the germ theory led to a greater understanding of the causes of infection. Less than a hundred years ago infection was such a common companion of childbirth in some communities, notably among poor hospital patients, that its symptoms were termed childbed, or puerperal, fever (referring to the puerperium, the approximate 6-week period after delivery). Standards of cleanliness in most nineteenth century hospitals were nonexistent, and the suggestion that illness might be spread by the contaminated hands of physicians and medical students met with much opposition and scorn. Nevertheless, despite much difficulty and even persecution certain individuals began to persuade the medical world that puerperal fever was really a contagion borne by many hands and common objects.

Chief among these medical pioneers was an Hungarian, Ignaz Philipp Semmelweis (1818-1865), whose sad and fascinating biography should be read by every obstetrical nurse. The American poet-physician, Oliver Wendell Holmes (1809-1894), is probably more remembered for his "Chambered Nautilus," but medical historians record his concern with the maternal

3

FIG. 1-3. Louis Pasteur (1822-1895), the brilliant French chemist and bacteriologist who confirmed that puerperal fever was caused by bacteria. (Courtesy The Radio Times Hulton Picture Library.)

FIG. 1-2. Ignaz Semmelweis (1818-1865), a pioneer in the struggle against puerperal fever. Modern obstetricians and mothers are greatly in his debt. (From Bettmann, O. L.: A pictorial history of medicine, Springfield, Ill., 1956, Charles C Thomas, Publisher; courtesy The Bettmann Archive, Inc.)

mortality and his widely criticized paper entitled "The Contagiousness of Puerperal Fever." The famed French chemist, Louis Pasteur, confirmed that childbed fever was indeed caused by bacteria and was contagious in character.

Improvement of techniques and teaching

Second, there has been a vast improvement in obstetrical techniques and teaching. With the acceptance of the germ theory, new concepts of care were evolved. Britain's Joseph Lister, the Father of Antisepsis, began to combat infection by chemical means and new wound-dressing techniques. Students of obstetrics were given

FIG. 1-4. Joseph Lister (1827-1912), the Father of Antisepsis, used carbolic acid spray in his operating room. (Courtesy The Radio Times Hulton Picture Library.)

more clinical instruction at the bedside, and their "experience" was not so confined to the printed page or the dissecting table. New tools such as improved obstetrical forceps, sutures, and syringes and antibiotic medications, laboratory clinical tests, transfusions, and anesthesia were developed. Hospitalization of the laboring or delivered mother and her child became an asset.

Development of prenatal care

Third, and probably most significant, has been the development of *prenatal care* and extended obstetrical services by private and governmental public health facilities. It is with pride that nurses relate that prenatal care began as a nursing contribution instigated by the Instructive Nursing Association of the Boston Lying-In Hospital in 1901. From one visit prior to delivery, prenatal care has now developed into the close supervision of the expectant mother considered necessary today. Prenatal care has been extended to more and more Americans through the services of public health departments, visiting nurses, and nurse midwives as well as private clinics and individual doctors. However, despite these efforts many women in the United States still do not obtain adequate prenatal care. Much education is still needed in this area.

Change and progress in child care

Naturally, the same factors that improved maternity care have helped to enhance the lives of children of all ages. However, pediatrics, the study and care of children in sickness and health, is a more recent speciality than obstetrics. Until the 1800's there was little formalized recognition of the special needs of children, the medical and surgical problems peculiar to childhood, or the different ways in which infants and children, in contrast to adults, respond to the presence of disease.

Development of pediatrics

In 1802 the first children's hospital was founded in Paris, France. In 1855 the first children's hospital in the United States was established in Philadelphia. But in most regions sick hospitalized children often were still quartered with ill adults, sometimes in the same bed! Gradually, the consideration of pediatrics as a separate study was initiated, and as medical schools recognized the unique qualities of the childhood period, nursing schools followed their lead and offered special classes in pediatric nursing, general hospitals established pediatric departments, and more separate treatment centers for children were inaugurated. An early leader in the recognition of the special needs of children was Abraham Jacobi, first president of the American Pediatric Society and founder of the first clinic operated exclusively for children.

Responses of a changing society to children's needs

Change in itself does not automatically guarantee progress, and certainly the vast technological changes of the late nineteenth and early twentieth centuries did little to improve the immediate outlook of a great number of the world's growing children. The new demands of the rapidly accelerating industrial revolution, often untempered by regard for the individual, child or adult, caused sudden urban congestion, and while standards of living rose for some, many times the industrial laborer suffered from deprivation and exploitation. Some of those laborers working in the mills, factories, and mines were children. Two early major events, the inauguration of the White House Conferences and the establishment of the Children's Bureau, reflected a definite improvement and promotion of a better life for all children.

White House Conferences. Since 1909, at the beginning of each decade the very important national White House Conferences have been held (Fig. 1-5). These have focused attention on the current prominent needs of children and youth. Delegates of private and governmental agencies at local, state, and federal levels concerned with maternal and child care as well as

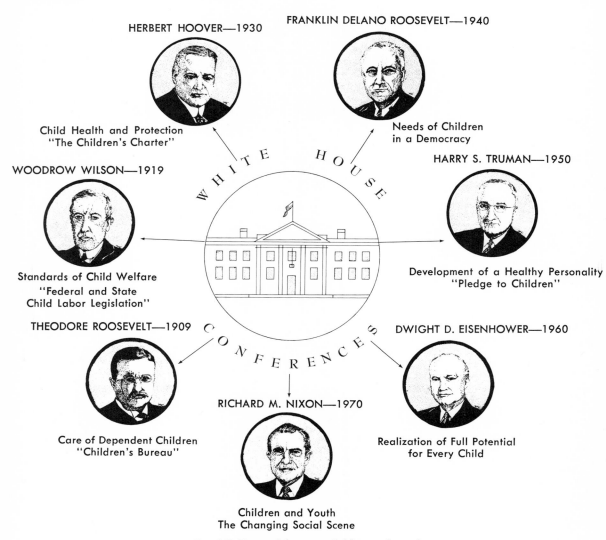

HERBERT HOOVER—1930

Child Health and Protection
"The Children's Charter"

FRANKLIN DELANO ROOSEVELT—1940

Needs of Children
in a Democracy

WOODROW WILSON—1919

Standards of Child Welfare
"Federal and State
Child Labor Legislation"

HARRY S. TRUMAN—1950

Development of a Healthy Personality
"Pledge to Children"

THEODORE ROOSEVELT—1909

Care of Dependent Children
"Children's Bureau"

DWIGHT D. EISENHOWER—1960

Realization of Full Potential
for Every Child

RICHARD M. NIXON—1970

Children and Youth
The Changing Social Scene

WHITE HOUSE CONFERENCES

Fig. 1-5. National focus on children and youth.

selected youth representatives meet for serious evaluation of these needs and ways in which they can be met. One of the most significant documents in the history of child care was prepared at the 1930 White House Conference on Child Health and Protection. Entitled "The Rights of the Child as an individual in the State," it has been called the "Children's Charter."

Children's Bureau. It is principally because of the problem of child labor that the Children's Bureau, founded in 1912 as a result of the support of the first White House Conference on Children and Youth, was initially placed under the jurisdiction of the Department of Labor. Later when the Department of Health, Education, and Welfare was created in 1953, it became part of the responsibility of this cabinet post. In its founding legislation, as amended, the Children's Bureau is charged with the responsibility "to investigate and report on all matters pertaining to the welfare of children and child life among all classes of our people. . ." to carry out research, demonstration and training func-

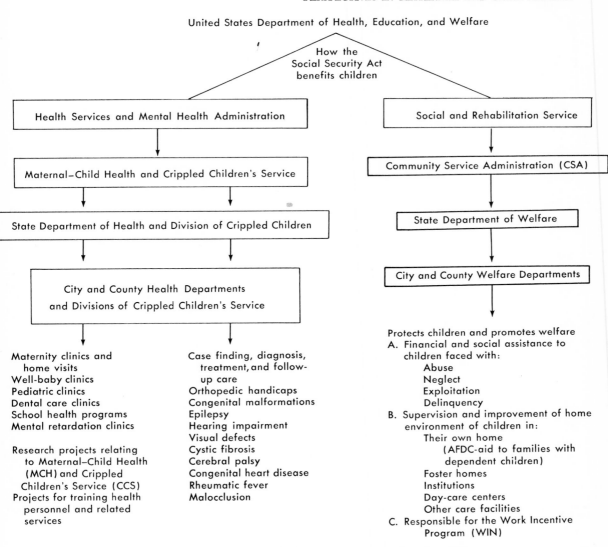

FIG. 1-6. Ways in which the federal Social Security Act benefits children.

tions, to help coordinate the programs for children and parents throughout the Department of Health, Education, and Welfare, to promote programs for youth, and to identify areas requiring the development of new projects.

Social security legislation. The Social Security Act, passed in 1935, has been amended twice recently (1965 and 1967). It established the principle that all people in the United States, through the federal government, share responsibility with the state and local governments for help-

ing to provide essential community services for children (Fig. 1-6). To back up this principle, the Social Security Act authorizes Congress to appropriate funds each year to be given to the states to help them extend and improve their maternal and child health, crippled children's, and child welfare services. Whether a child is eligible for such aid depends on his problem or diagnosis and the financial position of his family.

Head Start Project. Continued organized public concern for the health and welfare

7

of children has resulted in great progress in society's efforts to protect their rights and promote their well-being. One of the most recent advances has been the establishment of Project Head Start.

Project Head Start is a comprehensive program launched by the Office of Economic Opportunity in the summer of 1965 and delegated to the Department of Health, Education, and Welfare in July, 1969. It is designed particularly for preschool children from disadvantaged backgrounds to help them develop their full potential. It provides a daily program of learning activities, nutritious meals, medical and dental care, and psychological, social, and economic services for these children and their families. Parental participation is a vital requirement of the program.

The Parent and Child Center Program (part of Head Start) is a demonstration project providing a full range of services to disadvantaged families having at least one child under 3 years of age. It is planned to provide practical encouragement and assistance to parents in overcoming economic and personal problems and learning the importance of their role in child development. Although the value of Head Start and its benefits to society as a whole are not established at this time and are the subject of much discussion, there is no question that it has been very helpful to individual children and families.

Office of Child Development. In July, 1969, the Office of Child Development was established within the Department of Health, Education, and Welfare. It administers the activities and programs of the Children's Bureau and Project Head Start. It also coordinates and serves as an advocate for all children's programs throughout the federal government in an attempt to improve the wide range of services for children, youth, and their families.

Private volunteer programs. Numerous private voluntary organizations are interested in certain specific diseases or conditions and provide considerable funds for research, diagnosis, and treatment. The Na-

tional Foundation is now particularly interested in birth defects. The Cystic Fibrosis Research Foundation, the American Cancer Society, the Muscular Dystrophy Association, the American Heart Association, the Epilepsy Association of America, and the National Association for Retarded Children are all examples of such private voluntary groups. Other private social agencies help by providing essential community services, such as adoption, care of the unwed mother, counseling and psychiatric services, homemaking and recreational facilities.

International organizations. On an international scale two organizations under the auspices of the United Nations immediately come to mind. Perhaps the first is the United Nations International Children's Emergency Fund, called the United Nations Children's Fund since 1950, although the former initials, UNICEF, have been retained. This worthy organization, supported entirely by voluntary contributions, was established in 1946 primarily to meet the distress of children caused by war. It has now greatly expanded its scope. It currently includes not only the distribution of food, clothing, and medicine but also the provision for education and training of needed national workers in the health field. In 1962 UNICEF sponsored maternal and child health projects in ninety-six countries. It is the world's largest international agency devoted to children. In October, 1965, it was awarded the Nobel Peace Prize for its exceptional contributions toward the well-being of children all over the world.

The second United Nations–sponsored agency is the World Health Organization (WHO) formed in 1948. It helps coordinate efforts for disease control, provides a method of sharing new information in the fight against disease, and cooperates with UNICEF in promoting maternal and child health.

In 1956 the General Assembly of the United Nations approved another important statement in the history of child care, "The Declaration of the Rights of the Child."

The continuing challenge

In spite of significant progress made during the past decade, much remains to be done. Although our nation is more affluent than ever before, 30 million Americans continue to be burdened with poverty, hunger, illness and despair.

These are some of the many challenges still to be met in our society that profoundly affect the quality of our basic unit, the family and the child it produces. Continued effort must be exerted to strengthen this unit and lend stability, depth, and purpose to our daily lives so that individually and collectively we and coming generations may enjoy creatively the best that life can offer.

Role of the nurse

The modern obstetrical or pediatric nurse finds herself working in an area that demands increasing knowledge, skill, and appreciation. Her responsibilities embrace an understanding of the reproductive process, its possible complications, care of the mother and her growing child in health and illness, ability in health teaching, an appreciation of the role of the family, and a knowledge of community resources. Each patient is an individual with particular needs. For the alert nurse there is abundant opportunity for real challenge and achievement.

2
Antisepsis and asepsis vs. infection

The recognition that living things too small to be seen by the unaided eye could cause disease was a tremendous medical-surgical advance. However, the application of this discovery to everyday patient care was and is just as exciting since it is in this area of application that the struggle against pathogenic microorganisms is most dramatic. It is no exaggeration to say that the nurse often finds herself in a crucial position in these efforts to halt the activity of potentially dangerous organisms. She is directly involved in the prevention and treatment of infectious disease in both the obstetrical and pediatric areas, although prevention is emphasized in the hospital maternity section and treatment in the children's area.

The nurse will recall that infection, or the invasion of living tissue by disease-producing organisms, is usually accompanied by tissue reaction characterized by redness, heat, swelling, pain, and loss of function. This reaction, called inflammation, may also result when tissue is injured by noninfectious agents such as chemicals, wind, sunlight, and mechanical laceration. However, in the event of infection other signs and symptoms are usually present in addition, including the local formation of pus, an increase of white blood cells circulating in the blood, increased respiratory and pulse rates, a general feeling of illness, and possibly chills and fever. These indications are extremely important for the nurse to observe and report as part of the fight against pathogenic bacteria.

We will now define and discuss some terms often used to describe techniques employed by medicine and nursing against infection.

Key vocabulary

antisepsis literally means "against infection or decay" and usually involves procedures using chemicals that hinder the growth and development of mircoorganisms without necessarily destroying them.

antiseptics refer to different agents, usually chemical, that hinder the growth of or kill microorganisms. They are often used on or in living tissues.

asepsis broadly defined literally means "without infection or decay." It refers to the absence of living infectious or pathogenic microorganisms or to procedures that produce such an absence. It implies the use of special techniques to minimize contact with and transfer of any pathogenic microorganisms. It means that all objects, inanimate and animate, must be regarded from a particular perspective; that sterile objects must be touched only by that which is sterile; that clean objects must touch only that which is clean; and that dirty objects must touch only that which is dirty. If anything dirty touches that which is clean or sterile, everything becomes dirty. If anything clean touches that which is sterile, that which is sterile becomes only clean. In a surgical setting such objects are referred to as "contaminated." One often hears the terms "medical asepsis" and "surgical asepsis." Clear-cut definitions for these terms are difficult to formulate. Some authors use medical asepsis as a synonym for the isolation techniques used in the treatment of contagious diseases. Others use it as descriptive of all procedures and practices that help limit the transfer of disease-causing microorganisms from one person or locality to another. The term "surgical asepsis" is usually employed when sterile materials are used in a sterile manner to protect an especially exposed patient from inadvertent infection. Such a patient would be anyone having any type of operation or treatment in which the normal body barriers, such as the skin and mucous membranes, are in danger of being damaged, are being repaired, or are being deliberately breached. The surgical patient and some typical medical patients, depending on their individual needs, must be treated using surgical asepsis. In an attempt to provide for as safe an environment as possible in the hospital, both antiseptic and aseptic procedures are employed.

disinfectants refer to agents (usually antiseptics that have been strengthened or concentrated) that under certain conditions kill infectious or pathogenic microorganisms. The term "disinfected" is reserved for inanimate objects because disinfectants are too strong to be used on living tissue without producing injury. Some disinfectants destroy only vegetative (nonspore) forms of microorganisms; others destroy spores as well.

sterilization used in this sense refers to processes through which all microorganisms, beneficial or pathogenic, vegetative or spore forms, are killed, and an object is rendered sterile.

Common antiseptics

Many different types of chemical antiseptics and disinfectants are used in the hospital. This is because the *ideal* disinfectant is nontoxic to human tissue, does not produce allergies, is harmless to all products treated, kills both spores and vegetative forms, affects a wide variety of organisms, and is convenient, rapid, inexpensive, and, unfortunately, nonexistent! The nurse must be familiar with the uses, properties, and preservation of such products she is asked to handle and apply. She should remember that all antiseptics, taken in large enough doses, are poisons.

Some early disinfectants, such as phenol (carbolic acid) were derivatives of coal tar. Semmelweis used chloride of lime solutions, and chlorine solutions are still utilized. In fact, one of the more widely used antiseptics is a chlorinated diphenol known as hexachlorophene. This is commonly incorporated in many products, such as pHisoHex, Septisol, Genteel, and deodorant bar soaps.

Chlorine solutions are frequently found in the home where they may be employed as bleaches, disinfectants, and deodorizers. Chlorine and some other kinds of antiseptics, for example, hydrogen peroxide, deteriorate with exposure to heat. For this reason they are packaged in opaque or darkened, tightly capped containers and should be stored away from sources of warmth.

Some antiseptics are so strong that care must be taken not to reapply the medication too frequently. This is especially true of solutions of iodine and mercury; frequent repeated painting of the same area may cause chemical burns. Use of iodine on areas that perspire may cause blistering. For this reason iodine should not be applied to the axillae, perineum, soles of the feet, or palms of the hands. Some antiseptics and cleansers are dangerous when used together, for example, ammonia and chlorine products. The use of products containing both these chemicals produces an irritating gas.

Some antiseptics are diluted to various concentrations with water; these are called aqueous solutions. Other antiseptics are diluted or made up with alcohol; these are referred to as "tinctures." Tinctures become stronger with time because the solvent, alcohol, gradually evaporates.

Alcohol itself is an antiseptic. Isopropyl alcohol is a good product for skin cleansing prior to injections because it is a fat solvent and cuts through the oil normally found on the skin's surface. Alcohol may also be used for disinfection if the article is clean and completely immersed for a sufficiently long period of time. Alcohol has the disadvantage of causing pain when applied to injured tissue and of rapidly undergoing evaporation. However, this last characteristic is not always detrimental. It makes the product helpful in controlling body temperature and a 25% to 50% solution is used to sponge feverish patients.

Another antiseptic-disinfectant that has been used with some frequency is benzalkonium chloride, also known by the trade name Zephiran. It is one of the quaternary ammonium compounds, is usually employed in concentrations of 1:750, and may be used as either an aqueous solution or a tincture. It is often used in operating or delivery rooms to maintain the sterility of previously heat-sterilized lifting or transfer forceps employed in the arrangement of sterile supplies. It may also be used in the disinfection of certain cutting instruments such as scissors, needles, and scalpel blades or appliances that may be dulled or injured if subjected continuously to the moist heat of the pressure steam sterilizer (autoclave). If Zephiran is used in contact with metal, a rust preventive is added to the solution. The presence of soap reduces the effect of Zephiran. Therefore skin should be rinsed of soapy materials before the application of Zephiran.

Other solutions that are commonly used in disinfection or antisepsis are combinations of formaldehyde and alcohol or Zephiran. Iodophor detergents containing iodine such as 2% Amphyl, Wescodyne, or Betadine are favored by many.

Chemical vapors may also be used. Some hospitals have special ethylene oxide gas chambers designed for use in the disinfection of "sharps."

The use of chemical solutions or vapors to render objects safe for patient care has been termed "cold sterilization." However, objection has been made to the word "sterilization," since the end product is often not sterile in the true sense but only disinfected. The time interval needed to assure satisfactory results differs, depending on the type and concentration of the solution used as well as the organisms combated. In recent years there has been a real effort to use disposable needles, syringes, and other equipment difficult to sterilize properly or expensive to maintain.

Methods of sterilization

The most efficient method of sterilization, provided that the object to be sterilized can withstand the method, is the use of saturated steam under pressure. However, there are other methods in use that do not require such expensive equipment and may be satisfactory under certain conditions.

Open flame

The open flame is often used for emergency sterilization. The usual situation involves the extraction of a superficially placed sliver, accidentally acquired in a primitive setting. Drawbacks include the formation of carbon on the object sterilized (such as a needle) and the transfer of heat along the entire length of the metal object. In certain communities, the inside of a metal bowl is sterilized by rinsing its interior in alcohol, leaving a small residue in the bottom and setting the alcohol aflame with a long matchstick. This practice, although very dramatic, is not recommended.

Dry heat

Dry heat is capable of true sterilization and has been frequently used, especially to sterilize "sharps" or cutting instruments because the procedure does not dull surface edges. It is also recommended for most glass syringes because it will not erode the ground glass surfaces. However, dry heat must be maintained for a relatively long period to be considered adequate, since dry heat does not penetrate with the same rapidity as moist heat. Perkins lists the following temperature-time relationships to achieve sterilization:

320° F. or 160° C. for 1 hour (preferably 2 hours)
285° F. or 140° C. for 3 hours
250° F. or 121° C. for 4 hours*

Dry heat will cause damage to linens (scorching) unless carefully supervised, and any packages made must be quite small to be certain that the heat will completely penetrate. The object to be sterilized should first be clean and free from all oil or grease. An example of dry heat is the heat produced by the common kitchen oven. Hospital dry-heat ovens are more refined, but the principle remains the same. Such supplies as talcum powder and petrolatum are sterilized using dry heat.

---

*From Perkins, J. J.: Principles and methods of sterilization in health sciences, ed. 2, Springfield, Ill., 1969, Charles C Thomas, Publisher.

Moist heat

Moist heat is quite frequently employed for sterilization. The most common source is boiling water. The quantities of boiling water that the harassed father-to-be was instructed to prepare in days gone by were used to sterilize the physician's instruments and provide suitable cleansing solutions as well as give the male parent something to do and think about during such a period of stress. Syringes and small instruments are still quite commonly boiled in the home setting. Perkins, discussing this method, recommends that an object be subjected to a minimum exposure of 30 minutes in gently boiling water. Even with this instruction, he hesitates to call the end product "sterile" in the strictest sense, since boiling water destroys pathogenic organisms but cannot be relied on to destroy resistant spores. Other authors consider periods of 10 to 20 minutes complete exposure to boiling water usually sufficient to kill vegetative forms of bacteria on clean equipment. The time of "sterilization" must be computed *after* the water has come to a boil. Vigorously boiling water is not more effective than a gently bubbling surface and soon boils away. The addition of alkalies, such as sodium carbonate (sal soda), to make a 2% solution (4 teaspoons to a quart) decreases the time necessary for boiling. Most authors say a period of 15 minutes is sufficient when such chemicals are added.

The use of "hard water" to boil objects may form a deposit that may interfere with assembly and use of the object, for example, syringes. The formation of such deposits may be reduced by the addition of a weak acid such as vinegar. However, if sodium carbonate is added to water to speed disinfection, weak acids should not be used.

The objects to be sterilized must be completely immersed and should be added to the water after boiling has begun to minimize the possibility of rust formation and damage to objects. If total immersion is impossible because of the bulk of the object or impractical, as in the case of liquids, provision may be made for constant contact by the free-flowing steam generated from the water to those parts not under the surface by use of a tightly fitting lid and a sufficient supply of water. This method should be recognized as another form of disinfection employing free-flowing or streaming steam. It is used in some baby formula "sterilizers" and in so-called bedpan and dish sterilizers. The process does not result in true sterilization but, again, only in disinfection. When practical, boiling the articles totally immersed is preferable.

Steam under pressure

The bulk of hospital supplies, linen, and instruments are sterilized in pressure steam sterilizers, or autoclaves. The household pressure cooker is a small version of the hospital autoclave.

Structure of the autoclave. The typical hospital autoclave is a double-walled metal chamber (Fig. 2-1). The space between the outer and inner walls is the steam jacket. Steam is released from its source, usually a hospital pipe system, into the jacket to heat the inner walls of the sterilizer. When the inner chamber is appropriately packed and its door tightly shut, the saturated steam under pressure is then released into the inner chamber to contact directly the articles to be sterilized. Since the inner wall of the sterilizer has been previously heated by the steam within the enclosing jacket, condensation is kept at a minimum, and the load does not become too wet. The saturated steam flows forward from an entry near the top at the rear of the inner chamber, forcing the air present to leave through an outlet located at the lower front. Nothing should interfere with the free circulation of the steam through all the layers and to all surfaces of the material to be sterilized. Nothing should impede the evacuation of the air from the chamber prior to timing of the load for sterilization. Air in the chamber will cause uneven temperatures within the chamber and inaccurate processing. The outlet must be regularly and frequently cleaned to help pre-

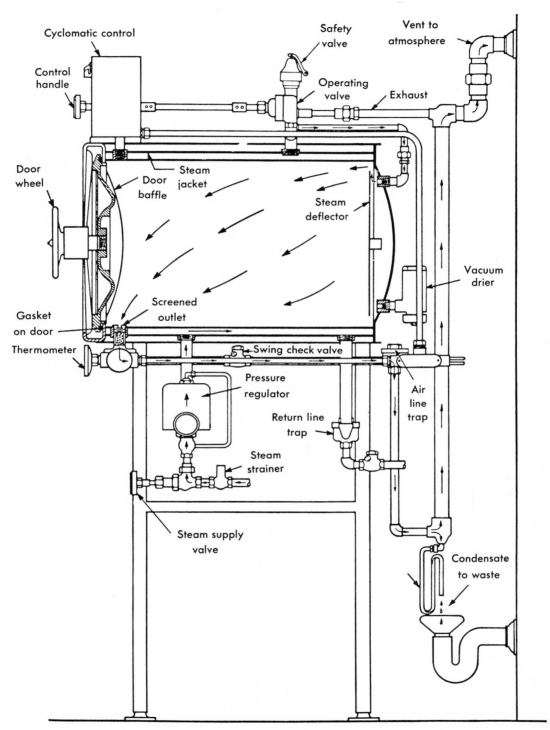

FIG. 2-1. Double-chambered autoclave sectioned from top to bottom to observe the steam flow. (Courtesy American Sterilizer Co., Erie, Pa.)

vent problems in the evacuation of chamber air and to assure proper automatic closure when the chamber is filled with steam. New models use a vacuum to expel air.

The temperature obtained in the autoclave, not the pressures used to secure these temperatures, actually causes sterilization to take place. The usual temperature level desired on standard autoclaves is 250° to 254° F. (121° to 123° C.). To achieve this, pressures of 15 to 17 pounds are necessary. Some autoclaves are especially built to withstand higher pressures and attain increased temperatures. Such so-called high-pressure sterilizers usually operate at pressures of 30 pounds at temperatures of 270° F. The resulting increased temperature completes sterilization in shorter periods of time. The time interval necessary to achieve sterilization depends on the type of article to be treated and the size and density of the load. Times may range from 3 to 60 minutes, depending on the article, how it is packed, and the type of autoclave used.

Preparation of supplies. All articles to be autoclaved must first be clean to be considered sterile after autoclaving. It is very important that all soil be removed from every surface of an instrument. Special attention must be paid to the "biting surfaces" of hemostats and forceps and the joints of all moving instruments. Soil can coat an object, leaving the undersurface unsterilized. To be sterilized, all surfaces of an object must be subjected to the required temperature for a sufficient time. Therefore all instruments should technically be open during sterilization to gain proper exposure. Containers must be left ajar in such a position that the circulating steam can easily enter and leave the receptacles. Canisters must not be tightly packed. Bulky trays and linen supplies must be carefully assembled and loosely arranged on end in the sterilizer rack not too close to the door or rear of the chamber to assure free circulation of the hot steam.

Articles that must be sterilized and then stored in a sterile manner, using fabric wrappers, must be wrapped twice in double-thickness muslin. Wrappers that are reused continuously without interim washing, even though clean, may by becoming very dry cause the steam to lose moisture, reduce its penetrating power, and interfere with sterilization. This loss of moisture may lead to overheating and damage to the goods especially fabrics. Small articles may be successfully sterilized wrapped in layers of steam-permeable paper or glassine bags.

After the load has been timed at the appropriate temperature for the appropriate interval, the steam is expelled (exhausted) from the chamber. At times use of a vacuum aids the drying process. When the chamber pressure gauge returns to zero, the operator may carefully loosen the door wheel and open the door about ¼ inch.

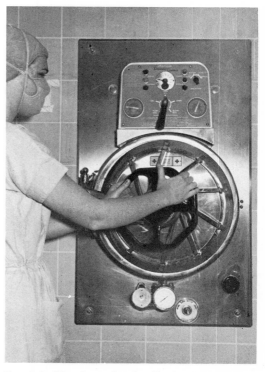

Fig. 2-2. "Cracking the door" of a high-pressure autoclave. Note the position of the nurse. (Courtesy Grossmont Hospital, La Mesa, Calif.)

This is termed "cracking the door." To avoid being burned by the escaping steam the operator should stand behind the hinged door when opening the autoclave. (See Fig. 2-2.) The door is left just slightly open until the steam from the chamber is dissipated and the articles have begun to dry—about 10 minutes for wrapped goods.

Operation of the autoclave. The operator should be familiar with his particular sterilizer and follow the manufacturer's instructions. However, the operation of an autoclave that has not been equipped to cycle through the various phases of the sterilization process automatically may be basically reviewed and outlined as follows:

1. Open the steam supply valve to release steam into the steam jacket if it is not already opened. Check the temperature of the steam jacket on the appropriate gauge.
2. Load the sterilization chamber properly.
3. Close and secure the chamber door tightly.
4. Open the operating valve to allow steam from the jacket to enter the sterilization chamber.
5. Time the load when the appropriate temperature is reached, depending on the type of sterilizer in use (standard models, 250° F.; high-pressure models, 270° F.).
6. Evacuate the steam from the chamber using exhaust and vacuum techniques appropriate for the type of materials and model of sterilizer.
7. Wait until the chamber pressure gauge records zero.
8. Open the chamber door cautiously a "crack."
9. Maintain the steam in the jacket to help dry the materials in the chamber.

Manual operation of an autoclave entails more risk of error through human failure. The use of an automatically cycling sterilizer, such as those equipped with a Cyclomatic control, reduces some risks of human error. When the Cyclomatic control has been *properly* set for automatic

control, the operator must only turn the operating handle to "sterilize" and check that proper temperature is attained. The load is processed and timed automatically. Whether or not the process will be set to include fast or slow evacuation or exhaust of the steam from the sterilization chamber will depend on the type of materials to be sterilized.

When the sterilizer is unloaded, care should be taken in the way certain objects and packs are handled, cooled, and stored. Muslin packs are usually left in a well-ventilated room on open racks to avoid rapid condensation of moisture and wetting. If

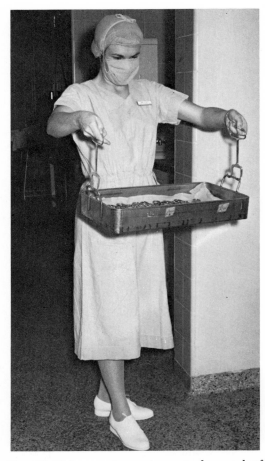

FIG. 2-3. This nurse is carrying a sterilizer rack of instruments from the autoclave to a sterile table using sterile handles, or lifts. (Courtesy Grossmont Hospital, La Mesa, Calif.)

a wrapper containing sterile supplies becomes wet, everything within the wrapper must be considered contaminated, since live microorganisms may have been absorbed into the interior of the pack. When needed, trays containing unwrapped sterile supplies may be handled with sterile lifts and carried to the sterile surface where they will be used (Fig. 2-3). If newly sterilized unwrapped instruments will not be used soon, the door of the autoclave must be kept closed to maintain their sterility, since prolonged exposure to air currents would cause contamination.

Wrapped sterile articles should be dated and routinely rotated to reduce outdating and waste. The date of sterilization of shelf supplies should be regularly checked.

Testing sterilization. From time to time it is necessary to test the efficiency of the sterilization process. The use of heat-sensitive tape to help secure the last outer cover of a pack or tray aids in helping to determine whether an object has been exposed to the heat of the autoclave. However, this tape does not indicate whether or not the necessary temperature penetrated the whole package long enough to produce sterility of the entire contents.

Although they are helpful indicators, even the placement of certain other heat-sensitive devices, such as a pellet of sulfur enclosed in a glass rod in the center of a pack, does not *assure* sterility, since the time during which the pack was subjected to the critical temperature, as well as the quality of steam present, is unknown. Steam-sensitive indicators, which are reported to change color progressively as different temperatures and periods of exposure are attained, have been introduced (Fig. 2-4). An example is the Aseptic-Thermo Indicator Steam-Clox. The use of time-temperature graph records, which may be installed to visually record the temperatures achieved during specific periods of time, is also a safeguard in alerting the operator that mechanical failure has occurred.

The most universally recommended test of sterilization procedures involves bacteriological studies as well as a basic understanding of autoclave operation. A known living spore-forming microorganism is introduced into the center of a pack prepared

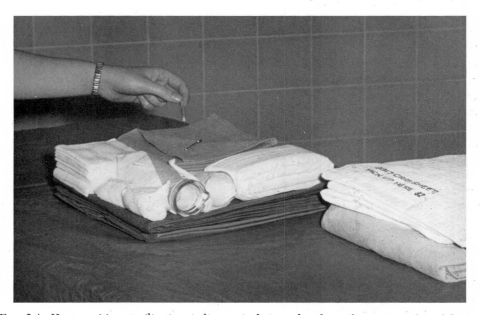

FIG. 2-4. Heat-sensitive sterilization indicator is being placed in the center of a delivery pack prior to autoclaving. The indicator will be checked for color change when the pack is opened for use. (Courtesy Grossmont Hospital, La Mesa, Calif.)

for sterilization. The laboratory usually prepares little strips of spore-bearing material that are strategically positioned. Then the packs containing the microorganism are placed in the autoclave along with other packs in a representative load. One test pack should be placed in the coolest portion of the autoclave near the front and bottom of the chamber not far from the outlet. Another should be near the center of the load. After the routine sterilization procedure has been completed, the special strips are carefully removed aseptically and returned to the laboratory. There the presence of any microorganism surviving the autoclave procedure may be detected. However, this method of sterilization control necessitates considerable time.

Less common sterilizing methods

Other methods of sterilization are theoretically possible but for the most part practically unfeasible in the hospital setting. They involve the use of electron beams or ultrasound. The vibrations of ultrasound are capable of sterilization, but large-scale use of this force is now financially prohibitive in most situations.

Principles and practice of aseptic technique

It is of no use to sterilize supplies unless one knows how to handle them in such a way as to maintain this hard-won quality. Because of this fact we will now consider the principles and practice of aseptic technique in more detail. The practice of asepsis is not really difficult if the appropriate equipment and supplies are available and conscientious, knowledgeable persons are responsible for their use and care. Sister Mary Louise, in her informative text, *The Operating Room Technician,* lists four simple rules summing up aseptic technique:

1. Know what is sterile.
2. Know what is not sterile.
3. Keep the two apart.
4. Remedy contamination immediately.°

°From Louise, Sister M.: The operating room technician, ed. 2, St. Louis, 1968, The C. V. Mosby Co.

Achieving these results requires order, organization, and a constant awareness of factors that could influence the safety of supplies or the working environment as a whole.

Environmental controls

An unsafe working environment ultimately means an unsafe patient. Wiping down shelves and lamps in the delivery room area with a cloth dampened with disinfectant does not sound too exciting to most people. Yet it is a very necessary way of helping to provide surroundings appropriate to the practice of asepsis. It is also an excellent way of learning where everything is in an area and checking for outdated supplies. All shelf contents should be returned to exactly the same position to guard against loss of time in finding necessary materials.

The nurse herself forms part of the environment in any situation. Her health, or rather lack of it, may pose a threat to good technique. Respiratory and skin infections can become key factors in unfortunate patient-personnel contacts.

Gowning

It is not practical or probably necessary for the nurse to wear special clothing in all situations to follow sterile technique. However, in relatively confined areas of high risk such as the operating and delivery room suites, it is now general practice for all staff to wear hospital supplied uniforms, usually called "scrub suits or gowns," within the circumscribed area. Appropriate cotton cover gowns are also worn when leaving the area for duties elsewhere in the hospital. The elimination of the use of personal outer clothing in such services is just one more step in the effort to promote asepsis. In addition, when one enters the delivery-operating areas, the hair must be adequately covered. If sterile goods are opened to the air in these areas, a mask must be worn (Fig. 2-5). It should be changed frequently and always after sneezing or coughing. When a mask is used, the danger of droplet contamination from the mouth and nose is not as great

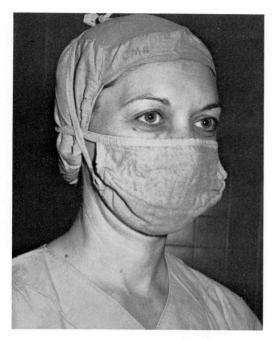

FIG. 2-5. Nurses working in the delivery room area should wear caps capable of covering their hair. When sterile supplies are uncovered, a mask covering both nose and mouth should be worn. (Courtesy Grossmont Hospital, La Mesa, Calif.)

as in the case of unmasked personnel doing bedside procedures. However, it is still a good plan to minimize unnecessary talking in areas where sterile fields are exposed.

In certain situations the personnel directly or indirectly contacting operative sites wear sterile cotton overgowns and gloves to provide greater protection against contamination. This is standard procedure during surgery and delivery and allows the operators greater ease of movement without undue concern about contamination of the vulnerable area. In other areas of the hospital such as those providing bedside care, faithful handwashing, the addition of sterile gloves, or the careful use of certain setups may be the only barriers needed to provide safe care. The barriers employed in the practice of asepsis depend on both need and practicality.

Gloving

At the bedside, sterile gloves are often worn to carry out catheterizations and dress wounds. They may act as a two-way barrier—to protect both the nurse and patient from contamination. In the delivery room the circulating nurse may put on gloves before cleansing the patient's perineum in as clean a fashion as possible immediately before the delivery. When gloves but no gown are used, the usual technique employed to put them on in a sterile manner is shown in Fig. 2-6.

Sterile scrubbing

If a nurse, doctor, or technician must gown and glove, then a sterile hand and arm scrub routinely precedes the actual gowning procedure. An antiseptic such as pHisoHex, Septisol, or Betadine is commonly employed. Most areas where such skin preparation is routine provide foot and knee controls at the scrub sinks to dispense the tap water and antiseptics and avoid possible hand contamination during the procedure. Sterile brushes are used. The following procedure is suggested:

1. Wash the hands and forearms well with an approved antiseptic such as pHisoHex, using finger friction and water to form a good lather. Clean fingernails.
2. Rinse.
3. With a sterile brush moistened with water and antiseptic, start scrubbing the fingers, the interdigital spaces, the palm, and the back of the hand, using approximately fifteen brush strokes for all areas.
4. The scrub continues with the wrist, the brush circling the arm and gradually climbing in this rotating fashion toward the elbow. Add more water and antiseptic as needed. Discard the brush.
5. Scrub the other hand and arm similarly, using another brush.
6. Rinse both hands and arms under the running water, holding the hands above the elbows to prevent water from less clean areas from flowing toward the fingers.
7. Dry with sterile towels, **proceeding** from the hand upward, always keep-

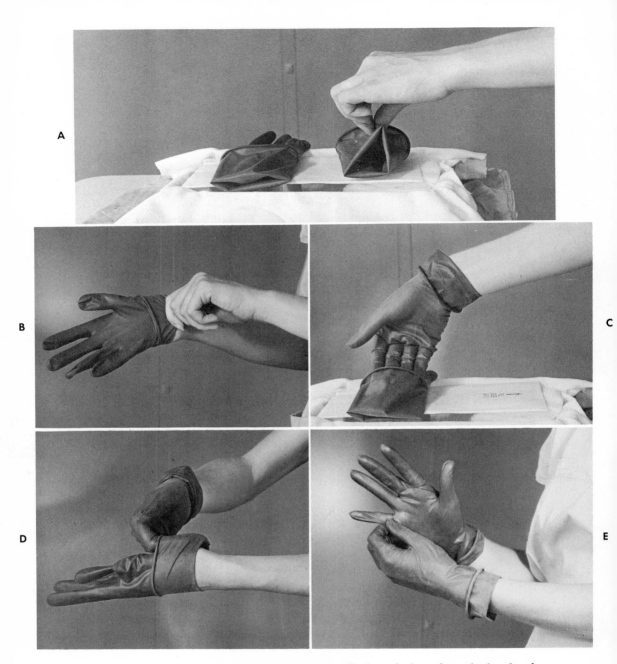

Fig. 2-6. Gloving procedure. A, Sterile gloves usually lie side by side with the thumbs on top at the outside edges, the left glove on the left and the right glove on the right. Pick up the glove by pinching the cuff folded down over the palm of the glove. If one is right-handed, he usually slides on the right-hand glove first. Your bare fingers may touch any area of the glove that represents the inside of the glove. B, Slide your hand in with a rotating motion while pulling on the turned down cuff. C, Pick up the second glove with your gloved hand by sliding your sterile fingers *under* the turned down cuff. D, Place your other hand into the glove, sliding and rotating your hand as you pull out and up against the inside of the cuff with your gloved fingers. Keep your thumb back out of the way. Remember, your arm and the top of the cuff are contaminated and must not be touched with your fingers. When only gloves are worn, it is permissible to retain narrow cuffs at the tops of the gloves, but they, of course, are not sterile and should not be treated as such. E, After you are gloved you may adjust the fingers. Learning to glove takes time, patience, and usually more than one pair of gloves. (Courtesy Grossmont Hospital, La Mesa, Calif.)

ing the towel's surface between the fingers and the skin.

8. Using a hexachlorophene-containing antiseptic, the scrubbing procedure should take about 4 to 5 minutes.

Those who put on sterile gowns pick them up carefully from a sterile table with their scrubbed, dried hands without touching anything else. The gowns are folded inside out previous to sterilization so that this maneuver does not contaminate the outer surface of the gown. They push their hands and arms partially through the sleeves, touching only the inside of the gown with their hands. Then the circulating nurse helps complete the gowning procedure by pulling on the inside of the gown to draw the sleeves completely on (Fig. 2-7). She then secures the back ties and tugs on the hem to straighten the gown, if necessary. The gown is technically sterile above the waist including the arms and shoulders but not including the back or neckband. However, just because certain areas are considered nonsterile does not mean that the nurse deliberately touches them!

The gowned physician or nurse may then be gloved by a worker already gowned and gloved. He may glove himself using the procedure previously described, releasing the cuffs of the rubber gloves carefully over the gown sleeves after both hands have been covered. He may use yet another approach called the "closed glove technique." If this latter method of gloving is used, the circulating nurse must be requested not to draw the sleeves over the fingers when assisting with the gowning process. The sterile gloves are handled through the slightly protruding sterile gown cuff, fitted over this cuff, and drawn over the fingers. Once introduced to this

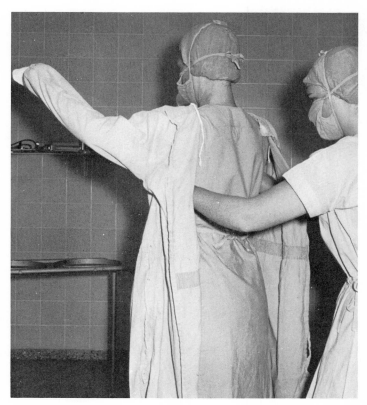

FIG. 2-7. Physicians do not always stand still for the gowning procedure. So, watch out! (Courtesy Grossmont Hospital, La Mesa, Calif.)

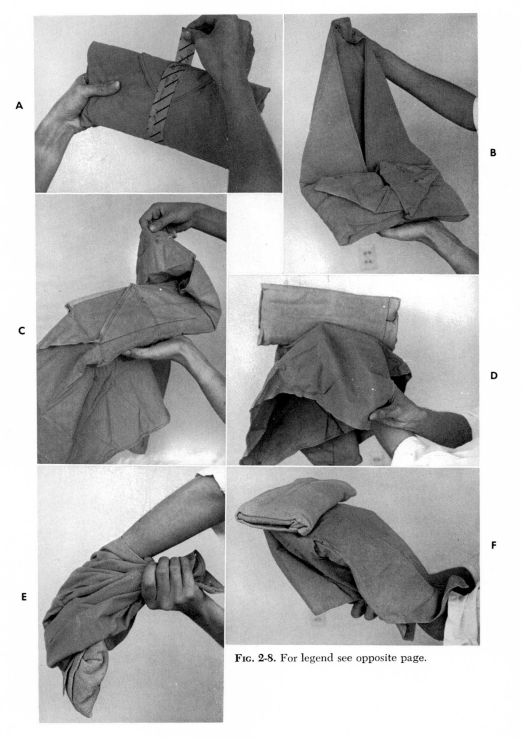

FIG. 2-8. For legend see opposite page.

Fig. 2-8. Opening sterile packages. **A,** Remove the heat-sensitive tape closing the package and check the tape for color change. Start unwrapping the package with the point of the wrapper facing you. In this way the part of the package next to you will remain covered and protected for the longest period possible. **B,** Pull back the point and let it drop down after assuring yourself that the outside of the dangling wrapper will not contaminate any possible nearby sterile surface. **C,** Pull back the two side folds by the little turnbacks designed for your use. Uncover the end on the side of the supporting under hand first, then the side next to the active hand. If you are preparing the inner package for a drop onto a sterile surface, stabilizing the pack by bringing your thumb over the top of the wrapper before completely exposing the inner pack is sometimes very helpful. **D,** Pull back the last fold covering the inner wrap to expose the sterile surface. The inner pack can now be picked up by a gloved associate or it can be "scooted" onto a sterile table while the ends of the outer wrapper are held back to prevent contamination. If the hand-thumb grip is used, the pack can be dropped in the manner pictured. Care must be taken not to get too close to a sterile table or field while adding supplies. (Courtesy Grossmont Hospital, La Mesa, Calif.)

method many workers prefer it to the older procedure, believing that there is less chance of inadvertent contamination.

Handling sterile supplies

Opening packages of sterile goods. To maintain the sterility of supplies, the nurse must learn how to open packages of sterile goods properly. Most square or rectangular packages are wrapped in the same way. The photographs in Fig. 2-8 illustrate the opening of a medium-sized package containing a sterile drape that may be "handed" to a gowned and gloved associate or dropped on a sterile table for use.

Packages containing fragile sterile supplies that one may hesitate to drop onto a sterile field may be placed on a clean surface and carefully unwrapped in basically the same manner. The object is then lifted

Fig. 2-9. The use of sterile transfer forceps to remove round needles and cutting needles from cold sterilization. Note that the lid of the container is turned upside down if it is not held in the hand. (Courtesy Grossmont Hospital, La Mesa, Calif.)

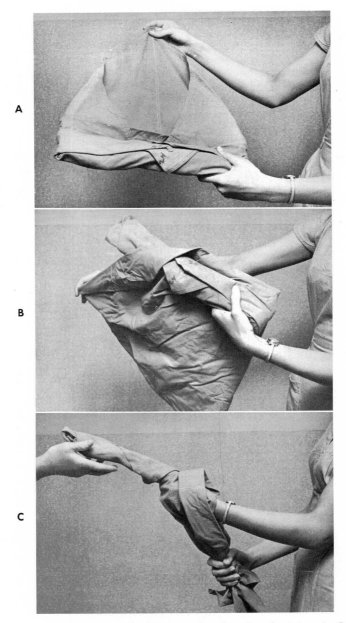

FIG. 2-10. Steps in unwrapping sterile forceps to hand to the physician. **A,** Grasp one end of the package, remove outer tape, and unwind outer wrapper. **B,** Pull back the inner turnback at the top of the package and continue to uncover the inner wrap (rather like peeling a banana!). **C,** Grasp carefully all dangling ends of the outer wrap and pull them out of the way toward your wrist. Do not touch the inner wrap! (Courtesy Grossmont Hospital, La Mesa, Calif.)

from the sterile inner wrapper by sterile transfer forceps (Fig. 2-9).

Using transfer forceps. The use of transfer forceps in the handling of sterile supplies is as safe as the technique employed for their care. Such forceps may also be called sponge sticks, lifts, tongs, or pickups. The forceps and their holding canister are steam sterilized periodically. The holding canister is filled with an antiseptic solution (often Zephiran, 1:750) to maintain the sterility of the lifts. When these forceps are used, care should be taken not to touch the ends of the instrument on any exposed inner side of the holding canister, since the area above the level of solution cannot be considered sterile because of prolonged exposure to the air. Some specially designed forceps and canister combinations include a lid, reducing the danger of this complication. Sterile transfer forceps should not be held below the level of the waist, and the points should always be pointed down. If the points of wet transfer forceps are elevated, drops of the antiseptic may run down the shafts of the instrument to the nonsterile surface near the handles. When the points are again lowered, these same drops, now contaminated, can run down the shafts to contaminate the points.

General considerations. When approaching a sterile field with an open tray or a complete table setup, take care to avoid accidentally brushing or touching the area. When passing a sterile field, keep a safe distance away and, if possible, face the field. Never turn your back on a sterile area. Avoid turning your back toward an associate who is gowned and masked in a sterile manner.

If contamination of a sterile area does occur, the event must be immediately reported. It is no terrible sin to contaminate, although it is unfortunate. It is a sin to contaminate a sterile field, know it, and do nothing about it when something could be done. No one at the time will see those organisms introduced into the sterile area, but later on the patient may feel the effects of their insidious activity. Everyone on the medical-nursing team should be glad to have breaks in technique or inadvertent contamination called to their attention in order to correct the situation.

It perhaps should be noted that occasionally in emergency situations sterile technique becomes secondary. If a baby decides to be born before the world is properly prepared to greet him, the physician will not let him drop to the floor because he has not finished putting on his sterile gloves! However, asepsis is not to be disregarded lightly, and as soon as possible steps should be taken to try to rectify the lapse.

Being trusted for the application of the principles of antisepsis and asepsis is no small responsibility. It is a challenge that leads to the development of another perspective and sensibility highly important in the life of a nurse.

UNIT I

SUGGESTED SELECTED READINGS AND REFERENCES

Berry, E. C., and Kohn, M.: Introduction to operating room technique, ed. 3, New York, 1966, McGraw-Hill Book Co.

Bookmiller, M. M., Bowen, G. L., and Carpenter, D.: Textbook of obstetrics and obstetric nursing, ed. 5, Philadelphia, 1967, W. B. Saunders Co.

Brooks, S.: Programmed introduction to microbiology, St. Louis, 1968, The C. V. Mosby Co.

Children's Bureau: Services for children, how Title V of the Social Security Acts benefits children, Washington, D. C., 1967, U. S. Government Printing Office.

Close, K.: Selecting priorities at the White House Conference on Children, Children 18:42-48, March-April, 1971.

Davis, M. E., and Rubin, R.: Obstetrics for nurses, ed. 18, Philadelphia, 1966, W. B. Saunders Co.

DeKruiff, P.: Microbe hunters, New York, 1926, Harcourt, Brace & World.

Dunlop, R.: Abraham Jacobi, the children's physician, Today's Health 48:58+, April, 1970.

Falkner, F.: Infant mortality: an urgent national problem, Children 17:82-87, May-June, 1970.

Ferris, E. B.: Microbiology for the nurse: unit-lesson text-workbook for practical nursing, Albany, N. Y., 1967, Delmar Publishing Co.

Fitzpatrick, E., Eastman, N. J., and Reeder, S. R.: Maternity nursing, ed. 11, Philadelphia, 1966, J. B. Lippincott Co.

Frobisher, M., Sommermeyer, L., and Fuerst, R.: Microbiology in health and disease, ed. 12, Philadelphia, 1969, W. B. Saunders Co.

Fuerst, E. V., and Wolff, L.: Fundamentals of nursing, ed. 4, Philadelphia, 1969, J. B. Lippincott Co.

Harmer, B., and Henderson, V.: Textbook of the principles and practice of nursing, ed. 5, Philadelphia, 1960, The Macmillan Co.

Hasselmeyer, E. G.: The infant mortality problem in the United States, J. Prac. Nurs. 19:26-29, Jan., 1969.

Hecht, J. H., and McGarry, B. D.: The state of the nation's children, Parents' Mag. 44:47, Jan., 1969.

Hilliard, M. E.: The changing role of the maternity nurse, Nurs. Clin. N. Amer. 3:277-288, June, 1968.

Hunt, E.: Infant mortality trends and maternal and infant care, Children 17:88-90, May-June, 1970.

Hunter, G. T.: Health care through Head Start, Children 17:149-153, July-Aug., 1970.

Kretzer, M. P., and Engley, F. B.: Effective use of antiseptics and disinfectants, RN 32:48-53, May, 1969.

Ledney, D. M.: Nurse-midwives: can they fill the OB gap? RN 33:38-45, Jan., 1970.

Louise, Sister M.: The operating room technician, ed. 2, St. Louis, 1968, The C. V. Mosby Co.

Marlow, D. R.: Textbook of pediatric nursing, ed. 3, Philadelphia, 1969, W. B. Saunders Co.

Memmler, R. L.: The human body in health and disease, ed. 3, Philadelphia, 1970, J. B. Lippincott Co.

Mendelsohn, R. S.: Head Start—success or failure, Clin. Pediat. 8:684-687, 1969.

Mumford, E.: Poverty and health, Nurs. Outlook 17:32-35, Sept., 1969.

Oettinger, K. B.: The growth and meaning of White House Conferences on Children and Youth, Children 7:3, May-June, 1960.

Oettinger, K. B.: This most profound challenge, U. S. Department of Health, Education, and Welfare, Welfare Administration, Children's Bureau, Washington, D. C., 1965, U. S. Government Printing Office.

Perkins, J. J.: Principles and methods of sterilization in health sciences, ed. 2, Springfield, Ill., 1969, Charles C Thomas, Publisher.

Reeser, F. E.: Aseptic methods in the operating room, Ass. Operat. Room Nurses J. 8:38-44, Oct., 1968.

Sutton, A.: Bedside nursing techniques, ed. 2, Philadelphia, 1969, W. B. Saunders Co.

Weinstein, L.: Problem with infections mounts as resistant organisms increase, Hosp. Top. 47:97-98, May, 1969.

Wheeler, M. F., and Volk, W. B.: Basic microbiology, ed. 2, Philadelphia, 1969, J. B. Lippincott Co.

White, L. S., and Nelson, Sister S. L.: Practical approach to microbiology, ed. 3, Philadelphia, 1968, F. A. Davis Co.

Yeager, M.: Operating room manual, ed. 2, New York, 1965, G. P. Putnam's Sons.

UNIT II

3

The female bony pelvis

To understand the events of labor and delivery we must be acquainted with the first journey the fetus takes—the all-important journey of a few inches through the mother's birth canal. Since this canal is shaped largely by the bones of the pelvis, we will begin with a discussion of its formation and contours.

The word pelvis means basin. We encounter the word at least twice when we study human anatomy. It is used in describing the cavity in the kidneys into which the urine drains before flowing down the ureter. It is also used to describe the bony ring located between the trunk and thighs, joining the spine above and the femurs below. This is the pelvis to which we refer now.

Anatomy

The pelvis is formed by the two innominate bones and the sacrum and coccyx. Each innominate bone, however, is the end result of the fusion of three once-upon-a-time distinct bones: ilium, ischium, and pubis.

Landmarks and joints

The names of these three bones often recur as we describe the following interesting pelvic landmarks:

anterosuperior iliac spines the lower front end of the iliac crest line.

iliac crests the hip bones. Convenient for book or baby balancing!

iliopectineal line (linea terminalis, brim) divides the upper or false, pelvis and the lower, or true, pelvis.

ischial spines two important landmarks in determining the depth of the fetus in the passageway. The location of the presenting part of the fetus in the pelvic canal in relation to the ischial spines is termed its "station." If the presenting part is at the level of the ischial spines, its station is said to be 0, or zero. If it is above the ischial spines, it is termed minus so many centimeters (for example, −1 or −2 cm.). If the presenting part is below the ischial spines, its location is termed plus so many centimeters (for example, +1 or +2 cm.). Naturally, it is important for the nurse to be able to interpret this information. When a patient in labor nears full cervical dilatation and has a station of +2 cm., the nurse must realize that if the mechanism of labor is normal, it will probably be only a relatively short time before the infant will be born.

ischial tuberosities major bony sitting support; important in measuring a transverse diameter of the pelvis.

pubic arch formed by the lower border of the symphysis pubis and the ischial bones.

sacral promontory the internal junction of the last lumbar vertebra and the sacrum; important in obtaining an internal obstetrical measurement, known as the true conjugate, conjugata vera, or C.V.

sacrococcygeal joint located between the sacrum

27

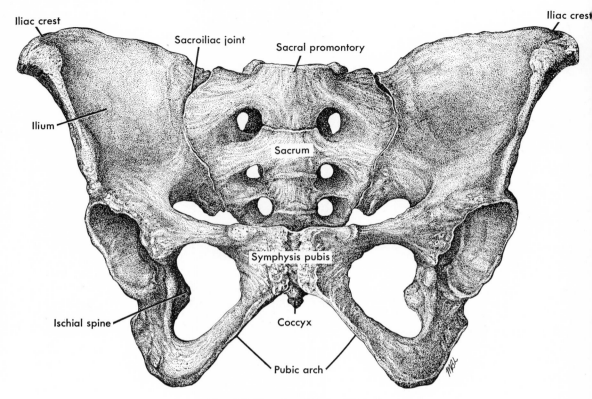

FIG. 3-1. Female pelvis, anterior view.

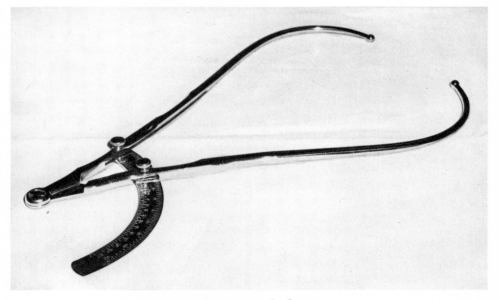

FIG. 3-2. One type of pelvimeter.

and coccyx, retains limited mobility, which may offer additional room for the passage of the fetus by bending the coccyx slightly backward. Some authorities say that as much as 1 inch is occasionally gained in this way at the outlet.

sacroiliac joints found at either side of the sacrum joining with the iliac bones.

symphysis pubis junction of the pubic bones.

True and false pelvis

The *false pelvis,* formed chiefly by flaring wings of the iliac portions of the innominate bones, helps guide the fetus into the true obstetrical canal. Its measurements may indicate possible difficulties in the structure of the true pelvis just below. The *true pelvis* is of real concern to the obstetrician. In its journey the fetus must adapt to its different diameters and shapes to successfully reach the outside world.

Inlet and outlet

The entrance to the true pelvis is termed the "inlet." Its shape is traced, in part, by the iliopectineal line. It is wider from side to side than from front to back. Therefore the head usually enters the true pelvis with its longest diameter (which is from front to back) pointed from side to side or in transverse position. Mechanically, it is either easier or absolutely necessary.

The exit of the true pelvis is termed the "outlet." The outlet is wider from front to back than from side to side. To pass through the outlet, the head, in most cases, must turn to accommodate its longest diameter to the longest diameter of the exit. This turning is called *internal rotation.* The canal formed by the true pelvis forms a slight curve near the outlet and has been likened in shape to the letter J.

Pelvic differences

Classifications. No two pelves are exactly alike although they may be classified according to their measurements. The most common classification concerns the shape and dimensions of the inlet. The typical female pelvic inlet is labeled "gynecoid." The typical male inlet is "android." Unfortunately, some women have android-type pelves. A look at a male pelvis should tell you at least one reason why the masculine member of the family would not bear children. The inlet is heart shaped and angular. The whole pelvic structure is heavier and more confining than that of the female. The pubic arch, under which every fetus should pass, is steep and narrow. In contrast, a typical woman's pelvis is relatively light and commodious, and the pubic arch is shallow and wide. Occasionally, a woman's pelvic inlet will be abnormally flat or platypelloid, with a decreased anteroposterior diameter or other abnormalities. These problems may necessitate a cesarean section, or abdominal delivery. But whether a birth will terminate abdominally or vaginally will depend on several factors: the type of passageway, the size and position of the fetus, the strength

A   B   C

Fig. 3-3. Types of pelves. **A,** Normal female pelvic inlet (gynecoid); **B,** flattened female pelvic inlet (platypelloid); **C,** typical male pelvic inlet (android).

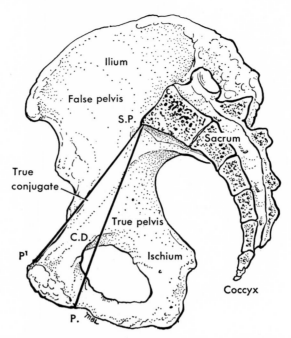

FIG. 3-4. Female pelvis, sagittal section. **C.D.**, Diagonal conjugate; **P¹**, inner superior border of the pubis; **P.**, outer inferior border of the pubis; **S.P.**, sacral promontory.

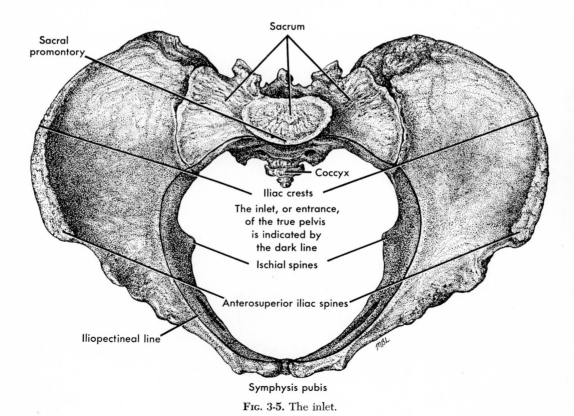

FIG. 3-5. The inlet.

of the uterine contractions, and the condition of the laboring mother.

Causes of abnormalities. A history of certain conditions may alert the physician to expect trouble because of pelvic abnormalities. The five main causes of abnormal pelvic measurements are (1) heredity (characteristic familial problems, dwarfism), (2) infections (poliomyelitis, osteomyelitis, tuberculosis of the bone), (3) poor nutrition (rickets), (4) accidents (fractured pelves), and (5) poor posture and exercise habits.

Methods of measurement

The three basic ways a physician may measure a pelvis are as follows:

1. Externally, with instruments known as pelvimeters. Common measurements secured in this way are the distance

   a. Between the anterosuperior iliac spines (I.Sp., average 26 cm.)
   b. Between the iliac crests (I.Cr., average 29 cm.)
   c. Between the depression formed by the junction of the sacrum and the last lumbar vertebra in the back and the anterior part of the symphysis pubis in the front. This measurement is the external conjugate, or Baudelocque's diameter (E.C., average 20 cm.)
   d. Between the ischial tuberosities (Bi. Isch., average 11 cm.)

2. Internally, with a lubricated gloved finger

   a. Between the sacral promontory and the outer inferior border of the pubis. This measurement is the diagonal conjugate (C.D., average 12.5 cm.)

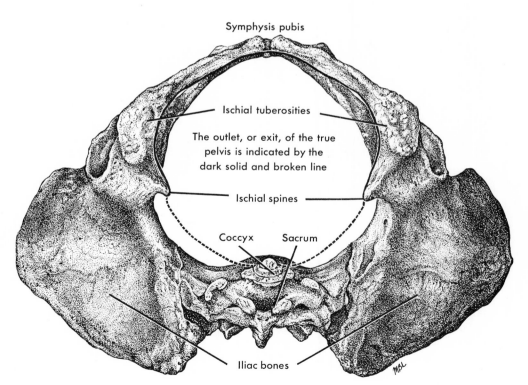

Symphysis pubis

Ischial tuberosities

The outlet, or exit, of the true pelvis is indicated by the dark solid and broken line

Ischial spines

Coccyx   Sacrum

Iliac bones

Fɪɢ. 3-6. The outlet.

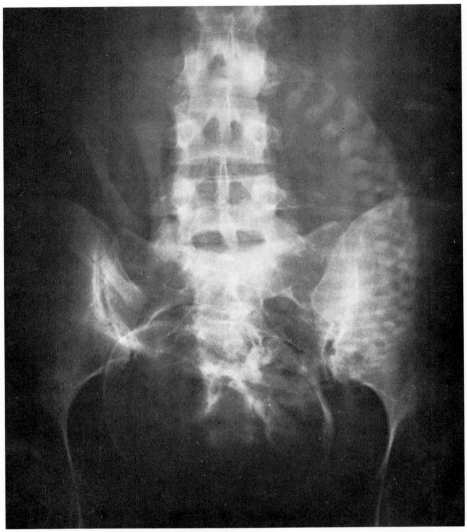

Fig. 3-7. Photograph of x-ray film. Pelvimetry showing a cephalic presentation. (Courtesy Grossmont Hospital, La Mesa, Calif.)

b. *Note:* from the preceding measurement the true conjugate or conjugata vera (C.V., average 11 cm.) is determined. This measurement is an estimate of the real anteroposterior diameter of the inlet of the pelvis. It is obtained by subtracting 1.5 cm. (an estimate of the thickness and tilt of the pubic bone) from the C.D.

3. By x-ray pelvimetry used with caution only during the latter part of pregnancy to prevent radiation damage to the fetus

There has been a trend in the last fifteen years for physicians working in areas well supplied with adequate hospital facilities to discontinue the determination of external pelvic measurements except perhaps an evaluation of the pubic arch. In fact, some believe that if cephalopelvic disproportion becomes a practical problem it can be eval-

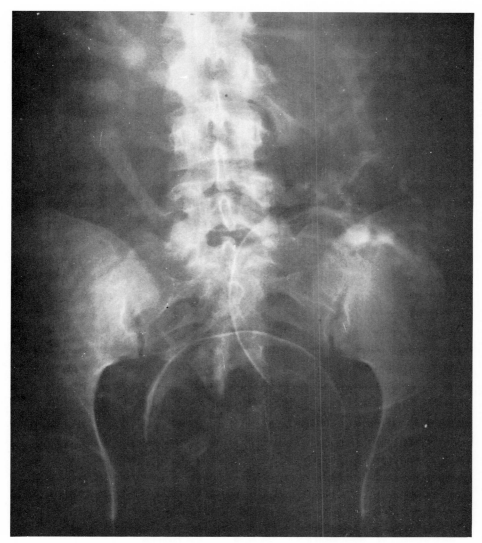

FIG. 3-8. Photograph of x-ray film. Pelvimetry showing twins. (Courtesy Grossmont Hospital, La Mesa, Calif.)

uated and faced best at the time of labor using the more refined diagnostic and treatment facilities available in the hospital.

A knowledge of the structure of the obstetrical passageway is basic to an understanding of the mechanism of labor and the problems faced by the physician. So far we have only discussed the bony pelvis. We shall continue in the next chapter with a consideration of the soft structures involved—the muscles of the pelvic floor and the organs they support.

4

The female pelvic organs—their relationships and support

The pelvis, through which the fetus must pass, contains many soft tissue structures vital to normal body function. These structures are supported by layers of muscle, fibrous coverings called *fasciae,* and various ligaments and tendons. They help to cushion the passage of the fetus through the hard, bony canal, help direct its descent, occasionally impede its progress, and may sustain damage at the time of birth.

Soft tissues of the vulva

Looking at the external female genitalia as they are observed when the patient is on her back with her knees flexed, we discover the superficial relationships of many of these vital soft tissue organs. The vulva, or external genital area, includes the following structures:

1. *Mons veneris* (Mount of Venus—mons pubis). A fatty pad over the symphysis pubis, which after puberty becomes covered with curly hair in the form of an inverted triangle extending between the legs.
2. *Labia majora* (larger lips). Two fleshy, hair-covered folds, extending on each side of the midline from the mons veneris almost to the anus. In a child or a woman who has not borne a child, these folds almost completely cover the structures between. They correspond to the two halves of the scrotum in the male. Their inner surfaces are rich in oil and sweat glands.

3. *Labia minora* (small lips). Two smaller, more delicate folds of tissue, located just under the labia majora. These small folds are somewhat erectile and are also supplied with oil and sweat glands.
4. *Clitoris.* A small, sensitive, erectile structure located at the anterior junction of the labia minora. Actually, folds of the small labia surround the clitoris, the top fold forming a fleshy hood, or *prepuce,* and the lower fold, the *frenulum.* The glans clitoris, the only part of the clitoris visible, corresponds to the male glans penis.
5. *Vestibule.* The triangular space between the labia minora in which we find the openings of the urethra, the vagina, and the *Bartholin glands.*
6. *Urethral opening.* The urethra, a tissue tube leading from the urinary bladder to the exterior, opens in the midline btween the clitoris and vagina. This opening usually appears as a dimple or slit and after delivery may be slightly displaced or more difficult to locate because of local swelling. On the floor of the urethra open two ducts that lead to *Skene's glands,* structures that have no known purpose but unfortunately may become infected rather easily.
7. *Vaginal opening.* The vagina, a large distensible tube or sheath, leads down and back to the uterine cervix.

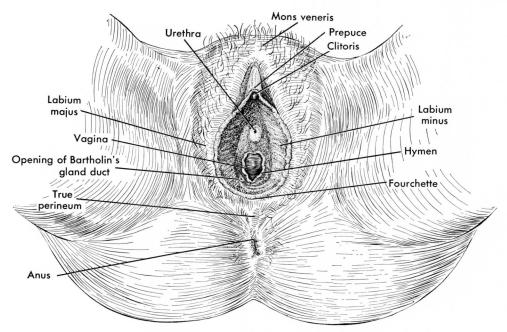

FIG. 4-1. Female external genitalia.

It serves as the exit point for menstrual flow, the female organ of intercourse, or coitus, and the soft tissue birth canal in labor and delivery. In virgins, it usually is partially covered by a membrane called the *hymen,* or maidenhead. However, absence of a hymenal membrane does not preclude virginity, since this tissue may be accidentally torn during childhood. On the other hand, the presence of the hymen is no proof of virginity, since it may be very elastic and fail to tear during intercourse. Rarely, the hymen completely covers the vaginal opening. This condition is termed "imperforate hymen" and is relieved by a hymenectomy.

8. *Bartholin's glands.* Two in number, the Bartholin glands produce a mucoid lubricating substance, which drains into the vestibule on either side of the vagina via two ducts during sexual stimulation. Occasionally, these glands become infected, and painful abscesses may form.

9. *Fourchette.* A tissue fold below the vaginal opening, formed by the fusion of the posterior edges of the labia minora, often lacerated by childbirth.

10. *Perineum.* Sometimes considered to be the entire body area between the patient's legs. However, when we speak of the *true perineum,* we mean that tissue block found between the posterior edge of the vagina and the anus or rectal opening. It contains the *perineal body,* a mass of connective tissue that forms the point of attachment for the muscles and fascia of the pelvic floor. It is this area that sustains the most frequent injury during delivery. The true perineum is a critical area of pelvic support. Such pelvic organs as the vagina, uterus, bladder, and rectum may be affected by its injury or inadequate repair. A look at Fig. 4-3, which shows these internal pelvic organs, will clarify their relationships and need for support.

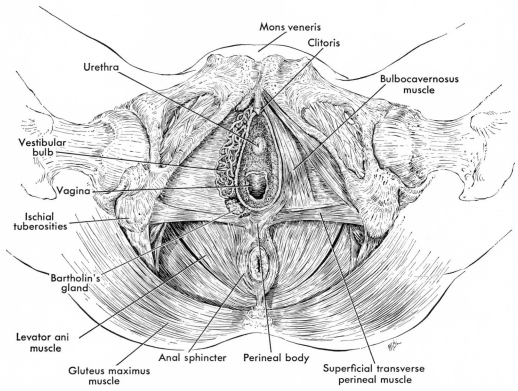

FIG. 4-2. Female pelvic floor in dissection from below. The coccygeus muscle is obscured by the gluteus maximus muscle.

Uterus and adnexa
Uterus and fallopian tubes

An adult, nonpregnant *uterus,* or womb, is a pear-shaped, hollow muscular organ about 3 inches long, 2 inches wide, and 1 inch thick. It serves as a protector and nourisher of the developing baby and aids in his birth. Attached to either side of the uterus are the *fallopian tubes,* also called the oviducts or uterine tubes, which help conduct the female sex cell to the uterus. The uterus may be divided into three main parts: the neck portion, or cervix, the main or central portion called the body or corpus, and the area above the oviducts, the fundus. Normally, the uterus is tipped toward the front of the body, resting on the urinary bladder just below. The cervix dips down into the posterior portion of the vagina from above. Vaginal and cervical tis-

sue ultimately join, forming two pouches, referred to as the anterior and posterior fornices (singular fornix). The posterior fornix is adjacent to a fold in the peritoneal lining of the pelvic cavity, termed the pouch, or cul-de-sac, of Douglas. Occasionally, because of infection of the pelvis or abdomen, pus may drain into this cul-de-sac and is aspirated vaginally or rectally by the physician.

Uterine support

Ligaments. The uterus is not only indirectly supported by the true perineum but also, along with portions of the oviducts and ovaries, is infolded in layers of the so-called *broad ligaments,* portions of the abdominal peritoneal lining. The lower portions of the broad ligaments are thicker and are sometimes called the *cardinal liga-*

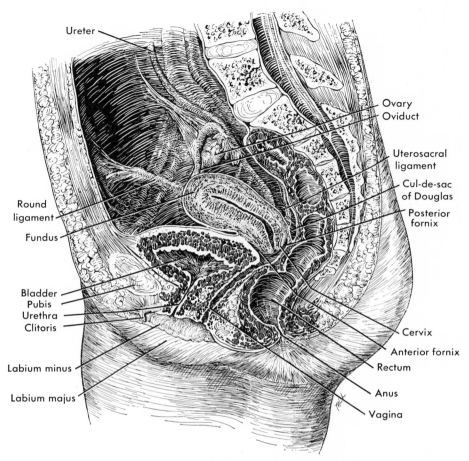

FIG. 4-3. Female reproductive system, midsagittal section.

ments. They connect the upper portion of the cervix to the lateral pelvic walls. The uterus is also positioned and stabilized by other fibrous attachments such as the *round ligaments* leading from the uterine walls toward the front, just below the fallopian tubes, down the inguinal canals, and to the labia majora. The round ligaments hold the uterus in its forward position. The *uterosacral ligaments* connect the posterior cervical portion of the uterus to the sacrum. The oviducts and ovaries and such soft tissue attachments are often referred to as the *adnexa,* or adjacent parts. The ovaries, two almond-shaped glands that produce female hormones and the female sex cells, or ova, are held one on each side of the uterus principally by the ovarian and broad ligaments.

Muscles. The deep muscles of the pelvic floor are arranged in such a way that they form a type of hammock pierced only by the urethra, vagina, and rectum. This muscle grouping, often termed the pelvic diaphragm, is formed by the branches of the large *levator ani* muscles and the *coccygeus* muscles. More muscles converge at the point of the previously described true perineum, reinforcing the levator ani. These are the *bulbocavernosus* muscle, the *transverse* muscles, and the *anal sphincter.*

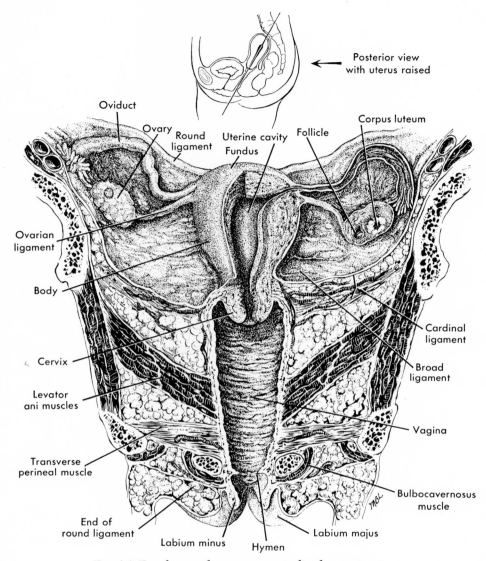

Posterior view
with uterus raised

Oviduct

Ovary

Round ligament

Uterine cavity
Fundus

Follicle

Corpus luteum

Ovarian ligament

Body

Cervix

Levator
ani muscles

Transverse
perineal muscle

End of
round ligament

Labium minus

Hymen

Labium majus

Bulbocavernosus
muscle

Vagina

Broad
ligament

Cardinal
ligament

FIG. 4-4. Female reproductive system, inclined posterior view.

Protection of the perineum

Various attempts are made to preserve or protect the muscles of the true perineum from tears (lacerations) at the time of delivery. The head of the infant is slowly extended by external, manual pressure to force the presentation of the smallest cephalic diameter. It is delivered slowly between contractions. Because the tissues of women bearing their first babies are not so easily stretched, many physicians, particularly in the United States, will perform a prophylactic perineal incision called an *episiotomy* to avoid an uncontrolled, jagged tear, reduce possible prolonged pressure on the baby's head, and speed delivery. Episiotomies may be performed in several ways. The midline, or median, episiotomy extends from the vagina straight down to the anus. It is said to be easier to repair

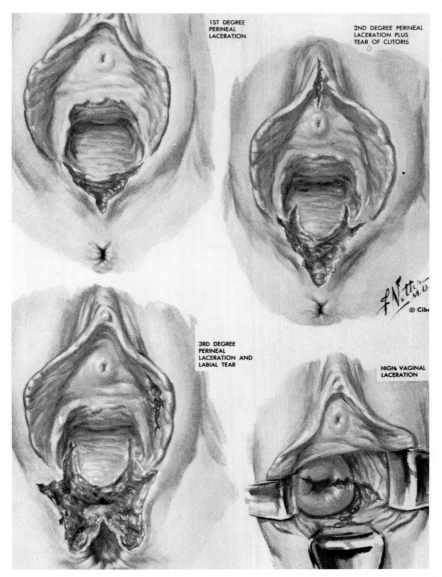

1ST DEGREE PERINEAL LACERATION

2ND DEGREE PERINEAL LACERATION PLUS TEAR OF CLITORIS

3RD DEGREE PERINEAL LACERATION AND LABIAL TEAR

HIGH VAGINAL LACERATION

FIG. 4-5. Obstetrical lacerations—vagina, perineum, and vulva. (From The CIBA collection of medical illustrations, by Frank H. Netter, M.D. Copyright CIBA.)

and more comfortable for the mother in the healing period, but it also may extend into the anal sphincter. Many physicians now use a combination episiotomy known as a mediolateral, which starts at the midline, but then angles off, missing the sphincter. Because of its angle, it is more difficult to repair and more painful during the postpartum period, since the suturing is done "on the bias." Episiotomies are so common now that most delivery room setups routinely include the instruments and supplies needed for their execution and repair. Low or outlet forceps are frequently used to speed delivery and lessen the pounding of the presenting part on the perineum.

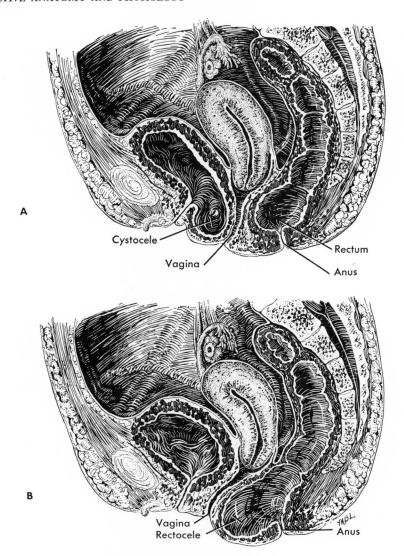

FIG. 4-6. A, Cystocele. **B,** Rectocele.

Perineal lacerations

In spite of precautions, occasional lacerations or episiotomy extensions will occur. Some maternal tissues tear more easily than others. Very large babies or unusual positions are a special threat to the perineum. Perineal lacerations are usually classified as follows:

First degree involving only the mucous membrane and skin

Second degree involving the mucous membrane, skin, muscles, and fascia of the perineal body, excepting the anal sphincter

Third degree involving mucous membrane, skin, muscles, and fascia of the perineal body, including the anal sphincter

Fourth degree involving mucous membrane, skin, muscles, and fascia of the perineal body, plus exposure and laceration of the wall of the rectum. Some-

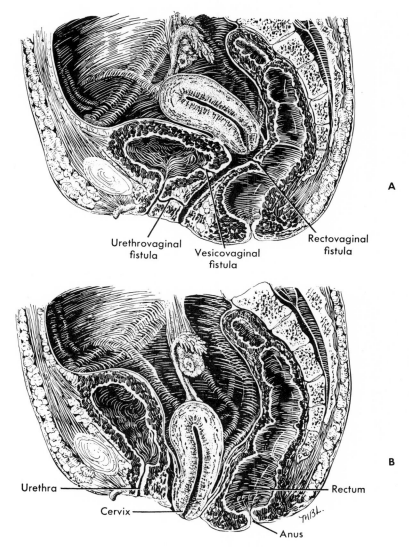

Urethrovaginal
fistula

Vesicovaginal
fistula

Rectovaginal
fistula

A

Urethra ——————

Cervix ——————

Rectum

Anus

B

Fig. 4-7. A, Fistulae. B, Prolapse of the uterus.

times such tears are still classified as third degree

Third- and fourth-degree lacerations entail considerable skill to repair and may have unfortunate long-term results.

Lacerations may involve areas other than the true perineum. Tears of the labia, interior vaginal wall, and cervix are not uncommon. All these areas should be inspected for such possibilities after a delivery.

Repairs

Prompt repair of an episiotomy or laceration usually follows the expulsion of the placenta, or afterbirth. Early suturing will lessen blood loss, help prevent infection, provide early restoration of adequate perineal support, and take advantage of any anesthetic that may be already administered. It is extremely important that the physician have good light for the repair. Occasionally, he may appreciate the help of a nurse who, reaching *under* the patient's sterile abdominal drape, holds the uterus up and away from the area to be sutured. For a description of the nursing duties involved in aiding the doctor during a repair and the nursing techniques used in perineal care after delivery, the reader is referred to the sections on nursing in the delivery room and postpartum areas.

Complications

If repair is nonexistent, inadequate, or improper, the patient is soon a possible candidate for hemorrhage, hematoma, and/or infection.

Later, as the weeks and years pass, certain pelvic displacements and malfunctions may show themselves. The patient may be troubled with urinary or fecal incontinence. She may suffer from a sagging of the pelvic musculature. When the tissue wall between the bladder and the vagina becomes abnormally relaxed, usually because of previous injury, the bladder drops out of place and pushes the anterior vaginal wall backward. The resulting abnormal condition is called a *cystocele.* A similar hernia-type abnormality involving the rectovaginal wall and a falling forward of the rectum is what is known as a *rectocele.* Small rectoceles or cystoceles are usually asymptomatic and are not surgically repaired. Large abnormalities of this type, however, may cause such complaints as a "dragging sensation" in the pelvis and such conditions as stress incontinence, urinary retention, and cystitis in the case of cystocele or constipation and hemorrhoids in the case of rectocele. A vaginal repair of these difficulties, or colporrhaphy, may be performed. If both a bladder and a rectal prolapse are surgically treated, the procedure is often called an A and P (anterior-posterior) repair. *Prolapse,* or a falling out of place of the uterus, often accompanies these other displacements. Occasionally, abnormal canals or tracts between two body cavities or a body cavity and the exterior develop as a result of obstetrical injury. These tracts, most often found between the vagina and the urethra or the vagina and the rectum are termed *fistulas* and are very difficult to eliminate. An adequate early repair of any obstetrical injuries to the passageway or its supports is very important to continuing good health.

It is well to note, however, that despite the many complications that can occur during this first journey taken by all mankind through the pelvic passageway, with proper care and management relatively few major difficulties actually materialize. Probably our first journey from internal to external space, though demanding for mother and child, is far less dangerous than the freeway trip we negotiate every afternoon going home from work.

5
The menstrual cycle

We have reviewed the anatomy of the pelvis. However, in order to study the physiology or function of the pelvic organs, we must discuss more than the contents of the pelvis itself.

Role of the pituitary gland

The proper functioning of the ovaries and uterus also depends on a gland located a considerable distance from the pelvic cavity but which empties its powerful products directly into the bloodstream, exerting influence on the body far beyond that expected, considering this gland's size and position. Remember, glands that empty their manufactured products directly into the blood circulation are called *endocrine* glands. Their products are termed "hormones." The gland outside the pelvis that is so important in ovarian and uterine function is the very busy *pituitary* located at the base of the brain. It, in part, is regulated by that portion of the brain called the hypothalamus. Some of the pituitary hormones help to regulate one of the events universal among women, *menstruation*.

Menstruation

Menstruation may be defined as the monthly elimination, through a bloody vaginal discharge, of a portion of the lining of the uterus that had been prepared to protect and nurture the fertilized egg in the event of pregnancy. Menstruation is also properly called menses, catamenia, or, more commonly, a period, or monthly flow. Terminology that implies that an undesirable condition or illness exists should be avoided because menstruation is not an ill-ness but an expected and necessary part of healthy mature womanhood. It may at times be individually inconvenient and troublesome, but it is the way all normal women function, and it declares the possibility of a type of growth unmatched in meaning and wonder by that provided by any other form of life.

Menarche

The advent of menstruation in a girl is a signal of impending physical maturity. This first menses is called *menarche*. It is one of the signs of "growing up." Menstruation occurs periodically all during the childbearing years, with the exception of periods of pregnancy and lactation, or breast feeding. The age of onset and termination differs from person to person but seems to be affected by heredity, racial background, nutrition, and perhaps climate. On the average, menarche occurs between 10 and 14 years of age. It is preceded by other body changes, such as the development of breasts, a rounding off of the many angles characteristic of the body of the preadolescent, and the appearance of axillary and pubic hair. Psychologically, a girl's interest turns toward members of the opposite sex.

The cycle

Menstruation occurs approximately every 28 days in most women and lasts about 5 days. The time between the beginning of one period and the beginning of the next is called the menstrual cycle, since it repeats itself every 4 weeks (Fig. 5-1). Day 1 is distinguished by the appearance of the menstrual flow.

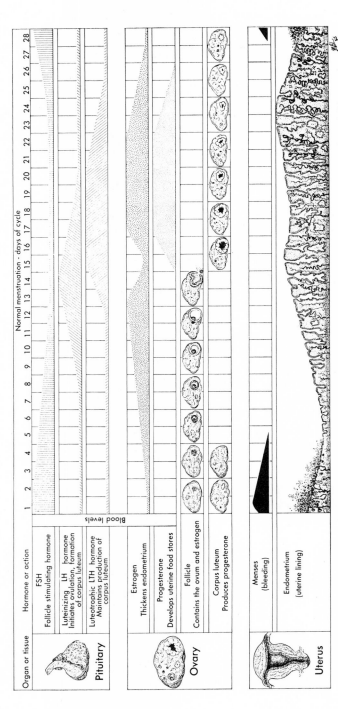

Fig. 5-1. Normal menstrual cycle. (Adapted from Physiology of normal menstruation, Schering Corp., Bloomfield, N. J.)

Anatomy and physiology

The physiology of menstruation is complex. As a student once remarked, "It is a good thing we don't have to understand the 'hows' and 'whys' of all our body's functions before it agrees to start to work!" However, a basic understanding of some of the relationships involved will increase our appreciation of the human body and its potential. Three organs are primarily involved: the pituitary gland, the ovaries, and the uterus. We will begin our explanation with a description of the ovaries.

The ovaries

The ovaries have two basic functions— first, the production of hormones (*estrogen* and *progesterone*), which help regulate the activities of the uterus and pituitary gland, bringing about the obvious changes that make a little girl a woman and, second, the formation of the microscopic eggs that carry the hereditary possibilities of her family heritage. United with a male sex cell, or sperm, the fertilized egg grows to become a new human being. These eggs are stored in varying degrees of immaturity in the underlying tissues of the ovary. Each month one egg develops to maturity within a protective tissue envelope called a follicle. This follicle and other ovarian tissue are filled with estrogenic fluid, which is secreted in large amounts into the blood to thicken the lining of the uterus. As the follicle develops, it pushes to the surface of the ovary to create a blisterlike bulge that may be clearly seen if the ovary is observed directly (for example, during surgery). The growth of the follicle in the ovary and the development of the egg, or ovum, it contains are not primarily the results of ovarian activity, however, but activity carried on by the ovary under the direction of that far-away master gland, the pituitary.

The pituitary gland

The anterior portion of the pituitary manufactures three hormones that govern the ovarian and, more indirectly, the uterine cycles. During the first and last days of the cycle, the pituitary secretes particularly large amounts of the *follicle-stimulating hormone* (FSH), which triggers and helps sustain the development of the follicle and ovum. Toward the middle of the cycle, a second potent pituitary product is released, the *luteinizing hormone* (LH), which furthers the development of the follicle and causes it to gently break open to expel the mature or ripe egg and begin its manufacture of progesterone. The rupture of the follicle on the surface of the ovary and the expulsion of the ovum is called *ovulation*. It occurs about the fourteenth day. After ovulation the mature egg is normally swept up into the fallopian tube to begin its journey to the uterus. After ovulation the empty follicle changes its name and alters its function. The walls of the follicle begin to thicken and form a yellow deposit about the size of a lima bean. This deposit is called the *corpus luteum* (yellow body). The name "follicle" is no longer used. The corpus luteum continues to produce estrogen but, in addition, manufactures another hormone, *progesterone*, initiated by LH and maintained by a third pituitary hormone, *luteotrophic hormone* (LTH). LTH, or prolactin as it is called in the postpartum state, is responsible for lactation.

Progesterone helps in the storage of foodstuffs in the wall of the uterus, built up and thickened by the action of estrogen. Progesterone, which means "a hormone designed to promote pregnancy," helps maintain the soft nutritious wall long enough to receive any fertilized egg and nourish it until the developing fetus is able to establish its more elaborate lifeline of placenta and umbilical cord. Progesterone is often given therapeutically to mothers who are having difficulty keeping their pregnancies and face the possibility of miscarriage. About the twenty-sixth day of the menstrual cycle, if no pregnancy has developed, the corpus luteum, lacking continued hormonal support from the pituitary, begins to degenerate. Approximately 2 days later the thickened lining of the uterus starts to disintegrate, having lost its progesterone and estrogen support.

Cycle control
Pregnancy

If pregnancy does occur, hormones released by the developing fertilized egg interrupt the normal menstrual cycle by maintaining the level of estrogen and progesterone and inhibiting ovulation.

Artificial hormonal control

In recent years oral estrogen- and progesterone-like compounds, which simulate to some degree the changes in the uterine lining and the regulation of ovarian and pituitary activity occurring during pregnancy, have been used to control ovulation and aid in planned parenthood. (See discussion of contraception, Chapter 19.)

Ovulation and menses

The menstrual flow consists of less than 60 ml. of cellular debris, mucus, and blood. Its appearance signals the advent of another cycle. It is interesting to note that ovulation may not occur each time the menstrual cycle repeats and is not dependent on menstruation. The occurrence of ovulation can be detected by the careful recording of rectal temperatures taken before arising in the absence of a temperature-causing disease. Just before ovulation, the temperature drops to the lowest level found in the first half of the cycle. This drop is followed by an abrupt rise of perhaps one half of a degree Fahrenheit, indicating ovulation has occurred. This information has also been used in trying to plan pregnancies, since the most fertile period is during this temperature change.

Problems
Dysmenorrhea

The most common menstrual disturbance is dysmenorrhea, or painful menstruation. Although most women observe some discomfort (for example, pelvic congestion, fatigue, or irritability), severe cramping and incapacitation should not be the rule. Repeated experiences of dysmenorrhea should be evaluated by a physician. Occasionally, a physical cause may be found, such as an abnormal narrowing of the cervical opening, poor uterine positioning, the presence of pelvic tumors, or possible glandular imbalance. Dysmenorrhea may be caused or aggravated by constipation. Its possibility is also greatly increased by fatigue and emotional upset. The maintenance of meticulous hygiene, proper diet, and good mental health is of prime importance to the body's total response during menstruation. Excellent teaching aids dealing with the anatomy, physiology, and hygiene of menstruation are now available through public health departments and private commercial outlets.

Treatment of dysmenorrhea, of course, depends on the cause, but moderate exercise, fresh air, a serene philosophy, prevention or relief of constipation, possible application of heat to the pelvis, and mild sedatives or muscle relaxants usually help greatly. Because it has been found that many times dysmenorrhea is not experienced if a menstrual cycle does not include ovulation, contraceptive preparations containing estrogen or estrogen-progesterone combinations are occasionally prescribed with good effect. However, if the contraceptive action of the medication or possible side effects present problems, this method of treatment may not be appropriate.

Disturbances in flow

Other types of menstrual disorders should at least be defined. *Amenorrhea* means the abnormal absence of menses. *Menorrhagia* refers to abnormally excessive flow. *Metrorrhagia* identifies the presence of bloody vaginal discharge between periods. All these conditions should be investigated by a physician.

6

The male parent—his contribution

The role of the mother in the creation of new life has often been emphasized, but the role of the responsible male parent is also very important. Truly for an emotionally, socially, and physically healthy child both marriage partners must make considerable contributions of time and effort. This does not mean that if these contributions are absent the child will never achieve a happy, productive life, but if he does, he does so "in spite of" instead of "because of" his early family life. For the mature parent, capable of giving as well as receiving, parenthood is a demanding responsibility but one that gives a deserved sense of fulfillment and pride.

The male role in the initial physical creation of his offspring is relatively brief but no less miraculous because of its brevity. The male reproductive system is an intricate mechanism worthy of study.

Anatomy and physiology
Puberty

Puberty, or the maturation of the reproductive system, occurs late in the male when compared to the female. The development of the male sex organs and secondary sex characteristics takes place, on the average, two years later. It involves such changes as the enlargement of the larynx and the deepening of the voice, the appearance of axillary, pubic, and facial hair, the development of increased musculature, the production of semen, and the normal occurrence of nocturnal emissions, or "wet dreams." Finally, there is a psychological change, and the boy who could not stand girls rather suddenly finds them quite attractive.

Genetic considerations

Perhaps a brief digression concerning genetics, the study of inheritance, is now in order. All cells that compose living things, animal or plant, have within their nuclei the potential of inheritance not only for the species but also for the individualized representatives of that species. Each living thing has a certain number of threadlike strands (chromosomes) of transmittable characteristics (genes) within the nuclei of its tissue cells. This number is constant for each species. For example, human beings have forty-six chromosomes in each body tissue cell. However, because the child necessarily inherits qualities from both parents and the body tissue chromosome count must be unaltered for the species, the sex cells of the male and female are different from the rest of the cells found in the body. Through a special process during their growth the chromosome count is reduced by half. When male and female sex cells unite, fertilization, or conception, takes place, and the species' chromosome count is restored in the new developing representative of the race.

Male organs of reproduction (Figs. 6-1 and 6-2)

The male sex cells, or spermatozoa, are manufactured in two oval endocrine glands called *testes* (singular testis), or *testicles*, located in a fleshy pouch suspended from the abdomen called the *scrotum*. In addition to the manufacture of sperm, the testes also manufacture a hormone called *testosterone*, which is responsible for the appearance of male characteristics even as estrogen in the female is responsible for

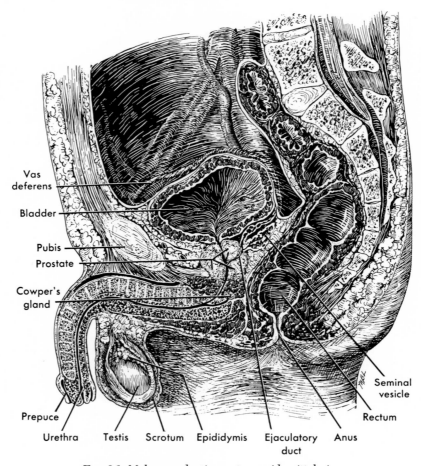

Vas deferens

Bladder

Pubis

Prostate

Cowper's gland

Prepuce

Urethra   Testis   Scrotum   Epididymis   Ejaculatory duct   Anus

Seminal vesicle

Rectum

Fig. 6-1. Male reproductive system, midsagittal view.

feminine qualities. The testes are found in the abdominal cavity proper during part of fetal development, but before birth they usually migrate to the scrotal sac via the inguinal canal. Occasionally, this migration does not occur, and a condition known as undescended testicles, or cryptorchidism, may exist. If this persists, sterility may occur, since the higher temperature of the abdominal cavity seems to interfere with the manufacture of sperm. If the condition continues, malignant changes are occasionally diagnosed.

Attached to the top of each testis is a coiled structure called an *epididymis,* which is actually an extension of the tubules of the testis where sperm are formed.

In the epididymides (plural of epididymis) the male sex cells mature. Each epididymis is in turn attached to a long tube called the *ductus deferens,* or *vas deferens,* which with associated nerves and blood vessels travels up the inguinal canal as the *spermatic cord.* The ductus deferens eventually loops downward in back of the urinary bladder. Attached to the ductus in this area is the *seminal vesicle.* This small pouch secretes a product that is added to the spermatozoa and aids the motility of the sex cell. The tube leading forward from the point of attachment of the seminal vesicle is called the *ejaculatory duct.* It joins the long urethra after passing through tissue of the *prostate gland.* Three paired glands

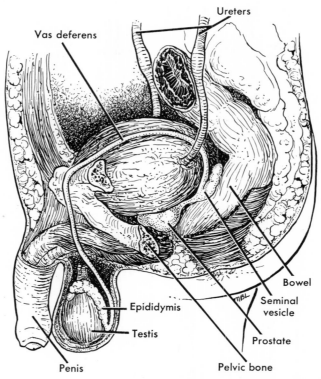

FIG. 6-2. Male reproductive system, sagittal view with partial dissection.

add secretions to the spermatozoa traveling from the testes to the exterior to form *semen,* or *seminal fluid:* the seminal vesicle, the prostate (already mentioned), and the bulbourethral, or Cowper's, gland, which opens into the urethra proper. These secretions regulate the acidity of the semen and influence the sperm's motility and life-span. As a result of sexual excitement and subsequent ejaculation of semen, approximately 250 to 500 million sperm are released at a time from the penis, the male organ of intercourse, through the urethral meatus.

When not sexually stimulated, the penis serves as the excretory organ of the male urinary system. The urethra opens at the tip of the penis in a sensitive portion called the *glans.* The glans is hooded by a fold of skin called the *prepuce,* or *foreskin,* which is at least partially removed if a circumcision is performed.

Sex determination

Because there has been considerable consternation in the past concerning the sex of certain heirs, perhaps it should be pointed out that the potential sex of the child is determined by the type of sex cell contributed by the male that penetrates the ovum, or egg. Only the male sex cells, the spermatozoa, may carry the Y chromosome, which dictates the conception of a boy. When the sperm that unites with an ovum carries the Y chromosome, a boy will result, but if the sperm that fertilizes the egg carries an X chromosome, a girl will result. There is some evidence that suggests that the acidity or alkalinity of the vagina may influence the type of male sex cell that survives.

"Our humanity"

Although few people would deny that a baby is a human being, it must be agreed that the true process of reproduction of the human race does not end at conception or at birth. It only enters another phase. Just how "human," in the best sense of the word, the child becomes depends on the human-ity he observes and feels about him within his own family circle—what he finds within the lives of his mother and father that he values as true and lasting.

UNIT II

**SUGGESTED SELECTED READINGS
AND REFERENCES**

Anthony, C. P.: Structure and function of the body, ed. 3, St. Louis, 1968, The C. V. Mosby Co.

Anthony, C. P.: Textbook of anatomy and physiology, ed. 8, St. Louis, 1971, The C. V. Mosby Co.

Crouch, J. E.: Functional human anatomy, Philadelphia, 1965, Lea & Febiger.

Davis, M. E., and Rubin, R.: DeLee's obstetrics for nurses, ed. 18, Philadelphia, 1966, W. B. Saunders Co.

Fitzpatrick, E., Eastman, N. J., and Reeder, S. R.: Maternity nursing, ed. 11, Philadelphia, 1966, J. B. Lippincott Co.

King, B. G., and Showers, M. J.: Human anatomy and physiology, ed. 6, Philadelphia, 1969, W. B. Saunders Co.

Memmlers, R. L.: The human body in health and disease, ed. 3, Philadelphia, 1970, J. B. Lippincott Co.

Netter, F. H., and Oppenheimer, E., editors: The Ciba collection of medical illustrations, vol. 2, The reproductive system, Summit, N. J., 1954, Ciba Pharmaceutical Products, Inc.

Rorvik, D. M., and Shettles, L. B.: You can choose your baby's sex, Look 34:88-98, April 21, 1970.

UNIT III

THE PERIOD OF GESTATION

7

Embryology and fetal development

The event of *conception* (Fig. 7-1), the union of the male sex cell (sperm) and the female sex cell (ovum) within the mother, sets into motion a period of growth unequaled at any other time in the life of the individual.

The ovum, just after *fertilization*, or conception, occurs, is not quite as large as the dot used to complete a sentence, but, within approximately 9 calendar months or 266 days, that particle of life will increase in size approximately 200 billion times and become the highly complex structure and personality known as a baby.

Embryology
Early beginnings

Fertilization normally takes place in the fallopian, or uterine, tube. The single cell soon becomes two, then four, then eight, multiplying until keeping count would be impossible. The egg assumes the bumpy appearance of a mulberry and for that reason is called a *morula* as it journeys down the tube in search of a warm, safe place to grow. The journey from ovary to uterine cavity, where nesting, or *implantation*, takes place, involves about 7 days. At the end of this time the fertilized egg burrows into the soft uterine lining. The outer surface of the egg is covered by fingerlike tissue projections called *chorionic villi*, which aid in the process of implantation. They also manufacture hormones that signal the corpus luteum in the ovary to continue to manufacture progesterone and estrogen to prevent menstruation and additional ovulation. The aggregation of cells begins to form a definite pattern. A hollow develops in its center, and the microscopic embryo forms, suspended within this hollow by a slender stalk that later becomes the umbilical cord.

Placental development and role

Fairly soon a "supply and disposal system" across the uterine wall is initiated through a special intermediary organ called the *placenta*, or *afterbirth*. The placenta, a miraculous structure, forms from part of the chorionic villi that extended from the outside of the egg. Attached to the uterine wall, it obtains the food and oxygen necessary for the growth of the fetus from the mother's blood. Through the process of osmosis, hormones and protective substances called antibodies also cross over the placental link to the fetus via the umbilical cord. Then, too, the placenta handles waste products brought to its tissue from the fetus, allowing the carbon dioxide and other metabolic wastes to pass over from the fetal circulation to the maternal bloodstream. The mother and fetus do not share

THE MENSTRUAL CYCLE

- Menstruation
- Ovulation

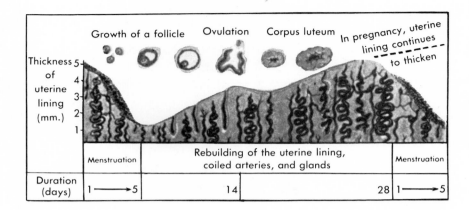

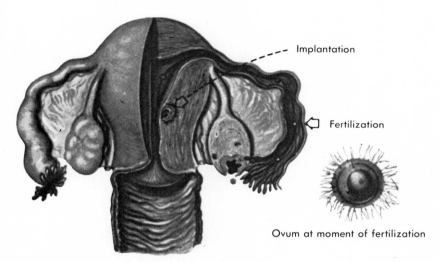

FIG. 7-1. The event of pregnancy. (Courtesy Carnation Co., Los Angeles, Calif.)

a common bloodstream. The fetus manufactures its own blood. Normally, the whole blood of the mother and that of the fetus stay within their own designated though closely related channels. Blood flows from the placenta to the fetus via a large umbilical vein in the cord. The two arteries in the cord, wound about the umbilical vein, carry the waste to the placenta.

"Bag of waters"

As the embryo develops, the chorionic villi, facing the interior of the uterus not involved in the formation of the placenta, fall off the spherical covering, leaving a transparent sac made up of two membranous layers called the *chorion* and *amnion*. The inner layer, the amnion, secretes a salty liquid known as amniotic fluid in which the fetus may be said to float. It helps to control the environmental temperature of the fetus as well as shield it from bumps and pressure. Perhaps weightlessness is not such an extraordinary condition for mankind after all! This amniotic sac is commonly known as the bag of waters.

THE FIRST THREE MONTHS

Actual size,
3/14 inch

At end of four weeks

Heart pulsating and pumping blood. Backbone and spinal canal forming. No eyes, nose or external ears visible. Digestive system beginning to form. Small buds which will eventually become arms and legs are present.

At end of eight weeks

About 1 1/8 inches long.
Weighs about 1/30 ounce.
Face and features forming; eyelids fused.
Limbs beginning to show distinct divisions into arms, elbows, forearm and hand, thigh, knee, lower leg, and foot.
Distinct umbilical cord formed.
Long bones and internal organs developing.
Tail-like process disappears.

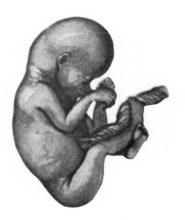

At end of twelve weeks

About 3 inches long.
Weighs about 1 ounce.
Arms, hands, fingers and legs, feet, toes fully formed. Nails on digits beginning to develop.
External ears are present.
Tooth sockets and buds forming in the jawbones.
Eyes almost fully developed, but lids still fused.

FIG. 7-2. Growth of the fetus the first three months. (Courtesy Carnation Co., Los Angeles, Calif.)

Normally, it persists intact until the time of labor and delivery.

The fetus (Figs. 7-2 to 7-5)

At the end of 8 weeks of growth, the embryo is recognizable as a small, unfinished human, and its name is changed to fetus, meaning "young one." It is less than 2 inches long and weighs a fraction of an ounce. Although rudimentary, body systems are formed and working. The cal-cified skeleton has even begun to be established.

At 12 weeks. By the close of the third month the sex of the fetus may be clearly discerned if it is directly inspected. Needless to say, there is always considerable curiosity regarding the sex of the developing fetus. However, there is still no *completely* safe way to discover the sex before birth. Nevertheless, a technique has been introduced that makes possible the sex identification before delivery if it is genetically important. Amniotic fluid is aspirated from the bag of waters and examined for cellular content and chromosome determination.

At 16 weeks. At 16 weeks' *gestation,* or pregnancy, the fetus has increased considerably in size. It is approximately 6 inches long and weighs about 4 ounces. The uterus will be correspondingly larger, and moth-

er's maternity clothes may make their debut.

At 20 weeks. At about 20 weeks, expectant mothers usually report feelings of life known as *quickening.* Elbows, feet, and hands punch and twitch as the fetus attempts more vigorous exercise in its confining temporary home. It is now about 10 inches long and weighs approximately 8 ounces. About this time the examining phy-

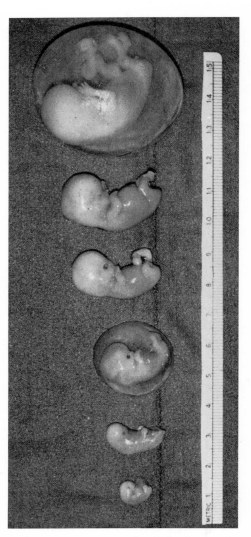

FIG. 7-3. Progressive growth of the human fetus (measured in centimeters). Two amniotic sacs are pictured still intact. (Courtesy Jeanne I. Miller, M.D., Modesto, Calif.)

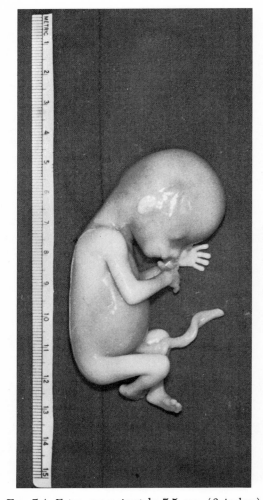

FIG. 7-4. Fetus approximately 7.5 cm. (3 inches) long at almost 3 months' gestation. (Courtesy Jeanne I. Miller, M.D., Modesto, Calif.)

sician may begin listening for the fetal heart tone, which, although present before, was too faint to be heard.

At 28 weeks. A child born after 28 weeks' gestation may occasionally survive, although his body systems are extremely im- mature. Each additional day the fetus is able to remain in the uterus until maturity is reached, at a little less than 40 weeks of gestation, is of benefit. Each day increases its ability to withstand the demands of ex- trauterine life and to adjust to the tremen-

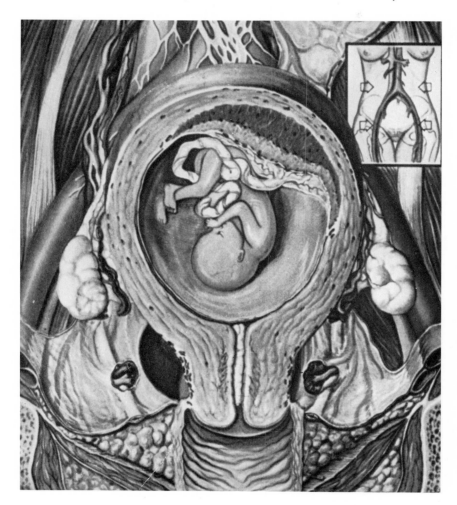

THE UTERUS:

> The fetus may develop within the uterus head down as shown or head up, and it may rotate completely before birth. It lives throughout its uterine life within the "bag of waters." The fluid filling this sac serves many purposes. It prevents the walls of the uterus from cramping the fetus and acts as an excellent shock-absorber. At term, there is usually about a quart of amniotic fluid.

Fig. 7-5. Pelvic relationships in early pregnancy, frontal view. (Courtesy Carnation Co., Los Angeles, Calif.)

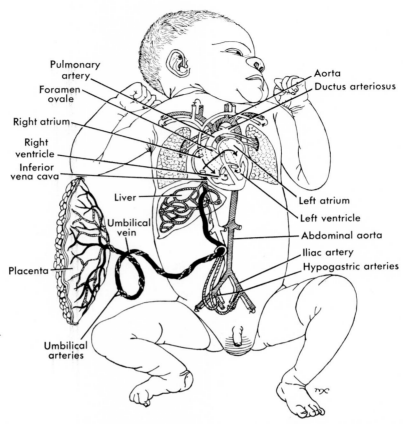

Pulmonary artery
Foramen ovale
Right atrium
Right ventricle
Inferior vena cava
Liver
Umbilical vein
Placenta
Umbilical arteries
Aorta
Ductus arteriosus
Left atrium
Left ventricle
Abdominal aorta
Iliac artery
Hypogastric arteries

FIG. 7-6. Fetal circulation. The darker the blood in the vessels, the greater its oxygen content. (See text for blood-flow pattern.)

dous circulatory, respiratory, and digestive alterations that must take place at birth.

Fetal circulation

A diagram of fetal circulation is shown in Fig. 7-6 to give a better understanding of the circulorespiratory changes. The umbilical vein extends from the placenta to the fetus, entering the body at the umbilicus. It travels upward, branching through the liver to eventually join the inferior vena cava. There its richly oxygenated blood mixes with the oxygen-poor blood flowing from the lower extremities and abdominal cavity toward the heart. The blood enters the heart via the right atrium, as in postnatal circulation, but because the pulmonary circulation is unnecessary to oxygenation, much of the blood entering the heart

from the inferior vena cava crosses directly to the left atrium through the fetal shunt, or interatrial opening, called the *foramen ovale*. This blood then is guided into the usual circulation pattern, left atrium → left ventricle → aorta.

Blood entering the right atrium from the superior vena cava, draining the head and upper extremities, flows for the most part into the right ventricle and is eventually pushed into the pulmonary artery. However, the trip to the lungs is superfluous at this time, and another shunt, the *ductus arteriosus*, is employed. This short duct leads from the pulmonary artery to the aorta. Relatively little blood flows to the lung fields and back to the left heart via the pulmonary veins.

The blood flow down the aorta is eventually channeled into the iliac arteries to the hypogastric arteries that join with the umbilical arteries leading to the umbilical cord and placenta.

The pulmonary circulation becomes established within a relatively short time after birth. The umbilical cord is cut, and the blood vessels it contains become occluded. The foramen ovale closes, and the ductus arteriosus collapses and becomes a liga-ment. Life indeed changes, and it is never the same again!

• • •

Interest in the developing fetus has accelerated in recent years. A new branch of medicine, "fetology," is being explored. Even now, the time is envisioned when this small patient may undergo corrective procedures.

8
Signs and symptoms of pregnancy

All the activity initiated within the uterus with the onset of pregnancy cannot be kept a secret for long. Widespread changes take place in the body, creating various signs and symptoms that possess varying degrees of importance in the diagnosis of pregnancy. These signs and symptoms are usually arranged, according to their accuracy, into three groups: the presumptive, probable, and positive signs of pregnancy.

Presumptive signs

The presumptive signs or symptoms of pregnancy are those that, taken by themselves, could easily be an indication of other conditions.

Amenorrhea. Although absence of menses may be an early sign of developing pregnancy, it certainly is not always. Amenorrhea may occur as a result of sudden changes in environment or occupation, emotional upset, malnutrition, fatigue, hormonal disorders, and the menopause.

Nausea and vomiting (particularly in the morning). Nausea and vomiting, presumably the results of changes in hormone levels in the body in the first weeks of pregnancy, are obviously not confined to this cause, being a common accompaniment of gastrointestinal tract irritation and emotional stress.

Frequent urination. Frequent voidings, usually of small amounts, are common during the first and last weeks of pregnancy because of the particular pressure of the uterus on the bladder. But frequency may also be present because of excitement, large fluid intakes, or irritation of the urinary tract.

Breast changes. Tingling, swelling, and tenderness involving the breasts are also found rather early in pregnancy. But a minimal amount of such symptoms may be experienced during each menstrual cycle just before menses. Color changes causing a deepening of pigmentation in the breast or production of breast secretion (colostrum) are considered good signs of pregnancy in a woman who has not been pregnant previously but have little value in a woman who has had children recently or has been nursing. Tiny nodules on the nipple and areola, which are enlarged lubricating glands called tubercles of Montgomery, are often seen.

Quickening. Quickening, meaning the first time life or fetal movement is felt by the mother, can sometimes be imitated by peristalsis or gas and wrongly interpreted. By the time quickening is felt (at approximately 5 months) other more definite signs should be manifest.

Fatigue. Fatigue, often included on the list, is a very widespread complaint even in nonpregnant women.

Probable signs

The probable signs of pregnancy are more certain, but not infallible. They usually include the following: changes in the shape of the abdomen, changes in the reproductive organs, and positive pregnancy tests.

Changes in shape of abdomen. Changes in abdominal contour may be accompanied by pink stretch marks, or striae (Fig. 8-1), but the striae themselves reflect sudden weight gain and not necessarily pregnancy,

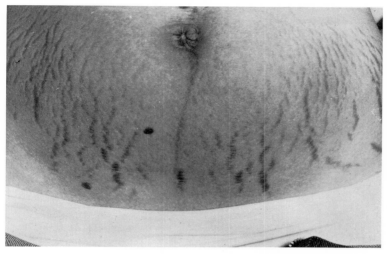

FIG. 8-1. Striae (stretch marks). (Courtesy Mercy-Guadalupe Clinic, San Diego, Calif.)

FIG. 8-2. Hegar's sign.

and the shape of one's abdomen may depend on dietary willpower rather than gestation. It may also be influenced by the growth of tumors. The development of a dark line extending from the sternum to the pubis in the midline, called the *linea nigra,* is considered by some a probable sign if the patient has not been pregnant before. This line is most often seen in brunettes.

Changes in reproductive organs. The enlargement of the uterus, rather than an increase in abdominal circumference, is a more definitive sign of pregnancy. Nevertheless, uterine tumors or inflammation may cause an increase in size. Because of the increase in blood supply to the area at about 8 to 10 weeks after conception, a violet tinge to the cervical and vaginal

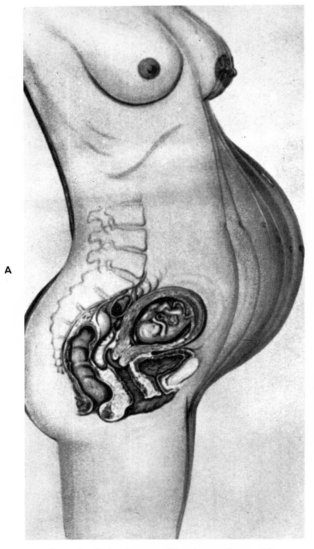

A

3rd
month

Your baby is now about 3 inches long and weighs about 1 ounce. It may continue to develop in the position shown or may turn or rotate frequently. The uterus begins to enlarge with the growing fetus and can now be felt extending about halfway up to the umbilicus.

Baby's hands are fully formed even at 12 weeks with fingers and nails all distinctly present.

FIG. 8-3. Growth of the fetus within the mother, with progressive silhouette changes. A, Pregnancy of 3 calendar months. B, Pregnancy at 5 calendar months. C, Pregnancy at 7 calendar months. D, Pregnancy at 9 calendar months. (Courtesy Carnation Co., Los Angeles, Calif.)

mucous membranes can be detected *(Chadwick's sign).* Since such a color change may occur in any condition causing pelvic congestion, some authors list it as only a presumptive sign. At about 6 to 8 weeks' gestation, a special softening of the region of the uterus between the body and the cervix, called the *isthmus,* occurs. It is determined by a simultaneous abdominal and vaginal examination, a bimanual examination illustrated in Fig. 8-2. This softening is termed "Hegar's sign."

Positive pregnancy tests. Pregnancy tests are based on the fact that the chorionic villi of an implanted ovum secrete a gonadotropic hormone, which is excreted in detectable amounts in the urine. The first tests were biological. A concentrated amount of urine obtained from a morning specimen, voided after a period of fluid limitation, was injected into a laboratory animal. The animal was then observed for changes in its reproductive cycle. Rabbits, mice, and frogs were used.

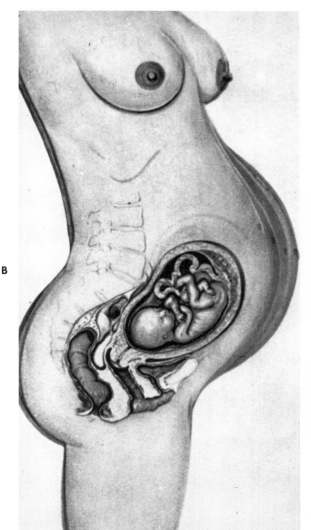

B

5th
month

Your baby measures about 10-12 inches long and weighs from ½ to 1 pound. It is still bright red. Its increased size now brings the dome of the uterus to the level of the umbilicus. The internal organs are maturing at astonishing speed but the lungs are insufficiently developed to cope with conditions outside the uterus.

The eyelids are still completely fused at the end of five months. Some hair may be present on the head.

FIG. 8-3, cont'd. For legend see opposite page.   *Continued.*

More recently, chemical tests have been perfected that no longer require laboratory animals. The presence of human chorionic gonadotrophic hormone causes certain changes in the test materials that may be read in minutes or hours, depending on the individual test selected. These tests are reactive much earlier than those employing animals, sometimes as early as 4 days after the expected date of menstruation. However, because they are only about 95% accurate, with possibilities of both false negatives and false positives, all positive pregnancy tests are considered "probable" and not "positive" signs of pregnancy. Pregnancy tests are generally not used just to satisfy curiosity—time will do that. A firm diagnosis of pregnancy can usually be made after the eighth week. But in those fairly rare cases when a pregnancy outside the uterine cavity (ectopic pregnancy) or a possible abnormal growth of the ovum,

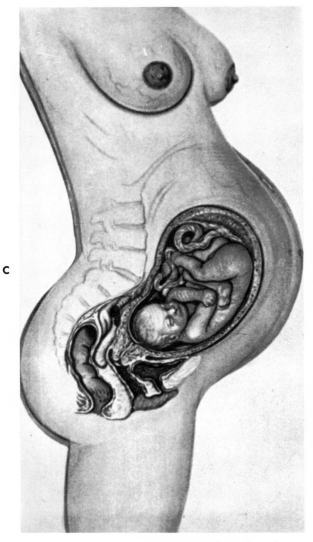

C

7th month

The baby's weight has about doubled since last month and it is about 3 inches longer. However, it still looks quite red, is covered with wrinkles which will eventually be erased by fat. At seven months the premature baby at this stage has a fair chance for survival in nurseries cared for by skilled physicians and nurses.

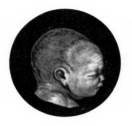

The seven month baby is wrinkled and red.

FIG. 8-3, cont'd. For legend see p. 60.

called *hydatidiform mole,* is suspected or pelvic surgery is contemplated, pregnancy tests are of real diagnostic value.

Positive signs

There are three positive signs of pregnancy.

1. Presence of a fetal heart tone, usually heard at about 4½ months
2. Fetal movement detected by a trained examiner

3. Visualization of the fetal skeleton on x-ray film (usually not done during early pregnancy because of the possibility of radiation damage to the fetus)

Progressive fetal growth (Figs. 8-3 and 8-4)

The growth of the embyro and fetus makes progressive changes in the contours and silhouette of the expectant mother. The

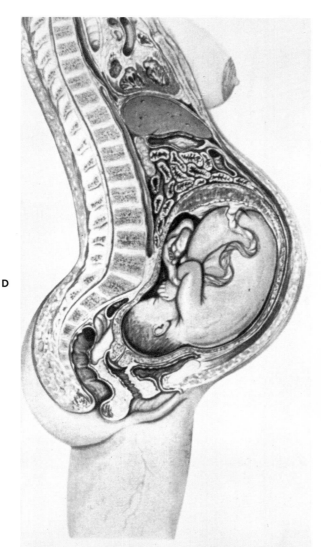

D

9th month

At birth or full term the baby weighs on an average about 7 pounds if a girl and 7½ pounds if a boy. Its length is about 20 inches. Its skin is white or pink but still coated with the creamy coating. The fine downy hair has largely disappeared. Fingernails may protrude beyond the ends of the fingers.

The size of the soft spot between bones of the skull varies considerably from one child to another but generally will close within 12 to 18 months.

FIG. 8-3, cont'd. For legend see p. 60.

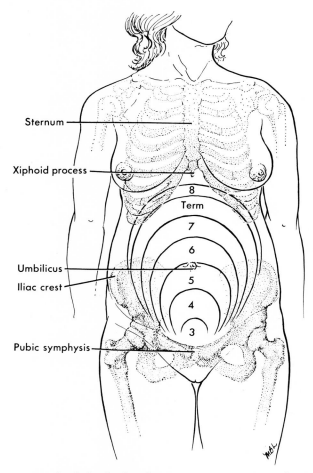

Sternum

Xiphoid process

8
Term
7
6
Umbilicus
Iliac crest
5
4
3

Pubic symphysis

Fig. 8-4. Progressive growth of the fundus during pregnancy, measured in calendar months. Note that the fundus is lower at term than at 8 months' gestation.

fundus, or top of the uterus, is felt about halfway between the top of the pubic bone and the umbilicus at approximately 3 calendar months. It is found at the umbilicus at about 5 calendar months. Near term, it is almost at the level of the tip of the sternum. A woman expecting her first baby usually experiences a sudden relief from shortness of breath about 2 weeks before her delivery when the fetus "drops," and *lightening* occurs, taking pressure off the diaphragm.

The increasing size of her temporary boarder puts greater demands on her respiratory, circulatory, and urinary systems.

Her intestines and stomach suffer from crowding and compression. Increasing size necessitates changes in wardrobe, creates a typical posture of pregnancy, and finally makes the heretofore simple process of tying shoes almost impossible.

In some women a bronze-type pigmentation, or heightening of color, appears on the face, especially over the nose and forehead, probably caused by different hormonal levels. This has been called *chloasma*, or the *mask of pregnancy*. But, as we have seen, progressive fetal growth is really impossible to mask. There is no such thing as a light case of pregnancy!

9
Prenatal care

When she suspects she is pregnant, a woman should consult a physician to gain optimum care even during the early months of pregnancy. Since women are not certain they will become pregnant and often are not aware of the fact of pregnancy until after several weeks of gestation have elapsed, the earliest prenatal care is always the responsibility of the woman herself. Her general health habits and physical condition before a physician is ever consulted are of considerable importance. When the diagnosis of pregnancy is established, provision for regular medical supervision and suitable plans for the baby's arrival must be made.

In the physician's office and the hospital setting expectant mothers are given certain professional labels by the staff to help in anticipating their needs and to briefly describe their obstetrical past. This terminology, with certain modifications, is used throughout their care. It consists of a series of prefixes and suffixes to help describe the number of times the patient has been pregnant and the number of times she has carried a child to a viable age (usually considered 28 weeks or more). The word elements are as follows:

gravida (a suffix) the number of pregnancies a woman has had. The term comes from the same root as gravity, which causes us to have weight. Pregnancy brings weight too.

para (a suffix) the number of viable deliveries a woman has had. This usually means how many babies she has carried 28 weeks or more; in most areas the birth of twins or triplets would only be considered as one de-livery. Both abdominal and vaginal deliveries re recorded in "para" counts.

nul (a prefix) means none. A *nulligravida* has never been pregnant. A *nullipara* has never delivered a viable child.

prim (a prefix) from primary or first. Combined with gravida, it reads *primigravida* and means a woman who is having or has had one pregnancy. Combined with para, it reads *primipara* and technically means a woman who has had one delivery of a viable child. However, once she is admitted into the labor-delivery suite, attending nurses usually refer to a woman who is carrying her first child but is not yet delivered as a primipara or "primip" to differentiate her from a woman who has been through the birth process.

mult (a prefix) meaning many or at least more than one. Combined with gravida it reads *multigravida* and means a woman who has had more than one pregnancy. Combined with para it reads *multipara* or "multip" and technically means a woman who has borne two or more viable infants. Actually, in the labor-delivery room suite the term is applied to a woman who has delivered one viable child or more, to differentiate her from a "first timer." Sometimes women who have had six or more deliveries are called "grand-multips."

Goals and importance of prenatal care

The term "antepartal or prenatal care" as used by doctors and nurses refers to the planned examination, observation, and guidance of an expectant mother. The goals are as follows:

1. A pregnancy with a minimum of mental and physical discomfort and a maximum of gratification
2. A delivery under the best circumstances possible
3. A normal, well baby

4. The establishment of good health habits benefiting all the family
5. A smooth, guided postpartum adjustment

It is well to remember that the extension of prenatal care is the primary factor in the improvement of maternal morbidity and mortality statistics. Women should be taught its importance.

The first visit

Usually prenatal care is formally begun shortly after the second menstrual period is missed. But in a broader sense, a woman is being prepared for her experience of childbearing and nurturing long before she steps into the physician's office. Her basic physique was determined by her parents before her birth. Her environment has left its physical and emotional imprint. Her own family circle and close friends have greatly influenced her attitude toward pregnancy and the challenges and responsibilities of motherhood. In a very real sense, prenatal care, negative or positive, has gone on in the life of a young woman long before she becomes pregnant. Today there is much controversy regarding the need for sex education, what should be taught by whom, and at what age level. Sex education and preparation for marriage and parenthood are taught—sometimes negatively by default. Children and young people do not live in a vacuum.

But enough philosophizing. What, in more detail, does formal prenatal care entail? Perhaps it would be easiest to describe the visits of the future mother to the physician's office. In most cases the most lengthy visit she makes is her first.

The first visit to the physician is usually a particular time of stress. Some women are very concerned because they want very much to be pregnant. Some are anxious about the nature of the examination and the tests to be made. Others may be concerned because they had not planned to have a child. Family financial problems may be mounting. A number of small children may already be part of the family, stairstep style, and the mother may feel for a while like the proverbial "old woman in the shoe." Health problems at home may cause worry. Previous unfortunate obstetrical experiences and half-believed gossip concerning pregnancy and childbirth may nag. The marriage may be undergoing a period of instability or even dissolution. All these possible situations tend to heighten the emotional content of the visit.

Setting and "climate"

The "climate" of the first as well as subsequent visits to the doctor is all important. A nurse who has the responsibility of greeting and caring for these patients has a key position. A cordial, respectful environment in which the patient feels personally important to the office staff and physician is a goal to be sought.

Preparation for the visit is usually made by a telephone call to the office. At this time it is customary for a new patient to be asked to bring a sample of the first voided urine on the day of the appointment if her visit will be made early in the morning. When the time of the appointment arrives, it is hoped that the prospective patient will not have to wait too long, but because of the very nature of a physician's practice, particularly one who must deal with the unscheduled flights of "Mr. Stork," some waiting is almost unavoidable. However, some of this time can often be put to excellent use. The nurse or receptionist can start to make contact with the patient and make her feel welcome. Brief information cards for office use may be completed. Frequently changed, attractive bulletin boards may emphasize good nutrition, available immunizations against disease, good grooming, maternity wardrobe styles, and approved courses for preparation for childbirth and child care. Up-to-date pamphlets on maternal and child care may also be available. Not all reading material should be pregnancy oriented, however. Just because a woman is pregnant does not mean that is all she wants to think about! When waits are protracted, an offer of coffee or fruit juice may be appreciated. The way to the public rest room should be clearly indicated, since frequent urination is an often encountered annoyance, and general nervousness will usually exaggerate this symptom. Just before the pelvic examination, the patient should have an opportunity to empty her bladder to ease the examination and to allow a more accurate measurement of the height of the fundus.

Vital signs and history

Before actually seeing the physician the patient is usually weighed and her temperature, pulse, and respiration checked by the nurse. In some clinics, nurses may also take the blood pressures and medical and

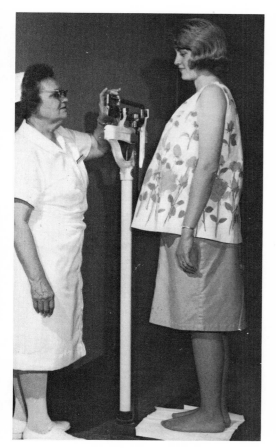

Fig. 9-1. Nurse weighing patient without shoes —every ounce off helps! (Courtesy Grossmont Hospital, La Mesa, Calif.)

obstetrical histories of new patients, but most practitioners prefer to complete the blood pressures and the histories themselves. A carefully secured history is very important in helping to determine any special emphasis needed in the care of the patient. What previous medical or surgical difficulties has she had? Any problems involving mental or emotional instability? Any family problems that may affect her toleration of the stress of pregnancy? The record of previous pregnancies, miscarriages, premature births, or full-term deliveries is extremely important as well as the history of current signs or symptoms. Many physicians believe the time spent is well worth the greater opportunity to evaluate the patient.

Pelvic examination

The visit usually continues with the determination of the presence of pregnancy. Each physician has his own routine, but it is our opinion that the pelvic examination should be done first in the schedule of the physical to alleviate the additional anxiety of waiting and avoid a filling bladder! The nurse, by her manner and efficiency, can help the patient immensely.

Preparation. An adequate gown, which gives reassuring coverage but opens in such a way to make a physical examination easily possible, is desirable. A drape that makes the patient feel covered even if she is not is a real aid. The hips should extend about 1 inch over the edge of the table with the feet supported in stirrups. Various drapes may be used. A nurse should always be present during the examination to give reassurance to the patient and protect the physician from criticism. Necessary instruments should be ready (Fig. 9-2): warmed speculum, spatula or applicator, and/or vaginal pipette with rubber bulb, slides and preservative for cervical cancer detection, long swabs or cotton balls, sponge sticks, both sterile and clean rubber gloves, lubricant, and paper tissue wipes. A good light and a convenient stool must be provided. If the patient is able to let her knees

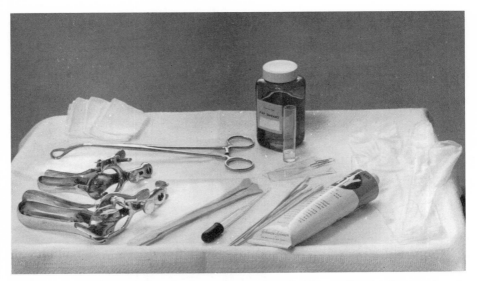

FIG. 9-2. Typical pelvic tray (sterile gloves are not shown). The small test tube contains physiological saline solution for wet mount of vaginal discharge.

fall outward and relax, the examination will be less difficult. Having her breathe through her open mouth usually helps promote relaxation, although there is some danger of hyperventilation in very tense patients.

Progression. The pelvic examination yields considerable information. The physician first inspects the external genitalia. Next, if a Papanicolaou smear for cancer detection is desired (and it is almost always part of the routine), a warmed, but unlubricated, bivalve speculum is inserted to reveal the cervix. Specimens of secretion may be aspirated from the posterior fornix with the pipette or secured with the applicator or spatula from the cervix and placed thinly and evenly on a slide or two. These slides must not be allowed to dry out but should immediately be placed in a fixative (usually equal parts of 95% alcohol and ether). The physician will then observe the cervix and vaginal mucosa for any abnormalities or unusual discharge. He may obtain specimens of any discharge for future study. Fungous infection caused by *Candida albicans* or infection initiated by microscopic animals, or protozoa, called *Trichomonas vaginalis* is fairly common.

The mucosa will be checked for Chadwick's sign, a violet tinge caused by increased circulatory congestion in the area.

After general inspection of the vulva, cervix, and vagina, the speculum will be gently removed and a digital examination will be made with the lubricated gloved hand. At this time the physician will feel the size and position of the uterus and perhaps try to elicit Hegar's sign, the softening of the uterine isthmus, through vaginoabdominal pressure. He will palpate the pelvic contents to try to identify any abnormal masses or tumors. Usually before completing his examination he will attempt to measure the *diagonal conjugate* to estimate the size of the pelvic canal and will evaluate the position of the ischial spines and tuberosities. In most cases, at the end of the vaginal examination a rectal examination is carried out. Most of the time the doctor can report at the end of the pelvic examination whether or not the patient is actually pregnant.

Determination of delivery date

The most common method of determining the date of delivery involves a record of the menstrual cycle. The patient is asked

Grossmont Hospital

Date 6/18/66

Gravida: II   Para: I

Age 26   Race Cauc   Religion Cath.

Occupation homemaker   Mar. Status M

PRESENT PREGNANCY ____ L.M.P. 4/21/66 E.D.C. 1/28/67

FAMILY HISTORY ____

A. MEDICAL (Tbc, Ca, Diabetes, etc.) ____
uncle has diabetes
parents L+W

B. OBSTETRICAL (Twins, Dystocia, etc.) ____
grandmother had twins

HUSBAND'S HEALTH asthma
PAST HISTORY Rubella, rubeola, mumps
no surg.

MENSTRUATION - Onset 13 ____ Interval 28 da.
Duration 5 da. Amt. mod. Pain 1st da.

✓ DRUG SENSITIVITY Phisohex ? ✳

TRANSFUSIONS none
PREVIOUS PREGNANCIES or Miscarriages:

Date	Term	Complications	Sex	Wt.	Labor
'65	FT	none	♂	7 30z	16 hrs.

PHYSICAL EXAM. - Ht. 5' 6½" Present Wt. (140)
Usual Wt. 135   Ideal Wt. 125
Gen. Appearance alert ____ Skin clear
EENT neg
Neck neg
Breasts neg
Heart neg   B.P. 128/84
Lungs clear
Abdomen neg.

Extremities slight varicosities - left leg
PELVIC EXAM: Outlet parous
Cervix Chadwick's
Uterus enlarged
Adnexae no masses.
I.S. ____ I.C. ____ I.T. ____ E.C. 20 B.T. ____ D.C. 12.5
Sacrum ____ Spines ____ Coccyx ____ Arch ____
P. S. adequate. Type Pelvis gynecoid

Address 3972 South Telford Ave S.D.
SPECIAL PROBLEMS ____
Anesth: Saddle
Pediatrician; Dr. Petersen
Nursing

QUICKENING: ____
LABORATORY: ____
Urinalysis neg.
Blood - Hgb 12   WBC ____ RBC Hct 40
Type O   Rh (negative)
Serology negative ____ Date 6/3/66
SPECIAL-(Smear, Cytology, B.T., C.T., etc.) ____
Pap. - neg.
X-RAY on file PHD 3/23/66

PRENATAL COURSE

Date	Wk	Wt	Urine	BP	Fundus	Pos	FHT	Remarks
6/18/66		140	0	128/84				
7/14/66		142	0	128/80				nausea
8/12/66		139	0	118/78	13			nausea
9/15/66		139	0	126/78	16		x	
10/3/66		144	0	124/80	20	LOT	x	water wt.

NOTES (Phone Calls, Medications, etc.) ____
Bendectin for nausea.

Examined by _G. B. Baldwin_   M.D.

Name—Last Merton	First Mary	Middle Ann.	Hospital No.
Location in Hospital	Clinic or Service	Attending Physician	

PRENATAL RECORD

FIG. 9-3. Sample prenatal form. (Courtesy Grossmont Hospital, La Mesa, Calif.)

to name the *first* day of her last *normal* menstrual period. The doctor then counts back 3 months and adds 7 days to calculate the estimated date of confinement (EDC). (Confinement is a rather old term used to indicate the period of labor and delivery.) For example, if a patient said that her last normal menstrual period occurred between May 7 and May 12, 1971, her EDC would be February 14, 1972. This method of calculation is called Nägele's rule. Of course, if the patient cannot remember the vital statistics involved, calculation may be more difficult. In that case, the size of the uterus may be interpreted, or the time of the intercourse that preceded conception may be known. Occasionally, *quickening* may be used as a measurable landmark, but it is not too reliable. However, even Nägele's rule offers only an estimation. It is said that only 4% of all babies arrive "on time" using this schedule, whereas 60% appear 1 to 7 days early or late.

Complete examination (Fig. 9-3)

The first prenatal visit to the physician may continue with a complete physical examination, or the physician may only talk with the patient, giving appropriate guidance and information, and making arrangements for a more detailed physical examination during the following visit.

The physician is interested in much more than his patient's pelvis. He checks her blood pressure; listens to her heart and lungs; examines her mouth, eyes, ears, nose, and throat; observes and palpates her breasts, alert to any abnormalities; and perhaps inquires about her preference for feeding the infant. The abdomen is palpated with the knees flexed for greater relaxation of the abdominal wall, and the extremities are checked for bruises, swelling, and enlarged veins.

At the conclusion of the physical examination, arrangements are made for the necessary laboratory and x-ray tests. A pelvic x-ray examination is not ordered because of danger of harm to the young developing child, but a chest x-ray film may be in order

to rule out chest diseases. A sample of venous blood is drawn. A complete blood count may be ordered or perhaps only a hematocrit to determine the amount of hemoglobin present in the blood in relation to its volume. A pregnant woman may be or may become anemic. A serology test for the detection of syphilis is performed. A determination of main blood group and Rh status is made. The urine specimen brought in the same morning or secured later at the office is tested for albumin and sugar. Many physicians order a complete urinalysis initially.

Guidance

After all these procedures have been completed, if they take place during one visit, the patient is usually tired. Long-winded instructions and explanations are not properly assimilated. Perhaps the best method of imparting needed information is through the use of some kind of prenatal instruction booklet that has been approved by or perhaps even written by the patient's doctor. Some doctors program a series of teaching films that individuals or groups can view while they are waiting to see him. Such guidance is absolutely necessary, but all of it need not come the first visit. However, some time should be spent answering questions that have been bothering the patient and giving some general instructions regarding dietary requirements, weight reduction, if needed, and the situations that should be reported to the doctor.

Reportable signs and symptoms

The physician should indicate the signs and symptoms that must be reported in a manner that will not be too alarming to the patient. They may or may not be significant, but only the physician is capable of deciding their importance, and he must be notified of their presence. They include the following:
1. Bleeding from the vagina at any time
2. Uncontrollable leaking of fluid from the vagina
3. Unusual abdominal pain or cramps

4. Persistent nausea or vomiting, especially in the second or third trimester
5. Persistent headache or any blurring of vision
6. Marked swelling of the ankles and especially of the hands and face
7. Painful or burning urination
8. Chills or fever

Then, armed with information, the patient may make an appointment for her next visit. Before her return she can jot down questions that come up about which she needs to be reassured.

Subsequent visits

During the first half of the pregnancy, expectant mothers most often visit their doctors every 3 or 4 weeks unless special needs become apparent. After 5 months, visits are usually scheduled every 2 or 3 weeks, and in the last month, checkups may be made every 1 or 2 weeks or more often.

Examination

The subsequent visits are not as long or involved. The patient is weighed by the nurse, and a urine specimen is checked for albumin and sugar. The blood pressure is recorded. These tests may reveal the beginnings of toxemia of pregnancy or diabetes mellitus. (Remember that the major signs of toxemia are elevated blood pressure, edema, excessive weight gain, and albuminuria.) The physician measures the height of the uterus to see if the pregnancy is progressing at the expected rate. He may repeat the pelvic examination during the first return visit. After about 4½ calendar months' gestation he may listen for the fetal heart tone. After 8 months' gestation he may palpate the abdomen to determine the presentation of the fetus. At about the same time, another hemoglobin determination is made to check for developing anemia. If Rh incompatibility is a possibility, an occasional Rh antibody titer may be run to check for a rising rate of antibodies in the mother's system. This may indicate whether the baby is Rh positive and alert the doctor to developing erythroblastosis fetalis. A newer, more reliable technique is the aspiration and analysis of amniotic fluid.

Guidance

During the initial and return visits a feeling of trust should be built up between the patient and the physician and his staff. The physician and nurse should be able to identify areas in which the expectant mother needs special help, whether it involves need for information, reassurance in her own capacity to be a good mother, possible help in organizing her household to achieve more rest and peace of mind, or simply provision for an interested human listener.

Nutrition. The area of guidance is large in prenatal care. Diet has already been mentioned, and it is of basic importance. Even in our supermarket economy malnutrition could be a real problem. The issue in most cases is not one of availability but of selection and, we might add, discretion. Good nutrition, with special attention to protein intake, helps prevent miscarriages and obstetrical complications.

To help all persons, not just pregnant women, eat wisely the National Dairy Council has described four basic food groups. If the diet selection for a day contains servings from each of the four groupings as indicated, the diet is balanced. These four groupings are illustrated in Fig. 9-4: milk, meat, vegetables and fruits, and breads and cereals.

Good dietary habits established in childhood aid the future mother to produce more healthy offspring and avoid obstetrical problems related to malnutrition.

Milk (and the calcium and protein it provides) is considered by most authorities as an important constituent of the expectant mother's diet. Diets in the last half of pregnancy should usually include a daily milk intake of 1 quart (either skimmed or whole). However, not all this requirement has to be taken without modification. The woman who does not care for milk per se is free to use flavoring, make what she does drink more concentrated in value through the addition of skim milk powders, use it in cooking for custards and puddings (but watch the calories!), or select a milk exchange of approximate equal value for calcium. For example, 1 slice of American cheese or 1 cup of creamed cottage cheese equals ⅔ glass of milk. If she cannot tolerate milk or is having muscle cramps due to phosphorus/calcium imbalance in the blood, calcium pills may be given, but in this case a fine, relatively inexpensive source of pro-

FIG. 9-4. A guide to good eating. (Courtesy National Dairy Council, Chicago, Ill.)

tein is lost. Milk is also usually reinforced with vitamin D, an important consideration in climates lacking sunshine.

Eggs are recommended particularly for the rich iron source found in the yolk. One or two per day, prepared either singly or in cooking, are advised. Although it may not be everybody's favorite, liver is also strongly favored in the diet because its high iron content is so important in preventing anemia.

Fruits and vegetables are important sources of vitamins, minerals, and roughage (if they are eaten unmodified). Constipation is a real problem for many pregnant women, and the use of bulk-producing foods, including whole grain breads and cereals, usually helps solve the problem. A high vitamin C (ascorbic acid) intake is advised for tissue building; the fruits especially helpful are grapefruit, oranges, lemons, limes, tomatoes, strawberries, cantaloupes, green peppers, and cabbage. Two servings a day of fruits in raw, cooked, or juice forms are recommended. Two portions of vegetables, emphasizing especially green and yellow types, are considered optimum.

Foods that contribute only calories are to be avoided. Sugar is a prime example. Foods high in sodium are not to be emphasized, since the sodium may help retain fluid in the tissues, causing edema. Ordinary table salt (sodium chloride) is the most common offender, so foods such as popcorn and potato chips are not desirable. Sodium may show up in unexpected places, and the pregnant woman having weight problems must be cautioned about the use of flavor heighteners containing monosodium glutamate and commonly used antacids for heartburn. In some cases the physician may want to limit sodium intake quite carefully; special printed diets from the Heart Association or of his own devising may be used.

In addition to dietary counseling, many physicians prescribe vitamin and mineral supplements to be taken in pill or capsule form. A few are adding fluoride to the list in an effort to help the fetus build decay-resistant teeth. The efficacy of this addition has not been proved.

Weight gain. The nutritional needs of pregnant women are similar in quality but, depending on their height, bony structure, and activity, may differ widely in quantity and caloric count. A woman's ideal weight as determined by her physician may even dictate that she lose weight during her pregnancy. If her weight is not too far from ideal, the average woman should aim at a gain of about 15 to 20 pounds. A bit more may be allowed if she is quite tall. If she gains more, her baby will not be appreciably bigger, but she may have a hard time regaining her figure after pregnancy. She will be more likely to develop backaches, more frequently have cardiovascular and toxemic complications, and perhaps experience a more trying labor. Normal weight gain averages about ½ pound a week after the first trimester and almost ¾ pound per week in the last 3 months. Any sudden weight increase should be suspected as a sign of developing toxemia or pre-eclampsia.

Smoking and alcohol. Mothers who smoke frequently bear smaller infants than do nonsmokers. However, there is no evidence that the low birth weight associated with smoking diminishes the infant's chance for survival. Other possible effects have not been sufficiently studied. Nevertheless, excessive smoking (more than 10 cigarettes per day) is discouraged. Of course, from the perspective of general maternal health, smoking is strongly suspect. Patients should be encouraged to decrease or stop the habit. The moderate use of alcohol, in itself, has not been associated with any known detrimental effects on the course of pregnancy or the health of the fetus.

General hygiene. There is more to good prenatal guidance than the question of diet. The mother-to-be will undoubtedly have questions regarding many other subjects. Sometimes she wants information regarding general hygiene—the need for rest, relaxation, and exercise. Pregnant women need to conserve their resources by getting adequate rest. They may not want to actually nap in the morning and afternoon, but at least they can sit down and put their feet up! Walking outdoors is wonderful exercise, available to all, but often neglected. Golfing, bowling, dancing, and even swimming, when not done to the point of fatigue, are fine. The more strenuous sports, however, are best left until the baby has been born and mother has had her 6 weeks' postpartum checkup.

Bathing. A woman is likely to perspire profusely during pregnancy, and frequent baths and showers are needed. Bathing may become a probelm in late pregnancy because of the woman's awkwardness, and great care must be taken that she not fall. Some physicans recommend that tub baths not be taken during the last months for this reason and that only sponge baths be used. Some have also forbidden tub baths late in pregnancy because of the possibility of infecting the vaginal tract and uterus. Most now consider this possibility highly unlikely.

Hair may need special attention because of the increased activity of the oil glands of the scalp. A permanent, if desired, will "take" during pregnancy.

Preparation for nursing. If the woman is planning to nurse her baby, the physician may advise certain routines to prepare her breasts for lactation. If she has inverted or flat nipples, the physician may prescribe the use of a manual breast pump or teach finger compression of the breast to draw out the nipple to make it easier for the newborn infant to grasp. He may advocate the expression of colostrum, the early breast secretion, in the last trimester of pregnancy to encourage milk production, help prevent engorgement, and toughen the nipples.

Some pregnant women, especially primigravidae, develop rather prominent pink stretch marks called striae on the abdomen and breasts because of the relatively sudden weight gain. Some people think that they are not so prominent if cocoa butter is applied to the skin. Certainly it does not hurt to use it if one does not object to the odor. These lines usually retract greatly after pregnancy and become scarcely noticeable.

Wardrobe. Never before has a mother-to-be had an opportunity for such an attractive, versatile wardrobe as today, and since maternity patterns are also available in the fabric stores, attractive clothing need not be expensive. Some of the styles and materials are so chic that nonpregnant window-shoppers have been heard to exclaim, "Oh! I forgot this store has maternity fashions only!" Maternity clothes should be lightweight, nonconstrictive, adjustable, and absorbent and should also provide a boost to the morale.

Probably more important physiologically than a cute dress or suit, however, are adequate, supportive underclothes. It is espe-

FIG. 9-5. Pregnancy may be in fashion! Many attractive outfits are available.

cially important that the pregnant woman have good breast support to prevent fatigue and maintain a good figure. She will not be able to go through her entire pregnancy with the same size brassiere! If she plans to breast-feed her baby, nursing bras are a fine investment. A maternity corset is not always advised. The tendency in the last few years is to counsel its use only for older multiparae if needed. Primigravidae and younger multiparae are usually told to practice certain exercises during pregnancy (especially the "pelvic rock, or tilt") that will improve posture and strengthen muscles. However, a light maternity girdle may be used with satisfaction. Specially designed garter belts are available. No constrictive round garters should be used because of interference in the blood's circulation from the legs.

If a woman has been accustomed to wearing high-heeled shoes, it will probably be difficult for her to suddenly descend to fairly flat heels. However, as pregnancy progresses and her center of gravity moves forward, she will find lower heels much less awkward and more flattering to her total silhouette. She will want to avoid shoe styles with ties or buckles, since toward the end of her 260 plus days of waiting, tying shoes will not be easy.

Dental care. The old saying "for every child a tooth" is not true. But it is a good plan for the pregnant woman to have a dental checkup early in pregnancy so that plenty of time is available for any needed repairs. Dentists do not like to work on women who appear to have stopped by on their way to the hospital!

Douching. Most women wonder whether they should douche or not. Normal vaginal secretions are usually intensified during pregnancy. Many physicians believe that douching should not be done routinely but only for a specific condition with a low-pressure fountain syringe, gently introduced. The individual preference of the physician concerning the specific patient should be ascertained.

Employment. Many pregnant women are employed. Whether they continue their employment and for how long depends on several factors, one of which is the type of work in which they are engaged (heavy lifting, exposure to potential hazards of radiation or chemicals, or long hours of standing without relief). The employment of pregnant women in certain occupations is often restricted by state law, policies of the individual employer (dependent on his insurance coverage, previous experience, etc.), and the health of the employee (whether she is experiencing any complications).

Travel. Sometimes the question of travel presents itself. If a trip can be so arranged, it is best to travel during the middle trimester, since the danger of abortion is not so great and the threat of premature or unprepared-for deliveries is at a minimum. If trips must be made by car, they should allow for adequate rest stops and should be carefully paced. Most airlines require a doctor's certificate before allowing passengers pregnant 8 months or more to board.

Marital relations. Physicians routinely advise their patients regarding marital relations during pregnancy. Many counsel that intercourse be suspended during the first trimester (3 months) at the time when the menstrual period would have taken place if pregnancy had not intervened because of the increased danger of abortion at this time. If abortion has been a problem in the past, further restrictions may be advised. Sexual intercourse should also be eliminated during the last 5 weeks of pregnancy because of possible infection, bleeding, and premature labor.

Community education resources. In many communities, classes are offered to help expectant parents prepare for the changes pregnancy and parenthood will bring. They may be sponsored by the American National Red Cross, YWCA, public health departments, adult education programs, hospitals, or groups of physicians. Participation in such approved groups is recommended, especially for primigravidae. Some classes concentrate on imparting an understanding of the basic anatomy and physiology of

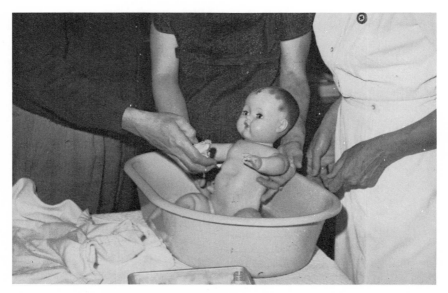

FIG. 9-6. The Red Cross nurse is instructing future parents about the importance of a good grasp on baby in the bathtub. The baby's head should be supported by the mother's forearm and his body stabilized by a firm finger hold of his far axilla and upper arm. (Courtesy American National Red Cross, San Diego Chapter.)

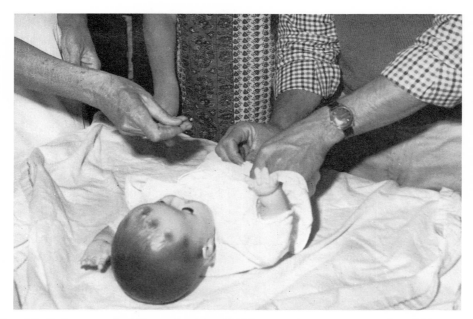

FIG. 9-7. Father must be able to do this too! (Courtesy American National Red Cross, San Diego Chapter.)

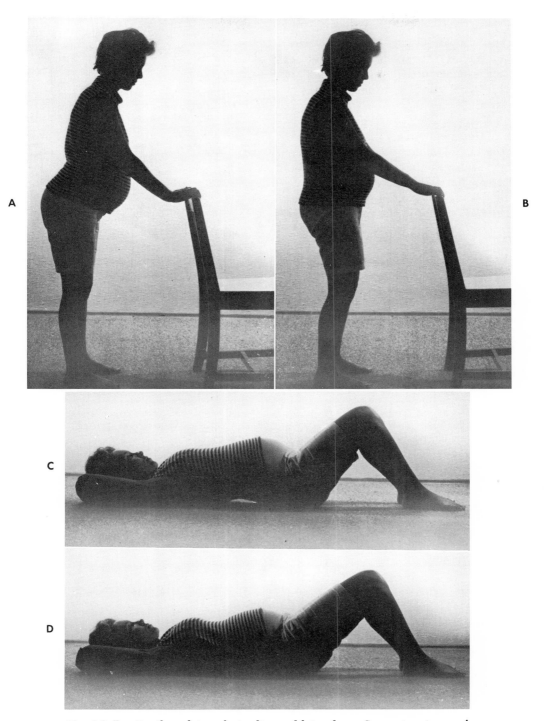

Fig. 9-8. Practice the pelvic rock standing and lying down. See posture improve!

reproduction; what to expect during the "waiting months"; what occurs during labor and delivery; how to prepare for baby—nursery, layette; how to bathe the newborn infant (Fig. 9-6); and how to prepare an artificial formula. Others emphasize exercises in training the body and mind for peak performance during pregnancy, labor, and childbirth and are usually led by a physical therapist especially interested in techniques promoting good posture, relaxation, and economy of effort (for example, the Lamaze technique, p. 131). In our opinion they are helpful to the expectant mother no matter what her preference may be regarding the use of analgesics or anesthetics.

Suggested exercises. Examples of four exercises often practiced at such sessions are included here because they have been found so helpful. These particular exercises are some of those described and outlined by Dr. John Seldon Miller in his very delightful and helpful *Childbirth, a Manual for Pregnancy and Delivery.* The following information is directly quoted from his instructions to the mothers-to-be:

Pelvic Rock. This is the most important exercise for comfort during pregnancy. It increases the flexibility of the lower back, strengthens the abdominal muscles, and shifts your center of gravity back toward your spine. It relieves backache, improves posture, and improves your appearance in late pregnancy tremendously. It should be practiced daily as an exercise, and in addition, once learned, you should always walk and stand with the pelvis tilted forward, thus providing your baby with a cradle of bone in which to lie. Then he won't be supported by your abdominal wall nearly so much with resulting and ever increasing stretching. . . . If you will learn this, you will not need a corset to support a sagging abdominal wall and a tired back. [See Fig. 9-8.]

First practice lying on your back, knees bent, feet flat on floor. You may put a small pillow under your head.

A. Tighten lower abdominal muscles and muscles of the buttocks. This will cause tailbone to be elevated, small of back pressed into floor. Do not lift buttocks off floor.

B. Relax abdominal and buttock muscles. As you do this, arch your back as high as you can.

C. Again tighten abdominal and buttock muscles, being sure that the small of your back presses tightly into the floor, your back becoming a straight line.

D. Do this five or six times daily. Do it before getting out of bed in the morning if your back feels stiff when you awaken.

Then practice it on your hands and knees, hands directly under the shoulders, knees under the hips.

A. Contract abdominal and buttock muscles and at the same time hump your back up as far as possible. Bend head down.

B. Slowly relax abdominal and buttock muscles and let yourself sag through the middle as you lift your head.

C. Repeat five or six times slowly.

Then practice it standing up.

A. Stand about 2 feet away from the back of a chair or other prop that is level with your hips.

B. Bend slightly forward from the hips, placing hands on chair back, elbows straight.

C. Rotate hips backward and sag with your abdominal muscles creating a real "sway back."

D. "Unlock" your knees, flexing them ever so slightly.

E. Slowly rotate hips forward, tucking buttocks under as if someone were pushing your buttocks from behind. In this position your pelvic cradle will be parallel to the floor.

F. After doing this three times, stand erect with buttocks tucked in, knees slightly flexed, arms

---

FIG. 9-9. Top: Layette possibilities. Types of diapers or related equipment. **A,** Large, colored, checked gauze diaper; **B,** waterproof lap pads (puddle pads); **C,** large white cotton diaper for wrap-around style using no pins for newborn infant; **D,** cotton diaper folded in kite style; **E,** "soaker" used for transition from diapers to training panties; **F,** snap diapers need no pins but may not fit as well; **G,** bird's-eye diaper—prefold style; **H,** reinforced contour diaper, often used in hospital newborn infant nurseries; **I,** plastic diaper holder—diaper folded into a thick rectangle and placed under two plastic strips; **J,** cotton prefold diaper opened out. (*Note:* Little boys need the diaper thickness in front, little girls in back.)

Bottom: There are a variety of disposable diapers on the market, which can be used with or without pins and with or without plastic overpants.

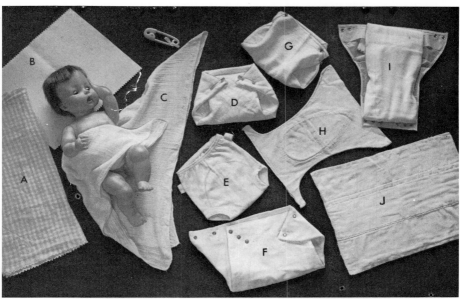

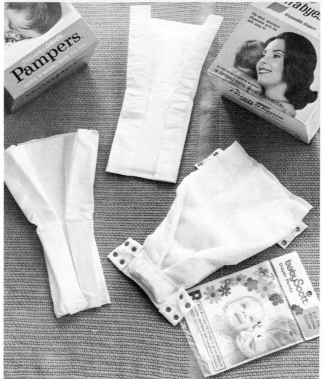

FIG. 9-9. For legend see opposite page.

at side, chest high. This is the ideal position for standing and walking, especially during the latter part of pregnancy. . . .

Abdominal Breathing. This type of breathing utilizes the diaphragm primarily to the exclusion of the chest muscles. It is the type of breathing singers use for perfect control and will be very helpful during the first half of labor. When you breathe with your diaphragm the abdominal muscles automatically relax, thus allowing the uterus to rise during contractions without tension against the tight abdominal wall. You may practice lying down, standing or sitting.

A. Place hands on abdomen.

B. As you inhale, elevate the abdominal wall. Expand your abdomen as far as you can.

C. As you exhale, allow the abdominal muscles to go down slowly.

D. Inhalation and exhalation should be of the same length. The chest should be completely still during the abdominal breathing.

E. Work toward breathing as slowly as possible— a slow, rhythmic inhalation and exhalation.

F. As you become more adept at this type of breathing, it will require less effort for you to expand your abdomen during inhalation.

This type of breathing, together with total relaxation, will often carry you through most of the first stage of labor. When it is no longer possible or effective in keeping you comfortable, you will switch to high chest breathing. This minimizes motion of the diaphragm and abdominal muscles.

High Chest Breathing.

A. Place hands on lower part of rib cage.

B. Inhale and exhale completely.

C. Start rhythmic, shallow breathing at a very rapid rate, approximately 100 breaths per minute. It may be helpful to punctuate this breathing pattern, at intervals, with a deep breath and continue shallow breathing. End by inhaling and exhaling completely.

D. Practice breathing for a minute at a time. Remember, it is very important to concentrate your attention on the chest and breathing rapidly, while simultaneously maintaining a high degree of total body relaxation.

Panting. You will pant during the actual delivery of your baby, letting the uterus do the work. This will prevent you from injuring yourself and it is probably better for your baby, too. Furthermore, if the baby's head is very low during the late first stage of labor, sometimes your urge to push prematurely becomes very great. Only by panting in this circumstance can you keep from pushing. Your doctor will of course instruct you as to when it is all right to push and when it is best to pant. As simple as panting seems to be, you should practice.

A. Place hands on breastbone.

B. Open mouth, allowing jaw to hang loosely.

C. Pant, making the breastbone move up and down. Pant slowly, deeply, and rhythmically.

D. Practice for 45 seconds at a time, at least once a day.*

The layettte. Provided finances are not too strained, preparing the layette for the new baby can be one of the most pleasurable duties of the expectant mother. For first timers, baby showers may also help in this regard but are not dependable. Contributors at such affairs should be told that the baby will grow and perhaps half the group, if it is sizable, could purchase basic clothes for the 1- to 2-year-old child. If the baby is not a "firstborn," then there probably will be considerable infant clothes left over from the last time. Babies usually do not wear out their clothes, but they do grow out of them.

A basic layette (Figs. 9-9 to 9-12), at least enough to start with, consists of the following items:

1. Six cotton shirts, short or long sleeves, depending on the weather (Stretch shirts cost more but can be worn by baby longer. Long sleeved shirts can have a fold-over cuff enclosing the hands rather than the string tie. To purchase a 3-month size is a waste of money.)

2. Four dozen cotton gauze, bird's eye or flannelette diapers if diaper service is not used; 1 dozen, if it is, or disposable diapers may be purchased (Disposable soft paper diaper liners are often favored.)

3. Two or three plastic diaper covers, to be used only if baby does not have any skin irritation

4. Four or five long gowns, opening down the front with grip fasteners

5. Two or three sweaters with no more than 10% wool content to prevent allergic skin rash

6. Three or four soft, light receiving blankets

---

*From Miller, J. S.: Childbirth, a manual for pregnancy and delivery, New York, 1963, Atheneum Publishers.

FIG. 9-10. Layette possibilities. Types of shirts and plastic diaper covers.

FIG. 9-11. Layette possibilities. **A,** Terry cloth matched set (shirt top, diaper cover, and cap); **B,** long gown or kimono; **C,** flannel matched set (shirt top, diaper cover, and bib); **D,** shortie gown; **E,** sacque.

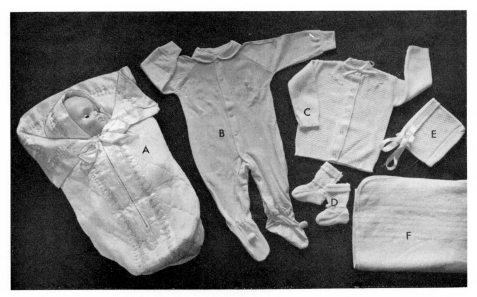

FIG. 9-12. Layette possibilities. **A,** Bunting; **B,** cotton knit one-piece suit; **C** to **E,** cotton knit sweater, cap, and booties; **F,** flannel receiving blanket.

7. One square heavy blanket for use outdoors
8. One cap
9. Booties if it is cold
10. One bunting if in a climate requiring such protection (The tendency is to overdress rather than underdress infants.)
11. Two or three waterproof squares for protecting surfaces from baby
12. Two washcloths used just for baby
13. Six cotton sheets, two crib blankets

Basic furniture needed includes a bed (a bassinet, although pretty, is unnecessary), a firm mattress, and cover. No pillow should be used because of the danger of suffocation. Some type of chest of drawers for storage, a covered diaper pail, and a large plastic tub or, if preferred, a canvas bathinette (this, too, is a frill) will be needed. A bath tray is a great convenience, but it does not have to be expensive. Any clean tray will do. On it should be a jar of cotton balls, a jar of safety pins, a mild soap and dish, a supply of baby oil or lotion, a box of paper tissues, and perhaps baby powder. But remember, baby lotion and powder are not to be used together, and powder should be used sparingly!

Even if baby is to be nursed, there should be equipment in the home for preparing artificial feedings, if necessary. In most cases, this means six 8-ounce formula bottles, nipples, a bottle brush, a bottle sterilizer or a large pan with a lid in which the bottles will stand upright, a quart measuring cup, measuring spoons, kitchen tongs, can opener, and funnel. Do not forget that mothers can often borrow such equipment.

There are many things on the market for baby, but many of those cute eye-catching gadgets and extras require money better spent elsewhere.

What to take to the hospital. There are other things the mother should have ready before that "special date" comes due. She should consider what she will take to the hospital with her. Usually, the following list suffices:

Two nightgowns (the short type is preferred)

Robe

Slippers

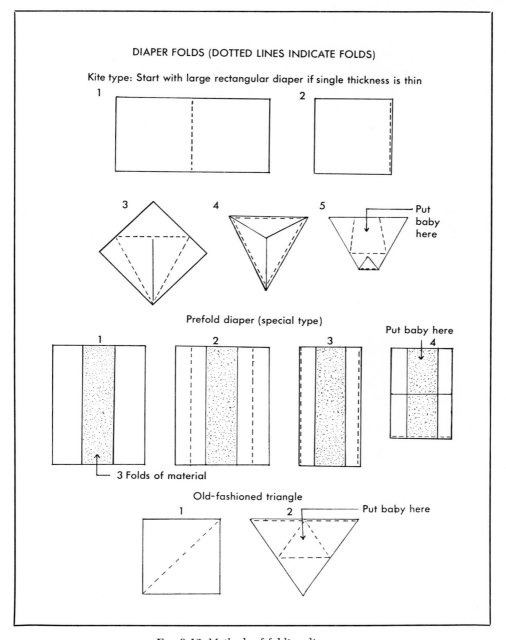

FIG. 9-13. Methods of folding diapers.

Two brassieres (nursing type if breast feeding)

One sanitary belt

Toothbrush, dentifrice, brush, comb, cosmetics, and hairpins

Deodorant

Shower cap

A good book

Writing materials, stamps, birth announcements, checkbook or cash for deposit at hospital, and insurance identification if applicable

"Going home" things for baby may be brought to the hospital later.

UNIT III
THE PERIOD OF GESTATION

Perspective

The period of pregnancy is a creative, productive period in a woman's life from many points of view. It should be a happy, truly expectant interval. But how a woman reacts to the challenge of pregnancy will be, in the main, determined by her basic emotional maturity or want of it. The doctor, the nurses, the clergy, and members of the community health agencies have an opportunity to help a patient mature in the understanding of herself and her role in life at this crucial time. If they help her, they are also helping the generation to come.

UNIT III

**SUGGESTED SELECTED READINGS
AND REFERENCES**

Apgar, V.: What every mother-to-be should know, Today's Health, 44:35, 77, Jan.-Feb., 1966.

Beebe, J. E., Pendleton, E. M., and King, E.: Bench conferences in a large obstetrical clinic, Amer. J. Nurs. 68:85-87, Jan., 1968.

Bookmiller, M. M., and Bowen, G. L.: Textbook of obstetrics and obstetric nursing, ed. 5, Philadelphia, 1967, W. B. Saunders Co.

Davis, M. E., and Rubin, R.: DeLee's obstetrics for nurses, ed. 18, Philadelphia, 1966, W. B. Saunders Co.

Druckemiller, S. D.: Order out of chaos, Amer. J. Nurs. 71:109-113, Jan., 1971.

Edwards, J.: Patient-oriented maternity nursing, Hosp. Top. 48:83, March, 1970.

Elliott, J. M.: Pica and pregnancy, Nurs. Clin. N. Amer. 3:299-305, June, 1968.

Fitzpatrick, E., Eastmen, N. J., and Reeder, S. R.: Maternity nursing, ed. 11, Philadelphia, 1966, J. B. Lippincott Co.

Gadpaille, W. J.: Is there a "too soon," Today's Health 48:34+, Feb., 1970.

Goodheart, B.: Sex in the schools: education or titillation? Today's Health 48:28+, Feb., 1970.

Ingelman-Sundberg, A., and Wirsen, C.: A child is born, New York, 1966, Delacorte Press.

Lerch, C.: Maternity nursing, St. Louis, 1970, The C. V. Mosby Co.

Linde, S. M.: Common problems of pregnancy . . . and what to do about them, Today's Health 46:50+, April, 1968.

Maternity Center Association: A baby is born, ed. 2, New York, 1960, The Association.

Michaelson, M.: In search of sanity: man in the middle, Today's Health 48:31+, Feb., 1970 (about sex education).

Miller, J. S.: Childbirth, a manual for pregnancy and delivery, New York, 1963, Atheneum Publishers.

Rubin, R.: Cognitive style in pregnancy, Amer. J. Nurs. 70:502-508, March, 1970.

Stone, A. R.: Cues to interpersonal distress due to pregnancy, Amer. J. Nurs. 65:88-91, Nov., 1965.

UNIT IV

PARTURITION

10

Presentations, positions, and progress

The relationship of the fetus to the obstetrical passageway is of great interest to both doctor and nurse. It will usually influence the length of labor, the preparation of the delivery room, and the type of complications possibly encountered.

Some common words are used in special ways to describe this relationship. For instance, in obstetrics one refers to the following terms: presentation, attitude, position, station, effacement, and show.

Presentation

The *presentation*, or *lie*, means the relationship of the length of the fetus to the length of the uterus. If the fetus is lying so that either the head, buttocks, or feet may be found just above or within the true pelvis, its presentation may be called longitudinal. If, instead, the body lies crosswise in the uterus, the term "transverse lie" may be used. A baby in transverse lie cannot be delivered vaginally without manipulation to a longitudinal presentation. At present, he may be delivered abdominally, since fetal manipulation or version is not always preferred or practiced with the increasing safety of the so-called cesarean section. Many times the term "presentation" is used synonymously with the phrase *presenting part*, that part of the baby which is coming through or attempting to come through

the pelvic canal first. Headfirst placement is referred to as a cephalic presentation. Feet or buttocks first is termed "breech." Approximately 96% of all deliveries are headfirst, or cephalic. About 3.5% are breech. Transverse presentations account for the remaining percentage. Presentation may be determined by abdominal palpation and rectal, vaginal, and x-ray examinations.

Attitude

The *attitude* refers to the degree of flexion of the body, head (Fig. 10-1), and extremities. The normal attitude is complete flexion. A well-flexed head presents the smallest cephalic diameter and fewer mechanical problems in descent and delivery. This "chin-on-chest" posture makes possible the *vertex* delivery so desired.

Position (Figs. 10-3 to 10-5)

The *position* technically is the relationship between a predetermined "point of reference or direction" on the presenting part of the fetus to the pelvic quadrants *of the mother*. It gives more detailed information about the fetus's progress through the pelvic canal as it seeks to adapt to the changing "topography." The maternal pelvic quadrants are identified as right and left posterior and right and left anterior (Fig. 10-2). They never change location, although the different perspectives from which they are viewed in illustrations and diagrams sometimes confuse the student. Sometimes the quadrants are seen from "below," that is, as they appear to the physician in front of the delivery table ready to receive the baby. Sometimes they are viewed from "above," from the vantage point of the unborn child entering the true pelvis. In some other diagrams, students miraculously look directly through the abdominal wall to view the fetus within the canal. The point of reference, of course, will vary according to the presenting part discussed and the amount of flexion present. In the event of a well-flexed cephalic or vertex presentation the point of reference employed is the occipital bone, or

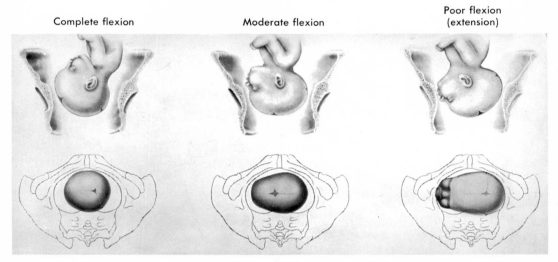

Complete flexion   Moderate flexion   Poor flexion (extension)

FIG. 10-1. Head diameters in various degrees of flexion. (From Phenomena of normal labor, Columbus, Ohio, 1964, Ross Laboratories, Publisher.)

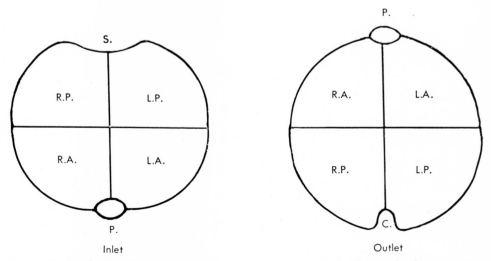

Inlet   Outlet

FIG. 10-2. Maternal pelvic quadrants stay the same; however, the student's perspective may change! C, Coccyx; P, pubic bone; S, sacrum.

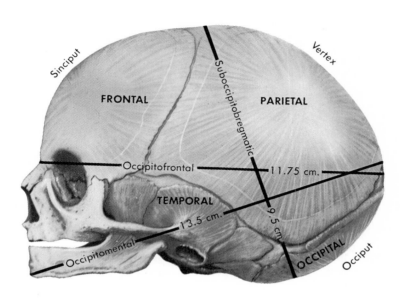

THE FETAL HEAD

Bones
    Frontal—2
    Parietal—2
    Temporal—2
    Occipital—1

Sutures
    Sagittal
    Frontal
    Coronal
    Lambdoid

Fontanels
    Anterior
    Posterior

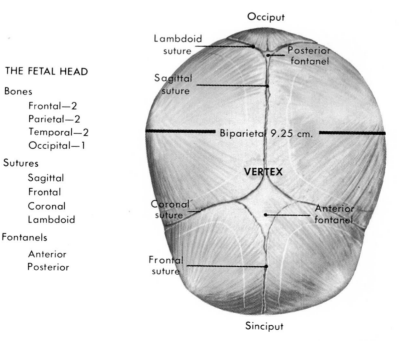

FIG. 10-3. Fetal head—physician's map. (From Phenomena of normal labor, Columbus, Ohio, 1964, Ross Laboratories, Publisher.)

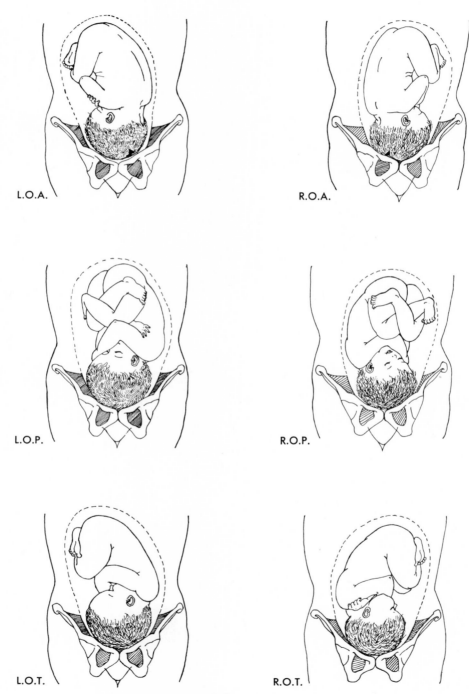

Fig. 10-4. Cephalic positions—vertex type.

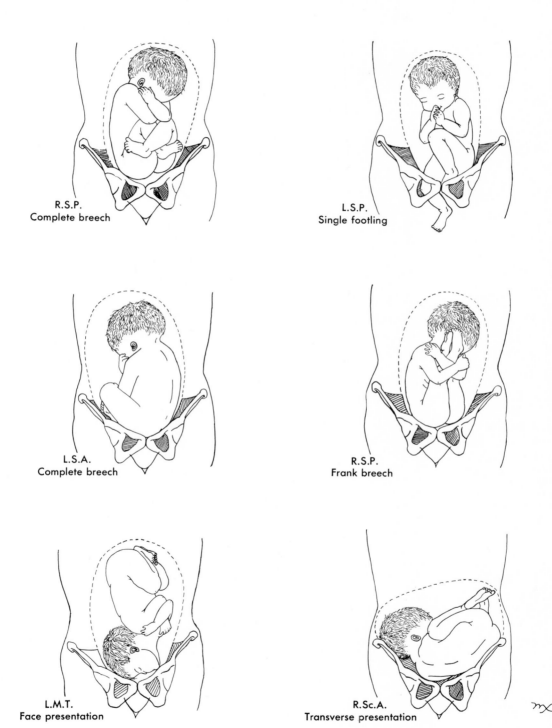

R.S.P.
Complete breech

L.S.P.
Single footling

L.S.A.
Complete breech

R.S.P.
Frank breech

L.M.T.
Face presentation

R.Sc.A.
Transverse presentation

FIG. 10-5. Various presentations and positions.

occiput. It is the most accessible to rectal or vaginal examination and identification. The vault of the fetal skull is made up of three paired bones and one single bone separated by tough but softer membranous seams, or sutures. It is fairly easy to follow these sutures with a gloved finger after sufficient cervical dilatation has occurred and determine the placement of the occiput. The sutures trace a Y, and the occiput is found between the top shafts of the Y just in back of the triangular posterior fontanel.

To simplify reference to the various positions possible, the descriptive phrase usually begins with either right or left followed by the point of reference used and the adjectives anterior, posterior, or transverse. Thus we refer to the most common vertex position as "left occiput anterior" or, shortcutting further, L.O.A. Each presenting part has the possibility of eight positions following the same pattern. Only the middle initial or code letters representing the point of reference need be changed. For example:

1. Right occiput* anterior   R.O.A.
2. Left occiput anterior   L.O.A.
3. Right occiput posterior   R.O.P.
4. Left occiput posterior   L.O.P.
5. Right occiput transverse   R.O.T.
6. Left occiput transverse   L.O.T.
7. Occiput at sacrum   O.S.
    Occiput posterior   O.P.
8. Occiput at the pubis   ⎫
    Occiput anterior   ⎬   O.A.
                   ⎭

Note that a transverse position is *not* the same thing as a transverse presentation, or lie. The letter "O" is usually employed only in the case of well-flexed or median vertex presentations (military). In the rare cases of cephalic presentations demonstrating more deflexion, other points of reference must be sought, since the occiput is no longer available or meaningful to the examiner. In a brow presentation, the letter "F" for fronto is used, referring to the area of the anterior fontanel. Brow presentations

---

*Sometimes the combining form "occipito" is used instead of the noun occiput.

are usually slow and difficult because of the increased diameter of the skull trying to force its way through the passageway. A cesarean section may be the procedure of choice. In cases of full extension of the head resulting in a face presentation, the letter "M" for mentum, or chin, is seen. Face presentations, although slow, usually terminate satisfactorily without intervention. The nursery nurse, however, will admit to her area a small person whose remarkable but temporary facial edema and distortion proclaim to all the staff his unorthodox entry into our world.

Breech presentations employ the sacrum or coccyx as a point of reference and the code letter "S." Breech presentations, of course, are varied. A complete, or full, breech in which the fetus sits tailor fashion with legs crossed is probably the most desirable obstetrically because there is less danger of prolapse of the umbilical cord and more consistent dilatation of the cervical canal. There are three varieties of the so-called incomplete breech. An incomplete breech may be *frank*, with the thighs flexed on the abdomen and the feet up against the face (sort of a foot-in-the-mouth posture), or it may involve one or both legs extended and presenting vaginally. These latter positions are termed *single* and *double footlings*, respectively.

A transverse lie, sometimes called a shoulder presentation, usually employs the scapula for reference with "Sc" as the code.

Station

Of course, another measurement related to the location of the fetus in the passageway is *station*. One may recall that station may be defined as the relationship of the presenting part to the ischial spines of the pelvis. When the presenting part is at the level of the spines, it is usually considered engaged, and the station is said to be 0. If the presentation is above the spines, it is usually considered high, and the station is said to be -1, -2, etc., an estimate of its location in terms of centimeters above the ischial spines. If the presenting part is

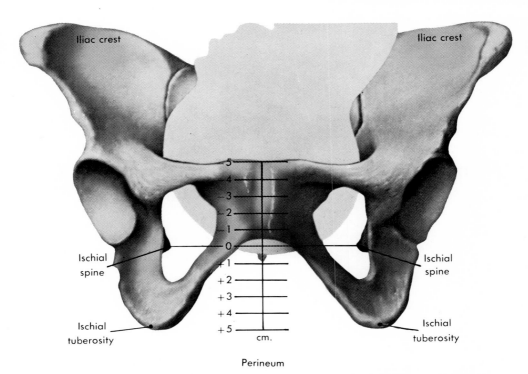

Iliac crest

Iliac crest

Ischial
spine

Ischial
spine

Ischial
tuberosity

Ischial
tuberosity

cm.

Perineum

FIG. 10-6. Stations of presenting part, or degree of engagement. The location of the presenting part in relation to the level of the ischial spines is designated *station* and indicates the
degree of advancement of the presenting part through the pelvis. Stations are expressed in
centimeters above (*minus*) and below (*plus*) the level of the ischial spines (*zero*). The head
is usually engaged when it reaches the level of the ischial spines. (From Phenomena of normal labor, Columbus, Ohio, 1964, Ross Laboratories, Publisher.)

below the ischial spines, we code the station as +1, +2, etc., again making the estimate in centimeters. A centimeter is a
little less than ½ inch. A plus station is
considered low. (See Fig. 10-6.)

Effacement and dilatation

One should not forget that the power accomplishing the shortening and thinning
(effacement) and dilatation of the cervix
to an opening approximately 10 cm. (or
about 4 inches in diameter) is provided by
the intermittent but increasingly frequent
and progressively stronger uterine contractions.

Show

Dilatation of the cervix is usually accompanied by what is called *show*. During
pregnancy, the mucus-producing glands

of the cervix have formed a mucoid deposit
in the cervical canal that helps protect the
interior of the uterus from the introduction
of infection. When the cervix begins to dilate, this mucoid material is discharged. As
the cervix continues to dilate, small capillaries in the cervix break and stain the
mucus with blood. The faster the cervix dilates and the closer it is to complete dilatation, the more abundant and red will be the
"show." However, it should not assume the
proportions or characteristics of frank
bleeding.

After complete dilatation is accomplished, then both abdominal and uterine
muscles contract to push the fetus to the
exterior. The mother has no control over
the contractions of her uterus; they are
under involuntary control. However, once
dilatation is complete, she may aid im-

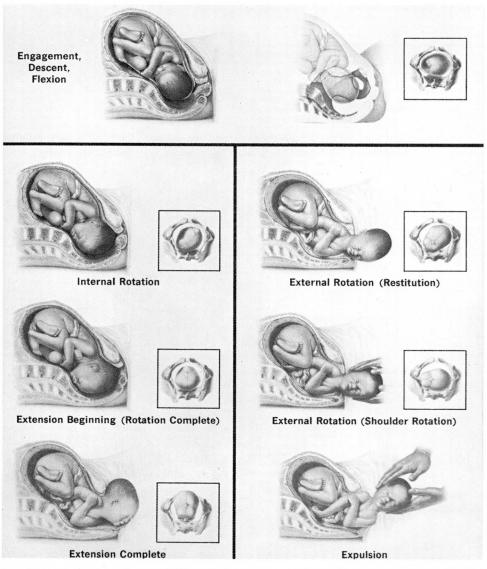

Engagement, Descent, Flexion

Internal Rotation

External Rotation (Restitution)

Extension Beginning (Rotation Complete)

External Rotation (Shoulder Rotation)

Extension Complete

Expulsion

FIG. 10-7. Mechanism of normal labor, L.O.A. position. (From Nursing education aid, No. 13, Columbus, Ohio, 1964, Ross Laboratories, Publisher.)

mensely by pushing with her abdominal muscles when her uterus contracts to help make the fetus descend in the pelvic canal.

Thus to help determine the progress of the passenger the physician is interested in the *presentation,* the body part that is trying to come first; the *position,* the relationship of the presenting part to the pelvic quadrants; and the *station,* the depth of the presenting part in the pelvic canal. If he knows these things plus the relative size of the pelvis and fetus, the condition of the soft tissue uterine exit called the cervix, and the quality and frequency of the uterine contractions providing the power, he has a good basis for his evaluation of the progress of the labor and the mechanisms involved.

Mechanism of labor

Textbooks usually speak of the cardinal movements in the mechanism of labor. In the vertex delivery they usually include the following: descent, flexion, engagement, internal rotation, extension, external rotation, and expulsion. The first *four* movements are not necessarily in order, since flexion may be present before descent and increase thereafter. Descent and internal rotation will also continue after engagement. These mechanisms may occur concurrently and defy a 1-2-3 order. (See Fig. 10-7.)

Descent, flexion, and engagement

In the case of a primipara,* a woman bearing her first baby, *descent* of the fetus into the true pelvis usually occurs about 2 weeks before the actual birth of the child. This descent is referred to as *lightening* and results in *engagement,* or passage of the largest diameter of the presenting part into the pelvic canal. Lay people remark about this change in fetal location by the phrase "the baby has dropped." The expectant mother, with less pressure on her diaphragm, happily finds that she can breathe more freely. The increased tilt and lowered location of the fetus produce a characteristic change in the maternal silhouette. In the case of a multipara,* a woman who has borne one or more children, descent and engagement may not occur until actual dilatation of the neck of the uterus, or cervix, begins.

Internal rotation

The amount of *internal rotation* necessary will depend on the position of the fetus and the way the head rotates to accommodate itself to the changing diameters of the pelvis. The most common rotation is that which involves the turning of the head to occiput anterior position. If the fetus begins its descent in L.O.T. or L.O.A. position, this rotation represents only a short distance of 45 to 90 degrees. If however, the internal rotation involves moving from a posterior position, it may mean a turn of 135 degrees. For this reason posterior positions usually entail a longer labor and more lower back discomfort for the mother, who will usually appreciate a nurse's firm, cool, intermittent sacral support. Occasionally, instead of rotating to an anterior position the occiput turns to the sacrum, and the child is born in O.S. position. This mode of delivery is usually slower and more dangerous to the maternal tissues. More often, the occiput will complete the longer rotation from the posterior position to the pubis. Sometimes the occiput lingers unduly in the posterior position or stops its rotation in transverse. The former situation is called "persistent posterior" and the latter a "transverse arrest." This can occur at almost any station or depth in the pelvic canal and may necessitate manual rotation or the use of rotation forceps by the obstetrician.

Extension

In a vertex delivery the head is delivered by *extension.* During descent it is normally forced into a flexed attitude by the pressure of the cervix, pelvic walls, and floor. Once the occiput has rotated to anterior position and occupies the pubic arch, the head cannot make any further progress unless extension is accomplished. This extension plus the natural curve of the lower pelvis is the reason that when the head is born it appears to push upward out of the vaginal canal. The rate of extension is gently controlled by the doctor. If the bag of waters (membranes) has not previously broken during labor, it must be artificially broken now by the doctor to avoid aspiration of amniotic fluid. To prevent uncontrolled tearing of the perineum, an episiotomy, or surgical incision extending the soft tissue vaginal opening, may be executed by the doctor just before the birth of the head.

---

*The words "primipara" and "multipara" in this section are used from the delivery-labor room perspective. More correct would be the terms "primigravida" and "primipara," but these are seldom employed in areas where we have worked.

External rotation (restitution, shoulder rotation) and expulsion

When the perineum slides over the chin of the baby and temporarily only the neck occupies the outlet, more room is available to the infant for head movement. Usually without coaxing by the physician the back of the baby's head will then turn to line up with his back, revealing the baby's position just before internal rotation of the head took place. This movement is called *restitution.* The turning movement of the head usually continues and influences the location of the back, helping to line up the unborn shoulders just beneath the pubis in anteroposterior position. This process of alignment is called *shoulder rotation.* Usually the top of the anterior shoulder is next seen just under the pubis—generally aided by the physician, who may exert gentle but firm downward traction on the head. Then the head is gently raised to clear the posterior shoulder, and the entire body follows without any particular difficulty. *Expulsion* of the infant is accomplished.

The three stages of labor

Labor is classically divided into three stages:

1. Stage one begins with the first true labor contraction, which begins the effacement and dilatation of the cervix, and ends when dilatation is complete—10 cm.
2. Stage two begins with complete dilatation of the cervix and ends with the birth of the baby.
3. Stage three begins with the birth of the baby and ends with the expulsion of the afterbirth, or placenta and membranes.

Approximate relationships

A wise nurse or doctor makes no specific predictions regarding the length of the stages of labor. However, Table 10-1 may be of some aid in estimating possible time intervals. A labor *without letup* lasting more than 24 hours is usually considered extended. The mother and baby must

TABLE 10-1. Stages of labor

	First stage	Second stage	Third stage
Primipara	8 to 20 hours	30 minutes to 2 hours	5 to 20 minutes (usually aided by oxytocics or manual pressure)
Multipara	3 to 8 hours	20 minutes to 1½ hours	5 to 20 minutes (usually aided by oxytocics or manual pressure)

be evaluated carefully for exhaustion or distress.

Third stage: special considerations

The third stage of labor is characterized by the separation of the placenta and its expulsion.

Placental separation. Separation of the placenta from the uterine wall is accomplished by the contraction of the uterus. The site of the placental attachment suddenly becomes reduced, but the placenta itself remains the same size, causing a separation of the two structures. The placenta slides down into the lower portion of the uterus and vagina. The physician watches for signs of placental separation, which include the following:

1. The rise of the uterus to the umbilicus or above—pushed up by the bulky placenta in the vagina
2. The increased firmness and rounded shape of the fundus
3. The lengthening of the exposed umbilical cord at the exterior as the placenta descends
4. The sudden appearance of moderate temporary vaginal bleeding originating from the site of the placental attachment at the time of separation

Placental expulsion. After the placenta is separated it may be pushed out by the mother as uterine contractions resume, and she is again instructed to "bear down," or, more commonly, she is assisted by the physician who carefully exerts abdominal pressure on the fundus from above, causing the placenta's expulsion. At times the physician may elect to help deliver the placenta through cautious intravaginal, intrauterine, or abdominal maneuvers. Manual extraction may be a necessity in cases of abnormally retained placenta or excessive uterine bleeding. Some physicians routinely carry out manual palpation of the uterine cavity after the delivery of the placenta in an effort to make sure that it is normal and empty. Visual inspection of the cervix is part of the usual follow-up. The expelled placenta is checked for abnormality and completeness.

The third stage of labor and those hours immediately following are probably the most dangerous for the mother because it is during this time that hemorrhages most often occur. In an effort to speed the separation of the placenta and lessen blood loss, oxytocics, medications that help contract the uterus, are often employed in the delivery room. The medications used will depend on the time during the delivery sequence their action is desired, the condition of the patient, the anesthesia used, and the personal preferences of the attending physician.

The satisfactory completion of the mechanism of labor and delivery as seen in all three stages is cause for congratulation. However, the whole drama of birth and adjustment is not completed—only Act I.

11
Labor and delivery

Normally, the onset of labor is the anticipated climax of 9 months of very constructive waiting. Under normal conditions each day has better prepared the fetus to make the transition from intrauterine to extrauterine existence smoothly, without undue strain. As the time of labor and delivery approaches, the mother should be alerted to certain "get set" signs, and she should be instructed when to call the physician and come to the hospital.

Signs of impending labor

Several signs and symptoms usually precede the onset of true labor—the opening of the cervix and expulsion of the baby and placenta. These hints of things to come are usually welcome. At the end of a full-term pregnancy the mother is quite willing to relinquish her lively and bulky boarder; however, she also has feelings of anxiety as she considers the actual period of labor and delivery.

Lightening. In a woman bearing her first infant, usually about 2 weeks before delivery a relative change in fetal location may be suddenly apparent. As the fetus "drops" into the true pelvis (a process called *lightening*) and the presenting part "becomes engaged" (the largest diameter of the presenting part passes the pelvic brim), she finds herself able to breathe more freely with less pressure on the diaphragm. Doctors expect primigravidae (women pregnant for the first time) to experience lightening and engagement before true labor begins. If it does not occur, the possibility of too small a pelvic inlet or too large a presenting part (fetal-pelvic disproportion)

may be considered. Women who have borne children previously may not undergo lightening until just before or during true labor.

Frequent urination. The woman may also find, alas, greater pressure on her bladder and may be troubled with *frequent urination.*

Energy. Many women experience a phenomenal "burst of energy" just before going into labor and want to clean the whole house. They should be advised to resist the impulse.

Uterine contractions. The uterus contracts and relaxes intermittently all during pregnancy, but its contractions are usually mild and not detected by the mother-to-be. However, in the last few weeks of waiting, these uterine contractions may become quite annoying, and contrary to what some texts declare, may be painful. The most discouraging aspect about these contractions of late pregnancy is that they are often only a rehearsal for the real thing. They do not serve to dilate the cervix and, therefore, are called false labor, or Braxton Hicks' contractions, after the British obstetrician who described them. Characteristics of false labor contrasted with true labor contractions include the following:

1. A duration of contraction that remains about the same, not becoming appreciably longer or more intensive as do true contractions.

2. A period between contractions that remains quite long and irregular. True contractions are regular, with a gradually decreasing interval.

3. Pressure or pain felt primarily in the

abdomen rather than in the small of the back.

4. A tolerance for walking during the contraction. In fact, walking may help relieve discomfort, whereas true labor contractions may be intensified by ambulation.

5. Show, or the appearance of a mucoid vaginal discharge tinged with blood, is absent in false labor but is usually present in true labor.

6. On rectal or vaginal examination the cervix is usually found to be long and closed in false labor but is effacing or dilating in true labor.

An expectant mother should be counseled to contact her physician about the onset of labor if (1) contractions are regular, becoming increasingly frequent and intensive; (2) show is present; or (3) the bag of waters, or membranes, ruptures.

The trip to the hospital

When the woman is instructed to go to the hospital depends on her reported progress, the distance she must travel, how many babies she has had, and the history of her previous labors. Usually, physicians want all their patients to be admitted as soon as the bag of waters ruptures or show appears. If these signs are absent, admission is advised when the contractions of primigravidae are regular at about 7-minute intervals. In the case of mothers who previously have had one baby or more, physicians usually want them hospitalized when contractions have achieved some regularity, but they do not wait until a certain frequency is reached. Women who have previously experienced a full-term normal delivery usually deliver more rapidly than those who have not. They are not encouraged to wait at home too long. If the onset of labor is suspected, the prospective mother should eat nothing and limit her intake of fluids until evaluated by the doctor to prevent possible aspiration at the time of delivery.

It is hoped that the ride to the hospital will not turn into a race nor be compli-cated with too many obstacles. Certainly, it is best to be able to be admitted without rush and confusion. Detailed planning for the journey should be made. The patient should be told by her physician or his office nurse before her entry what the admission procedures involve so that she may be more prepared for what will transpire.

Hospital admission

Admission directly to the labor room unit with a minimum of front office procedure is desirable. Usually only one signature is needed, that of the patient herself, for permission to perform the routine procedures necessary during labor and delivery. "Routine procedures" do not include a cesarean section. The husband or other accompanying family member may help complete any other office admittance procedure needed while the patient is being cared for in the labor room area. All women harbor anxiety regarding their hospital experience. Some patients are very nervous and fearful. The nursing staff should do everything in its power to alleviate this anxiety and make the patient feel welcome and secure. A gracious welcome to the patient and her accompanying family makes a lasting impression. Unfortunately, so does a rude, thoughtless, or disorganized admission experience. The patient does not want to hear about the current problems of the maternity service, past obstetrical experiences of former patients, or the personal histories of her attending nurses! Such recitals are indiscreet, impolite, and worrying to the patient and her family. The members of the immediate family should be shown a place where they can comfortably wait during the completion of the admission procedures. Ideally, this would include provision for a public telephone, magazines, perhaps a small, automatic coin-operated canteen for refreshments, and a television set. Once the admission is completed, most hospitals now allow and even encourage visitation of the patient by her immediate family during labor. However, most limit this contact to one person at the bedside at one time.

ROLE OF VOCATIONAL
OR PRACTICAL NURSE

The trained vocational nurse, as a part of the maternity staff, can make a real contribution to the well-being of the patient. Under the supervision of an experienced registered nurse, she can render valuable assistance to the department and the patient. We believe that the use of the prepared licensed vocational nurse (LVN or LPN) in nonsupervisory capacities in this department is legitimate and desirable but that it is a misuse of personnel to expect her to assume the role of a charge nurse or, on the other hand, to delegate to her only duties that can be accomplished by workers with less training.

The vocational nurse can provide valuable assistance in the admittance of the patient to the labor-delivery suite. After she arrives at the hospital, the patient is usually taken by wheelchair to the labor room area. The nurse helps the patient remove her clothes and put on a hospital gown and encourages the return of her clothes to her home. She makes special note of valuables, such as watches and eyeglasses. If the bag of waters has ruptured, the patient should not be allowed up. As soon as possible the patient is properly identified, preferably using a banding technique. If such a technique is used, the band should be carefully checked with the patient, who is initially asked, "What is your name?" The nurse asks the name of the attending physician and secures the patient's prenatal record if one is present at the hospital. With the supervising registered nurse, she may read the record to determine as much as possible about this patient before continuing with the admission. Important factors to check are (1) the obstetrical history—number of viable births she has had, previous difficulties, the rapidity of former labors, and Rh status; (2) the record of the current pregnancy—serology result, the expected date of confinement, and any

known allergies; (3) plans for the labor and delivery—type of anesthesia, accommodations desired, method selected for feeding the infant, and name of the doctor to care for the baby; and (4) marital status and, if it is questionable, plans for the baby, which should be determined with the utmost tact and discretion by one staff member only so that the patient need not be troubled by needless repetition of questions. Some of the necessary admission information will, by its very nature, be absent from the prenatal record. The admitting nurse must inquire when the contractions (if any) began, if any show has been noted, and if the bag of waters is known to have broken. The staff should know if the patient has recently eaten. In some maternity services a voided urine specimen is routinely obtained for urinalysis at the time of admission. In others, a specimen is secured on admission only if prenatal history prompts the physician to order it. Otherwise, a specimen is obtained at the time of the routine catheterization of the patient just prior to delivery. Some maternity services include weighing the patient in their admission procedure. Although most of the time a call will have previously been received from the attending physician regarding the admission, in some situations the nurse may want to know if the patient has contacted the doctor and if she has been examined by him. She will take the patient's temperature, pulse, and respiration. She will determine the blood pressure in the absence of a contraction and time the duration, interval, and intensity of her contractions. She will listen for and count the fetal heart rate and note the presence of amniotic fluid drainage and/or any show.

ROLE OF THE REGISTERED NURSE

The registered nurse having overall responsibility for the case greets the patient, noting any special needs. She palpates the patient's abdomen, evaluates contractions, and examines the patient rectally (sometimes vaginally, depending on local policy)

Catholic
Breast Feeding.
✱ Allergic to Penicillin   *Rh +*   *Saddle*

Name *Jones, Marilyn*   Age *24*   Doctor *Thompson*

Gravida *I*   Para *O*   Due date *5-10-66*

Date admitted *May 5, 1966*   Time *6:30* (A.M.)/P.M.   Walking ____ Wheelchair *X* Stretcher ____

STAGE OF LABOR ON ADMISSION: Not in labor ☐ Mild labor ☒ Active labor ☐ For induction ☐

Contractions began: Date *5-5* 19 *66* : *2* A.M. Now, every *6* minutes, lasting *35* seconds

Membranes: Intact ☒ Ruptured ☒ Time *2:14* P.M. Spontaneously ☒ Artificially ☐ By Dr. ____

Blood shown: None ☐ Moderate amt. ☒ Hemorrhage ☐ Temp. *98.8* °F. Pulse *88* Resp. *24* B.P. *118/76*

PRESENTATION: Head ☒ Breech ☐ FHT *140* Dilation *2* cm. Effacement *90* % Station *O*

DOCTOR NOTIFIED: Time *7:* A.M. ORDERS: (See order sheet) By *J. Smith* R.N.

First and second stages of labor: Date *5-5-66* Time first stage began *2* (A.M.)/P.M.

Date	Time	R or V	Dilat. Cm.	Eff. %	Stat.	Memb.	Pos.	FHT	Contractions	Examined by
5-5-66	8³⁰ A.M	R	4		O	I	LOA	144	q 5 min.	L. Thompson
	12 NOON	R	6		+1	I		144	4	J. Smith R.N.
	2¹⁵ P.M.	R	8		+2	R		136	3	J. Smith R.N.
	3⁵⁰ P.M.	R	Rim		+2	R		132	irreg. 2-4	N. Angelo R.N.
	4¹⁰ P.M.	R	C							

Date	Time	Medication, Diet, Fluids, Condition of Patient, etc.	Nurse
5-5-66	7¹⁰ A.M.	Synkdyvite 5 mgm. (IM)	J. Smith R.N.
	8³⁰ A.M	Demerol 50 mgm IM	J. Smith R.N.
	12 noon	Demerol 50 mgm IM	J. Smith R.N.
	2	Phenergan 25 mgm. + Demerol 50 mgm IM	J. Smith, R.N.
	4³⁰ P.M.	5% Dextrose / Water IV. (1000 cc) started left arm	M. H. Dupton RN

To Delivery Room at *4:15* A.M./(P.M.) Catheterized at *4:30* A.M./(P.M.) Specimen to laboratory *Yes*

DELIVERY DATE: *5-5* 19 *66* TIME *5:01* , P.M. SEX: MALE ☐ FEMALE ☒

TYPE DELIVERY: Spontaneous ☒ Vertex, Breech: Frank ☐ Footling: Single ☐ Double ☐ Forceps to ACH ☐
    Forceps: Low ☒ Mid ☐ Elective Low ☐ Operative ☐ Rotation-Forceps ☐ Manual ☐

Position: *LOA*

Cord: Clamped ☒ Tied ☐ Around neck ☒ *X1* OXYTOCIC: Ergotrate: ____ IV: ____ IM ____ Time ____ M.
Abnormalities: ____   ~~Pitutrin~~ *Syntocinon 1cc* IM/(IV) Time *5:12 P.M.*

THIRD STAGE OF LABOR: Placenta: Delivered Time *5:14* P.M. Expressed ☒ Extracted ☐

Complete ☒ Incomplete ☐ Schultz ☒ Duncan ☐ Blood Loss *250* cc.

Episiotomy, Kind: Midline ☒ Mediolateral ☐ : Right ☐ Left ☐ Catgut Type *Chr. 00b*

Cervix examined, Yes ☒ No ☐ Lacerated L. ☐ R. ☐ Elective bilateral repair ☐ Perineal laceration: 1 2 3

Transferred to Maternity Floor, Room No. *122* Time *5:40 P.M.*

Condition *Good*   Signed by *L. Thompson* , M.D.

GROSSMONT HOSPITAL

LA MESA, CALIFORNIA

LABOR RECORD

BALBOA PRINTING CO.

FIG. 11-1. Sample labor record. Another sheet for more detailed nursing notes is also used. (Courtesy Grossmont Hospital, La Mesa, Calif.)

to determine fetal station and presentation, determine the dilatation and effacement of the cervix, and determine the condition of the membranes and the position of the fetus. These last two are sometimes difficult or impossible to discern through the rectal-vaginal wall. If the rectum is not empty of feces, the results of the examination may be questionable. The position of the cervix may make the estimation of dilatation difficult. The patient's condition, progress, and reaction to labor are evaluated. The individual orders of the attending physician are consulted regarding types of analgesia and anesthesia and the expected delivery room setup. If no previous arrangement is known, the physician is called regarding the arrival of the patient at the maternity service, and any unusual vital signs and pertinent information gained from the rectal examination are relayed.

Unless the presence of true labor is doubted, the perineal shave may be completed. Whether or not an enema is given will depend on the progress and condition of the patient and the individual doctor's desires. Some form of vitamin K is usually given to prevent hemorrhage in the newborn infant. If analgesia is ordered, side rails should be in place. Which staff member carries out the necessary admission procedures depends on the patient's condition and needs.

PROCEDURES

Principles of the admission procedures should be discussed. It is impossible to describe in detail an admission that fits the needs of every hospital. There are many ways to accomplish similar aims. However, certain principles are followed in every good maternity service no matter where it may be. We will now discuss the admission shave, or "prep," the labor room enema, the timing of contractions, and the determination of fetal heart tone.

PERINEAL SHAVE

Purpose: To cleanse the external genitalia in preparation for delivery by shaving the pubic and perineal hair with an antiseptic and/or sudsing solution and safety razor in order to:
1. Prevent infection
2. Make possible episiotomy repair easier
3. Aid in postpartum observation and care of the area

Setup: Provides individual equipment for each patient or equipment that is used in such a way that no cross infection can take place. Provision should be made for:
1. Privacy
2. Adequate lighting
3. A waterproof pad under the patient's hips to protect the bed
4. A supply of clean, warm water
5. A sudsing antiseptic solution (pHisoHex)
6. A sharp safety razor
7. Two or three clean dry cotton balls or gauze compresses to help pull back on the skin as it is being shaved and to clean the labial folds
8. An irrigation pitcher and/or folded soft paper or cloth towels to help rinse off the soapy solution and dry the area
9. Several paper towels or a plastic sack to receive the waste in a convenient manner and intermittently help to clean off the razor
10. Clean plastic gloves for the nurse's use during the procedure

Procedure (complete or partial shaves may be ordered):

1. If possible, place light (wall or gooseneck lamp) on opposite side of bed from where you will stand so that no shadows are cast.
2. Screen the patient. The sheet may be over the lower legs and feet; the gown is turned up to just above the perineal hairline giving adequate space to work.
3. Have the patient bend her knees and drop her legs sideways—heels toward one another. Lather the pubic hair and, creating tension on the skin with a dry compress with one hand, shave with the other, placing your razor approximately at a 30-degree angle to the skin. Begin at the pubis and shave toward the perineum. Be sure to remove *all* hairs from the labia and cleanse away any collection of smegma (cellular debris found especially in the labial folds). Avoid getting any solution into the vagina. Wipe off prepped area with soft towel, folds dampened with water to remove the solution, which may be irritating. Use a different surface for each stroke (or irrigate the area) and dry with second soft towel, using same technique, never returning to the vulva after passing over the rectal area.
4. When the preparation of the perineal area is complete, turn the patient on her side to

FIG. 11-2. One example (Sterilon) of a disposable shave kit now being marketed.

finish the perianal region. Probably the most important area to clear is between the vaginal and anus, the *true* perineum, because this is the area cut during an episiotomy. Wipe off any residual solution.

5. Have your first "prep" checked so that you are certain what is expected of you. Even if it is your first "prep," you should not impress the fact on your anxious patient!

6. During the prep, if possible, try to gauge the frequency and quality of any contractions the patient may have, as well as how she is tolerating them. Report any vaginal discharge as to character and amount. Note: No perineal pads are worn during labor to cut down on the possibility of vulvar contamination resulting from the pad passing from the rectal to the vaginal area. However, the patient may have absorbent, protective bed pads under her hips.

DELIVERY ROOM ENEMA TECHNIQUE

Purpose: To empty the colon of feces in order to:

1. Help assure a clean delivery and prevent infection
2. Encourage contractions
3. Possibly provide more passageway for the child
4. Facilitate rectal examinations during labor

Setup:

1. Enema can or bag with appropriate tubing and clamp
2. Lubricant (K-Y jelly)
3. Protector for bed
4. Bedpan and tissue for patients not getting up
5. Paper towels to receive used tube
6. Ordered solution—usually a soapsuds enema made of water and castile soap. (Use a small amount of soap. You want a slightly milky solution, not billowing suds.) The solution should feel moderately warm. Fill the can and give as much as can be tolerated—usually about half (1,000 ml.). Note: Some physicians order the prepackaged phosphate enemas, which may be given in less time with less discomfort to the patient. Some believe that the results are not as satisfactory, however.

Procedure:

1. Explain procedure to patient.
2. Screen patient and place her in Sims's position on left side if possible. Drape with a sheet.
3. Place protector under hips.
4. Expel air from tubing.
5. Gently insert the lubricated tube approximately 2 inches, telling patient to take a

deep breath and bear down slightly; insert 2 inches more. (Occasionally, because of the position of the fetal head, more tubing must be inserted.) Hemorrhoids are common during pregnancy. Extra care and lubrication are necessary during the insertion if they are present. Hold the enema bag or can no higher than 18 inches from the rectum.

6. Stop the procedure when air is in danger of entering the tube via the enema can when it is almost empty.

7. If cramping results, you may clamp off the tube momentarily and lower the can. Instruct patient to breathe rapidly through an open mouth, "Pant like a puppy." Stop flow temporarily during a contraction.

8. Clamp the tube and withdraw.

9. Leave pan and tissue with patient if she cannot get up to expel the enema. She may be placed on the bedpan. Instructions should be given regarding proper use of tissue, that is, to wipe from front to back and discard! In some maternity services, cotton balls or antiseptic-impregnated towelettes are used, or perineal irrigations are administered following the enema. Patients are not allowed up if:
   a. Disoriented, sedated, weak, or in advanced labor
   b. Membranes are ruptured (there is danger of prolapse of cord)

10. Be sure necessary supplies are always replaced. Sterile supplies are wrapped in paper. Enema cans are sterilized between each patient, or disposable units are used.

11. Additional information.
   a. Enemas are not usually ordered for primiparous patients after a dilatation of 6 to 8 cm. or for multiparae above 4 to 5 cm. dilatation to avoid expulsion of the enema during delivery.
   b. Enemas should not be given to a frankly bleeding patient, since this will further encourage bleeding.

TIMING OBSTETRICAL CONTRACTIONS
Purpose:

1. To help evaluate the efforts of the uterus to dilate the cervix and expel the baby and to aid in determining the progress of the labor

2. To detect any abnormalities such as lack of uterine relaxation, which may reveal the onset of complications

3. To reassure the patient and her family by your presence and interest and at the same time render what assistance possible to help her better support her labor by:
   a. Encouraging and listening

   b. Rubbing her back or providing sacral support as desired
   c. Helping with relaxation, breathing, or pushing techniques as needed, according to the capacity of the patient to benefit
   d. Moistening her lips
   e. Changing pillowcases and replacing bed pads
   f. Watching for signs of the patient's changing needs (for example, the beginning of the second stage of labor)

Procedure:

1. Before going to the bedside, if possible, learn about each patient individually.
   a. Number of pregnancies and viable deliveries
   b. Her marital status and any special arrangements for the baby
   c. Any special complications or problems anticipated

2. The fact that you are feeling her uterus, as it contracts and relaxes under the abdominal wall, to measure her progress in labor should be explained unless she has previously had contractions timed.

3. Your hands should be clean and not too cold.

4. The term "contractions" should be used, not *pains*. Not all contractions are painful. Use of the word "pain" may interfere with maternal conditioning for childbirth.

5. If the pregnancy is full term, the fundus, where the strongest muscular contraction can be felt, will be located just above the umbilicus. The nurse's hand should rest lightly there to best detect the uterine contractions.

6. When the uterus contracts, it gradually becomes hard. The degree of hardness is called the *intensity* of a contraction. As the uterus contracts and the uterine muscle fibers shorten, the uterus may be seen or felt to rise in the abdominal cavity. It then gradually relaxes. The time that the uterus is discernibly firm or tight is called the contraction's *duration*. Usually contractions are easier to feel on multiparae than primiparae because of differences in abdominal muscle tone.

7. The term *"interval"* in the timing of contractions is used a bit differently than sometimes supposed. When one is asked to time the interval of a contraction, one times from the beginning of one contraction to the beginning of the following contraction.

8. The time between contractions is called the relaxation time, a period equally important. If the relaxation time is very short or non-

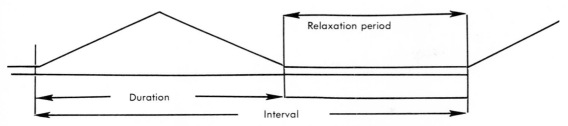

FIG. 11-3. Diagram of the contraction and relaxation of the pregnant uterus.

existent, the baby may suffer from lack of oxygen. A continuously contracted, hard uterus may be a symptom of abruptio placentae. Between contractions the fingers should be able to depress the abdominal wall, a sensation similar to depressing a foam rubber pillow.

9. The contraction and relaxation periods and the interval have often been diagramed as shown in Fig. 11-3. The straight line represents complete relaxation, and the curved line the actual state of the uterine musculature.

10. There is usually a relationship between the duration and frequency of uterine contractions and the dilatation of the cervix. It follows *somewhat* the pattern shown in Table 11-1 (1 inch = 2.5 cm.).

11. Recording of observations of contractions would include duration, interval, and intensity, as well as possible patient tolerance. For example, "contractions $\bar{q}$ 5 minutes for 35 seconds, mild in character. Patient tolerating labor well."

FETAL HEART TONE DETERMINATION
(Figs. 11-4 and 11-5)
Purpose:

1. To help detect the presence of fetal life at the time of admission.

2. To detect any possible fetal distress, as revealed by heart tone irregularity or too rapid or too slow a rate (120 to 160 beats per minute or 30 to 40 beats per 15 seconds is considered the normal range).

Materials: Several types of listening devices are used.

1. The Leffscope—a stethoscope with a large, heavily weighted bell.

2. The DeLee-Hillis head scope.

3. An ordinary stethoscope equipped with rubber bands to prevent the sound distortion that results when handling the bell directly.

4. Even a short cardboard cylinder will do!

5. In some hospitals, fetal heart monitors may be attached to the unborn infant's scalp or the mother's abdomen to provide a constant

TABLE 11-1. Possible uterine contraction and dilatation relationships

Cervical dilatation	Contraction	
	Duration	Interval
1. Fingertip to 2 cm.	20-30 seconds	6-8 minutes
2. 2 cm. → 4 cm.	30-35 seconds	5-6 minutes
3. 4 cm. → 6 cm.	40-50 seconds	4-5 minutes
4. 6 cm. → 8 cm.	45-60 seconds	3-4 minutes
5. 8 cm. → 10 cm.	50-80 seconds	2-3 minutes
(Most difficult period, fatigue, nausea, vomiting, irregular, intensive contractions)		(tends to be irregular)

check on fetal heart activity. Sometimes these monitors may also be constructed to measure intrauterine pressure or abdominal contour and thus indicate contraction activity as well.

Procedure:

1. Explain that you are checking on the fetus by listening to its heartbeat.

2. Make sure that no contraction is in progress or has just terminated.

   a. The fetal heart rate may decrease during a contraction, although some recent research disputes this.[*]

   b. The pressure of the fetuscope against the contracting and rising uterus is uncomfortable to the patient.

   c. If the fetal heart tone seems too slow or fast, then it may be desirable to check its rate or quality during a contraction.

3. After the heart tone is identified, listen for 15 to 30 seconds only, unless an irregularity or rate problem is found. Multiply to obtain the rate for 1 minute. Every separate beat

---

[*]Williams, B. L., and Richards, S. F.: Fetal monitoring during labor, Amer. J. Nurs. **70:**2384-2388, Nov., 1970.

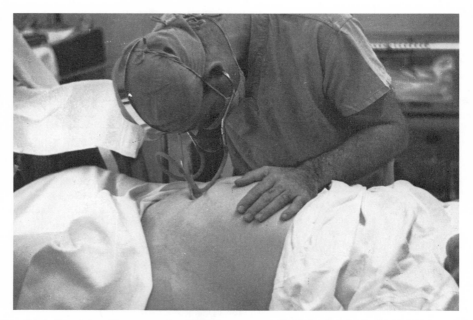

Fig. 11-4. Physician listens to the fetal heart tone (FHT) shortly before delivery. Note the location of the scope on the abdominal wall. (Courtesy Grossmont Hospital and Martin M. Greenberg, M.D., La Mesa, Calif.)

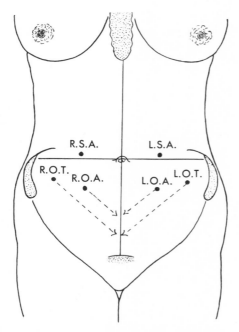

Fig. 11-5. Fetal heart tone locations on the abdominal wall indicating possible corresponding fetal positions and the effects of the internal rotation of the fetus.

heard should be counted. It will usually sound like a little watch. At first, much concentration will be needed to hear it.

4. A rate that is irregular, too rapid, or especially too slow is considered a sign of fetal distress. A fetal heart rate under 100 signals definite distress.

5. Be sure that friction noises from the fingers or the abdominal surface do not distort the sounds. Keep your fingers off the bell. Press firmly on the abdominal wall.

6. The area where the fetal heart tone may be heard the best is related to the following:

    a. *Presentation*—in headfirst or cephalic presentations the fetal heart tone is found in the lower abdominal quadrants, below the umbilicus. In breech presentations, the fetal heart tone is usually found at the level of the umbilicus or above.

    b. *Position*—if the back of the infant is toward the mother's left (L.O.A. or L.O.P. position), the fetal heart tone will probably be heard best on the mother's left. If it points to her right, the fetal heart tone will, in most cases, be heard best on her right. Just because a fetal heart tone can be heard in more than one place does not necessarily mean that more than one baby is involved. However, you may want to check by having another nurse listen simultaneously, using a finger-wagging technique to be sure that the rate heard in both areas is the same.

c. *Station*—as internal rotation and descent occur, the location of the fetal heart tone changes, swinging gradually from the right or left quadrants to the midline and dropping until, just before delivery, it is found just above the pubic bone.

7. It is recommended that the fetal heart tone be taken frequently during labor at half-hour intervals or less in the first stage of labor. In the event of problems it would be checked more frequently. The mother should be told at the time of admittance that a frequent check of the fetal heart tone is routine. Early in labor she or her husband may enjoy listening once, too.

8. Other sounds may be heard in the mother's abdomen as well. *Don't be confused.*

a. The maternal pulse may be heard. You should guard against reporting the maternal pulse as the fetal heart tone by feeling the mother's radial pulse at the same time as you are listening with a fetuscope. They should be different rhythms and rates.

b. The sound of the placental circulation can sometimes be identified. It is a "sh" sound, the same rhythm as the maternal pulse, called the placental souffle, or whistle. Sometimes the fetal heart tone can be heard at the same time in the background. Move the fetuscope about an inch and you will probably hear the fetal heart tone better.

c. Rarely you can hear a sort of soft, whistling sound occurring at the same rate as the fetal heart tone. This has been called the funic souffle, or cord whistle. Some think it is caused by a compression of the cord.

d. Many mothers-to-be are hungry, so you may hear peristalsis!

e. Occasionally, fetal hiccups may be detected. These may more properly be said to be felt rather than heard.

Continuing care and preparation

Once admission is completed, unless delivery is imminent, there is a prolonged period of waiting and observation in which the physical and emotional support of the patient and preparation for her delivery are paramount. Usually, the presence of her mother, husband, or other family member at the bedside is a source of support. If such visitation is not supportive or if it appears to antagonize or upset the patient, such observations should be reported to the charge nurse or doctor. Sometimes arrangements can be made for the visitor to have a "rest"!

EARLY LABOR

The patient in early labor (usually defined as up to 4 cm. dilatation) is characteristically alert, talkative, and nervous. She is usually most eager to cooperate with the doctor and nursing staff in attendance and responds readily to a calm, cheerful nurse who seems genuinely interested in her welfare. Her contractions, although perhaps uncomfortable, are tolerable. If her membranes are not ruptured and her contractions are not too frequent or intensive or show too remarkable, she probably will appreciate being able to be up and around for a while and not being automatically confined to her bed just because she has been admitted to the hospital. She should conserve her physical and nervous energy for the more demanding period of labor to come. Her temperature, pulse, respiration, and blood pressure should be taken at least every 4 hours, oftener if individual history or indications warrant it. Fetal heart tone should be checked at approximately half-hour intervals or less. The amount and character of any show or amniotic drainage, if present, should be noted.

Rupture of the membranes (spontaneous)

If the bag of waters breaks at any time while the patient is in the labor area (if not ruptured before admission), she should be instructed not to get out of bed or sit up steeply. Any visitors should be asked to step out while the nurse inspects the perineum for signs of a prolapsed cord, or in the case of advanced labor, evaluates signs of the advance of the presenting part (bulging perineum, appearance of the fetal scalp), and the amount and color of the amniotic fluid. If there is any meconium (infant stool) in the fluid, staining it a brownish yellow to gray-black, it should be reported immediately. Meconium-stained amniotic fluid in the case of cephalic presentation is considered a sign of fetal distress—the response of the fetus to oxygen lack. Such staining in the case of a breech presentation is usually not considered significant, since the pressure exerted on a breech during its passage through the pelvic canal may cause the discharge of meconium, and no real fetal distress may be involved. The appearance of old, dark blood or bright red, frank bleeding at any time during labor should also be reported. The fetal heart tone should be taken right after the rupture of the membranes to try to detect possible cord prolapse. The fact that the bag of waters appears to have rup-

tured should be reported to the head nurse immediately. Contractions should be frequently evaluated, depending on the progress the patient seems to be making.

Evaluation of progress

Rectal examination. Proof of the progress is usually gained through the performance of rectal (Fig. 11-6) or vaginal examinations. A nurse may perform either rectal or vaginal examinations or both if properly instructed, depending on the policies of the hospital for which she works and the wishes of the physicians involved. These examinations should be kept to a minimum because of the discomfort caused the patient, and, in the case of vaginal examinations, the

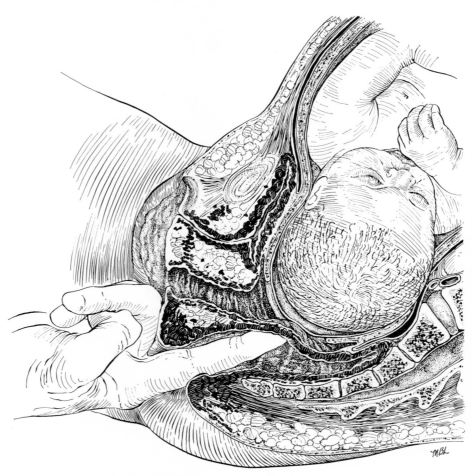

Fig. 11-6. Midsagittal section of the pelvis showing a rectal examination during labor. Note how the fingers are held away from the vagina to prevent contamination.

possibility of introduction of infection. Student nurses are not routinely taught the techniques of rectal examination. Student nurses in programs leading to registration are sometimes taught when it is known that the student is especially interested in the delivery room area and wants to continue working in obstetrics after her graduation. To instruct all students in the techniques would be useless because unless they are used frequently and much practice is gained, the ability to interpret what one feels is never obtained in the first place or easily lost. In addition, the patient has had the discomfort of duplicate examinations. The LVN is rarely given the responsibility of performing rectal examinations. This is usually considered the duty of the registered nurse. However, the LVN may be asked to assist a doctor when he examines a patient rectally. She does so by making sure that a supply of clean rectal gloves and lubricant is available and by chaperoning the patient and helping her to relax during an examination. Usually, if the patient drops her knees toward the outside and breathes deeply through her open mouth during the digital examination, it helps. Squeezing the nurse's hand seems to give some great satisfaction, too! After the examinations, the patient's rectal area should be cleansed of any leftover lubricant, and she should be encouraged as much as the circumstances permit.

Vaginal examination. The LVN or registered nurse may also assist the doctor in performing a vaginal examination.

Procedure. The way this procedure is carried out differs from institution to institution and physician to physician. In some instances, the patient is cleansed and draped as for delivery, and the doctor may scrub his hands with a brush before putting on sterile gloves. In other hospitals, the preparation may not be so elaborate. However, it seems to us that certain principles should always be observed. The vulva should be cleansed of any soil. The examiner's hands should be carefully washed. A sterile examining glove should be used. A sterile lubricant or disinfectant, such as pHisoHex, should be poured over the gloved fingers and vulva. Care should be taken in inserting the fingers not to touch anything but the actual vaginal canal, so that organisms from anal or other areas are not introduced into the canal. A vaginal examination can reveal information not detected by a rectal examination because the cervix and presenting part are felt directly by the fingers and not through the rectovaginal wall. It may help greatly in the determination of the type of presentation, position, and the condition of the bag of waters.

Rupture of the membranes (artificial). At times, in an effort to induce or hasten labor, the doctor will artificially rupture the membranes during a vaginal examination. This is done, however, only under certain conditions. The cervix should be effaced, and some dilatation must be present. The head should be engaged. The doctor ordinarily uses a sterile instrument with a small clawlike end. This may be an Allis, Iowa, or other type clamp. He ruptures the membranes between contractions and lets the fluid flow slowly out past his fingers to avoid having the cord swept out of place by a sudden gush of "water." Prolapse of the cord and its subsequent pinching between the presenting part and the bony pelvis is a complication to be feared and watched for. Immediately after the membranes have ruptured, the fetal heart tone should be taken to determine any distress of the fetus. The actual rupture of the bag causes no pain because there are no nerves in the membranes, but the pressure exerted in order to do the vaginal examination and position the instrument may cause the patient some discomfort. She should be especially encouraged during this period. If rupture of the membranes is anticipated at the time of a vaginal examination, the patient should be placed on several bed-protecting pads to catch the drainage. Some advocate placing the patient on a bedpan; however, the patient's discomfort is usually increased in such a position. The approximate amount (small, moderate, or large) of fluid expelled and its color should be noted and recorded. Remember, the appearance of meconium in the amniotic fluid during a head presentation is interpreted as a sign of fetal distress. After the examination, the patient should be made as comfortable as possible. The excess lubricant should be wiped from the vulva, using good technique (wiping from front to back with no return of a used sponge to the vaginal region). Dry protective bed pads should be in place. The patient should be instructed to say in bed.

INTENSIFIED LABOR:
CHARACTERISTICS AND CARE

As labor progresses, the patient experiences more frequent and intensive contractions. More and more her attention is focused on meeting their demands on her physical and psychological resources. If she has had training in relaxation and breathing techniques, these usually are of great aid. Abdominal and high chest breathing are described in Chapter 9, p. 78. If a laboring patient has had no previous training in these techniques, she may still benefit by some simple instruction in abdominal breathing. This usually eases the discomfort markedly. Rapid breathing techniques can also be taught, but if the mother-to-be is unfamiliar with the method she is likely to hyperventilate, and the normal proportion of oxygen to carbon dioxide in the blood will be upset. She may feel light-headed, and her fingers may begin to tingle. Such side effects should be avoided. If they appear, it may help if she breathes into a paper bag.

Probably the most difficult time during the labor and delivery, with the possible exception of the baby's actual expulsion, is that period just preceding complete dilation, the period of approximately 8 to 10 cm. dilatation. The laboring patient is now fatigued and usually discouraged. She wonders if she is ever going to have her baby and worries about her performance when she does. Although analgesics such as meperidine hydrochloride (Demerol) and tranquilizers such as hydroxyzine (Atarax)

may have been given, she still may be fretful concerning the outcome of her labor. Her contractions may be irregular, at times seeming to come "one right after another." Nausea and vomiting are common. She is usually most grateful for the presence of the nurse, who can help tremendously by offering firm back rubs, sacral support, cool, fresh pillowcases, damp clean gauze sponges to ease the dry mouth, or a cool cloth on the forehead. Husbands and mothers can often help with these simple methods of relieving distress. The nurse should offer the bedpan at intervals to the patient and be sure her bladder does not become distended. Distention may delay labor or, rarely, cause laceration of the bladder.

Signs of the second stage of labor

During this period, the patient needs to be frequently evaluated concerning the possibility of the onset of the second stage of labor, the period of expulsion. The doctor and anesthetist should be kept informed of the patient's progress. The second stage will ordinarily be heralded by (1) an increase in show, (2) an involuntary urge on the part of the patient to push or bear down with each contraction as the presenting part escapes the cervix and descends, (3) the fetal heart tone usually being heard just above the pubic bone in head presentations, and (4) late signs, including the bulging of the perineum, the dilatation of the anus, and the appearance of caput, or the fetal scalp. It is fervently hoped that a multipara will be in the delivery room and adequately prepared for the actual delivery before these last signs manifest themselves. Usually, multiparae are transferred to the delivery room at about 8 cm. dilatation to avoid a last minute race. However, women bearing their first babies, many times are not transferred to the delivery room proper before these last signs appear, since the period between complete dilatation and the delivery of the infant may be relatively protracted in the case of a primipara. Most hospitals in the United States do not welcome family members in the delivery room.

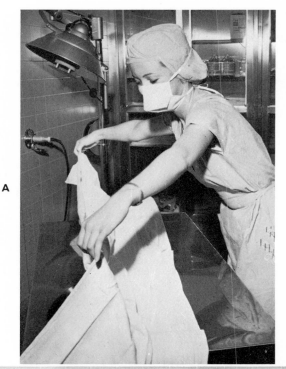

A

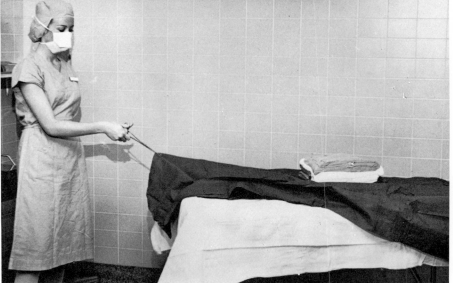

B

Continued.

FIG. 11-7. Preparation of the delivery room. **A,** Opening a sterile pack. The back portion of the pack is opened first to avoid leaning over uncovered sterile material. **B,** Unfolding the sterile table drape (this one happens to be paper). Note the distance of the nurse from the table and the use of sterile forceps. **C,** Lifting sterile instruments. For beginners this is a good grip. The instrument is balanced and the hand is far from the surface of the table. (Courtesy Grossmont Hospital, La Mesa, Calif.)

Pushing

Although she may wish to do so, a laboring patient should not be encouraged by the nurse to bear down or push before complete dilatation of the cervix is determined. To do so could cause greater fatigue for the mother, greater strain on the fetus, and possible injury to the cervix. Once complete dilatation has taken place, however, and all preparations for the delivery are made, pushing will be recommended. Unless experienced, the patient will probably have to be taught how to push to use her energy most efficiently. Most patients are quite relieved by pushing and cooperate well in following instructions, if they are not confused by too many instructors. The following aids and advice have been found to work well:

1. The patient is positioned on her back with her knees flexed. She may want to grasp her legs or the side rails or hand supports while pushing. The patient should be instructed to take a deep breath and blow it all out as she begins to feel a contraction. She then takes a second deep breath, which she holds.
2. She should close her mouth, put her chin on her chest, and bear down in the same manner as she would to move her bowels. If there are no contraindications, she is usually helped in this endeavor by being raised slightly by the nurse's hand and arm under her pillow.
3. If she "runs out of air" before the contraction finishes, she should be encouraged to take another deep breath and continue pushing. Short pushes are ineffectual.
4. Between contractions, she should be allowed to rest. The nurse may observe that once the second stage of labor has been entered, the contractions, although forceful, may be less frequent. There may be intervals of 3 to 4 minutes. This gives the working mother a welcome bit of respite. She may even snooze a bit between contractions.

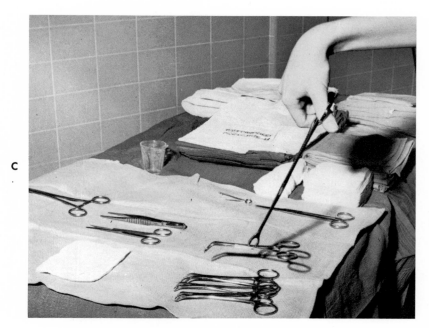

C

FIG. 11-7, cont'd. For legend see p. 109.

PREPARATION OF THE DELIVERY ROOM
(Fig. 11-7)

Before the second stage of labor is reached, the delivery room should be prepared for the actual birth of the baby. The responsibility of its preparation may be that of a trained vocational nurse. Hers is an important responsibility. To execute it correctly, she must have a clear concept of the principles of sterile technique, know where supplies are kept, know the patient's special needs and the attending physician's desires. She should have some idea when the room will be needed so that she can plan her work. The actual preparation of the delivery room will vary in different maternity services, but the basic needs to be met and the principles employed will be the same.

DELIVERY ROOM SETUP REMINDER

Purpose: The purpose of this procedure is three-fold:
1. To provide an aseptic field for the anticipated delivery and subsequent newborn infant and maternal care.
2. To assure the convenient placement and operation of all necessary articles to promote safety, speed, and confidence on the part of the staff in behalf of the physical and emotional care of the mother and child.
3. To aid in the necessary legal and statistical recording of the event.

Setup:
1. Personal preparation.
   a. Secure information.
      (1) Which doctor (for glove size, etc.).
      (2) Which delivery room.
      (3) Type of anesthesia to be used.
      (4) Special problems involving the patient (Rh-negative, preeclampsia, varicosities of the extremities, etc.).
      (5) Approximate time the room is needed.
   b. Wash hands.
   c. Put on mask. Be sure all your hair is covered by a cap. Remember, you should not wear clothes worn in areas outside the labor-delivery suite in the delivery room proper.
   d. Review in your mind the principles of sterile technique.
      Remember:
      (1) Touch sterile supplies only with sterile equipment!

      (2) As you handle the sterile transfer forceps, keep the points down and your knuckles away from the sterile surface being prepared.
      (3) As you work, keep back from the sterile tables. Never turn your back on a nearby sterile area.
2. Put out necessary sterile packs. Check outside tapes on packs for proof of sterilization if this type of tape is used. Check dates on packs to avoid outdated materials. Usually included are:
   a. The basic delivery pack with drapes and materials used on the patient or to accomplish the delivery. One such setup includes these sterile supplies:
      (1) Two drapes for the delivery supply table
      (2) One gown for the nurse caring for the baby
      (3) One drape for the interior of the incubator
      (4) One baby blanket
      (5) One gown and towel for the doctor
      (6) One set of drapes for the patient
         (a) One under-buttocks drape and pad
         (b) Two leggings
         (c) One abdominal drape
      (7) Two perineal pads
      (8) Four extra sterile towels
      (9) Eight gauze compresses
      (10) One gauze vaginal plug
      (11) One urine specimen bottle
      (12) One medicine glass for local anesthesia (if used)
      (13) One cord clamp
      (14) One Diak sterilization indicator, which should be checked early in the arrangement of the supplies for the proper color change
      Note: Added to these materials from room supplies will be:
         One pair gloves
         One aspirator bulb
         One catheter
         Appropriate needles and suture
         If the patient is Rh negative, a sterile collection tube for cord blood is added.
   b. The instrument pack (unless instruments are taken directly from a sterilizer). A typical pack may include:
      (1) One pair suture scissors ⎤ Because these are sharps and may become dull with autoclaving,
      (2) One pair episiotomy scissors ⎦ they may be wrapped separately or stored in disinfectant
      (3) Two curved Kelly's, for clamping the cord

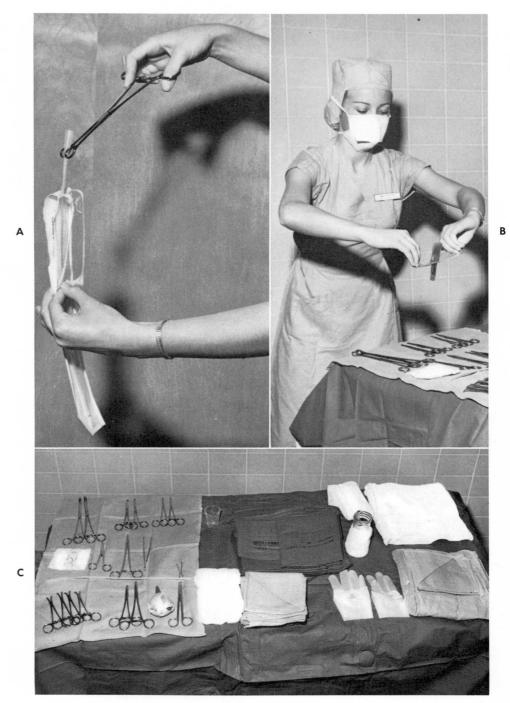

FIG. 11-8. A, Extracting a sterile catheter from a commercially prepared peel-back package. B, Dropping sterile suture from a commercially prepared peel-back package. C, One way to set up a basic delivery room table. (Courtesy Grossmont Hospital, La Mesa, Calif.)

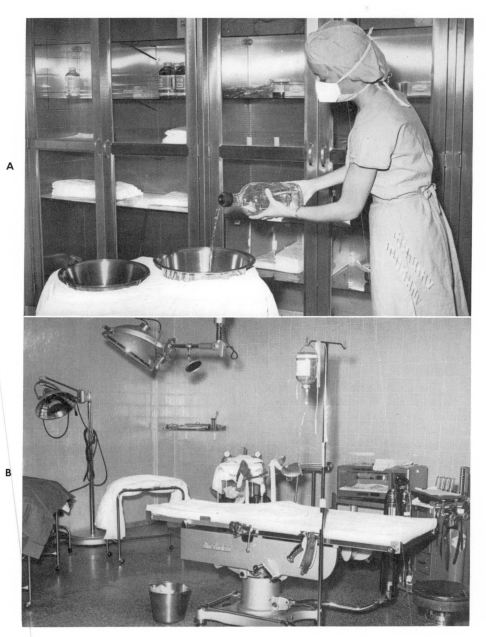

FIG. 11-9. **A,** When pouring sterile water into the "splash basin," hold the bottle high. **B,** The delivery room in readiness. Note covered sterile trays and tables, incubator, resuscitator, and anesthesia machine. (Courtesy Grossmont Hospital, La Mesa, Calif.)

(4) Four towel clips to help secure the drapes

(5) One needle holder

(6) One tissue forceps

(7) Two straight Kelly's

} To help in any repair necessary

(8) Two transfer forceps (pick-ups, ring forceps, sponge sticks)

(9) Two Allis clamps to help break the amniotic sac or aid in the repair of the perineum

Note: Other instruments may be requested (Gelpi retractor, Pelvi-fix retractor, etc.).

c. The basin-set pack, used to provide a sterile basin for the placenta and a sterbasin for lubricating obstetrical forceps, rinsing gloved hands, or cleansing the patient.

d. The perineal preparation tray will usually provide:

(1) A cleansing solution

(2) Sterile gauze sponges

(3) Sterile gloves or sponge sticks

(4) An antiseptic to be used on the skin after the cleansing of the area

e. The spinal anesthesia tray (if appropriate) usually containing:

(1) Two sterile towels

(2) Four gauze compresses

(3) One cup for antiseptic

(4) Three small sponges and sponge forceps for applying the antiseptic

(5) One syringe

(6) Several sizes of spinal needles plus stylets

Note: Added to this tray at the time it is opened for actual use are the doctor's gloves and the ordered anesthetic and antiseptic.

f. Any indicated obstetrical forceps are usually placed conveniently (still wrapped) in the room until called for, except Piper forceps used in breech deliveries for the aftercoming head. Piper forceps are usually unwrapped previously and placed on the supply table.

g. At the time of the delivery the necessary records are brought into the room for completion, and the identification procedures for mother and child are carried out.

TRANSFER AND IMMEDIATE PREDELIVERY CARE

The transfer of the patient to the delivery room should be as smooth as possible. If the patient has a strong desire to push and it is not appropriate activity at the time, she should be advised to pant through her open mouth. Care should be taken in the transfer of the patient from bed to cart to delivery table. In some maternity services, the bed itself is momentarily wheeled into the delivery room to avoid one change and speed the process. The patient can usually help considerably in the move to the delivery table if the staff is able to wait until a contraction is not present.

While the patient is being prepared in the delivery room, the doctor will be dressing and scrubbing for the administration of the spinal anesthesia, if used (analgesia and anesthesia are discussed in Chapter 12), or the delivery proper. The circulating nurse will uncover the sterile table and basin set and turn on the necessary operative lights. If no spinal anesthesia is used, the doctor usually advises the staff when he wants his patient placed in dorsal lithotomy position with her legs in supports.

Positioning

It is ideal to have two nurses assist in positioning, although it can be accomplished by one. To prevent strain on the patient's back, both legs should be raised or lowered at the same time. Coaching her to bend her knees as her legs are raised helps. Remember, if crutch or stirrup-type legs supports are used, you fit the supports to the patient, you do not fit the patient to the supports! The wrists of the patient are gently secured while she is on the table in order to prevent contamination of the sterile field and not primarily to restrict movement. Most modern delivery tables have some method of dividing in half, temporarily eliminating the foot portion of the table to allow the buttocks to hang over the end of the upper part of the table and the doctor to stand directly in front of the perineum. As soon as the patient's legs are adequately secured in the supports, the table is so adjusted. This is called "dropping," or "breaking the table."

Sterile perineal preparation

As soon as the table is dropped, the circulating nurse cleanses the abdomen, thighs, and complete perineal area with a soap or antiseptic solution. This procedure is the so-called "sterile prep." Again, it is carried out in different ways in different institutions. The principles are the same; the purpose is to help prevent infection and increase the visibility of the area involved. In performing the "prep" to prevent contamination of the birth canal, care should be taken that no sponge is used in the anal-rectal area and then returned to the vulvar region. Usually the first sponge is used to cleanse side to side from the pubic bone to the umbilicus. It is then discarded. The second and third are used to cleanse the thighs with an up-and-down motion from the labia majora to the midthigh. Each is

discarded directly after use. The fourth and fifth are used to clean the labia on the right and left of the vagina, avoiding the rectum, and then discarded. The last cleansing sponge passes directly over the vagina and anus. The patient is then usually rinsed and dried in a similar manner and sprayed or painted with an antiseptic such as benzalkonium chloride (aqueous Zephiran, 1:750). The purpose of the prep should be kept in mind. The object is not to go through so many prescribed motions but to get the patient clean. On the other hand, it must be performed rather swiftly, or the baby may be there before one is through. The gowned doctor is usually ready to drape for delivery as soon as the nurse is finished. Care should be taken that his hands or gown not be contaminated as she completes her "prep."

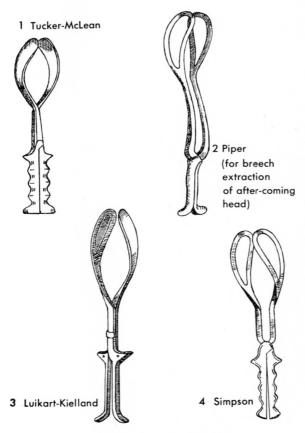

1 Tucker-McLean

2 Piper
(for breech
extraction
of after-coming
head)

3 Luikart-Kielland

4 Simpson

Fig. 11-10. Types of obstetrical forceps.

Draping

During the draping procedure, the circulating nurse provides a stool for the doctor, pushes the sterile supply table and double basin rack into position, adjusts the light, unwraps the forceps if they are desired, secures any additional supplies if needed, and begins her record of the delivery. A copy of one such record is included in Fig. 11-1.

After the patient is draped, no part of the exposed side of the sterile linen (or paper) covering the patient should be touched by anyone not properly gloved or gowned. If pressure must be exerted on the abdomen by a "nonsterile attendant" for any reason, she must reach under the sterile drape, avoiding the exposed perineum to accomplish her task. After the baby is born, if he is placed on his mother's abdomen, she may reach under the covering drape and, using the drape as a hand guard, hold on to an infant arm or leg to help give support while he is aspirated or the cord is tied. Babies can be very slippery.

DELIVERY

Forceps and episiotomies (Figs. 11-10 and 11-11)

If the mother is bearing her first infant, many doctors will assist her efforts by employing outlet forceps to lift out the baby's head. This assist may also be given multiparae. The forceps is applied after an episiotomy or planned incision of the perineum is performed and the bladder emptied by catheterization. Many times the episiotomy and judicious use of forceps considerably shorten the second stage of labor, especially when the use of general anesthesia makes it difficult or impossible for the patient herself to help push the baby. It also may avoid injury to the maternal perineum and the baby's skull. An episiotomy may be cut from the vaginal opening straight down toward, but not extending into, the rectum (midline). It may be cut at 5 or 7 o'clock position from the vaginal opening to extend sideways away from the anus (lateral). It may originate in the midline just above the anus, but then angle to the left

or right (mediolateral). The use of outlet (elective low forceps) is quite common. A midforceps is occasionally applied. The use of a high forceps is never recommended in modern obstetrics. It is too dangerous to mother and baby. Many babies are born

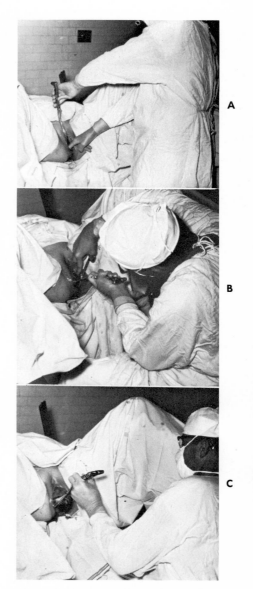

Fig. 11-11. A, Insertion of one forceps blade. B, A midline episiotomy (one blade of the forceps has been inserted). C, Use of outlet forceps. (Courtesy Wayne B. Henderson, M.D., San Diego, Calif.)

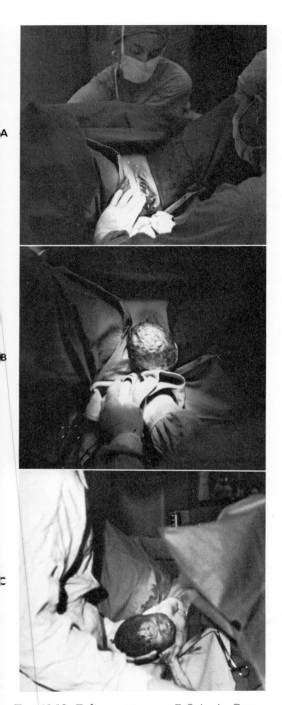

FIG. 11-12. Delivery sequence R.O.A. **A,** Crowning of the head. **B,** Delivery of the head. **C,** Delivery of the shoulders. (This time the posterior shoulder was delivered first.) The newborn infant's face is normally congested at the time of birth. (Courtesy Grossmont Hospital and Martin M. Greenberg, M.D., La Mesa, Calif.)

without any previous episiotomy or forceps application. Most physicians like to catheterize all patients before delivery to deflate the bladder and secure a urine specimen.

Delivery mechanisms (Figs. 11-12 and 11-13)

If a forceps is not used for the complete delivery of the head, it may be delivered manually between contractions by slow gentle extension. If the mother is awake and able, she may be asked to bear down between contractions to facilitate the actual passage of the head from the vaginal canal. After the head is delivered, the doctor checks to see if the umbilical cord is wound around the baby's neck. If it is, it must be slipped over the baby's head or clamped and cut to avoid strangulation or excessive pulling. Even before the entire body of the baby is delivered, the mouth may be aspirated to clear the airway. In order to deliver the shoulders, the doctor usually turns the baby's head to the side so that the occiput lines up with his back. He may then gently but firmly pull down to deliver the top (anterior) shoulder and then gently pull up to deliver the bottom (posterior) shoulder. Before one scarcely realizes it, all of the baby has been born. Further aspiration of the airway may be necessary, but normally the infant cries very soon. His umbilical cord is tied or clamped and cut, and he is handed to the nurse for further care in such a way as to protect the doctor's gloves and make a safe transfer.

The baby

Immediate care. The period immediately after birth is hazardous for the baby. Many adjustments must be made in his body to fit him for his new environment. He should be placed on his side and carefully and frequently observed. The nurse caring for the newborn infant should have freshly washed hands and wear a clean overgown. The nurse must provide warmth (usually in the form of an incubator or a heated blanket), observe his color and breathing

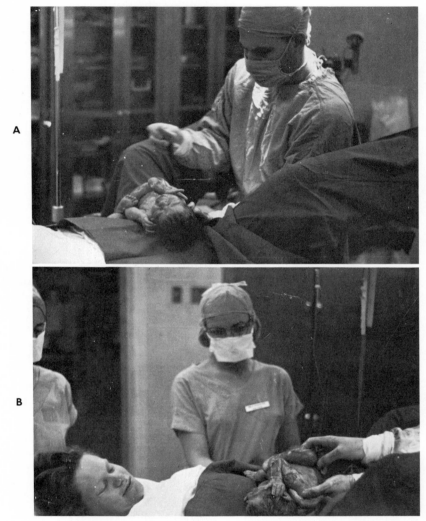

FIG. 11-13. A, Suctioning the airway. B, So here you are at last! (Courtesy Grossmont Hospital and Martin M. Greenberg, M.D.., La Mesa, Calif.)

pattern, and attach the identification approved by the hospital. During the same period of time, she usually performs the prophylaxis prescribed to prevent gonorrheal infection of the eyes. A penicillin preparation or silver nitrate, 1%, is used fol-

°There seems to be lack of agreement regarding the eye rinse to use after AgNO₃ instillation. Some nurseries employ saline because it forms a precipitate (silver chloride), which more quickly inactivates the irritating AgNO₃. Others consider the precipitate itself to be irritating and prefer to use water.

lowed by a rinse of sterile physiological saline or distilled water.°

Apgar evaluation. If the Apgar method of evaluating the newborn infant is used, the infant should also be scored for heart rate, respiratory effort, muscle tone, reflex irritability, and color, one and five minutes after birth. The highest score that can be given is 10. Dr. Apgar believes that few newborn infants conscientiously scored deserve a first rating totaling 10. She believes that a few babies are completely pink 1 minute after birth (see Fig. 11-14).

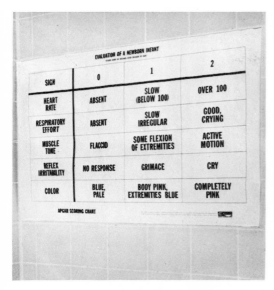

EVALUATION OF A NEWBORN INFANT			
SIGN	0	1	2
HEART RATE	ABSENT	SLOW (BELOW 100)	OVER 100
RESPIRATORY EFFORT	ABSENT	SLOW IRREGULAR	GOOD, CRYING
MUSCLE TONE	FLACCID	SOME FLEXION OF EXTREMITIES	ACTIVE MOTION
REFLEX IRRITABILITY	NO RESPONSE	GRIMACE	CRY
COLOR	BLUE, PALE	BODY PINK, EXTREMITIES BLUE	COMPLETELY PINK

APGAR SCORING CHART

FIG. 11-14. Prominently displayed on the walls of a delivery room is the Apgar Scoring Chart. (From Apgar, V.: J.A.M.A. **168**:1988, 1958.)

THIRD STAGE OF LABOR
Use of oxytocics

In most cases, some form of oxtyocic is ordered after the birth of the baby and/or after the delivery of the placenta. Oxytocin (Pitocin) hastens the delivery of the placenta. After delivery of the placenta, a form of ergot helps the uterus clamp down for a relatively long period to help prevent postpartum hemorrhage.

Delivery of the placenta (Fig. 11-15)

After it has separated from the uterine wall, the placenta may be delivered through the bearing down efforts of the mother if she is awake. More often it is expressed by the manual pressure exerted by the doctor on the fundus through the abdominal wall. This must be done very carefully, and only when the placenta has separated and the fundus is firm. Otherwise, hemorrhage or inversion, a turning inside-out of the uterus, may occur, a grave obstetrical complication.

Signs of placental separation are (1) the rising of the uterus to or above the umbilicus, (2) the rounding out and firming up of the top of the uterus or fundus, (3) the lengthening of the umbilical cord outside the vulva, and (4) a small gush of blood to the exterior. The placenta should be inspected to see if it was delivered in its entirety. Some doctors also perform an internal palpation of the uterus to assure themselves of its condition. In some hospitals, placentas that have not become contaminated with stool or were not born of women whose pregnancies were complicated by infectious disease, fever, or premature rupture of the membranes are saved and later processed by a pharmaceutical concern to extract the immune globulin they contain.

IMMEDIATE POSTPARTUM CARE
Lacerations

After the delivery of the placenta, any necessary perineal repair can be made (Fig. 11-16). Generally the same anesthetic used for the delivery can be employed. Sometimes a local anesthetic is administered. If this is used, the doctor will need a syringe (usually Pitkin), some infiltration needles, and the local anesthetic of choice as well as the usual materials involved in a perineal repair. He will want to sit down and be provided with a good light.

Lacerations of the perineum are described as first, second, or third degree. First-degree lacerations, involving a tear in the mucous membrane and skin only, are fairly common and usually of no permanent consequence. Second-degree lacerations include a tear into the muscles of the perineal block, but exclude the rectal sphincter. Adequately repaired, they usually heal well with little problem. Third-degree lacerations, however, are more difficult to repair and may result in permanent damage to the perineum and sphincter (review the anatomy of the pelvic floor).

During this time, if the mother is awake, she is cutsomarily shown her baby, after which he is taken to the nursery with the appropriate records of the delivery. If she is not alert, definite arrangement should be

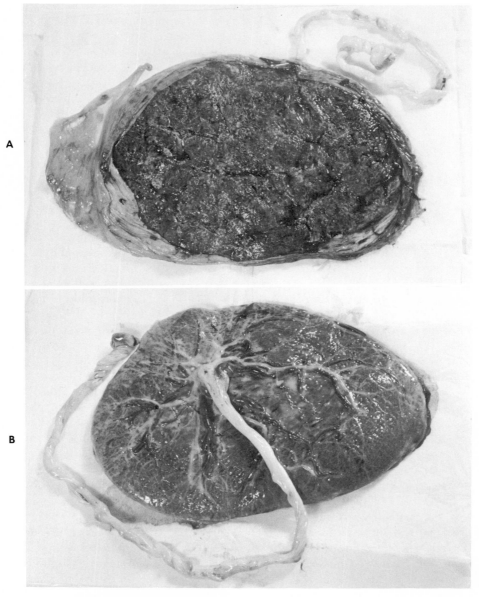

FIG. 11-15. Placenta. **A,** Maternal side showing cotyledons and membranes pulled to one side. The cord attaches on the opposite side. If this side appears first at the outlet, the placenta is said to have separated by Duncan's mechanism. **B,** Fetal side showing the insertion of the cord. If this side appears first at the outlet, the placental separation is by Schultz's mechanism. (Courtesy Grossmont Hospital and Martin M. Greenberg, M.D., La Mesa, Calif.)

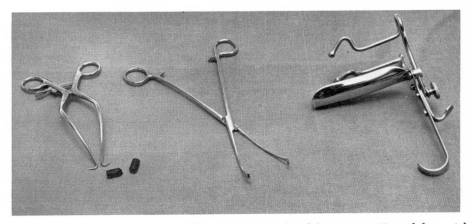

FIG. 11-16. Some instruments commonly used in the labor-delivery area. From left to right, the Gelpi perineal retractor used by some physicians during perineal repairs, an Iowa clamp used to rupture membranes during labor, and the Pelvi-fix or Tri-Blade retractor used occasionally during repairs. (Courtesy Grossmont Hospital, La Mesa, Calif.)

made for her to see the infant later as soon as she is able.

With the termination of the repair and the cleansing of the perineum, if needed, the head and foot of the delivery table are again realigned, and the patient's legs removed from the stirrups or supports. The perineal pads are attached, and a warm, clean hospital gown replaces the one worn by the patient during delivery. She is covered by a warm blanket. In some maternity services the initial preparation of the breasts of nursing mothers is done at this time also.

Observation

All during this early postpartum period, the patient is being observed for excessive bleeding and signs of shock. The blood pressure and pulse are frequently determined and the respiration observed. The uterus is palpated frequently to discover any relaxation of the fundus. If an intravenous infusion is in place (often used in conjunction with spinal anesthesia), it is carefully watched for rate of administration and possible infiltration. Many of these infusions contain an oxytocic and should not be given rapidly. Great care should be exercised that the needle is not dislodged during the transfer of the patient

from the delivery table to the cart. Several hands may be needed for this project if the patient has an intravenous infusion and is temporarily unable to use her legs properly because of the lingering effects of spinal anesthesia. The newly delivered mother may remain in the delivery room suite for a specified time for close observation near equipment that may be needed, or she may be transferred to a special postpartum recovery room. At the time of her various changes in location, special attention should be given to the transfer of her personal belongings. The husband and other family members should see her as soon after delivery as is appropriate, although they are not encouraged to have a long visit. Mother needs her rest!

SPECIAL SITUATIONS

Because questions always develop concerning them, we will now take time to consider some special situations that occasionally arise in the labor-delivery sequence.

Precipitate delivery

First to be considered is what is termed "precipitate delivery." This means a delivery that occurs with such speed and in such a situation that proper preparation and medical supervision of the event are lacking. A multipara with a relaxed perineal floor may have an extremely short period of expulsion. Two or three powerful contractions may cause the baby to appear with considerable rapidity. In this case, the nurse may be the only one at the bedside or delivery table to assist the patient. In no instance should she leave the patient alone. If it is obvious that the baby would be born before the delivery room is reached (for example, the patient is a para iii and the head is almost delivered), the nurse should do the best she can with what she has at hand. If present, any family member should be asked to step outside the room. The call light should be turned on. If there is time and it is available, an antiseptic lubricant such as pHisoHex may be poured over the perineum. The nurse should wash her hands or put on sterile gloves. A few towels are handy.

Birth of the head. The baby's head should not be forcibly held back, since this may cause fetal distress and aspiration, but it should be restrained to prevent a rapid exit from the vaginal canal. This restraint can usually be achieved by allowing the baby to deliver slowly against a guiding hand placed on the top of the advancing head. The fingers of the nurse should not enter the vagina. If the bag of waters is not broken, it must be pinched or torn to release the fluid and protect the baby from aspiration. The actual delivery of the head should be accomplished between contractions, the mother panting or lightly bearing down as needed to assist. As soon as the head is born, the nurse should wipe off the face and check to determine whether the cord is around the neck. If it is, she should slip it over the head or shoulders to prevent choking. Rarely it may be too tight to slip over with the fingers. If this happens, it is hoped that sterile clamps and scissors are available in the labor room or that a staff member has answered the light and brought the emergency pack containing the clamps and scissors necessary to cut the cord! The mother should firmly be instructed to pant through her open mouth and not push during this interval.

External rotation and expulsion. After the head is delivered and wiped and the location of the cord determined, if the back of the head has not already turned toward the mother's thigh, it should be turned in the direction of least resistance. There is no need to hurry. Next, the head should gently but firmly be directed downward to deliver the top shoulder. After the top shoulder is expelled, the baby is lifted up toward the pubic bone to release the bottom shoulder. The rest of the child is delivered without any particular problem. Before the expulsion of the shoulders, it is sometimes very helpful if the mother's hips can be elevated (for example, on a bedpan) by another person in order to give more room for the gentle up-and-down maneuvers described.

Immediate care of the baby. After the complete birth of the baby, care should be exercised that the airway be cleared. The baby should not lie in a puddle of amniotic fluid where aspiration can take place. He should be held upside down to "drain" without any tension being placed on the umbilical cord. After the airway is clear, he may be gently stimulated to cry, if necessary, and placed on his mother's abdomen —head slightly lower than his body. (Most of these babies cry immediately.) He should be wrapped in a towel or blanket for warmth. There is no haste to cut the cord, or for that matter to deliver the placenta. The cord can wait until proper sterile equipment is available. Usually the physician, who in the meantime has been contacted by the staff, completes the delivery of the placenta and repairs any possible lacerations. A calm, reassuring manner on the part of the nurse (even if she doesn't really feel so calm) is very helpful to the patient and all concerned. Usually no great permanent harm results from such an event, but every effort should be made to prevent its occurring. All patients should be frequently evaluated for progress during labor. Signs of the approach of the second stage of labor should not be ignored. In such deliveries, the advantages of antisepsis and asepsis are largely lost, there is greater danger of injury to the maternal tissues, danger of aspiration and injury to the baby, and acute embarrassment for the patient, not to mention the nurse.

Summary. Principles of emergency unprepared delivery no matter where it takes place include the following:

1. Keeping contaminating articles, including fingers, from the birth canal and providing as clean a delivery area as possible
2. Helping the head deliver slowly against a clean towel or hand and allowing its delivery between contractions to prevent perineal lacerations
3. Allowing the normal mechanism of labor to take place with a minimum of interference
4. Holding the newborn infant upside down to clear the airway—no tension on the cord
5. Gently stimulating the infant to breathe, if necessary, after placing the child on the mother's abdomen
6. Providing warmth for the newborn infant
7. Waiting for sterile supplies to be available to cut the cord
8. Waiting for delivery of the placenta unless professional aid is very long in arriving or excessive bleeding occurs (However, if no professional help is forthcoming, if the signs of separation of the placenta have occurred, if the uterus is firm, and if the mother experiences a return of contractions, she may be asked to bear down to deliver the placenta. It should be supported as it is born so that the membranes are not torn. It should be saved for later evaluation by a doctor.)

Induction of labor

At times in the labor suite there may be admitted a mother-to-be who is not in labor at all. She has come on appointment to have her labor induced.

Reasons for induction. There may be several reasons for an induction of labor: (1) a problem with erythroblastosis fetalis may have developed, (2) the mother may be diabetic, (3) the mother may have increasing symptoms of toxemia or placenta previa, or (4) the baby may be *definitely* late in arriving (postmaturity). Occasionally, induction is planned for the convenience of the patient or the doctor, although this is not usually considered a valid reason.

Methods and care. Candidates for induction of labor must be selected carefully, since it is not a procedure totally without risk to the mother and baby. In the past, prescriptions of castor oil and/or warm enemas were often made to start labor. But there are two main ways of inducing labor in the hospital today: the administration of pituitary hormones or their synthetic substitutes (most commonly Pitocin) and/or the artificial rupture of the membranes. Neither of these techniques will produce results unless the uterus has reached a certain stage of readiness for labor. The cervix must at least be partially effaced and soft and pliable. If the membranes are artificially ruptured and labor does not begin within 24 hours, the possibility of introducing infection must be faced. Posterior pituitary extract is very powerful and can cause violent uterine contractions. For this reason, mothers receiving this medication must be closely watched with very frequent checks of contraction patterns, fetal heart tone, and blood pressure. Today oxytocin (Pitocin) is probably most often administered by intravenous drip (usually 10 units of Pitocin per 1,000 ml. of 5% glucose in water) The rate of flow is usually ordered by the physician, who should be in the area while his patient is receiving such treatment.

Cesarean section

With the decreasing risk involved in the performance of cesarean section, the removal of the child through an incision in the abdominal and uterine walls, the operation is used more frequently in modern obstetrics.

Reasons for cesarean section. Sometimes patients admitted to the labor area will unexpectedly demonstrate symptoms that will advise the emergency use of the procedure: conditions such as placentae abruptio, placenta previa, fetal-pelvic disproportion, abnormal presentations, prolapsed cord, or uterine inertia (failure of the uterus to contract sufficiently to continue progress in labor). The most common cause for cesarean section in the United States, however, is not usually an emergency, but a previous cesarean section. It can be scheduled days in advance. But conditions that indicate acute fetal distress or maternal jeopardy demand the prompt and rapid preparation of the patient once the condition has been discovered and the course of action determined. A patient scheduled for an emergency cesarean section is subjected to much in a very few minutes. Everything should be done with as much calmness and dispatch as possible. The patient's morale should be supported as much as possible, because, if she is alert, she will probably be very frightened.

Preparation. The following procedures are routinely carried out:

1. Signing of the operative permit by the patient or responsible party
2. An abdominal-perineal prep, which starts at the nipple line and includes the entire abdomen from side to side as well as the perineal and rectal areas
3. Insertion of an indwelling catheter—sometimes done in surgery after anesthesia
4. Blood type and crossmatch and hemoglobin determination
5. Removal of any hairpins or hard objects from the hair; application of a surgical cap; removal of any extra jewelry, glasses, contact lenses, etc., to be given to the family; taping of wedding and engagement rings to the fingers, but not so as to impede circulation
6. Removal and safekeeping of any removable dentures
7. Removal of any nail polish from at least two or three fingers of each hand, in order that the anesthetist can check for cyanosis of the nail beds
8. Preoperative medications as ordered

The patient is given nothing by mouth as soon as cesarean section is contemplated, if this measure has not been instituted previously. An infusion may be started, although usually intravenous therapy is begun in the area where the actual section will take place.

Patients may be transferred to the operating room suite for surgery, or a delivery room may be prepared for the procedure. During all the busy preparations, any family members present should not be forgotten, and provision should be made for them to wait in as much mental and physical comfort as possible.

Discussion of the care of a cesarean patient after delivery is included in the section of the book treating the postpartum period.

Breech presentation

Another situation that is fairly often part of the labor-delivery experience is a breech presentation.

Incidence. You will recall that breech births make up approximately 3% of all deliveries. In former years, considerable effort was exerted in trying to turn these babies to a cephalic presentation before the onset of labor. Many were turned without too much difficulty only to revert back to a breech before the time of labor. Many practitioners now believe that if a baby is found to be a breech it is because of a valid anatomical or physiological reason, and there are fewer attempts to turn the child (a process called version).

Complications. Although a breech presentation would probably not be considered an abnormality, it involves more risk to the infant than a cephalic birth, and the mother is likely to have a longer and more tiring labor. As a rule there is greater possibility of prolapse of the umbilical cord during breech labor, and during the delivery of the body of the baby, it may be compressed against the pelvic outlet. The baby may try to take a breath before his head has been born and aspirate tenacious vaginal secretions. Occasionally, trouble is encountered in the extraction of the arms. Sometimes an unexpectedly large head may cause concern, and cerebral damage may occur. Although few maternity services today routinely provide a sterile scrub nurse in the delivery room, many physicians appreciate and request the help of such a nurse at the time of breech delivery. Such an attendant usually helps support the baby's body or may, when instructed, apply fundal pressure when it comes time for the delivery of the head. A special type of forceps called "Pipers" applied to the aftercoming head may be used at the time of a breech birth. They should always be on the sterile supply table when a breech delivery is anticipated. The delivery of the head is many times accomplished in such a way that the baby almost seems to do a guided half somersault over the mother's abdomen. A rather deep episiotomy is customary in breech deliveries. The baby may have edematous or bruised genitalia. In a minority of cases the doctor may elect to perform a cesarean section because of the general condition, history, or age of a patient.

Twins

Twins are another interesting feature of the obstetrical department. They occur about once every ninety pregnancies. There are two types of twins—fraternal and identical. Fraternal twins are the result of two simultaneous pregnancies developing from the fertilization of two separate ova by two distinct spermatozoa. They do not resemble one another any more than siblings resemble one another. They may be of the same sex or of opposite sexes. The placental circulation of each fetus is separate, although the adjoining placentas may be fused. Each fetus develops within its own amniotic and chorionic sac.

Identical twins result from the division of one fertilized ovum into two identical halves, which develop into two similar individuals of the same sex. The placental circulation is shared by the attachment of two umbilical cords. Each infant is encased in a separate amniotic sac but shares the chorionic sac with his twin. Fraternal twins are more common than those classified as identical. Twins are almost always premature, and the nursery should be alerted when a twin birth is anticipated. Occasionally, such an event is not anticipated, and the family, doctor, and nurse are surprised to receive a "bonus baby."

Preparations and complications. When twinning is expected, two sets of identifications should be ready with double newborn record sheets. Two sterile baby receiving blankets, two cord clamps, and two aspirator bulbs should be available. In almost half of all twin births both infants are cephalic presentations, but any combination of presentations and positions may exist. Occasionally, the babies' relative positions may cause problems in their delivery. Mothers of twins are more likely to suffer from toxemia of pregnancy and, because of the greater distention of the uterus, are more often victims of postpartum hemorrhage.

• • •

The nurse's experience in the labor-delivery room area can be a very satisfying, rewarding type of nursing. If skilled in the art of human relations and the observations and procedural techniques necessary to care for her patients, she can play an indispensable and gratifying role in a very crucial period in the life of a family. The alert student in this area can learn much and gain an appreciation and reverence of life that she will never forget.

12
Analgesia and anesthesia

Methods of pain relief

One should not leave the subject of modern childbirth without at least discussing briefly the most common methods being used to make the experience of labor and delivery easier and more comfortable for the mother. As we have seen these methods involve more than the administration of drugs; they also include ways available to help the patient to better understand the process of childbirth and to consciously cooperate with what her body is trying to accomplish. In most cases a clean, calm, quiet, dimmed environment, attention to the techniques of relaxation, the application of sacral support, the close supervision and encouragement of a concerned nursing staff and attending physician, and the companionship of those she loves will greatly decrease the need for the administration of analgesic and anesthetic drugs.

Key vocabulary

Five words perhaps should be defined for our use before a discussion of pain-relieving drugs is attempted.

amnesic a technique or medication that causes memory loss of varying degrees.
analgesic a technique or medication that reduces or eliminates pain.
anesthetic a technique or medication that partially or completely eliminates sensation or feeling. It may be local in extent or general, producing unconsciousness.
hypnotic a technique or medication that causes sleep.
sedative or **tranquilizer** a technique or medication that relieves anxiety and quiets the patient.

Obstetrical analgesia (first stage)

The prescription and administration of analgesic drugs during the first stage of labor is not without difficulty but is highly rewarding.

Special considerations

The physician must consider that he is caring for two patients. He must realize that many analgesics have a hypnotic effect not only on the mother but also on her unborn baby. He must so calculate the dosage and time of administration that the baby is not "sleepy" at the time of his birth and too drowsy to want to breathe on his own. Before delivery the sleepiness of the fetus is not so crucial because it does not have to breathe; it gets all its oxygen from the mother. But after birth this oxygen supply is no longer available. Failure to breathe or respiratory depression results in a condition known as asphyxia neonatorum. If a premature delivery is expected, the mother will be encouraged to carry through her labor with a minimum amount of analgesia. Happily, some antagonistic medications, for example nalorphine (Nalline), are now available to counteract the depressant action of drugs containing morphine and its derivatives on the newborn infant's respiratory system. However, doctors do not like to be forced to use them because occasionally they cause effects opposite from those desired and further depress the infant.

Another consideration that must be made in the administration of drugs during the first stage of labor is the possible effect of the medication on the progress of the labor. Given too soon, many analgesics may unnecessarily slow down or even stop contractions. Most physicians do not wish to give any drug before approximately 4 cm. dilatation has been achieved. Many patients will not need medication prior to or even after this dilatation has been reached.

Hypnotics and amnesics: effects and side effects

Many times, more than one drug will be used to gain the desired result. For example, the analgesic meperidine hydrochloride (Demerol) and the tranquilizer hydroxyzine (Atarax) are often given together with usually excellent results. The combination makes both medications more effective than they would be if given alone.

If an amnesic or hypnotic drug is given without an analgesic in the presence of pain, great restlessness can be produced in the patient. Amnesics such as scopolamine are usually accompanied by pain-relieving drugs such as meperidine hydrochloride. Scopolamine reduces anxiety and promotes amnesia for the period of labor. It is also used because it helps to dry the oral and bronchial secretions in preparation for future inhalation anesthesia and combats vagus nerve stimulation, which can cause irregularities in the heartbeat. However, the liberal use of the drug with barbiturate hypnotics such as pentobarbital sodium (Nembutal) or, at times, analgesics may cause disorientation. Many patients so medicated do not remember their labors, but their nurses usually do. Often the patients are so restless that it is difficult to minister to their needs. They require constant supervision to avoid injury in the labor room, and many hands may be rallied to place them in position for delivery. True, the patients are spared discomfort, but they also lose much of the creative feeling of having consciously participated in the drama of labor and usually are not sufficiently alert for many hours to welcome their babies after they arrive. Still, this method of pain relief during labor is followed by some physicians.

Trichloroethylene (Trilene) inhalations (Fig. 12-1)

Occasionally, a type of inhalation analgesia is offered during the latter part of the first stage of labor that is controlled by the patient herself. This is trichloroethylene (Trilene), a clear, blue liquid that readily assumes the form of a gas. It is placed in a cylinder that is equipped with a mask and a wrist attachment (the Duke inhaler). As the approach of a contraction is detected, the patient puts the mask to her face and breathes deeply. As the patient momentarily loses consciousness, her grip on the mask weakens, and the administration of the trichloroethylene comes to an end until needed again. The nurse should never "assist" the patient in holding the apparatus over her face because this may result in overdosage. Trichloroethylene may cause heartbeat irregularities, and it has the disadvantage of lingering in the body. A patient who has recently received it should not receive other anesthetics through a gas machine that employs soda lime to absorb carbon dioxide. Such use can cause the formation of very toxic gases.

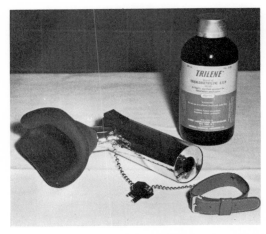

FIG. 12-1. The Duke inhaler used for self-administration of trichloroethylene (Trilene). (Courtesy Grossmont Hospital, La Mesa, Calif.)

Trichloroethylene is often used in conjunction with local anesthetics, especially when trained anesthetists are not available. For the most part, inhalation therapy is restricted to use in the second stage of labor.

Obstetrical analgesia and anesthesia (second and third stages)
General anesthesia

In obstetrics, a general anesthetic is usually inhaled (Fig. 12-2), although occasionally it may be administered intravenously.

Special considerations. When inhalation anesthesia is planned, it is very important to know how recently the patient has eaten because there is real danger of aspiration, obstruction of the airway (asphyxiation), and/or pneumonia. For the same reasons it is also important to remove any gum or

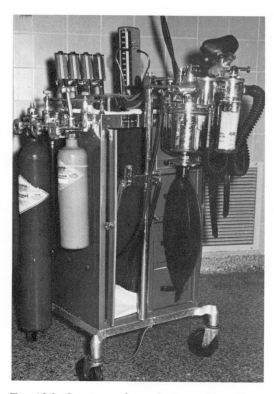

FIG. 12-2. One type of anesthetic machine. Gases commonly administered are nitrous oxide, cyclopropane, and oxygen. (Courtesy Grossmont Hospital, La Mesa, Calif.)

movable dentures from the mouth. Many gases used during anesthesia either support burning or are explosive. For this reason, delivery room nurses should routinely wear conductive footwear and clothing that will not build up static electricity and cause a spark. Nylon uniforms and underwear are not allowed. All equipment in the delivery room and the floor itself must be grounded. Periodic checks for conductivity must be made. Unnecessary, purposeless movement in the delivery room is discouraged; it is confusing and a possible explosion hazard. With the exception of the anesthetist, personnel should stay away from the gas machine or locale of gas administration during a delivery, since gases are concentrated in this area. Danger of explosion is probably greatest just at emergence (the completion of gas administration). During the period when a patient is being put to sleep (the period of induction), the delivery room should be as quiet as possible to make the induction smooth without patient distraction. Undue confusion and noise should also be avoided at the time of emergence.

All inhaled anesthetics, if given in sufficient concentration, will eventually pass the placental barrier to produce symptoms in the child. Therefore, they should not be started too far in advance of the expected birth of the infant. It is said that there is usually a margin of about 8 minutes before gas passes the placental barrier. General anesthetics may be accompanied or followed by nausea and vomiting. For this reason, it is routine to give a progressing patient in labor nothing by mouth. The nurse should be prepared for such problems and not offer unrestricted amounts of fluid or any solid food too soon after delivery. In case of vomiting, the patient's head should be turned to the side. Even better, if possible, is the maintenance of a side position.

Ether and chloroform, although still used in various areas of the United States, are not often administered in a hospital obstetrical area. Other medications are more advantageous and safe, although these newer agents may necessitate more complicated equipment and more trained personnel for their administration. Anesthesia is the province of the trained physician, anesthesiologist, or nurse-anesthetist. Nurses should not attempt to function in this area without skilled advanced training. The administration of anesthesia is not a nursing function.

The gases most often used in modern obstetrics in a hospital setting are oxygen, nitrous oxide, and cyclopropane. Oxygen must always be mixed with anesthetics to supply the body needs of the mother and her unborn child.

Nitrous oxide. Nitrous oxide (laughing gas) with oxygen is often given for analgesic effect at the period of expulsion during contractions. Administered in low percentages, it relieves the mother but still allows her to bear down with her contractions. Nitrous oxide may support combustion but is nonexplosive.

Cyclopropane. Cyclopropane is a useful fast-acting gas that produces fairly good muscular relaxation and allows a high oxygen concentration with a wide margin of safety for the mother and child. However, it is extremely explosive and may produce laryngospasm and heart irregularities. The danger of explosion persists after delivery in the immediate postpartum period because the gas is expelled from the body through the respiratory tract. Smoking should not be permitted in the postpartum room of this patient after her delivery.

Regional and local anesthesia

Regional anesthetics have enjoyed considerable popularity in recent years.

Saddle block. The use of low spinal, or "saddle," anesthesia has been particularly successful. The patient is supported on the edge of the delivery table with her back arched forward. The physician, using sterile technique, inserts a long spinal needle between the vertebrae at about the level of the iliac crests. The needle tip is placed in the subarachnoid space below the spinal cord proper. Its position is identified by the appearance of cerebrospinal fluid dripping from the needle's hub. Between contrac-

tions, an anesthetic that is heavier than the cerebrospinal fluid is injected into the subarachnoid space. Examples of anesthetics used include hexylcaine hydrochloride (Cyclaine), tetracaine hydrochloride (Pontocaine), and lidocaine (Xylocaine). The patient may be kept in a sitting position for 30 seconds after its instillation. She is then lowered to the delivery table to a position flat on her back with only her head elevated on two pillows. Such timing and positioning help localize the anesthetic at the correct level in the spinal canal. (See Fig. 12-3.)

Low spinal, or saddle-type, anesthesia deadens the abdominal and pelvic area below the umbilicus, and it usually affects the legs and feet as well. Classically, a "saddle" is only supposed to affect those areas of the body that would be touched by a saddle if a person were riding horseback. In practice, the anesthesia is usually more extensive. It begins to take effect immediately and gains maximum potency in about 8 to 10 minutes. How long it lasts depends on the medication used (1 to 3 hours). Because of vertebral abnormalities not all women can have spinals. A few are allergic to the type of medications usually injected. Sometimes lack of time or medical personnel able to do the lumbar puncture required precludes the use of a spinal anesthetic.

Much has been said about the aftereffects of spinal anesthesia. The so-called "spinal headache" is a complication often feared by patients. In fact, we have heard physicians counsel that the word "saddle" be used exclusively with patients because of anxiety that may have been previously built up concerning spinals. Actually, low spinal, or saddle, anesthesia does not deserve the poor reputation that it has in the minds of some members of the public. The incidence of postdelivery spinal headache has been estimated at less than 5% and is decreasing with the adoption of different techniques (for example, the use of an intravenous infusion to promote better hydration of the patient and the insertion of

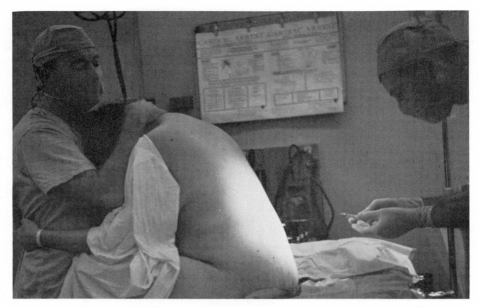

Fig. 12-3. Administration of a low spinal anesthetic. (Courtesy Grossmont Hospital and Martin M. Greenberg, M.D., La Mesa, Calif.)

only small-bore spinal needles to cut down on the possibility of cerebrospinal fluid leakage). Whether keeping the patient flat during the postdelivery period helps is debatable. Spinal anesthesia does entail certain other inconveniences, however. The mother must sit quietly while the procedure is carried out. This is difficult to do during the second stage of labor, even with the support of an understanding nurse. Saddle anesthesia does not stop contractions, but the patient does not feel them. She finds it difficult to push properly, and many times outlet forceps are used. Occasionally, a patient may experience a drop in blood pressure that may affect the baby's oxygen supply, or she may suffer from respiratory problems because of a high level of anesthesia. In the postpartum period the patient may find it more difficult to void spontaneously.

In the minds of many practitioners the negative aspects of this type of anesthesia are outweighed by its positive aspects. The baby is not in danger of being put to sleep by the anesthetic and of having a difficult time breathing at birth because of its action. The mother is awake. If she desires, she may see her baby born. She can hear his first cry—a real thrill. The regional anesthetics are safer than "gas" for a patient who has recently eaten, since nausea and vomiting during and after their use are minimal.

Caudal anesthesia. Other types of regional anesthetics are available. In considerable vogue for a time was *continuous caudal anesthesia,* or one-shot caudal, which introduces anesthetic agents into the sacral canal, where significant nerves travel outside the meninges or spinal cord coverings. This type of anesthetic can be used for pain relief during the latter part of the first stage of labor as well as during the second and third stages. However, its use involves the constant attention of an anesthetist and special apparatus. In the hands of the unskilled it can be dangerous, but this observation can be made of almost any nursing or medical procedure!

Pudendal block. Local anesthesia using direct infiltration of the perineal tissues or infiltration of those local nerve centers that serve to relay sensation initiated in the perineal area to the brain is probably the safest anesthesia for both mother and baby available today. A popular technique blocks four separate nerves by infiltration of a medication into specific areas using a long needle. It may be used in conjunction with nitrous oxide very satisfactorily. It is called a *pudendal block*. With its use, an episiotomy may be performed or outlet forceps applied. However, some women do not experience the relief they desire. This technique often causes some temporary bruising of the perineum.

Paracervical block. Another type of regional anesthetic that has been used less frequently but is favored in certain cases by individual physicians is the paracervical block. Approximately 10 ml. of local anesthetic is injected into the lateral fornices of the vagina at the junctions of the vaginal wall and cervix that correspond to the 3 and 9 o'clock positions on the face of a watch. This injection, usually performed with a special needle guard to prevent inadvertent deep infiltration, interrupts the sensory impulses traveling from the uterus to the spinal cord in the paracervical area. Anesthesia relieving the discomfort of uterine contractions develops in 3 to 5 minutes and may last approximately 1 to 2 hours. However, the procedure does not anesthetize perineal tissue and in most instances is not considered sufficient in itself to meet the total needs of the patient during the second and third stages of labor.

The paracervical block may be performed in the delivery or labor room when the patient has completed a cervical dilatation of more than 4 and less than 8 cm. Most patients report considerable benefit. When properly done, the technique, barring personal idiosyncrasies to the anesthetic employed, should have no adverse effect on the mother or child. However, when injections are repeated, temporary slowing of the fetal heart rate has been reported. Fetal heart tone should be checked fre-quently. Maternal blood pressure should also be taken regularly to detect possible medication reactions.

Education for childbirth

Modern trends in obstetrics favor a more alert patient during labor who is able to participate with dignity in her experience of childbirth. This means that there have been greater efforts made to educate the woman for her role, both psychologically and physically. Courses have been instituted to teach helpful techniques in posture, breathing, and relaxation, as well as impart basic information to the expectant mother. Many times her husband also attends some sessions in order to better understand and aid his wife.

The late English obstetrician, Dr. Grantly Dick Read, probably popularized the term "natural childbirth" in his book *Childbirth Without Fear*. In his writings and lectures he stressed that much of the fear felt by mothers-to-be was caused by a lack of knowledge of what was really happening and an ensuing feeling of helplessness. He declared that fear builds tension and that tension eventually produces pain. Because of this, much of his effort was spent in educating the future mother and prescribing exercises to better fit her body for labor and delivery. He stated that "Elation, relaxation, amnesia and exultation are the four pillars of parturition upon which the conduct of labor depends."* All his instruction was designed to strengthen these "pillars."

In 1952 the French obstetrician Fernand Lamaze became intrigued with the labor and delivery techniques based on Pavlov's theories of conditioned response he observed during a visit to the Soviet Union. When he returned to Paris, he introduced "psychoprophylactic" concepts into his practice to better prepare his patients for their maternity experiences and assist them to a conscious, rewarding participation in the

*From Read, G. D.: Childbirth without fear, ed. 2, New York, 1953, Harper & Row, Publishers.

birth of their children. Much of what he emphasized was also stressed by Dr. Read. However, the relaxation taught by Dr. Lamaze is based on the principle that a high level of concentrated cerebral activity can inhibit the reception of other stimuli. That is, the mind (psycho) could be induced to prevent (prophylaxis) the reception of unpleasant and painful sensations. Using the Lamaze techniques, the patient is educated (conditioned) to respond neuromuscularly to specific verbal cues. Intense preoccupation with certain muscular tension and release patterns, respiratory movements, and massage helps to attain these goals. A specially prepared labor coach, or "monitrice," may be assigned to assist and support the patient in her efforts to utilize her training.

The monitrice, the patient's husband, and the entire labor-delivery room staff should work as a team for the realization of a constructive, dignified, aware, satisfying parturition. The attending nurses should be calm, cheerful, and knowledgeable concerning the aims of the techniques employed. The details of the exercises used may differ but it is helpful if the delivery room nurses acquaint themselves with the psychoprophylactic programs that may be available in their communities and how the women have been taught. The mothers so trained for labor need nursing support and encouragement. The patient needs a nurse who will enhance, not disturb, her concentration during contractions; help evaluate and aid relaxation; render sacral support or pressure as directed; and be sincerely complimentary of the idealism and efforts manifested by the patient and her husband. In addition, the nurse should render the other nursing care services and watchful observation that all laboring patients require. Occasionally, symptoms of hyperventilation may be associated with some of the rapid-breathing techniques used. The patient may complain of tingling of the hands and feet, which causes her annoyance and loss of concentration. Slowing respirations or breathing into a paper bag helps relieve these problems. The absence of all forms of drug-induced analgesia or anesthesia is not a prerequisite of either the Read or Lamaze method, although this interpretation has been made. However, many patients do not use any drugs.

Those who have evaluated these techniques (cared for patients who were prepared as recommended) usually believe them to be of real value. The main problem seems to be securing enough time and personnel to adequately prepare the patient. The patient herself may find it difficult to attend instruction classes. Many people do not agree that these methods of caring for the childbearing woman are truly "natural childbirth." They look on them as "intensive education and preparation for childbirth." Some patients respond very well to the conditioning offered; others have personal histories or personality structures that make constructive participation in labor and delivery such as Read and Lamaze recommended very difficult or impossible. Both methods are advised only for those undergoing a normal labor and delivery. For those qualified candidates able to seek out a sympathetic practitioner and to undertake the intensive preparation involved, such a management of labor and delivery can bring many enduring rewards, not the least of which is a characteristically noisy, pink, new member of the family.

Hypnosis

No discussion of obstetrical analgesia and anesthesia can be undertaken without mentioning the possibilities of hypnosis. Admittedly the possibilities exist for the use of hypnotic suggestion in obstetrics, but little scientific research has been done in the field. More experience and training are needed before hypnosis can be evaluated as a method of pain relief in obstetrics.

From the foregoing it must be evident to the reader that no perfect means of pain relief applicable to all patients and situations has been found. But it is also clear that the physician has at his disposal many agents of worth, which, when used judiciously and backed up by good nursing care, will assist the patient tremendously.

UNIT IV

**SUGGESTED SELECTED READINGS
AND REFERENCES**

Allen, S.: Nurse attendance during labor, Amer. J. Nurs. **64:**70-74, July, 1964.

Bookmiller, M. M., and Bowen, G. L.: Textbook of obstetrics and obstetric nursing, ed. 5, Philadelphia, 1967, W. B. Saunders Co.

Davis, M. E., and Rubin, R.: DeLee's obstetrics for nurses, ed. 18, Philadelphia, 1966, W. B. Saunders Co.

Estey, G. P.: Natural childbirth—word from a mother, Amer. J. Nurs. **69:**1453-1454, July, 1969.

Fitzpatrick, E., Eastman, N. J., and Reeder, S. R.: Maternity nursing, ed. 11, Philadelphia, 1966, J. B. Lippincott Co.

Greiss, F. C., Jr.: Obstetric anesthesia, Amer. J. Nurs. **71:**67-69, Jan., 1971.

Hoff, F. E.: Natural childbirth—how any nurse can help, Amer. J. Nurs. **69:**1451-1453, July, 1969.

Hommel, F.: Natural childbirth—nurses in private practice as monitrices, Amer. J. Nurs. **69:**1447-1450, July, 1969.

Iorio, J.: Effective support during labor and delivery, RN **25:**70-78, 88, Feb., 1962.

Karmel, M.: Thank you, Dr. Lamaze, Philadelphia, 1959, J. B. Lippincott Co.

Maternity Center Association: Psychophysical preparation for childbearing: guidelines for teaching, ed. 2, New York, 1965, The Association.

Matousek, I.: Fetal nursing during labor, Nurs. Clin. N. Amer., pp. 307-314, 1968.

Miller, J. S.: Childbirth, a manual for pregnancy and delivery, New York, 1963, Atheneum Publishers.

Oxorn, H., and Foote, W. R.: Human labor and birth, New York, 1964, Appleton-Century-Crofts.

Read, G. D.: Childbirth without fear, ed. 2, New York, 1953, Harper & Row, Publishers.

Regan, W. A.: The legal hazards of OB nursing, RN **29:**37+, Feb., 1966.

Silverman, W. A., and Parke, P. C.: The newborn, keep him warm, Amer. J. Nurs. **65:**81-84, Oct., 1965.

Tryon, P. A.: Assessing the progress of labor through observation of patient's behavior, Nurs. Clin. N. Amer., pp. 315-326, 1968.

Ulin, P. R.: Changing techniques in psychoprophylactic preparation for childbirth, Amer. J. Nurs. **68:**2587-2591, Dec., 1968.

Williams, B. L., and Richards, S. F.: Fetal monitoring during labor, Amer. J. Nurs. **70:**2384-2388, Nov., 1970.

UNIT V

COMPLICATIONS ASSOCIATED WITH PREGNANCY AND DELIVERY

13

Minor problems of pregnancy

Once upon a time there was a French obstetrician named Mauriceau who declared that pregnancy was a disease of 9 months' duration. Although today we do not like the term "disease" applied to normal pregnancy, many minor discomforts are commonly associated with this period of waiting. Some were mentioned in Chapter 9. Now let us take a more detailed look at those discomforts and others not previously discussed.

Digestive difficulties

Nausea and vomiting. Probably the first discomfort noted by many pregnant women is nausea and vomiting—particularly in the morning, although it may occur at any time. Remember that it is a presumptive signal of pregnancy. This temporary condition is experienced by approximately 60% of pregnant women and is said to be linked with the great hormonal changes in the body at the onset of pregnancy. Emotional factors may also enter into the cause and effect relationship. The most successful preventative seems to be eating more frequent small meals instead of three rather large meals as is our custom. Liquids are tolerated better if taken between, instead of with, meals. Eating something dry and

high in carbohydrate value, like a few crackers or a piece of toast, before getting up also seems to help. If necessary, the physician may prescribe certain gastrointestinal tranquilizers that are also commonly used to combat motion sickness on boats and planes—medications such as dimenhydrinate (Dramamine). However, any use of medication by a pregnant woman must be carefully evaluated for need and closely supervised. Some medications may affect fetal development adversely. If the nausea persists and becomes severe, threatening the nutrition of the mother, then it is considered a rather serious complication called *hyperemesis gravidarum*, and it may necessitate hospitalization, the administration of intravenous feedings, and perhaps in some cases psychiatric counseling.

Other digestive complaints may be voiced by the pregnant woman, and considering the compression of the internal organs caused by the growth of the fetus, plus the hormonal changes in her body, it should not be surprising that such complaints may occur.

Heartburn. Heartburn, or *pyrosis*, an uncomfortable burning sensation felt behind the sternum often accompanied by gas and acid regurgitation into the mouth, has nothing to do with the heart. It only feels that way. It can be prevented or lessened with more attention to diet selection to avoid common gas-forming foods such as cabbage, cauliflower, Brussels sprouts, onions, cucumbers, radishes, turnips, and dried beans. A more serene, leisurely mealtime is also often helpful. Remedies usually include the administration of antacids with the physician's approval. Soda bicarbonate is not recommended because of its high sodium content, and several other proprietary antacids must be discreetly used, if at all, for the same reason.

Constipation. Constipation may also be a problem, especially if the woman has had such difficulty before pregnancy. Four things may help: a diet that includes plenty of roughage, abundant fluids, regular exercise, and a consistent time of day set aside for evacuation when she does not have to hurry. Mild laxatives may also be used, but an expectant mother should check with her doctor regarding the type and frequency of such medication. Taking a laxative is one way labor might be initiated.

Circulatory difficulties

Varicosities. Many pregnant women suffer from *varicosities,* also called varices, or varicose veins. They most often occur in the lower extremities and rectal area but may also occasionally involve the vulva and groin. These are surface veins, the walls of which are thin and greatly enlarged. They may appear as a swollen, purple, knotted network just under the skin. The affected lower extremities tire easily. The swollen veins may be more than a cosmetic problem, since occasionally

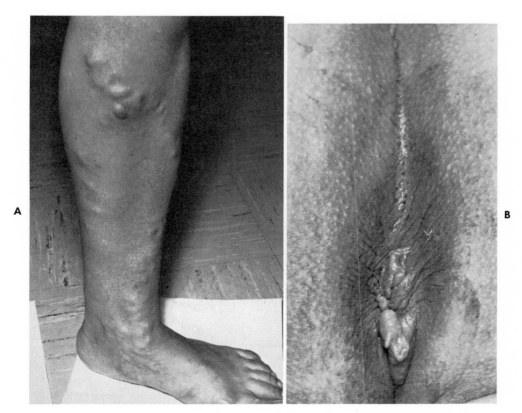

Fig. 13-1. **A,** Varicose veins of the lower extremity. **B,** Varicosities of the rectal area (hemorrhoids). (Courtesy Mercy-Guadalupe Clinic, San Diego, Calif.)

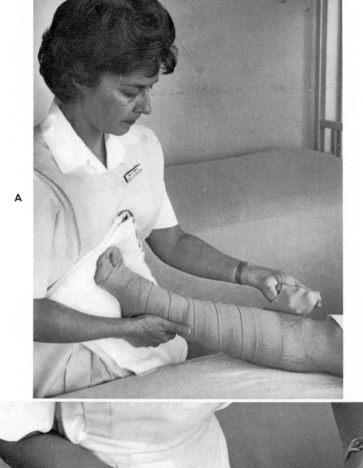

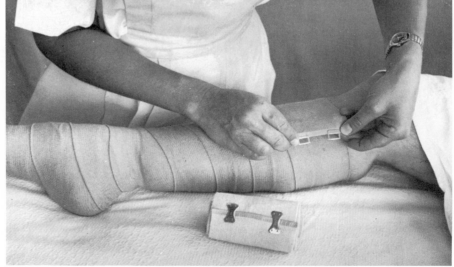

FIG. 13-2. A, When putting on elastic bandage around the lower leg, even tension is desired. B, Two types of fasteners are shown.

they may be injured, rupture, and bleed or become the point of origin for a blood clot, or thrombus. Most patients find relief by the application of elastic stockings or bandages that give the legs support and stimulate return circulation to the heart. Such bandages should be applied from the foot up, with an even tension, in order not to become in themselves obstructions to circulation. Ideally they are applied after the patient has had her legs elevated several minutes to drain the swollen veins. Because of mechanical interference in the return circulation of blood by the growing fetus, edema of the legs is fairly common in late pregnancy. However, it should always be evaluated by the physician, since it could also be a sign of toxemia. Pooling of the blood in the lower part of the body plus dilatation of the surface blood vessels may be one cause of the faintness experienced by many expectant mothers. (See Figs. 13-1 and 13-2.)

Hemorrhoids. Rectal varicosities are termed "hemorrhoids." They may be external or internal. They are produced or aggravated by the pressure of the developing fetus and/or constipation. They can be quite painful and occasionally become thrombosed or bleed. Most of the time surgical treatment is not contemplated during pregnancy because the condition usually disappears or vastly improves after delivery. Attention should be paid to the prevention of constipation. Witch hazel compresses or analgesic ointments such as dibucaine (Nupercainal) may help. Warm water sitz baths may also aid.

Muscle cramps

Muscle cramps are often experienced during pregnancy; they usually involve the calf muscle and can be agonizing. They are said to result from an imbalance in calcium and phosphorus in the body causing a form of *tetany*. Immediate treatment consists of straightening the leg by pushing down on the knee and pushing the ball of the foot up toward the knee. Preventive therapy includes increased calcium intake in the form of calcium lactate or gluconate with increased vitamin D intake. Some physicians using this regimen may limit the woman's intake of milk because of its high phosphorus content. Others will continue with the recommendation of a quart of milk per day but prescribe small quantities of aluminum hydroxide gel in the diet to trap dietary phosphorus in the intestine.

Leukorrhea

Increased mucoid vaginal drainage found in pregnancy is caused by the increased activity of the cervical glands. However, profuse, white, cream-colored, or yellowish drainage is abnormal and should be checked by the physician. A number of conditions can cause such a discharge, which is called *leukorrhea.*

Trichomonas vaginalis. Trichomonas vaginalis, a microscopic animal, is a common cause of leukorrhea. This organism may inhabit the vaginal canal without causing noticeable symptoms. However, during pregnancy the changes in the pH, or acidity-alkalinity, of the vagina may cause *Trichomonas vaginalis* to multiply rapidly and create annoying signs and symptoms. Typically these are an irritating, profuse, yellow vaginal discharge and vulvar itching or burning. The motile organism may be identified under the microscope in a hanging drop slide or occasionally by culture methods. *Trichomonas* is quite difficult to combat locally because of the structure of the vaginal folds, and many types of treatment have been attempted with some success. There is some evidence that drying and exposing the vaginal folds to air at intervals helps kill the organism, since it dislikes oxygen. But whatever method is used, great persistence and patience are needed to achieve success.

Candida albicans. Monilia albicans, or *Candida albicans* as it is more commonly called now, is another cause of leukorrhea quite difficult to treat. This organism is a fungus or yeast and is quite easily diagnosed by direct microscopic examination

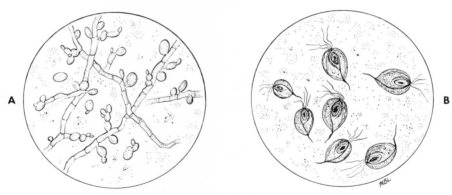

Fig. 13-3. Microscopic views. A, *Candida albicans (Monilia),* a fungus. B, *Trichomonas vaginalis,* a protozoon, or microscopic animal.

of the discharge or culture techniques. A *Candida* vaginal infection produces a cheesy, whitish discharge and local irritation. Like *Trichomonas, Candida albicans* can inhabit the body without any apparent signs or symptoms being produced but under certain conditions (especially with the use of broad-spectrum antibiotics) it may spread tremendously. The old remedy consisted of locally applying 1% gentian violet. The oral antibiotic nystatin has proved quite effective. It is given to prevent monilial overgrowth when broad-spectrum antibiotics are prescribed or to treat a current infection. The relationship of *Candida albicans* and thrush has been discussed in Unit VII. (See Fig. 13-3.)

Gonorrhea. It should not be forgotten that gonorrhea is still, unfortunately, an important disease in the community. Its incidence is increasing, particularly in the younger age groups. Profuse, purulent, yellow or greenish yellow vaginal drainage may signal the presence of the causative gonococcus. Particularly characteristic in such an instance is the involvement of the urethra, causing painful voiding. Gonorrhea may be cured by doses of penicillin or sulfonamide drugs. Sterility (caused by inflammation of the fallopian tubes) or even a threat to the patient's life because of a more widespread infection may be the result of poor or inadequate treatment. The danger of blindness in the newborn infant

of an infected mother has been discussed elsewhere.

Other causes. Leukorrhea may also be a symptom of the presence of cervical pathology such as polyps (fleshy growths), inflammation, and, occasionally, malignant changes. It can also be seen as a result of foreign body irritation in the vaginal tract.

Douching. Occasionally, as part of the treatment of leukorrhea, careful douching is advised if the pregnancy is not of more than 5 months' duration. If such advice is given (it should be given only by a physician), the nurse should be able to help the patient by giving more detailed or repeated instructions. Many times women are hesitant or embarrassed to admit they would like more information about the technique of douching. Some may not realize that they are not proceeding properly. Following are some factors that should be mentioned:

1. A fountain-type syringe with bag, tubing, and curved plastic or hard-rubber tip should be used. A bulb syringe is not efficient in treating the vaginal mucosa, and cases of air embolism introduced by the use of the bulb during pregnancy, although rare, have been reported in the literature.

2. All equipment should be personal and clean.

3. The douche should be done in a re-

clining position in the bathtub or on a bedpan or douche pan to allow the irrigating solution to contact the vaginal canal effectively. It should be administered only under low pressure. The bag should be no more than 18 inches above the hips.

4. Before douching, the external genitalia should be carefully washed so that organisms are not introduced into the vagina during the procedure. Care should be taken to wash first the genitalia and then the rectal area to avoid contamination.

5. The solution ordered should be warm but not hot. If powder or crystals are to be added to water to make the solution, they should be added and mixed in a container other than the douche can or bag to assure uniform distribution. One to two quarts of solution are needed.

6. The air should be expelled from the tubing before insertion.

7. The douche tip should be lubricated with water or a water-soluble jelly. Insertion of the douche tip should be *down* and *back* to follow the angle of the vaginal canal while in modified dorsal lithotomy position (the legs flexed and pulled up slightly toward the chest, with the knees dropped toward the outside). Sometimes the feet may be conveniently supported by each side of the tub. The douche tip should be inserted no more than 3 inches. The labia should not be closed around the douche tip because this may increase the pressure too much.

8. The irrigation usually takes about 5 minutes. Afterward all equipment, including the tub, if used, should be carefully cleaned.

14
Major problems of pregnancy and delivery

Coincidental diseases

It would be very convenient and extremely desirable if a pregnant woman could control her health by simply announcing, "Well now, I'm responsible for an unborn boy or girl so I just won't get sick for the next 9 months." But she can't. Pregnant women may have coincidental diseases and conditions that may complicate the pregnancy and call for specific therapy or regimens. Many times representatives of the various medical specialties such as endocrinology, cardiology, and urology must be consulted.

Diabetes mellitus. Diabetic mothers need special care in meeting their metabolic requirements and controlling their disease. The most common cause of fetal death is maternal diabetic acidosis. A large proportion of these women develop toxemia. They are more likely to have large babies and mechanical problems in the passage of their children. Placental insufficiency, perhaps related to degenerative vascular changes associated with diabetes, may cause the increase in births of stillborn and premature babies and hydramnios encountered by these patients. Diminished placental function may be detected during pregnancy through periodic evaluations of the amount of estriol in a 24-hour urine specimen. The physician may elect to try to initiate labor before term or perform a cesarean section, depending on the individual case involved. Children of diabetic mothers are more likely to suffer from respiratory distress syndrome (hyaline membrane disease). For a more detailed discussion of diabetes the reader is referred to the pediatric section of this book.

Cardiac problems. Cardiac patients are also individually evaluated to determine their capacity to tolerate a vaginal or abdominal delivery. They should be watched for any sign of possible heart failure. Such signals include increasing shortness of breath, cough, and rapid pulse.

Urinary problems. The pregnant patient with urinary tract disease is a real challenge to medical management, especially when kidney function is impaired. Pregnancy in itself puts a strain on the urinary system. The developing uterus may pinch or kink the ureters (particularly the one on the right because of the usual location of the uterus). Stoppage of normal urinary flow predisposes the system to infection (pyelonephritis). Infections are often caused by colon bacilli, but other organisms may also be responsible. If the kidneys are already damaged by previous pathology, the added load imposed by the excretion of fetal waste may be significant. Infection of the kidney may manifest itself in several ways: chills and fever, lower back pain, pain on voiding, as well as a urinalysis characterized by the presence of numerous white blood cells, bacteria, and, in more severe cases, perhaps red blood cells and albumin. Infection of the kidney usually responds well to such measures as bed rest, forced fluids, the application of heat to the lower back, and some type of sulfonamide therapy. When hospitalized, these patients are routinely on intake and output and have frequent blood pressure and daily weight determinations. Daily urinalysis is often ordered. Not all urinary tract or kidney disease is infectious. If it is, it is not always contagious in the usual sense. Many patients do not need isolation precautions to protect others. They themselves, however, must be protected from respiratory infections that may worsen their condition. Renal disease may be inflammatory or degenerative. It is closely connected with the condition of the blood supply to the kidneys, and any continuous process that interferes with this supply will, in time, present symptoms. Conversely, any significant damage to the kidney will reflect itself in a change in the circulatory system, particularly an elevation of the blood pressure as more and more pressure is exerted in an attempt to maintain adequate filtrations. The onset of significant hypertension is related to a worsening prognosis for both the fetus and mother. Patients whose renal disease is not caused by a current infection (for example, those suffering from glomerulonephritis) receive much the same nursing care as those with a diagnosed bacterial invasion, and antibiotics are often given prophylactically. There may be alterations in the diet, with sodium restriction and protein increase or decrease depending on the philosophy of the physician. Advanced renal disease may pose a real threat to both the mother and her unborn child.

Syphilis. Many states, although not all, require a premarital blood test to detect syphilis. A complete prenatal examination always includes a serological test for detection of syphilis, although the results may occasionally render false negatives or positives. At one time it was believed that the problem of syphilis had been largely solved because of these precautions and the successful introduction of the antibiotics in its treatment. Many so-called "L clinics," so named for *lues,* another name for syphilis, were closed. Education of the public and the related necessary casework regarding the venereal diseases (principally syphilis and gonorrhea), which were

responding so well to penicillin therapy, were not continued with the same diligence. Health workers were then very much concerned to find that national morbidity rates for syphilis had risen sharply. The reported cases of gonorrhea had also increased alarmingly. These increases were caused in part by the ill-founded sense of security regarding venereal disease and the cutbacks in federal, state, and local budgets helping in its control. They were also symptoms of the growing lack of purpose, restlessness, family breakdown, and moral laxity and resulting promiscuity, which have unhappily become major problems of twentieth century society.

Transmission. It should also be understood, however, that not all persons with a diagnosis of syphilis have been guilty of irresponsible conduct. The infectious agent, a corkscrewlike organism, or spirochete, called *Treponema pallidum* may also infect the innocent. A blameless marriage partner may contract the disease. The organism invades microscopic breaks in the mucous membranes. A fetus is susceptible to the mother's disease after the beginning of the fourth month of pregnancy. Up to that time a placental barrier exists that protects the fetus. Syphilis may be acquired through accidental inoculation by contaminated needles or exposure to infectious skin lesions on the part of professional personnel or other contacts, but this latter source of infection is rare. The infective organism cannot live for more than a few hours in an environment deprived of moisture, and it is destroyed by drying. It is also killed by many chemicals, including soap.

Stages. The disease is divided into three different stages of development, or progression. The first stage or period of initial body response usually manifests itself from 10 days to 10 weeks after exposure. The average time is 3 weeks. The characteristic lesion of the first stage of the disease is a relatively hard, raised, painless area crowned by a craterlike depression found at the area of entry known as a *chancre.* This lesion is not always seen, however. Sometimes it seems to be actually absent. At other times it is present but hidden from view in the folds of the vaginal or urethral canals. Rarely, the chancre may develop on the lips or breast. The chancre is highly infectious. The spirochete may be identified in its secretions in dark-field microscopic studies. However, at this time the serology test is usually negative. The chancre disappears after 3 to 8 weeks. The uninformed victim may think that the problem has also disappeared, but such is not the way of syphilis. The organisms have been multiplying and spreading throughout the body. Usually not long after the chancre vanishes the patient discovers other difficulties, and their advent signals the beginning of the second stage of the infection.

The second stage of syphilis is characterized by a bronze or rose-colored rash often called *rose spots.* Flattened, moist, wartlike lesions may also appear on the skin and mucous membranes called *mucous patches,* or *condylomata lata.* These are very infectious, containing the spirochete. The patient does not feel well and may have headache, sore throat, and aching joints and muscles. There may be spotty loss of hair. These signs and symptoms may, after several weeks, fade away never to return in the same way, or they may reappear at irregular intervals for a period up to 3 to 4 years. During the second stage of syphilis the serology test is routinely positive.

The third stage of the disease may occur anywhere from 2 to 20 years after the initial contact with the spirochete. Although the disease is present, it may produce no visible symptoms. About 20% of those patients in the tertiary stage do develop widespread serious disorders that interfere greatly with life. Soft tumors called *gummas* develop in the tissues that may ulcerate or form abscesses. Vital centers such as the brain, spinal cord, large blood vessels, and heart are often damaged. There may be gastrointestinal symptoms.

A patient may become mentally ill; such mental illness is called *generalized paresis.* He may be unable to walk normally because of central nervous system disease, and he has a typical body-jarring gait. The patient is usually not infectious at this stage. Routinely the serology test is positive. Adequate treatment with penicillin in the first or second stages brings an optimistic prognosis. Results of treatment in the third stage are questionable.

Congenital syphilis. The prenatal serology examination has been quite successful in warding off congenital syphilis by establishing treatment before the infant is affected. Some physicians repeat these blood tests later in pregnancy to combat developing infection and fetal damage. The disease may be prevented prenatally by treating the affected mother for syphilis before the eighteenth week of pregnancy.

The syphilitic baby may not be delivered alive. The untreated syphilitic mother characteristically has a high abortion rate. If born alive, the innocent child may suffer from various problems. Probably the most common characteristic of the syphilitic infant is the presence of a thick, almost continuous, sometimes blood-tinged nasal discharge associated with a sniffling sound on respiration. For this reason the manifestation is called "snuffles." The skin, especially over the palms of the hands and soles of the feet, may be blistered and peeling. There may be sore fissures around the lips and anus. The joints are sometimes very tender. The liver and spleen are usually enlarged. The causative organism has been found in some of the skin lesions and such a syphilitic infant should be isolated. Fortunately such full-blown cases of congenital syphilis are not common now in the United States. Other more permanent signs of the one-time presence of congenital syphilis are notched teeth, "Hutchinson's teeth," and a so-called "saddle nose." Penicillin is again the drug of choice in the treatment of congenital syphilis. (See Fig. 14-1.)

Gonorrhea. Gonorrhea is the most com-

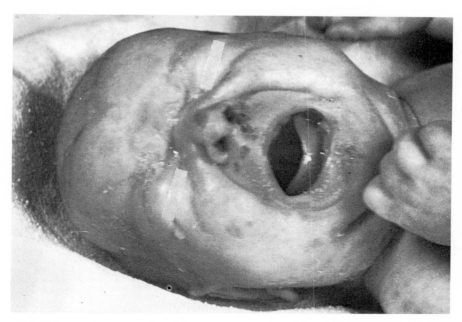

FIG. 14-1. Infant with congenital syphilis. Note excoriation of the upper lip caused by "snuffles" and fissures around mouth. (Courtesy W. W. Duemling, M.D., San Diego, Calif.)

mon venereal infection. In many communities it has now reached epidemic proportions, particularly among the teen-age and young adult population. Many city and county health departments accept minors for free venereal disease diagnosis and treatment confidentially, without parental consent, relying on their right under law to care for persons of all ages suffering from communicable diseases. However, only 15 states have laws that permit private and hospital physicians to treat minors for venereal disease without parental consent. Gonorrhea is caused by a coffee bean–shaped diplococcus, *Neisseria gonorrhoeae.* It usually produces an irritating purulent vaginal discharge and, since it often infects the Skene glands, may initiate burning on urination. The disease may spread up the reproductive tract and bring inflammatory changes. It may cause abnormal narrowing of the fallopian tubes and may be responsible finally for ectopic pregnancy (a pregnancy that develops outside the normal uterine placement) and/or sterility. Gonorrhea may also become a more gen-

eralized infection spread through the bloodstream and lymphatic system. It responds well to treatment with sulfonamides or penicillin. Gonorrhea may be contracted by common use of infected articles such as towels, clothing, or bathroom fixtures. These are the means by which some children may acquire a gonorrheal vaginitis. Infection of the eyes through contact at birth or later is a real possibility. Prophylactic newborn eye care is a legal requirement in all states because of this possibility.

Rubella. German, or 3-day, measles, technically known as *rubella,* is in itself a rather mild disease, but it has a deservedly bad reputation associated with pregnancy. If an expectant mother develops the disease in the first trimester (3 months) of her pregnancy, it is possible that her infant will be seriously damaged by the causative virus' action on the fragile developing fetal tissues. The disease can cause heart defects, congenital cataracts, deafness, mental retardation, bone diseases, and blood abnormalities. Young girls have been counseled in the past to purposely expose themselves to rubella before marriage to reduce the risk of fetal complications during pregnancy. It is gratifying to report that a safe and effective vaccine against the rubella virus was licensed for use in 1969. It has been used chiefly to immunize preschool and school-age children. This procedure will substantially reduce the number of susceptible persons remaining in the population who may serve as a reservoir of the virus for another outbreak. Administration to adult women is not recommended unless there is no possibility of pregnancy, since the vaccine's effect on an undetected embryo or fetus is unknown. The susceptibility of a woman to rubella can be tested by a blood test that measures antibody formation. This test may one day be offered as part of a premarital examination. One interesting recent finding reveals that newborn infants who have been infected with the disease may be themselves infective and should be isolated.

Tuberculosis. Tuberculosis, although not as common as formerly, is still a maternal-child health problem because the disease may be worsened by pregnancy and postpartum demands, and it may be contracted fairly easily by the newborn infant. Rarely, cases of infection of the fetus have been reported. A pregnant woman with tuberculosis should be under close medical supervision. Drug therapy and newer surgical techniques have made the outlook for tuberculosis patients much more optimistic. As a rule, gas anesthetics at the time of delivery are avoided. The infected mother should not breast-feed her infant because of his great susceptibility to the disease.

Diseases associated with pregnancy

The following complications are so grouped because they are of major importance and are associated only with pregnancy, labor, and delivery.

Hemorrhagic complications

The threat of hemorrhage is a very real consideration during all periods of pregnancy, delivery, and even postpartum. In the months of gestation, vaginal bleeding is always considered a potential menace to both the fetus and the mother. Hemorrhage, you will remember, is the most common complication of pregnancy.

Abortion. Spotting or bleeding during the early months is usually related to *abortion,* which is now defined as loss of the fetus before viability and does not itself imply any illegal proceedings.

Types. Abortions may be *spontaneous,* without any premeditation (called miscarriages by the public), or they may be *induced.* Most communities identify two types of induced abortion: legal abortions, which are done with the consent of society after medical consultation, and criminal abortions, which have no legal sanction and are often done clandestinely under poor conditions by unskilled operators. The extent of criminal abortion in the United States is difficult to estimate, but some writers believe that as many as 10,000 expectant mothers die annually because of its practice. The problem of criminal abortion is one of the factors that has brought about a change in the laws governing legalized abortion.

Other terminology is also used in describing an abortion. Physicians and nurses often use the adjectives "threatened" and "inevitable." A *threatened abortion* may possibly be halted. It may declare itself by uterine cramping or intermittent backache and spotting, but the loss of blood is relatively small, and the cervical opening remains closed. An *inevitable abortion* is characterized by severe or persistent contractions, moderate to abundant blood loss, and dilatation of the cervix. Loss of the fetus cannot be prevented. An *incomplete abortion* refers to the retention of some of the products of conception, most commonly a portion of the placenta. The uterus usually must be emptied by a mechanical dilatation of the cervix and gentle scraping of its walls by a curet. Such a procedure is called a dilatation and curettage, or "D and C." If it must take place at all, a *complete abortion* is desirable. In the case of a complete abortion, all the products of the pregnancy are eliminated from the uterus. Usually patients with the diagnosis of threatened or inevitable abortion are admitted to the gynecological service. However, if the viability of the fetus is debatable, the patient may be placed on the obstetrical service.

Women who have lost more than three pregnancies at about the same stage of development are said to be victims of *habitual abortion.* Sometimes a very young fetus will die in the uterus and remain there 2 months or longer before it is expelled, either through spontaneous processes or medical or surgical intervention. Such a situation is declared a *missed abortion.* In such cases the placenta usually remains attached to the uterine wall for an extended period of time, and the amniotic fluid is gradually absorbed, producing a type of fetal mummification or even petrification.

Nursing care. The nursing care of a woman diagnosed as having a nontherapeutic abortion would routinely include bed rest; observation for uterine cramping, loss of amniotic fluid, periodic pulse, and blood pressure determinations; careful determination of the presence and amount of vaginal bleeding (the physician may wish all pads and soiled linen saved to evaluate the extent of blood loss); and watchfulness to secure any passed tissue for diagnosis. Periodic checks for fetal heart tone should be performed if the fetus is over 4½ months' gestation, and vigilance for an elevation of temperature should be maintained. Orders would probably include hemoglobin and hematocrit checks, sedation, and hormonal therapy, depending on the condition of the patient. The use of progesterone may help maintain the pregnancy. Iron medication or blood transfusions may be indicated. Antibiotics may be employed. Inevitable abortion may be speeded by the use of drugs (oxytocics) to stimulate the uterus to contract or by surgical intervention, especially in the presence of hemorrhage. A patient who aborts must continue to be closely observed for complications for

several hours or days, depending on her general condition and the circumstances of her loss.

About 50% of all threatened abortions terminate as abortions. A large percentage of such fetal loss is associated with some defect in the developing child. Spontaneous abortion seems to be one way that nature tries to rectify a basic error.

The nursing care of a patient undergoing a voluntary legalized abortion in the hospital setting will be determined by the condition of the patient, the length of her pregnancy, and the method used by the physician to terminate her pregnancy. Termination may be secured by dilatation and curettage, aspiration techniques, or intra-amniotic saline injections. (See Chapter 19.)

Nurses caring for patients receiving hypertonic intra-amniotic salt injections should observe their patients carefully for signs of excessive blood sodium levels revealed by mental confusion, changes in the level of consciousness, and shock. Resuscitation equipment should be readily available.

Because of recent changes in the interpretation and content of abortion laws nurses working in gynecological, delivery, and operating room areas may be requested more frequently to assist in the process of legalized abortion. If the scruples of a nurse would dictate that she not participate, she may decline her services if by so doing she is not jeopardizing the immediate health or life of a patient (for example, she could secure another nurse to assist for whom abortion did not pose the same ethical problem). However, the nurse who declines to participate may be risking the loss of her employment.

Ectopic pregnancy. The term "ectopic pregnancy" refers to any pregnancy that does not occupy the uterine cavity proper. In the vast majority of pregnancies the migrating egg is fertilized by the sperm in the fallopian tube and nests or implants rather high on the walls of the uterine cavity. However, because of the anatomy and physiology involved, this progression does not always occur. Sometimes the tubes are abnormally narrow. This narrowing, or stenosis, may occur because of inflammation or tumor formation, or it may be congenital in origin. The tube may allow the sperm to ascend but be too narrow to allow the passage of the fertilized egg into the uterus. The egg may develop in the tube and cause rupture or eventually drop out the end to perish. In rare cases, it may continue growing as an abdominal pregnancy, which in unusual cases produces a full-term child who may survive if delivered through an abdominal incision. Pregnancies have also been found trying to develop in the ovary. The danger of hemorrhage in ectopic pregnancy is very serious. The amount of vaginal bleeding observed does not always reveal the true condition of the patient, since much blood loss can be hidden within the abdominal cavity. An ectopic pregnancy is most often tubal.

Symptoms. If tubal rupture or abortion occurs, the patient, who may or may not consider herself to be in early pregnancy, characteristically suffers severe knifelike pain in either lower abdominal quadrant. This may or may not be followed by spotting or bleeding.

The signs of shock that develop are out of proportion to the amount of blood loss apparent. The patient may exhibit the classic signs of circulatory shock: pallor; cold, clammy skin; rapid, weak pulse, which will slow if shock deepens; falling blood pressure (a systolic reading of 90 or under is usually considered "shock" depending on previous readings obtained); apprehension; loss of consciousness; and dilated pupils. Rapid surgical treatment and blood loss replacement are usually indicated. Estimates vary, but ectopic pregnancy is more common than usually supposed, occurring approximately once in 250 to 300 pregnancies. It terminates almost invariably with fetal loss, and the maternal mortality is alarmingly high.

Placenta previa. Two main types of obstetrical hemorrhage are associated with the location of the placenta and its attachment. In the condition known as *placenta previa,* the placenta implants low on the interior of the uterine wall. It may cover or impinge on the cervical opening. In the latter part of pregnancy, the uterine contractions, which are always taking place to some degree although they are not always felt by the mother, may loosen the attachment of this abnormally positioned placenta and cause bright red, painless bleeding. The presence of placenta previa in other cases may not be detected until the onset of true labor and the dilatation of the cervical canal. Because of the relative safety of cesarean section today, it is usually the treatment of choice. However, if the placenta is not implanted too low, bleeding is minimal, and the fetus is well but premature, some obstetricians may adopt a "wait and see" attitude and eventually deliver the patient vaginally. Infection and embolus are other possible complications of placenta previa that should be considered. Many hospitals now practice the "double setup technique" when treating a patient with placenta previa. Because vaginal or rectal examinations may worsen any bleeding present but are considered necessary for accurate diagnosis, these procedures may be delayed until preparations are completed for either a cesarean or a vaginal delivery in the same location as needed. X-ray diagnosis and detection of a low placental insertion by the use of radioactive tracers or ultrasonic techniques is sometimes available. Placenta previa is more common in women who are multiparous. (See Fig. 14-2.)

Abruptio placentae. The other type of hemorrhage related to placental attachment is one resulting from *abruptio placentae,* or placentae abruptio, also called premature separation of the placenta. In this condition the placenta is implanted in the correct place, but for some reason—high blood pressure, sometimes as part of the toxemia of pregnancy syndrome, local injury, hormonal imbalance, etc.—it becomes detached. Although its name in-

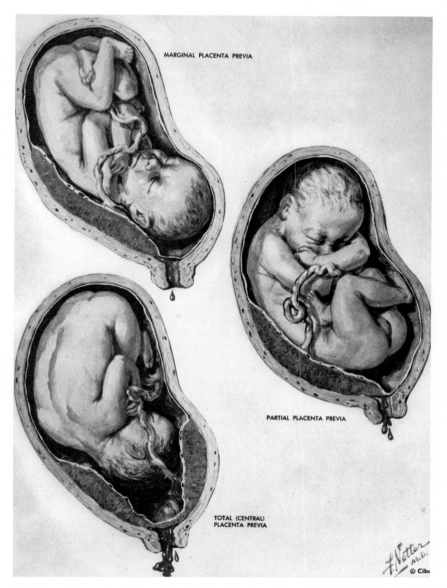

MARGINAL PLACENTA PREVIA

PARTIAL PLACENTA PREVIA

TOTAL (CENTRAL)
PLACENTA PREVIA

FIG. 14-2. Placenta previa. (From The CIBA collection of medical illustrations, by Frank H. Netter, M.D. Copyright CIBA.)

cludes the implication that the detachment occurs suddenly, this is not always the case. Separation of the placenta from the uterine wall may occur over a period of time. Detachment may occur first at the center of the placenta, resulting in hidden hemorrhage at first, or it may begin at the rim or outer portion, causing vaginal bleeding of varying amounts. Old blood, which has been trapped behind the separating placenta, appears dark when it finally escapes from the vaginal canal. Fresh bleeding usually is bright red in color. Bleeding from a premature separation of a normally implanted placenta may be severe enough to cause rapid maternal circulatory shock and danger to the fetus. (See Fig. 14-3.)

Symptoms. The first signs of abruptio

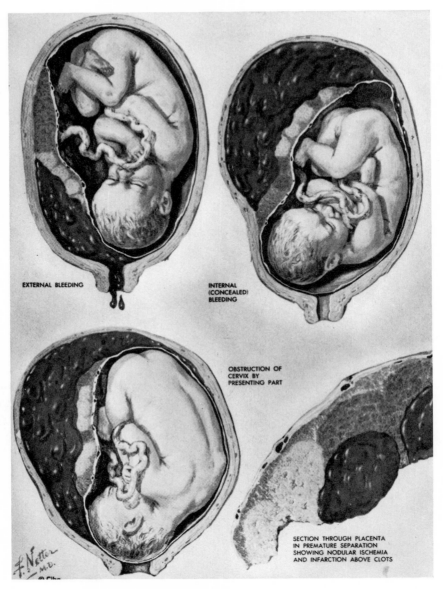

EXTERNAL BLEEDING

INTERNAL (CONCEALED) BLEEDING

OBSTRUCTION OF CERVIX BY PRESENTING PART

SECTION THROUGH PLACENTA IN PREMATURE SEPARATION SHOWING NODULAR ISCHEMIA AND INFARCTION ABOVE CLOTS

FIG. 14-3. Abruptio placentae. (From The CIBA collection of medical illustrations, by Frank H. Netter, M.D. Copyright CIBA.)

placentae during labor may be an alteration in the contraction pattern. The contractions are very strong and almost constant. Little relaxation period, if any, is detected. The uterus becomes boardlike, may enlarge with retained hemorrhage, and seems quite tender. There may or may not be external bleeding from the vagina. The fetal heart tone is either greatly accelerated or slowing. (Normal rate is approximately 120 to 160 per minute.) The fetus, in its struggle to obtain more oxygen, may be very restless and active. If the amniotic sac, or bag of waters, is ruptured, meconium may appear in the amniotic fluid—another sign of fetal distress. As shock from blood loss develops, the blood pressure falls, and the pulse increases and weakens. Abruptio placentae in its more severe forms is an obstetrical emergency. The treatment often, although not inevitably, includes delivery by cesarean section and blood replacement. A serious complication of abruptio placentae that has been encountered often enough to warrant mention is the development of afibrinogenemia, or an abnormally low fibrinogen level in the blood that makes normal blood clotting impossible. Treatment includes fibrinogen replacement, an expensive but lifesaving technique.

Hydatidiform mole. Another complication that may produce hemorrhage, although it is characterized by a much more unusual series of signs and symptoms, is called *hydatidiform mole* (usually shortened to hydatid mole—the other term is a mouthful to pronounce!). In this condition, for some unknown reason the fertilized ovum deteriorates, and instead of producing a fetus and normal placenta, an abnormal tissue develops, which usually does not include any clearly defined fetal structures. At times this tissue may resemble a cluster of small grapes, or it may be of tapioca consistency. Its presence may be suspected when a pregnancy seems to be growing abnormally rapidly (a 3-month pregnancy may equal the size of a 5-month gestation), when no fetal heart tone or movement is detected, and nausea and vomiting are excessive or persistent. Vaginal bleeding may be intermittent. X-ray examination may be used cautiously to confirm a tentative diagnosis. No fetal skeleton is demonstrated. Part of the abnormal tissue may be expelled from the uterus, and pathological examination may be possible. This growth rarely may erode the uterus and cause rupture. If not totally expelled or carefully removed, it occasionally becomes malignant, spreading to the lungs and other body parts. After the mole's removal, pregnancy tests are continued to see if any tissue is still active in the body and producing hormones. In the event of the diagnosis of hydatid mole, physicians may consider the advisability of removal of the uterus (hys-

terectomy) because of the possibility of the development of a malignant tumor, choriocarcinoma. Spreading choriocarcinoma, it is wonderful to relate, has been cured by the use of anticancer chemicals such as methotrexate.

Other causes. The causes of obstetrical hemorrhage previously discussed—abortion, ectopic pregnancy, placenta previa, placentae abruptio, and hydatidiform mole— are those that most often occur during pregnancy and/or early labor. However, they are not the only causes of significant blood loss associated with childbirth. Obstetrical laceration—vaginal, perineal, or cervical—and uterine inertia (abnormal postpartal relaxation of the uterus) leading to excessive bleeding from the site of former placental attachment can be important intrapartal and postpartal complications.

Care of the bleeding patient. Before leaving the topic of blood loss during pregnancy and labor, let us review the care of bleeding patients. Here are some important "do's" and "don't's" that all nurses should know. Although licensed vocational or practical nurses (LVN's or LPN's) should not have the total responsibility in such cases, they should understand the following basic considerations:

1. Never give a bleeding patient an enema as part of the "routine admit." A nurse never examines a bleeding patient rectally. The physician performs the examination if he wishes. Unnecessary manipulation in the area may increase the bleeding (especially in cases of placenta previa). Keep the patient on bed rest and give no food or fluids until ordered otherwise.

2. Observe the patient carefully and frequently.
    a. Take frequent pulse and blood pressure determinations. Systolic blood pressure readings of 90 or below are usually indicative of shock, but remember that a hypertensive patient may not have a pressure reading so low that it would routinely indicate shock but

may still be suffering from what would be, for them, hypotension. Compare, if possible, the results obtained with the patient's blood pressure reading on her prenatal record.

b. Check for type and amount of vaginal bleeding and/or amniotic drainage. If it is possible, save the evidences of bleeding for evaluation by the physician.

c. Check the fetal heart tone every 15 to 30 minutes, depending on the patient's condition. Remember, distress is related to irregularity and speed (too slow or too fast). (The normal fetal heart tone averages 120 to 160 beats per minute. Rates of 100 or below definitely indicate distress.) An unusually active fetus may signal difficulty.

d. Estimate the character of the contraction and relaxation period by frequent timing. Check for any special uterine pain or tenderness and for poor or absent uterine relaxation.

3. Keep the charge nurse and physician informed of any changes in the patient's condition.

4. Expect possible orders for hematocrit or hemoglobin determinations and cross match for blood transfusion. Know if any religious scruples would preclude transfusion (for example, if the patient is a Jehovah's Witness).

5. Maintain a calm, supportive manner, sensitive to the appearance as well as the reality of the situation.

Toxemias of pregnancy (Fig. 14-4)

One of the most common causes of maternal mortality is not, in itself, primarily a hemorrhagic disease, but it may finally contribute to the development of hemorrhage. Hypertension associated with toxemia of pregnancy may initiate abruptio placentae or, in severe cases, cause localized hemorrhages in the maternal liver, brain, and other organs. Sometimes one sees references to the toxemias of pregnancy, a purposeful use of the plural because the general health histories of the patients and pathological changes encountered are not always similar. In some classifications the toxemias of pregnancy refer to all complications occurring that include one or more of these classical signs: excessive weight gain produced by hidden or observed edema, hypertension, and the appearance of protein (albumin or globulin) in the urine. In severe cases, coma and convulsions may also occur.

Types. Toxemias that have an onset late in pregnancy (after 24 weeks' gestation) are usually referred to as acute, or true, toxemias. They are divided into two classes. Those that exhibit any of the previously listed signs with the exception of convulsion are called preeclampsias, whereas those that include coma and/or convulsion are called eclampsias. Hypertension or kidney disease that predates or is worsened by the presence of pregnancy is generally considered as a second separate category of the toxemias. Preeclampsia occurs in 6% to 8% of hospitalized obstetrical patients. Its incidence is increased in young primigravidae.

Pathology. The underlying mechanism of preeclampsia is not known but we do know that for some reason associated with pregnancy the affected patients retain abnormal amounts of sodium in their bodies and, since sodium holds water, they become edematous. We know that the arteries of the body go into spasm, causing hypertension and a reduction in the supply of blood to the kidneys, brain, and uterus. These spasms may also cause localized hemorrhages. Evidence of vascular spasm may be detected by ophthalmoscopic examination of the fundus of the eye. As the result of vascular spasms, changes take place in the filtration ability of the kidney, and protein is lost in the urine. In severe cases the rate of urine formation may decrease. Edema of the brain may eventually cause coma and convulsions. The condition then be-

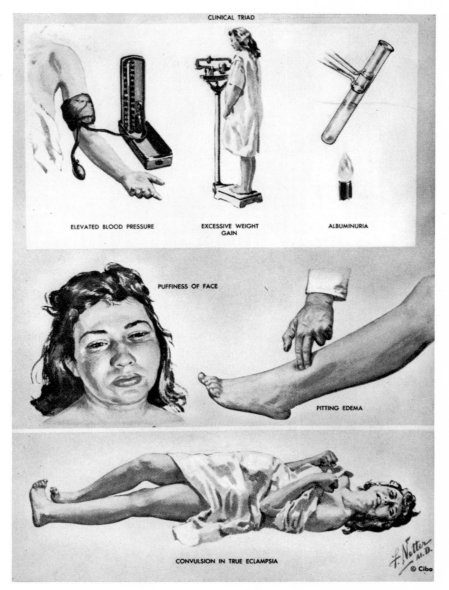

CLINICAL TRIAD

ELEVATED BLOOD PRESSURE

EXCESSIVE WEIGHT GAIN

ALBUMINURIA

PUFFINESS OF FACE

PITTING EDEMA

CONVULSION IN TRUE ECLAMPSIA

FIG. 14-4. Acute toxemia of pregnancy; symptomatology of preeclampsia and eclampsia. (From The CIBA collection of medical illustrations, by Frank H. Netter, M.D. Copyright CIBA.)

comes eclampsia. If the patient dies, death is usually caused by circulatory failure with pulmonary edema, cerebral hemorrhage, or complications of operative deliveries. About 10% to 15% of eclamptic patients expire.

Symptoms. Hypertension is usually the first sign detected. Several systolic blood pressure readings of 140 mm. Hg or above or a rise of 30 mm. Hg or more beyond the known overall normal level of the patient in question is significant. Also, diastolic readings of 90 mm. Hg or above or 15 mm. above the patient's usual diastolic pressure are noteworthy. A weight gain of over 1 pound a week during the last

12 weeks of gestation is thought to be suspicious, signaling fluid retention. Edema of the face and hands is more significant than swelling of the ankles, which afflicts most pregnant women to some degree in the last weeks of waiting. Since most women do not have the tools or the ability to take their own blood pressure, they should be told to report persistent headache, dizziness, or spots before the eyes, which may be symptoms of hypertension and edema of the retina. Other significant signs and symptoms of developing or worsening toxemia may be vomiting, epigastric pain, and decreased urine production.

Treatment. Treatment of preeclampsia or acute toxemia of pregnancy depends on the severity of the symptoms encountered. Regular, adequate prenatal care is the best insurance for control of the complication. In cases of mild toxemia, if a patient is conscientious in carrying out her physician's instructions, all treatment may be possible on an outpatient basis, but many physicians prefer to hospitalize their patients until symptoms are controlled. Treatment is directed toward relieving the edema and hypertension and restoring normal kidney function. To accomplish this a low-salt or sodium-restricted diet may be ordered. Calories may also be restricted. Many of the patients have weight increases not caused by water retention! A diuretic is usually prescribed.

When hospitalized, these patients are usually placed on bed rest in a quiet room. A sedative, usually phenobarbital, makes bed rest more tolerable. Their blood pressures are taken at least every 4 hours. A daily urinalysis is common. Intake and output should be observed. They are questioned regarding the appearance of any symptoms such as headache, blurred vision, abdominal pain, or nausea. Caloric and sodium dietary restrictions usually continue as does the administration of diuretics and sedatives. In those cases requiring rather severe sodium restrictions, distilled water may be substituted for cooking and drinking purposes. The rationale of treatment is to improve the condition of the mother to allow a vaginal or abdominal delivery at term. However, if her condition continues to deteriorate, induction of labor or a cesarean section may be carried out.

Preeclampsia may be defined as "severe" if one or more of the following signs and symptoms are present: blood pressure of 180/110 or more, albuminuria 3+ or more, urinary output of less than 400 ml. per 24 hours, cerebral or visual disturbances, pulmonary edema, or cyanosis. In the event of severe eclampsia the room should be dimmed and the toxemia tray containing a padded tongue blade, airway, percussion hammer (to test reflexes), emergency sedative, and diuretic drugs with appropriate equipment for their administration should be close at hand. An oxygen mask or cannula, a suction apparatus, and possibly emergency tracheostomy equipment should be nearby.

Fortunately, the incidence of convulsion is rare today—1 in 1,000 to 1,500 deliveries. However, this does not mean that the nurse can consider the possibility so remote that no precautions are taken. Abdominal pain, apprehension, twitchings, and hyperirritability of the muscles often precede convulsions. As soon as a convulsion manifests itself, a padded tongue blade or soft, rolled washcloth should be placed in the patient's open mouth between the teeth to prevent biting the tongue and help maintain an airway. If possible, the head should be turned to the side. Suctioning is rarely necessary. During the periods of rigidity and muscle contraction, the patient should be restrained only enough to keep her from hurting herself or rolling off the bed. The sides of the bed should be padded with pillows. Be aware that babies have been suddenly born during a convulsive episode. An eclamptic patient should never be left alone. Certain patients may convulse in response to loud noises, jarring of the bed, or bright lights. Conversation should be minimal.

To measure urinary output and character

more accurately, an indwelling catheter is often inserted and attached to a urinometer. The blood pressure cuff is left in place. Frequent pulse and respiration checks are made. The patient is heavily sedated (chloral hydrate, magnesium sulfate, or morphine may be used). Often a temperature elevation is associated with the onset of eclampsia. Rectal or axillary temperatures should be taken.

As soon as the patient's convulsions are controlled, the condition of the fetus (if the seizures occur before delivery) is ascertained, and plans for the birth are considered. The patient may deliver spontaneously. If the progress of labor is sufficient and the condition of the patients (mother and fetus) satisfactory, vaginal delivery may be done. However, a cesarean section may be the procedure of choice. After delivery of the baby, the possibility of convulsion diminishes with the passage of time. It has been said that no eclamptic seizure has occurred after 72 hours postdelivery.

Rupture of the uterus

Rupture of the gravid uterus may occur during late pregnancy but is most often reported during labor and delivery. The nurse should know under what circumstances this emergency is most likely to occur, the signs and symptoms most often seen, and the usual treatment pursued.

Uterine rupture is most frequently associated with previous uterine surgery (e.g., cesarean sections, myomectomies), injudicious application of obstetrical forceps, a tempestuous or prolonged obstructed labor (e.g., fetal-pelvic disproportion), grandmultiparity, and the use of oxytocin.

Typically, the patient experiences a period of strong, almost unremitting contractions that, in spite of their force, produce little progress in the descent of the fetus in the birth canal. The uterus becomes extremely tender, and a weakening of its lower segment may cause a distention above the pubic bone, which may simulate the appearance of a full bladder. At the moment of rupture the patient may exclaim that she had a sharp pain and "felt something giving way." If rupture is complete, that is, the wall of the uterus is torn through, contractions will suddenly cease. The patient, after experiencing momentary relief from the pain, will usually quickly develop signs of profound circulatory shock due to intraabdominal hemorrhage. Some of this blood loss may be visible vaginally. Signs and symptoms of rupture depend on the extent and depth of the tear, the location of the fetus, and the stage of labor in which the complication occurs. Occasionally, the onset of symptoms will be delayed. Almost all the unborn babies succumb, and one third of their affected mothers die. Treatment usually consists of immediate laporotomy, possible hysterectomy, antibiotics, and massive blood transfusions.

Amniotic fluid embolism

A complication that few women survive involves the spontaneous, accidental infusion of amniotic fluid into the endocervical or uterine veins after the bag of waters has ruptured. This may occur anytime during the labor-delivery and immediate postpartum period but has been most often reported near the end of the first stage of labor. Amniotic fluid containing particles of meconium, vernix, and lanugo may enter the large blood sinuses in the placenta through defects in the placental attachment. These emboli gain access to the mother's general circulation and lodge in the lungs. Although the entire disastrous mechanism is not clear, it would seem that this foreign material produces profound shock and intravascular clotting, leading to lowered fibrinogen levels in the blood and subsequent hemorrhage. It is important to note that this complication is more frequently associated with tumultuous uterine contractions and has been described in an excessively disproportionate number of cases in which oxytocin has been administered to initiate or stimulate labor.

Symptoms manifest themselves suddenly. The patient may complain of chest pain or dyspnea and become extremely restless and cyanotic, occasionally expectorating frothy, blood-tinged mucus. Profound circulatory shock from hemorrhage may occur rapidly. Fetal death may result, and maternal death is almost always the outcome. It is good to know that this complication is rare—occurring only once in several thousand deliveries. Emergency care includes intravenous administration of fibrinogen, blood, and other fluids and oxygen therapy. If the baby is not yet born, he is delivered as soon as possible.

Prolapse of the cord

When the umbilical cord precedes the presenting part of the fetus during labor so that the blood circulating within the vessels of the cord may be clamped off against the pelvis by the continued advance of the fetus down the birth canal, an obstetrical emergency exists. This condition, termed prolapse of the cord, occurs in approximately 0.4% of labors. It is typically associated with certain types of fetal presentations, maternal pelvic contours, or labor situations. For example, the nurse should be aware that this complication is more frequent during labors involving multiple pregnancies and breech or shoulder presentations. It is more common when pelvic distortion or asymmetry is present. To prevent prolapse of the cord, patients in labor whose fetal presentations are not engaged should not ambulate or sit up steeply after cervical dilatation has advanced. A sudden gush of amniotic fluid may push the cord down into the vagina or to the exterior. This is one of the reasons the fetal heart tone is always taken after the bag of waters ruptures spontaneously or is ruptured artificially by the physician. Sometimes the cord is clearly visible outside the vaginal canal. In other instances it has prolapsed but is not visible. It may only be felt. As long as pulsations are detected, blood is flowing in the cord. Periodic checks of the fetal heart tone are necessary, since any compression of the cord would usually cause detectable, abnormal alterations in its rhythm or rate. Other signs associated with fetal distress could be the passage of meconium in the case of a cephalic presentation and sudden agitated fetal activity.

Treatment is directed toward removing any real or potential pressure on the cord, the fetal lifeline. In the hospital, the patient is usually placed in a steep head-down (Trendelenberg's) or knee-chest position (Fig. 15-9). Close observation of the fetal heart tone is maintained. A fetal heart monitor would be very helpful. The nurse should never attempt to replace the cord. The administration of oxygen is not thought to aid the baby if oxygenation of the mother is adequate, since oxygen concentrations would already be maximal even if the supply system, the cord, is in jeopardy. Usually the only feasible treatment is cesarean section, carried out as quickly as possible—preferably within 30 minutes.

Illegitimate pregnancies and teen-age motherhood

Other problems meriting our consideration as nurses may be related to special circumstances surrounding the events of pregnancy, delivery, and the responsibilities of parenthood. They may not be physiological or anatomical problems per se, but they represent situations that may be associated with certain obstetrical complications and may profoundly affect the entire experience of the patient and her future adjustment to life's challenges. Two such situations that are creating increasing concern in our society are teen-age parenthood and illegitimate pregnancies. Although the two need not be related, they often are.

Those investigating the incidence of teen-age marriage in the United States report that in 1966, 40% of the nation's brides were 15 to 18 years of age.* One study indicates that one third to one half of all these marriages are associated with premarital preg-

---

*From Time 87:102, April 29, 1966.

nancy.* Some writers estimate that as many as 50% of these marriages terminate in divorce within four years.* This is not meant to imply that there are no successful marriages begun in teen-age years. It does, however, reveal that the chances for a satisfactory, continuing family relationship are slim. Teen-age marriages in modern American society too often are an attempt to solve or escape problems too serious and complex to be corrected by a wedding ring.

In 1966, over 72,000 girls under the age of 18 gave birth out of wedlock in the United States. The number who do so has been increasing for the past 5 years by an average of 4,000 a year.† In 1965 girls 15 through 19 years of age had an estimated 42% of the live births reported out of wedlock.‡ Many factors may be related to the incidence of early marriage and/or illegitimate births. These factors most often involve family conflicts, social and economic deprivation, individual psychological problems, and/or a lack of education and appreciation regarding the role and responsibilities of sexuality in the family and society. Communities are now becoming more aware of the needs of the young parent, married or not. Not long ago few services were available to meet these needs. Some programs have been instituted in recent years that make it possible for the pregnant girl's formal education to continue. These programs also may supervise prenatal care; prepare the girls for their experiences during pregnancy, labor, and delivery; possibly increase mothering skills; and assist them with needed personal and vocational planning. In the instance of illegitimate birth, attempts are made to avoid a defeating repetition of similar behavior.

A few agencies make efforts to work with the unwed father, as well as the mother.

Physicians and nurses are learning more about the needs of the teen-age obstetrical patient, both in and out of the hospital setting. Needless to say, most teen-age maternity patients need a great deal of supportive care, careful instruction, and explanation to enable them to gain constructively from their experiences. A punitive attitude toward these patients on the part of the nursing staff does not aid the individual girls or help solve the larger problems involved.

The nurse should realize that the incidence of toxemia of pregnancy is higher in this age group, especially for girls in their early teens. This increased incidence may be related to the poor dietary control exhibited by many of these young girls. These patients also have an especially large number of low-weight babies. The delivery room nurse will be interested to know that teen-age multiparae are more prone to precipitate labor than any other group of obstetrical patients. For the teen-ager who has experienced a forced marriage or an illegitimate pregnancy, the trauma of the situation is mainly psychological. Her misdirected search for identity, freedom, love, or recognition places her in a role for which she is ill prepared, faced with decisions the outcome of which will unavoidably influence her the rest of her life. (See the unwed mother, p. 176.)

• • •

This unit, with its rather dismal recital of the minor and major complications of pregnancy and labor, may seem frightening to the student anticipating marriage and founding a family. She may be reassured. It is the purpose of a text to point out the unusual as well as the commonplace. It is the business of a nurse to know about the possibility of these problems although some of them she may never encounter—either personally or professionally.

*Semmens, J. P., and Lamers, W. M., Jr.: Teenage pregnancy, Springfield, Ill., 1968, Charles C Thomas, Publisher.
†Howard, M.: Comprehensive service programs for school-age pregnant girls, Children 15:197, Sept.-Oct., 1968.
‡Daniel, W. A., Jr.: The adolescent patient, St. Louis, 1970, The C. V. Mosby Co.

UNIT V

SUGGESTED SELECTED READINGS
AND REFERENCES

Beckner, F. J.: How do you respond to the unwed mother? RN 33:46-53, Aug., 1970.

Bookmiller, M. M., and Bowen, G. L.: Textbook of obstetrics and obstetric nursing, ed. 5, Philadelphia, 1967, W. B. Saunders Co.

Cassidy, J. T.: Teenagers in a family planning clinic, Nurs. Outlook 18:30-31, Nov., 1970.

Cianfrani, T., and Conway, M. K.: Ectopic pregnancy, Amer. J. Nurs. 63:93-95, April, 1964.

Davis, M. E., and Rubin, R.: DeLee's obstetrics for nurses, ed. 18, Philadelphia, 1966, W. B. Saunders Co.

Elder, M.-S.: Nurse counseling on sexuality, Nurs. Outlook 18:38-40, Nov., 1970.

Fitzpatrick, E., Eastmen, N. J., and Reeder, S. R.: Maternity nursing, ed. 11, Philadelphia, 1966, J. B. Lippincott Co.

Fiumara, N. J.: Venereal disease, Pediat. Clin. N. Amer. 16:333-345, 1969.

Garnet, J. D.: Pregnancy in women with diabetes, Amer. J. Nurs. 69:1900-1902, Sept., 1969.

Golab, S.: V.D., the unconquered menace, RN 33:38-45, March, 1970.

Malo-Juvera, D.: What pregnant teenagers know about sex, Nurs. Outlook 18:32-35, Nov., 1970.

Pannor, R.: The forgotten man, Nurs. Outlook 18:36-37, Nov., 1970.

Pannor, R., Evans, B. W., and Massarik, F.: The unmarried father. (In press.)

Sarrel, P. M.: Teenage pregnancy, Pediat. Clin. N. Amer. 16:347-354, 1969.

Semmens, J. P., and Lamers, W. M., Jr.: Teenage pregnancy, Springfield, Ill., 1968, Charles C Thomas, Publisher.

Smith, E.: An oasis for pregnant teen-agers, RN 33:56-61, March, 1970.

Sommer, C.: When your OB patient is in the ICU, RN 32:464, Aug., 1969.

Ziring, P. R.: Current status of the rubella problem, Cardio-Vasc. Nurs. 6:47-50, July-Aug., 1970.

UNIT VI
POSTPARTAL AND POPULATION PROBLEMS

15
The postpartal period

The postpartal period, or puerperium, is usually considered to be the interval extending from the birth of the baby until 6 weeks after. It is characterized by the return of the reproductive organs to their approximate prepregnant positions and the development of lactation. Of course, some mothers, not wishing or unable to nurse their babies, do not experience the full development of this latter characteristic. The return of the reproductive organs to the nonpregnant state is called the process of *involution*.

Admission

PREPARATION AND TRANSFER

The basic care of the postpartum patient is an extention of the care given in the delivery room after delivery. The patient arriving on the postpartum ward is put to bed in a unit previously prepared for her. The bed will be turned down, and bed protectors will be in place to catch extra vaginal drainage. Near at hand will be a sphygmomanometer, stethoscope, and individual unit equipment such as towel and washcloth set, wash and emesis basins, soap, bedpan, back care lotion, breast and perineal pads, and newspapers or paper bags for pad discard. If the patient has an intra-venous infusion, some sort of support for the bottle will also be needed.

The transfer of the patient from the stretcher to the bed may require two or three people, depending on her condition. Side rails are applied. Before the delivery room nurse leaves the area she checks the patient's fundus to determine if it is firm and makes sure that any pertinent information concerning the patient is told the postpartum charge nurse as she transfers the patient's records. Care is taken to properly oversee the patient's personal effects and not lose anything in transit.

OBSERVATION

The postpartum nurse continues to check the condition of the patient every 15 to 20 minutes for at least 2 hours to determine the following (Fig. 15-1):

1. Blood pressure, pulse, and respiration
2. Type and amount of vaginal discharge (lochia) and the appearance of the perineum
3. Consistency and location of the fundus
4. Signs of urinary distention
5. General condition of the patient: color, feel of her skin (warm or cold, dry or clammy), level of conscious-

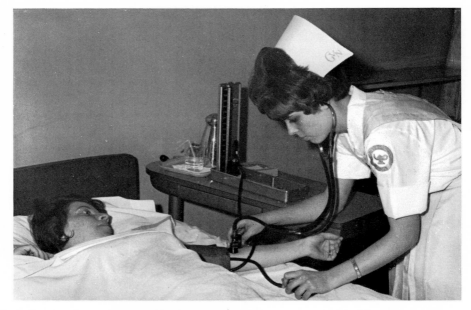

Fig. 15-1. Another postpartum blood pressure check. Pulse, respiration, blood pressure, fundus, and lochial checks should be made every 15 to 20 minutes. (Courtesy Grossmont Hospital, La Mesa, Calif.)

ness (drowsy, apprehensive, unresponsive), and the presence of nausea or vomiting

6. Rate of flow and condition of any infusion present

Observation for signs of hemorrhage

Blood pressure, pulse, and general condition. Occasionally the blood pressure will be elevated at the time of transfer. This condition may be the result of the excitement of the delivery and seeing the baby. It may be related to the type of oxytocic the patient received or is still receiving per intravenous feeding. It may be a sign of toxemia. All elevations over 130 mm. Hg systolic or 90 mm. Hg diastolic should be reported orally to the charge nurse.

The blood pressure may be low. Any pressure 100 mm. Hg systolic or below should definitely be reported. Other pressures that may not be that low but are not hypertensive and continue to fall should be reported for evaluation. Many patients with a systolic reading of 90 mm. Hg or below are going into circulatory collapse or shock. Such a falling blood pressure would be accompanied by an initially rising pulse. However, if the patient continues in shock, the pulse will gradually slow, weaken, and have a thready quality. Abnormally dilated pupils, pale, cyanotic, or clammy skin, apprehension, and an unconscious state are also signs of shock.

Some postpartum patients have a relatively slow pulse, but it has a good quality and is not associated with other signs of shock. This pulse rate (usually in the 60's) is not significant.

Lochia. The attending nurse is also interested in the amount of vaginal drainage, or *lochia.* As she checks the patient's drainage she is sure to check under the patient's hips, since much of the drainage may not be observed on the perineal pad but seeks lower dependent areas. Immediately after delivery the lochia should be moderate in quantity and dark or bright red in color— a quality called *rubra.* (About 2 days later the lochia changes to a pinkish brown, called *serosa.*) The patient will usually wear two perineal pads that have to be changed once or at the most twice during her routine 2-hour postpartum check. These should always be removed and applied from front to back to avoid contamination of the perineum. The saturation of a greater number of pads would be considered abnormally excessive. When estimating blood loss and its significance, the general condition and size of the patient must be evaluated. Usually a 450 to 500 ml. blood loss is considered hemorrhage.

Fundus. The first consideration related to blood loss is the condition of the uterus. Is the fundus firm and contracted? Is it at or below the umbilicus? If a fundus is large, soft, or boggy (seems to contain excess blood), it should be gently massaged with a circular motion until firm, while one hand is held against the top of the pubic bone to prevent the uterus from being inverted or prolapsed. If clots are suspected, once the fundus is *firm* it may be gently grasped and positioned in the middle of the abdomen. Pressure is then exerted in the direction of the pelvic canal to push out to the exterior the clots that were emptied from the uterus into the lower uterine segment and vagina during the period of massage. Students should not attempt to express clots alone until instructed individually. In the event of excessive vaginal bleeding, massage is the first measure employed to control vaginal hemorrhage.

It is surprising how quickly the uterus responds to simple massage in most cases. The nurse can easily feel the uterine muscle tighten. This tightening of the uterine muscle to make a firm fundus is essential. It pinches off the large vessels that brought blood to and from the placental sinuses before the placenta separated and was delivered.

Postpartum hemorrhage. In cases in which the uterus does not contract or remain contracted, the presence of placental fragments in the uterus may be suspected. If bleeding continues to be excessive and the uterus remains firm, a cause other than uterine relaxation must be sought to explain the blood loss. Excessive bleeding may develop because of a previously undetected cervical or vaginal laceration, or it could be the result of a defective suture or repair. In many cases of abnormal bleeding the patient will be returned to the delivery room to facilitate inspection of the uterus and vaginal canal. In some cases a dilatation and curettage of the uterus or the insertion of vaginal or, more rarely, uterine packing may be undertaken. If no lacerations or abnormal tissue retention are evident, treatment is usually confined to the administration of additional oxytocics such as ergot or its modification, methylergonovine (Methergine). Such treatment will combat the lethargy of the uterine muscles known as uterine inertia. Blood transfusions may be required. Patients who have had many children, multiple pregnancies, or large babies should be especially observed for the development of uterine inertia.

The location and consistency of the fundus are important. A high, soft fundus makes nurses think of possible uterine bleeding; a high, firm fundus more often indicates urinary retention. A distended bladder, located just below the uterus, will cause the fundus to rise (usually to one side and most often to the right). After the completion of the third stage of a normal full-term labor, the fundus should be found below or possibly just at the umbilicus. Any higher position is suspect.

The position of the fundus is usually coded by counting finger widths above or below the umbilicus in the following manner. If the fundus (which usually feels somewhat like a large cantaloupe through the abdominal wall) is two finger widths above the level of the umbilicus, it is recorded as +2. If it is located one finger width below the level of the umbilicus, it is recorded as −1. A recording of 0 may indicate that the fundus is found at the level of the umbilicus, but usually nurses write "@ umbilicus." A typical record of the condition of the fundus would be "Fundus: firm −2 central." The first day after delivery the fundus is usually felt at the umbilicus or below at −1 or even −2 posi-

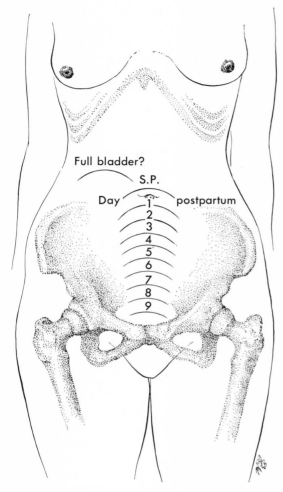

Full bladder?

S.P.

Day   postpartum

1
2
3
4
5
6
7
8
9

FIG. 15-2. Involution of the uterus, showing the various positions of the fundus. **S.P.**, Level just after separation of the placenta from the uterine wall before its delivery.

tion. The location of the fundus may be influenced by the size of the patient's baby, the condition of her uterine muscle, the content of the urinary bladder, and such abnormal conditions as retained placental fragments and the development of uterine infection. Normally the uterus undergoes involution at the rate of about one finger width a day. At the end of 10 days it is usually down behind the pubic bone again and not palpable. (See Fig. 15-2.)

Multiparae often complain of "aftercramps" caused by the contraction of the uterus in the process of involution. They are more often bothered by cramping than primiparae, who usually possess better muscle tone. Nursing mothers may experience more aftercramps because of the stimulation of the uterus during the process of nursing. Mild analgesics usually relieve the discomfort.

Observation for signs of urinary distention

The most common cause of a high fundus is a full bladder. Even when a woman is catheterized just before delivery, she may have a full bladder fairly soon after admittance to the postpartum area, especially if she is receiving or has had intravenous infusions. Sometimes the baby arrives so quickly that the physician is unable to catheterize the patient before delivery. The postpartum nurse should be aware of this.

Other signs of urinary distention are a puffy area just above the pubic bone, complaints by the patient that she feels she should void but cannot, or the voiding of small amounts—less than 200 ml. This is called "dribbling" and usually indicates a full bladder that is capable of contracting only partially to release limited amounts of urine. A distended bladder is to be avoided because it jeopardizes normal bladder tone and may lead to the development of residual urine, an amount that routinely remains in the bladder and is not voided. Residual urine may become an excellent medium for bacterial multiplication. A distended bladder may also interfere with the normal contraction of the uterus and predispose the patient to hemorrhage. A distended bladder may be painful and add to the aftercramping experienced by some patients.

Encouraging voiding. Voidings of postpartum patients are usually measured until two voidings of over 300 ml. are recorded and a fundus check after the voidings indicates that the patient is emptying her bladder well. To check the efficiency of a bladder the physician will sometimes order a catheterization for residual urine. It is important that all the equipment necessary be at the patient's bedside before she voids so that the catheterization may proceed without delay.

If a patient is suspected of having a full bladder, every effort should be made to help her void without resorting to catheterization, which may cause inflammation even in the best of circumstances, especially if repeated. Several techniques to encourage voiding may be useful.

If the patient cannot get up to the bathroom because of her general condition, because she has delivered too recently, or because she has had a saddle type of anesthesia and does not as yet have an ambulation order, the problem of initiating natural voiding is more difficult. Many patients find it difficult to use the bedpan. The time that physicians allow their patients to ambulate postpartum differs widely. Patients who have received spinal anesthesia may be kept in bed, flat or with a pillow, for a period of 6 to 24 hours after delivery. The restriction in ambulation and posture is chiefly an effort to reduce the possibility of "spinal headache." Whether the restriction actually prevents the headache, however, has been debated. Patients who have had a general anesthetic are usually ambulated at the end of 8 hours. Those who have had local or no anesthetic usually are allowed up with aid as soon as they wish. Sometimes if a physician knows that a choice must be made between catheterization and probable success in voiding, he will choose to order earlier ambulation. "Saddle" patients also have more problems voiding because they have lost normal feeling in the bladder area.

If a bedpan must be used, it should be warmed. Patients who have had a saddle type of anesthesia may be raised just enough so that their hips are not higher than their heads while positioned on the pan. Privacy should be maintained, and, if possible, water should be left running into a washbowl to provide psychological stimulation. If an order is available, giving a "pain pill" such as oxycodone (Percodan) about 20 minutes before the bedpan is offered often helps solve the problem. Having the patient blow bubbles through a straw into a glass of water or pretend to blow up a balloon while she is on the bedpan sometimes helps relax the sphincter muscle. Pouring a measured amount of warm water or pHisoHex solution over the perineum may help the patient void. If not, it will help clean off the area prior to catheterization. Encouraging the patient to drink *large* amounts of fluid before she has voided normally will, at times, add to rather than relieve the problem and is not recommended.

Catheterization technique. If none of the preceding methods bring about the desired result, catheterization must be carried out. The nurse should know whether a specimen should be saved for laboratory analysis. The technique of catheterization and the materials used will differ from hospital to hospital. There are several presterilized disposable catheterization sets available from commercial sources that a number of hospitals are using. In other institutions a central supply service or, rarely, the nurse on the maternity area herself assembles and sterilizes the equipment. The following instructions are only general in character to make allowances for the different setups used, but they include principles that should be understood as well as review information for the student.

CATHETERIZATION: POSTPARTUM AREA

Purposes:
1. To relieve urinary distention
2. To obtain a "sterile" specimen for laboratory examination
3. To check for residual urine not expelled at the time of voiding
   (In this case the catheterization must be done immediately after the patient voids.)
4. To instill medications into the bladder
5. To maintain an emptied bladder during surgical procedures—generally with the use of a retention catheter (Foley)

Materials needed:
1. A sterile tray containing:
   a. A drape (to provide a field)

b. Antiseptic and cotton balls for cleansing
c. One or two No. 14 straight catheters
d. Lubricant
2. Gloves (properly sized)
3. Adhesive tape and rubber band
4. Provision for the collection of the urine obtained; specimen bottle, if needed. If an indwelling catheter is ordered, add the following sterile equipment:
   a. No. 14 Foley catheter
   b. Five-milliliter syringe filled with sterile saline
   c. Drainage tubing and bottle or bag
   d. Safety pin
5. A protective bedpad under the patient's hips
6. A good light, well placed
7. A bath blanket for adequate draping. The diamond drape is recommended
8. Paper for perineal pad disposal
9. Perineal pads
10. Waste basin or plastic bag

Procedure:

1. Check the physician's orders regarding catheterization.
2. Assemble and position equipment.
3. Explain in simple terms what is going to be done for the patient and that she will feel better as a result of the procedure.
4. Provide privacy and *lighting*.
5. Wash your hands, remove the perineal pads; wash your hands again and drape the patient.

6. Carry out routine perineal care if indicated.
7. Actual catheterization:
   a. Open the sterile tray, conveniently located (Fig. 15-3).
   b. Lift the perineal drape to expose area.
   c. Make provision for the disposal of waste and collection of urine.
   d. Put on sterile gloves.
   e. Lubricate catheter, if not already done. (Do not occlude eyes.)
   f. Prepare cotton balls with antiseptic if not done previously.
      (How and when this is done will depend on the packaging available.)
   g. Place sterile field up to patient and position sterile tray.
      (If the sterile tray is not compartmentalized or equipped to receive more than a few cubic centimeters of the expected urine, a basin or bedpan must be previously placed nearby to be positioned once the flow of urine has started.)
   h. Expose the upper vestibule.
      (1) With the hand closest to the patient's head as you stand facing the bedside, gently part the labia majora *and minora* to expose the upper vestibule.
      (2) You *must* get sufficient exposure to identify the urethral meatus, but you must be gentle. Remember, many patients have stitches in the true perineum just below the vagina.

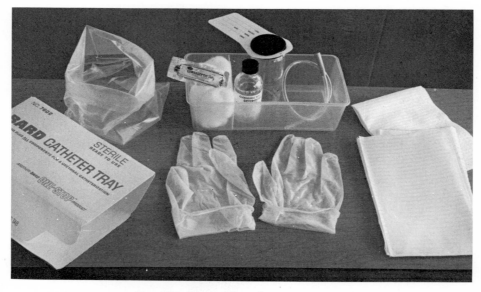

FIG. 15-3. Disposable catheterization tray.

(3) Some of the newly delivered "saddle" patients will have little feeling in the area; others will be very sensitive.

(4) *Remember,* once your hand has touched the patient, it is contaminated.

(5) Sometimes, holding the labia back with a cotton ball under one supporting finger helps maintain the position.

(6) Technically, if you let the labia close after having washed the crucial area with antiseptic, the area must be rewashed, since it has been contaminated by the enfolding tissue; therefore, it is important to maintain the labia in a drawnback position.

i. Gently cleanse the upper vestibule:

(1) Gently wipe down one side of the urethra; discard ball in waste disposal. Some techniques provide a forceps on which to mount the ball. Others use a forceps for picking up and inserting the catheter.

(2) Gently wipe down the other side of the urethra; discard ball.

(3) Gently but firmly cleanse the urethra (wiping down with the cotton ball at the same time as you lift up against the tissue with your other hand; this helps smooth the area immediately surrounding the meatus and visualize the urethra). The urethra is usually located midline just above the vaginal opening and may look like a little slit, dimple, or inverted V. Use more cotton balls as necessary.

(4) Guard your fingers against touching the tissue or drainage while cleansing the area with your "sterile hand."

j. Insertion of the catheter:

(1) Pick up the catheter about 3 inches from the tip.

(2) Ask your patient to take a deep breath at the moment of insertion. This distracts her and helps loosen the urethral sphincter.

(3) The female urethra is about 1½ inches long. No more than 4 inches of the catheter should ever be inserted, to avoid bladder puncture. If obstruction is encountered, the catheter should never be forced. There may be an abnormality of the canal (presence of a tumor, stricture, etc.),

or you may not have properly identified the meatus.

(4) A slight downward incline of the catheter may aid insertion as the urethral canal slopes downward when the patient is in dorsal recumbent position.

(5) Urinary flow should come within a few seconds. If it does not, ask the patient to cough and *gently* press on the area above the pubis; this may start the flow. If it still does not appear, reposition the catheter, pulling it out slightly. If it still does not come, you may be in the vaginal canal instead of the urethra, or your patient may have an empty bladder!

(6) Any time you touch a nonsterile object, perineal tissue that has not been antiseptically prepared, or the vaginal canal with a urinary catheter, it is contaminated, and another sterile catheter must be used.

(7) If 600 to 700 ml. of urine are collected and the bladder is still not empty, most physicians do not object if you clamp off the catheter in a sterile manner, tape it to the inside of the thigh, and return to drain and remove it in half an hour. (Removing a large amount of urine suddenly by artificial means may cause shock.) It is better not to have a bladder become distended with such an amount of urine in the first place. However, if the bladder does contain more urine, the preceding is perhaps the best procedure.

(8) If a Foley insertion is ordered, inflate the bulb with the sterile saline solution as soon as the catheter is in place. Gently tug on the Foley catheter to make sure it is positioned correctly and the bulb is inflated. Connect the drainage tubing attached to a collection bottle or bag. Stabilize the catheter by a strip of adhesive tape attached to the inner thigh of the leg, which is away from the doorway of the patient's room. Lead the tubing underneath the patient's knee or over her thigh (according to her physician's preference) and over the side of the bed to the collecting bag or bottle. Stabilize the drainage tubing, using a safety pin and rubber band attached to the sheet to as-

sure direct gravity drainage to the urine collector. There should be no dependent loops in the tubing. All patients with an indwelling catheter are on intake and output determinations.

k. Always measure the amount of urine obtained and record it. Note also the color of the urine. Note whether a catheter was left in place and if a specimen was obtained and sent to the laboratory.

l. When withdrawing a catheter, pinch the tube and ask the patient to take a deep breath.

m. Make the patient comfortable; dry and straighten her legs before caring for equipment or measuring output.

n. If the procedure was carried out for distention, the patient's ability to void should continue to be evaluated. She should still be on "output" and any complaints of frequent or painful urination reported.

o. A few physicians desire the instillation of a prophylactic urinary antiseptic just before the withdrawal of the catheter at the conclusion of a catheterization.

Continuing care

The necessity for good aseptic technique during all procedures in the postpartum area is readily understood when it is realized that within the uterine cavity, easily accessible to microorganisms from the exterior, is an open "wound," the former place of placental attachment. This diminishing, but still easily infected, area is well supplied with veins and arteries. It provides an ideal entry into the general body circulation and the possibility of septicemia.

You will remember that not too many years ago infection was the leading cause of maternal mortality. Childbed, or puerperal, fever was a real threat. It still is, if we are not enlightened and conscientious in our techniques.

PERINEAL CARE

Postpartum perineal cleansing is given in countless ways in maternity services across the nation. Techniques range from the use of separate sterile irrigation setups by a masked nurse each time needed by the patient, to teaching the mother which way to wipe with a clean washcloth. The accept-

ance of a technique should be based on whether it is safe, adequate, simple, inexpensive, and aesthetically satisfying to all concerned. The principles involved in perineal care should be the same whether it is done by the nurse or the patient herself.

Perineal cleansing

Perineal cleansing is performed to prevent infection, eliminate odor, observe the area and lochial flow, and ease the patient. Any equipment used by the patient should be absolutely clean and should not be used by another. Equipment used by more than one patient should be sterilized between patients. Hands should be washed before and after care. Care should be taught in cleansing the perineum and in removing and applying perineal pads so that soil cannot be introduced to the vulva. This means, for both nurse and patient, stroking from front to back once only with each cotton ball or cleansing surface. It means that the nurse will routinely remove and apply perineal pads from front to back, but this is a bit hard for mother to do! It is better to teach her to attach both ends to her sanitary belt, and then draw the belt up snugly into place so that the pad will not slip. The pad should be changed each time she uses the toilet. Some maternity services issue plastic squeeze bottles of antiseptic solution or warm tap water plus cellulose wipes to each mother for self-care. Others issue pitchers and furnish appropriate solutions. Still others provide individually wrapped, moist towellettes impregnated with rapidly drying antiseptic. Whatever is offered, the principles must be understood. No "pour-off" technique should be used if the patient has a vaginal packing. The patient will be cleansed with moist cotton balls or towelettes instead.

Episiotomy and first- and second-degree lacerations

For patients who have had episiotomies or laceration repairs, perineal care usually involves more than just cleansing. In these cases many hospitals also provide an anti-

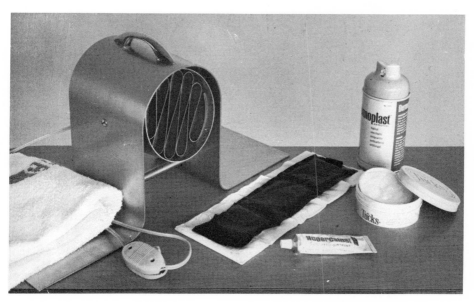

FIG. 15-4. Aids in relieving perineal discomfort through local application: the perineal lamp (the hood is draped with a towel when used), a perineal ice pack (unwrapped for better viewing), Nupercainal anesthetic ointment, Dermoplast antiseptic-anesthetic spray, and Tucks (lightweight witch-hazel–impregnated compresses). (Courtesy Grossmont Hospital, La Mesa, Calif.)

septic, analgesic perineal spray such as Dermoplast or ethyl aminobenzoate (Americaine). Most maternity services also routinely offer a perineal heat lamp several times a day for 20-minute intervals. The heat lamp is used to improve circulation, promote healing, and ease discomfort. It is usually not applied until several hours after delivery because it may stimulate additional bleeding if given too early and is not a real need in the first 12 hours or so. When applying heat lamps, care must be taken that they are not too close to the patient, even when a low-watt lamp is used. The thighs of blondes, redheads, or other fair-skinned patients should always be draped before the lamp is used.

Patients with standard episiotomies and first- and second-degree lacerations usually respond very well to the combination of irrigation, heat lamp, and analgesic spray offered. However, many such women still would prefer to stand rather than sit during periods of waiting. It is thoughtful to place pillows protected by plastic-backed pads

on hard chairs. Advising the mother to tense her buttocks and tuck in her pelvis before sitting down often helps too, or she may prefer to sit sideways and lean like the classical Tower of Pisa!

Other local analgesics may also be ordered, such as dibucaine (Nupercainal) ointment and witch-hazel compresses such as Tucks. (See Fig. 15-4.)

Third-degree lacerations

Mothers who have had third-degree perineal lacerations (extending into the rectal sphincter) may need more help. Great caution must be exercised in giving patients who have had such problems any type of enema, suppository, or cathartic, since the suture line may not only involve the sphincter but also may extend into the rectum itself. Oral analgesics may be needed.

Application of cold to the perineum

Occasionally a patient has a swollen perineum after delivery, or a physician may consider swelling of the perineal tissues likely in a certain case. An order for the application of cold compresses or ice packs may be written. An ice pack should be wrapped with sterile, waterproof material and a fairly thin, sterile, absorbent outer layer and applied directly to the perineum. This must be done to protect the patient against cross infection and still render the cold desired by the physician. It may be held in place by an encircling sanitary pad. Various perineal ice packs are now available. They need to be fairly comfortable, durable, and able to provide cold for reasonable periods. If no such pads are available to the nurse, she may fill a rubber glove with cracked ice and water, close it tightly and wrap it in a light, disinfected plastic covering and a sterile towel. Ice packs must be changed frequently. The perineal area should be frequently observed for developing hematoma or increased swelling.

AMBULATION

As previously stated, the ambulation of the postpartum patient is determined by the orders of the attending physician. His orders depend on the type of anesthetic given during delivery and the general condition of the patient. Early judicious ambulation of postpartum patients has lessened the incidence of respiratory, circulatory, and urinary problems, helps prevent constipation, and promotes the rapid return of strength. But whenever the patient is first allowed out of bed, *the nurse should not leave her alone!* These patients often become dizzy and faint. If the patient does become faint, ease her onto a chair, her bed, or even gently to the floor, but do not leave her to seek help. If she is on a chair, support her with her head lowered to her knees. No matter how many days post partum, the nurse should always evaluate her ambulating patient.

The first time the postpartum patient gets up she may experience a sudden temporary gush of vaginal discharge. This is not significant. It reflects the patient's change in posture after being several hours

recumbent when the uterine drainage was not as efficient.

BATH AND BREAST CARE PROCEDURES

The postpartum bath given the afternoon or morning after delivery is a procedure designed to permit observation and instruction as well as provide comfort and protection against infection. The postpartum patient is likely to perspire profusely. It is one way the body has to rid itself of excess fluids. In most cases mothers have only one such bed bath during their hospital stay. On succeeding mornings they take showers.

The postpartum bath differs from the routine bed-bath procedure followed in other hospital areas. It recognizes that the new mother's body includes two areas that are easily infected: the breasts and the perineum, which leads to the internal reproductive tract. If initial breast care is not given to nursing mothers in the delivery room area, it will be incorporated into this bath. Following is a suggested postpartum bath procedure.

POSTPARTUM BATH PROCEDURE

Materials:
1. Clean wash basin
2. Clean washcloth and towel set
3. Soap and/or antibacterial cleanser (pHisoHex)
4. Bath blanket
5. Clean bra or breast binder
6. Breast pads

Procedure: After the preliminaries necessary before all bed baths:
1. Start washing the breast area first, whether the mother is nursing or not.
   a. Wash in a circular manner from the nipple outward.
   b. Instruct the mother to follow this same order of bathing during her shower the next day.
   c. If the mother is planning to nurse, especially observe the nipples for inversion, fissures, and cleanliness. Some hospitals will include the use of an antibacterial cleanser such as pHisoHex in the breast care of nursing mothers.
   d. Dry the area and cover with a clean towel.
2. Continue the bath by washing the face,

neck, hands, arms, axillae, abdomen, and back.
3. Give a back rub. This is much appreciated!
4. Apply bra or breast binder and breast pads.
   a. If patients may wear their own bras, be sure they are large enough and clean. Otherwise, apply a supporting breast binder until the patient can have another bra brought in.
   b. All patients should have some type of adequate breast support and breast pads whether they are nursing or not.
   c. In applying the bra or binder be sure the breasts are not pushed down against the chest wall. They should be elevated and lifted toward the opposite shoulder.
5. Wash the feet and legs; do not rub vigorously or massage because of the danger of embolus.
6. Perineal care is usually done at the completion of the bath as a separate procedure. At this time the principles of perineal self-care are taught.

Anatomy of the breasts

A greater understanding of the importance of breast care, the technique of nursing an infant, and the principles involved in pumping the breasts may be gained at this time by a brief description of the anatomy involved.

The breasts, or mammary glands, are normally two in number. Each breast is divided into segments, or lobes, which in turn are divided into lobules (smaller lobes). These contain the actual milk-producing glands known as *acini*, or alveoli—as indicated in Fig. 15-5. The breasts are richly supplied with blood vessels, lymphatics, and nerves.

Each segment of the breast radiates from the central colored portion known as the *areola* that in turn rings the sensitive erectile tissue known as the *nipple*. Milk ducts from the acini travel toward the areola and open out onto the surface of the nipples. There are usually 15 to 20 such openings on one nipple.

As each major milk duct approaches the areola it widens temporarily, forming a small reservoir, or sinus. When a mother pumps her breasts manually, she obtains the best flow if she first presses the breast tissue back with her thumb and fingers

and then squeezes the breast. Properly holding the breast with one hand during nursing not only allows the baby to breathe more comfortably but also encourages the secretion of milk.

When the order is given that a mother's breasts be pumped, it is usually done to maintain or encourage her milk supply. It is not advised to relieve engorgement, since emptying the breasts stimulates more milk production.

Breast engorgement

Breast engorgement usually occurs about the third day postpartum and is often regarded by mothers as the result of the "milk coming in." However, not all the tenderness and swelling results from the presence of more milk. It is, for the most part, the result of the increased venous and lymphatic congestion in the breast tissue. During this period of engorgement, which is experienced by all mothers to some degree whether or not they are nursing, the breasts may feel hard and nodular. Lay people often call this "caked breasts." This uncomfortable and often painful condition usually subsides in about 2 days. In the meantime the nurse can encourage her patient by explaining that soon the breasts will be less congested and more comfortable. She can aid the patient by providing good breast support to be worn continuously and by applying wrapped ice caps intermittently to the area as ordered. Analgesic drugs may also be prescribed to relieve the pain. Some type of estrogenic compound such as stilbestrol is routinely prescribed to nonnursing mothers to relieve congestion.

Pumping the breasts

A mother may pump her breasts manually as described or use a hand or electric pump as shown in Fig. 15-6. Whatever method is used she should be supported comfortably in a sitting or side position with her hands and breasts freshly washed. Any equipment that would touch her breasts should have been sterilized before use. If the milk is to be saved for the baby, it should be collected in a sterile container, using aseptic technique. The mother should be instructed how to empty her breasts using the method that is ordered or preferred. If the electric breast pump is used, the nurse must make sure that the suction is not too great. It should be increased gradually. Four to 6 inches of pressure is plenty! A record of the amount of milk obtained should be kept in the patient's chart. Mothers sometimes are distressed at the color of their milk. They should be assured that

human breast milk looks weaker or more bluish than cow's milk but that it is perfectly suited for baby.

Breast infections

Infections of the breast are not as common today as formerly, but occasionally they still occur. Most infections are introduced at the nipple area, which may be fissured or cracked because of poor nursing techniques or exceptionally fragile breast tissue. If such a complication develops, it

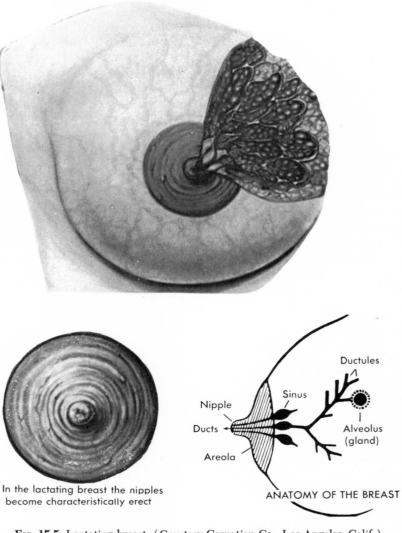

In the lactating breast the nipples become characteristically erect

ANATOMY OF THE BREAST

Ductules

Sinus

Nipple

Ducts

Areola

Alveolus (gland)

FIG. 15-5. Lactating breast. (Courtesy Carnation Co., Los Angeles, Calif.)

is usually not found while the patient is in the postpartum area because of early discharge practices. It becomes the subject of an office call and, rarely, an admission to another part of the hospital for excision and drainage of an abscess. Fortunately, most cases of infectious mastitis do not progress as far as abscess formation. The nurse should always observe the patient's breasts or inquire about their condition. Signs of inflammation or cracked and bleeding nipples should always be re-

ported. For the latter, a nipple shield (Fig. 15-7) is sometimes ordered and periodic exposure to warm air (perhaps the local use of a hair dryer) and application of an antiseptic analgesic breast cream may be advised. Breast infections are most often caused by the organism *Staphylococcus aureus*. Any patient with such an infection should be isolated and moved from the maternity service. The application of cold or heat to the breasts may be ordered. The treatment prescribed will depend on the

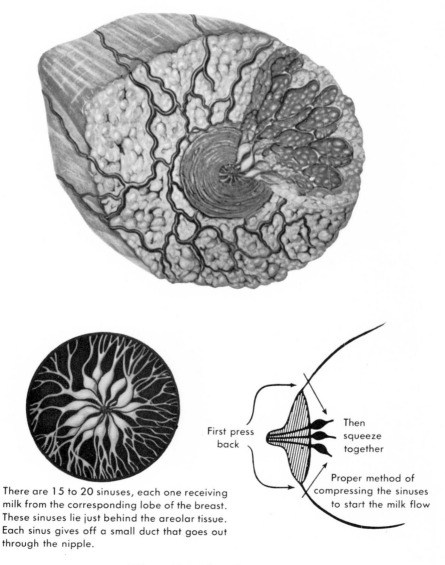

There are 15 to 20 sinuses, each one receiving milk from the corresponding lobe of the breast. These sinuses lie just behind the areolar tissue. Each sinus gives off a small duct that goes out through the nipple.

First press back

Then squeeze together

Proper method of compressing the sinuses to start the milk flow

FIG. 15-5, cont'd. For legend see opposite page.

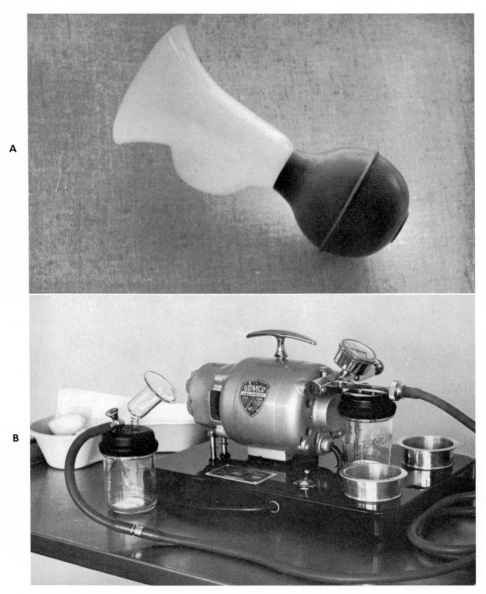

FIG. 15-6. **A,** Hand breast pump. **B,** Electric breast pump. (Courtesy Grossmont Hospital, La Mesa, Calif.)

stage of the infection. Systemic antibiotics are commonly given.

ELIMINATION

Constipation may be a problem to the postpartum patient; it may be caused by diminished intestinal and abdominal muscle tone. Physicians often order a mild laxative the evening of the first or second post-partum day. If this medication does not produce results, a gentle enema is often scheduled. It may be a tap water and soapsuds solution or the newer phosphate-type enema in disposable packaging. Since many of these patients suffer from hemorrhoids or have adjacent episiotomy or laceration repairs, one must be very careful in the insertion of the well-lubricated enema

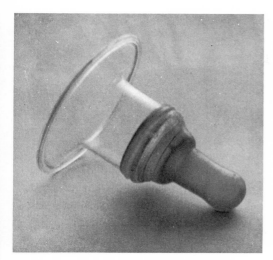

Fig. 15-7. Nipple shield. (Courtesy Grossmont Hospital, La Mesa, Calif.)

tip. Early ambulation has been credited with preventing much constipation.

SUPPORTIVE CARE AND EDUCATIONAL OPPORTUNITIES
Aims of postpartal hospitalization

The postpartal hospital stay should ideally provide safety, rest, and constructive encouragement to the recent parturient. However, in some areas the actual hospitalization period is so brief that it is quite difficult to realize the ideal. Brief postpartal hospital experiences are largely motivated by economics and availability of accommodations. It is not unusual in some maternity services to see a mother going home with her baby 2 days after her delivery date. Discharge in the third postpartum day is almost routine in many parts of the United States. The pendulum has swung a long way since the time of mother or grandmother, when 5 and 10 days passed by before the new mother stirred from her bed!

The fact that the pendulum of postpartum management needed to swing is not debated. Certainly early ambulation and self-care techniques have reduced the incidence of many complications associated with prolonged bed rest, such as thrombo-

phlebitis, pneumonia, and subinvolution of the uterus. However, the shortened postpartal stay necessitates a prenatal reevaluation of the needs of the new mother and her provisions for help in the home setting. The average primipara has had less opportunity than her counterpart of past generations to learn the arts and crafts of child care in her own family circle while growing up. In many cases her first responsible contact with a newborn infant arrives the day she takes her own baby home from the hospital. Many times she has adequate and loving help at home. Too many times she does not.

Educational resources

There do not seem to be enough hours in the hospital day to teach a new mother what she needs to know about herself and her baby and still give her sufficient time to regain her strength and composure. Of course, in the case of a multipara perhaps educational needs are not as great, but the primipara cannot gain the assurance desired in a 3-day period even if hospital classes and practice sessions could be held all day long and she could attend them all.

At present the answers seems to lie in greater utilization of the prenatal courses offered by community agencies such as the YWCA, Red Cross, or public health departments, wider involvement of the visiting nurse, greater availability of rooming-in facilities in hospitals, and a greater awareness on the part of all postpartum staff members of their teaching roles.

The vocational nurse would probably not find herself involved in any formalized classroom teaching, but the quality of nursing care given, the importance she places on personal hygiene (her own and her patient's), and the skill she develops in observing, listening to, and responding to her patient's needs will make her an important teacher nonetheless.

Of course, in places where postpartum stays are longer and facilities and staff are available actual classes in baby care, bathing, formula preparation, and nursing tech-

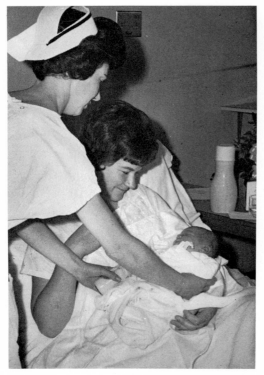

FIG. 15-8. Nurses can do a great deal to reassure new mothers. (Courtesy Grossmont Hospital, La Mesa, Calif.)

niques may be offered to mothers. If the prerequisites are present, the maternity department should not neglect its opportunity.

Rooming-in

The so-called rooming-in plan is especially well adapted to provide learning opportunities for the new mother who desires to have this closer contact with her infant. The baby is kept at the mother's bedside or in an adjoining cubicle close at hand most of the day. If the mother so desires, her baby may be returned to a special part of the newborn nursery for the night or specified periods. A nursery nurse may be assigned to go to the patient's unit, bathe the baby, and help with any questions that the mother may have. She may return at feeding times and when called to assist in any way necessary. As the mother feels

stronger and more confident, she is invited to participate in her child's care. The postpartum nurse washes her hands and wears an overgown when caring for the mother, her unit, or the baby. Visitors are usually restricted to the father. He must wear an overgown during the visit and wash his hands when entering. In this way he, too, is able to know his child better before discharge. Rooming-in is not desired by all parents. Some mothers, especially multiparae, welcome the brief period when they will have little direct responsibility for child care. Others may feel too nervous to have the baby at the bedside for extended visits. This method of care however, when available, offers excellent teaching and learning possibilities.

• • •

The new mother is usually an exceptionally good source of questions. Some the nurse will be able to answer immediately. Others she must refer to the physician.

One of the first things the mother wishes to investigate after she has seen her baby and recovered some of her strength is her own weight loss. She is usually dissatisfied with her initial loss the first time she steps on the scale and needs to be reassured that under normal conditions she will lose from 15 to 20 pounds total over a period of weeks. However, to help regain a good figure she must regulate her caloric intake to her metabolic needs. The weight gained during pregnancy in normal conditions is caused by the size of the infant, the weight of the placenta (about 1 pound), the amniotic fluid (about 1½ pounds), the increased size of the uterus (about 2 pounds), breast enlargement (about 2 pounds), and increased circulating and tissue fluids.

Sometimes students are a bit taken aback when they see postpartum patients ambulating for the first time. They confide to one another that Mrs. Smith does not look as though she has delivered yet! Multiparae, because of the repeated stretching of the abdominal muscles, particularly need time and effort to regain a nonpregnant-appear-

FIG. 15-9. Knee-chest position.

ing shape. Occasionally a hernia develops because of the separation of the rectus abdominus muscles, which are supposed to support the abdominal contents. This condition adds to the "pregnant look." A number of years ago the use of straight or many-tailed scultetus abdominal binders for support was common. Now they are not often ordered unless the abdomen is particularly pendulous or the patient requests them for increased comfort. If a scultetus binder is ordered in the postpartum period, it should be applied upside down with the wrapping starting at the top to avoid forcing the uterus up and out of place.

Nowadays it is thought better to rely on the abdominal muscles for support and to build up their strength instead of advocating indiscriminate use of abdominal binders. Various postpartum exercises are recommended to restore muscle tone as well as improve circulation and regain general strength. These exercises are graded according to difficulty, ranging from deep breathing and gentle range of motion to the assumption of the so-called knee-chest position (Fig. 15-9), leg lifts, and "bear walks." The progression of exercises and when they are to be used is up to the attending physician. The knee-chest position is claimed to be especially helpful in preventing the uterus from falling backward out of place (retroversion) and supposedly aids in uterine involution.

Mothers often ask what they may do when they return home. They should be advised to increase their activities gradually, avoid fatigue, and avoid lifting heavy objects and older children. They should be encouraged to have midmorning and midafternoon rest periods. There is a tendency for a newly delivered mother to try to do too much and then regret it. Even while in the hospital the provision for rest is sometimes limited. Nurses should make every effort to provide their patients with a restful environment. Showers and shampoos at home are allowed as soon as desired. Some physicians allow tub bathing equally as early. Others permit tub baths 2 or 3 weeks after delivery. Douches and intercourse should be deferred until the routine postpartum checkup by the physician is completed, usually at the end of 6 weeks.

In the interim, patients should be made to feel welcome to contact their physicians if any problems arise. However, a good physician-patient chat and the distribution of printed instructions and hints for a smooth adjustment to life with baby before discharge cuts down on much avoidable phoning and/or office visits. Problems that should be reported when noted include pain or localized tenderness in the legs, increased vaginal flow, painful breasts or cracked nipples, painful urination, backache, and fever.

In the case of nonnursing mothers, menses usually return in 5 to 8 weeks. The nursing mother may not experience menstruation until several weeks after the weaning of her infant. This does not mean, however, that she cannot become pregnant during this period.

DISCHARGE

The discharge of the mother and child from the maternity service is an exciting time for the family. A calm and, literally, collected patient the morning of discharge is rather the exception despite all efforts to smooth the departure. Before the patient leaves, any instructions concerning the mother or baby to be carried out after discharge must be clarified.

The baby is brought to the room after all other arrangements have been completed and the mother is ready to go. Her bags are packed, and she is dressed as she wishes to travel home. Great care should be taken that all her belongings leave with her.

The baby is identified again and dressed for the short trip outdoors to the car. The mother is discharged in a wheelchair. The nursing staff sincerely wish to both a "bon voyage."

Special considerations

Postpartum hemorrhage, the most common, serious problem in postpartum, has been previously discussed on pp. 158 and 159.

Toxemia of pregnancy has been discussed on pp. 150 to 153.

THE CESAREAN SECTION PATIENT

Let us now discuss some of the exceptional conditions that students encounter in their postpartum experience. First, let us consider the patient who has had a cesarean section. In many hospitals such a patient is kept in a recovery room for several hours before returning to general nursing care. If her cesarean section was anticipated, she may have been admitted initially to the postpartum unit and prepared for surgery by its staff. For information regarding the preparation of a patient for cesarean section, please see p. 123, where the topic was discussed in relation to complications of labor and delivery.

The physical care of the postcesarean section patient is similar to that of any patient who has had abdominal surgery. However, in addition, this patient has become a mother. She needs special attention to her postpartal needs.

Nursing care

Immediate observation. The care she receives on transfer is an extension of the postoperative care she received in surgery or the recovery room. Blood pressure, pulse,

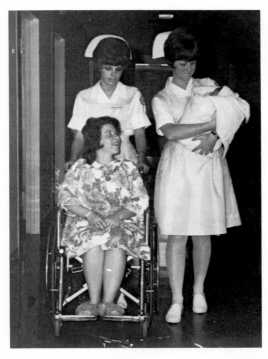

Fig. 15-10. Soon you'll be in your own little bed!

and respiration rate should be taken at least every 20 minutes for a minimum of 2 hours and until stable. Students are again reminded that a systolic blood pressure reading of 90 mm. Hg or below is usually considered a sign of circulatory shock. A falling blood pressure and a rising pulse are among the first signs of difficulty. Other signs of shock include pallor, cold, clammy skin, apprehension, disorientation or unresponsive behavior, and dilated pupils. But do not wait to observe all the classic signs of shock before seeking help should you have the responsibility of helping with such a patient! As is the case with all surgery patients, the dressing should be observed for drainage and any staining reported. The abdominal dressing is not the only site to be watched for signs of hemorrhage, however. The lochia must be observed and evaluated. As a rule cesarean section patients have less lochial flow. After the placenta is extracted during surgery the uterus is inspected and gently sponged, emptying the cavity of some of the drainage that would otherwise be expelled vaginally. The fundus is not routinely palpated because of the presence of the dressing and the recent incision.

The patient usually receives intravenous fluids during the first 24 to 48 hours. The first ordered fluids may contain an oxytocic to cause the uterus to contract. The intravenous infusion should be frequently observed for rate of flow and signs of infiltration. An indwelling Foley catheter is usually maintained for 24 hours or until the intravenous fluids are discontinued. The catheter should be checked for rate of flow and the type of urine being obtained. The tubing should be stabilized and without dependent loops.

Dietary considerations. At first, the patient is usually given nothing by mouth, and then she is gradually given a progressive surgical diet based on her toleration of oral feedings. This would mean progressing from sips of water to a clear liquid, a soft diet, and then to a regular diet, over a period of approximately 3 to 4 days.

Because of their reputations as gas formers, milk, ice water, and citrus juices are many times omitted from the diet along with other notorious foodstuffs such as green peppers, cauliflower, and Brussel sprouts. Some observers believe that drinking through straws may also increase flatus. A new surgical patient or a patient with an intravenous infusion or an indwelling catheter should be on intake and output determinations.

Ambulation. Although orders to get the patient out of bed may not be written until the day after surgery, planned movement in bed should be carried out. The patient is periodically encouraged to deep breathe and cough as soon as she is put to bed from surgery. She is turned at least every 2 hours. How long she remains flat depends on the anesthetic used (usually spinal), her general condition, and her physician's orders. When she is first allowed out of bed, she should briefly dangle her feet and then stand and march in place; during the second attempt she walks with the nurse's support. Walking the patient to a chair two steps away for a 15-minute period of sitting is not considered the best interpretation of "ambulate the patient"! The sitting position does not aid the circulation in the lower extremities. It is very important to follow orders for progressive ambulation. Just because a patient is hesitant does not mean that ambulation should not be carried out. The nurse does not need to reiterate all the complications that the physician is seeking to avoid by early ambulation. Usually if she simply states that it will help the patient feel stronger faster and help prevent or relieve flatus, the needed initiative will be provided.

Abdominal distention. Abdominal distention caused by trapped flatus can be quite distressing to any patient who has undergone abdominal surgery. Many times it is the chief complaint of the cesarean section patient. Although the medications ordered for postoperative pain may be used, such as morphine or meperidine hydrochloride (Demerol), it is still much better to try to eliminate the distention. As part of her care the nurse should evaluate the condition of the abdomen. Is the area just above the dressing hard, bloated, and tender or is it soft and relatively flat? Ambulating the patient may help relieve distention—so may intermittent, small enemas, the Harris flush technique, or insertion of a rectal tube. Also helpful are suppositories, laxatives, or the use of neostigmine. Occasionally, strange to say, the use of carbonated drinks helps the patient to "bring up air" more easily and gain relief. In severe cases a nasal gastric tube connected to suction may be inserted.

Sutures. The cesarean patient will receive perineal irrigations for cleanliness and comfort, but no sprays or heat lamps are used, since there are no sutures in the perineal area. But there are abdominal sutures, clips, or adhesive "butterflies" that are usually removed about the fifth or sixth postoperative day.

Complications

Cesarean sections result in a relatively low maternal mortality rate—less than 0.2%. Neonatal mortality, however, is quite high. The results depend on the condition of the mother and the fetus, the equipment available, and the skill of the operator and nursing staff. The most common serious maternal complications reported are thrombosis and embolism. Occasionally afibrinogenemia complicates the recovery. Most physicians advise no more than three cesarean sections for one patient, although more have been performed. Many physicians believe that once a cesarean section has been performed, subsequent pregnancies should be delivered abdominally because of the danger of rupture of the previous uterine scar. Others believe that a trial labor is justified if obstetrical indications for cesarean section do not persist.

THE SORROWING MOTHER

Not all mothers admitted to the postpartum area leave with healthy babies. Some leave without a child because the infant did not survive birth or died in the early hours of life. Some leave alone because their infant is premature or has some abnormality. Still others leave alone because they are not going to keep their babies; they will be placed for adoption. It is especially sad when a new mother who has waited for her child with anticipation finds that for all her waiting and care there is either no child or a child with gross deformities. Mothers of stillborns are usually placed in an area where they will be far from the nursery and away from baby traffic. Supportive nursing will be much needed by these women. See p. 236.

Nurses on the postpartum floor should be alerted by the nursery when a baby is not "doing well." Good communications between the nursing and medical staffs concerning what has been told patients regarding their infants is essential. Discretion should be practiced by all nursing personnel.

THE UNWED MOTHER

At times, conditions surrounding pregnancy and delivery call for "confidential" or "no information" treatment of a patient. For numerous reasons, knowledge of the presence of the patient in the hospital may not be wished to be shared. The patient may be unmarried. Her child may have been conceived before marriage took place. Her husband may not have fathered the child. A patient may simply want a quiet hospital period without undue publicity attached to legitimate pregnancy. Some of these patients will choose to have their babies adopted; others will keep them. "Confidential" or "no information" patients are often cared for in a separate unit or wing.

Several community agencies are engaged in helping the unwed mother and her child. The Salvation Army operates residential and casework facilities as do the Florence Crittenton Homes and various church-related and public organizations. Public welfare departments assist with adoption arrangements when desired. It is not the function of the nurse to judge patients who have illegitimate pregnancies. Her function is to meet these patients' postpartum needs as much as possible. The circumstances in which most of these patients find themselves are symptoms and not the cause of basic difficulties in their lives. The nurse may privately disapprove of the conduct of such a patient and its almost inevitable consequences, but she should not reject the patient herself. This patient needs kindness probably as never before. Constructive help by professional social work personnel to aid the patient face the situation and evaluate its causes is indicated (see p. 154).

POSTPARTUM "BLUES"

As body hormonal levels change and the responsibilities of an enlarging family and infant care rather suddenly make themselves felt, most newly delivered women experience at least some degree of depression, commonly called postpartum "blues." The nurse may enter a patient's room for a routine check and find her previously exuberant mother trying to wipe away some tears. While providing some tissues and gently asking what she may do to help, the nurse is often told that the patient does not really know why she is crying. "The tears just come." The knowledge that mothers sometimes are a bit depressed after delivery is usually reassuring to the patient. "Blues" commonly are not prolonged.

POSTPARTUM PSYCHOSIS

Labor and delivery is often a physically and emotionally exhausting period even for the normal, healthy woman. For a small minority the entire period of pregnancy is a great strain because of other basic unsolved psychological problems. During the postpartum period these patients may show the development of definite signs of mental illness. They may become withdrawn, disinterested, and/or belligerent and suspicious. They are often victims of unreasonable fears. In severe cases they may become dangerous to themselves and others. Any signs of such behavior or inability to cope with reality should be reported and evaluated by the patient's physician. Psychiatric help may be indicated. Many times these patients have had histories of previous emotional instability or mental illness.

PUERPERAL INFECTION

The term "puerperal infection" may be used to describe any infection of the reproductive tract during the puerperium. However, more technically speaking, a patient is considered to have a puerperal infection if she has a fever of 100.4° F. or more on 2 successive days during the first 10 days post partum, excluding the first 24 hours—unless another source of the temperature rise is determined.

The appearance of a puerperal infection is always a serious development. It may involve the perineum proper, the uterine lining (endometritis), or the pelvic area outside the uterus (parametritis). It may extend via blood vessels and lymphatics to areas relatively far removed, as in the case of septic thrombophlebitis of the leg. It is most often localized, but it can become a generalized peritonitis or septicemia. It can be caused by several different organisms, but the usual microorganism implicated is the streptococcus or staphylococcus. If such an unfortunate complication should occur, all effort should be made to determine the original source of the infection. Such detective work involves a knowledge of the history of the patient, the personal health of attending personnel and visitors, and/or the nursing and medical techniques used.

Accompanying signs and symptoms

Along with the appearance of fever, pelvic infection is often accompanied by abdominal tenderness or pain, foul smelling lochial drainage, an abnormally large uterus, and the presence of chills. The patient may complain of general malaise and lack of appetite and display a rise in pulse rate. Such signs and symptoms should be reported immediately. Detection of a puerperal infection should initiate isolation procedure and again, if possible, the removal of the patient from the maternity service proper. Such a diagnosis may also affect the nursing procedures in the care of the infant and the infant would not be allowed to visit his mother.

Treatment of a case of pueperal infection will depend on the extent of involvement. Antibiotics to which the causative organisms are sensitive will be ordered. In cases of pelvic infection the patient will most often be placed in Fowler's position to encourage drainage of the affected area.

Extension of infection

Observation for signs of the extension of the infection or generalized peritonitis should be constant. Such indications would be increased abdominal tenderness and distention and nausea and vomiting, as well as the previously listed symptoms.

Thrombophlebitis. Not all cases of thrombophlebitis involve the presence of infection, but many do. Clots may form anywhere in the body where a slowdown in circulation, a repair of damaged tissue, or a plugging of bleeding vessels occurs. During the postpartum period, clots or thrombi may form in the pelvis or the lower extremities. They may stay localized and interfere with local circulation, set up areas of inflammation, or actually become foci of infection. Rarely, they may break away from the original site of formation and travel about in the circulation. Then they are called emboli (singular, embolus). These clots are particularly dangerous because they may enter some small but vital vessel and cause grave damage or even sudden death. This most often occurs in the case of an embolus or emboli in the lung field or brain.

A common site of thrombophlebitis is the thigh or calf. Sometimes circulation is so impeded that the leg swells considerably, is extremely painful, and may demonstrate red streaks or locally inflamed areas. The skin may be so tense that it appears particularly white. The appearance of the enlarged white extremity gave femoral thrombophlebitis its oldtime lay name of "milk-leg." It often occurred at the time of engorgement and to the uninformed appeared to be white because it was "full of milk."

Treatment of femoral thrombophlebitis varies considerably depending on the philosophy and experiences of the physician in charge. Some will order elevation and the application of heat with a heat cradle or pad. Others will order ice packs. Antibiotics may be indicated. Some may prescribe anticoagulants to cut down on the formation of further thrombi. The nurse must recognize that use of anticoagulants on a postpartum patient increases the possibility of postpartum hemorrhage significantly. Her observations of any abnormal bleeding would need to be quickly reported. Blood pressure would need to be taken periodically. Prothrombin determinations by the laboratory would be expected.

An order for Ace bandages or other elastic-type leg supports is common. Applied correctly, they help speed the venous circulation back to the heart and discourage the formation of clots. No massage of the legs is permitted for fear of dislodging previously formed clots. Ambulation is only ordered dependent on the day-by-day progress of the patient revealed by the presence or absence of fever and her general condition. Thrombophlebitis may occur in all degrees of severity. Some physicans automatically order Ace bandages applied to the legs of their patients who have had difficulties with varicosities, as a preventive measure.

• • •

The postpartum stay is brief in many parts of the United States. However, the nurse can do much, even in this short interval, to aid the patient to face her increased responsibilities with added knowledge, skill, energy, and assurance.

16
Population, ecology, and reproduction

Any text focused on maternal and child health published in the decade of the 70's would be neglecting a crucial area of concern and controversy if it did not include at least a brief consideration of the topics of population, natural resources, and environmental protection. These subjects are vitally linked with such obstetrical and pediatric interests as genetic counseling, birth planning, abortion, sterilization, fertility, and adoption. Because discussion of birth planning has often been part of postpartal counseling, these topics are included in this unit. However, it is readily understood that they represent a much broader area of concern, involving more than this particular interval in an individual's life.

For many centuries, some of these subjects were deemed either irrelevant, irreverent, or simply outside the possibility of human control. The idea that the entire earth could become seriously impoverished or poisoned by mankind was foreign to most human thought. A rather simple optimism existed that as one resource became scarce, another would be prepared to take its place. Problems of ecology, the balance of nature, were considered to be largely theoretical or curiosities of only local importance.

Now, of course, one can hardly pick up a popular magazine or scientific journal without encountering a discussion of some aspect of this very complex problem. In fact, some people have already grown weary of the theme and request a respite. Some believe that the ecological crisis has been overstated and is being used to di-

vert attention from other international and domestic issues that cannot afford to be slighted. However, the wish to avoid appropriate analysis and any subsequent necessary action must not be granted if we are to be reckoned responsible ancestors by those who live after us.

Let us consider some of the factors that have made those engaged in predicting the shape of tomorrow's world extremely uneasy. They revolve about the realization that although the earth's resources are finite, or limited, the demands for her bounty are steadily increasing. (See Fig. 16-1.) Note that the world population projected by the United Nations for the year 2000 is more than twice that of 1960. The reason for this vast increase is the decrease in infant and maternal mortality and the lengthening of the average life-span. Also sobering is the prediction that the major areas sustaining this population growth will be the underdeveloped countries, where often a large percentage of the people already live on the border of starvation. Although some have expressed the opinion that methods will be found to substantially increase food production and provide the nourishment necessary, a look at the current doubling time of our planet's population should cause us to reject this theory. It is presently estimated that our current world population, barring intervention, will double in approximately 37 years. The doubling time for the population of the United States was estimated in 1968 to be 63 years. Even if interplanetary colonization were soon feasible, we would, at this

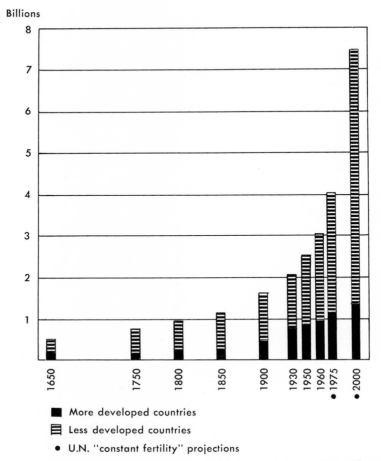

Billions

Fig. 16-1. Growth of world population. (Courtesy Planned Parenthood-World Population, New York, N. Y.)

rate, still eventually face an unmanageable population growth.*

Other threats to earth's inhabitants besides starvation should be identified. An increasing population uses more and more raw materials of all kinds. When the supply of an article is limited, intense competitive activity may develop in an effort to obtain its control. A nation whose population is rapidly increasing and whose vital resources are curtailed has frequently become a militant nation. As peoples double and triple in number, both goods and services are stretched to the point where they can no longer meet basic human needs, and more mental and physical illness is to be anticipated. Is mankind expecting famine, war, and disease to automatically solve our population problem? There must be other more acceptable alternatives! To preserve a worthwhile world for our children these should be intensively and extensively explored.

The options would all seem to involve a conscious, orderly limitation of the number of persons who are to inherit our earth. Such a limitation may be achieved in various ways, and there is much debate regarding the efficiency and morality of the techniques employed. The basic methods,

*Ehrlich, P. R.: The population bomb, New York, 1968, Ballantine Books, Inc., pp. 17-26.

all of which have been used at some time, are (1) abstinence, (2) contraception, (3) premeditated abortion, (4) sterilization, (5) infanticide, and (6) adult murder.

Attitudes, both public and private, concerning the desirability and methods of birth planning have undergone considerable modification in the last 40 years. Changes have been particularly marked in the last decade. Of the methods just listed, infanticide and adult murder are, of course, unacceptable to all. Abstinence, although very efficient when practiced, appears difficult to maintain. Its use within the context of marriage, except for special circumstances for agreed periods, may be questioned. Three methods seem to have gained some acceptance by segments of modern society today. They are contraception, abortion, and sterilization.

All human beings do not accept the same explanation of the origin and meaning of life, nor do they agree concerning the order of life's priorities. A number of diverse codes of behavior or morality of varying usefulness to present society and the individual are observed. When the morality of an individual or group clashes significantly with the concepts of right or wrong held by another person or group, the parties involved may label the activities of the other "immoral." In reality, probably any evaluation of human conduct considered controversial would include more than the two points of view. Indeed, one might say that in addition to the perspectives of those persons engaged in a dispute, there is also the perspective of truth that some would declare is reserved to God alone.

Philosophical differences in viewpoint cause various groups or individuals to endorse, tolerate, or condemn certain techniques of population control or family planning. These philosophical considerations include convictions regarding (1) the ultimate purpose and potential of the individual and mankind as a whole, (2) how the developmental state of the unborn child affects his status as a person or soul, (3) the rights of the unborn vis-à-vis those who have already begun extrauterine existence, (4) the purposes of the marriage relationship and sexual intercourse, (5) the responsibility and ability of the individual to make and implement decisions involving personal conduct, and (6) the role of Deity in the affairs of man.

Various religious groups have spoken regarding these matters at different times. Though most agree concerning the importance of the population problem, they are not agreed regarding the morality of the methods proposed to ease it. Because of the size and structure of the Roman Catholic Church and the historical authority of the papacy, the encyclical letter of Pope Paul VI, Humanae Vitae, or "Of Human Life" has been much discussed. Within this document, Pope Paul states that ". . . the Church, calling men back to the observance of the norms of the natural law, as interpreted by their constant doctrine, teaches that each and every marriage act . . . must remain open to the transmission of life." He does, however, recognize that "If . . . there are serious motives to space out births, which derive from the physical or psychological conditions of husband and wife, or from external conditions, it is then licit to take into account the natural rhythms . . . for the use of marriage in the infecund periods only. . . ."* Periodic abstinence or continence of married couples is approved. Premeditated abortion, even for therapeutic reasons, and sterilization of either sex is prohibited. There is much dialogue concerning these considerations in the Catholic church today. Evangelical Christian and Jewish representatives, though usually assuming positions of greater acceptance and in numerous instances endorsing birth planning, are not of "one mind"—lacking unity regarding the propriety of different contraceptive techniques and the practices of abortion and sterilization.

---

*From Encyclical Letter of Pope Paul VI: Of human life, 1968.

Contraception

Contraceptive techniques or methods used to temporarily prevent birth are usually considered to fall into three main categories: (1) those that prevent fertilization, (2) those that prevent ovulation, and (3) those that prevent implantation. Strictly speaking, the last is not a method of contraception, since the egg may be fertilized but unable to embed itself into the uterine lining to maintain life.

The first efforts to limit birth were designed to prevent fertilization. These methods included premature withdrawal of the penis before ejaculation during intercourse (coitus interruptus), the selection of infertile periods for sexual relations, and the use of various kinds of barriers by the man or woman to prevent the entry of the sperm through the cervical opening. Barrier techniques included the use of the penile sheath, "prophylactic," or condom, the insertion of various cervical caps or diaphragms, and/or the application of spermicidal chemicals. The method that involves the prevention of ovulation is the use of "the pill" for which there are numerous chemical formulas. Although the mechanism is not clear, the intrauterine contraceptive devices seem to help prevent the implantation of a fertilized egg. A brief description of these methods follows.

Methods used to prevent conception

1. Coitus interruptus (withdrawal, "being careful"). This is probably the oldest type of birth control practiced. It has been accused of being related to the incidence of pelvic congestion and frigidity in females and enlargement of the prostate and impotence in males. However, these charges have not been proved, and the method is used by many couples.

2. The "rhythm technique." This method depends on the identification of the infecund period of each individual woman's menstrual cycle, which is best determined by an extended, careful calendar history of her menses and her basal body temperature patterns. Such combined procedures are prudent, since menstrual cycles differ so much from woman to woman and, indeed, at various times in the experience of one woman. Ovulation may not always be correctly detected even with the help of these procedures. The use of a calendar alone to estimate the time of ovulation or the period of greatest fertility reduces protection considerably. Any calculation of an infecund period must consider that sper-

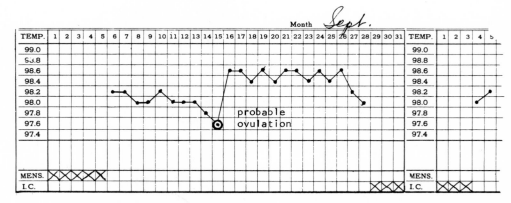

Fig. 16-2. Basal body temperature graph. Normally, ovulation is signaled by a drop in basal body temperature of about half a degree Fahrenheit followed by a rise of 1 degree or more. This relative elevation continues until about 2 days before the menstrual flow reappears. If pregnancy occurs, the temperature remains within a relatively high range. Basal body temperatures must be taken consistently, either rectally or vaginally before *any* activity directly on awakening each morning.

matozoa live approximately 72 hours after deposit and that an ovum is available for fertilization for an estimated 24 hours. This method involves temporary abstinence during the period of risk. The Catholic Marriage Advisory Council recommends the inclusion of days 10 through 19 of the menstrual cycle. The detection of ovulation by changes in basal body temperature is illustrated in Fig. 16-2.

3. Condom. The most widely used birth control device in the world, the condom was probably first employed to prevent the spread of venereal disease. It must be carefully applied to the penis after erection. It can be used in conjunction with chemical contraceptives, which may also serve as lubricants.

4. Cervical caps and diaphragms. Use of these devices was first reported in the 1800's. Cervical caps may be made of rubber, metal, or plastic. They fit closely over the cervix. Diaphragms are latex domes with spring rims (Fig. 16-3). They are positioned over the cervix between the pubic bone and posterior vaginal wall.

Both devices must be used in conjunction with spermicidal cream or jelly. They hold these chemicals in place over the mouth of the uterus. Caps and diaphragms must be fitted by a doctor or technician. The patient's ability to insert them properly must be checked, and detailed education regarding their use is necessary. Because of anatomical differences not all women can be fitted satisfactorily. Some women find it distasteful to insert the device. These barriers should be inserted no longer than 3 hours before intercourse and should remain in place at least 6 hours after intercourse.

5. Chemical contraceptives used alone. These substances are available in the form of creams, jellies, suppositories, foams, and aerosols. They must be applied immediately before sexual relations and be allowed to remain in the vagina for 6 hours after intercourse. Couples sometimes complain that they are irritating to tissues and "messy" to use.

6. Vaginal sponges. These may be made of natural or synthetic materials and have been used in conjunction with spermicidal

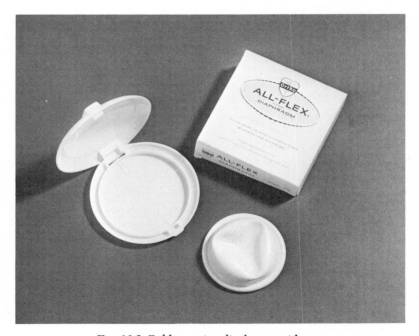

FIG. 16-3. Rubber spring diaphragm with case.

chemicals. They may be bulky and possibly irritating.

7. Douches. Vaginal irrigations are not recommended as a means of contraception. Sperm may enter the cervix 90 seconds after ejaculation. Douching may help to force sperm into the uterus.

Methods used to prevent ovulation

In recent years various combinations of estrogens and progesterone-like compounds have been introduced in tablet form that, when taken orally as directed, are designed to prevent the escape of the ovum from the ovary. They simulate pregnancy in this regard. Another associated action of these substances that helps prevent pregnancy in the rare instances when ovulation is not inhibited involves the decrease in and the thickening of cervical mucus, making the uterus less hospitable to spermatozoa. "The pill" was first accepted for general use by prescription in the United States in 1960. It is now the most popular method of contraception in this country. If the standard technique of administration is followed, a woman is given a special dispenser to help her keep a record of her medication. She takes one tablet every day after supper, beginning the fifth day of her monthly flow, for 20 or 21 days (depending on the type of pill), then she discontinues the tablets. Usually menstrual-like vaginal bleeding results from 1 to 3 days later. She begins her medication again on the fifth day of this period. There are two main types of pills and programs that may be prescribed. One prescription uses one type of tablet (the combination) that includes both estrogens and progesterones throughout. The other includes two types of tablets to be taken in special sequence—first an estrogen only, then the last five days, a combined pill like those previously described. Sequential hormone therapy is supposed to cause fewer side effects but may be slightly less reliable.

Frequently reported problems associated with oral contraception include nausea, occasional vomiting, breast tenderness, acne, headache, increased weight gain, and irreg-

ular vaginal bleeding. Paradoxically, however, some women are placed on the pill, not primarily for contraceptive protection, but because its use may eliminate or reduce dysmenorrhea and symptoms of premenstrual tension. It may also improve acne. It appears that there may be a certain risk of a more serious nature associated with the use of the pill. Research is now going forward to evaluate the danger to the patient of blood clot formation, phlebitis, and embolism. The question has been raised whether the dangers of pregnancy in certain cases outweigh the possible perils of the pill itself.

Disadvantages involved in its use include (1) the need for ability and motivation to proceed with its administration faithfully and (2) its expense. Advantages include its high reliability, the fact that its use is removed from the actual sex act, and the patient's ability to stop therapy and conceive.

Methods that may prevent implantation

Authorities are not agreed as to how the intrauterine devices (IUD) may prevent birth. It would seem, however, that the mechanism involved interferes in some way with the fertilization process, the readiness of a fertilized ovum to implant, and/or the ability of the uterine wall to receive the egg. IUD's are not new, but only within the last decade have they been used with much success. Those inserted in the early 1900's often caused tissue damage and infection because of their placement or design. Their use was largely abandoned by physicians. However, since the advent of polyethylene and improved designs, they have been a particularly popular method for controlling birth in populations who lack the finances, skill, or opportunity to use other techniques. IUD's must be positioned by a proficient physician or technician. They are not usually appropriate for women who have not borne children. They may still be associated with uterine cramping and bleeding and, in rare instances, infection and perforation. IUD's may be spontane-

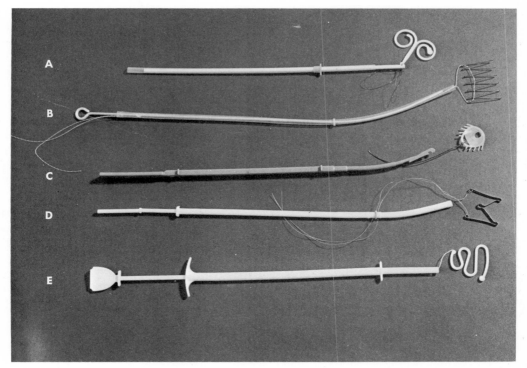

FIG. 16-4. Various types of intrauterine devices with their inserters. A, Saf-T-Coil; B, Majzlin spring; C, Dalkon shield; D, "M" device; E, Lippes loop.

ously expelled. However, once inserted they require little care and unless expelled, they may remain in place for months or years without untoward symptoms. Occasionally, failure of the device may be noted in the delivery room when it is identified by the attending obstetrician after the birth of a baby. (See Fig. 16-4.)

Reliability of contraceptive methods

An evaluation of the efficiency or reliability of the various methods of contraception is difficult to present in statistical terms because in some instances data collection and analysis has posed particular problems. However, all discussions consulted considered oral contraception the most effective. (Some writers claimed 100% success when the pill was "taken as prescribed.")* All discussions also rated the

*Guttmacher, A. F.: Birth control and love, Toronto, 1969, The Macmillan Co., p. 35.

IUD as second-most reliable. Contraceptive techniques perhaps can be ranked for effectiveness as follows, with the recognition that more research is needed:

Most reliable	"The pill"
Highly reliable	Intrauterine devices
	Condom
	Diaphragm with jelly or cream
	Cervical cap
Moderately reliable	Aerosol vaginal foam
	Rhythm, using basal body temperature
	Jelly or cream alone (nonfoaming)
	Suppositories
	Intravaginal tablets (foaming and nonfoaming)
Less reliable	Withdrawal
	Rhythm (calendar computation)
	Vaginal sponge
Least reliable	Douche

It is plain that there is no perfect method applicable to all persons and circumstances,

185

and research continues. Equally clear is the trite observation that a method must be used consistently to be effective.

Abortion

If a pregnancy occurs that for medical, psychiatric, economic, or social reasons is unwanted by those who would have the responsibility of bearing and caring for the child, the possibility of terminating the intrauterine life is sometimes considered. At times such an interruption may be accomplished in optimal surroundings with legal sanction. In many instances it is performed without any such sanction under very poor circumstances, which may result in the mother's mental or physical injury or even death. It has been estimated that approximately 1 million criminal abortions occur each year in the United States.* Until 1967 the only way that a woman could procure a legal abortion in most states was through a statement of medical agreement that continuation of the pregnancy would be a threat to her life. (A few states also considered the *health* of the mother in the wording of relevant legislation.) Laws condemning abortion where written approximately a hundred years ago when the operation was dangerous, even under the best auspices, and in unskilled hands was often catastrophic. Community concepts concerning population growth, the roles of women and children, and meanings and rules surrounding sex, pregnancy, and childbirth also influenced this legislation. Since 1967 several states have modified their statutes to include other reasons for abortion such as the mother's physical and mental health, probable serious deformity of the baby, and cases of incest or rape. Most recently, New York State and Hawaii have made a private decision between a woman and her physician the criterion for abortion. However, applicants in Hawaii must meet nonviability and residency requirements, and legal abortions cannot be performed in New York if pregnancies are over 24 weeks'

*Lader, L.: Abortion, Boston, 1966, Beacon Press, p. 2.

duration. Nurses should be familiar with the laws of the area in which they practice and how they have been interpreted. Legal sanctions regarding this problem are currently undergoing rapid change.

The following methods of abortion are employed in hospital settings if the pregnancy is of less than 3 months' duration:

1. Dilation and curettage. The cervical canal is progressively dilated, and the products of conception are gently scraped from their uterine attachments. This method is used most frequently.

2. Aspiration. The uterine contents are dislodged by the use of a specially designed suction catheter. This method was introduced in mainland China in 1958 and is gaining in favor. The procedure is rapid (approximately 5 minutes), and blood loss is minimal.

Methods used if the pregnancy is of greater duration are as follows:

1. Hysterotomy. This is a type of cesarean section, but it is performed when a nonviable fetus is present. It usually involves a hospitalization and recovery period similar to that of a cesarean section.

2. Intra-amniotic injections. About 200 ml. of amniotic fluid is aspirated from the bag of waters using a vaginal or abdominal approach. This fluid is usually replaced by an equal amount of concentrated (20%) salt solution. An antibiotic may also be instilled. The hypertonic salt solution kills the fetus and usually initiates uterine contractions within a day or two.

Abortions performed in the first trimester are statistically less dangerous physically than a tonsillectomy or a full-term delivery. Obviously, interruption of a pregnancy after 3 months is a more difficult and hazardous procedure. The psychological impact of abortion, though perhaps not immediately apparent, is a critical consideration. The nursing care of the abortion patient is briefly discussed in Unit V.

Sterilization

In some instances an individual or couple, for health, genetic or social considerations, may wish to permanently discontinue the capacity to have children. Any process that produces this result may be termed "sterilization." The written consent of a spouse, although not usually a legal requirement, may be requested by the hospital or physician. Such procedures may be performed without interfering with the ability to participate in sexual relations or diminishing any masculine or feminine characteristics previously present. Either the male or female may be sterilized. Sterilization of a woman is more complex. Usually it involves an abdominal procedure, ligation, or tying, and often the excision of sections of the fallopian tubes. Sterilization of the male by vas ligation or vasectomy is accomplished without entry into the abdominal cavity. It may be an office procedure. Twin surgical incisions are often made in the area where the scrotum joins the body, just over the vas. The ducts are tied and separated. Portions may be excised. After the operation the male does not become sterile immediately, and follow-up sperm counts should be made to determine when contraceptive techniques are unnecessary.

Although sterilization procedures are performed to be permanent, occasionally a man or woman may regret his or her decision. In some cases the tubes may be rejoined and reproductive ability regained, but sterilization should be viewed initially as a lasting intervention. However, occasional spontaneous failures of sterilization techniques have been reported. At this writing, sterilization is illegal in Utah except for medical necessity.

• • •

This section has been a discussion of methods used to limit population. In some instances they have been used to control the types, as well as the number, of persons living in our world. The power to control population is staggering in magnitude and implies the application of value judgments that would seem beyond the ethical capacity of small influential groups. It is hoped that voluntary action based on intensive research and education will be forthcoming and that the democratic process of action through representation will continue to function.

Genetic counseling

One fairly recent attempt to advise individuals on the probable inherited potential of their offspring and thus make possible more enlightened decisions regarding family size is the establishment of genetic counseling services. There is no coercive action associated with the information given. What persons do with the knowledge they gain is a personal choice. Through the use of the services of a genetic counselor the geneology of the client or couple may be investigated. This is particularly helpful when a hereditary problem has been identified in a person's family, but the potential incidence of the defect is unknown. The investigation may include tissue studies to determine chromosomal patterns and biological constituents. Examples of inheritable conditions that are genetically dominant (needing only one affected parent to pass on the trait to all children) are Marfan's syndrome (arachnodactyly), osteogenesis imperfecta, and myotonia congenita. Examples of inheritable conditions that are genetically recessive, (needing genetic support from both parents who may or may not be affected) are cystic fibrosis, galactosemia, phenylketonuria, and sickle cell anemia. Counseling by the service may also be of value in cases of possible alteration or damage of an individual's genetic components.

Subfertility or infertility

In a world where population increase is a major problem it may seem inconsistent to be concerned about the inability of a man and wife to conceive. Yet the capacity to have children of one's own lineage is particularly desired by and meaningful to most persons even if they are not ruling monarchs or shahs! Some authorities have stated that a marriage may be regarded as infertile when pregnancy has not occurred after a year of periodic intercourse without the use of contraception.

Occasionally, instruction concerning the fertile period and the rhythm technique in reverse is all that is necessary. However, anatomical or physiological problems may exist. If infertility is present, it may be caused by problems associated with either or both sexual partners. Statistically when a definite cause is determined, the male is found to be the cause as often as the female. Alan Guttmacher, President of Planned Parenthood Federation of America, has estimated that one third to one half of childless couples could be helped to have children if they received "prompt investigation and treatment."*

This investigation usually begins with an evaluation of the reproductive capacity of the man. Recent semen samples are examined microscopically to detect abnormalities in the number, form, and motility of his sperm. If few or no sperm are found, a testicular biopsy and x-ray studies may determine if the spermatozoa are being manufactured but lack transport because of a blockage of his reproductive system. If this is the case, surgery to relieve the obstacle is sometimes possible. If sperm are not being produced or are limited in quantity, hormonal therapy may be helpful. Attention to the general overall physical and emotional condition of the patient may also prove rewarding.

Evaluation of the capacity of the female to conceive is more complex because of the difference in anatomy. A complete physical examination is usually followed by a determination of the ability of the woman to ovulate. Several methods may be used; these include detection of a characteristic pattern of basal body temperature reading (Fig. 16-2), microscopic examination of a biopsy of the endometrium, or lining of the uterus, and investigation of the viscosity of the cervical mucus. If ovulation is established, examination of the patency of the

fallopian tubes through dye and gas studies may be performed. The uterine cavity, the vaginal canal, and the type and action of cervical and vaginal secretions may also be investigated.

If ovulation does not occur, hormonal therapy as well as general measures to improve health may be helpful. One example of a hormonal product that stimulates ovarian function is follicle-stimulating hormone (Pergonal). This medication has been known to promote the maturation of more than one ovum during the menstrual cycle, causing the development of multiple births (e.g., quadruplets and quintuplets). Since these infants are usually of low birth weight and very fragile, multiple births are not an unmixed blessing to even the most eager parents.

The surgical intervention to open blocked passageways that must be traversed by the ascending sperm or the descending egg may also be performed with varying success depending on the area to be treated. Sometimes the diagnostic procedures used to detect fallopian tube obstruction also serve as therapy, causing the removal of minor blocks in the oviducts. Medical treatment of pelvic inflammatory disease may enable conception to occur.

How intensively solutions for infertility will be sought depends on the ages of the couple, their continued interest, cooperation, and financial resources. At times, persistent failure to conceive because of certain defects of the male can be circumvented through artificial insemination techniques using the husband's sperm. More rarely, semen from an anonymous, healthy, normal male may be employed. Adoption or foster parenthood, although sometimes not available to couples and often involving long waiting periods, may be a satisfying alternative. There are certainly many children already on earth who need loving care.

• • •

Never before in the history of our world have the questions of population, ecology,

---

*Guttmacher, A. F.: Birth control and love, Toronto, 1969, The Macmillan Co., p. 236.

and reproduction appeared more pressing than in this last half of the twentieth century. It behooves all our citizenry to be informed concerning the problems to be faced and their possible solutions. All those engaged in the provision of maternal and

child health, whether within or outside the hospital setting, need to be especially involved in striving to increase the possibility that a newborn boy or girl will not only be well and well-formed, but also welcome.

UNIT VI

SUGGESTED SELECTED READINGS
AND REFERENCES

Abortion and the changing law, Newsweek **75**:53, April 13, 1970.

Abortion, the lonely problem, RN **33**:34-43, June, 1970.

Bookmiller, M. M., and Bowen, G. L.: Textbook of obstetrics and obstetric nursing, ed. 5, Philadelphia, 1967, W. B. Saunders Co.

Burt, J. J., and Brower, L. A.: Education for sexuality: concepts and programs for teaching, Philadelphia, 1970, W. B. Saunders Co.

Carner, C.: Don't be surprised by after-baby blues, Today's Health **45**:33-35, Dec., 1967.

Contraception and abortion, Christianity Today **13**: entire issue, Nov. 8, 1968.

Cooke, R. E., Hillegers, A. E., Hoyt, R. G., and Richardson, H. W., editors: The terrible choice: the abortion dilemma (based on the proceedings of the International Conference of Abortion), New York, 1968, Bantam Books, Inc.

Davis, M. E., and Rubin, R.: DeLee's obstetrics for nurses, ed. 18, Philadelphia, 1966, W. B. Saunders Co.

DeBell, G., editor: The environmental handbook, New York, 1970, Ballantine Books, Inc.

Demarest, R. J., and Sciarra, J. J.: Conception, birth, and contraception, New York, 1969, McGraw-Hill Book Co., Inc.

Edwards, J.: Wrong and right approaches in maternal care, RN **33**:65-81, Jan., 1970

Ehrlich, P. R.: The population bomb, New York, 1968, Ballantine Books, Inc.

Encyclical Letter of Pope Paul VI: Of human life, 1968.

Findlay, E., and Capes, M.: Figure control for your postpartum patient, RN **32**:38-41, Jan., 1969.

Fitzpatrick, E., Eastman, N. J., and Reeder, S. R.: Maternity nursing, ed. 11, Philadelphia, 1966, J. B. Lippincott Co.

Gardner, R. F. R.: Christian choices in a liberal abortion climate, Christianity Today **14**:766-768, May 22, 1970.

Golub, S.: Genetic counseling: heading off birth tragedies, RN **32**:38-47, 72-73, Nov., 1969.

Gonzales, B.: Voluntary sterilization, Amer. J. Nurs. **70**:2581-2583, Dec., 1970.

Guttmacher, A. F.: Birth control and love (wholly revised and greatly expanded edition of the

Complete book of birth control, Ballantine Books, Inc., 1961), Toronto, 1969, The Macmillan Co.

Hendrick, W.: An elderly primigravida takes a "refresher course" in obstetrics, Amer. J. Nurs. **70**:787-789, April, 1970.

Hershey, N.: Abortion and sterilization, status of the law in mid-1970, Amer. J. Nurs. **70**:1926, Sept., 1970.

Hershey, N.: Abortion: a stormy subject, RN **33**: 53, Sept., 1970.

von Hildebrand, D.: The encyclical humanae: a sign of contradiction, Chicago, 1969, Franciscan Herald Press.

Hogan, A. I.: The role of the nurse in meeting the needs of the new mother, Nurs. Clin. N. Amer. **3**:337-344, June, 1968.

Hubbard, E.: How to solve breast-feeding problems, RN **33**:46+, March, 1970.

Irwin, T.: The new abortion laws: how are they working? Today's Health **48**:21, March, 1970.

Lader, L.: Abortion, Boston, 1966, Beacon Press.

Leroux, R., Barnes, S., Gottesfeld, K., West, D., and Tolch, M.: Abortion, Amer. J. Nurs. **70**: 1919, Sept., 1970.

Meek, L.: Maternal emotions and their implications in nursing, RN **32**:38+, April, 1969.

Morley, G. W.: The important "ten B's" of postpartum hospital care, Hosp. Top. **44**:107, Feb., 1966.

Newton, N.: Maternal emotions, New York, 1955, Paul B. Hoeber, Inc.

Noonan, J. T., Jr.: The church and contraception: the issues at stake, New York, 1967, Paulist Press Deus Books.

Peel, J., and Potts, M.: Textbook of contraceptive practice, New York, 1969, Cambridge University Press.

Sine, I. K., and Cameron, J.: Relief of afterpains, Nurs. Clin. N. Amer. **3**:327-336, Sept., 1968.

Tyler, E. T.: "The pill"—is there a danger? Today's Health **46**:24, May, 1968.

Wallace, H. M., Gold, E. M., and Dooley, S.: Relationships between family planning and maternal and child health, Amer. J. Pub. Health **59**:1355, 1969.

Wrage, K.: Man and woman, Philadelphia-London, 1969, Fortress Press; William Collins Sons & Co., Ltd. (This book is a translation of Mann und Frau, Grundfragen der Geschlechterbeziehung, Gütersloh, Germany, 1966, Gütersloher Verlagshaus Gerd Mohn.)

UNIT VII

THE NEWBORN INFANT

17

The normal newborn infant

The newborn infant is a marvelous creation, the result of approximately 40 weeks of intensive growth and development never to be equaled at any future period during his life. A passive participant in the drama of birth, his present and near future is almost totally dependent on the physical care, emotional support, and mental stimulus given his inborn potential by his immediate environment. The human newborn does little for himself. In his egocentric way he waits impatiently for his needs to be met by others as if no other needs exist, and indeed as far as he knows they do not.

Although newborn infants have shared similar environments during their approximately 9 months of prenatal life, even this basic experience is not identical. True, all lived in the warm, watery environment of the amniotic sac, but not all infants receive identical portions of nourishment or oxygen. Their genetic backgrounds, greatly influencing basic body strengths and weaknesses, are very unlike. The stresses and strains of each delivery are not always duplicated. Babies are individuals; each is different, and there is a wide range of shapes, sizes, and behavior patterns that despite their variations must still be labeled "normal." So although we often speak of the typical newborn infant, we

must realize that in reality he exists only within the pages of some text.

Qualifications of nursery personnel

The nursery nurse caring for the newborn infant has a tremendous responsibility. Her observational capacity must be keen because these little persons cannot express themselves in the same ways as the older child or adult. Her technique and skills should be based on scientific principles, precise yet gentle. Her health must be frequently evaluated to be certain that she is not a source of infection to her susceptible charges. Her ethics must be above question as she cares for these small future citizens.

The typical newborn infant

Having explained that a baby is really an individual, we will now describe the general appearance, anatomy, and physiology of the "representative" newborn infant. First some statistics are in order. For unknown reasons there are approximately 106 male infants born to every 100 female infants. It can be said, however, that the male newborn infant appears to be more fragile than the female, having a higher mortality rate. The average male newborn infant weighs about 7½ pounds or 3.400 kg., whereas the average female weighs about half a pound less, or 3.180 kg. The average male length is 20 inches, half an inch longer than his female counterpart. Of course, these figures are just averages, and much depends on the hereditary background of the child. Negroes and Orientals usually have smaller babies, whereas Caucasians tend to have larger children.

When uninitiated persons see a newborn infant for the first time, certain reactions are fairly standard: "He seems to be all head." "Where is his chin?" "Nurse, my baby has flat feet!" "Boy! He sure is red." "Will his skull always be that shape?"

THE HEAD

The head of a newborn infant represents one fourth of his total length, but in adulthood the head equals only one eighth of the individual's total height. The newborn infant's head circumference equals or exceeds that of his chest or abdomen, and the normal limits of his head size are from 33 to 37 cm., or 13.2 to 14.8 inches. No wonder its relative size causes comment! (See Fig. 17-1.)

The shape of baby's head can also cause a mother or father needless concern. Cesarean section babies and even breech babies usually have quite rounded "normal appearing" heads. But infants who are delivered vaginally in cephalic presentations, particularly those who are firstborn, usually undergo considerable head sculpture, or *molding*. This molding is caused by the compression of the head in the pelvic canal during labor. The infant skull, because of the soft membranous seams separating the skull bones, has the possibility of becoming shaped in its journey through the canal. In response to the pressure of the cervix and bony pelvis, the head usually elongates, and the skull bones may even overlap in places. This phenomenon is called *overriding;* the molding lasts for only about a week or less.

The fontanels, or soft spots, where sutures cross or meet are particularly noteworthy. There are two that are easily felt and identified: the anterior diamond-shaped fontanel through which a pulse is sometimes visible, hence the name fontanel, or "little fountain," and the smaller posterior fontanel just in front of the occiput. The larger fontanel closes at 9 to 18 months of age. Occasionally it is the site of "cradle cap," or "milk crust," also called seborrhea. This occurs when the mother or nurse is fearful of cleaning this soft area, and secretions from the oil glands and cellular debris build up. Actually the cartilage covering the fontanels is quite tough; the mother should be assured that no harm will come from shampooing the area well. The posterior fontanel is so small that it is closed at 2 to 3 months of age.

There are two other temporary conditions involving the head that may manifest themselves and cause parental anxiety. These are usually caused by the continued pressure of the undelivered head against

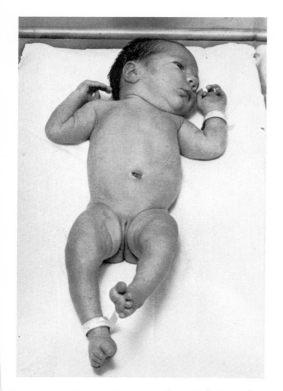

FIG. 17-1. Representative newborn infant, 3 days old. Note the size of the head relative to total length. (Courtesy Grossmont Hospital, La Mesa, Calif.)

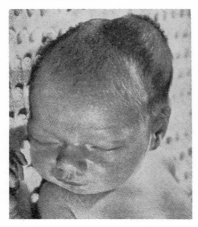

FIG. 17-2. Cephalhematoma over the parietal bone. (From Davis, M. E., and Rubin, R.: DeLee's obstetrics for nurses, ed. 17, Philadelphia, 1962, W. B. Saunders Co.)

the partially dilated cervix. The first and less important is called *caput succedaneum,* or caput. Caput is an abnormal collection of fluid under the scalp on top of the skull that may or may not cross suture lines, depending on its size. It is usually absorbed over a period of days and requires no treatment. The second condition is *cephalhematoma* (Fig. 17-2), caused by a collection of bloody fluid under the first covering layer (the periosteum) of a flat cranial bone. Since cephalhematoma is located within the bone structure, it cannot cross suture lines. It usually develops when labor is particularly prolonged and the passageway is tight in relation to the needs of the passenger, causing bruising against the pelvis. As a result of the trauma, small blood vessels under the periosteum break. A cephalhematoma may not be apparent at the time of birth because of the presence of a more inclusive caput. Like caput, cephalhematoma, although temporarily disfiguring, is not harmful and requires no treatment. In fact, many believe that aspiration of the swelling should not be attempted because of the danger of infection.

GENERAL BODY PROPORTIONS

Parents are often amazed to see the small size of the child's face compared to

his total head size. The facial bones are underdeveloped and the chin almost nonexistent. The baby's neck is usually short and creased and difficult to clean unless the head is tipped backward and unsupported while the child is held at his shoulders. The torso of the normal newborn infant displays a relatively small thorax and a soft, rather protuberant abdomen. The genitalia are small but may be swollen. The extremities are quite short in relation to body length. The feet are always flat because of the presence of a fatty pad that normally disappears as the child begins to exercise and purposefully use his feet.

EARS AND EYES

The ears may be folded and creased and seem out of shape because they contain little hardened cartilage. The infant usually responds to sound within hours after birth. The eyes may not track properly and may cross (strabismus) or twitch (nystagmus). These symptoms are usually not considered significant unless persistent beyond the age of 6 months. The irises are slate blue, and true eye color is usually not determined until 3 to 6 months of age. It is difficult to tell what a baby is able to see. We do know that the pupils react to light, that soft light apparently attracts a newborn infant's gaze, whereas bright light is annoying. Blinking is an inborn protective reflex. The lacrimal glands evidently function only minimally at birth, and the newborn infant's cries are characteristically tearless. Occasionally, an eye discharge that is caused by eye irritation initiated by the prophylactic against *ophthalmia neonatorum* (a condition that results from a gonorrheal infection in the mother) is apparent. The prophylactic, which is required by all states, is usually silver nitrate, 1%, or penicillin ophthalmic ointment or drops. The reason for the eye irritation should be explained to the parents.

SKIN

The skin of the newborn infant is subject to numerous conditions and manifestations that always elicit questions.

Vernix caseosa. The skin of the fetus is protected from its watery environment by a soft, yellowish cream named *vernix caseosa,* or "cheesy varnish." This is an accumulation of old cutaneous cells mixed with an early secretion from the oil glands. Sometimes the baby is thickly covered with vernix at birth. Sometimes it is found in abundance only in the body creases. Some nurseries remove only a minimum of vernix at the time of the initial bath, preferring to leave a thin coating, which will eventually be absorbed or wear off, to further protect and lubricate the infant. Other newborn nurseries meticulously remove all vernix, considering that its protective role has largely ended.

The skin of the newborn infant is quite thin. The more immature he is the less developed will be his layer of subcutaneous fat. For this reason, babies not many hours after birth, when oxygenation is optimal, tend to be quite red. The smaller the baby, the more tomato colored he will tend to be —especially when upset and crying. Nurses should be aware that Negro babies are quite fair at birth and darken gradually.

Lanugo. A relatively long, soft growth of fine hair is often observed on the shoulders, back, and forehead of the newborn infant. In fact, the infant at times may seem to have sideburns. The more premature the infant the more conspicuous this extra growth of hair tends to be. It is called *lanugo* and falls away and disappears early in postnatal life.

Toxic erythema. Another skin manifestation that can be quite puzzling but is altogether harmless is a condition known to the nursery staff as *toxic erythema.* The adjective "toxic" perhaps should not be used, since there has never been any poison proved to be associated with the cause. In fact, the cause is unknown. Some authors list it as a possible allergic response and call it instead *erythema allergicum.* The lesions consist of red blotches that quickly develop hivelike elevations, which may later become blisters containing clear fluid. These may appear on the day of birth and

persist for days or weeks. They are most often seen on the trunk but may appear elsewhere. They are not contagious and are most often seen on vigorous, healthy babies. No treatment is needed.

Mongolian spots. Babies of Negro, Indian, Mongolian, or "Mediterranean" ancestry often exhibit blue-black colorations on their lower backs, buttocks, anterior trunks, and, rarely, fingers or feet. These are not bruise marks or signals of ill treatment, nor are they associated with mental retardation. These so-called *Mongolian,* or *Asiatic, spots* disappear in early childhood.

Jaundice. The skin of the infant on about the third day may begin to take on a yellow cast. This icterus, or jaundice, is not in most cases considered to be pathological but is thought to be associated with the destruction of red blood cells that are no longer needed in as great a number as when external respiration via the lungs was impossible in utero. However, if jaundice is present before 36 hours of age, the possibility of Rh factor or main blood group incompatibility (AB-O) most certainly should be recognized and determined. Indeed, no matter what the age of the baby, the fact that the baby is jaundiced should be reported and evaluated because there is nothing magical about the number 36, and although it is not common, difficulty could occur later. The jaundice caused by the expected erythrocyte destruction is seen to some extent in almost all newborn infants and has been termed *physiological jaundice.*

Petechiae. Another possible signal of trouble associated with the skin that usually turns out to be a false alarm is the presence of petechiae, or small blue-red dots on the body, the result of the breakage of minute capillaries. If present, these dots are usually seen on the face as a result of the pressure exerted on the head during birth. Nevertheless, if petechiae are accompanied by jaundice or begin to increase measurably after birth, one may consider a diagnosis of blood disease.

Milia. Small pinpoint white or yellow

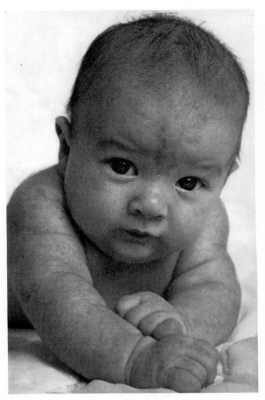

FIG. 17-3. This infant exhibits telangiectasia between the eyes and on the lower forehead. The skin of the arms also shows a slight amount of "mottling," a circulatory pattern common during periods of inactivity and exposure.

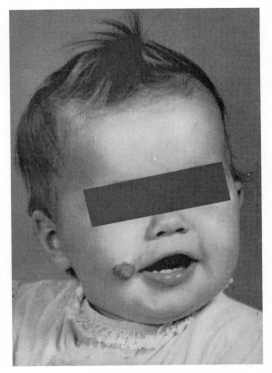

FIG. 17-4. Lesion on the right cheek of this little girl is a slowly disappearing strawberry mark.

dots are common on the nose, forehead, and cheeks of the newborn infant. They are clogged sweat and oil glands that have not yet begun to function normally and are called *milia*. They will disappear with time and under no circumstances should they be expressed.

Birthmarks. Small reddened areas are sometimes present on the eyelids, midforehead, and nape of the neck. They are probably the result of a local dilatation of skin capillaries and abnormal thinness of the skin. Because of the frequent involvement of the nape of the neck they are sometimes called "stork bites," but another name often heard is *telangiectasia* (Fig. 17-3). Some writers term such an area *nevus flammeus,* an unfortunate choice of terminology, since this term is also used for the so-called

port-wine stain, which is disfiguring and difficult to treat. Whatever the choice of terms, however, the parents should be told that in most cases these small areas fade and disappear altogether. Some are noticeable only when the person blushes or becomes excited.

Other birthmarks are sometimes seen. The so-called strawberry mark may not be present at birth but may develop days or weeks later. It is characterized by a dark or bright red raised, rough surface, and since it is formed by a collection of capillaries at the skin's surface it may be classed as a blood vessel tumor, or *hemangioma.* The first signs of a strawberry mark may be a grouping of red dots that eventually coalesce, forming the clear-cut raised lesion. Many times this mark will disappear spontaneously in early childhood without treatment. However, some such hemangiomas tend to increase in size rather than subside, and some seem so disfiguring to the parents that efforts to remove the lesion are made at an early age. The application of dry ice at brief intervals or actual surgical excision, depending on the location of the strawberry mark, are methods of removal. A "wait-and-see" attitude is advocated, since many such lesions regress spontaneously. (See Fig. 17-4.)

Additional birthmarks that may sometimes cause concern are various flat or raised, frequently pigmented irregularities of the skin that are generally termed moles or *nevi* (singular, *nevus*). For the most part these lesions are benign, causing only occasional cosmetic difficulties. Nevertheless, there is a type of blue-black mole that is considered precancerous, and any such lesion must be evaluated by the physician to ascertain its true character.

VITAL SIGNS IN THE NEWBORN INFANT

Temperature. The newborn infant's body temperature drops immediately after birth from a reading approximately equal to that of his mother to a subnormal range. His heat-regulating center and circulatory system have not yet matured, and his body temperature rapidly reflects that of its environment. Placed in a warm incubator or wrapped in warm blankets his temperature usually reaches "normal" (98.6° F. or above, rectally) within 8 to 12 hours. Maintaining body warmth as much as possible in the immediate postnatal period may be critical to the well-being of an infant; therefore special efforts have been initiated to provide warmth to newborns in many delivery rooms. A newborn infant's feet and hands are bluish, and circulation is particulary poor in his extremities. For this reason one should not attempt to judge an infant's temperature by feeling his feet or hands. Evaluating the warmth of his trunk is more accurate. Newborn infants are sometimes overheated by overzealous nurses or mothers who put too much clothing or

bedding on or around them. Since the newborn infant is not yet able to perspire effectively (his sweat glands are not functioning adequately), he breaks out in a pinpoint reddish rash. This is sometimes called *prickly heat,* or *miliaria.*

Pulse. It is very difficult to take a radial pulse on an infant. For this reason all "pulse" readings are routinely taken with a stethoscope over the heart region, either through the chest or back. The reading is called an *apical pulse.* Newborn infants' pulse rates usually range between 120 and 160 per minute (the same as the fetal heart tone range).

Respirations. Newborn infants' respirations are irregular and usually abdominal or diaphragmatic in character, ranging from thirty to eighty breaths per minute. If respirations at rest are persistently sixty or more per minute, the rate is usually considered abnormal, and further respiratory evaluation is required. At no time are costal or sternal retractions considered normal in the newborn infant. Retraction, or a sucking in of the chest wall in the rib or sternal area on inspiration, is an indication of respiratory distress.

A nurse is seldom called on to take the blood pressure of an infant. However, occasionally such orders are written. With a cuff 1 inch wide, the average blood pressure at birth is 80/46 mm. Hg. Such a blood pressure is often difficult to determine and many times is inaudible. If it is unheard, the nurse is allowed to record the systolic reading at the point where the needle on the aneroid sphygmomanometer began to "twitch." Students should know that as a person grows older pulse and respiratory rates decrease, whereas blood pressure readings rise.

SURVEY OF THE NEWBORN INFANT'S BODY SYSTEMS
Gastrointestinal system

Mouth. The newborn infant's mouth is of great interest to parent and physician and should be carefully examined for gross abnormalities such as cleft lip and palate.

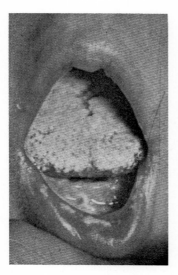

FIG. 17-5. Thrush. (From Potter, E. L.: Pathology of the fetus and the newborn, Chicago, 1952, Year Book Medical Publishers, Inc.)

However, certain small structural differences in the normal newborn infant may need to be explained to the first-time parent to alleviate anxiety. Near the center of the hard palate little, white, glistening spots may be occasionally observed. These are called *Epstein's pearls*. They mark the fusion of the halves of the palate and will disappear in time.

Sometimes the mother has heard of an oral infection called *thrush* and thinks that Epstein's pearls are an indication of this infection. Thrush, or oral moniliasis, caused by a fungus called *Candida (Monilia) albicans,* is a coating on the tongue and cheeks that looks something like milk curds (Fig. 17-5). But it does not dissappear when water is given to the infant as do true milk curds. The white patches adhere to the mucous membrane, but when they are forcibly lifted by an applicator, a raw, red, sore surface is revealed. These sore lesions may discourage appetite. The organism causing thrush is found frequently in the vaginal canal of women where it may or may not cause symptoms. The child may contact the fungus during his passage down the pelvic canal or while nursing if the mother's nipples or the nursing bottles are contami-

nated. The organism is very prevalent and may be especially troublesome in the debilitated patient. The use of broad-spectrum antibiotics kills off much normal intestinal flora but allows *Candida albicans* to abnormally multiply. Babies receiving such therapy may develop thrush. The fungus can involve other parts of the gastrointestinal or respiratory tract as well as the mouth and occasionally may cause a diaper rash. Treatment of thrush, the oral form of infection, is usually quite simple. It responds to application of gentian violet, 1%, or nystatin (Mycostatin).

The gums of the newborn infant may at times appear quite jagged, and the rear gums may be whitish. Although the deciduous teeth are semiformed, they are not erupted. If a tooth is present at birth, it usually is an "extra," which has little root. These so-called "rice teeth" are sometimes pulled to prevent aspiration when they loosen.

The cheeks of the newborn infant have quite a chubby appearance because of the development of fatty sucking pads that persist until food is obtained in other ways.

Mothers are often quite worried about the possibility of tonguetie or a restrictively short frenulum at the base of the tongue. Actually problems in food manipulation or speech are rare because of this condition.

Stomach and intestines. The fetus has no need for a digestive system of its own. All its food is provided predigested via the placental circulation. A good share of the waste products created are eliminated through the same circulation. After birth, however, digestion is a different story.

The capacity of the newborn infant's stomach at birth probably varies from 1 to 2 ounces and increases rapidly. The feeding usually begins to leave the stomach before the total taken is completed. It is common for the infant to swallow air as he feeds, especially when bottle fed. Swallowed air in the stomach may cause difficulty in continuing the feeding or it may cause vomiting later. Air passing into the intestines may cause colic (abdominal cramping). Bottle-fed babies need to be bubbled frequently. Newborn infants are usually bubbled after every ounce of formula. The older infant is bubbled once halfway through the feeding and again at the end of the feeding. Nursing babies are usually bubbled once or twice during a feeding. Immediately after the feeding, a little milk may come up with a bubble. This is termed regurgitation and is not significant.

The first stool of the newborn infant is meconium, a greenish black, tarry, odorless, but very tenacious material. It consists of old lining cells of the gastrointestinal tract, swallowed amniotic fluid debris, and early tract secretions. The first stool should appear in a maximum of 24 hours. If it does not, malformation of the gastrointestinal tract is strongly suspected. Meconium continues to be the normal stool for about 2 days, then the products of digestion of the offered milk begin to change the color of the stool. It becomes first brown and then yellow-green and more loose in consistency. These are the *transitional* stools. Later the stool will become yellow as more milk product digestion takes place. The stools of formula-fed babies are characteristically lemon-yellow and curdy. The stools of breast-fed babies have a more yellow-orange color, are usually softer, and during the first few weeks are more frequent.

Circulatory system

In fetal life the circulatory system serves also as a modified respiratory system, since oxygen is not obtained through the breathing of air into the lungs of the baby but through the successive pulsations of the vein in the umbilical cord leading from the placenta attached to the uterine wall. Carbon dioxide is also eliminated through this attachment via the two umbilical arteries.

At birth, of course, this type of respiratory function is not continued, since the cord is cut and/or the placenta soon becomes detached. The fetal circulation, which is designed to channel blood flow to functioning organs and largely avoid the lung fields, is rerouted after birth (see discussion of fetal circulation, pp. 56 and 57). The two fetal shunts that direct blood flow away from the pulmonary circulation normally close, apparently because of changes in internal pressures and vascular reflexes resulting from loss of the maternal oxygen source and subsequent lung expansion. The opening between the two atria of the heart, the *foramen ovale,* shuts, closing off the blood flow to the left atrium from the right heart and forcing more blood into the right ventricle. The *ductus arteriosus,* the fetal vessel between the pulmonary artery and aorta, collapses, obliging the pulmonary artery to send its total contents on to the lungs.

The circulation of blood in the baby at birth is not at the same stage of development throughout the body. The hands and feet are typically blue. At times the entire body of a baby at delivery may be quite blue because the fetal blood has a relatively low oxygen content, and a momentary disturbance of the placental circulation may occur before expansion of the lungs is possible. However, as soon as the airway is cleared and a healthy cry is elicited, the skin "pinks up" dramatically. Although significant, color is the least important of the characteristics or vital signs to be considered when using the Apgar scoring method in evaluating a newborn infant's need for resuscitation aid (Fig. 11-14). If a newborn infant is chilled or inactive for a period of time, a mottled pattern may be seen on the skin—particularly on the extremities. This purplish mottling called *cutis marmorata* is transitory in nature and soon disappears.

Newborn infants' blood pressure readings and pulse rates have been mentioned in previous paragraphs.

Vitamin K is often given to newborn infants to prevent hemorrhage because of the natural low prothrombin level in this period of life. It is especially recommended for those suffering from hemorrhagic disease of the newborn, infants born of complicated deliveries, or premature infants. However, it has been found that too high a dosage (usually over 5 mg.) may be accompanied by an increase in jaundice and in some cases kernicterus (the yellow staining of the basal ganglia of the brain, causing possible cerebral damage). In some maternity services vitamin K is given to the mothers in labor for the sake of the baby. If it is given intramuscularly at least 2 hours before delivery, the baby is considered to have received an adequate dosage.

At about the third day of life the "extra" blood cells with which the baby is born are no longer needed and are destroyed in greater numbers. The liver cannot cope with the increase of red blood cell breakdown products, and they are found at higher levels in the blood. One particular breakdown product circulating at high blood levels, bilirubin, temporarily tints the skin. This phenomenon has been called *physiological jaundice*. It usually does not persist beyond the first week of life.

There are three blood vessels in the umbilical cord—one vein and two arteries. These are fairly easily seen in the cut umbilical stump. Recently, considerable interest has developed in counting these vessels at the time of the nursery admission, since if only two vessels are found, there seems to be a significant incidence of internal congenital defects (malformed kidneys, heart, etc.).

The vessels of the umbilical cord are fairly soon occluded through the formation of a clot and contraction of the vessels at its end. However, if the cord is manipulated often, the clot may become dislodged, and bleeding through the cord stump may occur if the ligature or cord clamp is loose. Large cords that contain a great amount of gelatinous connective tissue, called *Wharton's jelly*, must be especially watched for bleeding, since the cord will shrink in diameter and the clamp or ligature may become ineffective. There are no sensory nerves in the cord. The baby does not feel it when the cord is clamped or cut. The

umbilical cord drops off, and the place of attachment heals in about 1 week.

Respiratory system

Although the fetus may make some occasional shallow lung movements in utero, the lungs serve no respiratory function, since the oxygen supply is secured through the placental circulatory system from the mother. Until the first breath of air is taken, the air sacs (alveoli) in the lungs are in an almost total state of collapse, or *atelectasis*. This is as it should be, however, because we would not want the lungs to fill with amniotic fluid or other liquids. In fact, one of the physician's main concerns at delivery is the possible aspiration by the baby of thick secretions before the airway can be cleared, thereby plugging or irritating the respiratory tree.

As mentioned in the section discussing the vital signs of the newborn infant, the baby's respirations are normally irregular and diaphragmatic or abdominal in character—the chest and abdomen rising together. The respiratory rate is highly variable, depending on activity, usually ranging between 30 and 80. Persistent respirations under 30 or over 60 at rest should be especially evaluated.

Babies normally are nose breathers and do not breathe through open mouths. Cyanosis of other than the hands and feet, costal or substernal retractions, flaring nostrils, and expiratory grunts heard with or without a stethoscope are all possible signs of respiratory distress.

The most frequent cause of respiratory difficulty in the first few minutes or hours of birth in the United States is the too liberal use of sedatives, tranquilizers, analgesics, and anesthetics that not only affect the mother but also pass over the placenta to the baby, making him sleepy and disinclined to take his first breath.

We do not know exactly why a baby takes his first breath, but we believe the following are significant factors:

1. The buildup of carbon dioxide in the fetal bloodstream caused by the be-

ginning separation of the placenta from the uterine wall and the pressure of the uterine contractions

2. The decrease of oxygen in the fetal bloodstream
3. The rapid change in the baby's environment at the moment of birth
4. The direct handling of the baby for the first time in his life

Urinary system

The newborn infant's renal system does not have the ability to concentrate urine to the degree of the older child or adult. Water is not reabsorbed as freely by the nephrons, and a newborn infant may become dehydrated rather easily. A newborn infant with profuse diarrhea or vomiting is in imminent danger of dehydration.

Uric acid is found in relatively large amounts in the urine of the newborn infant. Occasionally this substance may "crystallize out" as it cools in the diaper, leaving a pink stain like "brick dust."

It is important to record all infant voidings in the delivery room or nursery. Although the newborn infant may not void a large amount or often at first, it is very important to note the fact that he is able to void normally.

Endocrine system and genital area

The endocrine system of the newborn infant is supplemented by maternal hormones that have crossed the placental barrier. These maternal contributions, presumably the estrogenic hormone, luteal hormone, and lactogenic hormone, when withdrawn from the baby through the act of birth, bring about certain phenomena that may cause parents concern and should be explained. The maternal hormones crossing to the fetus may affect the breasts of both male and female infants, causing swelling, which is particularly noticeable about the third day of life. This condition is usually called *gynecomastia*. The breast secretion sometimes seen has been given the interesting name of *witch's milk*. The breasts may continue to be swollen for about 2 or 3 weeks, but gradually the congestion subsides without treatment. The breasts should not be squeezed; this only increases the possibility of infection and injures the tender tissue.

Maternal hormones acting on the miniature uterus of the female newborn infant may set the stage for *infantile menstruation*. The hormones help thicken the infant's tiny endometrial lining. Withdrawn at the time of birth, they no longer maintain this thickened uterine lining, and a tiny menstrual flow may be observed. Usually only a few blood spots are seen on the diapers. The entire process may terminate in one or two days. This bleeding should not be profuse, and any considerable blood loss may be an indication of hemorrhagic disease. White mucoid vaginal discharge in the newborn infant is also thought to be stimulated by maternal endocrine secretions. The genitalia of both the male and female may be swollen. Hymenal tags that regress spontaneously may be seen on the female. Breech infants may have particularly swollen genitalia because of the prolonged pressure on the area. In male infants the scrotum most often contains the testes, although sometimes the descent of one or both is delayed. The foreskin may adhere to the glans penis (phimosis). Circumcision may be advised.

Whether or not the thymus gland should be included in the endocrine system has long been debatable. However, since this lymphoid tissue is most often discussed with the full-fledged members of this group, it will appear under this heading in our presentation. At birth, the thymus gland, located under the sternum and above the heart, is larger than a baby's fist. It is now thought to initiate the body's complex immunity reactions by producing special defensive cells that are distributed to the spleen, bone marrow, and lymph nodes. After puberty, however, the thymus is atrophied, and the change in the gland's size is thought to either stimulate or reflect the development of sexual maturity. Pressure on the respiratory tract from a large thymus has, in the past, been cited as the cause of occasional infant suffocation. The belief that many such cases of "crib death" were caused not by the size of the thymus but by a very virulent, swift-acting microorganism attacking the respiratory tree or other unknown factors is more recent.

Neuromuscular system

The nervous system of the normal newborn infant is very immature. Essential activities for maintenance of life and protection are largely reflex in character—inborn reactions making life possible until the nervous system and associated muscles can "grow up" to the demands of more complex living. Inborn reflexes that normal newborn infants possess include the rooting, sucking, and swallowing reflexes employed in eating and the protective reflexes such as coughing, sneezing, gagging, blinking, and perhaps crying. Certain muscular reactions in newborn infants are also reflex.

The most commonly tested muscular reflex is a total body response known as the Moro reflex, normally present during the first 3 months of life. It is elicited when the

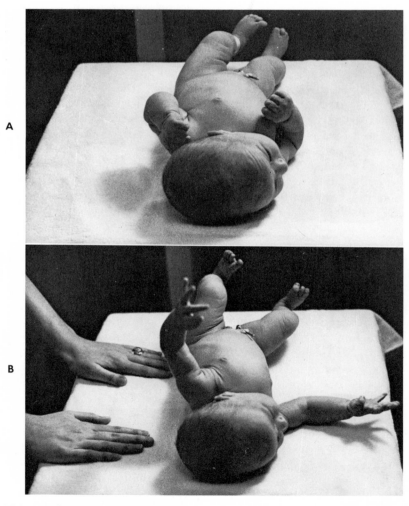

FIG. 17-6. A, Infant at rest. B, Typical Moro reflex, stimulated by jarring the table. (Courtesy Mead Johnson Laboratories, Evansville, Ind.)

baby is startled, usually by a sudden jarring of his support such as occurs when the physician abruptly pounds on the examining table with his fist. The infant responds by throwing out his arms sideways and drawing up his legs with the soles of his feet in opposition. The absence of the Moro reflex in the newborn infant may indicate brain damage. (See Fig. 17-6.)

Another often-seen reflex position is called the tonic neck reflex. The child assumes a modified fencer's position while on his back. The arm and leg on one side of the body are extended while the opposing arm and leg are flexed. The fists are shut and the toes curled. The head is turned toward the extended arm, which incidentally is usually the dominant side. This reflex position may be seen quite commonly until about 4 months of age. Grasping is also an inborn reflex.

The immaturity of the nervous system is demonstrated by the unstable temperature regulation of the newborn infant and his inability to pursue purposeful activity. He may "see" but be unable to interpret what he sees. He may "hear" as soon as the fluid commonly found in the middle ear is absorbed but be unable to sort out the sound and make it meaningful. The sense of taste is quite well developed. The sense of smell is rather hard to evaluate, but evidently some newborn infants can detect the smell of breast milk. Cutaneous sensation is highly developed. Pressure, temperature, and pain are increasingly felt by the infant. The newly born react to cuddling, caresses, and skillful, gentle handling with greater relaxation and acceptance of care.

The newborn infant at first sleeps about 20 hours per day, waking to be fed, bathed, changed, repositioned, and briefly entertained. Usually he stays in the position in which he is placed, since he seldom has the ability to turn himself. However, no baby should be left alone on an unguarded table or bed. Accidents can happen! The order of peripheral nervous system development and muscular coordination proceeds from the head region to the arms and then the legs. Later, the finer activities of the hands and feet are perfected.

Intellectual devlopment is difficult to assess in the newborn infant, but we are reassured when all the normally present reflexes are active. We are concerned when a baby fails to suck well, lacks good muscle tone, or is lethargic and unresponsive to care.

• • •

All in all, the newborn infant is quite an invention, and the succeeding months of his life will include some of the most perplexing, exasperating, and wonderful hours ever experienced by any family lucky enough to welcome him into their home.

18
Care of the normal newborn infant

Universal needs

Every newborn infant, be he a tiny Congolese born in some remote African village or an heir of modern American suburbia, has certain needs that must be met for him to thrive and take his place in society. Some of these needs take priority; some can be met simultaneously; and still others are important but need not be rushed. Following are listed nine universal needs of the newborn infant; the first two must be met in order:

1. A clear airway
2. Established respiration
3. Warmth
4. Protection from hemorrhage
5. Protection from infection
6. Identification and observation
7. Nourishment
8. Rest
9. Love

A clear airway

The first two needs must be met immediately or the baby will not survive, and no amount of oxygen, mouth-to-mouth resuscitation, or intermittent positive pressure will stimulate a newborn infant to breathe if his airway is not open. Conversely, if his airway is not clear but filled with amniotic fluid, meconium particles, blood, etc., and he does try to take a breath and inhale, he may plug, irritate, or contaminate his respiratory tree. The airway may be cleared as follows:

1. Wiping off the child's face at birth of the head
2. Holding the child's head down to drain immediately after birth, while gently compressing the throat toward the mouth to milk out secretions
3. Gentle suction of the mouth and nose by a small, soft, short bulb aspirator or a soft rubber catheter attached to a DeLee trap
4. Visualization of the larynx with a laryngoscope and suction with an endotracheal catheter by trained personnel in unresponsive cases

Established respiration

With the introduction of closed-chest cardiac massage techniques and appliances to electrically stimulate heartbeat, perhaps "established respiration" should read "established respiration *and* heartbeat." However, for this discussion it will be assumed that heart action is present and adequate. If respiration does not occur spontaneously after the airway is clear, the child should be stimulated to cry. This may be done by slapping the heels, lightly spanking the buttocks, rubbing the back gently, or gently suctioning the nose with a soft catheter. Any rough treatment or such procedures as alternating hot and cold baths is now considered to add to the child's problems rather than offer a solution. If breathing is not initiated soon, methods of breathing for the infant must be employed. Sometimes this means the use of intermittent positive pressure via mask and bag (for example, the Ambu). Sometimes the operator will blow directly through a patent endotracheal tube. In some cases an appliance such as the Ohio-Kreiselman resuscitator (Fig. 18-2), equipped with a mask able to deliver oxy-

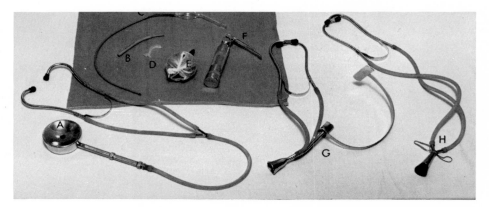

FIG. 18-1. Equipment used to detect infant distress or treat asphyxia. **A,** Leffscope; **B,** endotracheal catheter; **C,** DeLee trap for suction; **D,** newborn infant–sized airway; **E,** rubber aspirator bulb; **F,** laryngoscope; **G,** DeLee-Hillis overhead fetuscope; **H,** standard stethoscope equipped with rubber bands. (Courtesy Grossmont Hospital, La Mesa, Calif.)

gen at intermittent premeasured pressures, may be used. Also the much publicized mouth-to-mouth resuscitation may be attempted. No matter what method is used, it must be emphasized that an airway must be maintained through proper head positioning and/or the use of a small oropharyngeal airway to keep the tongue from falling back and obstructing the pharynx.

Carbon dioxide therapy to stimulate respiration is contraindiacted, since there has already been a carbon dioxide buildup in the blood, and more would further depress the respiratory center. When a child is breathing poorly on his own, is cyanotic, or is being resuscitated, an oxygen-enriched environment is recommended. However, it should be noted that premature infants should not be exposed to long-term oxygen concentrations of more than 40% because of the danger of the man-made disease, *retrolental fibroplasia*. Excessive oxygen in the very small infant can cause spasm of the blood vessels in the retina and greatly impaired vision. However, for emergency purposes higher concentrations can be used for brief periods, if clearly needed. A good rule to follow, no matter what size baby is involved, is to use just enough oxygen to relieve symptoms and no more.

Warmth

Warmth is provided to the infant in most delivery room settings through the use of an incubator or by wrapping the infant in a warm blanket. Some maternity services use wrapped hot-water bottles placed at the sides of the crib or under the crib mattress. If hot-water bottles are employed, they should be used with great caution because of the danger of leakage and burning. In emergency situations, placing the baby against the mother's body will provide considerable warmth.

Recently the importance of maintaining an infant's body heat immediately after delivery and in the extended neonatal period has been emphasized. The temperature of the infant affects his oxygen consumption, the incidence of apnea, and the acid-base balance of his blood. In the instance of a sick infant, the provision of appropriate heat may be critical. Infant warmers utilizing an overhead radiant heat panel are now available and used in some delivery rooms and nurseries. They provide controlled warmth coupled with ready accessibility of the infant for examination and therapeutic measures. (See Fig. 18-3.) When the infant warmer is used, only a diaper is positioned on the child.

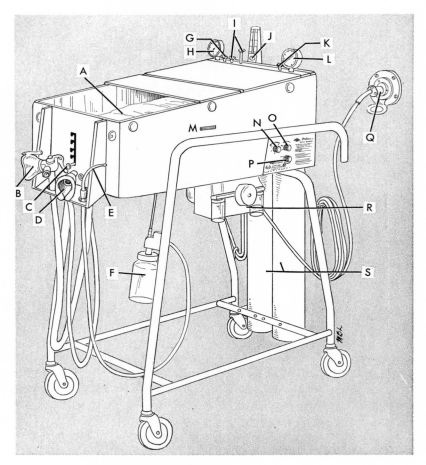

FIG. 18-2. For legend see opposite page.

The way in which the baby is dressed will depend on the temperature of the nursery or rooming-in area. Hospital nurseries are usually kept at temperatures ranging from 72° to 78° F., with a humidity concentration of approximately 55%. The increased humidity helps the babies retain body warmth and helps keep respiratory mucous membranes moist. Some babies are perfectly warm in only a cotton shirt and diaper, covered by a light cotton blanket. Premature infants in a controlled environment, such as that provided by the Isolette, may wear no clothing. In some models of incubators the temperature of the artificial environment may be automatically controlled by the baby's own skin temperature

through the use of a heat-sensitive probe taped to the baby. The temperature setting of other appliances is adjusted manually, depending on the results of intermittent rectal temperature readings.

Temperature determinations are usually taken rectally with a stubby thermometer for 3-minute periods once or twice a day unless closer surveillance is indicated. The thermometer and baby are always supported in such a way that no injury could occur to the rectum.

Protection from hemorrhage

Today, most babies born in hospitals have their cords clamped with a type of compressive metal band rather than tied

Fig. 18-2. Use of the Ohio-Kreiselman resuscitator (series 24). **A,** Bassinet (a mattress especially designed for use in the bassinet is available. The manufacturer does not recommend that any other pad be used except for the possible addition of a thin cotton cloth covering. The mattress is secured by fabric tapes, looped around the outside knobs near the top of the front and sides of the resuscitator); **B,** resuscitative-inhaler unit (oxygen with positive pressure); **C,** control to lower or raise the head position of bassinet; **D,** oxygen inhalation mask (free-flowing oxygen); **E,** metal aspirator (suction) tip; **F,** suction trap bottle; **G,** resuscitator (positive pressure) control knob (preset); **H,** resuscitator (positive pressure) gauge; **I,** controls to lower or raise foot portion of bassinet; **J,** oxygen flowmeter control knob; **K,** aspiration (suction) control knob (preset); **L,** aspiration (suction) gauge; **M,** bassinet thermonometer; **N,** thermostat control settings (1 to 8); **O,** "on-and-off" switch for heating unit; **P,** "on-and-off" switch for suction; **Q,** electrical plug and outlet; **R,** resuscitator motor; **S,** twin oxygen cylinders.

Procedure: The following items should be checked for readiness:

1. Routinely check that the tank oxygen supply is sufficient by slowly turning on the cylinder valve and observing the pressure dial at rear of resuscitator.
2. Check that the power cord is properly secured in electrical outlet (**Q**).
   a. Maintain constant warmth of the resuscitator bassinet. Keep heater switch (**O**) "on." If the thermostat (**N**) is kept on setting 8, this should produce a bassinet temperature of 92.5° F. at a room temperature of 70° F. For every 5-degree increase in room temperature, the bassinet temperature will increase 2.5 degrees. For each setting that the thermostat is lowered, the temperature will be reduced approximately 2.5 degrees. For example, a setting of 7 on the thermostat in a room temperature of 70° F. will produce a bassinet temperature of approximately 90° F. Check the thermometer mounted on the right side of the unit.
   b. Turn suction pump switch (**P**) to "on." Check maximum suction (aspiration) pressure by holding thumb over end of aspirator tip (**E**). Adjust knurled knob adjacent to vacuum gauge (**K**) until desired suction setting is obtained. The lowest effective suction is to be used. Attach aspiration catheter to aspirator tip. Usually a No. 8 catheter is used for nasal suction, No. 10 or 12 for pharyngeal-tracheal suction.
   c. Positive pressure is controlled by presetting the resuscitator control knob. A safety relief valve is located on the resuscitator inhaler body (be sure to see instructions with model). Oxygen is given under pressure at no more than 16 to 20 cm. of water or 12 mm. Hg.

Operation: The following items are necessary for operation of the resuscitator:

1. If resuscitation procedures are necessary and intermittent positive pressure is to be used, the infant is positioned on his back in sniffing position; a small towel under the shoulders may help. The airway is previously cleared with the suction and a small oropharyngeal airway put in place. The resuscitation mask is placed over the child's face and the handle depressed for approximately 2 seconds. Afterward, the handle is released for about 2 to 3 seconds to allow for the deflation of the child's lungs. Resuscitation measures are continued until voluntary breathing is established. Resuscitation efforts should be synchronized with any beginning respiratory efforts made by the child. At times, further investigation of the airway may be necessary. A laryngoscope may be needed and an endotracheal tube inserted. Attachments are available that may connect the tube with the resuscitation apparatus.
2. If inhalation therapy is desired with free-flowing oxygen, assure clear airway and adjust knob on front of flowmeter to 4 to 5 liters per minute. Place inhalation mask gently next to the infant's face. Remove the mask occasionally to observe the airway for obstruction.

Note: Licensed vocational or practical nurses should understand the operation of the resuscitator and be ready to be of assistance in an emergency. Because different models will vary, nurses are advised to read carefully the instructions accompanying their apparatus.

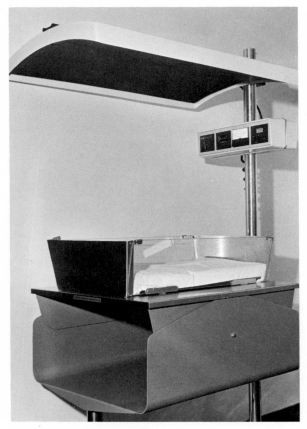

Fig. 18-3. Radiant infant warmer. A "thermister" may be attached to the baby to monitor skin temperature. The crib sides of the unit may be removed to allow greater accessibility to the infant during procedures (e.g., exchange transfusions, resuscitation). The bed tilts. (Courtesy Children's Health Center, San Diego, Calif.)

with the woven cotton umbilical tape used for so many years. These commercial clamps have proved to be quite satisfactory, and although the cord must still be frequently observed for bleeding, incidences of difficulty are extremely rare. When a ligature of any kind is being used, it is usually tied approximately 1 inch from the abdominal wall in a depression in the cord made by a previously placed hemostat, if one is available. The tie is secured by a square knot for stability and checked frequently during the first few hours to detect any loosening or bleeding (Fig. 18-4).

Protection from hemorrhage in the newborn infant also becomes important when caring for the male infant after circumci-

sion, to be discussed later in this chapter. In an effort to decrease the possibility of abnormal cerebral pressure and subsequent intracranial bleeding, newborn infants in their beds are not placed in as steep a head-down position as was popular several years ago when it was quite common to tilt the nursery bassinet on a steep incline for the first 12 hours to aid in the drainage of mucus from the respiratory tree. Vitamin K to decrease coagulation time is routinely adminstered in many hospitals.

Protection from infection

Protection of the newborn infant from infection is a constant challenge to the delivery room and nursery nurses. It involves

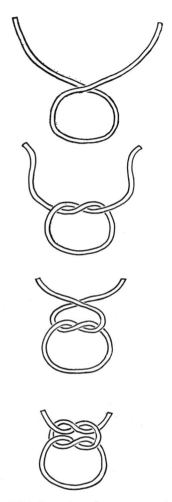

FIG. 18-4. Steps in making a square knot.

tion of the infant from infection involves the use of some prophylactic against ophthalmia neonatorum caused by the gonorrheal organism. Usually this prophylactic (silver nitrate, 1%, or penicillin ophthalmic ointment or solution) is instilled in the delivery room, unless the child's condition or delivery circumstances dictate a more rapid transfer of the child to the nursery. Care must be taken in administering the drops or ointment; no pressure should be put on the eyeball itself. Occasionally, if the eye area has not been previously touched, shading the baby's eyes from the light will cause them to open spontaneously, making instillation comparatively easy. This helpful reaction does not always occur, however. The nurse pulls down on the lower lid to instill a drop of $AgNO_3$ into the conjunctival sac, guarding her clean fingers with a corner of the sterile drape or gauze compress to prevent slipping on the skin surface. This instillation is followed by a brief irrigation with sterile physiological saline or distilled water (see footnote, p. 118). All the while the nurse guards the child from cold and continues to observe his color and respiration patterns.

In the nursery the infant has his own individual bassinet and should also have his own bath equipment, supply of linen, and layette (Fig. 18-6). He should be bathed in his own bed and not on a common bathing table. The scale used for determining weight should be protected and balanced and handled in such a way that no cross infection could take place. Technique papers may be used if necessary. Any instruments or appliances that must be used for more than one infant because it is not feasible to supply individual equipment must be carefully disinfected or sterilized after use. This would apply to stethoscopes, circumcision boards and instruments, resuscitators, etc.

Staff members should wear simple, hospital supplied and laundered scrub gowns on duty, keep their fingernails short, restrict jewelry, and evaluate their own health. No personnel should assume responsibility in a nursery if suffering from a res-

the entire environment of the baby and the techniques used in handling and nourishing him. It even can be said to reach back to the prenatal period when we strive to prevent any contamination of the fetus by organisms that are able to pass over the placental barrier (viruses, spirochetes). The baby, while in the hands of the delivering physician, is considered and maintained sterile. The physician clamps and cuts the cord aseptically. Then the baby is usually handed to a circulating nurse who, having carefully washed her hands and put on a clean overgown, receives him for further care without contaminating the physician's sterile gloves.

In all states of the United States, protec-

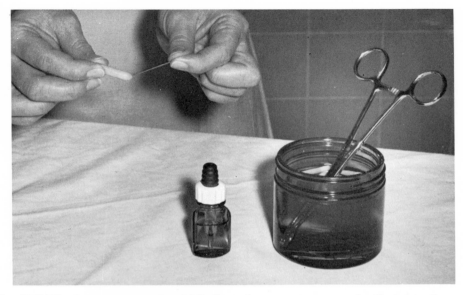

FIG. 18-5. Piercing a wax ampule of 1% silver nitrate preparatory to instillation in the eyes of a newborn infant. The bottle in the foreground contains sterile water. (Courtesy Grossmont Hospital, La Mesa, Calif.)

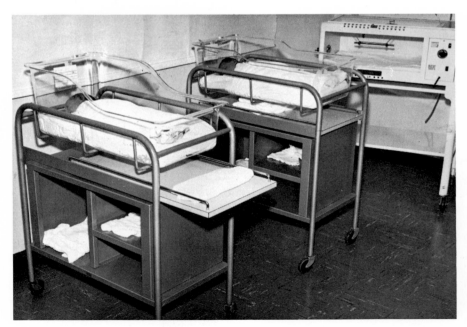

FIG. 18-6. Individual nursery units reduce the possibility of cross infection. (Courtesy Grossmont Hospital, La Mesa, Calif.)

piratory or skin infection or diarrhea. Some hospitals require that nursery staff have periodic or irregular nose and throat cultures. However, since the flora of the human respiratory tract is so changeable, this measure has not been carried out with any sense of having proved anything conclusive in relation to the future safety of the nursery.

Personnel entering the nursery should scrub their hands and arms above the elbow with an antibacterial product such as pHisoHex or Septisol before starting patient care. Hand washing is mandatory after the care of each baby or his unit and in the care of the same baby after changing a soiled diaper and proceeding with further needs. The hands should always be washed before treating the cord. The cord can become the site of serious infection. It should be observed for signs of inflammation and drainage. A nurse who leaves the nursery area should wear a cover gown to protect her clean nursery gown. If her gown should become soiled in the nursery with urine, regurgitation, or stool at any time, it should be changed. Unless wrapped in a protective blanket or on a protective cover, the infant should be held away from the nurse's gown during care and feedings to protect the nurse's dress from becoming a source of cross contamination to other infants. Precautions not necessary at home are a must when many infants from many backgrounds and family units are being cared for in a small area, such as the hospital nursery.

To help protect these youngest of our citizenry, professional organizations such as the American Academy of Pediatrics, hospital accreditation boards, and local public health and safety officials take an active part in making recommendations and requirements governing the construction, maintenance, and operation of the nursery as well as other parts of the hospital. They are concerned about the floor space available, the distance between bassinets, the type of ventilation, the control of temperature and humidity, the provision for adequate lighting, the safety of electrical ap-

pliances, the elimination of possible fire hazards, appropriate dressing and hand washing facilities, and safe formula preparation as well as optimum techniques. The maternity floor should be separate from other hospital services, and personnel should not be borrowed from other services where infectious sources may exist. Newborn infant nurseries are usually divided into several units sufficient unto themselves and are rotated, the newborn infant of one date going into one nursery, those born another date into another. This facilitates observation of the newborn infant and routine terminal cleaning of the rooms. It is also a further method of controlling any possibility of infection.

Identification and observation

Identification of the infant may be accomplished in various ways, but it should always be done beyond doubt before the baby leaves the delivery room. In case of multiple births, the infants should be identified immediately after birth so that no confusion will result. Identification that can be easily counterchecked, such as the use of double or triple bands, is recommended.

Admission bath. Although some newborn infants receive their first bath in the delivery room or its annex, most infants have their "admission bath" in the nursery after being checked-in, identified, weighed, and measured. Some infants are not bathed completely until several hours after birth when the body temperature is higher. Newborn infants are covered with varying amounts of vernix and blood. They may also be soiled with meconium. During the admission bath the nurse usually seeks to remove this soil, reaffirm identification, inspect the infant more carefully than was possible in the delivery room, take his temperature, dress him appropriately, and tuck him into bed. An admission bath may make use of a mild soap solution, an antibacterial product, or oil. Mineral oil is used relatively infrequently for total cleansing purposes now, since it is thought that it may interfere with the proper functioning of the skin by suppressing the action of the oil glands, it has no antibacterial action, and it temporarily stains clothing. The following description tells what may occur during the admission bath, although details may differ from hospital to hospital. The nurse's hands are freshly washed before she starts.

ADMISSION BATH

Materials:

1. Basin of warm water
2. Mild soap or antibacterial product
3. Washcloth or paper mesh squares
4. Approximately 6 sterile cotton balls
5. Alcohol, 70%, or other antiseptic for cord care
6. Applicators for cord care
7. Two towels or soft diapers for covering and drying
8. Individual thermometer
9. Small plastic comb
10. Laundry hamper
11. Appropriate clothing, diaper, shirt, and receiving blanket

Procedure:

1. The newborn infant is usually wrapped partially with a towel or coverlet to prevent chilling.
2. The eyes may be wiped with cotton balls moistened with sterile water if necessary.
   a. Irrigation or wiping starts at the nose and proceeds outward to try to prevent unwanted drainage from the inner canthus of the eye down the lacrimal duct to the nose. (One cotton ball is used for each wipe.)
3. The face is cleaned with a soft washcloth or paper mesh square dipped in clear water. No soap is necessary, as it may be drying to the skin.
   a. If necessary, the opening of the nose is cleared with water-moistened, firmly twisted wisps of cotton (remember, babies are nose breathers).
   b. The external ears may be gently wiped with water-moistened cotton balls, but the canal is never probed.
4. The head is gently but efficiently sudsed and rinsed over the wash basin.
   a. A football hold on the baby is best.
   b. A small comb, gently used, helps to lift out particles of vernix that are difficult to dislodge.
5. The bath is continued, washing, rinsing, and drying the neck, chest, arms, hands, abdomen, and back.
   a. The recently clamped cord and its base are avoided. Many nurseries today put

no gauze dressing on the cord whatsoever and have found that it dries much faster and has no greater incidence of infection for having been left exposed.
   b. Some nurseries do not insist that every bit of vernix found in skin folds be removed at the time of the initial bath but certainly all blood and meconium should be. Special attention should be paid to the neck creases.
   c. After turning the baby on his side to wash, rinse, and dry, a clean, dry, partially folded towel may be placed under the washed portion of the infant to be completely unfolded when his "bottom half" is clean.
   d. A small undershirt may be put on at this time, rolled up away from the cord to conserve warmth until the bath is complete.
6. The temperature is taken.
   a. If a rectal temperature is to be taken, it should be completed before bathing the buttocks and genitalia, since the stubby rectal thermometer used in most nurseries often initiates a stool.
   b. Usual time is 3 minutes or until the mercury stops rising.
7. The bath is continued, washing the legs, feet, and then the buttocks and perianal region.
8. The nurse's hands are again washed and the ordered antiseptic applied with an applicator to the cord end and the inner rim of the skin cuff surrounding the base of the cord. The vessels in the cord may be counted at this time.
9. The genitalia are inspected and cleansed with cotton balls previously moistened with clear water.
   a. In the case of a baby girl the cotton balls may be wiped gently from front to back between the labia, never using a ball more than once.
   b. In the case of a baby boy the foreskin may be retracted gently if possible and the glans carefully wiped. It should never be forced and if retracted should be immediately replaced.
10. The diaper is put on and the infant is tucked into bed. The crib identification card is checked against his own personal identification.
    a. Newborn infants are frequently propped on their right sides with a rolled blanket. In the older infant a right-side position is supposed to be better because of the aid gravity gives to the flow of food from the stomach and because any air or bubble remaining will rest near the

entrance of the stomach and be more easily expelled.

b. No newborn infant should be placed on his back because of the danger of aspiration.

c. Newborn infants are frequently placed head down on a *slight* incline to encourage mucous drainage.

d. In some hospitals the newborn infant is not dressed until shown to the parents and waiting relatives through a nursery window.

11. Notations regarding voidings, stool, or any pertinent observations should be appropriately recorded.

All during the bath procedure the nurse is inspecting and evaluating the infant. As she cleans the eyes she watches for discharge, conjunctival hemorrhage, or areas of opacity. As she feels the head she checks the contour, the relative size of the fontanels, and the presence of areas of swelling. Pushing down on the chin she peers into the mouth. Continuing in her bath procedure she evaluates respirations, counts and separates fingers, and judges skin turgor and muscle tone. As she washes each part she inspects. She is not trying to diagnose, but she wants to be able to report significant findings so that the pediatrician or general practitioner may be called if necessary. Every new baby should be completely examined by a physician within 24 hours of birth, and the condition of some may necessitate a much earlier examination.

Inspection bath. The following days the bath of the newborn infant serves two main purposes—inspection and stimulation. An example of this procedure follows.

DAILY INSPECTION BATH
Materials:

1. Each infant should have his own individual unit including:
   a. Thermometer
   b. Diapers, shirts
   c. Linen supply
   d. Blankets
2. Paper mesh squares or two washcloths
3. pHisoHex
4. Alcohol, 70%, or other cord antiseptic
5. Applicators for cord care
6. Scales and scale paper, technique paper
7. Scratch paper and pencil
8. Laundry hamper
9. Amphyl solution, 1%, or other disinfectant for equipment cleanup

Procedure:

1. Wash your hands with pHisoHex, check crib for materials needed.
2. Identify the baby.
3. Remove the infant's clothing and drop into hamper.
4. Take a rectal temperature—leave thermometer in place until the mercury stops rising.
5. Wash hands; place the baby on a clean paper mesh square on scale; weigh, using technique papers to handle scale weights and pencil.
6. Apply alcohol to the cord at the base by the skin margin and at the tip.
7. Replace the baby in the crib on the scale paper and wash his face with a paper mesh square and clear water. Wash the rest of the baby with pHisoHex and water solution in the following order: external ears, head, neck, arms, front of body (avoiding the cord), back, legs and feet, lower back and anus. Some nurseries rinse the pHisoHex, others do not. Pat dry. (Genitalia are cleansed as necessary with newly washed hands and a separate paper mesh square or cotton ball.)
8. Dress the infant and change the bed as necessary.
9. Place the baby on his abdomen, head to one side. Tuck one blanket over the infant.
10. Record weight, temperature, general condition, stool, and urine on work paper. Loose, watery stools should be reported.
11. Hands should be washed before and after each baby's care and after caring for the anal-genital area before proceeding with additional tasks with the same child. Hands should also be washed before removing a cord clamp.
12. Avoid chilling the baby during the procedure.
13. All equipment that becomes contaminated while weighing should be washed with disinfectant before it is reused. Scales, cart, and all equipment are washed with disinfectant at the end of daily care.
14. As you bathe the infant, inspect for the following:
    a. Color—jaundice
    b. Rash
    c. Petechiae
    d. Bruise marks
    e. Swellings on the head
    f. Condition of the mouth
    g. Condition of the eyes (cleaned only if a discharge is present)
    h. Condition of genitalia

    i. Condition of the cord (signs of inflammation, discharge, bleeding)

    j. Signs of possible paralysis or spasticity

    k. General level of alertness and activity

    l. Indications of respiratory distress

    m. Possible congenital malformations

Lifting and holding. The positioning, handling, and transport of young babies can sometimes be very frightening to new mothers or beginning student nurses. It is almost as if they expect to see sawdust leaking out of a tiny joint after touching the child. Both need to be reassured of their ability to learn to care for their charges and to learn comfortable and safe methods of handling a baby. A baby does not break, and knowledge of certain principles will help to give him greater support and confidence.

The newborn infant usually tries to maintain his fetal position. With a little coaxing —a pat here, a little pressure there—he usually readily assumes his unborn posture. This is sometimes useful to the pediatrician trying to evaluate the placement of a foot or the line of a mandible.

The newborn infant has one continuous anteroposterior spinal curve and no real control of his head movements, although in prone position he may raise his head slightly and briefly. Whenever the baby is lifted or transported, his head, being so large and heavy in relation to the rest of his body, must be supported for comfort and to prevent muscle strain. For safety all lifts must have at least two contact points so that if one fails another still is available. Babies, even small ones, can be wriggly and sometimes slippery. Following is one of the most common methods of lifting an infant on his back from his bed (Fig. 18-7):

1. Facing the soles of his feet, lift his legs and buttocks slightly with one hand by grasping the feet, ankles separated by a finger.
2. Slide the opposite hand, palm up, under the full length of the baby until finally the entire back and head are supported.

A second method follows:

1. Facing the baby's side, slide one hand from the side under the head and neck to grasp the farther arm. The head is supported by the forearm, or the head and neck may be supported by the grasping hand.
2. With the other hand reach under the legs to grasp the farther thigh or grasp the feet holding one finger between the ankles. This is a good lift for weighing the baby or putting him into a tub.

A baby should not be lifted by his arms. When head stability is attained at about 3 months of age, the child may be lifted by grasping his trunk with both hands below the arms. A newborn infant should not be left alone flat on his back. He may be propped with a rolled blanket along his back to maintain a side position or may be placed on his abdomen with his head turned to one side. Some newborn infants, when placed in this position for protracted periods, seem to object and rub their knees

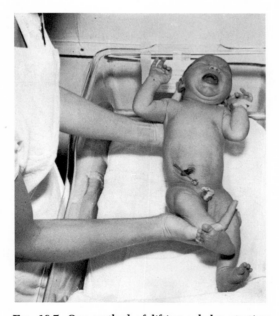

FIG. 18-7. One method of lifting a baby, starting from a side position. The head and upper back are supported by one hand, the legs by the other. Note that the baby is gently grasped. (Courtesy Grossmont Hospital, La Mesa, Calif.)

up and down on the linen, causing reddened shins. Baby beds should have firm mattresses regardless of the style. No pillow should be used. A child should not always be placed in the same position, since this can distort the shape of his head or chest or cause localized baldness.

There are many ways that babies have been carried. Some ways are better than others in giving the one who carries and the carried a greater sense of safety and support. Three ways are common in the United States and are recommended:

1. The traditional cradle hold: The child's head is cradled in the bend of the elbow; the forearm reaches around the outside of his body to grasp the outer leg with the fingers. The nurse's opposite hand and forearm helps support the back and buttocks. This additional support may be momentarily withdrawn if the hand is needed for a task. (See Fig. 18-8.)

2. The football hold: About half the length of the baby's body is supported by the nurse's forearm with his head and neck resting in her palm. The rest of baby's body, legs, and buttocks are firmly wedged between the nurse's elbow and hip. This is a fine secure hold, and it was definitely designed to provide the mother or nurse with a free hand. (See Fig. 18-9.)

3. The shoulder hold: The baby is held up against the chest and shoulder. The palm of one hand supports the baby's buttocks. The other hand keeps the head and back from sagging. Two

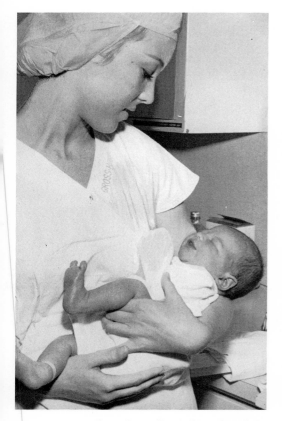

FIG. 18-8. Traditional cradle hold. This baby was a wriggler! (Courtesy Grossmont Hospital, La Mesa, Calif.)

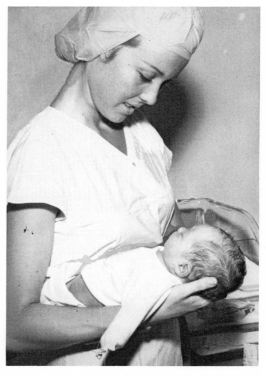

FIG. 18-9. Football hold. (Courtesy Grossmont Hospital, La Mesa, Calif.)

FIG. 18-10. Shoulder hold. (Courtesy Grossmont Hospital, La Mesa, Calif.)

hands are needed to support the baby's back correctly. This is the old hold used often for bubbling the baby. (See Fig. 18-10.)

Newborn infants love to be cuddled, and the way they are handled, touched, and fed are ways we can show love and respect for them as individuals and as very important members of humanity.

Nourishment

Nourishment is the least pressing of a newborn infant's needs, but eventually it becomes paramount. In modern society there are two ways of meeting this need—breast feeding and formula feeding.

Breast feeding. Breast feeding, of course, has an ancient biological basis and is still the most universally recommended way of providing infant nourishment. A mother should carefully consider its advantages when deciding how she will feed her infant.

Advantages. Putting the baby to breast contributes to the mother's well-being in that the stimulation of the infant nursing causes the recently emptied uterus to contract and helps in the return of this organ to its proper size and position, a process called involution. Many investigators believe that the baby receives certain immune factors through the breast milk that help protect the baby against diseases to which the mother may have been previously exposed. However, this has not been proved. It is agreed that as a general rule breast-fed babies have fewer respiratory infections and alimentary tract disturbances. Certainly, when environmental hygiene is poor, breast feeding is to be preferred over the great possibility of the contamination of artificially prepared feedings.

The observation that cow's milk was first designed for calves, whereas mother's milk is specifically designed for babies is indisputable. The curd of human milk is softer than that of cow's milk and is easier for a baby to digest. Breast-fed babies have fewer allergy problems. At first, breast-fed babies have more frequent stools than formula-fed youngsters. The stools are yellow-orange and aromatic but not necessarily offensive. Later on they may have fewer stools than their formula-fed counterparts. There is no preparation time necessary except that of washing the breasts, and in the long run, successful nursing is less expensive. If the mother nurses her baby, the return of menstruation will probably be delayed until 6 to 8 months after the birth of the baby, but nursing is no guarantee that pregnancy will not occur. However, the nursing mother may experience such a sense of fulfillment and motherliness in her role that this becomes the primary reason she continues to nurse.

Problems. But there are other considerations, and to say that breast feeding has all the advantages and no negative aspects would be unfair and untrue. The nursing mother must have a good diet to maintain her resources and provide sufficient nourishment for her infant. She needs increased fluid intake to maintain her milk production. Her diet should also include at least 1½ quarts of skimmed or whole milk in liquid form or cooking mixtures per day to protect her personal calcium supply and avoid possible *osteoporosis*, or weakening of the bony skeleton. Calcium in the form of medication can be supplied if necessary, but a balanced diet containing calcium-rich foods would give her other healthful nutrients as well, benefit the whole family unit, and eliminate the need for pills. Some foods eaten by the mother have been said to cause the nursing baby abdominal distress such as cramping or diarrhea, but no one food seems to affect every baby. Probabilities are chocolate and "strong" vegetables such as cabbage, Brussels sprouts, and asparagus. Other notorious "gas formers" should be approached with an attitude of caution, but some babies do not seem aware of any deviation in diet. Certain drugs taken by the mother may pass through the milk to the baby and cause difficulty; however, most must be taken in considerable quantity to cause symptoms. One exception is the drug thiouracil used in treating hyperthyroidism. It actually becomes more concentrated in the maternal milk and may affect the infant severely. Certain laxatives are equally as effective on baby as on his mother and should be avoided or used only very judiciously. Common medications to be avoided include cascara, milk of magnesia, Epsom salt, and Ex-lax, but not inert mineral oil. It is wise to counsel mothers to remind their physicians that they are nursing when receiving new prescriptions. Recently concern has been expressed regarding the amount of DDT found in some human milk samples. This is part of the general environmental problem of our time.

Some cultures teach that an intake of low-percentage beer or, for those more affluent, the addition of champagne to the diet increases milk production. We are convinced that it is not the beer or champagne as such that may produce results, but the fact that they come in liquid form and for

some people produce a feeling of relaxation and ease. It is true that a tense, worried mother may have difficulty in maintaining an adequate milk supply.

Mothers who must or who prefer to work outside the home may find it difficult to maintain breast feeding, depending on the demands of their employment. To maintain a milk supply the breasts must be stimulated and emptied at fairly frequent intervals. A nursing mother may manually empty her breasts when unable to feed her infant because of separation, but this procedure may not always be convenient. The nursing mother needs good breast support. The typical nursing bra, with the lift-down cup, is usually efficient and easily used. Occasionally, specially manufactured plastic-backed squares of absorbent material are tucked over the breast when excessive drainage is foreseen, or some mothers use a freshly laundered handkerchief, strategically placed, to prevent soiling.

To be completely successful most nursing mothers must really want to nurse, be convinced of its advantages, and receive instruction in the prenatal period regarding the care and normal function of their breasts as well as encouragement and assistance in the postpartum period. If a woman has flattened or inverted nipples, they should be treated during this period of preparation by massage and possibly suction as directed by her physician. In some localities groups of mothers particularly interested in promoting nursing have formed organizations to help the new mother or mother-to-be. La Leche League, founded in Illinois in 1956, is an international organization that is very dedicated and active in this field.

Contraindications. Even though some mothers may want to nurse, occasionally the condition of the mother or baby makes it inadvisable. Maternal illness that is particularly protracted, severe, or contagious in nature may preclude any breast feeding. A former tubercular patient is usually not allowed to nurse because of the drain on her own resources, the possibility of reactivating the disease and infecting the very susceptible infant. Likewise, an involved cardiac patient or a patient with established renal disease may be discouraged from nursing. Mentally disturbed mothers would probably not be allowed the close contact needed for feeding their infants either artificially or by breast unless closely supervised. A mother with severely cracked nipples or breast abscess may find it best to terminate nursing. With proper initial management such conditions are increasingly uncommon.

The condition of the baby may influence the decision of whether or not to nurse. Small premature infants usually do not have the strength to suckle at breast, but they may benefit from the expressed maternal milk. For this reason, mothers of premature infants may wish to maintain their milk supply for the immediate use of the baby in the hospital (to be given per gavage) and for later use when the baby goes home. Other babies, unable to suckle, may benefit from maternal milk—for example, the child with a cleft lip or palate whose defect is too large to allow suction and who is in danger of aspiration. In a few communities maternal milk banks have been established for the benefit of babies with special feeding problems. Milk that is expressed for use of a baby must be carefully handled to safeguard its purity, and a mother expressing milk to be used by her baby needs to be instructed meticulously to prevent contamination.

Techniques. The breast-feeding mother and her baby should be comfortably positioned. The mother may lie on her side with a pillow to her back or sit up in bed or on a chair. A mother sitting up in bed usually finds it more comfortable to place the baby on a pillow in her lap. This brings the infant closer to the breast with less strain. Nursing mothers should carefully wash their hands and breasts before beginning. In the hospital, because of the many different babies and mothers involved, the cleanliness of the mother has become quite a ritual. Before feedings the hands may be washed with soap or detergent and water. After this initial washing nothing else is touched except necessities such as bedcovers, pillow, and bra. Next the hands may be wiped with a prepackaged, sterile paper towel dampened with alcohol or benzalkonium chloride (Zephiran). The breasts previously washed are again cleaned with Zephiran sponges or other agents, starting at the nipple and wiping in a circular fashion outward, and a clean surface is prepared for the wrapped baby to lie on.

When putting the baby to breast, the nurse and mother have some powerful allies—inborn reflexes and hunger. If it is the first time at breast or a relatively new procedure for the baby, gently expressing a drop of milk on the tip of the nipple will serve as an appetizer and help give him the basic idea. If the breasts are engorged, expressing some milk before beginning to nurse will relieve the tension of the breast and make it easier for baby to grasp the nipple. Most babies resent having their mouth shoved at the breast to begin nursing and protest. It is infinitely better to rely on the rooting reflex. When the baby's cheek is touched to the breast, he almost invariably turns his open lips to seek the nipple. The mother should compress the breast with her thumb and forefingers while the baby nurses to regulate flow and draw the breast away from his nose, making it easier for him to breathe. The baby must nurse with the nipple plus almost the entire areola in his mouth in order to suck successfully and preserve the good condition of the nipple. Cracked or fissured nipples generally originate from two causes: allowing the baby to chew on the end of the nipple or to nurse too long at one time. Different maternity services have different nursing schedules, but most do not advocate allowing the baby to nurse more than 2 or 3 minutes at a time the first day. Each succeeding day the nursing time is gradually increased to 5 or 10 minutes or longer depending on the state of the nipples and the baby's desires. Fair-skinned, blonde and redheaded mothers should be espe-

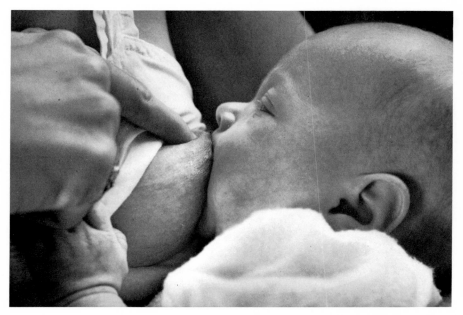

FIG. 18-11. Feeding time for a breast-fed baby. Note that the nipple and almost all the areola are within the baby's mouth.

FIG. 18-12. It is possible to nurse an infant unobtrusively.

cially careful about nursing too long because their delicate skin may need greater protection. Once nursing has been established the infant gets most of his nourishment the first 10 minutes at breast. The rest of the time he spends satisfying his sucking reflex and enjoying the whole procedure. Twenty minutes is usually the maximum time allowed. The first few days the baby obtains an "introductory milk" called colostrum, which has a laxative effect and supposedly contains protective antibodies. Maternal milk becomes "complete," that is, possessing its characteristic content, several weeks later.

When removing the baby from the breast, remember that he is capable of considerable tenacity. You may gently pinch the nose to convince him that it is best to let go, pull down on the chin or corner of the mouth, or press the breast away from the baby's mouth, but please do not just pull!

It must be emphasized that the greatest aid to milk production is frequent stimulation and emptying of the breasts. If the breasts are not emptied, milk production will dwindle. Probably the ideal maternity accommodations for a nursing mother, particularly if the child involved is her first, is the rooming-in plan or a modification of rooming-in. In this setting the baby may be put to breast as desired and is not limited to 4-hour feeding schedules followed by most hospitals. Breast-feeding methods also differ in various hospitals. Some alternate breasts, emptying one side for one feeding, emptying the other for the next. Other maternity services advocate putting a child to breast on one side, allowing him to empty the breast, and changing him to the other breast for a few minutes to stimulate milk production. Perhaps the most important consideration is that the breast be emptied. If it is not emptied by baby, the mother should empty it manually or with the aid of a pump to maintain milk production. For a brief presentation of breast anatomy and more details of breast care, see the section on postpartal care (p. 167).

Breast-fed babies, like formula-fed babies, must be bubbled to get rid of swallowed air. Sitting the infant up or holding him over a protected shoulder while gently rubbing his back, plus patience, produces results for both breast and bottle babies.

Artificial feeding. Today, with our knowledge of nutrition and our increased understanding of food processing and preservation, it is no tragedy if a child is not breastfed. He need not be threatened with malnutrition or disease. While mothers should be told the advantages of breast feeding, they should not be considered or made to feel like maternal failures if they cannot or choose not to nurse. To assume such a position is unrealistic and unkind. To force a mother to nurse against her will may cause an unhappy cycle of rebellion, failure, and regret and make those few mothers who cannot or should not nurse feel lacking in maternal virtue. Some have schedules difficult to combine with nursing, some are concerned that their youngsters get enough to eat, and some have felt like failures nursing in the past. For others the process of nursing is physically unattractive. Many are the healthy children who have been formula fed in our society. A loving mother cuddling her baby while tilting a milk-filled bottle need not consider herself to be a "poor mother."

Comparison of cow's milk and human milk. A comparison of the components of cow's milk and human milk gives a clue to formula preparation in the event that breast feeding is not undertaken.

	Cow's milk	Human milk
Protein	3.5%	1.25%
Fat	3.5 to 4%	3.5 %
Carbohydrate	4 to 5%	7.5 %
Salts (calcium, phosphorus, and potassium principally)	0.75%	0.20%

Most formulas seek to modify cow's milk to make it as much as possible like human milk. To do this, cow's milk is usually diluted to decrease the protein and add additional carbohydrate. The most commonly used formula has an evaporated milk base. Remember, evaporated milk is twice the strength of whole cow's milk.

Sample formula. Following is one commonly used beginning formula prepared for a 24-hour period of six feedings for a newborn infant:

> 6 ounces evaporated milk
> 18 ounces water
> 1 tablespoon Dextri-Maltose No. 1
> or ½ tablespoon Karo syrup
> Divided into six feedings of 4 ounces or eight feedings of 3 ounces.

This is a very dilute formula, equal to only 12 calories per ounce. Some nurseries that normally discharge their newborn infants when they are only 3 days old exclude the sugar, making the formula equal to 11 calories per ounce. The formula must be strengthened as the child grows to meet his metabolic needs. These are determined by his body weight and expected rate of growth and activity. Following is an example of a stronger formula:

8 ounces evaporated milk
16 ounces water
2 tablespoons Dextri-Maltose No. 1
or 1 tablespoon Karo syrup

This mixture equals 17 calories per ounce.

Human milk, when "complete," has almost the same caloric count as whole cow's milk, approximately 20 calories per ounce. However, most young babies do not tolerate the proportions of ingredients found in whole cow's milk and must have a modification. A so-called full-strength, 20-calorie-per-ounce formula would be as follows:

13 ounces evaporated milk
19 ounces water
4 tablespoons Dextri-Maltose No. 1
or 2 tablespoons Karo syrup

The general practitioner or pediatrician is the one to guide the use of infant formulas. There are now a wide variety of possibilities available. In addition to the different strengths of evaporated milk formulas with a variety of possible carbohydrates—Dextri-Maltose, Karo syrup, table sugar (sucrose), etc.—there is a shelfful of the so-called proprietary formulas premixed to various specifications. These may come in liquid or powder form and are usually constituted by the addition of warm, sterile water. Their use saves some preparation time and bother, but they are more expensive. Examples of nationally known and frequently used proprietary formulas are Similac products (Similac powder, Similac liquid, and Similac powder with iron), Enfamil powder, Dryco powder, and SMA powder. When the infant is allergic to milk products, commercial meat-base formulas or soybean feedings may be used, such as Sobee or Soyalac liquid. A number of companies are manufacturing disposable prefilled nursing units (Fig. 18-13). Some hospitals use commercial baby formula services.

Preparation of the formula. There are three ways of preparing infant formula: the standard or aseptic method, the terminal sterilization method, and the tap water method. Most hospitals use a combination of the first two because of their increased exposure and greater responsibility. They may assemble the entire formula supply aseptically and then sterilize it at the end of the procedure. Such precautions are not necessary in the home. Figs. 18-14 and 18-

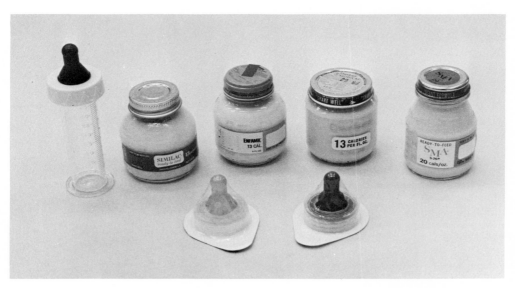

Fig. 18-13. Some types of disposable bottles and formulas currently available.

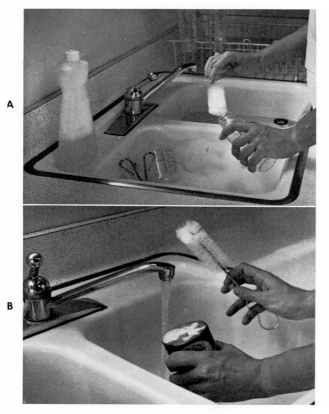

Procedure:

A and **B**, Washing. Wash all the equipment to be used, including the top of any can to be opened; rinse everything with hot water and drain dry.

Fɪɢ. 18-14. Formula preparation—aseptic method.

Materials:

Large container with lid for boiling equipment and rack for bottles
Lifts or forceps for handling equipment
Quart-sized measuring pitcher
Large mixing spoon
Measuring spoons
Knife (if powdered carbohydrate is used)   } Sterilized together
Funnel
Six or seven formula bottles (one extra is handy for an
    additional supply of formula or sterile water)
Can opener
Eight nipples, rings, and discs, if appropriate   } Sterilized together
Saucepan for sterilization of nipples
Teakettle containing boiled water for formula
Watch, clock, or timer
Formula ingredients as ordered by the physician
Bottle brush
Soap or detergent

FIG. 18-14, cont'd. Formula preparation—aseptic method.

C, Preparation for disinfection, Plan 1. If the container has a tight lid, flowing steam will disinfect the contents of the container. Empty bottles should be placed upside down in the container in a small rack, alongside the measuring pitcher containing other necessities. Water should be poured to a depth of 2 to 3 inches in the bottom of the container and inside the pitcher to assure sufficient steam.

D, Preparation for disinfection, Plan 2. If no container with a tight lid is available, the parts of the equipment to be sterilized should be completely covered with boiling water (theoretically only handles to be touched later by the hands should protrude). The formula bottles are filled with water and placed upright in a rack in the large container to prevent them from floating to the top of the water and breaking. In this setup the glass measuring pitcher is pictured in the center, and the smaller utensils are positioned inside with the lifts, handles up.

Preparation for disinfection, Plan 3 (not illustrated). A small bottle "sterilizer" may be used, but an additional large container will be needed for the rest of the equipment.

Continued.

15 illustrate the first two methods. Ever since the problem of nipple clogging was solved, terminal sterilization has been more widely used. It is simpler and, for the family's use, equally effective.

FORMULA PREPARATION—

TAP WATER METHOD

This method of formula is to be recommended only to intelligent parents who understand its limitations and who will not abuse its simplicity. It is a good method to know in emergencies.

Materials:

Capped formula bottle	Saucepan
Nipple	Can opener
Bottle brush	Spoon
Soap or detergent	

Procedure: (Not illustrated). Using canned milk.
1. Boil the nipple in the saucepan for 5 minutes.
2. Add enough carbohydrate (if ordered),

Text continued on p. 227.

Fig. 18-14, cont'd. Formula preparation—aseptic method.

E, Disinfection. Time the heating phase of aseptic formula preparation from the time steam appears. The usual recommended time for the treatment of empty clean bottles is 10 minutes. (For other uses, longer periods are usually recommended. See discussion on asepsis.) If it is necessary to cover the equipment entirely with water, it will take considerable time for the equipment to cool sufficiently to allow handling. A pot holder may be used to handle the forceps, but one must be careful not to get burned. Lift out the bottles and other equipment carefully using the forceps. Do not touch the inside of the pitcher or bottles with your hands. Place the small equipment on the inside of the lid. Boil the nipples, rings, and discs in a separate saucepan for 5 minutes. To reduce wear, do not place the rubber nipples in the water until it is boiling.

F, Mixing. Add the correct amount of boiled water to the pitcher and measure out the ordered carbohydrates and canned milk; stir.

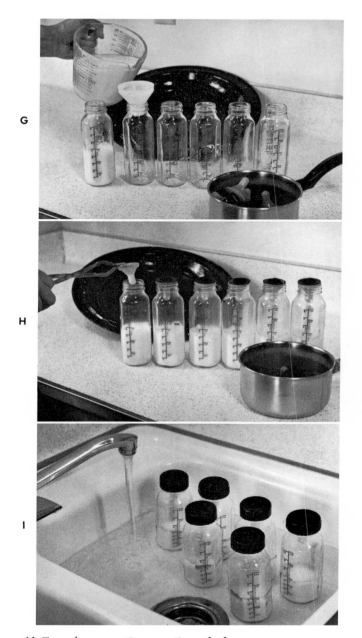

Fig. 18-14, cont'd. Formula preparation—aseptic method.

G and H, Assembly. Pour the prepared formula through the funnel into the bottles. Cap without touching the nipple; cover loosely.

I, Cooling. Cool the formula by placing the bottles in cool water to the level of the formula. Tighten the nipple covers or caps and place the bottles in the refrigerator. The aseptic method is a fairly complex way to prepare formula, but some mothers prefer it nonetheless, especially if they have had difficulty with clogged nipples or their babies have formulas that should not be heated for long periods (for example, acidified or cultured milks or some special vitamin-reinforced formulas).

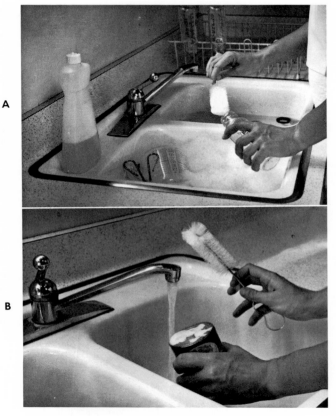

Procedure:

A and **B,** Washing. Wash all the equipment to be used, including the top of any can to be opened; rinse everything with hot water and drain dry.

FIG. 18-15. Formula preparation—terminal method.

Materials:

Small bottle "sterilizer" or container with a tight lid large enough for bottles
Quart-sized measuring pitcher
Large mixing spoon
Measuring spoons
Knife (if powdered carbohydrate is used)
Funnel
Six or seven formula bottles (an extra is handy for an additional supply of formula or sterile water)
Can opener
Eight nipples, rings, and discs, if appropriate
Watch, clock, or timer
Formula ingredients as ordered by the physician
Bottle brush
Soap or detergent

Fig. 18-15, cont'd. Formula preparation—terminal method.

C, Mixing. Mix the formula with clean, not "sterile," equipment. Add the correct amount of clean, warm water to the pitcher and measure out the ordered carbohydrate and canned milk; stir.

D and E, Assembly. Pour the formula into the clean bottles and place the clean nipples on the bottles; cap loosely.

Continued.

FIG. 18-15, cont'd. Formula preparation—terminal method.

F, Preparation for disinfection. Place bottles in sterilizer on rack or washcloth. Pour 2 to 3 inches of water in the bottom of the container.

G, Disinfection. Time the heating phase for terminal sterilization for 25 minutes after the steam appears.

H, Cooling. Move the container from the burner to cool without lifting the lid. When the sides of the sterilizer are cool enough to be comfortable to the hands, the lid may be lifted, the caps on the bottles tightened, and the formula refrigerated.

canned milk, and warm water from the tap if water is approved (otherwise boil the water) to a meticulously clean formula bottle for one feeding. Mix with a clean spoon.
3. Place nipple on bottle.
4. Feed *immediately;* do not save formula from one feeding to the next or for more than an hour.

Sterilization of formula is necessary because milk is such an ideal medium for the nourishment and growth of other living things besides human babies. Microorganisms not at all compatible with baby's digestive system may multiply rapidly in milk if it is improperly "sterilized" or is left open to air and warmed for an extended period. Once a bottle has been opened, it should be used fairly soon and under most circumstances should not be saved to use over again. The typhoid organisms used to be fairly common contaminants of milk and milk products before pasteurization became widespread. Because of baby's susceptibility, sterilization is carried out in most households until he is about 6 months old or is drinking milk from a cup and putting all kinds of things unbidden into his mouth. If there is any question about the purity of the milk or water supply, sterilization should be continued longer.

Techniques of feeding. Feeding an infant his formula can be a very enjoyable experience. The hands should be clean, the milk should be tepid (no sensation of hot or cold, just slightly warm) falling on the inside of the nurse's wrist.

Experiments using cold formula for feeding the newborn have demonstrated no untoward effects even on premature babies. However, personally we find it psychologically difficult to give a young infant a *cold* meal. Many nurseries are discarding formula warmers because of problems with elevated bacterial count on the equipment. They are offering feedings at room temperature. The rate of nipple flow should be almost one drop per second when the bottle is inverted. Nipple holes may be enlarged by a hot needle mounted on a cork. Vigorously sucking babies should be given a resistant nipple. Babies who tire easily and prema-

ture babies do better on a soft, pliable nipple. Be sure the nipple is on top of the tongue, and do not push it too far back—it may stimulate the gag reflex. Babies seem to drink best when held on a definite incline. Recent studies have indicated that such positioning minimizes the possibility of retrograde infection through the eustachian tubes to the middle ear as well as helps prevent aspiration. The neck of the bottle should always be tipped so that it is full of milk and the baby swallows less air. Bubbles may be expelled by gentle rubbing of the baby's back while he is held upright against the shoulder or is supported in a sitting position on the nurse's or mother's lap. This may be done after each ounce with very small babies or halfway through and at the end of the feeding for larger babies. Some babies, particularly finger suckers, may be best bubbled before feedings as well. Newborns should be carefully observed before and during feedings for indications of any abnormality in the digestive or respiratory tracts. Prefeeding coughing, cyanosis, and excessive mucus may be associated with anatomical abnormalities. Regurgitation of a feeding through the nose and mouth should be reported at once. Most babies are offered water before they are put to breast or fed formula to evaluate their ability to drink without difficulty. (See Figs. 18-16 to 18-18.)

After feeding, the infant should have his diaper changed if needed and be placed on his right side or abdomen to sleep. The amount taken should be recorded in nursery records. The newborn infant may take only 1 ounce the first day and 2 to 3 ounces per feeding on the second and third days. See Table 18-1 for usual formula amounts and number of feedings.

Evaluation of nutritional status. There are numerous ways of judging if a newborn infant, whether formula- or breast-fed, is receiving enough to eat.
1. Observing his behavior; does he seem content, or is he a short sleeper and irritable? (Note that babies cry for reasons other than hunger pangs; for

example, if they are wet, too tightly bundled, too warm, or have gas pains.)

2. Watching for signs of dehydration from poor fluid intake.
   a. Dark, concentrated urine; dry, hard stools.
   b. Dry skin with little "bounce."
   c. Low-grade fever. (Note that the most common cause of low-grade fever is dehydration, although the nurse does not want to overlook the possibility of infection.)
   d. In severe cases, sunken fontanels.
3. Measuring intake.
   a. This is routinely done on bottle babies.

b. If measuring is ordered, breast-fed babies are weighed directly before the feeding and directly after the feeding, before any diapers are changed.
   c. Intake should be evaluated in terms of a 24-hour period and not individual feedings.
4. Measuring weight gain.
   a. This method is of little use in the nursery because of the short hospital stays of most newborn infants in the United States (approximately 3 days).
   b. All babies lose weight directly after birth, and we are not concerned unless the weight loss ap-

FIG. 18-16. Various types of nipples. A, Regular; B, soft rubber, for premature infants; C, crosscut; D, winged; E, cereal (with large hole).

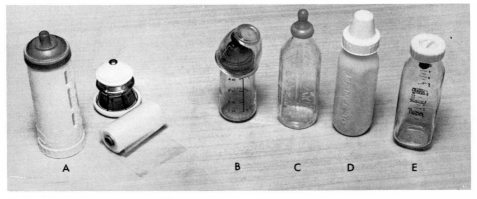

FIG. 18-17. Various types of bottles. A, Playtex Nurser equipment (bottle holder, nipple, expander, and plastic sterile bottles); B, bottle featuring large nipple and measuring cup cap (Hygeia); C, narrow-necked Pyrex bottle; D, plastic bottle (Even-Flo); E, glass ring-and-disc–type bottle (Davol).

proaches 10% of the birth weight. Babies may not begin to gain again until the fourth or fifth day of life.

c. After weight gain is reestablished, a gain of about an ounce a day is average, equalling about 6 ounces a week; at the end of 5 months most babies have doubled their birth weight.

Rest and love

The birthday of a child is certainly a special occasion, and, although the child needs to be protected against infection and overexposure, the way that the child is introduced to the parents and other members of the family is of great importance. If at all possible, both the father and the mother should have an opportunity to see the in-

TABLE 18-1. Suggested schedule on an approximate 4-hour basis*

Age	Ounces per feeding	Number of feedings	Time of feedings
First week	2 to 3	6	6, 10, 2, 6, 10, 2
Two to four weeks	3 to 5	6	6, 10, 2, 6, 10, 2
Second to third months	4 to 6	5	6, 10, 2, 6, 10
Fourth and fifth months	5 to 7	5	6, 10, 2, 6, 10
Sixth and seventh months	7 to 8	4	6, 10, 2, 6
Eighth to twelfth months	8†	3	7, 12, 6

*From Williams, S. R.: Nutrition and diet therapy, St. Louis, 1969, The C. V. Mosby Co., p. 384.
†4 oz. milk may be given midafternoon.

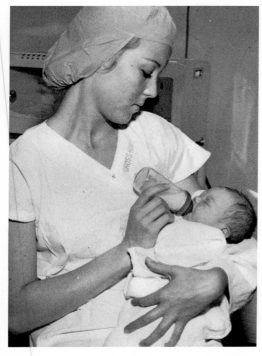

FIG. 18-18. The nipple should always be full of formula. An upright position is often preferred. (Courtesy Grossmont Hospital, La Mesa, Calif.)

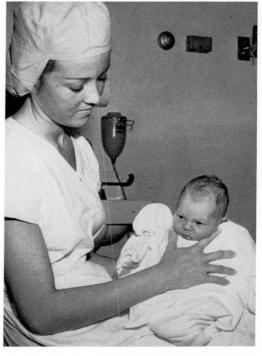

FIG. 18-19. Let's hear a "thank you!" (Courtesy Grossmont Hospital, La Mesa, Calif.)

fant without hurry directly after birth, and if they are around, grandparents, adult aunts and uncles, etc. should be able to see baby through a glass window, too. If the viewing area is outside the actual maternity area, smaller members of the family should also be invited to see little brother or sister. Some new nurseries have a covered walk outside the nursery windows that is ideal for this adventure. The newborn infant may receive all other things, but if he does not receive true love, he will not thrive.

Special needs
Baptism

Sometimes other occasions of special meaning and deep significance occur in the nursery. Catholic parents and occasionally Protestant families may request the baptism of their child while he is in the nursery. When the child is in no immediate danger, a member of the clergy involved should always be called. Most hospitals have appropriate utensils available. If doubt exists concerning what should be in readiness, the clergy may always be consulted. Some will bring their own articles. Most require only a pitcher of pure water. If the child is a member of a Catholic family and appears to be in immediate danger of death, a nurse may baptize the baby. It is preferable that a nurse of the Catholic faith should do so, but any adult may do so. In performing the baptism, she should pour water on the head or face of the child while saying, "I baptize thee in the name of the Father, and of the Son, and of the Holy Ghost." A record of the baptism should be made in the nurse's notes and the parents notified. This simple but deeply meaningful act can be of great comfort to the family.

Circumcision

Many male infants in the United States are circumcised as a hygienic measure, regardless of their religious backgrounds. However, the circumcision of a Jewish infant has religious import as well. Among Orthodox Jews it is undertaken by an ordained circumciser called a "mohel." This ceremony is usually performed after the child leaves the hospital on the eighth day of life. The child is then officially named.

Circumcision entails the surgical removal of all or part of the foreskin, or prepuce of the penis. Advocates of the procedure believe that it decreases irritation of the area from an accumulation of debris under the foreskin and may help avoid cancer. Other practitioners declare that it is unnecessary and, a possible source of infection and hemorrhage.

Each physician usually has his own preferences regarding the technique used, but the following setup list and procedure may help in anticipating his wants.

CIRCUMCISION PROCEDURE (FIG. 18-20)
Materials:
1. Sterile setup including:
   a. One circumcision drape
   b. Two 4 × 4 squares (flats or gauze compresses)
   c. Two cotton balls
   d. Three small hemostats (mosquito clamps)
   e. One Yellen (Gomco) clamp, 1.3 or 1.1 cm. in diameter
   f. One scalpel handle and added blade
   g. Possibly needle holder, needle, and suture materials (chromic 000)
   h. One grooved director and probe
   i. One thumb forceps
2. Sterile gloves, appropriately sized.
3. Ordered antiseptic for skin preparation.
   a. Tincture of benzalkonium chloride (Zephiran), 1:750
   b. Tincture of thimerosal (Merthiolate)
4. Dressing materials.
   a. Petrolatum-impregnated gauze
   b. Tincture of benzoin application
5. A circumcision board, diapers, pins, or special restraining halter that ties over the board.

Procedure:
1. Preliminary.
   a. Obtain a signed permit from parent before procedure.
   b. Properly identify the baby. Check for possible reasons for not proceeding with the operation (presence of inflammation, tendency to bleed). Clean diaper area.
   c. Restrain gently but firmly on a padded circumcision board.

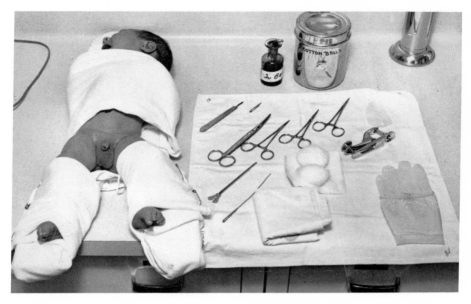

FIG. 18-20. One circumcision setup with the infant restrained on a circumcision board. A thumb forceps is also often needed. (Courtesy Grossmont Hospital, La Mesa, Calif.)

d. Assure good light. A stool or chair may be appreciated by the operator.

e. Prepare a sterile nipple stuffed with glucose-saturated gauze to pacify baby.

2. Technique.

a. The technique of circumcision differs considerably from physician to physician. Rarely local anesthetic will be given, but most physicians seem to feel it may cause more problems than it solves (distortion of tissues) and consider the operation of such short duration, performed in an area which, at this age, has a low level of sensitivity, that it is not truly necessary.

b. The Yellen (Gomco) clamp may be used to cut off circulation, and the foreskin excised. Sutures may or may not be used.

c. The foreskin may be freed from the glans with probe, cut away, bleeders controlled and sutured.

d. A nonconstrictive dressing is applied.

3. Aftercare.

a. Notice of the recent circumcision should be attached to the crib.

b. Frequent checks should be made to determine possible swelling and bleeding.

c. Voidings should be carefully charted. There is a danger of urinary retention.

d. The area should be kept clean; soiled or displaced dressings should be replaced with clean materials.

e. The infant is positioned on his side.

Rarely, circumcisions are performed in the delivery room, but most are performed the third or fourth day of life. Sometimes they are performed not long before the baby's discharge home. In this event, the mother should be carefully instructed regarding observation and care of the area.

Discharge procedure

Discharge is an exciting, trying time for most mothers. It is strongly advised that first-time mothers do not depend on the brief period of their hospitalization to learn all about baby and his needs. Many new mothers know very little about the child they are taking home and need much more instruction and reassurance than the nursery or postpartum nurse is able to provide or the patient is able to assimilate in so brief a time. This is one reason why prenatal courses in child care and preparation for motherhood are so important and should be emphasized during her antepartum period. Another assist that may be available to the new mother is the home guidance of the visiting nurse who, in cooperation with her physician, helps her

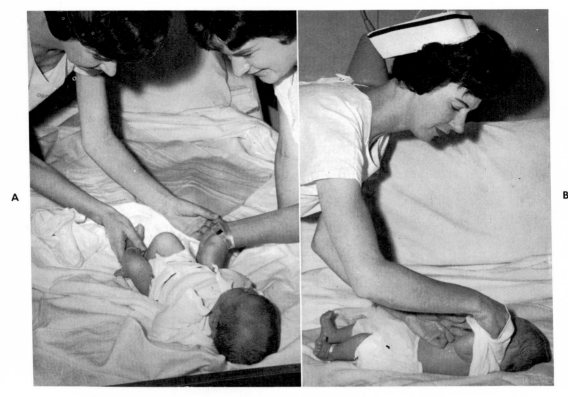

A   B

FIG. 18-21. A, Identification of the baby before hospital discharge using the double-banding technique. B, Dressing the baby in his own clothes for discharge. (Note the method of placing the sleeve over the infant's hand and arm.) (Courtesy Grossmont Hospital, La Mesa, Calif.)

feel confident doing such rather scary things as preparing formula, sponge bathing a new baby, or, after the umbilicus heals, putting him into a tub for the first time. Many times a grandmother, other relative, or neighbor can help.

Before the actual time of departure, the physician's order for discharge is checked and home orders reviewed. The mother's belongings are packed and clothes are put out for the infant. Mothers should have ready at least two diapers, pins, a baby shirt, kimono, and receiving blanket or comparable wardrobe. The baby is usually brought in from the nursery wrapped only

in a blanket and dressed at the bedside. Identification should be established, the discharge of the baby signed and witnessed, the baby unwrapped, viewed, and dressed in his own clothes (Fig. 18-21). If the mother wishes it, a supply of formula may be available to take home to tide her over until formula can be made. Before saying goodbye to the family, the nurse should make sure discharge instructions are understood and preferably written out. Before leaving the infant, she should take one last peek at his face to assure herself of his condition. Then, no matter what she may desire, she must let him go.

19

Infants with special needs—prematurity and abnormality

This chapter is included to help the student appreciate some of the more common abnormalities or conditions encountered during her practical experience and to help her to more intelligently assist in the care of infants who have these conditions. Some of the conditions discussed are found and treated in the nursery and pose few or no problems later. Other anomalies by their very nature call for prolonged therapy and correction long after the neonatal period, infancy, or, indeed, childhood has passed.

The premature infant
(Figs. 19-1 and 19-2)

The first group of babies with special needs to be discussed is the premature infants. The most common definition of prematurity is based on weight. Usually, babies having a birth weight under 5½ pounds or 2,500 grams are considered premature. However, in reality some of these babies have completed a term gestation and are underweight because of genetic or intrauterine factors. When this is the case, the terms "low birth weight" or "small for gestational age" are more accurately applied rather than "premature." The survival rate of these infants depends on their general condition as well as weight. Some of them are quite vigorous, whereas others of the same weight are feeble.

It would be much more scientific if the prenatal period were included in the total months considered when computing the age of a child. To compare a 1-month-old, small, premature infant with a 1-month-old child of normal gestation is grossly unfair. The premature infant is indeed born too soon. Just how much too soon is many times difficult to determine. As a general rule, assuming that the estimated birth date is fairly accurate, babies are considered premature if born before the end of the thirty-seventh calculated week of gestation. Infants of less than 28 weeks' gestation have been known to survive, but this is rare. Actually, in determining the status of the small infant, birth weight, heredity, possible length of gestation, clinical appearance, and behavior all must be considered. Although some babies cannot be classified premature by the scale or calendar, they are judged underdeveloped and treated as "premies."

Role of the nurse

The licensed nurse who wishes to work with premature babies should seek more supervised advanced training than is possible in her basic course. The nursery care of these infants must be very gentle, deft, and precise, and the ability to properly evaluate their behavior and reactions takes an extended period of time to acquire. However, although as a student she may not have the opportunity to be involved in the direct nursing of many premature infants, she should understand the nature of the problems encountered in such nursing. The first cause of infant mortality, remember, is prematurity.

233

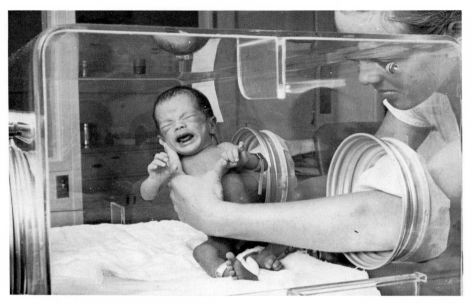

FIG. 19-1. This baby is technically premature if only his birth weight is considered. However, his Oriental ancestry influenced his size; he is probably a "finished product," although he weighs less than 5½ pounds. (Courtesy Grossmont Hospital, La Mesa, Calif.)

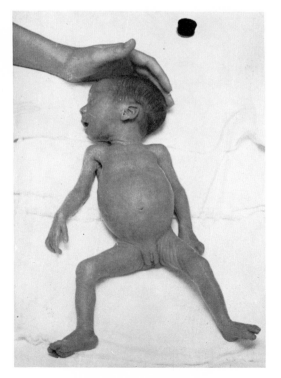

FIG. 19-2. Typical premature infant. (Courtesy Grossmont Hospital, La Mesa, Calif.)

Causes

The causes of prematurity or low-birth weight infants are not always known. However, it is recognized that there is a higher incidence of these infants born to mothers of lower socioeconomic status. This may be related to the extent of medical supervision available, the obstetrical complications encountered, nutrition, and general health practices. Young teen-age mothers have a higher rate of low-birth weight babies. Multiple births are almost always associated with prematurity. Heavy smoking seems to be an etiological factor. Approximately 10% of all deliveries in the United States are premature.

Appearance and activity

The typical premature infant has a "wrinkled old man" appearance resulting from lack of subcutaneous fat. He has a good supply of long, soft body hair called "lanugo"; his head and abdomen are relatively large; and his thorax is small. There is little molding of the skull. His respirations are usually quite irregular, and he may be surprisingly active.

Nutrition

Sucking and swallowing reflexes may be weak or absent in very small infants, necessitating feedings by gavage or the insertion of a stomach tube. Stronger "premies" may do well fed from a rubber-tipped dropper or a soft rubber nipple. Although the subject of premature feeding schedules and techniques is controversial at the present time, usually, the smaller the baby, the longer his first oral feeding is delayed to allow more time for recovery from the trauma of birth, clearance of respiratory passages, and reduction of edema. Some nurseries wait 24 hours or longer before even feeding water or glucose solution orally. When such nourishment is given, it is offered in extremely small amounts of 2 to 5 ml. at a time. Most premature infants are put on a 2- or 3-hour feeding schedule. Intravenous feeding of the premature is in the process of evaluation.

The premature baby tolerates fat poorly. For this reason, his formula is often based on skimmed milk. His diet later is supplemented by iron administration. The danger of overfeeding the premie is very real. Overfeeding may increase abdominal distention, cause respiratory embarrassment, and trigger vomiting, which may involve aspiration. The infant must be bubbled frequently. After a feeding the baby's head and chest may be elevated by tilting the incubator mattress tray to discourage emesis and aspiration.

Special needs

The maintenance of body temperature is a real challenge in the care of premature infants. Because of the immaturity of the temperature-regulating center in the brain, little stability is seen. The baby must be specially assisted in his efforts to keep warm. Usually, this aid is provided by the use of a plastic home called an incubator. This valuable piece of equipment should also be able to regulate humidity and oxygen concentration, as well as provide a way to constantly observe the naked infant. It is necessary to limit oxygen concentration to less than 40% unless a temporary emergency condition exists or the child cannot tolerate concentrations this low. Oxygen concentrations should be determined regularly every 2 hours. This is done to prevent blindness produced by long exposure to a high-oxygen environment. The veins in the retinas of the eyes dilate and hemorrhage. The retinas partially or completely detach from the inner surfaces of the posterior chambers of the eyes. They become fibrous masses behind the lenses, unable to receive visual stimuli. This condition is called retrolental fibroplasia.

The premature infant is especially susceptible to injury and must be handled with extreme gentleness and discretion (he needs his rest to grow!) He is particularly prone to injury at the time of birth and may suffer from intracranial hemorrhage and brain damage. A large percentage of cerebral palsied children, who exhibit some form of spasticity, or lack of muscle control, were premature. Lack of muscular coordination and mental retardation may stem from brain injury, prolonged lack of oxygen caused by delayed or interrupted breathing at the time of or subsequent to birth, or bilirubin deposits in the brain tissue due to the inability of the immature liver to handle red blood cell breakdown satisfactorily. Jaundice is a significant finding.

"Premies," because of their abrupt debut, are said to be deprived of antibody protection given by mothers to full-term infants. They are also less prepared to manufacture their own antibodies. They are easy victims of infection and must be scrupulously guarded.

Significant immaturity of the respiratory system is an often encountered finding. Failure of lung tissue to expand, or atelectasis, is often reported. *Hyaline membrane disease, or developmental respiratory distress syndrome,* is found in a high percentage of premature babies, particularly those delivered by cesarean section, and in children of diabetic mothers. (These babies, although large, appear to be physiologically immature and should be treated similarly to premature infants.) This disease is the commonest cause of death in premature infants. The origin and pathological mechanisms of respiratory distress syndrome in the newborn are not clearly understood, nor is there agreement concerning the optimum treatment of its small victims. The disorder may be classified as slight, moderate, or severe in character, with corresponding gradation in prognosis. The clinical signs usually manifest themselves within a few hours after birth. They include increasing respiratory rate at rest (over 60), which in more severe cases is associated with progressively worsening thoracic retractions, cyanosis, flaring nostrils, expiratory grunting, developing exhaustion, and episodes of apnea.

Some investigators consider that the problem is related to increased pulmonary resistance when the onset of breathing should be initiating expansion of and decreased circulatory pressure in the lung fields. The causes of the development of this abnormally elevated pulmonary pressure are just now being determined. It appears that immaturity of the lungs precludes the formation of a chemical (lecithin), which is normally produced by more developed lung tissue. Lack of this agent increases alveolar surface tension and air sacs once inflated collapse again completely. The infant becomes progressively unable to create the elevated pressure necessary to reinflate the airless alveoli, and respiratory distress increases. Eventually a protein or hyaline membrane forms in the alveoli.

Recently a chemical analysis of the amniotic fluid surrounding the fetus has made it possible to evaluate the maturity of the fetal respiratory system. Better estimates of fetal age help reduce the incidence of respiratory distress syndrome secondary to early elective cesarean section. In the delivery room, careful attention to the preser-

vation of the body heat of the high-risk infant may aid the maintenance of normal acid-base balance and enhance respiratory mechanisms. Increased oxygen and humidity may be helpful. The condition of severely involved infants can be observed more accurately by frequent analysis of the gas content (oxygen–carbon dioxide) of the baby's blood. This may be best achieved by the insertion of a small catheter into an umbilical artery or the umbilical vein. Because of the possibility of such catheterization and the need to preserve its vessels, the umbilical cord is cut long in some hospitals. This is not essential, however. To combat acidosis, solutions of sodium bicarbonate may be given via these catheters by the physician. Infant ventilation is often maintained by machine. The premature infant is best nursed in a neonatal intensive care unit with equipment designed and personnel trained for his special needs—if he is lucky enough to be born where one is available.

• • •

The care of the premature infant is a heavy responsibility; life is enclosed in a fragile package. Yet some of the celebrated figures of history, who have made vast contributions to mankind, entered the world in just such an unfinished state— such men as Sir Isaac Newton and Sir Winston Churchill. Do not underestimate the "premie"!

Abnormalities of the newborn infant

One would wish that each baby born would be perfect in every detail—physically, intellectually, and emotionally ready to meet the challenge of life without an initial obstacle or defect. Sadly, such is not the case. Approximately one in sixteen of all children born have some kind of serious abnormality, causing disfigurement or resulting in physical or mental handicaps or a shortened life.

The birth of a handicapped or ill child is always a distressing time for the family. Feelings of anxiety, guilt, frustration, and exhaustion are common. Parents at first may be unable to believe that their child is abnormal, and when the realization comes, grief may be intense. Problems in organizing the family to meet the unexpected demands created by the necessary trips to the hospital, doctor, and therapist and the extra financial burden it all entails can seem almost without end to the often perplexed and unprepared parents.

Although the vocational nurse is not in a position to give professional guidance to people to mobilize the total resources of the family and community to meet the needs involved, she should recognize the pressures under which they are operating. She should know how much has been told the mother regarding her child and be extremely discreet in her conversations. She should be supportive in allowing the parents to express themselves and in relaying any problems that seem to be causing worry to the charge nurse or physician. It is *very important* that the parents not feel isolated in their attempt to adjust to the reality of their child's imperfection. In an attempt to prevent isolation the nurse can be a vital liaison between the family, medical staff, clergy, and community resource personnel.

Birth injuries

Cerebral hemorrhage. The most common type of birth injury is *intracraninal hemorrhage*. As noted previously, it is most often seen in premature infants but can be diagnosed in full-term babies as well, particularly those who had a traumatic passage to this external world. Symptoms or signs of hemorrhage within the skull may manifest themselves suddenly or gradually. They may include irritability, listlessness or cyanosis, marked irregular respiration, varying degrees of paralysis, lack of appetite or poor sucking reflex, tremors, convulsions, projectile vomiting, unequally dilated pupils, tense or bulging fontanels, and a high, shrill cry. These kinds of symptoms could arise from other causes such as intracranial abscess, cerebral edema, tumor, or developing hydrocephalus—in fact, from anything that would increase the pressure within the skull. Diagnosis is usually made through the history and observation of the infant. Sometimes the bleeding is mild and stops of itself, and the child recovers with little or no effects. Sometimes pressure is so intense it must be relieved by aspiration of the subdural space or surgery. Sometimes brain damage is permanent, or death results from the condition.

The infant is usually placed in an incubator with the head slightly elevated in an attempt to relieve pressure. Rarely, a spinal tap may be done for the same reason or as a diagnostic aid. Vitamin K to relieve bleeding tendencies may be prescribed. Sedatives such as phenobarbital may be ordered in case of tremor. It is very important for the nurse observing the infant to be able to accurately describe the type of tremor, convulsion, or abnormal behavior pattern seen; her description of the part of the body affected—one or both sides—how long it lasted, and what, if anything apparent, occurred just beforehand may be able to help the physician localize the area of bleeding. The child is kept as quiet as possible.

Fractures. Fractures may occur at birth. The most frequently broken bone is the clavicle, or collarbone. It usually heals without treatment. Fractures of long bones are uncommon; they may be splinted. All broken bones normally heal rapidly during infancy.

Facial paralysis. Temporary or even permanent paralysis occasionally results from nerve injury during delivery. Facial paralysis may be caused by forceps pressure. The side of the face affected does not move, and the eye may remain open. This condition usually disappears gradually.

Erb's palsy. Injury to the brachial plexus, the network of nerves that branches to supply the nervous control of the upper extremities, may cause the arm on the affected side to hang limply from the shoulder and rotate internally and the hand to partially close with palm facing outward.

The infant cannot raise his arm. This injury, called Erb's palsy, is usually not permanent. Permanent spasticity, tremor, and lack of coordination can result from brain damage caused by trauma or lack of sufficient oxygen.

Hydrocephalus

Hydrocephalus is a defect that results from the accumulation of abnormally large amounts of cerebrospinal fluid within the cranium, causing abnormal enlargement of the immature skull (Fig. 19-3).

Types. There are a variety of causes of hydrocephalus. A congenital structural defect may exist in the cerebrospinal fluid drainage system, preventing the flow of the fluid from the ventricles of the brain into the subarachnoid space and into the venous system. Such blockage may also occur as the result of developing brain tumor or abscess. This type of blockage produces · noncommunicating hydrocephalus. Occasionally, the flow of cerebrospinal fluid from the ventricles to the subarachnoid space is normal, but the absorption of the fluid into the venous system is abnormal and inadequate because of an obscure de-

velopmental defect. This situation, described as communicating hydrocephalus, may occur as a sequela to meningitis or subarachnoid hemorrhage. It sometimes coexists with a congenital defect called *myelomeningocele,* a herniation of a part of the spinal cord elements and its coverings through an abnormal opening in the back of the bony spine. The hydrocephalus usually becomes more evident after the myelomeningocele is surgically repaired. Circulation pathways outside the brain for the cerebrospinal fluid that had previously been available may be disturbed or unavailable.

Early recognition and treatment. The infant responds to mounting cerebrospinal fluid pressure by a progressive symmetrical increase in head size. Other manifestations noted shortly after birth include bulging of the fontanels, separation of sutures, distended scalp veins, irritability, and vomiting. A downward displacement of the eyes and skin tension giving the pupils a "setting-sun" appearance is a late symptom.

Early reduction in ventricular size is essential if the child is to have the best chance of becoming a useful individual.

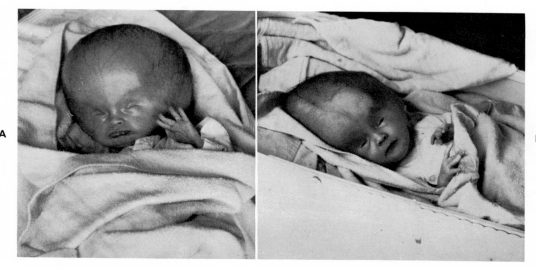

Fɪɢ. 19-3. **A,** This baby with advanced hydrocephalus is 4½ weeks old. However, he was delivered 7 weeks early per cesarean section. **B,** The same child at 3 months of age. The cranium has collapsed. He died at 5½ months of age.

The treatment of hydrocephalus is influenced by the degree of intracranial pressure, the level of obstruction, and any associated major congenital defects found. Spontaneous arrest occurs in 30% to 40% of children affected but usually does not occur until the hydrocephalus is well advanced. By this time a useful existence may be impossible.

Although many types of shunt procedures may be performed, to date, the most satisfactory way of effectively reducing ventricular size is by shunting the fluid from the ventricles into the vascular system.

Ventriculoatrial shunt. The insertion of silastic tubes and valves that allow one-way flow of fluid has led to the successful shunting of cerebrospinal fluid into the jugular vein and right atrium (Fig. 19-4). A burr hole is made in the skull, and a small tube is directed into the lateral ventricle of the brain. Through a small neck incision the cardiac tube is inserted into the right atrium via the internal jugular vein. The

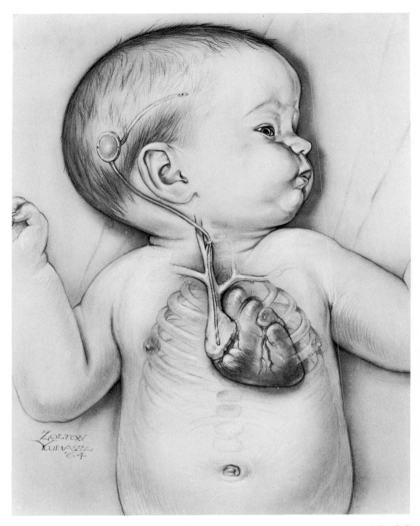

FIG. 19-4. Pudenz valve—one type of shunting device that drains cerebrospinal fluid from the ventricles of the brain into the right atrium. (Courtesy R. H. Pudenz, M.D., and the Heyer-Schulte Corp., Santa Barbara, Calif.)

ventricular and cardiac tubes are then connected to the flushing device situated beneath the skin and behind the ear. The flushing device is shaped to fit into the burr hole with its flange overlying the surrounding skull. Under normal operating conditions cerebrospinal fluid flow is unobstructed. The flushing devices differ on the various tubes used. In the Pudenz-Mishler double-lumen device the ventricular cardiac catheters are flushed when the reservoir is compressed. Pumping the functioning shunt permits highly effective flushing in both directions. Obstruction of the ventricular tube, the commonest cause of shunt malfunctions, may be cleared by occluding the easily felt atrial catheter with finger pressure and compressing the reservoir. Thus the flushing device serves a dual purpose; it flushes and checks the operation of the entire system. In postoperative care, a daily check by manually depressing the skin (pumping) over the reservoir of the flushing device and watching for refill will determine if the shunt is functioning properly.

Postoperative care. When the infant is wide awake, dextrose in water is offered by mouth. If it is tolerated, formula may be given. It is important that the nurse observe the baby before the shunting procedure to compare and evaluate his postoperative condition. To avoid respiratory complications the child must have his position changed at least every 2 hours. The head should be placed carefully to avoid pressure on the cranial wound, which might predispose the skin to break down. The fontanel should be less tense and slightly depressed. If the fontanels are sunken, the child is kept flat. If the fontanels are full or bulging, his head is elevated. Pulse and respiration determinations and pupil equality checks are done frequently. The nurse must be constantly alert for any signs of increased intracranial pressure such as slowed pulse and respirations, lethargy, irritability, vomiting, and tense fontanels. Head circumference should be measured at the widest diameter daily. Any abnor-

malities detected by those observations, signs of faulty functioning of the flushing device, or an elevated temperature should be recorded carefully and immediately called to the attention of the physician.

Complications. The tubing may become plugged, infection may occur, and growth of the infant may cause the tip of the cardiac tube to become displaced. These conditions usually require frequent revisions of the shunt. Insertion of a foreign body (in this case, the cardiac tube) into the bloodstream may cause thrombus formation. Debilitated infants seem to be prone to infection. Although most children do benefit from a shunt procedure, improved methods of controlling infantile hydrocephalus will continue to be sought.

Continued care. When surgical intervention cannot be considered, nursing care of the child with advanced hydrocephalus takes considerable gentleness and patience. The head may be extremely large with widely separated cranial bones, broad sutures, and bulging fontanels. Despite the plasticity of the infant skull, pressure on the brain usually causes some degree of mental retardation. There may be wide swings in body temperature, tremors or convulsions, lack of appetite, or vomiting. Check the tension of fontanels, and check for other signs of increasing intracranial pressure daily.

Attention must be given to preventing pressure sores on the scalp by frequent turning and soft pillow supports. When not being supervised directly, the child should be positioned on his side or abdomen with his head turned to the side to prevent aspiration. Support for the head must always be given during feedings, and the nurse may find it more comfortable for baby and less tiring for herself to place a pillow on her arm for head support and to rest her elbow on the chair arm. After feeding and bubbling, the infant should be left as quiet as possible to prevent vomiting. Malnutrition and infection are frequent complications for these unfortunate babies.

Cranial stenosis and microcephaly

Other congenital deformities of the skull may be found, but happily they are rare. The sutures of the skull may prematurely close (cranial stenosis), causing abnormal pressure on the brain and possible mental retardation, as well as an asymmetrical distorted appearance of the head, if unrelieved. In another instance the brain may fail to continue growing, and a severely retarded, *microcephalic* individual may result. Very rarely, a child may be born without a developed brain and lack the usual cranial covering of the brain. This condition is called *anencephaly;* the infant soon dies.

Mental retardation

Mental retardation is an extremely common problem. It affects approximately 3% of the general population. Good prenatal and delivery care helps prevent some of the possible causes (birth injury, anoxia). Some types of mental retardation can be prevented or aided by dietary supervision or hormonal therapy.

Intelligence classifications. Because of the many problems that have been identified in trying to determine a person's intellectual capacity by testing devices, the concept of I.Q., or intelligence quotient, has lost much of its former significance. The mental age score attained by an individual in testing may be influenced by his motivation and environment, as well as the test presentation itself. Nevertheless, I.Q. scores are still often obtained. They represent a special testing score (mental age) divided by the individual's chronological age and multiplied by 100. Table 19-1 shows certain ranges of I.Q., representing various degrees of intelligence. The terms in parentheses are no longer recommended. However, since they are still sometimes seen, they are included for the sake of completeness.

Down's syndrome. A type of mental retardation associated with certain physical characteristics that has undergone considerable investigation is that of Down's syndrome, or mongolism. The most common of the three types known is called "trisomy 21" because it is associated with an abnormal chromosome count in the baby's body cells. Although in the past these children have been described as "Mongolian idiots," they are not really Orientals, and certainly not all are retarded to such an extent. They include the profoundly to mildly retarded.

Mongoloid children are usually identified in the nursery, but some are diagnosed later. Characteristically, infants with Down's syndrome are short; they have relatively small skulls, flattened from front to back; their birth weights are usually low; and their behavior is lethargic. The most

TABLE 19-1. Intelligence classifications

Classification	Intelligence quotient	Performance level
Profound retardation (idiot)	I.Q. 0 to 24	Unable to attend to personal needs; always requires supervision. 0- to 2-year-old behavior
Severe retardation (imbecile)	I.Q. 25 to 50	May be trained to meet personal needs but not self-sustaining 3- to 7-year-old behavior
Moderately severe retardation (moron)	I.Q. 50 to 75	Self-sustaining in simple jobs with supervision
Mild retardation (borderline)	I.Q. 75 to 90	
Average	I.Q. 90 to 110	What most of us are
Above average	I.Q. 110 to 130	What most of us would like to be
Gifted	I.Q. 130 to 150	
Genius	I.Q. 150 and above	These people have problems in adjustment, too

reliable signs of mongolism are exaggerated epicanthic folds, which make the eyes slant up and out; short hands and fingers with the little finger bent in; a deep, horizontal crease across the palm; and a large space between the great and small toes. Physicians will examine the eyes in an effort to detect small white dots on the iris, which, when present, are helpful in making a diagnosis. Decreased muscle tone and excessive joint mobility are also significant findings. (See Figs. 19-5 and 19-6.)

After the newborn period, other signs manifest themselves, such as delayed eruption of teeth, fissured tongue, and retarded intellectual and physical development. These youngsters often have congenital heart malformations and umbilical hernias. If they survive long enough, they usually possess rather affectionate, placid person-

alities. Many times, depending on home circumstances and the individual needs of the child, they can remain with the family, and care outside the home community is not necessary. No one knows for sure the true cause of this condition, but trisomy 21 is found most often in cases in which the mother is near the end of her reproductive life. One type of Down's syndrome is hereditary.

Phenylketonuria. Another type of mental retardation that is much less common and has been publicized a great deal is that produced by an inherited error in metabolism of a certain amino acid, or protein, called *phenylalanine*. The disease is called PKU, a short way of saying phenylketonuria. It results when an enzyme normally produced by the liver is missing or inadequate. Unless appropriate measures are taken, poisons build up in the bloodstream

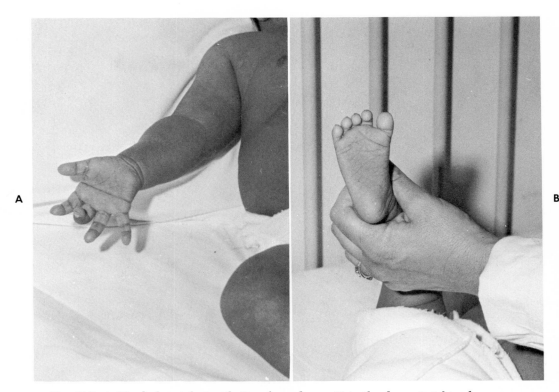

Fig. 19-5. **A,** Hand of an infant with Down's syndrome. Note the deep, straight palmar crease. **B,** Same infant's foot. Note the exaggerated space between the big and little toes. (Courtesy U.S. Naval Hospital, San Diego, Calif.)

that, after a few months, begin to produce noticeable damage to the brain. A high level of the potentially poisonous substance can be detected in the blood serum of the newborn infant, but a few weeks are usually needed before the offending chemical is found in the urine. Blood tests to detect the disease may be done the third day of life just before discharge from the hospital; urine examinations are not valid until later. Treatment consists of eliminating as much as possible of the offending protein from

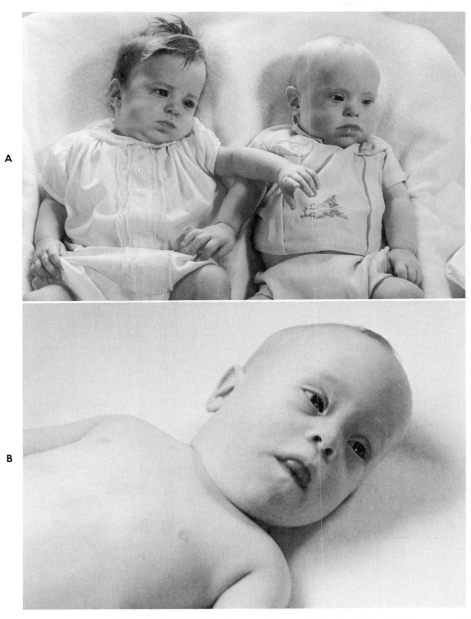

FIG. 19-6. **A,** These children are brother and sister (fraternal) twins. The little boy manifests Down's syndrome, his sister is unaffected. **B,** Close-up of the little male twin. Note the large tongue and typical eyes.

the diet for an indeterminate time. Since phenylalanine is found in many protein foods, the diet is extremely curtailed, and synthetic protein foods are necessary. Results of treatment have been highly gratifying.

Galactosemia. Galactosemia, another rare metabolic error that may produce mental retardation, involves the metabolism of galactose (p. 628).

Cretinism. Cretinism, or infantile hypothyroidism, may also be a cause of mental retardation. The thyroid hormone is absent from the time of birth. Prenatally, the infant is supplied with thyroid by his mother. The signs of hypothyroidism develop gradually.

The typically affected baby has a large tongue that, because of its size, may protrude from his mouth, causing problems in feeding. His cry is hoarse; his hair is coarse, and his skin is dry (no perspiration is observed); constipation is a continuous problem; and growth is retarded if the condition is untreated. Occasionally, inexperienced observers may have difficulty distinguishing the condition from that of Down's syndrome (mongolism).

If cretinism is diagnosed early by studies of the thyroid gland or the iodine content of the blood and the child is given hormone replacement therapy, he usually progresses fairly normally, although slight intellectual retardation may persist.

Spina bifida

Spina bifida, a condition briefly noted in the discussion of hydrocephalus, may exist in several degrees of severity. The term "spina bifida" simply means "divided spine" or that a portion of the posterior wall of the spine is missing.

Types. The defect may be so small that it offers no difficulty and is discovered only when an x-ray examination of the spine is done for other reasons. This type of defect is called "spina bifida occulta," or "hidden divided spine." The second main type of spina bifida (meningocele) involves a protrusion of only the meninges of the spinal cord through the opening, usually causing a tumor on the lower back that contains cerebrospinal fluid. The child usually develops normal urinary and intestinal control and suffers from no paralysis, but the tumor is a cosmetic problem and its possible injury

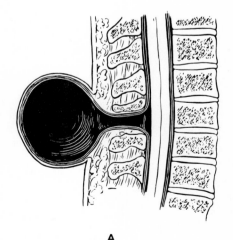

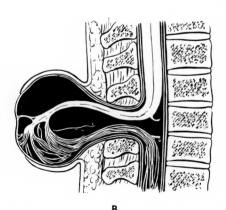

| A | B |

FIG. 19-7. **A,** Section of the spinal cord and vertebral column showing a meningocele. Note that no nervous tissue protrudes through the defect into the sac. **B,** Section of the spinal cord and vertebral column showing a myelomeningocele. Nervous tissue is found in the herniated meningeal sac. (From Benz, G. S.: Pediatric nursing, ed. 5, St. Louis, 1964, The C. V. Mosby Co.)

always poses the problem of infection of the meninges or brain. A third type of spinal defect has been called *myelomeningocele,* or meningomyelocele. In this condition the meninges protrude through the spinal opening, and nerve tissues are also found in the herniated sac. Children with this problem are often troubled with persistent incontinence, partial or complete lower extremity paralysis, and sensory disturbance. Hydrocephalus frequently accompanies this defect. (See Figs. 19-7 to 19-9.)

Nursing care. The nursing care of the

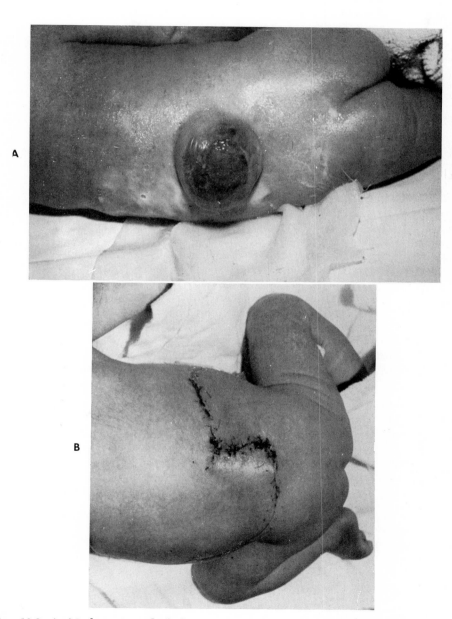

Fig. 19-8. **A,** Myelomeningocele before surgery. (An antibacterial dressing was used.) **B,** Repair of the same patient. (Courtesy M. C. Gleason, M.D., San Diego, Calif.)

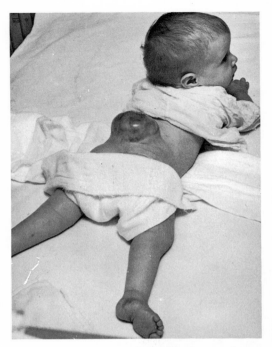

Fig. 19-9. This youngster's myelomeningocele was repaired shortly after this photograph was taken. (Courtesy Children's Health Center, San Diego, Calif.)

child with either meningocele or myelomeningocele is challenging. Before surgery, the sac, or tumor as it is sometimes called, must be protected from injury and infection. The child must be adequately nourished and should be assured of loving care. To protect the sac, the child is usually positioned on his abdomen or carefully propped on his side. Because of the usual position of the tumor, no diapers are pinned in place. To avoid putting strain or pressure on the sac, the nurse must be extremely careful in lifting the infant. Slipping her hands and forearms palms up under the leg and chest area to grasp the farther thigh, arm, and shoulder seems to be a safe, effective way of lifting and moving the smaller infants. Caution must be taken putting these children in sitting position even when no direct pressure is exerted on the tumor. Sometimes the sac is so low on the spine that the sitting position puts too much tension on the area. A positioning device

called a Bradford frame may be used. This consists of a metal framework that rests on the bed and elevates the baby on a divided, padded canvas support. The perineal area and sac are placed directly over splits in the canvas, and a bedpan is positioned directly underneath. Plastic strips hanging from the opening of the frame help direct urine and feces into the pan. This device helps protect the area from soil and pressure.

When being fed, the infant may be propped on his side with his head elevated, held by one nurse with his head over her shoulder while fed by another nurse holding the bottle or, his condition permitting, held in a sitting position with no pressure on the sac.

Meticulous skin care must be observed and pressure areas prevented. Occasionally, to avoid infection, the tumor area will be irrigated periodically with a mild antiseptic. It may be covered by sterile petrolatum or medicated strips and gauze compresses. A foam rubber ring with a hole large enough to admit the tumor may be placed over the sterile compresses and wrapped in place with an elastic bandage. Treatment depends on the tumor's size, location, and condition. The sac should be observed for variance in size and tenseness as well as ulceration. The head of a child with any type of meningocele usually is regularly measured to try to detect developing hydrocephalus. The sensation and movement of the lower extremities are evaluated as care is given.

After surgery (usually a flap-type procedure done in stages) the prone position is maintained, at least until the sutures are removed. There may be no dressing over the incision, and a dry incision and body warmth may be maintained by a carefully positioned gooseneck lamp or the use of an incubator. Although surgery rarely improves function, it certainly improves the child's appearance and facilitates care. The care of a patient with spina bifida, complicated by a herniation of nerve tissue elements, continues for life. Many orthopedic procedures may have to be completed before the child achieves even the ability to walk with braces. Many spina bifida babies also have clubfeet. Urinary complications are the rule rather than the exception. An artificial bladder may be developed from an excised part of the ileum with an opening on the abdominal wall to avoid the problems created by the continued long-term use of indwelling catheters as the child grows. The prevention or treatment of decubiti is a real concern. The child needs constant psychological and emotional support, as well as physical assistance, to attain a healthy personality capable of giving as well as receiving from his environment.

Cleft lip and cleft palate

Cleft lip and cleft palate are fairly common congenital malformations. They appear approximately once in every 500 to 1,000 births. They constitute a failure in the embryonic development of the child, and the hereditary factor is often found to be significant. Cleft lip is found more often in males, whereas females more often have cleft palates. Cleft lip, quite commonly called harelip, may vary from a single notching of the border of the lip to a deep split extending through the lip to or into the nose. It may exist on only one side of center or be found on both sides. It may create a problem in feeding, dentition, and appearance but fortunately usually has an excellent prognosis. A cleft lip is usually repaired very early—as soon as the infant's condition is sufficiently stable, at approximately 2 months of age or before. A cleft palate may involve lack of fusion of only part of the hard or soft palate or may extend along the entire roof of the mouth. Cleft palate is repaired later according to the child's individual needs.

Before taking their baby home to await surgery for cleft lip or palate, the parents must receive detailed instructions regarding his care and have several opportunities to feed the infant with supervision. The baby usually has difficulty sucking nor-

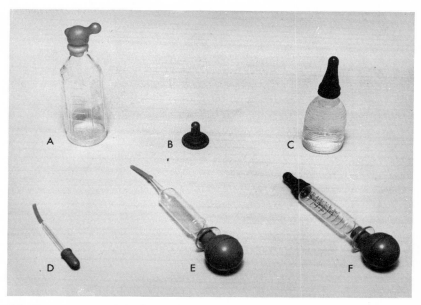

Fig. 19-10. Various types of feeding aids for cleft palate babies. **A,** "Ducky" nipple (the hump fits into the defect); **B,** soft "premie" nipple is often used; **C,** lamb's nipple; **D,** rubber-tipped medicine dropper; **E,** rubber-tipped Asepto syringe; **F,** Brecht feeder. (Courtesy Children's Health Center, San Diego, Calif.)

mally, since he cannot create the necessary vacuum in his mouth. He may be fed slowly with a rubber-tipped Asepto syringe, a rubber-tipped medicine dropper, or a Brecht feeder, no faster than his capacity to swallow (Fig. 19-10). Occasionally, the defect is so placed or is so small that a regularly shaped soft nipple with a large hole may be used. Rarely, a specially molded cleft-palate nipple with an extra built-in hump that fits the cleft in the palate and makes sucking possible is employed. Because of their shape, these are sometimes called "ducky nipples." Occasionally, soft, long lamb's nipples are tried, or the child may be fed off the end of a small spoon. Levin gavage is avoided if at all possible. The baby is fed in an upright position to help prevent aspiration and, in the case of cleft palate, to prevent regurgitation through the nose. The method of feeding that is most successful and clos-

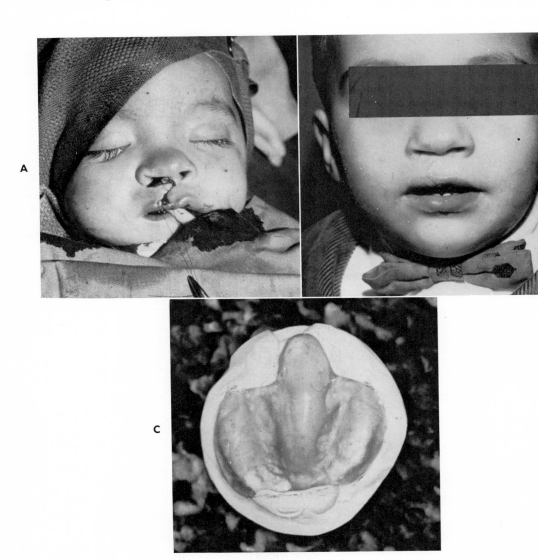

FIG. 19-11. A, Closure of a unilateral complete cleft lip. B, Same child 13 months later. C, Palate prosthesis resting in a plaster-of-Paris mold. The prosthesis is used until a child is old enough for optimal palate repair. (Courtesy M. C. Gleason, M.D., San Diego, Calif.)

est to that used by a normal baby is the method of choice. Since these babies swallow more air than usual, they should be bubbled frequently. This will lessen the possibility of emesis or unattended "wet burps" and subsequent aspiration. Some children with cleft palate are fitted early with a prosthesis to help guard against nasal regurgitation, aid in the formation of speech patterns, and maintain anatomical relationships important to the final repair.

The success of plastic surgery depends on the extent of the defect, the developmental stage of the individual, the repair techniques available, the skill of the surgeon, the standard of nursing care, and the cooperation of the parents. A cleft palate is much more difficult to repair, and the child may have to undergo several procedures at different ages. (See Fig. 19-11.)

Nursing care of the patient with cleft lip. After surgery for a cleft lip the infant should have his arms restrained to prevent damage to the suture line or pulling on an indwelling gavage tube. Elbow or wrist restraints may be used. Very young infants may have their arms restrained adequately by pulling their long shirt sleeves past their hands and pinning the sleeves to their diaper. Periodically, these restraints should be removed one at a time to provide needed exercise and inspection of the arms. The indwelling, nasally inserted Levin tube is used to provide feedings for several days to lessen the lip motion that would take place if a nipple were placed in the mouth, thus helping to safeguard the suture line. A soft nasal packing may be in place in the opposite nostril to prevent bleeding of the operative site and help "mold" the nose properly. It is removed after approximately 2 days. (See Fig. 19-12.)

The suture line should be kept clean, and no crust should be allowed to form because crusting enlarges the scar. Various solutions are used for cleaning, depending on the physician's preference; examples are hydrogen peroxide, warm sterile water, or physiological saline solution. Tightly wrapped, sterile cotton applicators or small gauze sponges mounted on forceps may be used to remove blood. Such maneuvers

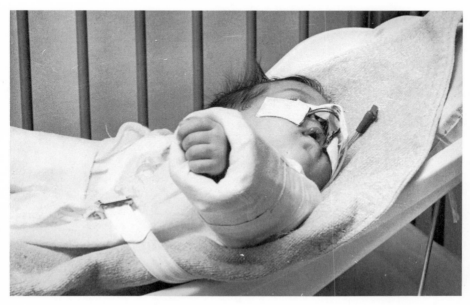

FIG. 19-12. Infant with a newly repaired cleft lip. Note the Logan bow, gavage tube, and elbow restraints. The child has a palate prosthesis in place. (Courtesy Children's Health Center, San Diego, Calif.)

must be done gently but persistently. Soaking the area for a brief period with a saturated applicator or sponge before any motion over the area is attempted aids considerably. Afterward, the lip should be gently dried, and any protective covering ordered should be applied. Sometimes an antibiotic ointment is used, or a small "mustache" of petrolatum gauze may be left on the lip.

A Logan bow may be employed to prevent lateral tension on the suture line. This metal loop arches over the suture line and is held in place on both cheeks by pieces of adhesive tape. When a Logan bow is used, the indwelling gavage tube is usually taped to its arch to prevent tension on the nose and eliminate the use of more adhesive tape on the skin.

Every effort should be made to keep the child happy—not just because we want a child to be happy, which we do, but because a happy child cries less and puts less strain on his repair. The parents should be allowed to cuddle the infant and, as soon as feasible, participate in feedings under supervision. Usually, the tube is removed about the third postoperative day. The child may then be fed by Asepto syringe, Brecht feeder, or a rubber-tipped medicine dropper, and graduated to a soft nipple when sucking is allowed. The ability to suck is usually markedly improved by the repair.

Nursing care of the patient with cleft palate (Fig. 19-13). As stated before, repair of a cleft palate is usually more difficult than repair of a cleft lip. A series of operations may be needed. A cleft palate is also a more serious defect, considering the impairment of function it produces. Not only is feeding difficult, involving possible problems of aspiration and dental placement, but speech is often nasalized, and infec-

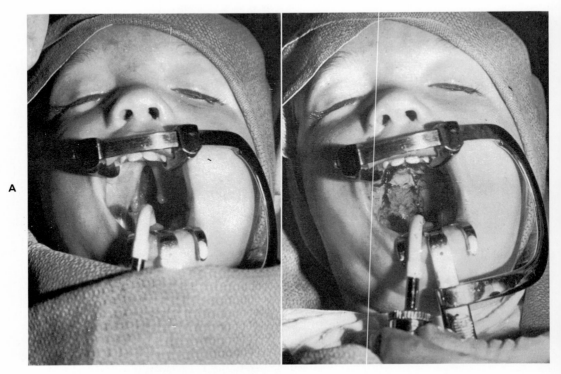

Fig. 19-13. A, Cleft palate just before surgery. B, Closure of the cleft palate. (Courtesy M. C. Gleason, M.D., San Diego, Calif.)

tions of the respiratory tract and middle ear are common. The child who has undergone palate surgery may also be gavaged the first 2 or 3 days, or he may be fed from a cup or side of a spoon. Nothing is introduced into the mouth that may endanger the suture line, and, unless the child is old enough to understand and cooperate, arm restraints must be used. The diet progresses from clear liquid to full liquid to soft food over a period of approximately 1 week. The mouth should be rinsed with water at the end of a meal.

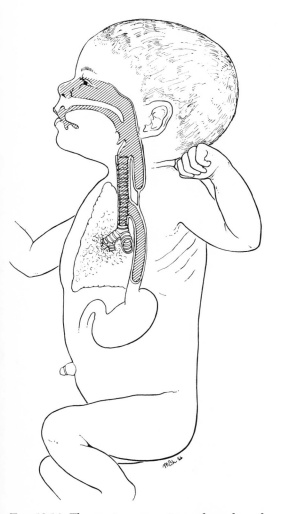

FIG. 19-14. The most common type of esophageal atresia involves an upper esophageal segment ending in a blind pouch and a lower tracheo-esophageal fistula. There is great danger of aspiration.

The problems of the child with cleft lip, cleft palate, or both are occasionally so complex that the combined therapy of a plastic surgeon, pediatrician, orthodontist, speech therapist, child psychiatrist, and medical social worker may be needed. For this reason, clinics for those with cleft lip and palate are found in most large cities.

Other digestive tract abnormalities

Other abnormalities of the digestive tract are found with enough frequency to at least merit mention, especially since they are so serious in nature. There can be lack of development or faulty development of the esophagus; the esophagus may end in a blind pouch (esophageal atresia) or lead directly into the trachea (tracheo-esophageal fistula) (Fig. 19-14). There may be a tubal connection with the trachea leading to the stomach but only a blind esophageal pouch above. Such gross defects must be discovered early, before the child aspirates or formula in large amounts reaches the lungs via an existing fistula. Any significant sputtering, cyanosis, or drooling at the time of the first water feeding should be reported immediately. Some nurseries, as part of their admitting examination, have initiated a gentle soft catheter probe of body orifices to detect congenital structural abnormalities. A small catheter is passed up the nasal passage to the nasal pharynx. It is then passed nasally or orally to the stomach.

Occasionally the infant's rectum ends as a closed or blind pouch or connects to an adjacent canal (urethra, vagina) via a fistula (Fig. 19-15). The possibility of this defect is one reason observation of the stools of the newborn is so important. Many times a temporary colostomy, an abdominal exit for the contents of the colon, must be made. Later the creation of a normally placed functional rectal opening will be attempted.

Omphalocele (Fig. 19-16) is an absence of the normal abdominal wall in the region of the umbilicus that may allow a portion of the intestinal contents to be clearly ob-

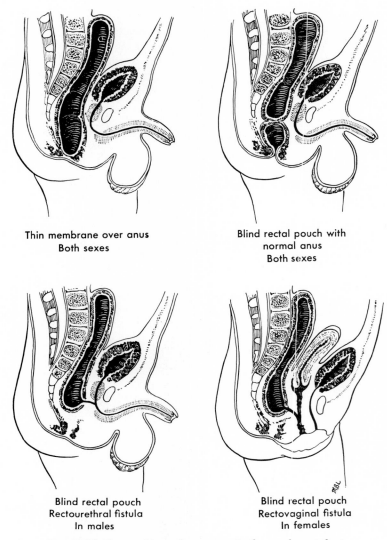

Thin membrane over anus
Both sexes

Blind rectal pouch with
normal anus
Both sexes

Blind rectal pouch
Rectourethral fistula
In males

Blind rectal pouch
Rectovaginal fistula
In females

FIG. 19-15. Types of imperforate anus in the newborn infant.

served, virtually unprotected, and subject to herniation and strangulation. The defect may be small or exaggerated. Its repair is usually considered a surgical emergency. Another type of hernia, involving the abdominal contents and causing respiratory distress as well as digestive problems, is the *diaphragmatic hernia*. In this condition an abnormally large opening is present in the diaphragm that allows part of the contents of the abdominal cavity to displace upward into the chest. Sometimes the entire stomach, as well as portions of the intestine, is found in the thorax, crowding the heart and lungs. This situation, too, is a surgical emergency.

Hypospadias

A fairly common malformation of the urinary system that is found in male infants is hypospadias (Fig. 19-17). The urethra, instead of traveling the entire length of the penis, opens out on the underside of the penis, either at its base or at varying distances from the tip. Sometimes the presence of hypospadias, coupled with other irregu-

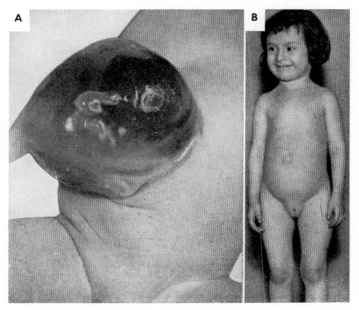

FIG. 19-16. A, Omphalocele before repair. B, After corrective surgery. (From Potter, E. L.: Pathology of the fetus and the newborn, Chicago, 1952, Year Book Medical Publishers, Inc.)

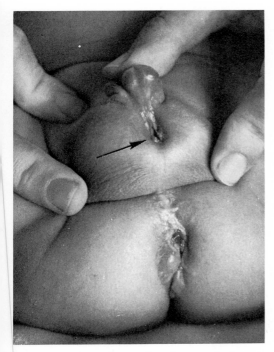

FIG. 19-17. This infant suffers from multiple congenital anomalies. The arrow indicates the opening of the urethra at the base of the penis (hypospadias). An imperforate anus was previously repaired.

larities of the external genital organs, leads to confusion in determining the sex of the infant, and cell studies and exploratory operative procedures may be necessary. The repair of well-defined hypospadias by the extension of the urethral canal is usually accomplished by a series of operative procedures before the child is of school age. Minor positional deviations of the urethral meatus may not require treatment.

Congenital heart deformities

Congenital cardiac conditions many times stem from the persistence of some part of the fetal circulation pattern, so it would be of benefit to review the basic circulation present before birth (Fig. 7-6). The foramen ovale may fail to close, resulting in an *atrial septal* defect. The *ductus arteriosus* may persist. Real structural deviations may also exist in many different combinations. A combination of four different defects, which causes such a degree of cyanosis that those suffering from it are termed "blue babies," is tetralogy of Fallot. Children with this diagnosis have a ventricular septal defect, and the aorta, instead of draining just the left ventricle, straddles the ab-normal ventricular opening. We say that it "overrides" the two ventricles. As if this were not enough, the pulmonary semilunar valve is narrowed or stenosed, and the right wall of the heart has to pump against such pressure that it becomes exceptionally thick or hypertrophied. The blood under such conditions is very poorly oxygenated. Open-heart surgery, with the use of the

heart-lung machine, now gives more hope of survival and the possibility of a more normal life.

Hemolytic disease of the newborn infant

A number of conditions can cause blood destruction in the fetus or newborn infant. Probably the most well-known cause is Rh factor incompatibility, which may initiate

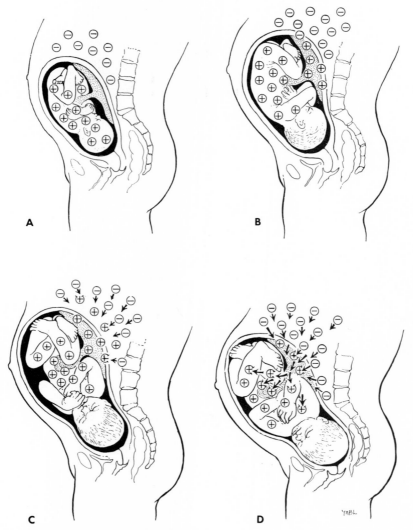

FIG. 19-18. Mechanism of erythroblastosis fetalis, which is caused by Rh incompatibility. **A,** Rh-positive child is carried by Rh-negative mother. **B,** Rh protein crosses the placental barrier and invades the mother's bloodstream. **C,** Mother's system manufactures antibodies to destroy the foreign Rh protein. **D,** Antibodies cross back over the placenta and destroy the baby's blood cells, which are intimately associated with his Rh protein.

the condition *erythroblastosis fetalis*. The Rh factor is a protein first identified in the blood of Rhesus monkeys. It is found in approximately 85% of the Caucasian population and in higher percentages among the Mongoloid and Negroid peoples. (See Fig. 19-18.)

Rh incompatibility. If a woman who lacks the Rh protein in her blood marries a man who also lacks it, no problem will exist because of the Rh factor for their offspring. However, if her husband is Rh positive and their child inherits Rh-positive blood from his father, trouble may occur.

Probable mechanism. Some of the baby's blood cells carrying the Rh protein may pass through a microscopic tear in the placental barrier and reach the mother's bloodstream. The mother's body automatically manufactures antibodies (protective substances) designed to destroy the foreign protein in her body. Some of these antibodies may also cross the placental barrier through microscopic defects and find themselves in the fetal circulation. There, they do just what they were designed to do. They destroy the Rh protein, or factor and, in so doing, also destroy the red blood cell to which it is attached. The fetus suffers from the effects of anemia and toxicity caused by the large amount of red cell breakdown products (chiefly bilirubin) circulating in its body. Making a valiant effort to supply more red blood cells, the fetal body forces out into its bloodstream immature, inadequate forms of red blood cells called erythroblasts. This is the reason the resulting disease is called by the term *erythroblastosis fetalis*. As the disease progresses, the liver and spleen become enlarged, and brain damage called *kernicterus* may occur because of the large amount of toxic bilirubin pigment circulating in the blood. If the pregnancy is not successfully terminated before fetal injury occurs and adequate treatment is not made available, a stillborn infant or neurologically handicapped child may result.

One of the first clinical manifestations of Rh factor sensitivity in the infant is the appearance of jaundice within 24 to 36 hours. The baby with a more severe case may be lethargic, suck poorly, and manifest spasticity.

However, not all mothers with Rh-negative blood have such sick babies. Sometimes the baby is also Rh negative and no such problem arises. Sometimes the number of antibodies the mother has produced in response to the baby's cells in her bloodstream is so small that no damage to the baby is detected. Usually, trouble is not encountered until the second or third infant. After several pregnancies, the titer of antibodies in the blood usually increases markedly. This titer may be measured during pregnancy; also the progress of the disease may be estimated by analyzing amniotic fluid aspirated from the sac surrounding the baby. These tests allow the physician to evaluate the health of the fetus and plan for the baby's delivery and care.

Often the question is asked, "Why doesn't an Rh-positive mother become ill when her unborn child is Rh negative?" The answer seems to be in the relative inability of the fetus to produce enough antibodies to attack the mother's blood cells in sufficient number.

Treatment. When the presence of erythroblastosis fetalis is determined in a newborn infant, exchange transfusion is carried out. The umbilical vein is used to achieve access to the baby's bloodstream per polyethylene catheter. A carefully measured amount of blood is slowly withdrawn and discarded by a syringe equipped with a complex of stopcocks. Then crossmatched, Rh-negative donor blood with a low Rh antibody titer warmed to room temperature is pushed slowly per syringe back into the baby's body as a replacement. This process is repeated many times until complete replacement is estimated to have occurred. During the procedure, close observation of the baby's vital signs and the blood volume exchange is essential. The baby must be kept warm, and oxygen may be administered. This treatment must occasionally be repeated, but the results are usually highly successful, and the child born in good condition and receiving prompt transfusion when needed has an excellent prognosis.

Recently, another method of treating erythroblastosis has been publicized that uses a new dramatic approach—intrauterine transfusion of those unborn infants that show signs of not being able to survive until viable. This procedure, now available at a few research centers, is not without risk but may be considered when no other real choice is possible.

The exposure of infants with elevated blood bilirubin levels to blue or fluorescent light to reduce the amount of circulating bilirubin is now being evaluated. The naked infant is positioned under the lamps with protective eye shields in place. He is turned periodically to increase body surface exposure. (See Fig. 19-19.)

Prevention. For the Rh-negative primipara who has never received Rh-positive blood in a transfusion or miscarried an Rh-positive infant, a recent wonderful discovery will prove beneficial. It has been found that passive immunization or ready-made antibody protection, given at a certain time, will destroy the invading foreign Rh protein and inhibit the natural formation of antibodies by the individual. If passive Rh_oD antibodies are injected intramuscularly into a previously unsensitized patient within 3 days after her delivery, the subsequent pregnancy has little risk of developing he-

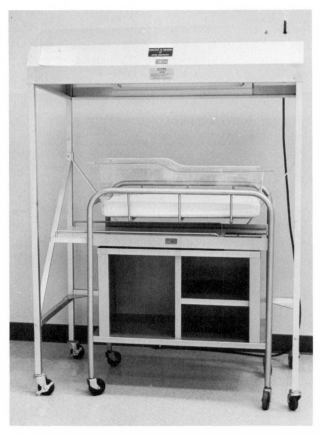

FIG. 19-19. One type of bilirubin lamp positioned over a crib. Light is provided by fluorescent rods. This treatment appears most successful in lowering bilirubin levels of jaundiced premature infants. This model is manufactured by the National Biological Corp., Cleveland, Ohio. (Courtesy Grossmont Hospital, La Mesa, Calif.)

molytic problems because of the Rh factor. This special passive immunization is marketed as Rh₀GAM. Unfortunately, it does not aid Rh-negative women who have already actively developed their own immunization against the Rh factor.

A mechanism similar to the Rh problem, but usually of a less serious nature, can operate when the mother has type O blood and the baby has type A, B, or AB. Such a situation is called "ABO incompatibility."

Orthopedic abnormalities

Orthopedic abnormalities are quite common in the newborn nursery. As a general rule, the earlier they are treated the better the prognosis.

Congenital dislocated hip. Early treatment is particularly important in the case of so-called congenital dislocated hip, which may indicate a partial or, more rarely, complete displacement of the head of the femur from a malformed hip socket or acetabulum. This abnormality is found eight times more frequently in girls than in boys. The first sign of difficulty is usually limitation of abduction of the hip joint involved.

Normally, when the infant is lying on his back, his flexed thighs and knees can be pushed outward and down to almost the level of the examining table—an angle of 90 degrees. This amount of abduction is not possible in the case of "congenital hip." X-ray examination confirms the clinical diagnosis. Complete dislocation may occur in the older child when weight bearing begins with standing and walking. This may cause such signs as a shortening of the leg, exaggerated gluteal folds on the affected side, limping, and limitation in abduction. Different methods of treatment are used, depending on the extent of the dislocation and the preference of the physician, but some form of abduction is usually employed. Continued abduction and pressure forces the head of the femur into the acetabulum and deepens the socket. Sometimes, in the case of an infant, a bulky double diaper or pillow forces the tiny legs sideways, and the child is kept in a prone position by restraints or pinning the diaper to the sheets. The Frejka, or pillow, splint, sometimes seen in clinics, is a type of harness attached to a pillow that helps hold

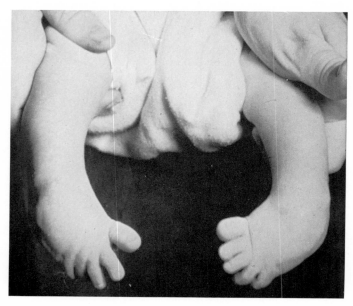

Fɪɢ. 19-20. Talipes equinovarus. (From Larson, C. B., and Gould, M.: Orthopedic nursing, ed. 7, St. Louis, 1970, The C. V. Mosby Co.)

the position of the legs when applied over the child's diaper and plastic protector. At times, such measures are not sufficient, and the child may be admitted to the hospital for gradual reduction of the deformity through the use of skin traction and the Putti board, or "A frame" (Fig. 33-2), or skin traction may be applied to both legs in suspension in such a manner that complete abduction will gradually be obtained. These traction treatments are followed by the application of plaster casts or abduction bars for continued treatment at home. For information regarding the nursing care of the child with "congenital hip," see Chapter 33.

Clubfoot (talipes). *Clubfoot,* or *talipes,* is a fairly common orthopedic deformity. It is not always congenital, since it can be the result of neurological or muscle disorders in later life, but, of course, in the newborn nursery all cases would be classed as congenital; many are hereditary. A clubbing of the foot can mean many types of distortion. The foot may turn in (talipes varus), may turn outward (talipes valgus), may turn down forcing the heel off the walking surface (talipes equinus), may turn up forcing the toes off the walking surface (talipes calcaneus), or a combination of these types of defects may occur. One or both feet may be involved. The most common clubfoot is *talipes equinovarus* (Fig. 19-20).

The feet of the newborn infant must be carefully evaluated. Not all apparent de-

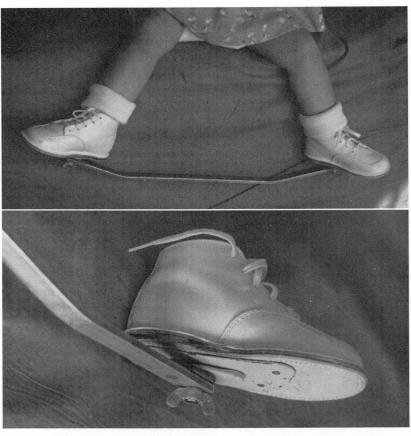

Fig. 19-21. Modified Denis Browne splint is often used to help maintain corrected positions of the feet. (From Larson, C. B., and Gould, M.: Orthopedic nursing, ed. 7, St. Louis, 1970, The C. V. Mosby Co.)

formities are true clubfoot. Some distortions are simply caused by intrauterine positions and not real structural differences. These feet can be corrected to neutral position in all elements of the deformity by manipulation during examination. A true clubfoot cannot.

The treatment of clubfoot depends on the individual case. Sometimes, simple exercises are prescribed, or foot braces, special shoes, or casts may be worn (even while the child is in the nursery!) (Fig. 19-21). In some cases subsequent surgery may be necessary. The type of surgery performed at a later period is usually a plantar stripping of the fibrous tissue of the foot and a lengthening of the heel cord or tendon of Achilles.

Syndactyly and polydactylism. Syndactyly, or webbing of the fingers or toes, is a very interesting anomaly, usually responding well to surgical separation. Syndactyly may accompany another digital abnormality called *polydactylism,* or the presence of extra fingers or toes. At times, these extra digits have no bony connection with the hand or foot and, when a ligature is tied around the fleshy stalk, cutting off circulation, the digit soon drops off. When a bony connection exists, surgery is necessary if gloves are to be worn with ease in later years.

Effect of contagious diseases

The effect of contagious diseases on the fetus and newborn infant is discussed in Unit V. Those considered are syphilis, gonorrhea, tuberculosis, and rubella (German measles).

• • •

Many are the abnormalities possible in the newborn infant, but when one considers the intricacies of life, the miracle is that more of them do not occur.

UNIT VII

SUGGESTED SELECTED READINGS
AND REFERENCES

Arnold, H. W., Barnard, B. L., Desmond, M. M., Putnam, N. J., and Rudolph, A. J.: Transition to extra-uterine life, Amer. J. Nurs. 65:77-80, Oct., 1965.

Atkinson, H. C.: Care of the child with cleft lip and palate, Amer. J. Nurs. 67:1889, Sept., 1967.

Behrman, R. E., editor: The newborn, Pediat. Clin. N. Amer. 17:entire volume, 1970.

Blake, F. G., Wright, F. H., and Waechter, E. H.: Nursing care of children, ed. 8, Philadelphia, 1970, J. B. Lippincott Co.

Bray, P. F.: Neurology in pediatrics, Chicago, 1969, Year Book Medical Publishers, Inc.

Cochran, L., editor: Care of the newborn, Nurs. Clin. N. Amer. 6:1-112, March, 1971.

Darnell, B.: We give our preemies family-centered care, RN 29:57-61, March, 1966.

Davis, M. E., and Rubin, R.: DeLee's obstetrics for nurses, ed. 18, Philadelphia, 1966, W. B. Saunders Co.

DeMarco, J. P., and Reed, R.: Care of the high-risk infant in the intensive care unit, Nurs. Clin. N. Amer. 5:375-396, Sept., 1970.

Downes, J. J., Vidyasagar, D., Morrow, G. M., III, and Boggs, T. R.: Respiratory distress syndrome of newborn infants, Clin. Pediat. 9:325-330, 1970.

Fitzpatrick, E. N., Eastman, N. J., and Reeder, S.: Maternity nursing, ed. 11, Philadelphia, 1966, J. B. Lippincott Co.

Griffith, J. F., and Ojemann, R. G.: Hydrocephalus: medical and surgical considerations, Clin. Pediat. 6:494-500, 1967.

Gustafson, S. R., and Coursin, D. B.: The pediatric patient, Philadelphia, 1969, J. B. Lippincott Co.

Hasselmeyer, E. G.: Maternal and infant well-being (a continuing feature), J. Prac. Nurs. 20:21+, Aug., 1970.

Hervada, A. R.: Nursery evaluations of the newborn, Amer. J. Nurs. 67:1669-1671, Aug., 1967.

Hill, L. F.: Infant feeding: historical and current, Pediat. Clin. N. Amer. 14:255-268, 1967.

Holt, L. E., Davies, E. A., Hasselmeyer, E. G., and Adams, A. O.: A study of premature infants fed cold formula, J. Pediat. 61:556-561, 1962.

Hubbard, E.: How we solve breast-feeding problems RN 33:46+, March, 1970.

Iffrig, Sister M. C.: Nursing care and success in breast feeding, Nurs. Clin. N. Amer. 3:345-354, June, 1968.

Kallaus, J.: The child with cleft lip and palate: the mother in the maternity unit, Amer. J. Nurs. 65:120, April, 1965.

La Leche League International: The womanly art

of breast feeding, Franklin Park, Ill., 1963, The Interstate Printers & Publishers, Inc.

Larson, G. I.: What every nurse should know about congenital syphilis, Nurs. Outlook **13**: 52-55, March, 1965.

Marlow, D. R.: Textbook of pediatric nursing, ed. 3, Philadelphia, 1969, W. B. Saunders Co.

Martin, L. W., Gilmore, A., Peckham, J., and Baumer, J.: Nursing care of infants with esophageal anomalies, Amer. J. Nurs. **66**:2463, Nov., 1966.

O'Grady, R. S.: Feeding behavior in infants, Amer. J. Nurs. **71**:736-739, April, 1971.

Pomeroy, M. R.: Sudden death syndrome, Amer. J. Nurs. **69**:1886-1890, Sept., 1969.

Pryor, K.: Nursing your baby, New York, 1963, Harper & Row, Publishers.

Ragsdale, N., and Koch, R.: Phenylketonuria, detection and therapy, Amer. J. Nurs. **64**:90-96, Jan., 1964.

Shepard, K. S.: Care of the well baby, Philadelphia, 1968, J. B. Lippincott Co.

Silverman, W. A., Parke, P. C.: The newborn: keep him warm, Amer. J. Nurs. **65**:81-84, Oct., 1965.

Spock, B.: Baby and child care, revised ed., New York, 1968, Duell, Sloan & Pearce, Inc.

Thompson, E. D.: Pediatrics for practical nurses, ed. 2, Philadelphia, 1970, W. B. Saunders Co.

Thompson, L.: Nursery infection—apparent and inapparent, Amer. J. Nurs. **65**:801, Nov., 1965.

Whitley, N. N.: Breast feeding the premature, Amer. J. Nurs. **70**:1909, Sept., 1970.

Zickefoose, M.: Feeding the child with a cleft palate, J. Amer. Diet. Ass. **36**:129-131, 1960.

Special aids

Mead Johnson Laboratories: Series of five pamphlets on "variations and minor departures in normal infants," Evansville, Ind., 1968.

UNIT VIII

GROWTH, DEVELOPMENT, AND HEALTH SUPERVISION

20
Physiological growth

Concepts of growth and development

As the child grows up he is constantly changing physically and functionally. This is the main factor that distinguishes the child from the adult. Growth is exhibited by all healthy children, although it may be impaired by malnutrition and disease. Growth is the one feature that sets apart "pediatrics" as a specialty.

Every nurse interested in the care of children needs to have a basic understanding of human growth and development. Such an understanding will be of great help in evaluating the physical, intellectual, emotional, and social behavior of the dynamic child patient.

TERMINOLOGY

The terms "growth" and "development" are closely bound together. Changes in structure (growth) are accompanied by changes in function (development). As a child grows in size he grows up or matures mentally, emotionally, and socially. Differences in the way a child thinks, feels, or acts are just as real as changes in size.

As growth and development proceed, various levels of maturity are observable. *Maturation* is the process whereby inherited tendencies begin to unfold, independent of any special practice or training.

Each child has his own built-in growth pattern. Some children have patterns that allow them to mature very rapidly; other children are very slow physically, mentally, and emotionally and are called late maturers. There can be a wide range in the growth and development rates of normal children. Mary enjoyed walking at 12 months of age; her sister was 15 months old when she took her first steps. Each child is born with an internal drive to mature as fast as he can. The child is his own best guide, and when he is ready, he will take each succeeding step toward maturity himself.

Because of similarities in children, cultures, learning methods, and child rearing practices, generalizations can be made concerning growth and development. Although these generalizations are not applicable in every case, they do provide valuable points of departure in understanding and dealing with groups. This discussion of growth and development follows the child through an orderly sequence beginning with the prenatal phase and continuing through babyhood, childhood, and adolescence.

PRINCIPLES

The normal growth of a child through the successive periods of babyhood, childhood, and adolescence is guided by certain

TABLE 20-1. Progressive stages of development

Stages of life	Divisions of life stages	Chronological age
Prenatal		
Conception to birth	Germinal	Conception to 10 days' gestation
	Embryonic	10 days to 2 months' gestation
	Fetal	2 months' gestation to birth
Babyhood		
Birth to 1 year	Newborn (neonate)	Birth to 1 month
	Infancy	1 month to 1 year
Childhood		
1 to 12 years	Toddler	1 to 3 years
	Preschool	3 to 6 years
	School	6 to 10 years
	Preadolescence	10 to 12 years
Adolescence		
12 to 19 years	Early adolescence	12 to 16 years
	Late adolescence	16 to 19 years

basic principles. They may be stated as follows: (1) growth occurs in an orderly sequence; (2) growth, although continuous, is characterized by spurts and periods of relative rest; (3) growth progresses at different rates, the speed of growth being highly individualized from child to child; (4) different body structures grow at different rates at different ages; and (5) growth is a total process involving the "whole child."

Orderly sequence

Growth occurs in an orderly sequence and is continuous. The sequence of growth is the same for all children, even though some children do things earlier than others. Children generally creep before they stand and stand alone before they walk. The *average* child talks before he reads and usually reads before he can write. One child will read at 4 years of age, and another will read at 6 years of age. What happens at one stage influences what happens in the next stage; each stage in the development of the individual is an outgrowth of an earlier stage. During the first year the baby babbles; as he grows, he begins to say simple words. The toddler uses words in phrases, and the preschooler uses words in short sentences. No child speaks clearly before babbling, and each stage in the sequence can surely be anticipated.

Continuity

Growth continues from the moment of conception until the individual reaches maturity, but at no time is growth even and regular. There are spurts and rest periods within the same child even though there are no real interruptions until growth is completed. Growth is greatest during the prenatal period and is still rapid during babyhood (infancy) and early childhood. It is slow but constant in middle childhood. It shows a spurt during early puberty and then tapers off in the latter part of puberty.

Differences in growth rates

Children who are tall at one age are tall at other ages, just as those who are short remain short. The rate of growth is consistent, and each child has his own unique growth timetable. A child who develops rapidly at first will continue to do so. Jimmy sat alone at 6 months of age and walked alone at 9 months of age. His brother John sat alone at 8 months and walked alone at 15 months. Even in the same family no two children grow at the same rate.

Variation of growth rates for different body structures

Not all parts of the body mature at the same time. The brain attains its adult size when the child is about 6 or 7 years of age, but it certainly does not attain organization until many years later! Different phases of physical and mental growth occur at their own individual rates and reach maturity at different times.

Growth as a total process

The child does not grow physically one day and mentally the next day. He grows physically, mentally, socially, and emotionally at the same time. The child develops as a whole being. Changes in interest and mental growth are closely related to growth in walking and talking. Growth is a total process involving the whole child, not just his body, his mind, or his emotions. Each child passes slowly and almost imperceptibly from stage to stage, preserving a patterned integration of behavior throughout his life.

INFLUENCES AND LIMITATIONS

Growth is an inborn characteristic in every normal child and is continuous until about 20 years of age. Sometimes growth is retarded temporarily, but unless the process is deterred for a long period the expected potential, although perhaps delayed, is usually achieved. Every child's growth (pattern, rate, rhythm, and extent) is governed by endocrine, genetic, and environmental factors. These factors must be considered when evaluating physical retardation or overgrowth in any child.

Endocrine influences

Widely distributed throughout the body are small, ductless glands that secrete substances directly into the bloodstream. These complex chemical substances, called *hormones*, control and integrate various body activities. Normal growth is an expression of the precise balance of hormones secreted by the anterior pituitary gland, thyroid gland, gonads (testes or ovaries), and adrenal cortex. Any slight derangement involving either a decrease or an increase of any hormone may throw the system out of balance, causing abnormalities such as idiocy, dwarfism, gigantism, sexual precocity, and sterility. In more severe situations glandular malfunction may produce life-threatening syn-

dromes such as diabetic acidosis and Addison's disease.

Genetic influences

Heredity. An understanding of the process of conception provides some appreciation of the characteristics a child inherits from his parents. The story of the development of a new life, the uniting of two single microscopic cells to become a complex, integrated human being, is a story of miracles.

Within the chromosomes of the *zygote,* or fertilized egg, are a large number of smaller units called *genes.* These genes are handed down from the parents to the child; they control hereditary traits. Each hereditary trait is passed on through a gene or a combination of genes. Like the chromosomes, the genes are also in pairs; for example, there is one gene for hair color in one chromosome and another gene for hair color in a related chromosome. These genes interact in a number of complex ways.

The sex and inherited characteristics of a baby are established at the moment of conception when the male sex cell, the spermatozoon, penetrates the female sex cell, or ovum. Within a fertilized cell are twenty-two chromosomes plus an X chromosome from the female and twenty-two chromosomes plus an X or Y chromosome from the male. Half the chromosomes are given by the mother and half by the father. Ova contain only X chromosomes. If an ovum is fertilized by a sperm cell containing a Y chromosome, the resulting child will be a male. However, if the sex-determining chromosome contributed by the father happens to be an X chromosome, the offspring will be a girl. The father's contribution is the crucial factor in sex determination. The fertilized cell divides first into two cells, then four; this division of cells is repeated over and over as the individual grows.

Sexual differences. Certain general sexual differences in growth occur at different ages. Boys are usually larger than girls until 6 years of age. Girls tend to weigh more than boys until puberty. At all ages the muscular development of boys is more advanced than that of girls.

Racial characteristics. Certain racial characteristics in growth and stature may have a genetic basis. Significant differences have been noted among different groups. Children of the Oriental race are usually shorter than those of the Caucasian race. Negro children seem to manifest a more rapid bone maturation than do Caucasian children. However, when socioeconomic conditions are the same for Negro, Caucasian, and Oriental children, no marked difference in skeletal development is apparent.

Inborn errors of metabolism. Anomalies of the genes may lead to faulty development. Glycogen-storage disease, galactosemia, and improper protein metabolism causing phenylketonuria (PKU) originate in one or more mutational events. The genetic constitution of an individual is so altered in any of these conditions that normal growth and development are disrupted.

A genetic mutation of grave consequences is Tay-Sachs disease. Apparently healthy at birth, the infant, after about 6 months of life, becomes apathetic and displays definite developmental arrest, wasting, and mental deterioration; early death results.

Environmental influences

Environment and heredity are two great interrelated forces in the growth of the child. From birth onward, children show distinct marks of individuality. Some children are active, some lethargic; some are outgoing and aggressive, others shy and timid. Some children demand attention; others seem to be self-sufficient. A child not only interprets his environment in terms of his inherited tendencies and mental ability but also in terms of good health and good emotional balance. A strong, happy child will make the best use of his environment and will be most able to deal with obstacles or defects in his surround-

ings. The environment is vitally important to growth. An environment that provides satisfying experiences fosters growth.

Home and family. To develop naturally and wholesomely, the child needs devoted mothering and a family setting that is loving, permissive, accepting, and understanding. Such a home is one in which the child has a mother and father who love each other, love the child, and fulfill his basic needs. At birth the child has basic needs for the maintenance of life. Proper food, love, shelter, and protection increase the child's capacity to grow and develop. Lack of affection alone will result in little or no smiling, loss of appetite, poor sleep, failure to gain weight, and persistent respiratory infections. Numerous studies indicate that children deprived of love, parents, and home fail to thrive.*

Nutrition. The growing child is vulnerable to many nutritional inadequacies. Disturbed patterns of skeletal development caused by the lack or overabundance of one nutrient exemplify the need for "balance." A well-balanced diet is essential for the development of bones and teeth, good skin, and general physical well-being (Table 20-2). Clarification of the nutritional needs of children and a general abundance of high-quality foods have simplified the feeding of infants and children. Despite this, nutritional inadequacies may occur in the midst of plenty through faulty dietary habits, food fads, or psychic tensions centering around mealtime and the feeding situation.

Overnutrition rather than undernutrition seems to present more problems in the United States. However, a severe form of protein deprivation, kwashiorkor, is common in underdeveloped countries of South America and Africa. Kwashiorkor is found among children under 4 years of age. Characteristically, these children lag in growth and in skeletal development.

Disease. Illness is both a physical and

---

*Brady, S.: Patterns of mothering, New York, 1956, International Universities Press, Inc., p. 97.

TABLE 20-2. Clinical signs of nutritional status*

	Good	Poor
General appearance	Alert, responsive	Listless, apathetic, cachexic
Hair	Shiny, lustrous; healthy scalp	Stringy, dull, brittle, dry, depigmented
Neck (glands)	No enlargement	Thyroid enlarged
Skin (face and neck)	Smooth, slightly moist; good color, reddish pink mucous membranes	Greasy, discolored, scaly
Eyes	Bright, clear; no fatigue circles beneath	Dryness, signs of infection, increased vascularity, glassiness, thickened conjunctiva
Lips	Good color, moist	Dry, scaly, swollen; angular lesions (stomatitis)
Tongue	Good pink color, surface papillae present, no lesions	Papillary atrophy, smooth appearance; swollen, red, beefy (glossitis)
Gums	Good pink color; no swelling or bleeding, firm	Marginal redness or swelling, receding, spongy
Teeth	Straight, no crowding, well-shaped jaw, clean, no discoloration	Unfilled caries, absent teeth, worn surfaces, mottled, malposition
Skin (general)	Smooth, slightly moist, good color	Rough, dry, scaly, pale, pigmented, irritated, petechiae, bruises
Abdomen	Flat	Swollen
Legs, feet	No tenderness, weakness, or swelling; good color	Edema, tender calf, tingling, weakness
Skeleton	No malformations	Bowlegs, knock-knees, chest deformity at diaphragm, beaded ribs, prominent scapulae
Weight	Normal for height, age, body build	Overweight or underweight
Posture	Erect, arms and legs straight, abdomen in, chest out	Sagging shoulders, sunken chest, humped back
Muscles	Well developed, firm	Flaccid, poor tone; undeveloped, tender
Nervous control	Good attention span for age; does not cry easily, not irritable or restless	Inattentive, irritable
Gastrointestinal function	Good appetite and digestion; normal, regular elimination	Anorexia, indigestion, constipation, or diarrhea
General vitality	Endurance, energetic, sleeps well at night; vigorous	Easily fatigued, no energy, falls asleep in school, looks tired, apathetic

*From Williams, S. R.: Nutrition and diet therapy, St. Louis, 1969, The C. V. Mosby Co., p. 372.

a psychological hazard for the young child. Arrested growth is the obvious effect of fever and anorexia. Prolonged illness causes a definite decrease in the rate of growth and height as well as decreased ability to function. Any disease that interferes with physical activity and metabolic processes over a long period will deter normal progress.

Although there may be some growth loss during a minor illness, a subsequent growth spurt will compensate for the temporary setback.

Uncontrolled diabetes always results in retarded growth in both height and weight. A chronic heart disability associated with anoxia hampers growth as also do malabsorption syndromes such as cystic fibrosis and celiac disease.

Growth and development depend on each other and represent a continuous process of interactions between genetic potential on one hand and environment on the other. The kind of environment a child lives in will determine whether or not he will realize all his inborn capacities for physical, social, mental, and emotional growth. Although nothing can make a child do more than his inborn capacities permit, he must have a favorable environment to develop and learn as fast as his growth patterns allow.

Physical growth

Although all phases of growth are continuous and take place concurrently, for convenience and clarity discussions of the main aspects of growth and development will be presented separately. Since physical growth is most obvious, it shall be discussed first.

Physical growth may be divided into four well-defined periods:
1. The period of very rapid growth during babyhood
2. The period of slow, steady growth during the childhood years
3. The period of the growth spurt during puberty
4. The period of decreasing growth and attainment of maximum height

The greatest increase in growth usually occurs during the early part of babyhood. Small, steady gains continue during the slow periods. This general pattern of growth is characteristic of all the body systems with two exceptions. The nervous system grows rapidly during infancy, then decelerates, and after puberty ceases growing; the reproductive organs, on the other hand, grow very slowly until sexual maturation, which occurs during the pubertal spurt.

Measurements of height and weight are commonly used to show that a boy or girl of a particular age and height should weigh within a certain number of pounds. In the course of development, observable trends in height and weight imply that one can draw certain conclusions regarding these aspects of growth. In connection with growth, norms can be successfully determined for a group of children and may serve as a point of reference for making comparisons. However, any table of averages should be interpreted with caution.

Although these tables may accurately state averages, they do not necessarily state what is desirable for individuals. (See Fig. 20-2.)

The best method of evaluating a child's general growth progress is by comparing the child with himself from time to time. A large number of observations and measurements recorded periodically demonstrates the individuality of the child's own progress. The grid, a special graph devised by Wetzel,* has become a common instrument for evaluating the individual's progress.

Height

Infants average about 20 inches in length at birth. During the first year of life the child grows about 10 inches. Five inches are added during the second year, and the child grows 3 inches per annum during the preschool period. From the sixth to the tenth year of life the annual gain is reduced to approximately 2 inches. The maximum growth rate occurs during the pubertal period at the approximate time of sexual maturity. Growth in height reaches a peak for boys at about 14 years of age and a year or so earlier for girls. It ceases sometime before the twenties. (See Fig. 20-1.)

Puberty occurs at widely different ages. An early pubertal growth spurt is associated with an early cessation of growth. Individuals who mature late tend to grow for a longer period of time and ultimately become tall adults.

Weight

At birth the infant weighs about 7½ pounds. This weight doubles by the end of the fifth month of life, and by 1 year the birth weight has approximately tripled. A sharp drop in the rate of gain occurs after the first year. The child characteristically appears lanky and even skinny. During the preschool years the weight rises

---

*Wetzel, N. C.: The baby grid. An application of the grid technique to growth and development in infants, J. Pediat. 29:439-454, 1946; Benz, G. S.: Pediatric nursing, ed. 5, St. Louis, 1964, The C. V. Mosby Co.

Text continued on p. 272.

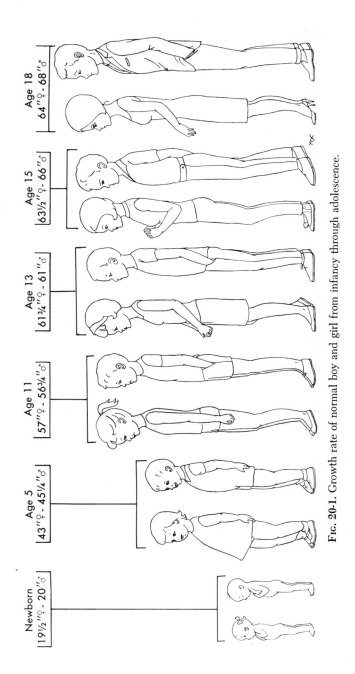

FIG. 20-1. Growth rate of normal boy and girl from infancy through adolescence.

INFANT GIRLS

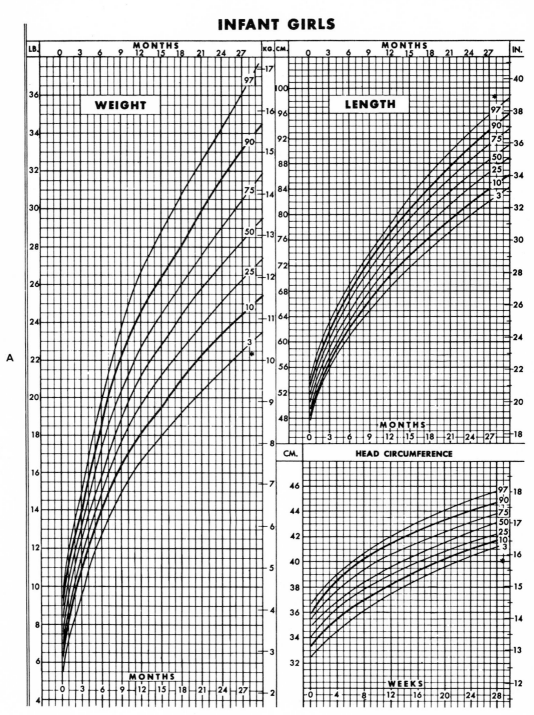

FIG. 20-2. A to **D,** The percentiles on these charts are based on repeated measurements of children under comprehensive studies of health and development by Harold C. Stuart, M.D., and associates, Department of Maternal and Child Health, Harvard School of Public Health, Boston, Mass. The charts were constructed by the staff of the department for use at the Infant's Hospital. (Reproduced with permission of the Children's Hospital Medical Center, Boston, Mass.)

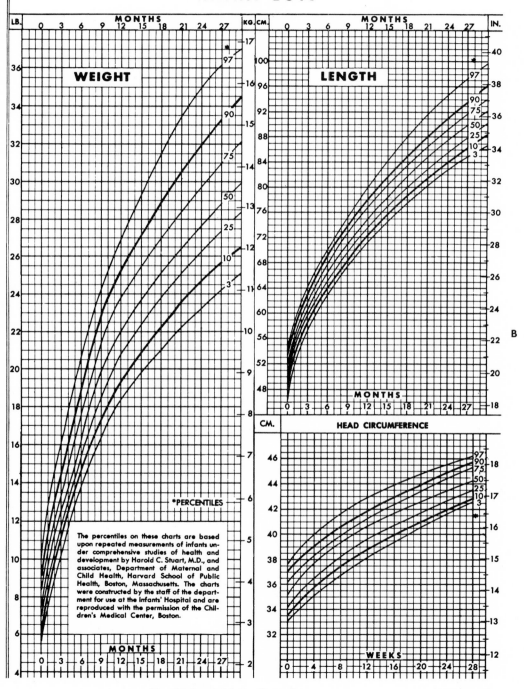

INFANT BOYS

WEIGHT

LENGTH

HEAD CIRCUMFERENCE

*PERCENTILES

The percentiles on these charts are based upon repeated measurements of infants under comprehensive studies of health and development by Harold C. Stuart, M.D., and associates, Department of Maternal and Child Health, Harvard School of Public Health, Boston, Massachusetts. The charts were constructed by the staff of the department for use at the Infants' Hospital and are reproduced with the permission of the Children's Medical Center, Boston.

FIG. 20-2, cont'd. For legend see p. 268. *Continued.*

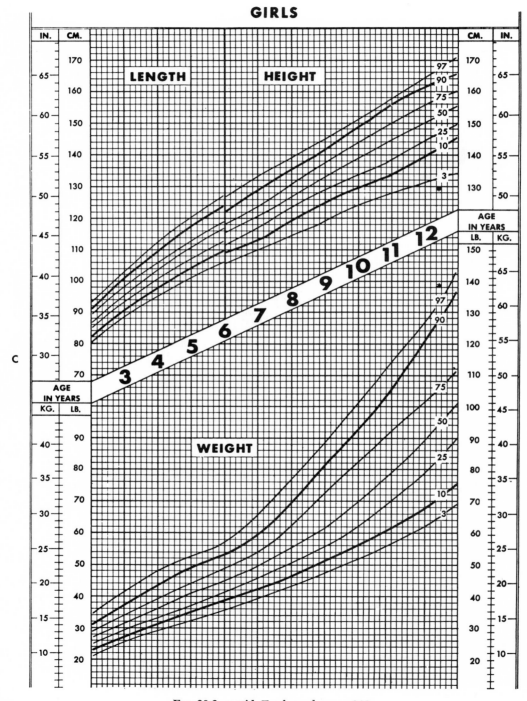

FIG. 20-2, cont'd. For legend see p. 268.

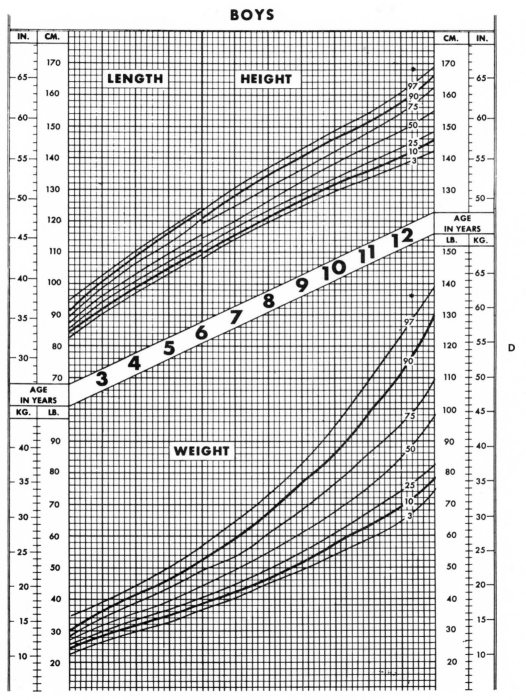

FIG. 20-2, cont'd. For legend see p. 268.

slowly, averaging about 5 pounds each year.

During the school years the weight gain is slightly increased. Weight varies more than height, since it is readily susceptible to external factors such as dietary intake.

Generally, boys are taller and heavier than girls except in the years preceding puberty. A rapid gain in weight usually occurs in both sexes during puberty, cor-

responding closely with the gain in height. Girls begin their preadolescent growth spurt at about 10 to 12 years of age, 2 years earlier than boys. Girls also reach their adult proportions sooner than boys.

Body proportions (Fig. 20-3)

There are distinct changes in body proportions between birth and maturity. The small child not only differs from the adult

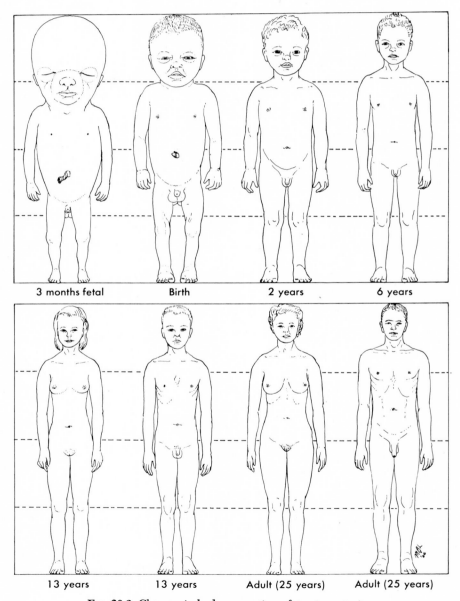

| 3 months fetal | Birth | 2 years | 6 years |

| 13 years | 13 years | Adult (25 years) | Adult (25 years) |

Fig. 20-3. Changes in body proportions, fetus to maturity.

in size but also in body form. At birth the head is relatively large, about one fourth of the total body length, whereas in the adult it is about one eighth of the body length. The arms and legs are relatively short. During infancy the trunk is longer than the extremities. The midpoint of the total length of the infant is at the umbilicus, whereas in the adult it is at the symphysis pubis.

During puberty, adult proportions are attained, and the characteristic mature body shape for each sex becomes differentiated. The straight leg lines of the young girl become curved by 15 years of age. Her hips grow wider, but her shoulders remain narrow. The boy's shoulders become broader, whereas his hips remain narrow.

Body proportion and build, or physique, is unique to the individual. Within his own general pattern—slender, stocky, muscular—the child's body build seems to be constant.

Bone development

During the early days of fetal development, bones begin as simple connective tissue. Later, this tissue becomes cartilage. By the end of the fifth month of gestation, certain mineral salts, especially calcium phosphate, are deposited in the cartilage, causing it to harden. Cartilage is gradually replaced by bone; this process is called *ossification*. During the early years of life, cartilage persists between the diaphysis (shaft) and epiphyses (ends) of long bones. Bones grow in length by a continual thickening of the epiphyseal cartilage. (See Fig. 20-4.)

As the child grows, changes occur in the texture, size, and shape of the "old" bones, and new bones appear. The process of skeletal maturation is perhaps the best evidence of general growth. Bone development continues in an orderly sequence and is completed by the third decade of life.

Bone age can be determined by x-ray examination of certain joints. The information gained is compared with a standard.

The x-ray films are studied to detect the following:

1. The appearance of new bones
2. Changes in the contour of the ends of bones
3. The union of the epiphyses with the bone shaft

Growth of the long bones is complete when the epiphyses and diaphysis are fused.

Bone development of the hand and wrist is a good index of the individual's progress in skeletal growth. Since boys lag behind girls in bone development at all ages, separate standards are used.

At birth the ends of the arm and wrist bones (epiphyses) are not developed; the carpal bones are not present. Shortly thereafter, the carpal bones and epiphyses gradually appear, and changes in the size and contour of the ends of bones continue through the school years. Bone development of the wrist and hand is complete at the seventeenth year of life for girls and 2 years later for boys.

Tooth development (Fig. 20-5)

The foundation of a child's tooth structure is formed early in fetal life. At birth, all the temporary (deciduous or baby) teeth and the first permanent teeth (6-year molars) are developing in the child's jaw. Dentition is characterized by wide variation.

It is not always possible to predict exactly when the first tooth will erupt, but it is possible to predict with some accuracy which teeth will erupt first. The two lower central incisors usually appear first, between 5 and 7 months. The upper central incisors appear next. Most children have six teeth at 1 year of age and all twenty deciduous teeth by 2½ years of age.

There is a wide variation in the pattern of temporary tooth shedding and permanent tooth eruption. Before the appearance of the first molars (6-year molars), all the permanent teeth are growing and maturing. During this time the roots of the temporary teeth are disappearing by the

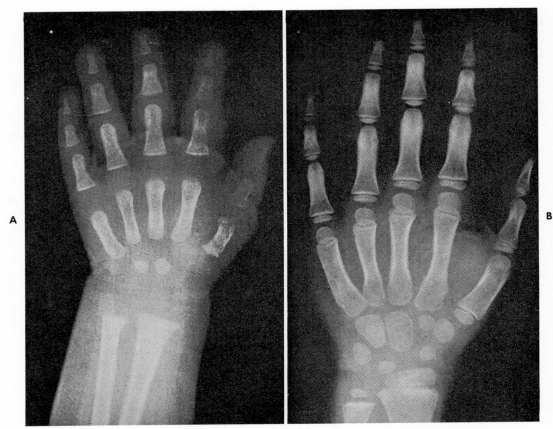

FIG. 20-4. Progressive ossification of the hand of a white female. **A**, Age 3 months. **B**, Age 6 years 3 months. **C**, Age 11 years 3 months. **D**, Age 16 years 3 months. (From Todd, T. W.: Atlas of skeletal maturation, St. Louis, 1937, The C. V. Mosby Co.)

process of resorption. Only the crown of the temporary tooth is left when the permanent tooth below is ready to erupt. The loose tooth then drops out. The care and preservation of the temporary teeth are important. Unless they are beyond repair, temporary teeth should not be pulled out. They contribute in large measure to proper alignment and good health of the permanent teeth.

Tetracycline antibiotics have an adverse effect on newly formed bones. The drug stains developing teeth with a yellow-brown material. Tetracyclines also cross the placenta. After the fourth month of gestation, the deciduous teeth of the developing fetus are also affected. Such dis-coloration of the teeth may be avoided by *not using* the drugs during pregnancy and the first 8 years of life.

Motor growth

As the child's body grows he acquires the ability to function in increasingly complex ways. Motor changes accompany physical growth. Motor abilities involve various types of body movements that result from the coordinated activity of nerves and muscles. Maturation of the nervous system and learning are interrelated in the acquisition of motor abilities.

Motor development is the process of learning, controlling, and integrating muscular responses. Great advances in body

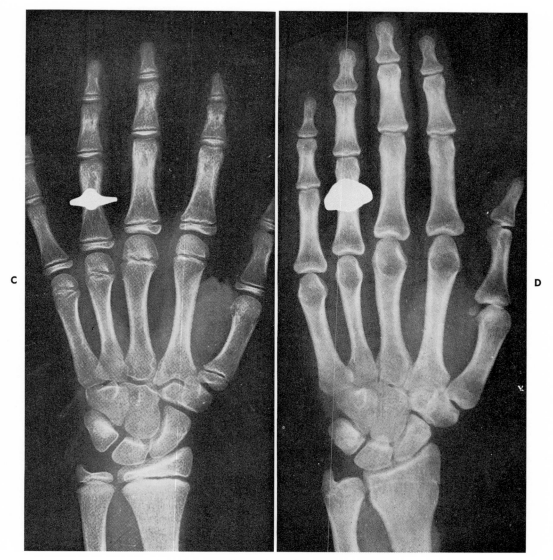

C

D

FIG. 20-4, cont'd. For legend see opposite page.

control and locomotion are accomplished during the first 2 years of life. At first an uncoordinated, helpless infant, the child is soon able to sit, stand, walk, reach, and grasp.

Like other phases of growth, motor development unfolds in an orderly sequence that is closely related to the maturation of the nervous system. It follows a definite sequence. Characteristically, motor development begins in the head region of the

individual and moves downward toward the feet (cephalocaudal). Development also tends to proceed from the center of the body toward the extremities (proximodistal). The sequence of motor development is similar for all children, but the rate at which the development progresses varies with each individual child.

Prehension and locomotion provide examples of the usual sequences in the course of motor development.

275

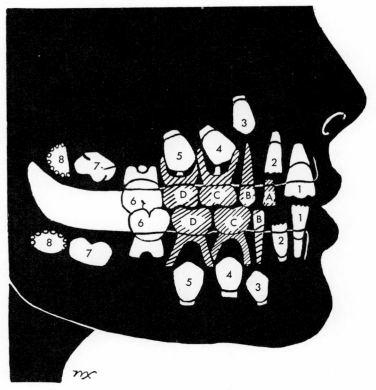

Fig. 20-5. Illustration of 7-year-old child with good occlusion. Deciduous teeth. **A,** Lateral incisors; **B,** cuspids; **C,** first molars; **D,** second molars. Permanent teeth. **1,** Central incisors; **2,** lateral incisors; **3,** cuspids; **4,** first bicuspids; **5,** second bicuspids; **6,** first molars; **7,** second molars; **8,** site of wisdom teeth.

TABLE 20-3. Usual pattern of dentition

Teeth	Lower (mandibular) appear at age	Upper (maxillary) appear at age
Deciduous		
Central incisors	5 to 7 months	6 to 8 months
Lateral incisors	12 to 15 months	8 to 11 months
Cuspids (canines)	16 to 20 months	16 to 20 months
First molars	10 to 16 months	10 to 16 months
Second molars	20 to 30 months	20 to 30 months
Total per jaw—10		
Total set—20		
Permanent		
Central incisors	6 to 7 years	6 to 7 years
Lateral incisors	7 to 9 years	8 to 9 years
Cuspids (canines)	8 to 11 years	11 to 12 years
First bicuspids	10 to 12 years	10 to 11 years
Second bicuspids	11 to 13 years	10 to 12 years
First molars (6-year molars)	6 to 7 years	6 to 7 years
Second molars (12-year molars)	12 to 13 years	12 to 13 years
Third molars (wisdom teeth)	17 to 22 years	17 to 22 years
Total per jaw—16		
Total set—32		

FIG. 20-6. Developmental progression of prehensory behavior. **A,** 3 months—looks at cube. **B,** 5 months—looks and approaches. **C,** 6 months—looks and crudely grasps with whole hand.

Continued.

Prehension

The development of the ability to oppose the thumb to the fingers in picking up an object is preceded by reaching, grasping, and raking movements. Early attempts in reaching also involve eye-hand coordination. Effective use of the hands for picking up small objects or for grasping is called prehension. The developmental sequence proceeds from eye-hand coordination in grasping to reaching without looking, from large muscle activity of the arms and shoulders to fine muscle activity of the fingers, and from a crude pawing closure to a closure of the fingertips in a refined fashion.

FIG. 20-6, cont'd. Developmental progression of prehensory behavior. **D,** 9 months—looks and deftly grasps with fingers. **E,** 12 months—looks, grasps with forefinger and thumb, and deftly releases. **F,** 15 months—looks, grasps, and releases to build a tower of two blocks.

Gesell tested prehension by placing a little red cube before a baby. He described the grasping sequence as follows (Fig. 20-6):

Development progression in grasping

1. 12 weeks   Looks at cube
2. 20 weeks   Looks and approaches
3. 24 weeks   Looks and crudely grasps with whole hand
4. 36 weeks   Looks and deftly grasps with fingers
5. 52 weeks   Looks, grasps with forefinger and thumb, and deftly releases
6. 15 months   Looks, grasps, and releases to build a tower of two cubes*

---

*From Gesell, A., and Ilg, L. B.: The child from five to ten, New York, 1946, Harper & Row, Publishers.

Locomotion

The ability to walk alone is also attained gradually after a sequence of developments that can be traced back to the first days of life. Moving from place to place and walking are examples of gross motor skills. Complete establishment of this control usually takes most of the first year for early walkers and 15 to 16 months for those who mature later.

The walking sequence begins when the baby is able to hold his head up, and it is half accomplished when he can sit alone. When an infant is able to change from a prone to a sitting position, he tends to begin to creep. He usually creeps to an object or person, where he pulls himself to a standing position. Gradually he stands alone and finally walks independently.

Birth
Keeps his legs tucked up under him and bears his weight on his knees, abdomen, chest, and head.

2-3 months
Extends his legs and lifts his chest and head to look around.

5-6 months
Can sit up with support, hold his head up, and is alert to surroundings.

6½-7½ months
Sits up alone and steadily without support. Legs are bowed to help balance.

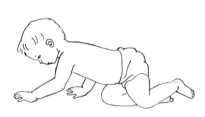

8-9 months
Creeping; the trunk is carried free from floor. With practice, rhythm appears and only one limb moves at a time.

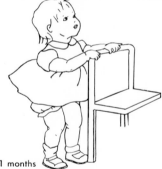

9-11 months
Pulls himself up and stands holding onto furniture. Feet far apart, head and upper trunk carried forward.

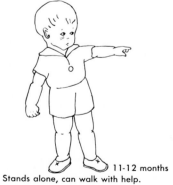

11-12 months
Stands alone, can walk with help.

12-14 months
Walks alone on wide base with legs far apart.

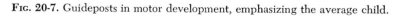

Fig. 20-7. Guideposts in motor development, emphasizing the average child.

The motor sequence (Fig. 20-7)

1. ½ to 1 month — Lifts head
2. 2 to 3 months — Raises chest
3. 3 to 4 months — Turns from side to back
4. 5 to 6 months — Sits with support
5. 6 to 7 months — Rolls from back to abdomen
6. 6½ to 7½ months — Sits alone
7. 8 to 9 months — Creeps
8. 9 to 11 months — Pulls self up
9. 11 to 12 months — Walks with help
10. 12 to 14 months — Walks alone

Prehension and locomotion develop independently of any teaching. Knowledge of these motor abilities "just comes." Each skill follows an orderly sequential course whose rate is little affected by environmental factors.

As each skill develops, opportunity to use it and practice it is necessary. This means that the child needs plenty of space for walking, objects to pick up and handle, and, most of all, he needs health, vigor, freedom, and encouragement to venture. The nurse who understands the development of motor skills will not restrict the child to his crib but, rather, encourage his full capacity for motor growth!

21
Psychological growth

We have seen from our discussion in Chapter 20 that the physiological growth of a child—his physical and motor development—is of great importance. Indeed, as nurses, our most immediate concern is expressed in meeting the pressing physical needs of the individual. However, these needs, although significant, do not represent the total requirements of a human being. To experience the potential intended for them as individuals, people must mature psychologically. Furthermore, they must incorporate within their lives a philosophy that will bring satisfying meaning and purpose to their activities and a moral sensitivity to the needs of their world, which will lead to constructive contributions to society. Mankind has seen too often the results of the activities of half-made men, near-perfect physical specimens who have nonetheless brought havoc and misery to millions of people. These men, although only partially developed, do not recognize their needy state. Lacking the humbleness that enlarged perception grants, they struggle for power. If they gain power, and many times they do, the entire race may suffer. The psychological (that is, intellectual, emotional, social, and spiritual) growth of an individual is at least as important as his physical well-being. Many would say it is more important.

Intellectual development

Of all the factors influencing the overall development of the child, his intelligence seems to be the most important. Superior intelligence is associated with superior development, whereas inferior intelligence is associated with retarded development.

A child's intelligence will affect his observation, thought, and understanding. It strongly influences the level of difficulty at which the child is able to function efficiently and the scope of his activities.

Many changes take place in the intellectual life of the child as he develops from infancy to adulthood. At birth the centers of higher intellectual activity in the brain are not fully developed. Furthermore, the sensory acuity necessary for these higher intellectual functions is likewise immature. The mental world of the newborn infant seems to consist primarily of experiences arising through direct physical contact with the environment and through the sensations that originate within his own body. New experiences expand his mental world and are interpreted in the light of previous learning.

Beginning as early as the first year of life, children exhibit the ability to imagine and to engage in make-believe activities. Such make-believe activities aid in exploring the real world, organizing experiences, and solving problems. Through make-believe, the child is able to participate in a wider range of experiences and partially overcome his own limitations. Such fantasies are a necessary and normal part of learning.

As growth proceeds, the ability to concentrate develops. The child's span of attention is likely to be longer during activities that he has chosen or that are at least related to his own desires.

The development of a child's ability to reason is gradual and continuous. Although there are changes with age in the range and complexity of the problems that engage the attention of children, the development of reasoning power is not characterized by distinct stages. The young child is concerned with events related to his own immediate experience and well-being. As he grows, he becomes increasingly able to occupy himself with more remote issues and deal with abstractions. Such changes can be noted in connection with the enlargement of the meanings associated with various terms in the language he uses, the interest and ability he eventually displays in facing social issues, and his ability to relate to events in the world beyond his immediate experience.

Emotional growth

Every infant, child, and adult possesses the drive to express himself in some way. The reaction that accompanies either the satisfaction or frustration of a basic need may be termed an "emotion." Another way of describing an emotional response is to define it as a psychological reaction caused by internal or external stimuli. Although emotions are not identical to basic drives, they are related. The basic drives can be physical, social, intellectual, or personal. Emotional experience includes feelings, impulses, and physical and physiological reactions. For example, if a baby's needs are fulfilled, he is happy, joyful, contented, or loving; if a baby's drives are frustrated, he is anxious, fretful, frightened, or angry. Physiological changes initiated by emotions may stimulate a person to violent action.

All emotions cause a physical response. But just as no two persons think or act alike, no two react to the same emotion in the same way. For example, because of fear one person may feel belligerent, another anxious, or still another depressed. As soon as one begins to experience emotion, physiological changes take place. Manifestations of these changes include facial expressions, laughter, and crying.

Emotions appear early in life. Even during the first days of life the infant's need to satisfy his physical needs is accompanied by emotional response. The infant usually reacts by crying or kicking. Soon the baby finds a given stimulation pleasant or unpleasant. When the infant is hungry or uncomfortable, an unpleasant state results, which he makes known by crying or restlessness. When his wants are satisfied, a pleasant state of well-being ensues, which is evidenced by cooing, gurgling, or sleep. Thus the emotional responses of the infant are initially stimulated by physiological needs.

Through a combination of maturation and learning, more specialized responses soon occur. By the end of the first year, emotions of fear, rage, excitement, anger, and joy become recognizable; and facial expression, vocalization, and body movement become part of the child's emotional equipment. Changes in the expression of the emotions continue progressively throughout the childhood years.

Love. Love is the most important of all the emotions because it is the foundation on which all positive relationships are built. The child's first love is centered on his mother, since she is the one who initially loves and serves him. The child's capacity for affection and love develops gradually from this early association. During the normal course of development the child transfers a part of his affection to other individuals who share his pleasures and achievements. Eventually this love will grow to form the nucleus of another family—his own. A child who receives loving and affectionate care is prepared to give as well as receive love. His security is not simply a passive thing but a safe feeling that lets him be venturesome in the belief that people will be good to him.

Fear. Fear is aroused naturally when the infant experiences any startling, sudden occurrence such as a loud noise, an unexpected jar, or a fall. These threats to

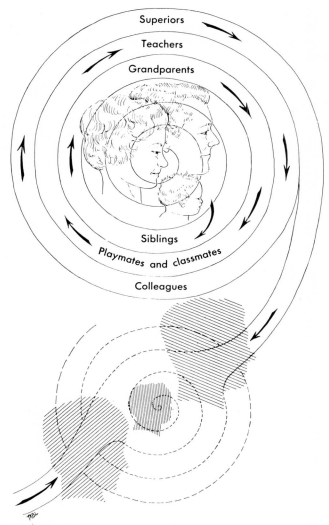

Superiors

Teachers

Grandparents

Siblings

Playmates and classmates

Colleagues

FIG. 21-1. During the normal course of development the child transfers a part of his affection to other individuals who share his pleasures and achievements. Eventually this love will grow to form the nucleus of another family—his own.

security are characterized by crying and general body distress. The young child acquires other fears that are associated with objects and persons in his immediate environment. As children become older, fearful responses become increasingly specific; they are expressed by withdrawal from the fearful situation. Later, children learn to avoid situations that cause anxiety.

Once a child becomes afraid in a certain situation, any repetition of the same or similar situation will reproduce fear. How-

ever, if the boy or girl learns that the situation is not truly hazardous, the fear diminishes and/or disappears. Reasonable fear is a valuable safeguard against many dangers. Fear acts as a check on behavior. A person may be driven to action by anger, hate, or jealousy, but his conduct is held within reasonable bounds through the fear of consequences. In other words, fear may act as a negative guide to more orderly behavior.

Anger. Anger denotes a variety of emotional states that range from turbulent rage to milder forms of resentment. In infancy, anger arises primarily through interference with body movement or gratification of basic needs such as feeding. Crying, screaming, biting, hitting, and kicking are expressions of anger. In early childhood, anger may take the form of numerous acts of disobedience and resistance. When the child learns to talk, he gains command of new ways to express his anger. Children may find outbursts of anger useful for attracting attention to themselves and for obtaining a desired end. Children are even more likely to give vent to anger when suffering from lack of sleep, hunger, or fatigue.

Anger may be controlled in small children by guarding the child's general health and physical condition and by providing regular meals, sleep, and time with his mother and father for pleasurable experiences. Parents can also aid by maintaining poise and self-control, refusing to be manipulated by theatrical displays of emotion (temper tantrums), and encouraging a friendly home atmosphere.

Jealousy. Jealousy is an emotional response compounded of anger, fear, and love. It is an emotion that, in general, seems to arise when persons or objects threaten to take away something, share something, or interfere with that which is felt to belong to oneself. In the young child, jealousy tends to develop when the child is threatened by possible loss of love as a result of the presence of a newborn brother or sister. Because of the mother's preoccupation with the infant, the older child may equate loss of time and attention with loss of love. He sees the younger sibling as a rival and becomes jealous. The reaction of the child may be positive and result in either aggression toward or competition with the new baby. Thus the jealous child may resort to hitting the baby or may turn to infantile habits to gain the attention he desires. A negative reaction may consist of withdrawal from competition or repression. For example, a child

may sulk or refuse meals. The expression of jealousy varies with age. Behavior caused by such personal envy gradually becomes less direct and less openly violent; it is more subtle but no less real.

The factors precipitating emotions and the reaction patterns they initiate have typical stages of development and can be traced just as the other stages of growth and development. The emotional responses of individuals not only vary in form and intensity from person to person but also from age to age. The emotions identified and the reactions they stimulate are closely related to the individual's maturity and life experience. Emotions always find an outlet; if the most desired expression is blocked, another, perhaps less desirable, is substituted. This observation has many practical applications and is basic to the understanding of many behavior problems and the concept of psychosomatic illness.

Social behavior and moral values

An individual's characteristic response to social situations is a useful way of describing personal-social behavior. Personal-social behavior includes all the modes of behavior that characterize the child's own individuality.

The dynamic interaction of a child's thoughts and feelings that produces his characteristic responses to his environment comprise his "personality." Personality includes one's intelligence, physique, habits, and appeal to others. As a child grows older, his ways of responding become more and more characteristic of himself. The first social group for a child is his family, a group that plays an important role in establishing his attitudes and habits.

The major source of personality growth for the child resides in the maturity and harmony of his parents. The parents provide the models that the child consciously and unconsciously emulates. Home is the place where the child learns, even as a tiny infant, what people and life are like.

At home he learns friendliness, confidence, security, belonging, loving, and sharing as these are reflected in the people in his immediate environment.

The awakening of social behavior manifests itself as the baby grows alert to his surroundings and is able to distinguish between persons and objects. During the first weeks of life the infant reacts instinctively to his immediate surroundings and those persons, particularly his mother, who care for him. The infant who is primarily concerned with satisfying his basic needs does not readily make distinctions between people and things. Soon, however, he begins to respond to the presence of others and their behavior toward him. The baby's awareness of persons around him grows out of the simple responses he gives as they care for him and supply his wants. For example, if a baby is handled gently and lovingly, his natural response will be a happy one such as cooing, smiling, or tranquil rest. If a baby is treated roughly with impatience, agitation, and frustration, he will respond accordingly, perhaps with fretful crying, kicking, or enraged screaming. Thus certain forms of social behavior begin to develop as the child responds to those in contact with him.

Early in babyhood the child imitates those about him, both adults and other babies, in order to become a part of the family or social group. At about 3 months of age the baby first imitates facial expressions, such as smiling and wincing. Gestures and movements such as waving "bye-bye," shaking the head, or throwing a kiss develop at approximately 6 months of age.

A happy, smiling child is a good indication that his social development is progressing well; and the framework for this positive, outgoing nature is built most firmly by parents who have made their child feel loved in the early months and years of life. The way people work and play, their ability to enjoy other people, and how they feel about tackling new things (even the foods they prefer or will not touch) have had beginnings early in life's experience. People can change, but the effects of early childhood experiences are likely to persist.

Probably the most important medium of socialization is language. Socrates said, "Speak that I may see thee." The early vocalizations of the infant quickly develop from throaty noises at 4 weeks of age to three-word sentences at 2 years of age. The young baby rapidly recognizes the urgency to verbalize as he becomes part of the social group. Although language at first consists of object naming and identification, it soon becomes a vehicle for the transportation of ideas. Hence hand in hand with language development goes the development of understanding.

In the first few weeks of life the infant has no understanding of his environment. Gradually, as language ability increases as a result of maturation and learning, the child becomes more able to understand what he observes. It is important to note, however, that no two children can be expected to have the same understanding of an object or situation, since no one has exactly the same intellectual abilities or experiences. If an infant is handicapped in sensory development through deafness or blindness, he will be handicapped in language growth and understanding. To the extent that a child is deprived of such sensory stimulation, his personal and social behavior is proportionately delayed or impaired.

The child learns the values and expectations of his culture through the examples and teachings that are provided by the key adults in his life. One of the important functions of the family is to help provide the appropriate learning experiences for the child during his first few years, whereby the primary drives will bring forth socially acceptable behavior. The child must learn to satisfy his needs in a culturally conforming manner. The hazards involved in this learning are great. Effective training helps build secure personalities whose capacities for adjustment to the needs of others is sufficient to assure wholesome and mutually satisfying relationships throughout life.

It is largely in the home that the child's basic moral and spiritual concepts are developed. Community agencies, school, and church make significant contributions, but they do not usually occupy the primary position in the child's esteem that is held by the home. It is trite, but true, to say that it is the parents' behavior and not their words that is the influencing factor. To re-word an old saying, "What they are speaks so loud that the child does not hear what they say."

In the development of a human being, physical growth, psychological development, and moral sensitivity should not proceed independently of each other. They are like branches of the same tree, which, when mature, provide strength, protection, meaning, and beauty to both the individual and his community.

22
Ages and stages

Many books have been written to describe the physical, motor, and psychological changes that take place as an individual goes through the process we call "growing up." Table 22-1 is designed to aid the student in the rapid identification of some of the outstanding characteristics of certain ages and the common challenges and problems they experience. The performance times noted are averages only. Individual children may be exceptions to the rule. (See Figs. 22-1 to 22-16.)

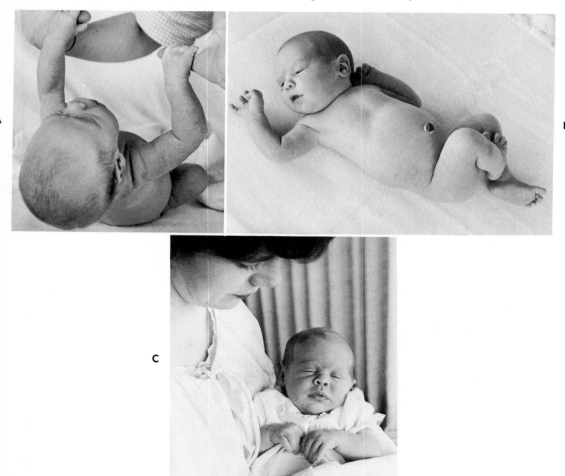

FIG. 22-1. Newborn infant: **A,** grasp reflex is strong; **B,** tonic neck posture is readily assumed; **C,** sleeps most of time.

TABLE 22-1. Ages and stages of maturation

Age	Physical growth	Motor development	Nutrition	Common behavior, activities, and problems	Basic psychosocial challenges*
Babyhood, 0-1 yr.					
Newborn (birth-1 mo.)	Average weight, 7½ lb.; average height, 20 in. (grows 10 in. during first year Pulse: 110-150 Respiration: 30-50	Readily assumes fetal position; Moro reflex present Raises head but not stable Can turn head from side to side	Breast milk or formula; supplementary vitamins and water (6 or more feedings daily) Schedule for introduction of semisolid foods depends on infant and physician Small amounts of thin pablum offered at 3-4 wk.	Sleeps about 20 hr. a day Cries when hungry Displays impassive face Regards face of an adult	In each stage of child development a central problem has to be solved, temporarily at least, if child is to proceed with vigor and confidence to next stage; each type of challenge appears in its purest form at a particular stage of child development
1-3 mo.	Average weight gain, 1 oz. per day (5-7 oz. weekly)	Activity diffuse and random Specific activities limited to reflexes Cries with tears Raises chest (3 mo.)	Pureed fruits and vegetables offered at 4-6 wk.; pureed meats at 3 mo.	May have periods of colic Responsive social smile; attentive to voices and light Coos Eyes can follow moving object 180 degrees	
3-6 mo.	Birth weight doubled at 5 mo.	Turns from side to back at 3-4 mo. Reaches out at objects Rolls over; Moro reflex absent at 5 mo. Sits with support	Egg yolks offered at 4 mo.	Sleeps through the night; 8-12 hr. Laughs aloud Babbles Recognizes mother Puts things in mouth	
6-11 mo.	First deciduous teeth appear	Sits alone Crawls Creeps Pulls self to standing position	Gradual substitution of home-mashed, cooked vegetables and junior foods, depending on dentition	Recognizes and avoids strangers at 6-8 mo. Responds to name Develops crude pincer grasp and hand transfer at 7 mo. Holds bottle at 7 mo. Well-defined pattern of sleep Has special blanket or cuddly toy Playpen useful Begins to feed self at 10 mo.	*Trust vs. mistrust:* As infant grows older, he acquires increasing awareness of himself as individual who can be happy and satisfied or frustrated and anxious; when he senses he is loved (i.e., his needs are gratified), he is happy, content; he begins to develop a basic sense of trust, which is fostered by a warm and loving mother-child relationship; discontinuities in care bring frustration and pain; child may then develop basic mistrust that may last throughout life

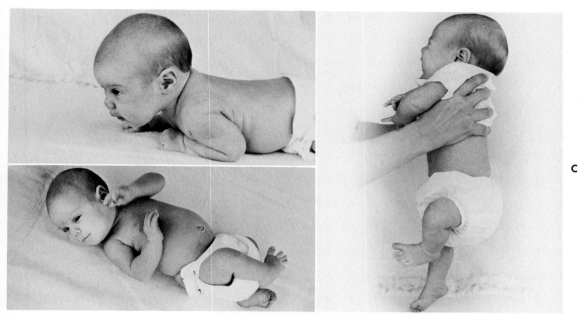

FIG. 22-2. At 1 month: **A,** lifts and turns head when supine; **B,** activity is diffuse and random; **C,** dance reflex when held upright.

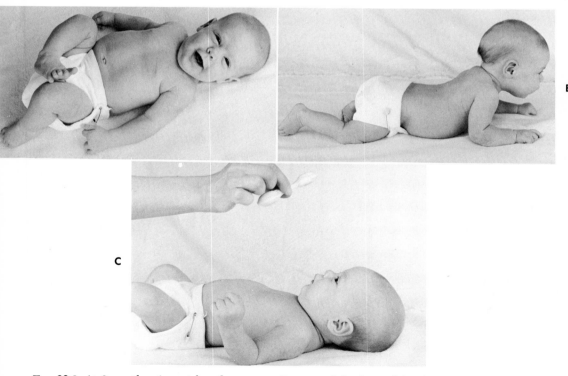

FIG. 22-3. At 2 months: **A,** social smile appears; **B,** can arch back, good head control; **C,** eyes follow objects.

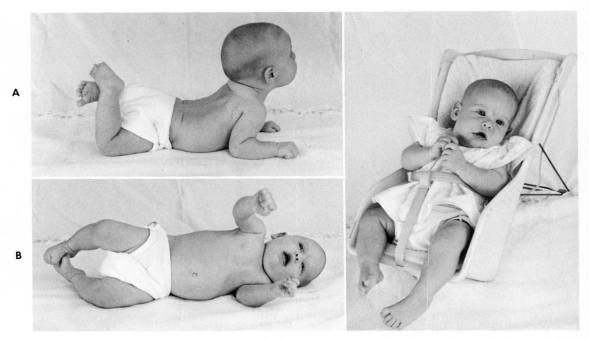

FIG. 22-4. At 3 months: **A,** raises head when prone, on forearms; **B,** turns from back to side; **C,** sits for short period when supported.

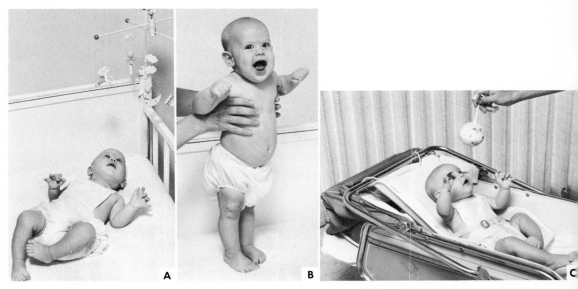

FIG. 22-5. At 4 months: **A,** gazes straight up, symmetrical posture predominates; **B,** pushes with feet when held erect; **C,** reaches and grasps at objects.

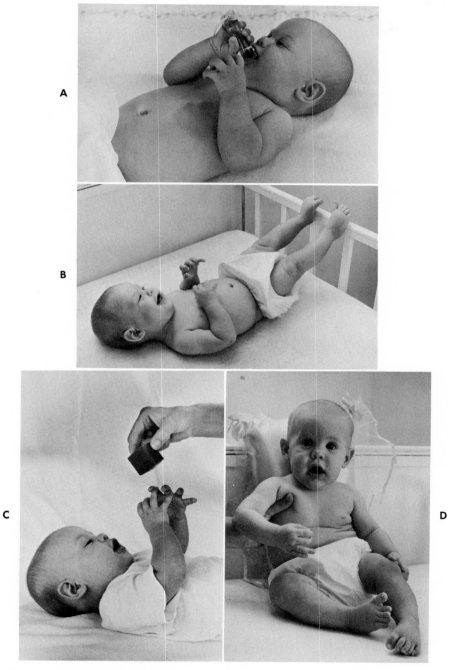

Fɪɢ. 22-6. At 5 months: **A**, manipulates and chews small objects; **B**, pushes with feet when supine; **C** and **D**, alert to surroundings.

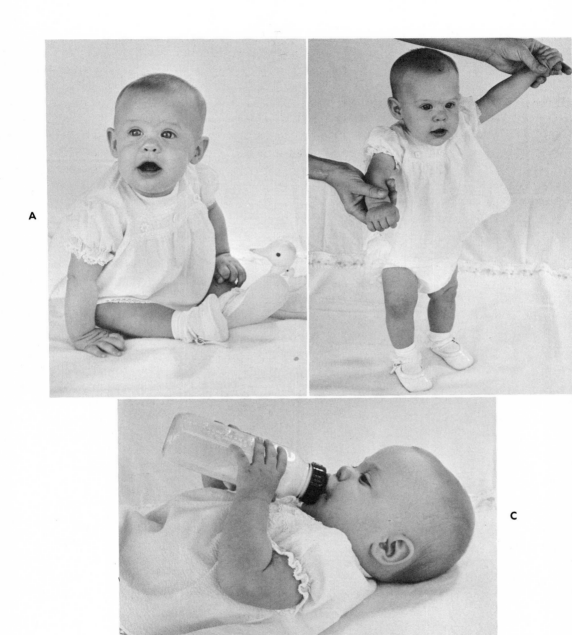

Fig. 22-7. At 6 months: **A**, sits alone, leaning forward on one hand; **B**, sustains own weight for short periods; **C**, places two hands around bottle.

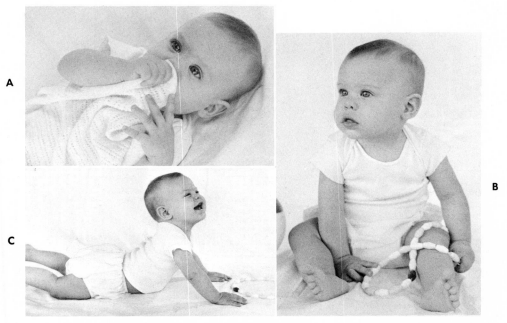

FIG. 22-8. At 7 months: **A**, sleeps with favorite blanket and thumb in mouth; **B**, sits alone without support; **C**, propels self forward on belly (crawling).

FIG. 22-9. At 8 months: **A,** bubbles, gurgles, loves to play with adults; **B,** content in playpen for short time; **C,** can lean forward and straighten up; **D,** tires easily.

FIG. 22-10. At 9 months: **A,** hand preference appears; **B,** can pull self to standing position; **C,** propels self forward on all fours, trunk above and parallel to floor (creeping).

FIG. 22-11. At 10 to 11 months: **A,** can sit indefinitely, good balance, straight back; **B,** drinks from cup with ease; **C,** cruises around, holding on to furniture.

FIG. 22-12. At 12 months: **A**, walks with assistance; **B**, stands alone on wide base; **C**, good finger-thumb opposition.

Table 22-1. Ages and stages of maturation (continued from p. 288)

Age	Physical growth	Motor development	Nutrition	Common behavior, activities, and problems	Basic psychosocial challenges
11-12 mo.	Birth weight tripled; height 29-30 in.; growth slows	Stands and walks with help. Drinks from cup. Picks up small objects with fingers	Eats 3 meals per day	Vocabulary of 2 or more words. Begins bowel training. Plays spontaneously	
Toddler, 1-3 yr.					
12-15 mo.	Has 6 teeth. Pulse: 100-140. Respiration: 26-34	Walks alone with wide stance and short steps. Can throw object. Prehension complete (15 mo.)	Enjoys finger foods; appetite normally decreases	One nap per day. Cooperates in dressing. Very active, assertive, and independent. Says "no, no"	Trust, cornerstone of a healthy personality, usually established by end of first year
15-18 mo.	Anterior fontanel closed. Abdomen protrudes	Plateau of motor development. Walks upstairs holding on. Seldom falls. Increasingly mobile	Small, attractive servings desired	Negativism begins. Vocabulary of 5 words. Follows simple commands. Thumbsucker. Into everything—accident hazard high. Pulls toys. Carries special toy or blanket. 10 words of jargon	*Self-esteem (autonomy) vs. shame and doubt:* Child's energies now centered around asserting that he is an individual with his own mind and will; he has to have right to choose; he wants to do more and more for himself; feelings of self-esteem, pride, and independence develop; with guidance from his parents and others, he learns to make decisions and to become more self-reliant; those who guide growing child wisely will be firm and tolerant of him and will avoid shaming him and causing him to doubt his sense of worth
18-24 mo.	Walks well. Seats self	Uses spoon ineptly	Introduce new food when child is hungriest	Fleeting attention span. Bowel control may be achieved	
2 yr.	Pulse: 90-120. Respiration: 20-35. 16 teeth. Weighs 26-28 lb.; grows 3-4 in. during second year	Runs up and down stairs alone. Opens doors. Self-feeding improves	Do not insist that child eat—but prevent snacking to sharpen appetite	Parallel play is characteristic; has difficulty playing *with* others and sharing. Bedtime ritual. Uses sentences of 3-4 words. Names 3 pictured objects	

Continued on p. 301.

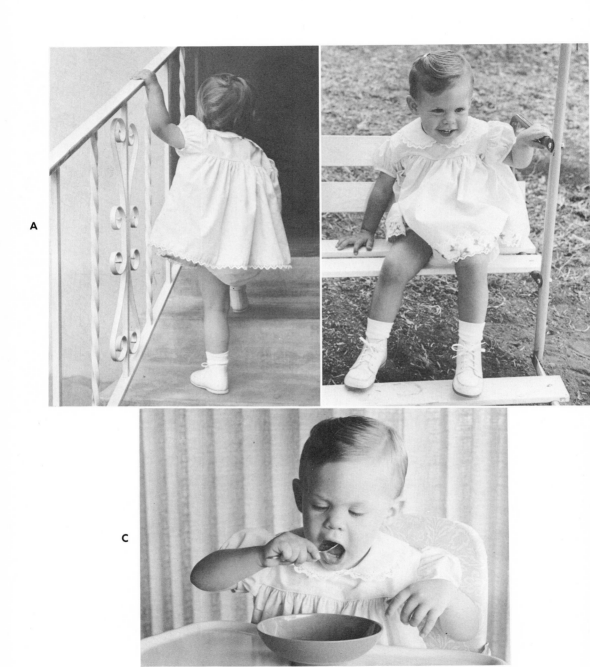

Fig. 22-13. At 15 months: **A**, climbs up stairs, holding on; **B**, plays outside; **C**, uses spoon to feed self.

FIG. 22-14. At 18 months: **A,** pets and friends are nice; **B,** loves to push and pull toys; **C,** needs independence but supervision too.

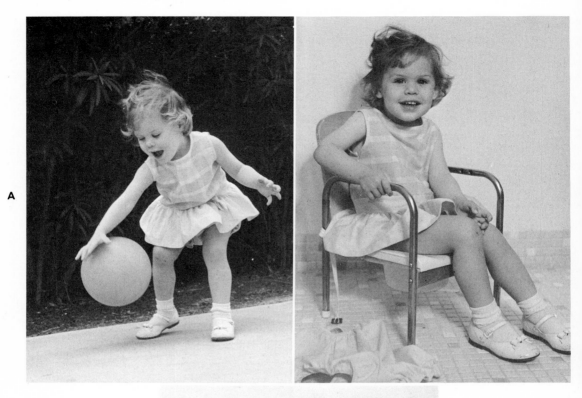

A

C

FIG. 22-15. At 24 months: **A**, muscular coordination greatly advanced; **B**, verbalizes toilet needs; **C**, drinks from straw.

Table 22-1. Ages and stages of maturation (continued from p. 297)

Age	Physical growth	Motor development	Nutrition	Common behavior, activities, and problems	Basic psychosocial challenges
2½-3 yr.	Full set of baby teeth	Increasing motor control Jumps	Mealtime should be happy time	Enjoys kiddie cars, large balls Vocabulary of 300-350 words Knows full name and sex Daytime bladder control Temper tantrums Discipline by firm, kind supervision and distraction	
Preschooler, 3-6 yr.					
3-4 yr.	Period of relatively slow growth; gains less than 5 lb. per year; height increase averages 3 in. per yr.	Uses stairs with alternating feet Strings large beads Hops on one foot	In hospital, toddlers and preschoolers often eat well together with supervision Habitual good nutrition brings current and future benefits	Relatively stable age Talks in sentences Vocabulary of 900 words Possibly has nursery school experiences May display sibling rivalry Sensitive observation of sex differences and parental attitudes toward sex Usually has nighttime bladder control Asks questions constantly Understands "taking turns" Beginning of religious awareness and training Foundations of spiritual-moral values	*Initiative vs. guilt:* Knowing that he is a person in his own right, child of 4 or 5 wants to find out what kind of person he can be; he imagines what it is like to be grown up; little girls want to be like "mamma" and boys like "daddy"; he imitates parents and yearns to share in their activities; by this age, conscience has developed; an age of avid curiosity and consuming fantasies, which lead to feelings of guilt and anxiety; initiative must be fostered and care taken that young child not feel guilty because he dared to dream
4-5 yr.		Climbs and jumps well Increasing finger dexterity		Relatively unstable age Can use blunt scissors, lace shoes, brush teeth May have imaginary playmate	
5-6 yr.	Begins to lose temporary teeth	Improved coordination; can hop, skip, and jump rope		Relatively tranquil age Kindergarten experience Enjoys group activities and conformity Prints first name Dresses and undresses without help Talks constantly	

Continued on p. 304.

Fig. 22-16. At 36 months: **A,** can brush teeth and wash hands; **B,** can put shoes on; **C,** can pump swing with legs; **D,** attempts to sing simple songs; **E,** knows age and sex, good balance; **F,** motherliness, enjoys parallel play.

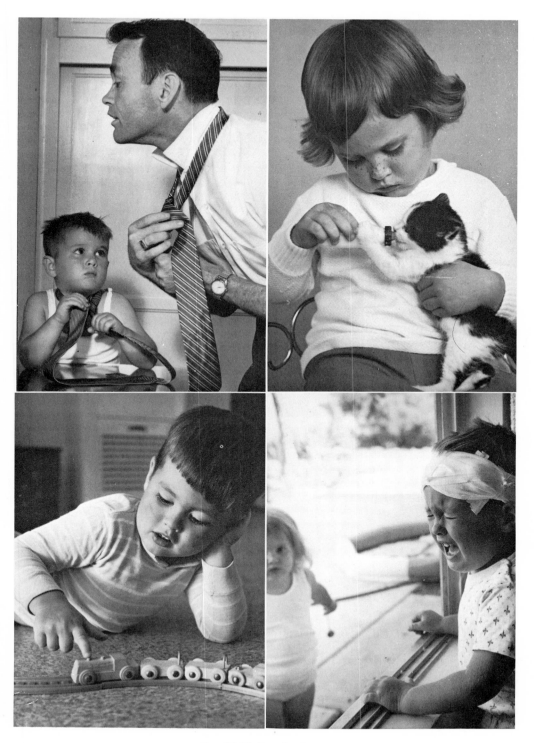

FIG. 22-17. Preschoolers.

Table 22-1. Ages and stages of maturation (continued from p. 301)

Age	Physical growth	Motor development	Nutrition	Common behavior, activities, and problems	Basic psychosocial challenges
Young schoolchild, 6-12 yr.					
6 yr.	6 yr. molars—first permanent teeth Annual growth of 2 in.	Good balance; increased dexterity Advanced throwing Roller-skates Swims	Home schedules must allow time for adequate breakfast before school Supervision of lunch habits needed; to preserve appetite and protect teeth, avoid sugar and rich foods	Period of transition from home to school, usually stressful Can tie shoes Skilled with oral language Begins to print Religious interest increases	*Industry vs. inferiority:* Preoccupation with fantasy subsides; child wants to be engaged in real tasks that he can carry through; in learning to accept instruction and win recognition by producing "things," he develops sense of adequacy and accomplishment; when child does not receive recognition for his efforts, he develops sense of inadequacy and inferiority
7 yr.		Can walk straight line	Frequent oral hygiene needed	Usually stable age Enjoys solitary or group play; begins to prefer own sex Learning to tell time	
8 yr.		Movements more graceful; manual skills more complex	After-school lunch of fruit and milk	Eager, curious age; many projects, not always completed Begins to write rather than print	
9 yr.		Balances on one leg with eyes closed		Peer group very important; clubs, gangs, hero worship pronounced Competitive sports valued	
10-12 yr. (also called preadolescence or puberty)	Growth spurt; girls may show beginning sexual development—widening hips, budding breasts, pubic hair, and occasionally menses			Group activities intensify; sociable and sensitive to power of suggestion; has high aspirations, critical of parent and self	

Continued on p. 306.

FIG. 22-18. Young schoolchildren.

Table 22-1. Ages and stages of maturation (continued from p. 304)

Age	Physical growth	Motor development	Nutrition	Common behavior, activities, and problems	Basic psychosocial challenges
Adolescence *Early adolescence, 12-16 yr.* 12-14 yr.	Slow, continuous growth Secondary sex characteristics appear Girls mature earlier than boys	Hands and feet out of proportion; self-conscious; awkward	Search for independence may be reflected by nutritional rebellion and fad diets	Participation in organizations may continue Interest in opposite sex increases Boys involved in sports Constantly challenges existing society	*Identity vs. diffusion:* Adolescent seeks to establish a sense of identity; if a good foundation has been laid (including building blocks of trust, autonomy, sexual identification, initiative, and learning), he will be able to integrate childhood identifications, basic biological drives, native endowment, and opportunities offered in social roles to feel secure regarding his part in society; self-diffusion or lack of a feeling of identity may be temporarily unavoidable because of the physiological changes and psychological upheavals in this period
14-16 yr.				Emotionally unstable; alternately depressed and exuberant Problems in self-knowledge, adjustment, and relations with opposite sex; ambivalence toward parents Activities reflect preparation for adult roles of citizen, homemaker, wage earner, and parent Increasing concern with philosophical and religious questions	
Late adolescence, 16-19 yr. 16-19 yr.	Adult size and proportions usually attained	Male physical strength and athletic ability highly prized	Boys have tremendous, unwise appetites Girls are weight conscious; erratic food consumption Good nutrition still requires parental encouragement and provision	Need for acceptable self-image and self-respect Age of many problems, difficult decisions; school expenses; continuing education, work, or military service; courtship and marriage plans; responsibilities of citizenship, political and religious affiliations	*Intimacy vs. isolation:* When a young person feels secure in his identity, he is then able to establish warm, meaningful, constructive relationships with others and eventually a love-based, mutually satisfying sexual relationship with a member of the opposite sex; when individual is unable to relate to others, he may develop deep sense of isolation

Fig. 22-19. Adolescents.

23
Preventive pediatrics

The valuable "ounce of prevention" that we all have heard mentioned so often is frequently measured in cubic centimeters, drops, or minutes spent with the physician and nurse for regular health supervision. The maintenance of an individual's optimal physical and mental health is a major goal of the physician and nurse.

Child health supervision is an extension of the prenatal care received by the mother and the developing fetus. Such supervision is designed to detect the presence of deformity or disease, to provide help in interpreting nutritional requirements and assuring proper food intake, to protect against certain preventable infectious diseases, and to offer appropriate counseling regarding child rearing practices and commonly encountered child behavior patterns. Records of the child's individual health history are maintained, and his personal growth and development are often plotted in graph form. Health supervision may be carried on by the private physician, a public facility, or a child health conference.

The infant usually is scheduled to visit his physician once a month until his first birthday. During this period growth changes are rapid, and modification of infant care is frequent. The toddler (1 to 3 years) and preschooler (3 to 6 years) should be checked by a physician at least once a year. Special attention should be directed toward detection of any hearing impairment, visual defect, or orthopedic difficulty. Professional dental supervision should be started before any real problem is apparent, at about 3 years of age.

The school-age child in our society, because of his multiple community contacts and the activities of public health nurses in many schools, usually receives more consistent health supervision than the preschool child. Even so, the school-age child should have an annual physical examination and appropriate help and counseling as his growth and development level require.

The following topics of study are fundamental to the consideration of preventive pediatrics. It is hoped that these introductory discussions of basic nutrition, immunization, and child safety will encourage the student to continue investigation of the positive approach to health with increasing interest and reward.

Self-feeding and basic nutrition

Feeding and eating can be very natural. It is well to remember that a number of studies have indicated that infants and children select food of the right type at the right time and in the right amounts if it is available to them from the beginning of the self-feeding process. Babies accept solid foods and feed themselves when their neuromuscular progress permits them to do so.

PHYSIOLOGICAL GUIDES
Hunger vs. appetite

Babies have a rhythmical pattern of hunger contractions characterized by discomfort, restlessness, and crying. The rhythm of hunger contractions differs in each baby, but they usually reappear every

3 to 4 hours. Babies should be fed according to their hunger rhythms, since rigidly prescribed feeding schedules ignore these hunger patterns. The normal young infant's nutritional needs can be met adequately the first 3 months by breast feeding or formula plus vitamins. The amount of milk or formula consumed varies from day to day, but in general most infants take 2 to 3 ounces of formula per pound of body weight, distributed over a 24-hour period. When sucking stops and the healthy infant falls asleep, the hunger-appetite mechanism has been satisfied. The infant should not be coaxed or forced to take more milk, regardless of the amount remaining in the bottle.

During infancy, hunger prompted by physiological needs chiefly controls food intake. Before 6 months, an infant will take almost any liquid consistently. However, in the latter half of the first year, preferences related to taste, appearance, and custom (that is, appetite) become important. Maternal diet, likes, and dislikes begin to condition the child's eating habits. By 1 year the baby shows definite preferences and dislikes. If the conditioning process has not been adverse, appetite may be trusted as a physiological index of the infant's nutritional needs. In this happy situation it is believed that if a baby refuses an essential food, he should not be forced to take it, since he will accept it later when he needs it.

DEVELOPMENTAL GUIDES
Protrusion reflex

The protrusion reflex manifests itself when the infant pushes out solid food placed on the anterior third of his tongue. This response, common during the first 9 weeks, disappears by the fourth month of life. It does not interfere with the baby's bottle or breast feeding because any nipple empties into the back of the mouth. However, it makes early feeding of solids difficult. The disappearance of the protrusion reflex is the neuromuscular indication for the introduction of semisolid food. A number of investigators believe that the practice of giving pureed food before 2½ or 3 months of age produces neither beneficial nor harmful results, but rather attests to the remarkable adaptability of the infant to whims of his caretakers.

Getting the baby to accept the spoon willingly is an important learning process that proceeds slowly. Usually, new food should be offered first, while the baby is hungry. However, a *very* hungry baby may refuse a new food because of his urgent desire for milk and his low frustration tolerance.

Place a small amount of food on the baby's lips to get him accustomed to the taste. The first solid food introduced is usually cereal and should be almost as thin as milk. Solid food may be introduced as early as 3 weeks but need not be stressed until the protrusion reflex has disappeared.

Self-feeding

Hand-to-mouth self-feeding begins before 1 year of age. If the baby is prevented from feeding himself when he is neuromuscularly ready, the acquisition of this skill may be delayed for weeks or months. A 6-month-old child can usually put his hands around a supported bottle and guide it to his lips. If permitted, the 7-month-old may hold the bottle by himself. At 8 months he can feed himself a cookie. Chewing motions appear at about 8 or 9 months and are the neuromuscular indications that lumpy foods can be introduced whether the teeth are present or not. Chopped foods should be introduced gradually. If undigested food appears in the stool, one should wait a week and try again. By 9 months, an empty plastic or metal cup may be placed on the baby's tray for practice. At 10 months of age he can begin practice with a spoon. Shortly after 12 months he can use a cup well, and by 18 months he can use a spoon skillfully. Self-feeding is usually accomplished between 12 and 18 months and consists of a mixture of feeding skills using the spoon, hand, or cup.

BASIC NUTRITION CONCEPTS

A happy child with good health reflects good eating habits. Good nutrition is like a good insurance policy. During the course of a lifetime it pays dividends in the form of a well-developed body with good muscles, smooth skin, glossy hair, and clear, bright eyes. As the dividends accumulate, one finds that appetite, digestion, and elimination are good. Finally, the policy (good nutrition) matures as one enjoys a high level of health in old age.

All systems and tissues in the body depend on proper nourishment for their existence and maintenance; this nourishment is obtained from the foods we eat and drink. Our food must perform three functions within the body:

1. Provide heat and energy
2. Build and repair the tissues of the body
3. Regulate the body processes

Substances essential to perform these vital functions are the following:

1. Oxygen
2. Water
3. Carbohydrates
4. Proteins
5. Fats
6. Minerals
7. Vitamins

Oxygen

Oxygen is so vital to the activity of the body cells that without it, life would cease immediately. The natural source of oxygen is fresh air. Through the activity of the respiratory system, oxygen enters the circulating blood, which carries it to every living cell. An abundance of fresh air is desirable at all ages.

Water

Second only to oxygen, water is necessary for life. Without water, death ensues in just a few days. Water comprises about 70% of the body weight. It is a basic constituent of all cells and is a major component in blood, lymph, spinal fluid, and the various body excretions such as urine and sweat. During infancy, considerable water is lost through the kidneys and skin. To keep pace with normal fluid losses, the infant must receive a daily intake of at least 150 ml. per kilogram (2¼ ounces per pound). The infant is subject to conditions causing water loss, notably fever, vomiting, and diarrhea. Unless water intake is increased during these abnormal states, symptoms of dehydration and its grave consequences appear rapidly.

Carbohydrates

Carbohydrates serve as the body's primary source of heat and energy. Examples of carbohydrate-rich foods include grains, fruits, vegetables, and sweets. (Pure sugar is 100% carbohydrate.) Carbohydrates not utilized for heat and energy are stored in many of the body's organs (especially in the liver and muscles as glycogen), or they are converted to fatty tissue. Glycogen is readily converted in the liver to glucose when carbohydrate is not available in the food consumed. Since immediate heat and energy requirements have priority over tissue growth and repair, the body is also capable of utilizing tissue fat and protein to furnish its energy needs. It is therefore important to have sufficient carbohydrates in the diet to meet these needs adequately, thus sparing protein for its primary use of building and maintaining tissues.

The waste products of carbohydrate metabolism are excreted from the body in the form of carbon dioxide and water.

Protein

Every living cell and almost all body fluids contain protein. Protein is necessary for the growth, repair, and maintenance of all body tissues. Immune bodies, which help the body resist infection, contain protein. Enzymes and hormones also include protein in their composition.

The end products of protein digestion are amino acids—small units, which, when properly reassembled, form the needed body protein. Of the many amino acids known, nine are essential for normal growth and body maintenance. Amino acids are found in varying amounts in various forms in foods.

Proteins are divided into three groups: complete, partially complete, and incomplete. The complete proteins contain all nine essential amino acids. A dietary supply of these amino acids is necessary because they cannot be synthesized by the body. Proteins from animal sources such as meats, poultry, fresh eggs, milk, and cheese provide the essential amino acids. Gelatin is 100% protein from an animal source but is not a complete protein.

Partially complete proteins are found in cereal products and vegetables. They contain many amino acids but not all the essential ones. When protein intake is not sufficient, the result is a slow rate of growth and increased susceptibility to bacterial infections.

Incomplete proteins such as corn and gelatin are incapable of either maintaining or supporting life. When incomplete proteins are the only source of protein, malnutrition, or marasmus, results.

Children will receive adequate amounts of protein in meat, milk, and eggs. The overall protein value may be improved when both animal and vegetable protein are eaten together. Since there is no storage of amino acids in the body, it is essential that food contain sufficient amounts. Amino acids not needed by the body tissues are returned to the liver, where approximately half are converted into urea, a waste product excreted by the kidney, and half are changed into glycogen or fatty tissue and stored to meet future energy requirements.

Finally, it is important to note that all nine essential amino acids work together. New tissue cannot be formed unless all the essential amino acids are present in the bloodstream simultaneously. Therefore it is imperative that some form of complete protein be included at each meal.

Fats

Certain fatty acids found in dietary fats are necessary to maintain good nutrition. These essential fatty acids permit normal growth and the health and maintenance of normal skin. Fat also provides the vehicle of absorption of the fat-soluble vitamins, A, D, E, and K. Unless dissolved in fats, these vitamins cannot be retained in the body in adequate amounts.

Fats are found in both animal and vegetable foods. Egg yolks, butter, meat, soybean oil, cottonseed oil, corn oil, and olive oil are good sources of the essential fatty acids. It is important that one of these sources be included in the daily diet, since the essential fatty acids cannot be synthesized from other fats. The waste products of fat metabolism, like those of carbohydrate metabolism, are carbon dioxide and water.

If fat intake is inadequate, the child may not receive the essential fatty acids required to prevent the formation of certain types of skin lesions. The rapidly growing young infant is highly susceptible to this deficiency and will develop dryness and thickening of the skin with chafing and desquamation if the cause is unrelieved.

Energy requirements

Whenever work is to be performed by the body, energy is needed. The body must be supplied with fuel in the form of food in sufficient amounts to meet the energy requirements of that individual. To determine how much food a child needs, it is necessary to know the child's metabolic rate, or "rate of heat production." The unit of heat in metabolism is called a Calorie. (It may be defined as the amount of heat needed to raise the temperature of 1 liter of water 1° C.) A person's *basal* metabolic rate (BMR) is described as the minimal amount of heat produced by body cells when the body is at rest with only vital processes such as circulation and respiration functioning. Several factors—size, age, sex, hormonal levels, and body temperature—influence the BMR. The *total* metabolic rate of a person represents the total amount of heat produced by the body in a given time (usually 24 hours) under normal conditions. The total metabolic rate of a child represents the amount of food his body must burn not only to keep alive and awake but also to continue his physical activity, to support growth, to supply specific dynamic action (ingestion and assimilation of his food), and to replace calories lost. (See Fig. 23-1.)

Total energy expended determines the need for calories. The fuel values of energy-producing foods are as follows:

Carbohydrates   4 calories per gram
Protein   4 calories per gram
Fats   9 calories per gram

The average distribution of calories in a well-balanced diet is as follows:

Carbohydrates   50%
Protein   15%
Fats   35% (or less)

If the number of grams of carbohydrate, protein, and fat in a food is known, the caloric value can be determined by multiplying each by the appropriate fuel value.

When food is not available, the body's nutritional reserves and tissues are consumed to meet its need for caloric energy.

Carbohydrates stored as glycogen in different body organs are consumed first; fat deposits are consumed next. Usually, fat in the extremities is consumed before fat located in the trunk. Fat in the cheek pads is consumed last. Recessed cheeks in young children usually indicates severe malnutrition.

Minerals

Calcium   Phosphorus
Magnesium   Manganese
Sodium   Chloride
Potassium   Molybdenum
Iron   Selenium
Iodine   Fluoride
Copper   Arsenic
Zinc   Cobalt

The preceding list indicates minerals that are essential to many body structures and functions. The actions of minerals are interrelated in the body, and often one mineral is combined with another to complete the reaction. (For example, in the bones, calcium and phosphorus function together, and sufficient vitamin D is necessary for the proper utilization of calcium.) Most

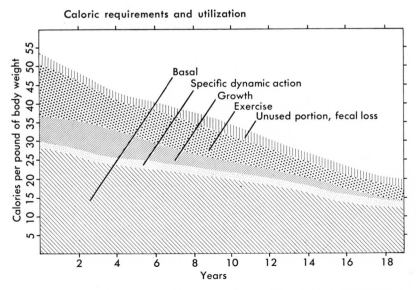

FIG. 23-1. To determine the total caloric requirements of a child, multiply his weight in pounds by the number of calories for his age.

of these minerals are readily obtained from a well-balanced diet. Two minerals, calcium and iron, require special attention. Deficits of the other minerals do not ordinarily arise from inadequate intake. However, large amounts of minerals may be lost through vomiting and diarrhea.

Iron. One of the most vital elements in the body is iron. It is a component of hemoglobin, the oxygen-bearing element in the blood. Iron is required for growth, and the need for iron varies with the rapidity of growth at different periods of infancy and childhood.

TABLE 23-1. Significant vitamins

Vitamin	Function	Effects of deficiency
A	Promotes good eyesight	Night blindness
	Aids in maintaining resistance to infections	Frequent infections
	Maintains skin integrity	Dry, rough skin; papular eruptions
	Helps form and maintain mucous membrane	Burning, itching eyes
	Helps in formation of bone and teeth	Retarded growth; thin and defective tooth enamel
B complex		
B_1 (thiamine)	Aids in maintenance and function of nervous system	Beriberi
		Listlessness, fatigue, and irritability
	Regulates appetite; normal digestion	Anorexia, vomiting, and diarrhea
	Promotes a feeling of general well-being	Generalized weakness; gross symptoms of neuromuscular, digestive, and cardiovascular impairment
B_2 (riboflavin)	Aids in eye adaptation to light	Photophobia; impairment of visual acuity; cataracts
	Provides essentials for metabolism of carbohydrate, fat, and protein	Impaired formation of blood cells
	Necessary for normal growth	Anemia
Niacin (nicotinic acid)	Essential for normal function of digestive tract and nervous system	General poor health
		Gastrointestinal changes—loss of appetite, nausea, vomiting, abdominal pain, red tongue, ulcers and fissures of tongue
		Dermatitis
		Nervous system manifestations—headaches and dizziness, impairment of memory, and neurotic symptoms
C (ascorbic acid)	Important role in formation, maintenance, and repair of teeth, bones, and blood vessels	Scurvy
		Loose teeth; faulty bones; slow growth
	Facilitates absorption of dietary iron	Weakness and irritability
	Maintenance of normal blood hemoglobin levels	Delayed healing of wounds
		Cutaneous hemorrhages
D	Enhances absorption of calcium and phosphorus	Rickets
		Retarded growth and lack of vigor
	Plays a vital role in formation of normal bone	Variety of bone deformities—large head, pigeon chest, kyphosis, and curved long bones
	Promotes tooth development	Teeth erupt late and decay early

TABLE 23-2. Food intake for good nutrition according to food groups and the average size of servings at different age levels*

Food group	Servings per day	Average size of servings					
		1 yr.	2-3 yr.	4-5 yr.	6-9 yr.	10-12 yr.	13-15 yr.
Milk and cheese (1½ oz. cheese = 1 cup milk)	4	½ cup	½-¾ cup	¾ cup	¾-1 cup	1 cup	1 cup
Meat group (protein foods)	At least 3						
Egg		1 egg	1 egg	1 egg	1 egg	1 egg	1 or more
Lean meat, fish, poultry (liver once a week)		2 tbsp.	2 tbsp.	4 tbsp.	2-3 oz. (4-6 tbsp.)	3-4 oz.	4 oz. or more
Peanut butter			1 tbsp.	2 tbsp.	2-3 tbsp.	3 tbsp.	3 tbsp.
Fruits and vegetables	At least 4, including:						
Vitamin C source (citrus fruits, berries, tomato, cabbage, cantaloupe)	1 or more (twice as much tomato as citrus)	⅓ cup citrus	½ cup	½ cup	1 medium orange	1 medium orange	1 medium orange
Vitamin A source (green or yellow fruits and vegetables)	1 or more	2 tbsp.	3 tbsp.	4 tbsp. (¼ cup)	¼ cup	⅓ cup	½ cup
Other vegetables (potato, legumes, etc.) *or*	2 or more	2 tbsp.	3 tbsp.	4 tbsp. (¼ cup)	⅓ cup	½ cup	¾ cup
Other fruits (apple, banana, etc.)		¼ cup	⅓ cup	½ cup	1 medium	1 medium	1 medium
Cereals (whole grain or enriched)	At least 4						
Bread		½ slice	1 slice	1½ slices	1-2 slices	2 slices	2 slices
Ready-to-eat cereals		½ oz.	¾ oz.	1 oz.	1 oz.	1 oz.	1 oz.
Cooked cereal (including macaroni, spaghetti, rice, etc.)		¼ cup	⅓ cup	½ cup	½ cup	¾ cup	1 cup or more
Fats and carbohydrates	To meet caloric needs						
Butter, margarine, mayonnaise, oils: 1 tbsp. = 100 calories		1 tbsp.	1 tbsp.	1 tbsp.	2 tbsp.	2 tbsp.	2-4 tbsp.
Desserts and sweets: 100-calorie portions as follows: ⅓ cup pudding or ice cream, 2 to 3 in. cookies, 1 oz. cake, 1⅓ oz. pie, 2 tbsp. jelly, jam, honey, sugar		1 portion	1½ portions	1½ portions	3 portions	3 portions	3-6 portions

*Adapted by Bennett, M. J., and Hansen, A. E., from Four groups of the daily food guide, Institute of Home Economics, United States Department of Agriculture, Publication No. 30, Children's Bureau, United States Department of Health, Education, and Welfare, Washington, D. C., 1945.

TABLE 23-3. Recommended dietary allowances and important dietary sources of the nutrients*

Age and weight (Boys and girls 25-75th percentiles)	Calories†	Protein (gm.)	Calcium (gm.)	Iron (mg.)	Vitamin A (I.U.)	Thiamine† (mg.)	Riboflavin† (mg.)	Niacin‡ (mg.)	Ascorbic acid (mg.)	Vitamin D (I.U.)
1 yr. (22 ± 2 lb.)	1020	42	0.6	5.4	2325	0.47	1.0	3.4	40	300
2-3 yr. (30 ± 5 lb.)	1320	48	0.8	6.1	3225	0.64	1.0	7.3	51	400
4-5 yr. (39 ± 6 lb.)	1720	67	1.0	8.4	4270	0.85	1.5	11.7	60	500
6-9 yr. (56 ± 15 lb.)	2130	76	1.1	11.4	5140	1.2	2.0	19.3	88	600
10-12 yr. (81 ± 20 lb.)	2480	93	1.4	13.0	4590	1.4	2.5	23.0	102	600
13-15 yr. (108 ± 27 lb.)	2580–3080	100	1.4	14.4	5540	1.5	2.5	23.7	107	600
		Milk Cheese Eggs Meat Fish Poultry Legumes Cereals Nuts	Milk Cheese Greens Clams Canned salmon	Liver Meat Egg yolk Greens Cereals (whole and fortified)	Liver Butterfat Egg yolk Fish liver oils Fortified margarines Precursors from green and yellow foods	Liver Pork Other meat Milk Cereals (whole and fortified) Wheat germ Legumes Nuts	Milk Meat Eggs Fish Greens Cereals (whole and fortified)	Meat Fish Poultry Liver Cereals (whole and fortified) Greens Peanuts	Citrus fruits Tomatoes Berries Cantaloupe Cabbage Greens	Fortified milk and margarine Fish liver oils Skin exposure to ultraviolet light

*From Recommended dietary allowances, Publication 1694, Food and Nutrition Board, National Academy of Sciences—National Research Council, Washington, D. C., 1968.

†Selections from fat and carbohydrate group included for caloric values, but not for other nutrients.

‡Based on the following: thiamine, 0.5 mg./1,000 calories; riboflavin, 0.025 mg./gm. of protein; niacin, 6.6 mg./1,000 calories

Iron deficiency leads to the development of anemia, or insufficient hemoglobin for the needs of the body. Anemia causes few deaths but contributes seriously to the weakness, ill health, and substandard performance of many children throughout the world. The greatest incidence of iron-deficiency anemia occurs in infants and young children. Both cow's milk and breast milk contain insufficient iron. When the stores present at birth become depleted (at about 3 months of age), iron-deficiency anemia develops unless a supplement is given. The addition of iron-containing pablum or cereal offered at about 3 weeks of age prevents this anemia and the need for additional iron supplements. Foods rich in iron are liver, meat, and egg yolk.

Calcium. Relatively large amounts of calcium are required to perform many vital functions in the body. Calcium is essential for normal heart action and is an important element in the blood-clotting mechanism. Calcium builds bones and teeth and is necessary for normal muscular-skeletal action. When there is insufficient calcium in the diet, the blood will use the calcium in the bones to maintain the normal composition of the blood. Bowed legs and rickets may result. Hypocalcemia may cause neonatal tetany, crying, muscle twitching, and convulsions. Unrelieved, it may end in death.

Milk and milk products are good sources of calcium.

Vitamins

Fat-soluble vitamins	Water-soluble vitamins
	C
	B complex
A	Thiamine (B_1)
D	Riboflavin (B_2)
E	Niacin
K	Folic acid
	Pyridoxine (B_6)
	Biotin
	Pantothenic acid
	Cyanocobalamin (B_{12})

Vitamins are organic compounds found in minute quantities in foods. They participate as catalysts in almost all metabolic processes and are vital to growth and good health. Vitamins A and D are the only two vitamins stored in the body. Excessive intake of these two vitamins will result in toxic manifestations such as skin lesions, liver enlargement, and bone spurs. Any vitamin may be lacking, causing disturbances in the pattern of growth, metabolism, and development of the child.

The best sources of vitamins are found in the natural foods. A well-balanced diet containing the Basic Four Food Groups (Fig. 9-4, p. 72) will assure an adequate supply of vitamins. Six vitamins merit special consideration. The same foods that supply these vitamins supply all other vitamin needs. (See Table 23-1.)

Summary

Digestion refers to those processes that prepare food for assimilation into the bloodstream or lymphatics of the body, but metabolism refers to all the changes that occur in the utilization of those nutrients by the cells and the generation of heat and energy. Amino acids, essential fatty acids, vitamins, and minerals are utilized primarily for cell growth and repair. They are also utilized in the formation of enzymes, hormones, and other body substances. Carbohydrates and fats are utilized primarily for caloric energy (that is, to supply fuel to keep the body warm) and mechanical energy for performing the body's work. When caloric needs are not met by fats and carbohydrates, protein is then utilized for energy. Adequate intake of carbohydrates and fats will spare protein for cell growth. Therefore it is necessary that the diet contain a balance of all six substances—carbohydrate, fat, protein, vitamins, minerals, and water—as each one plays its own vital role in the processes of growth and development.

Immunization

The brilliant success achieved in conquering the classic contagious diseases of childhood is attributed to immunization. Through immunization a person is able to build up defenses against certain infectious diseases. When a person is able to resist a certain disease, he is said to be immune. He is immune because antibodies are present that injure or destroy the disease-producing agent or neutralize its toxins. Immunization (artificial) is the process whereby certain substances called *antigens* are injected into the body to stimulate the production of antibodies. Immunization is the best and cheapest method of preventing illness. In fact, it is the most routine procedure in preventive pediatrics.

Because the mechanisms for developing immunity are immature in the young infant, he is very susceptible to some infections. The protection he has against infection is obtained from his mother, if she is immune. Any passive immunity acquired from the mother lasts about 4 to 6 months and may protect the child against diphtheria, tetanus, measles, and poliomyelitis. Since there is great variability in such passive protection in the young infant and no passive immunity against pertussis (whooping cough), immunization should be initiated as early as possible. Potent antigens may be given at any time with success. Combined antigens reduce the number of injections, enhance the action of each, and establish a desired immunity within the first 6 months of life.

Current practice begins immunization when the infant is between 8 and 12 weeks of age. A "triple toxoid" of diphtheria, pertussis, and tetanus antigens in one injection and a concurrent feeding of oral polio vaccine are given. The "triple toxoid" DTP is repeated three times at intervals of not less than 1 month. The necessity to prevent the high mortality from pertussis (whooping cough) in infancy is the main reason for the early start in basic DTP immunization. However, pertussis vaccine is not considered to be as satisfactory as diphtheria and tetanus toxoids. It does not provide absolute protection.

After the initial series of immunizations, "recall" or "booster" doses are given to stimulate high antibody levels and maintain maximum immunity. Children who have received three doses of "triple toxoid" (DPT) and oral polio vaccine (OPV) should be given a booster dose at 15 to 18 months of age after completing the primary sequence. Subsequent booster doses are recommended at 4 and 6 years of age. Active, up-to-date immunization produces a degree of resistance in children comparable to that which follows the natural infection.

Precautions

1. Needles and syringes must be sterile before use.
2. Injection site and rubber stopper should be cleaned with an antiseptic solution such as 2% tincture of iodine.
3. Toxoids and vaccines (antigens) containing alum are given intramuscularly, preferably into the midlateral thigh or deltoid muscles.
4. Systemic and severe local reactions after an injection call for a delay or decrease in succeeding doses.
5. After vaccination the site should remain clean and dry until the crust falls off.
6. Aspirin, 1 grain per year of age (up to 5 grains), may be given 2 hours after the injection. This dosage may be repeated as needed *not more than five times at 4-hour intervals* without medical consultation.

Contraindications

1. Acute upper respiratory and other infections—interval between injections may be prolonged and does not interfere with final immunity.

2. Neurological disorders—begin at 2 months of age with one tenth the recommended dosage of DPT and OPV and follow the schedule for normal children. If a convulsion or central nervous system reaction occurs, immunization may be delayed until after infancy and then begun cautiously with fractional doses of separate antigens.

3. Eczema and other acute forms of dermatitis—smallpox vaccination is withheld

TABLE 23-4. Recommended schedule for active immunization and tuberculin testing of normal infants and children[*][1]

2 mo.	DTP—trivalent OPV[2,3]
3 mo.	DTP[3]
4 mo.	DTP—trivalent OPV
6 mo.	Trivalent OPV[2]
12 mo.	Tuberculin test[4]—live measles vaccine[5]
15-18 mo.	DTP—trivalent OPV—smallpox vaccine[6]
4-6 yr.	DTP—trivalent OPV—smallpox vaccine[6]
12-14 yr.	Td—smallpox vaccine[6]—mumps vaccine
Thereafter	Td every 10 yr.[7]—smallpox vaccine every 3-10 yr.[6]
	Rubella vaccine[8]

[*]From Report of the Committee on the Control of Infectious Diseases, Red Book, 1970 edition, American Academy of Pediatrics, p. 5. Readers must consult the publication to obtain details of immunization procedures. DTP = diphtheria and tetanus toxoids combined with pertussis vaccine. Td = combined tetanus and diphtheria toxoid (adult type) for those over 6 years of age in contrast to diphtheria and tetanus (DT) containing a larger amount of diphtheria antigen. OPV = trivalent oral poliovaccine.

[1]Handling, storage, and dosage of immunizing agents; sites, routes of administration, and courses should follow product (package) information.

[2]Trivalent OPV is recommended, but monovalent OPV may be substituted; the order of monovalent virus-type feeding is type 1 followed by type 3 and then type 2.

[3]If DTP dose is not given to the infant at 3 months, it should be given at 4 and 5 months or at 4 and 6 months.

[4]Frequency of repeated tuberculin tests depends on risk of exposure of the child and on the prevalence of tuberculosis in the population group; tuberculin testing annually up to 4 years of age, thereafter annually or every 2 years is recommended.

[5]Live attenuated measles vaccine with or without immune serum globulin (measles)—ISG—or further attenuated measles vaccine without simultaneous administration of ISG is recommended. Killed measles virus vaccine is not recommended. Tuberculin testing preferably should be performed within 2 to 3 days prior to administration of measles vaccine, and the test should be read on the day of anticipated administration of the vaccine. (This constitutes optimal practice but is not mandatory.) Measles vaccine should be given to all children with a positive tuberculin reaction only after initiation of antituberculosis therapy.

[6]Any licensed smallpox vaccine may be used. The reaction should be read and recorded.

[7]The 10-year interval for tetanus boosters may be calculated from each dose given for prophylaxis (injury). Prophylactic use for wounds is a matter for clinical judgment. Individuals who have had the initial series and booster doses may be expected to have adequate protection for at least 1 year after the last dose without receiving an additional booster dose.

[8]Present recommendations call for use of live rubella virus vaccine between age 1 year and puberty.

because it may produce eczema vaccinatum. Children with eczema must live in another setting when their siblings at home are vaccinated because of the danger of cross infection.

4. Steroid therapy—immunization procedures are deferred during the administration of steroid drugs because antigenic response is depressed.

Rubella virus vaccine

The principal objective of rubella (German measles) control is preventing infection of the fetus. This can best be achieved by eliminating the transmission of the virus among children, who are the major source of infection for pregnant women. All children between 1 year of age and puberty should receive the *live rubella virus* vaccine. The primary target is children in kindergarten and the early grades. Pregnant women *should not* be given live rubella virus vaccine because it may cause an inapparent maternal infection that may damage the fetus.

Mumps virus vaccine

The principal objective is prevention of mumps in preadolescent males and young male adults. Live attenuated mumps virus

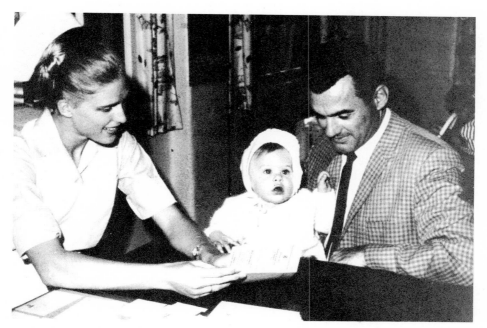

Fig. 23-2. Immunizations should not be given without follow-up instructions to the parents. This nurse is explaining the World Health Organization immunization record and what to do if certain signs and symptoms develop after Mary Ann's inoculation. (Courtesy U. S. Naval Hospital, San Diego, Calif.)

vaccine is recommended for all susceptible children and especially for preadolescent males and men who have not had the disease.

Tetanus toxoid

Recall injections after injury may be considered. Boosters as requirements for admission to camps and schools are *not* necessary. The immunity conferred by tetanus toxoid is extremely long lasting. The recommended schedule (Table 23-4) should be followed. Combined tetanus-diphtheria (Td) adult-type injections given at 10-year intervals and reliably recorded will eliminate the need for annual boosters and minimize the incidence of toxoid reactions.

Nursing responsibilities

The office nurse can do a great deal by her efficient, yet kindly, manner to help parents realize the importance of continuing the immunization program. She should

be sure that the parent knows what type of injections the child is receiving. She should be aware of any allergies that the child has demonstrated and learn if there have been any noteworthy reactions to previous immunizations. A continuous written record of the type of protection the child has received and the dates of administration should be given the parents. The date and time of the next appointment should be clearly understood. (See Fig. 23-2.)

The nurse's good-humored recognition that the medicine does sting a bit and that a sincere "ouch" is not out of place may help wary youngsters. A matter-of-fact, positive attitude rather than an overly solicitous manner seems to offer more support to the parent and child.

Sometimes it is worthwhile to inquire about the current status of the parents' immunizations. Maybe Mom and Dad should be getting injections too! The proverbial daily apple really is not too successful in

319

preventing illness, but regular immunization is a proved and necessary protection for both young and old.

• • •

Immunization is so important that information about the procedure should be given in prenatal classes. New parents are very concerned about "doing what is right" for their child. Before going home from the hospital, the mother and father should be reminded again about the immunization program. Although immunizations are usually given by the private practitioner or his nurse as part of the baby's regular health checkups, parents of modest means should be told of community resources where free immunization services are available.

Child safety

Successful prevention and treatment of infectious diseases and nutritional disorders have resulted in a marked decrease in child mortality rates. The greatest threat to the health and well-being of the child today is the accident. An estimated 15,000 to 16,000 children under 15 years of age die annually in the United States from accidents.

Accidents kill more children than the next six leading causes of childhood death combined.

	Death rates Ages 1 to 14
Accidents	22.9
Cancer	7.1
Congenital malformation	4.4
Pneumonia	3.7
Heart disease	0.9
Homicide	0.8
Meningitis	0.8*

The magnitude of the accident problem is further stressed by the fact that 17 million children suffer nonfatal injuries every year. Many of these children are crippled or permanently disabled for life. Of course,

---

*Deaths per 100,000 population, National Center for Health Statistics, 1967.

not all childhood accidents are brought to the attention of medical personnel. Perhaps an additional 25% of children up to 14 year of age have significant but unreported injuries. Thus the conservative figure of 17 million childhood injuries emphasizes a serious national problem.

Accidents

An accident is defined as "an unpremeditated event resulting in a recognizable injury." The most common accidents that injure children consist mainly of cuts, piercings with instruments, blows from objects, animal bites, and injuries related to motor vehicles. Motor vehicles are the major cause of accidental death. Also ranked among the leading causes of fatal accidents are drownings, fires, and poisonings. (See Fig. 23-3.)

Certain factors seem to be influential in causing childhood accidents. (1) Approximately half of all the fatalities occur in children under 5 years of age. (2) Boys at all ages have more accidents than girls. (3) The nonwhite population has a considerably higher incidence of accidents than does the white population. (4) Most accidents occur during the spring and summer months. (5) A higher percentage of accidents occur in the home, especially during the preschool period. (6) The child between 1 and 2 years of age is most vulnerable to accidents of all sorts. (7) Some children are accident-prone. Combinations of certain personality characteristics and environmental influences predispose a child toward repetitive accidents.

Prevention. Accidents do not just happen; there is always a cause. Good safety habits could eliminate many of these causes. Gains in safeguarding the lives of children depend on accident prevention.

In the past, much emphasis has been placed on two particular approaches to accident prevention: (1) elimination of specific environmental hazards peculiar to different age groups and (2) alterations of the child's behavior through safety education. A glance at the data of the past years

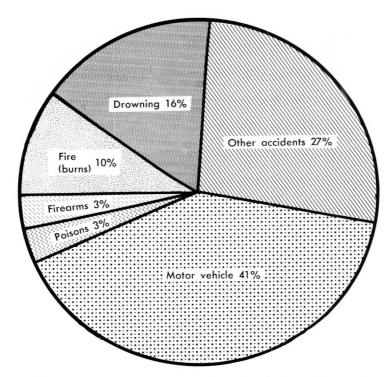

Fig. 23-3. Major causes of accidental death in children from birth to 14 years of age. (Reports of Vital Statistics Division, National Center for Health Statistics, 1969.)

shows a continued increase in the actual number of accidents.

Our vital statistics indicate the number of children injured and the kinds of accidents causing the injuries. However, they do not provide sufficient detail about each individual case to fully describe the complete situation of each accident. This prevents the making of valid conclusions concerning accident causation and prevention in childhood. Often, vital information is not recorded. This is undoubtedly why specific recommendations for the prevention of certain injuries have not always been effective.

To date, there is no single approach to accident prevention. "Accidents" are the result of a large number of complex mechanisms. Like other illnesses, they can be conquered only through systematic investigation. To understand the nature and cause of accidents, several factors must be considered simultaneously: the host (the child who is affected), the agent (the object that

is the direct cause), and the environment (the situation in which the accident takes place). This is known as the epidemiological approach to the study of accidents.

Although a great deal remains to be learned about the interaction of these major factors, the existing knowledge has led to the following new principles aimed at accident prevention:

1. Control of the agent whenever possible (e.g., use of child-protective caps on medicine bottles and household products)
2. Recognition and protection of a vulnerable host (young, inquisitive children, especially boys, and children with a past history of accidents)
3. Control of the environment, or milieu (e.g., consistent love and discipline)

Alerting and instructing parents. All parents should be made aware of the dangers confronting the child at each stage of his development, particularly the toddler and

TABLE 23-5. Accidents common at various stages of development

Typical behavior	Type of accident	Precaution and safety education
Infant		
Sleeps most of time	Suffocation	Use a firm mattress, no pillow; destroy plastic covers and filmy bags
Wiggles and rolls	Falls	Never leave child unattended on a table, sofa, etc.; keep crib bars up
Helpless in water	Drowning	Never leave alone in bathtub or near pools
Sucks on objects	Choking; ingestion of foreign objects	Keep small objects out of reach, especially pins or other sharp objects; buy toys too large to swallow
	Poisoning	Keep medicines and poisons in a locked cabinet
Toddler		
Roams all over house Climbs into things	Falls	Use gates on stairways; keep windows and doors locked; fence in yard
Takes things apart	Cuts	Provide large, sturdy toys without sharp edges or small removable parts; keep sharp instruments and knives out of reach
Curious about everything	Burns	Needs constant supervision; never leave hot coffeepot or running water unattended; turn pot handles inward; keep matches locked up; treat flimsy clothing with fire-retardant (7 oz. borax, 3 oz. boric acid, 2 qt. hot water)
Pokes and probes with fingers	Electric shock	Keep electrical appliances out of reach; cap unused light sockets with safety plugs
Chews everything	Poisoning	Keep medicines, cosmetics, and household poisons out of reach
	Ingestion of foreign objects and aspiration	Keep small objects such as coins, beans, needles, pins, jewelry, and doll's eyes out of reach
Enjoys playing in water	Drowning	Keep away from unattended pools, ponds, etc.; stay with child while in bathtub; fence in bodies of water
Rides tricycle	Motor vehicle accidents	Be firm and instruct child to keep clear of driveways and out of streets
Likes to ride in car and wants to go everywhere with mother		Instruct child in proper car safety; keep car doors locked and use safety belts; never allow child to sit or stand in front seat of a car or allow him to put hands or head out of window
Preschooler		
Ventures out into neighborhood		Teach child safety rules and demonstrate principles by good example; enforce obedience
		Do not overprotect—the preschooler can begin to protect himself, and overprotection deprives him of experience he needs in growing up and learning independence
Inquisitive	Burns	Teach him danger of open flames and hot objects
Rides bicycle Plays ball	Motor vehicle accidents	Instruct him in proper traffic safety rules—look both ways before crossing street, walk, never run across street, go with traffic light and walk in crosswalk, and never dart into street to go after a ball
Climbs trees and fences	Falls	Teach him good footing and proper handholds when climbing
Enjoys playing in water	Drowning	Begin swimming instruction; never let child play around unsupervised pools

TABLE 23-5. Accidents common at various stages of development—cont'd

Typical behavior	Type of accident	Precaution and safety education
Preschooler—cont'd		
Plays rough; runs up and down stairs	Blows; cuts	Check play areas for hazards
		Store dangerous tools and equipment in a locked cupboard
	Poisoning	Teach him not to taste unidentified foods, especially berries
		Lock up poisons; store in labeled bottles
		Discard old medicines down drain before putting containers in trash
Early school age, 6-9 yr.		
Adventurous	Motor vehicle accidents	Needs intensive instruction in safety rules
Will try anything	Drowning	Encourage swimming safety
Loyal to his friends	Falls	Point out importance of fun and not getting hurt
		Needs to know consequences for failing to follow rules
	Burns	Teach him to avoid smoldering fires; bottles and cans may explode and cause fatal injuries
		Teach him danger of matches and fires
		Teach proper use of chemistry sets
	Firearms	Point out serious consequences of playing with Dry Ice, fireworks, etc.
Late school age, 10-14 yr.		
Rides bicycle constantly	Motor vehicle accidents	Enforce safety rules; explain reasons for them
Plays away from home, often in hazardous places	Drowning; burns; explosions	Know where child is at all times
Has lots of energy and enjoys strenuous play	Sprains; contusions	Point out importance of fun and not getting injured
Enjoys working with father's tools	Lacerations	Show boys how to work around house safely (they should not use power tools unless tools are in good condition and they have knowledge of their use and safety); use proper equipment and keep it in good condition

preschooler (Table 23-5). Parents need to realize fully the normal child's search for adventure and his ignorance of consequences. They should know that fatigue, hunger, family discord, and anxiety increase the likelihood of an accident. A wise and loving parent will know that discipline is a fundamental prerequisite for accident prevention. Children should be taught that disobedience leads to unpleasant consequences that are not limited to punishment. The discipline of obedience rapidly becomes the only reliable method for ensuring protection of the school-age child.

All children and families should be instructed in safety. Community educational efforts aimed at accident prevention should include information on burns, water safety, road safety, and the use and proper storage of potentially toxic household chemicals, medicines, and tools and equipment. Individual responsibility and alertness multiplied to assure intelligent community involvement is needed.

Snakebite poisoning (Fig. 23-4)

An emergency requiring immediate medical attention is snakebite. About 7,000 individuals are bitten annually by snakes in this country. Half this population is under 20 years of age. Only a few cases end fatally, but most of those who die are children. Fortunately, most snakebites are inflicted by nonpoisonous snakes.

The majority of poisonous snakebites are inflicted by copperheads and rattlesnakes.

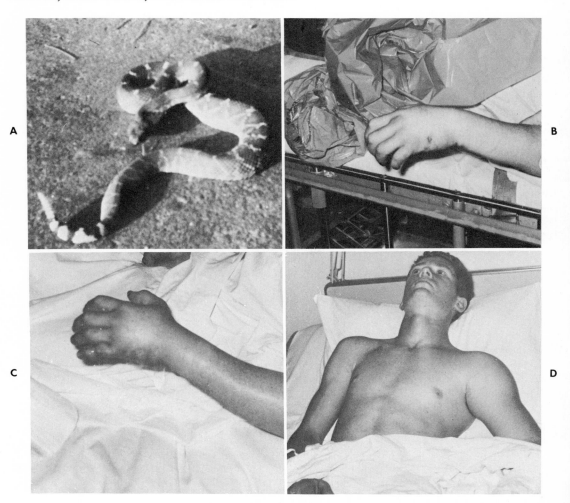

FIG. 23-4. **A,** Rattlesnake that bit the hand of the teen-age boy shown here. **B,** 20 minutes after bite. Note large white area around fang marks caused by tissue reaction. **C,** 8 hours after bite. Extensive swelling and bleeding present. **D,** Entire arm and shoulder is three times normal size. **E,** 48 to 72 hours after bite. Blisters have formed where the venom accumulated. **F,** Blisters are debrided. **G,** 4 weeks after healing. Note muscle loss and difference in size of the two hands and arms. (Courtesy W. T. Soldman, Jr., M.D., La Mesa, Calif.)

If the snake was not seen, diagnosis of a bite from a poisonous snake is established on the basis of fang marks, pain, and a white wheal at the site of the injury. Within 15 minutes the involved area becomes reddened and edematous. Swelling of the entire part increases and extends rapidly. Poisonous venom may interfere with blood coagulation. The venom may contain tetanus bacteria from the snake's diet of rats and rabbits. Local damage at the site includes the destruction of blood vessels, blood cells, nerve sheaths, and muscle tissue. Subcutaneous hemorrhage causes the skin to become dark and purplish, and blisters form in associated areas where the venom has concentrated. Forty-eight hours later, sanguinous fluid oozes from the blisters and in the more severe cases, necrosis of the limb may occur. Systemic symptoms may include hemorrhage, nausea, and vomiting. The reaction of the patient to a

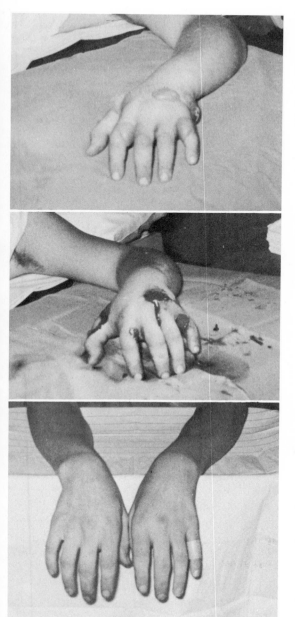

FIG. 23-4, cont'd. For legend see opposite page.

part. The victim should lie down in the shade. No stimulants should be given although drinking water is permitted and encouraged. (Of course, if one were unfortunate enough to be bitten while hiking alone in an isolated area, one would have no choice but to "walk out" to seek aid. One should not be hiking alone in the first place!) Local incisions and suctioning of the wound are *not* to be attempted. The use of a broad, soft tourniquet is recommended if it is applied only tight enough to restrict venous flow and is loosened and reapplied periodically. The best first-aid measure is to very carefully, quietly, and quickly take the victim to the nearest source of antivenin.

A polyvalent horse serum antivenin affords protection against a large variety of poisonous venoms. If skin testing indicates that the patient can tolerate the serum, a large dose of antivenin is administered intramuscularly and sometimes intravenously. The antivenin accumulates rapidly at the site of the toxin injection. Additional vials are given as necessary to keep local pain, swelling, and systemic symptoms under control. The patient should be observed for allergic reactions.

Nursing measures that lessen the effects produced by the poison include immobilization of the affected part and bed rest. Other measures that may help to prevent complications include antibiotic therapy, tetanus toxoid, and whole blood transfusions. After the acute phase, surgical debridement of the vesicles may be necessary. Continuing physical therapy and perhaps reconstructive surgery may be needed.

Poison ingestion

The variety and number of toxic substances children have been known to swallow are fantastic. The most frequent poisons are found in the medicine cabinet and under the kitchen sink. Often parental negligence has been directly responsible for the loss of a child's life. The majority of accidental poisonings in childhood are preventable.

snakebite will depend on a number of factors, including the amount of venom injected, the site and size of the bite, and the physical condition and emotional state of the victim.

First-aid measures include immediate rest and immobilization of the affected

Each year approximately 500 children die as the result of accidental poisoning, and an estimated 500,000 to 2 million children are involved in poisoning accidents. The major number of accidental poisonings occur in children under 4 years of age. This is the "age of curiosity," and these children are not selective about what they ingest. A number of nonfatal poisoning victims are left with permanent disabilities such as esophageal stricture or hepatic or renal damage.

Precautions. The following suggestions must be repeated until parents learn:

1. Keep all drugs, poisonous substances, and household chemicals in a locked cupboard out of the reach of little hands.
2. Do not transfer or store poisons or inflammable materials in food containers or bottles.
3. Never tell children that flavored medicine is candy (not even vitamins). Always refer to medicine as medicine!
4. Discard old medicines in drain before throwing away container.
5. Always read label before giving medicine.
6. Always return medicine to its proper place.
7. Do not underestimate the curiosity and abilities of children.

Emergency treatment. All accidental poisonings in young children are treated as an urgent emergency. Call the physician immediately and bring the child and the poisonous substance to a hospital emergency room. Supportive and symptomatic treatment should be initiated immediately, even though the specific poison substance may not be known.

Immediate management. The following immediate action should be taken in the case of poisoning:

1. Identify and remove the poison
2. Administer the antidote
3. Administer other supportive treatment

Removal of poison. In most cases the immediate necessity is to empty the child's stomach, even if hours have passed since the ingestion. *If not contraindicated,* emesis should be induced if possible. Removal (after prevention) is the most important aspect of poison management. However, emesis should not be induced in the event of the ingestion of corrosives (lye or strong acids), strychnine, or any hydrocarbons (kerosene, gasoline, fuel oil, paint thinner, and cleaning fluid). Neither should it be initiated if the child is unconscious or convulsing.

1. To induce vomiting, first have the child drink a glass of milk or water, then stroke your finger on his posterior oral pharynx to stimulate the gag reflex. The child's head and shoulders should be lowered to prevent aspiration of the vomitus.
2. An emetic drug such as *syrup of ipecac* (never the fluid extract), 15 ml., may be used. If vomiting does not occur, administration should be repeated *once only* in 15 to 30 minutes. Packaged in 1 fluid ounce containers, syrup of ipecac may be sold without prescription for first-aid use. Gagging may also be helpful when syrup of ipecac fails to induce immediate vomiting. An apomorphine injection is used often in the hospital as an emetic.
3. Gastric lavage is usually reserved for the unconscious child, the child who has ingested large amounts of hydrocarbons (to prevent aspiration or chemical pneumonia), and the child who has not vomited after two doses of syrup of ipecac. Severe cardiac disturbances result from an overdose of syrup of ipecac. A gastric tube with a large lumen is inserted, and the stomach is irrigated with copious amounts of tap water. Because of the time lapse in getting to the hospital and because the stomach normally traps material unaccessible to the lumen of the tube, chemical emesis is now favored over gastric lavage.

Specific measures can be instituted as

soon as the particular poison is identified. In most cases of acute poisoning, the physician can identify the agent by a quick history of the incident or by the label on the container. The poison container should always be brought to the hospital with the child.

Poison Control Centers. Information about poisons and emergency treatment of poison ingestion may be obtained immediately by telephoning the nearest Poison Control Center. Over 250,000 toxic or potentially toxic *trade name* products are on the consumer market. Federal law requires that the ingredients of drugs, pesticides, and caustic products be clearly stated on labels. However, many household products frequently involved in accidental ingestions are not required to be so labeled. To assist the physician with his very grave problem of identification, Poison Control Centers have been established in key areas of the United States. These centers are usually associated with medical schools or large hospitals equipped with laboratories, library, house staff, and faculty. They are available to dispense information 24 hours a day. They also serve as treatment centers and are actively engaged in programs of public education to prevent accidental poisoning. The Poison Control Centers give information to physicians only. Other persons calling receive first-aid instruction and are advised to call the physician at once.

Administration of antidote. Antidotes should be given immediately after emesis or lavage to render any remaining poison inert or prevent its absorption. Specific antidotes are not available for all poisons. Among the few available antidotes is dimercaprol (BAL, British antilewisite). Dimercaprol is a good antidote for mercury, antimony, and lead poisoning. Activated charcoal is a powerful physical antidote that adsorbs most poisons to itself. It should *not* be used with other substances that may interfere with its adsorptive capacity or with which it may interfere (syrup of ipecac). Large doses of the adsorbent should be used, especially when a large dose of poison has been ingested.

An antidote should be put in the Levin tube before its removal from the stomach. The specific antidote is given if one is available. The so-called "universal antidote" (two parts burned toast, one part milk of magnesia, and one part strong tea) is neither universal nor an antidote. The three ingredients "neutralize" each other—hence it is ineffective.

In the event of caustic ingestion, immediate administration of water or milk to dilute the poison has been advised. Both emesis and lavage are contraindicated because of possible further tissue injury.

Supportive treatment. Overtreatment by emetics, sedatives, and stimulants is dangerous and should be avoided. Overtreatment may result in more harm than the ingestion of the poison. Keep the patient comfortable, warm, and dry. Assure a clear airway and fresh air. Mouth-to-mouth resuscitation may be lifesaving.

Salicylate (aspirin) poisoning. More children die from accidental ingestion of salicylates (aspirin, sodium salicylate, oil of wintergreen) than from any other products. Seventeen percent of all accidental deaths resulting from poisoning are attributed to salicylate intoxication.

The widespread use and availability of salicylates are prime factors in overdosage. The use of salicylates is so commonplace that parents and sometimes physicians underestimate the toxicity of the drug. Salicylates act rapidly but are excreted slowly. A small dose repeated frequently may accumulate to cause a severe state of salicylate poisoning.

Candy-flavored aspirin was invented to obtain an accurate, small dosage and improve the taste, but children should never be told that medicine is candy; flavored aspirin should *never* be left within a child's reach.

A common but grave error occurs when the parent mistakenly gives the child a teaspoon of oil of wintergreen instead of cough medicine. One teaspoon of oil of wintergreen contains as much salicylate as

Fig. 23-5. Pink pills are *not* candy. Keep medicines in a locked cabinet.

60 grains of aspirin. It represents a *fatal* dose in most cases.

Clinical signs. There are many clinical signs of salicylate poisoning in children. In cases of acute poisoning the first manifestation is hyperpnea with an increase in respiration depth. Severe acidosis, electrolyte imbalance, and dehydration follow. Other common symptoms include restlessness, extreme thirst, fever (usually 103° F. or higher), profuse sweating, tremors, bleeding, delirium, convulsions, pulmonary edema, and coma. Cerebral hemorrhage may occur.

Treatment. The treatment of salicylate poisoning is always immediate emesis or lavage. Parents should attempt to induce vomiting as soon as the discovery is made. The physician or nearest Poison Control Center should be called for emergency instructions. The child is usually ordered to the hospital. The parents are requested to bring with the child any implicated container, loose pills, and sometimes the material vomited.

Gastric lavage is carried out in the hospital emergency room. A blood specimen

Fig. 23-6. Young children will eat and drink anything regardless of taste. Keep household poisons in a *locked* cupboard.

is ordered immediately to determine the level of salicylate intoxication. Treatment of salicylate intoxication is aimed at correcting electrolyte imbalance. Measures are instituted to promote the rapid excretion of salicylates in the urine. Parenteral fluids are given both to combat dehydration and to facilitate prompt excretion of salicylates from the body. Salicylate excretion is greatly increased by small doses of acetazolamide (Diamox). Acetazolamide renders the urine alkaline moments after administration; this, in turn, favors the excretion of salicylates.

Nursing care. Nursing care for salicylate poisoning is supportive. Fever is reduced by cool sponges; hourly urinary output is recorded and pH of the urine tested with

FIG. 23-7. Use firm discipline to keep child out of driveway and street.

FIG. 23-8. Even shallow water is dangerous for the unattended child.

Fig. 23-9. Always turn handles of pots and pans to the back of stove.

Nitrazine paper. Accurate hourly output notations will help determine amounts of parenteral fluids necessary. Temperature, pulse, and respiration are checked every 15 minutes until stable; oxygen is given as necessary. Exchange transfusions or dialysis may be considered in severe, life-threatening intoxication.

Poisoning is one of the most common pediatric emergencies. It is always difficult to treat. In more than half the cases the poisonous substances have been carelessly handled and stored by adults. The child often was improperly supervised. As part of the growing-up process, children investigate their environment. This investigation includes feeling and tasting, and these activities are always dangerous. However, opportunities for investigation must be available.

Parents must take time to answer questions, show their children how things work, and help them learn to do things safely for themselves. Patience and supervision will teach the child what he wants to know and show him the way to safety, too.

Fig. 23-10. Knives are highly dangerous. Keep them out of the toddler's reach.

Misuse of drugs

The abuse of drugs by youth in our society is a major and growing social and personal problem. The average age level of drug users is dropping steadily. Many junior-high and grade-school children are now frequent offenders.

The magnitude of the problem is revealed by the fact that in New York City in 1970 more deaths were caused by heroin

FIG. 23-11. Needles, buttons, and pins are easily swallowed. Keep them away from the toddler.

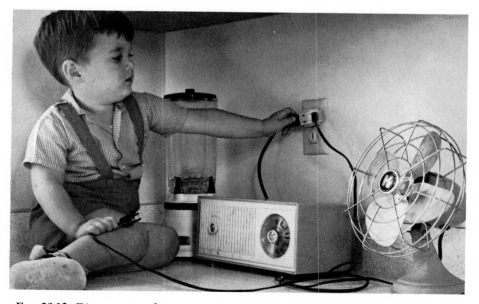

FIG. 23-12. Disconnect appliances not in use. Plug outlets and avoid hurts and burns.

use than by any other factor in the 18 to 35 age group, including accidents and disease. These statistics bode ill for the future if current trends continue.

The subject of drug abuse cannot be treated in any detail in this text, but students are encouraged to learn more concerning the causes, prevention, and treatment of this problem. Because of the severity and widespread nature of the difficulty, it is likely that pediatric nurses will encounter a variety of different situations related to drug abuse. One usually thinks of teen-age involvement with hallucinogenic drugs, but recently two toddlers were admitted to a pediatric emergency room after ingesting an unknown number of "LSD pills." Treated with chlorpromazine (Thorazine), they did respond favorably.

Drug reactions vary. A heroin overdose produces a severe depression, whereas an amphetamine overdose will result in hyperactivity and overstimulation. Violent psychological reactions, varying from hallucinations to severe psychoses (paranoia) may result from LSD use. Immediate medical attention is essential. Nurses should be alert for any unusual behavior not typical of the individual or his age group. Such signs include abnormal dilatation of the pupils, excitability, talkativeness, profuse perspiration, staggering, mental confusion, disturbances in perception, and general personality changes. The nurse can best assist these patients by a calm, supportive manner and a quiet atmosphere. She should make a careful attempt through conversation to make the patient aware of reality.

Sincere concern by the nurse for the addict can, in some cases, help build a communication bridge back to society that will help rehabilitate the individual. Unfortunately, such successes have been less frequent than the failures.

Child abuse

The term "child abuse" includes many types of physical, mental, and emotional neglect or injury. Hundreds of children are killed annually, and thousands of others are permanently harmed at the hands of adults, usually their parents.

Affected children commonly manifest abrasions, lacerations, skull fractures, intracranial bleeding, and multiple long bone fractures in various stages of healing, as well as personality disturbances and mental impairment. One type of child abuse in which the victim is characterized by severe physical injury and neglect has been called the *battered child syndrome*. Neglected, battered children brought to the hospital are typically under 3 years of age, frequently boys. They are many times born out of wedlock, unwanted, mentally retarded, and/or physically malformed. The children are often too young or too afraid to talk.

Parents of such children are described as emotionally immature and unready to accept the responsibilities of parenthood. Often, they are burdened by adverse social conditions, financial strain, and personal frustration. Some have reversed roles with their children, expecting them to provide love, gratification, and fulfillment to meet their own needs. Many of these parents were rejected and battered in their own childhood. They are repeating familiar parental behavior experienced in their young years.

Recognition. Certain clues may help identify these children. When first admitted to the hospital, neglected and battered children shut their eyes, turn their heads away, and cry irritably, in contrast to well-nurtured children who characteristically cry loudly and reach out for their parents. The skillful observer may recognize the difficulty when parents offer no reasonable explanation regarding the character, circumstances, or nature of the trauma sustained.

One 2½-year-old boy entered the hospital to have his leg "checked" (Fig. 37-3, p. 532). He weighed 19 pounds, one front tooth was missing, a fingernail was pulled off, his head and face were covered with skin lesions, and his right femur was severed.

The only information offered by his mother was, "He was very clumsy and stumbled in the yard." Two weeks passed before he would turn to look at anyone. His parents visited once in a period of 2 months. Suspicion should always be aroused when any of the following are noted: abnormal uncleanliness, malnutrition, multiple soft tissue injuries or burns in various stages of healing, and illness obviously caused by a lack of medical attention. Often, the behavior of the child shows he has no real expectation of being comforted or helped.

Reporting. Because parental neglect and abuse is difficult to understand, it may go unrecognized. Children may recover from their injuries and go home, only to be battered again. The alert nurse is usually the first to suspect that a child has been abused. She should carefully chart what she observes and *report* the situation to the physician at once! Every state requires that the physician report his suspicions to the police department or to the appropriate child protection service in the community. After a written report has been submitted, the case is carefully investigated. The physician participating in good faith in making a report is immune from civil or criminal liability. Willful refusal to report child neglect or abuse constitutes a misdemeanor.

Protection. As part of public comprehensive child welfare services, most communities have established "protective services" for neglected and abused children. The purpose of a protective service is not only to provide care and protection for the child but also to help parents who "want to be good" but for some reason are unable to assume their role. Why else do parents bring their neglected and battered children to the hospital? They always run the risk of punishment. Could an abused or neglected child be their way of actually asking for help?

Management of this serious problem may range from professional counseling and the introduction and explanation of various community services involved in child care to criminal court action. Juvenile courts have power over "neglected children," but according to recent studies, criminal prosecution is a poor means of preventing child abuse. Usually, criminal proceedings divide the family and cause parents to hate and despise their children. Legal action is only advisable when all other means of protection and prevention have failed.

UNIT VIII

SUGGESTED SELECTED READINGS AND REFERENCES

Bellam, G.: The first year of life, Amer. J. Nurs. **69:**1244-1246, June, 1969.

Benz, G. S.: Pediatric nursing, ed. 5, St. Louis, 1964, The C. V. Mosby Co.

Breckenridge, M. E., and Murphy, M. N.: Growth and development of the young child, Philadelphia, 1969, W. B. Saunders Co.

Breckenridge, M. E., and Vincent, E. L.: Child development, ed. 6, Philadelphia, 1969, W. B. Saunders Co.

Brody, S.: The developing infant, Children **13:**158-160, July-Aug., 1966.

Colella, R. F. A.: Dental care, Pediat. Clin N. Amer. **15:**325-336, 1968.

Coleman, A. B., and Alpert, J. J., editors: Poisoning in children, Pediat. Clin. N. Amer. **17:**entire volume, 1970.

Committee on the Control of Infectious Diseases, Report of, American Academy of Pediatrics, 1970.

Daniel, W. A.: The adolescent patient, St. Louis, 1970, The C. V. Mosby Co.

DiPalma, J. R.: Status report on immunization, RN **33:**69-77, Sept., 1970.

Drug menace: how serious? U. S. News and World Report **25:**38-42, May, 1970.

Egan, M. C.: Combating malnutrition through maternal and child health programs, Children **16:**67-71, March-April, 1969.

Erikson, E. H.: Childhood and society, ed. 2, New York, 1964, W. W. Norton & Co., Inc.

Fargel, H. C.: Teenage drug abuse, Clin. Pediat. **8:**123-125, 1969.

Frazier, C. A.: Those deadly insects, RN **34:**49-55, April, 1971.

Fremon, S. S.: New ways to measure intelligence in infants, Parents Mag. & Better Family Living **46:**39-41+, April, 1971.

Gellis, S. S., and Kagan, B. M.: Current pediatric

therapy, ed. 4, Philadelphia, 1970, W. B. Saunders Co.

Gesell, A., and Ilg, L. B.: The child from five to ten, New York, 1946, Harper & Row, Publishers.

Green, M., and Haggerty, R.: Ambulatory pediatrics, Philadelphia, 1968, W. B. Saunders Co.

Green, M., and Richmond, J. B.: Pediatric diagnosis, Philadelphia, 1962, W. B. Saunders Co.

Gregg, G. S.: Physician, child-abuse reporting laws, and injured child, Clin. Pediat. 7:720-725, 1968.

Gustafson, S., and Coursin, D.: The pediatric patient, Philadelphia 1969, J. B. Lippincott Co.

Helfer, R. E., and Kempe, C. H.: The battered child, Chicago, 1968, University of Chicago Press.

Hill, L. F.: Infant feeding: historical and current, Pediat. Clin. N. Amer. 14:255-268, 1967.

Illingworth, R. S.: The prevention of accidents, Clin. Pediat. 6:286-287, 1967.

Illingworth, R. S.: How to help a child to achieve his best, J. Pediat. 73:60-68, 1968.

Jones, J. G.: Preventing poisoning accidents in children, Clin. Pediat. 8:484-491, 1969.

Marlow, D. R.: Textbook of pediatric nursing, ed. 3, Philadelphia, 1969, W. B. Saunders Co.

Meyer, R. J., and Klein, D.: Childhood injuries, A report of the Second National Childhood Injury Symposium, Pediatrics supp. 44:entire volume, 1969.

Morrison, S. T., and Arnold, C. R.: Patients with common communicable disease, Nurs. Clin. N. Amer. 5:143-155, March, 1970.

Nelson, W. E., Vaughan, V. C., and McKay, R. J.: Textbook of pediatrics, ed. 9, Philadelphia, 1969, W. B. Saunders Co.

Nowlis, H. H.: Why students use drugs, Amer. J. Nurs. 68:1680-1685, Aug. 1968.

Paulsen, M. G.: Legal protections against child abuse, Children 13:42-48, March-April, 1966.

Ramirez, E.: Help for the addict, Amer. J. Nurs. 67:2348-2353, Nov., 1967.

Russell, F. E.: Injuries by venomous animals, Amer. J. Nurs. 66:1322-1326, June, 1966.

Sarrkot, M., and Smith, D. E.: Drug problems in the Haight-Ashbury, Amer. J. Nurs. 68:1686-1689, Aug., 1968.

Shirkey, H. D., editor: Pediatric therapy, ed. 3, St. Louis, 1968, The C. V. Mosby Co.

Skillenger, W. S.: Treatment of poisoning in children, Amer. J. Nurs. 65:108-112, Nov., 1965.

Wetzel, N. C.: The baby grid. An application of the grid technique to growth and development in infants, J. Pediat. 29:439-454, 1946.

Williams, S. R.: Nutrition and diet therapy, St. Louis, 1969, The C. V. Mosby Co.

UNIT IX

THE CHILD, THE FAMILY, AND THE HOSPITAL SETTING

24

Preparation for hospitalization

Not too many years ago the preparation of a child and his parents for the experience of hospitalization did not receive much consideration. Emphasis was placed on the child's disease rather than the fact that he was a particular person of certain capabilities and potentials who happened to be ill. Typically, the parents brought little Mary Lou to the pediatric ward, signed some papers, and said a rather hasty and usually tearful good-bye. In some cases Mary Lou was placed in a special semi-isolation admission area to be observed for 24 to 48 hours for the possible onset of contagious disease before being transferred to the main pediatric ward. Little was done to prepare her or her parents for this sudden change in their pattern of living.

Today, although we still have a great deal to learn about the child, his needs, and family relationships, we do recognize that the old approach and many of the old methods were incomplete and unnecessarily traumatic for all concerned. The modern nurse recognizes that the family may have a great deal to offer the hospitalized child, and when properly prepared and supported, the parents may be able to help the child during a difficult but, we hope, also a potentially constructive period in his heretofore brief experience with life.

Preparation of the parents

The heart of the problem in preparing the child for hospitalization lies in the preparation of his parents, who are then best able to help their child. It is imperative that parents receive sufficient knowledge of the child's illness so that they readily understand the need for hospitalization. It is also necessary for parents to have some understanding of the tests and treatments to be given and the risk and discomfort involved.

A child's morale will inevitably reflect his parent's outlook. When parents are inadequately prepared, they cannot adequately prepare their child. It is extremely important that the parents have sound information about the child's illness, confidence in their physician's recommendations, and the devoted interest of warm, intelligent, and understanding nurses.

Preparation of the child

According to his level of understanding, the child should be told why it is necessary for him to go to the hospital. Truthful assurance is the best guide. The truth is less frightening to a youngster than the ideas his imagination can invent. Children who are not given the true reason for hospitalization often believe that they have been punished or sent away because they have

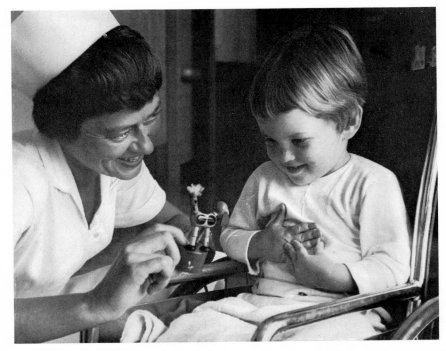

FIG. 24-1. No child is greatly disturbed permanently by hospitalization when sympathetic nurses educated in child care are available. (Courtesy Children's Health Center, San Diego, Calif.)

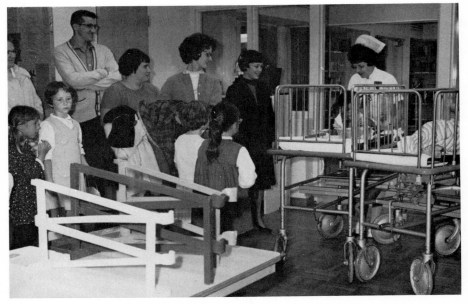

FIG. 24-2. Inviting the child and his parents to visit the hospital before admission helps them to know what to expect. (Courtesy Children's Health Center, San Diego, Calif.)

been naughty. Of course, if the truth is to be supportive, the child must have trust in his parents and other authority figures, trust based on previous experience of their trustworthiness. Such an attitude cannot be established in a day. Its foundation is laid during the first year and perpetuated through each stage of life.

Telling a child about surgery is a highly individual matter. Information about the impending operation will depend on his age, his level of understanding, and his emotional makeup. Usually a brief, simple explanation of what is wrong and what must be done to change it or make it better will help the child develop a sound and healthy attitude. A detailed and accurate explanation of the operation is not necessary; the child needs the truth, but not always the whole truth. The belief that an

event has been explained relieves tension.

Pediatric units in hospitals throughout the United States have developed methods to prepare parents and children for hospitalization. Colorful booklets and pamphlets, telephone calls, hospital tours, preadmission or orientation parties, and the use of television sets all have lessened the trauma of admission to the hospital. Advising parents of procedures and inviting the child and his parents to visit the hospital before admission help the child to know what to expect.

A child should know in advance what the hospital is like. He should be told simply and in a matter-of-fact manner about such things as the differences between hospital beds and beds at home, the use of the bedpan and urinals, the baths in bed, the special schooling, the playroom, and the food service. If 4-year-old Jimmy knows in advance about the big, wiggly scale that he must stand on to see how heavy he is and some of the other things that will happen at the hospital, he is less likely to be shocked when he faces them directly.

It is not always possible, necessary, or desirable for the child to know everything that will happen. All the child needs to know is enough to assure him that what happens is according to plan and that Mother will be at his side whenever possible. When she cannot be there, kind friends, physicians, and nurses will help care for him until he can go home again.

Liberal visiting hours and rooming-in facilities have made it much easier for the parents to continue their supportive role and counteract any sense of isolation or desertion the child may harbor.

Need for consistent mothering

Florence Erickson states that a child has a pronounced need for consistent mothering.* Even before his first birthday, he is

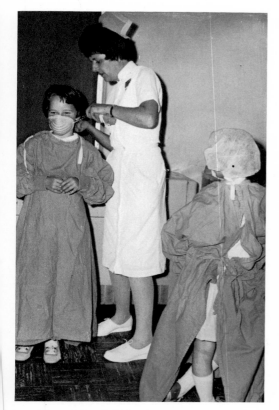

FIG. 24-3. If the child knows in advance what will happen, he is less likely to be shocked when he faces the situation directly. (Courtesy Children's Health Center, San Diego, Calif.)

*Erickson, F.: Therapeutic relationship of the nurse to the parents of a sick child. In Current concepts in nursing care, Columbus, Ohio, 1965, Ross Laboratories.

very much aware of strangers and becomes frightened if Mother leaves him. Until the child is about 5 years of age, he develops an extreme separation anxiety when away from his home or family. Older children become anxious too, especially when separation is complicated by illness, but ordinarily their anxiety is decreased by age and experiences away from home.

A sick child needs his mother; the mother, in turn, needs desperately to be of help to her child. Extended visiting hours and rooming-in arrangements should allow the mother to help with such routines as bedmaking, feeding, temperature taking, bathing, and dressing. These chores help Mother feel that she is important and that she is making a contribution to the health of her child. Most important, the child's social and emotional needs are met through his own parents. No one can easily take the place of a child's parents, especially the place of "Mom."

Aim of the hospital

The aim of the hospital is to provide a child-centered ward specifically organized to meet the needs of hospitalized children. Play programs, guided group experiences, and social, educational, and recreational programs accompanying everyday nursing routines can help meet the physical, emotional, and social needs of the hospitalized child. A milieu similar to the home is designed to help the child to be happier in a relatively normal environment, get well more quickly, and go home sooner.

Plans for the trip

Allowing the child to share in the planning and even to pack his own suitcase is very rewarding; telling him that his old clothes will be patched and washed while he is away reassures him that he will come home again. If a child has a favorite toy or object, he should take it with him to the hospital. Often a toy will give him comfort and some security when a situation is strange and perhaps frightening.

No matter how well a child is prepared for hospitalization he may still cry at the prospect of treatment, needles, and pain. Explain to the parents that this is a natural reaction and encourage them to stay with

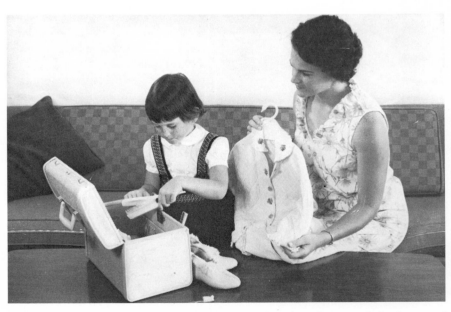

Fig. 24-4. Allowing the child to share in planning and packing her own little things is both reassuring and rewarding.

their child, since they are best able to comfort him with the thought that he will feel better when it is over. Usually Mother's presence helps the child to weather each interference as it comes and greatly reduces the risk of emotional trauma.

In this environment the nurse is available to give advice and explanation as necessary, helping, through the mother, to keep the situation as secure as possible for the child. No child is greatly disturbed in any permanent way by hospitalization when free contact with parents is permitted, sympathetic nurses educated in child care are available, and every attempt is made to attune the administration to recognize the needs of the child-parent unit.

25

The adverse effects of hospitalization

Considerable evidence has shown that the child often views hospitalization as desertion by his parents and thus may be profoundly affected by his hospital experience. When parents of a young child are unable to come to the hospital, the hospitalized child is exposed to numerous traumatic factors resulting in frustration of those inborn needs that are normally met in a family environment. As a result, the child may fail to thrive physically, socially, and psychologically. In extreme cases, maternal deprivation may be manifested as a general marasmus, or wasting away.*

Nurses, physicians, and parents have voiced an increasing concern for the hospitalized child. Much has been learned about the stresses a child faces when he becomes sick and is hospitalized. Hospitalization can be one of the most fearful experiences of childhood, with important, harmful aftereffects. The emotional aftermath of hospitalization may appear in such forms as night terrors, fears, negativisms, regressions to earlier, more babylike behavior, and protracted hostilities. In some cases the emotional aftermath does not appear until later in life.

Adverse effects of hospitalization are recognized in children who fail to cooperate with hospital staff or fail in relations with other hospitalized children. Irritability and anger are often seen in physically sick children. With the growing recognition of the possible traumatic effects of hospitalization, pediatric units have adopted a variety of measures to decrease the adverse effects of illness and hospitalization on children. Examples of these measures include hospitalizing children only in cases of unavoidable necessity, preparing children and their parents for the hospital stay, allowing rooming-in for mothers (especially for mothers of children under 5 years of age), providing playrooms for ambulatory children, bringing toys from home, liberalizing visiting hours, urging parents to be present when the child awakens from surgery, and helping children act out their operations or express their feelings in play situations.

A concern for the welfare of the total child requires not only preventing or neutralizing the possible traumatic effects of hospitalization but also trying to discharge the child from the hospital in a stronger condition emotionally as well as physically. The child needs to be helped to develop effective mechanisms to cope with the crises of hospitalization. The nurse can best accomplish this goal by first supporting the mother, who in turn reassures the child by her continuous, loving relationship. Working closely with the child's parents, the nurse discusses plans for the child's care. Learning from parents how a child behaves —the things he likes and dislikes—can be very helpful to the sympathetic and understanding nurse.

Separation anxiety
The young child

Studies have pointed out that between 1 and 4 years of age the risks involved with parent-child separation are greatest. These

---

*Beelicka, I., and Alechnowicz, H.: Treating children traumatized by hospitalization, Children 10:194-195, Sept.-Oct., 1963.

risks taper off beyond 5 years of age but never disappear entirely during childhood, since the child is incapable of emotional self-support. The mother of a young child who has been separated from his parents for a relatively long period can often confirm the pitiable behavior that seems to persist for months and, occasionally, even years later. Gradually, the child expresses his feelings of separation. He does this by his readiness to go with his mother as if never wanting to let her out of sight. He cries and is often excessively babyish, anxious, and easily angered.

By allowing parents to help care for their children in the hospital, nurses can be free to comfort, feed, and hold other children whose parents cannot be there.

Prolonged illness necessarily extends a child's separation from his parents, siblings, and familiar surroundings. Fear, anger, hostility, depression, and withdrawal are common manifestations of anxiety and tension provoked by long separation. The state of being ill is a stressful situation for most children. The disorder interferes with the child's usual activities, sources of pleasure, and capacities to achieve. Confinement to a hospital for a long time is hardly conducive to the fulfillment of childhood needs.

Separation anxiety is experienced by all children who have established a healthy mother-child relationship, especially by those under 4 years of age. The phenomenon of "settling in," or adjustment to hospitalization and separation, is deceptive. Robertson[*] found that children under 4 years of age experience three phases in the process of settling into the hospital: protest, despair, and denial.

At first the child *protests* the separation. He cries aloud for "Mama," shakes the crib, throws himself around, and is alert for any signs of his mother's return. The nurse may pick up the child and try to quiet him, but this is to no avail. Telling a child to stop crying only conveys to him that he is not

[*]Robertson, J.: Young children in hospitals, New York, 1958, Basic Books, Inc., Publishers, p. 48.

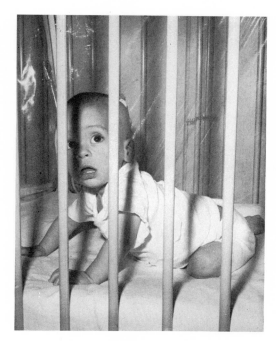

FIG. 25-1. Confinement to a hospital for a long time is hardly conducive to the fulfillment of childhood needs. (Courtesy U. S. Naval Hospital, San Diego, Calif.)

understood and adds to his feelings of helplessness. This phase may last for a few days or even up to 1 week.

During the phase of *despair* the child becomes apathetic and withdrawn, which is sometimes confused with acceptance. Instead of crying, he sobs. The hope of the return of his mother fades, but the wish for her return remains. During this quiet stage, distress seemingly has lessened, and the nurse presumes that he is "settling in." When his parents arrive, he turns his face away and cries aloud. He does not understand why he is in the hospital. He rejects his parents as they seem to have rejected him. Why has his mother failed him when he needs her most? Parents spend most of visiting time trying to get the child to take notice of them, and just as the child brightens up, they desert again. The child's piteous cries on the mother's arrival and departure lead the nurse to think that he is better off without his parents. The nurse who understands the reason for the child's

FIG. 25-2. Protest. The day after admission, the child (Marie, 2½ years old) cries aloud for "Mama," shakes the crib, and is alert for any signs of her mother's return. (Courtesy Children's Health Center, San Diego, Calif.)

FIG. 25-3. Despair. Four days after admission, the child has become apathetic and withdrawn. She does not understand why her mother has left her or why she is in the hospital. (Courtesy Children's Health Center, San Diego, Calif.)

behavior can be of great help to the mother who dreads coming back because she anticipates the distress of her child. The mother needs to realize how much her child needs her, and she should be encouraged to come often; when she leaves, she should be sure to tell the child when she will come back. It is unfair for a mother to tell her child that she is going for a cup of coffee. Children have lain awake all night waiting for mothers to return.

Gradually, *denial* follows despair. The child begins to show more interest in the surroundings, is more responsive to nursing attention, and actually denies the need for his mother. When his mother comes, he seems hardly to know her, is happy and gay throughout the visit, and may even wave good-bye. Because a young child cannot

tolerate the intensity of distress, he represses the need for his mother. After he returns home he often demonstrates disturbed feelings characterized by regressive, babylike behavior and is forever clinging to his mother, which only confirms that his complacency in the hospital was a facade.

The school-age child

The school-age child is not so prone to separation anxiety if his illness is short. The child has learned to rely to some extent on adults and other children when away from home. He can understand that hospitalization is a temporary situation and why his parents come only at certain times. School-age children seem more bothered by the disease process and its treatment. Imagination persists strongly throughout these years, and often fantasies and fears of mu-

FIG. 25-4. Denial. Eight days after admission, the little child cannot tolerate the intensity of distress, so she represses the need for mother. When her mother comes, she seems hardly to know her, is happy and gay. (Courtesy Children's Health Center, San Diego, Calif.)

tilation influence the degree of emotional reaction. Older children worry about the hospital costs. If by chance they feel responsible for causing their illness, their financial worries are intensified.

Long-term hospitalization imposes numerous anxieties on children of all ages. During a serious illness even an older child has a great need for his mother and can tolerate her absence only for short periods.

He needs to know that his parents will be there when he needs them most and that he is loved and missed.

Motor restriction

Each child comes to the hospital with his own individual makeup and achieved state of development, a unique past experience, and his own methods of dealing with anxiety. The nurse can encourage emotional growth by accepting the child as he is and by assisting him to continue in his present stage of development. For example, often a child is expected to conform to hospital rule by staying in his crib when, in essence, he has had the run of the whole house prior to hospitalization. Unless acutely ill, a child may refuse to stay in bed. The nurse should not arbitrarily urge the child to "stay there." She should be aware of the dangers of restricting the child to his crib when otherwise he could be ambulatory. For the toddler, sustained restriction of movement may lead to a severe state of anxiety and hostility. Whenever this basic urge is thwarted, the child becomes frustrated and angry and may regress. Every child has a motor urge. This drive is constructively handled by the wise nurse who is able to devise ways to allow the child freedom to move about safely.

• • •

This discussion has highlighted the psychological risks of hospitalization that are real and well documented. However, it is comforting to note that children usually are able to survive the event of hospitalization without significant emotional scars. It is largely the nurse's function to see that the original trauma is slight and the scars minimal.

26

The long-term pediatric patient

For most children the period of hospitalization is brief—a day or two, or perhaps a week. However, some youngsters become more accustomed to the children's treatment wing than to their own homes. The severely ill child who has a long, complicated convalescence and the child undergoing prolonged orthopedic correction are examples of the long-term pediatric patient.

These little patients should continue to grow physically, emotionally, intellectually, and socially despite illness. Three principles for nursing children with long-term illnesses may be suggested to encourage their growth: (1) maintain a basic sense of trust, (2) protect from fear, frustration, and pain, and (3) facilitate social contacts and contact with the outside world.

Maintain a basic sense of trust

Whether a child is well or sick, he is concerned with building and maintaining a basic sense of security. Experiences connected with the fulfillment of basic needs are prime sources for the development of this sense. Parents are best able to fulfill their child's basic needs and give a quality of care that enhances a sense of trust or feeling of security.

This sense of trust must be fostered during the admission process. When admitting the child to the hospital, the nurse routinely takes his pulse, respiration, and temperature. During this procedure she explains to the child what is being done, and she answers the parent's questions. Parents will judge the nurse's ability to care for their child at this time. When parents perceive the nurse as a secure (in her knowledge),

warm, and gentle individual, a trusting relationship begins. Fears about their child's hospitalization subside, and they begin to trust and have faith in the nurse. Parents begin to relax and may even talk about their many difficulties. Worries about an operation, the cost of surgery, and whether or not the child will recover are some of the problems they face. Although it is not always possible to remove all anxieties, the nurse can assist parents, step-by-step, to solve the concrete problems they face each day. Taking time to listen to parents and to answer their questions often relieves many fears. Frequent rounds, easy availability, and a willingness to help and explain make parents more comfortable. The parents' feelings of confidence and trust are carried over to the child.

Gradually, as the child's body becomes more dependable, he seeks within his environment ways of gaining active exercise and a greater range of sensory experiences. He investigates, listens, touches, and even tastes in these efforts. Of course, most important is not the fulfillment of these needs but the manner in which they are fulfilled.

Protect from fear, frustration, and pain

Children often are afraid of hospitals and fear what nurses and physicians might do to them. Parental threats of sending the child to the physician as punishment confuse the child and help develop the idea that illness may be a punishment. The necessary diagnostic measures and treatment procedures may cause great apprehension and physical discomfort. The nurse

FIG. 26-1. Parents are best able to fulfill the child's basic needs and give a quality of care that enhances a sense of trust. (Courtesy U. S. Naval Hospital, San Diego, Calif.)

can readily see from the responses of many children that long-term illness imposes difficult emotional adjustments to unpleasant and painful experiences. Unpleasant experieces can be minimized by giving the child every opportunity to talk about his fears. His questions should be answered truthfully, simply, and patiently. Preparing the child emotionally for a procedure is very helpful. However, a child should not be told of unpleasant procedures too far in advance. If too much time remains before the procedure, unconscious fantasies and fears may be activated.

Because a child is interested only in that which will affect him, information about a treatment must be focused on him—how he will feel and what he may do during the procedure. A painful procedure should be explained just before it is done. Telling the child that the injection will feel like a beesting will not necessarily result in acceptance, but the fact the nurse has been truthful shows him that she understands his reactions. Honest explanations will lessen a child's fears and will strengthen his trust and confidence in the nurse.

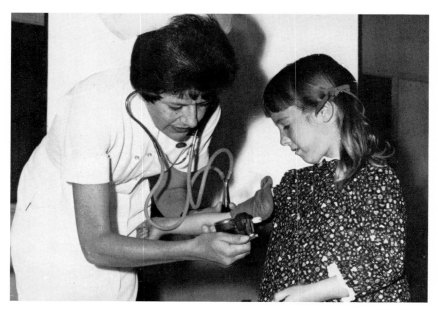

FIG. 26-2. Honest explanations will lessen a child's fears and strengthen the child's trust and confidence in the nurse. (Courtesy Children's Health Center, San Diego, Calif.)

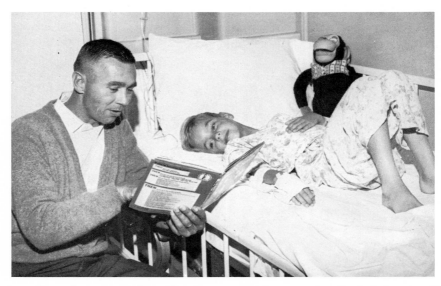

FIG. 26-3. Physical restoration from illness is not enough; to combat the isolation that illness inflicts, activities suitable to the child's physical condition must be encouraged. (Courtesy U. S. Naval Hosptal, San Diego, Calif.)

Protection against pain and feelings of distress will promote constructive uses of hospital experience. Friendly, comforting hands answering a child's cry, not forcing him to eat nor waking him from sleep, are sound nursing decisions that will enable the child to utilize his inner strengths to get well.

Facilitate social contacts and contact with the outside world

A common danger for a child who experiences a long illness and convalescence is that he may begin to feel dependent. His stay in the hospital may lessen his initiative because he gets so much satisfaction from being nursed. Adverse effects of hospitalization must be offset by educational opportunities in the hospital that provide experiences for growth and development. A well-rounded program of guidance, instruction, and recreation will develop self-respect, encourage initiative, and help fulfill the needs of the whole child.

Physical restoration from illness is not enough. Often a child is socially immature because he has come from a protected hospital environment. Emotional and social progress must match or even exceed physical improvement if a child is to be rehabilitated in the true sense. To combat the isolation that illness inflicts, the hospital should provide the child with experiences that are, as much as possible, comparable to those he would be experiencing if he were not hospitalized—his usual world of home, schoolwork, and recreation. These include activities suitable to his physical condition, especially those that bring him the companionship of children his own age.

Guidance. Guidance entails training and teaching the child how to live and care for himself. Naturally, it would be easier for the nurse to go ahead and do all the work, but by careful planning and suggestion, a constructive program can be devised with the child working along with the nurse. For example, during the early morning period, which is a busy time in the hospital, many boys and girls can be taught to take care of their personal belongings and attend to their personal hygiene. Success is a strong incentive to every boy and girl, and the child who feels he has succeeded in accomplishing something worthwhile develops more self-esteem and self-confidence.

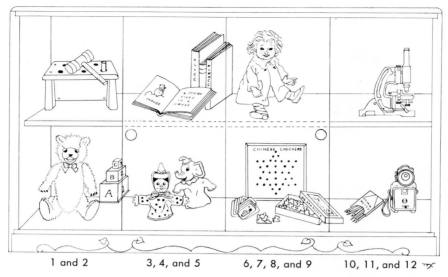

1 and 2   3, 4, and 5   6, 7, 8, and 9   10, 11, and 12

FIG. 26-4. Every pediatric ward should have a toy cupboard with toys arranged on shelves according to the different age interests. The nurse is better able to assist the child in play if she knows how to select toys, where to find toys, and what toys a child might like.

Each morning while observing the child, the nurse is confronted with questions about his illness, body, and medical procedures. One essential aspect of a constructive hospital experience is the creation of a balanced emotional climate in which it is possible to learn by asking questions. The nurse is uniquely qualified to educate the child about his body and illness. Talking with the child and answering his questions may calm specific fears and contribute to his long-range education and development.

Instruction. The public school system is responsible for providing education for all children, including children in the hospital. Pediatric hospitals should supply adequate space for educational facilities. The schoolroom should be large enough to accommodate a group of children in beds, wheelchairs, or carts. The nurse should arrange routine procedures and treatments to allow adequate time for a consistent educational program. A program can be planned to meet each child's need if the physician, nurse, teacher, social worker, librarian, and physical therapist meet together and discuss the overall progress of each child from week to week.

Recreation. Play periods are included daily as an integral part of the educational program. Play is a learning activity; play serves the child physically, mentally, emotionally, and socially. In play a child develops new physical abilities, and he acquires knowledge about himself and explores the feel, look, and taste of the world around him. He uses play to express what he is thinking and feeling, and through play he learns to relate and interact with others.

In the hospital a play program provides a warm, friendly atmosphere that will help the child develop normally while his body mends. A place to play, suitable materials, and other youngsters to play with are what children need. Because play is a child's way of learning, toys, materials, and equipment are learning tools. Paints, modeling clay, dolls, blocks, wood, games, books, and toys are the materials with which children rebuild the world to their size—a world they bring with them, a world of people, things, and feelings. Children will play wherever they are. A child's play is his occupation just as surely as teaching is his father's occupation. They only need space,

347

the right kind of toys, and friendly adults to help them.

A play program should be designed to protect children from the effects of separation from family, isolation, and reaction to medical procedures. Play offers healing for hurts and sadness. For example, dramatic play is recognized as an emotional release, and children who fear treatments are helped to release their pent-up feelings in their use of dolls and other toys. Janie, 5 years of age, confined to the hospital for a long time with a serious blood dyscrasia, picked up her doll one day and said, "Don't cry Janie, it isn't your fault. Mommy is going to come every day to take care of you." The attitudes and feelings that children reveal in their play are full of meaning. Every opportunity should be afforded the sick child to release his feelings, lest the effects of experiences in the hospital linger as he grows into adulthood. Unless the deep-lying impulses satisfied by play are allowed to be expressed in childhood, adult life suffers.

The nurse can help children choose the right kind of play material with which to have fun and find satisfaction. A few prin-

TABLE 26-1. Play-and-get-well chart

Age	Interest	Toys	Books
Infant (Birth-1 yr.)	Toys that attract the eye, make little sounds, and tempt grasping hands	Bright hanging objects; large plastic rings; string of gaily colored rings; rubber toys that squeak; tinkling bells	None (enjoys a song or lullaby)
Toddler (1-3 yr.)	Toys that enable parallel play, provide security and attention, and help development of muscle coordination	Nest of blocks; mallet and wooden pegs; trucks and cars; cuddly toy animals; large dolls; rocking horse; toy telephone; musical toys; kiddie car	Large linen picture books; nursery rhymes; ABC books; farm and zoo animal stories Likes the same story over and over again
Preschooler (3-5 yr.)	Toys that stimulate child's imagination and develop creative abilities	Nurse and doctor sets; trains and trucks; Tinker Toys; cabin logs; magnets; toy army men; record player; hand puppets; crayons and color books; dolls and clothes; simple puzzles; modeling clay; scrapbooks; cuddly toy animals	Dr. Seuss books; Golden Books; once-upon-a-time stories Enjoys stories about airplanes, trains, and police and fire stations Likes to look at pictures while being read to
Early school age (6-9 yr.)	Application of mental as well as physical skills Interest and enjoyment in playing with children of same sex Realistic toys that bring child into contact with world outside hospital	Craft sets; models; picture painting; stamp collection; string marionettes; spool knitting; beadwork Games such as Monopoly, checkers, and Clue Paper and pencil games; jigsaw puzzles; paper dolls	Comic books; riddle books; crossword puzzles; fairy tales; adventure stories; simple science book; how and why books; who-when-where books; *Highlights*
Middle school age (10-12 yr.)	Adaptable to group activities Combine companionship and challenge and coordinate work and play in teams	Card games; photoelectric football; science toys; chess; checkers Skill games such as sculpturing and wood carving Walkie-talkie; telescope; transistor radio; camera; television; picture viewer	Comic books; school textbooks; biographies; adventure stories Junior classics such as *Heidi, Little Women, Treasure Island, Robin Hood, Alice in Wonderland, Andersen's Fairy Tales, Aesop's Tales*

ciples that should be kept in mind when choosing toys are as follows:

1. Suitability for a particular age
2. Safety
3. Durability

Choosing the right play materials at the right time is not an easy task. However, an understanding of the wide variety of play interests can often give helpful clues.

Every child needs a well-balanced toy selection for all-around development. The choice should be planned to stimulate the following:

1. Social play
2. Dramatic play
3. Creative play
4. Manipulation and constructive play
5. Active physical play

Toy cupboards should be available in each ward and stocked with educational and instructive toys for children of all ages.

In a long-term hospital unit, a play therapist may be responsible for developing a play program. A well-organized play program should provide a daily schedule of activities in keeping with the ages, interests, and needs of all children in the pediatric unit.

Play is the working partner of growth. Activity is as vital to growth as medicine, food, and sleep. In the final analysis, what is the worth of a healed body if the mind is permanently limited from lack of opportunity to grow socially and emotionally?

Continuity of nursing care

The child who has a prolonged hospitalization may sometimes be greatly aided in establishing meaningful relationships if certain nurses on each shift are consistently assigned to his care. His unit should be made as homelike and personal as possible, but the nurse must remember to go through his small hoard of belongings periodically to restore order from chaos! The nurse caring for a child who has been a patient over a long period must guard against taking him for granted. She must discipline herself to observe this boy or girl with the same alertness she exercises when caring for other youngsters not so accustomed to hospital routine. Finding real ways that this type of patient can be a helper in the area is very rewarding to the child and the nurse. Depending on his age, capabilities, and interests, he may help show other boys and girls around the unit, make decorative tray cards or scrapbooks, help entertain 2-year-old Scott in the playpen, help stamp hospital record sheets, or perhaps assist with some tasks directed by central supply. However, in our age of disposables the manual tasks of assembly so constantly needed in the past in the maintenance of hospital supplies are not required so often.

The child who remains within the hospital for a protracted period presents a real challenge to the nursing skills, educational abilities, and psychological awareness of the staff and entire health team.

27

The dying child, his parents, and the nurse

Few nursing assignments are more challenging than helping a mother and father and their sick child who is afflicted with an illness that is invariably fatal. Since the nurse cannot change the reality of the tragic situation, she frequently feels sorrowful. Probably no human experience cuts so deeply into the center of one's heart as the loss of a child.

Understanding a child's concept of death will help the nurse know what to say. Understanding the ways in which his parents may react to the prospective death and one's own feelings about death will relieve some of the nurse's stress. This knowledge should enable the nurse to provide helpful support to the parents and the kind of tender reassuring care the child needs.

A child's concept of death

A child's concept of death is dependent to a considerable extent on his age, since there are different levels of understanding at different ages. Young children do not perceive of death as final or terminal. For children 3 to 5 years of age, death is denied; it is only a change of some kind and is not permanent. Children 5 to 9 years of age recognize death but cannot conceive of it as resulting from chance or a natural happening. Causation is personified. Death to them is like part of a game of cowboys and Indians. Everybody kills each other off, and then they resurrect themselves and play another game. Hence, when someone dies, in the child's mind the event is usually thought of not only as a deprivation but also as a personal abandonment. It may be considered a hostile act on the part of the person who died.

Children 9 years of age and older achieve a realistic concept of death as a permanent biological process. A child over 9 years old is capable of integrating the concept of "not being" if his parents can do so. However, he is comforted by the thought that his death (and theirs) is yet far away.

In view of the preceding information the nurse can readily understand the reasons why children need not be told of their fatal illness. Children generally accept, without obvious panic, the restriction imposed on them as a disease progresses. However, until their energy diminishes they want to do the same things that other children do. A very bright 3½-year-old boy was nearing the terminal phase of cancer. He seemed so weak that we had his breakfast brought to his cribside instead of serving it in the dining room where most of the little patients ate. For days he hardly ate at all. One morning he asked if his food was cooking. When his tray arrived, he cried aloud and would eat nothing. Knowing that he was hungry, we decided to prop him up and move his crib to the dining room. There he was able to finish every bite without assistance. Even near the end when vomiting occurred after eating, his cries on removal from the dining room could be heard by all. As the child's energy diminishes and death approaches, he has less interest in his surroundings and sleeps most of the time.

Children rarely manifest an overt concern about death, probably because they attempt to repress their anxiety concerning it. Nevertheless, the older child should be allowed to express his fears verbally if he is capable or through play media if he is not. Highly susceptible to the attitudes of his parents, the child will likely sense the gravity of the situation and will need to ventilate his feelings. Often the child should be reassured that his illness is not his fault and is not a punishment for anything he did.

What to tell the child

If by chance the older child does ask about dying, a statement such as, "You have a serious illness, but no illness is without hope and you should remember that,"* is likely to be believed and reassuring. If the child sees or asks about the death of another child, the nurse might say, "Johnny was very sick and died." This implies that the inquirer is not as ill as was his friend. Answer questions simply and always truthfully. Keep in mind the child's level of understanding.

Three stresses of terminal illness

In addition to having illnesses that cause considerable distress, children suffering from terminal illness are subjected to three stresses common to other hospitalized children, namely, separation from mother, traumatic procedures, and isolation. Modification of hospital routine and procedure must be considered.

Separation from mother. Depriving a mother and child of each other when permanent separation will soon take place would be particularly unfortunate. The child wants his mother. Encourage her to touch him. The warmth of physical contact is the most primitive and basic nonverbal comforting technique we possess. It can communicate a solace or comfort to the frightened child that words can never produce.

Traumatic procedures. When parents are helped to understand the reasons why tubes are inserted, intravenous feedings are ordered, blood is withdrawn, or other treatments initiated, they feel better satisfied. Parents are usually best able to console and protect their children from fear. Remember, the nurse is best able to help a child allay his fears through his parents. By helping parents to understand, you will have helped the child.

You can also help the older child by transferring his attention and concern from his incurable illness and focusing them on other *curable* problems or symptoms he may be experiencing. Listen with interest and attention to all his complaints, particularly ones related to intercurrent infections —rashes, etc.—that can be eliminated. These complaints should be treated intensively. The child can receive enormous reassurance and relief as your attempts to control them are successful. Wahl* calls this method of relieving anxiety "trading up." One month before his death, a 12-year-old leukemic boy stated that he had a cold. Because there was bleeding from all body orifices it was difficult to recognize his symptoms. However, once aware of the preceding information, we treated his cold vigorously. His attention was diverted from his never-ending bloody diarrhea and his many painful intravenous feedings and blood transfusions. Nearing the last stages of life, he succeeded in one last remission; "trading up" illnesses increased this boy's courage as he survived 4 more weeks.

Isolation. Finally, do not isolate the dying child from his friends, relatives, or staff. Usually you cannot conceal a child's death from other children in the ward. They know that "room 101" is the place where children go to die. Furthermore, the most dreaded possibility does not seem to be that of dying but that of dying alone. Children feel secure with other children, and they know nothing too terrible can happen when Mom is there. Encourage parents and relatives to say when they will come back. It implies a promise, "I will see you again, and you will have nothing

---

*From Wahl, C. W.: The dying patient, Consultant, Nov., 1961, Smith, Kline & French.

*Wahl, C. W.: The dying patient, Consultant, Nov., 1961, Smith, Kline & French.

to fear in the interim." Although relatives and staff are encouraged not to isolate the child, the nurse should not permit constant or unduly prolonged visits that the child may interpret as a "death watch."

Parental reaction

One of the most important roles in the management of the child with a terminal illness is the help that the nurse may provide to the grieving parents.

Integrating the event

Integrating the tragic event of death into their life experience is most difficult. The parents' reactions to the prospective death of the child may be likened to the mechanism of separation anxiety. However, it has much deeper meaning than most separation anxieties that parents and children face.

The mourning process

Anticipation of the forthcoming loss is often accompanied by mourning. The process of resigning oneself to the inevitable outcome usually begins before the child dies, and the parents must be allowed this period of mourning that involves a concentration of interest and energies, self-examination, self-condemnation, and guilt. The parents ask themselves and others, "Would it have made a difference if we had called the physician earlier? Did the child inherit the disease from one of us?" The nurse allows the parents to voice their guilt and reassures them by the gentle and understanding way she answers their questions.

The nurse can help relieve the suffering of parents who are mourning if she has insight into the feelings that they are experiencing. According to Bowlby,* there are three phases in the natural mourning process: protest, despair and disorganization, and hope and rebuilding. Mourning is the process of healing that helps us face and recover from loss. The normal healing process

takes a year or more. The clearest evidence of recovery is the ability to remember comfortably and realistically both the pleasures and disappointments of the lost relationship. The following predictable steps in the mourning process permit a judgment that healing has occurred: protest, despair and disorganization, and hope and rebuilding.

Protest. The first phase is characterized by a general tendency to protest or deny the diagnosis of disease or its fatal outcome. In trying to deny the facts, many strong emotions are brought into play—anxiety, yearning, anger, and guilt. Parents cannot quite believe that this could happen to their child. Often a parent's attitude is one of suspicion, hostility, and constant criticism. Hope for the child is stressed but in a nonspecific way. The parent tells himself, "Something will be discovered." He wants to try anything that might offer hope for a cure no matter how irrational it may seem.

Anxiety is manifested by an intense need to weep, an empty feeling in the abdomen, and loss of appetite. Along with anxiety goes yearning, longing for a sign that a cure will be found and the child will get well. Guilt feelings are constantly expressed in tears, "If only I had done this or that, if only I had notified the physician sooner." It is natural and necessary to cry, to be angry, and to be disorganized. These are all healthy signs of normal grief. It is a stage in the gradual process of accepting a great loss.

Involvement of parents in the physical care of the child is extremely important in facilitating parental adaptation. But although parental participation in the care of the sick child is desirable, it should not be at the expense of the emotional and physical well-being of the remainder of the family. (Siblings may be disturbed during this period and may require considerable parental support. Parents should be encouraged to divide their time among the various members of the family as the situation warrants.) Mothers and fathers usually want to be with their sick child

---

*Bowlby, J.: Process of mourning, Int. J. Psychoanal. **42:**331, 1961.

and need to feel that they personally have done everything possible for the child. Feelings of guilt are somewhat relieved by the expenditure of personal effort in the care of the child. Parents are allowed and encouraged to participate realistically in the physical care of the child by bathing, feeding, or entertaining him and escorting him to the laboratory and x-ray departments. Thus parents become integrated into the ward program, and communication with ward personnel is enhanced.

During the initial period on the ward, mothers physically cling to their children. They are involved solely in their care. After a while parents desire to help as effectively as they can with the care of other children. Assisting them to the playroom and reading to a group rather than just their own child are examples of this desire. Manifestations of this capacity (to help other children) marks a turning point in parental adjustment that reflects acceptance of the child's illness and ultimate death.

Despair and disorganization. Facing and accepting the reality of the fatal illness, parents feel helpless. Life is stripped of meaning. Active, realistic efforts to prolong the child's life are typical in this second phase.

The mother spends most of her time ministering to the needs of her sick child. During this time the nurse must be aware that the mother's attempts to cope with the situation may fluctuate from gentle, assured bedside care to inappropriate exhausting activity. At one moment she may express exaggerated gratitude to the nurses and medical staff, in the next she is overly critical. Her emotions may range from philosophical resignation to emotional sentimentality.

The reality of the fatal illness and its meaning begins more and more to penetrate the mother's consciousness. Her denial of the character of the illness may disappear, but hope of a cure persists. Her hope is more specific now, often related to particular scientific efforts.

During this period, mothers cling less to their children and encourage them to participate in ward activities. Parents should be encouraged to express their feelings of depression and defeat during moments away from the child. This helps them move beyond the initial shock and recognize some of the specific things they still have to offer their child. Every attempt must be made to enable parents to see the continuing value of their function as parents, despite their feeling of helplessness in the face of death.

As the child's physical energy begins to diminish, preoccupation with measures that involve treatment of the disease begins to subside, and parents are interested in relieving the child's discomfort and pain. Although they continue to hope that their efforts will save the child, the intensity of the expectation is gradually reduced. Emotionally they are separating themselves from the child.

Hope and rebuilding. The third phase is characterized by a calm acceptance of the child's impending death. Separation from the child is no longer an adaptive problem for the mother. Mother remains with the child whenever possible but with adequate consideration for the remainder of the family. For the first time, the mother expresses a wish that the child could die so that his suffering would end.

Many parents never reach this third phase of mourning during their child's illness. It may not be until after the child dies that the third phase begins. With the loss acknowledged and the depth of pain plumbed, new people, relationships, and activities become meaningful. Some parents take interest in such organizations as the Cancer Society, Cystic Fibrosis Association, etc. By so doing, the mourner is able to reduce preoccupation with self and the dead child. This allows the mother to reinvest feelings in her other love objects— her husband, her remaining children, or close relatives. The length of the grief reaction and how a person finally adjusts to his new social environment depends, Lindermann* says, on the success of what is called the "grief work." By this he means the transition of responsibility for the deceased to other areas of activity and the formation of new relationships and the readjustments this necessitates.

The nurse and the dying child
Feelings toward death

Awareness of one's feelings toward death is essential to acquiring the ability to give comprehensive nursing care to the dying child and his parents. Information about the child's concept of death and his parents' fears is not enough. To give sensitive and supportive care to the dying child, the nurse needs help in understanding her own fears about death.

Understanding the concept of death

Death is the most inescapable and realistic of all the fears that we face. Fear and anxiety lead to convictions of immortality on a conscious or unconscious level and are universal in all men. We recognize that other people must die but feel an inward assurance that it need never happen to us.

To learn about death, Wahl[†] suggests that we look at the unconscious mind. The mind may be likened to an iceberg. One seventh of it shows above the water (the conscious) and six sevenths lies below (the unconscious).

The unconscious is continually active. Its thought processes are illogical. To the unconscious mind, death is never possible in relation to the self. The unconscious is like the mind of the child before he learns to rationalize. Death is never the result of chance or natural happening. When a child has strong feelings of hostility toward a person, he might say, "I hate you, I wish you were dead." If by chance this person dies, the child concludes, "Because I wished this thing, it happened. Therefore I am responsible."

Death of loved ones is viewed as a deliberate abandonment on their part because of something the child has done. His mother and father died because they hated him. These are the kinds of concepts a child forms. Unconsciously, fear of death involves these same kinds of concepts in adult life.

Each person feels or reacts differently to the death experience. If this reality (death) is so painful that we handle it by immersing ourselves in it or utterly denying it, it will be difficult for us to fulfill our role as nurses. We ought to let ourselves recognize, at least to a limited degree, the awe and fear that all of us experience in the face of death. Fear of death is handled in several ways: (1) by a religious belief in immortality, (2) by a denial of the awe felt for death, (3) by withdrawal from the dying child, and (4) by the formation of various phobias or compulsions. The nurse is involuntarily influenced by illogical but protective defenses in the presence of impending death. However, if we are to help parents who are experiencing deep grief and distress, we are not to ridicule them or isolate ourselves from them. We are not to punish them in this way. We must become aware of our own feelings. We must try to better understand how we ourselves feel about death.

Courage

Nursing the dying child requires courage. The nurse must remember that courage is not the absence of fear but the willingness and ability to function in its presence. No good nurse is less human because she calls herself a nurse. Nurses who care for dying children and counsel their parents must preserve a sympathy and empathy and yet be free enough of emotional involvement to do their work commendably well. We should not become so

---

*Lindermann, E.: Symptomatology and management of acute grief. In Parad, H., editor: Crisis intervention: selected readings, New York, 1965, Family Service Association of America.
†Wahl, C. W.: Death, tape recording of lecture, UCLA, November, 1958.

personally involved with the dying child that we neglect the other children who have an equal need for nursing care.

Basic concepts of religion

The comfort the nurse can give to the parents of the dying child is important. Knowing their religious belief concerning death may be a great help. Often the nurse will observe that parents with deep faith in God find real comfort in their religious beliefs. For Catholics and Protestants who believe in personal immortality, there is great solace and comfort in the conviction that they will one day rejoin their loved ones.

In the Jewish faith the concept of immortality is not clearly defined. Judaism teaches that perhaps there is a life after death, but the only immortality of which man is certain is the immortality he achieves while he is still alive or through his descendants.

Knowing the basic concepts of the various religious faiths concerning death may be of great assistance to the nurse. The nurse is not expected to be a theologian nor should she attempt to share her religious beliefs concerning death unless she is asked, but the nurse can help the child and his parents by supplying physical and emotional support and the comfort of spiritual counsel by contacting any clergyman the parents desire. This spiritual advisor, especially one who has added to his religious training skills in personal counseling, can well be the one to whom a parent may turn. He can communicate comfort to parents when friends and relatives are helpless.

Death is inevitable but no less difficult because of its inevitability. Just as it may be the nurse's privilege to help parents and their infant at the event of birth, it may also be her privilege to ease and comfort a mother and father and a small human being who has come to life's last hours. May she do so with gentleness, reverence, and skill.

UNIT IX

**SUGGESTED SELECTED READINGS
AND REFERENCES**

Ambler, M. C.: Disciplining hospitalized toddlers, Amer. J. Nurs. 67:572-573, March, 1967.

Amend, E. L.: A parent education program in a children's hospital, Nurs. Outlook 14:53-56, April, 1966.

Aufhauser, T. R.: Parent participation in the hospital care of children, Nurs. Outlook 15:40-42, Jan., 1967.

Beelicka, I., and Olechnowicz, H.: Treating children traumatized by hospitalization, Children 10:194-195, Sept.-Oct., 1963.

Belmont, H. S.: Hospitalization and its effects on the total child, Clin. Pediat. 9:483-492, 1970.

Bergmann, T.: Children in the hospital, New York, 1965, International Universities Press.

Blake, F. G., Wright, F. H., and Waechter, E. H.: Nursing care of children, ed. 8, Philadelphia, 1970, J. B. Lippincott Co.

Blake, F. G.: The child, his parents and the nurse, Philadelphia, 1954, J. B. Lippincott Co.

Blake, F. G.: Immobilized youth: a rationale for supportive nursing intervention: Amer. J. Nurs. 69:2364-2369, Nov., 1969.

Bowlby, J.: Processes of mourning, Int. J. Psychoanal. 42:317-340, 1961.

Broadribb, V.: Foundations of pediatric nursing, Philadelphia, 1967, J. B. Lippincott Co.

Carpenter, K. M., and Stewart, J. M.: Parents take heart at City of Hope, Amer. J. Nurs. 62:82-85, Oct., 1962.

Dimock, H. G.: The child in hospital; a study of his emotional and social well-being, Philadelphia, 1960, F. A. Davis Co.

Dittman, L. L.: Child's sense of trust, Amer. J. Nurs. 64:91-93, Jan., 1966.

Engel, G. L.: Grief and grieving, Amer. J. Nurs. 64:93-98, Sept., 1964.

Erickson, F.: Reactions of children to hospital experience, Nurs. Outlook 6:501, Sept., 1958.

Erikson, E. H.: Childhood and society, New York, 1960, W. W. Norton & Co., Inc.

Evans, A. E.: If a child must die, New Eng. J. Med. 278:138-142, 1968.

Folck, M. M., and Nie, P. J.: Nursing students learn to face death, Nurs. Outlook 7:510-513, Sept., 1959.

Geis, D. P.: Mothers' perceptions of care given their dying children, Amer. J. Nurs. 65:105-107, Feb., 1965.

Geist, H.: A child goes to the hospital, Springfield, Ill., 1965, Charles C Thomas, Publisher.

Hagberg, K. L.: Combining social casework and group work methods in a children's hospital, Children 16:192-197, Sept.-Oct., 1969.

Haller, J. A., Jr.: The hospitalized child and his family, Baltimore, 1967, The Johns Hopkins Press.

Hewitt, H. E., and Pesznecker, B. L.: Blocks to communicating with parents, Amer. J. Nurs. 64:101-103, July, 1964.

Hott, J.: ℞: Play PRN in pediatric nursing, Nurs. Forum 9:288-309, 1970.

Jacob, N. M.: Unrestricted visiting in a children's ward, Lancet 2:584, 1969.

Jean, S. L.: Mental windows for hospitalized children, Children 13:182-186, June, 1949.

Jolly, H.: Play is work. The role of play for sick and healthy children, Lancet 2:487-488, 1969.

Koop, C. E.: The seriously ill or dying child: supporting the patient and the family, Pediat. Clin. N. Amer. 16:555-564, 1969.

Lascari, A. D.: The family and the dying child: A compassionate approach, Med. Times 97:207-215, May, 1969.

Lindermann, E.: Symptomatology and management of acute grief. In Parad, H., editor: Crisis intervention: selected readings, New York, 1965, Family Service Association of America.

Marlow, D. R.: Textbook of pediatric nursing, ed. 3, Philadelphia, 1967, W. B. Saunders Co.

Plank, E. N.: Working with children in hospital, Cleveland, 1962, Press of Western Reserve University.

Puner, H.: Choose toys for stages not ages, Parents' Mag. 45:50, Nov., 1967.

Ritchie, M.: The hospital schoolroom, Amer. J. Nurs. 63:77-79, July, 1963.

Robertson, J.: Young children in hospitals, New York, 1958, Basic Books, Inc., Publishers.

Rousseau, O.: Mothers do help in pediatrics, Amer. J. Nurs. 67:798-800, April, 1967.

Scahill, M.: Preparing children for procedures and operations, Nurs. Outlook 17:36, June, 1969.

Shore, M. F.: Planning for children in the hospital, Bethesda, Md., 1965, National Institute of Mental Health.

Smith, M.: Ego support for the young child, Amer. J. Nurs. 63:90-95, Oct., 1963.

Solnit, A. J., and Green, M.: The pediatric management of the dying child. Part II. The child's reaction to the fear of dying. In Solnit, A., and Provence, S., editors: Modern perspectives in child development, New York, 1963, International Universities Press, Inc.

Toys at work, Amer. J. Nurs. 65:68, Dec., 1965.

Wahl, C. W.: The physician's management of death and the dying patient, Proceedings of the Third World Congress of Psychiatry, 1960.

Wahl, C. W.: The dying patient, Consultant, Nov., 1961, Smith, Kline & French.

Wahl, C. W.: The fear of death. In Fulton, R., editor: Death and identity, New York, 1965, John Wiley & Sons, Inc.

Washington guide to promoting development in the young child, Seattle, 1970, University of Washington School of Nursing (mimeographed material available from the university).

Webb, C.: Symposium on the nurse and the ill child, Nurs. Clin. N. Amer. 1:73-120, March, 1966.

Webb, C.: Tactics to reduce a child's fear of pain, Amer. J. Nurs. 66:2698-2701, Dec., 1966.

Wu, R.: Explaining treatments to young children, Amer. J. Nurs. 65:71-73, July, 1965.

UNIT X

PEDIATRIC PROCEDURES

28

Hospital admission and discharge

First impressions are important, especially when a parent and his child are involved. At times hospitalization of a child may be planned, and a previsit to the pediatric department may be possible to reassure parents and patient, but for many families hospitalization comes as an abrupt, unscheduled, and basically frightening experience.

A cordial, smooth introduction to hospital life, extended by a nurse who is sincerely interested in the family involved, will do much to ease the anxiety inherent in the situation. All good nurses minister to more than the hospitalized patient's needs. They are alert to the needs expressed and unvoiced by all family members. However, perhaps nowhere more than in the care of the child is the nurse's response to the entire family so crucial. If the trust of the parent or guardian can be secured initially, the nurse has obtained vital cooperation, a less tense, more rested mother and father, and a more relaxed child. A few more minutes spent at the time of admission may save hours of time later on.

If first impressions are important, so are last contacts. The dismissal may be a really helpful period for the parent, or it may be a confusing "getaway." The following paragraphs are included to help the nurse function well in these two eventful situations.

Admission

IDENTIFICATION

The admitting nurse should be introduced or introduce herself to both the new patient and his parents. In many hospitals identification of the patient is accomplished through use of a bracelet, which should be checked for accuracy. Unfortunately, some of the children will be from broken homes. The mother's name or the father's name may be different from the child's. This should be clearly and discreetly noted to better understand the situation and avoid embarrassing incidents. To help the staff know their small patients better, many pediatric departments send out questionnaires to the parents of prospective patients requesting helpful information regarding the abilities, habits, likes, and dislikes of the child. Nicknames and special vocabulary used by the child are also investigated. It is good to know that 3-year-old Edmund Atherton Barnstow III responds to "Barney" and loves grape-flavored Popsicles.

QUALIFICATIONS OF A PEDIATRIC NURSE

The pediatric nurse should feel friendly toward and comfortable with children. She should wish for them the best the future can hold and gain great satisfaction in helping the child become better equipped to meet the demands of life. Her loving

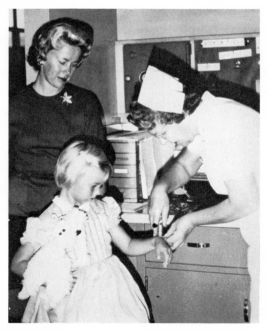

FIG. 28-1. "And here is your bracelet, Mary Lou." (Courtesy Children's Health Center, San Diego, Calif.)

concern for children should be expressed through a warm but not "gushy" approach. Children can readily detect people who genuinely care about them. Those nurses who find it difficult to work with children because of inexperience with or isolation from this age group need not feel that they will never function successfully in a pediatric area. But they must really want to learn to know children and think of them as persons and not as *problems*. If nurses are willing to be patient and alert, if they are adaptable and imaginative, and if they are capable of a kind, supportive love (rather than a smothering type of love that allows only dependence on the "lover"), then they possess the potentials for pediatric nursing, which will develop into a real asset in any children's treatment area.

Nurses many times find the pediatric area emotionally taxing. It is sad indeed to see a tender, innocent child suffer or a young boy or girl suddenly struck down by disease or death early in a life that had

been bright with promise. We do not know all the answers to the philosophical questions created by such circumstances, but we do know that these children and young people and their parents need help. There must be those who are willing to try to help them and are especially prepared to do so.

The nature of a pediatric nurse's responsibilities dictates that she possess an ample portion of both fortitude and *discretion*. She must think at least twice before she speaks; one can never withdraw a word once uttered. Detailed or crucial information about a patient must come from an authoritative source, such as the *nursing supervisor* or *attending physician*, and should only be given to those directly involved, usually attending personnel or parents. Well-meaning but curious casual inquirers should not be given diagnoses or progress reports. Finally, the nurse must develop the capacity for benevolent self-criticism and evaluation of her own actions so that she may constantly improve her ability to meet her patient's needs.

NURSE-PARENT ROLE

The newer concepts of pediatric care do not picture the pediatric nurse as an authoritarian dispenser of knowledge and skill, who alone has the ability to meet any need of the small patient. She is not a substitute mother, usurping the biological or legal mother's position. However, she is a practitioner who has the advantage of special practical and theoretical education and training not available to most mothers, and she is a person who cares about children, sick or well. The aims of the pediatric nurse and the child's parents should be basically the same—to help develop each child's potential to the optimum level and produce a creative, contributing member of society who finds high purpose in life and a role worth pursuing. The family learns from the nurse, and the wise nurse learns from the family.

The amount of parental participation in the care of the hospitalized child depends on the condition of the child and the response and abilities of the parents. To say that they should be allowed to do nothing when they have probably had total responsibility for the child until he was admitted to the hospital is often unrealistic and even unkind. On the other hand, if the mother gives the child his bath, feeds him, and completes his routine hygienic care alone, much valuable observation of the child is lost by nursing personnel. At times, instead of obtaining more relaxed, cooperative parents, an exhausted, worried mother and father may result. Perhaps, when the parent and child seem to gain much from parent participation in his hospital care, it is best to carry out such care with the nurse helping the mother and vice versa. Then cooperation is enhanced, observation and reporting is more accurate, and any legal complications of parental care are absent or minimized.

Some parents are unable to share constructively in the care of their hospitalized children. Others do not wish to participate. Occasionally, children may be more relaxed when mother and father do not participate. Parental anxiety caused by possible feelings of guilt, inadequacy, or frustration may be sensed by the child and cause him, in turn, to be anxious. In certain cases the child may be confused about the role of the parent when the mother is at the bedside and the nurse must minister to the small child. In this situation, asking the mother to take a brief rest period until the procedure is completed may benefit both parent and child. For the most part, however, the presence of the parents is a real asset to the child. The mother and father, depending on the condition of the child, can help and be helped by sharing in the admission of the child. They may aid by undressing him, positioning him for temperature readings, helping with feedings, and providing the comfort of their presence. However, no parent should be made to feel that unless he or she is at the bedside the child will not receive complete and loving nursing care. This would

cause many anxieties. Nor should parents be made to think that they are neglecting their duty to the child unless they are at the bedside almost constantly. The liberal visiting privileges now extended to parents in most pediatric hospitals are designed to ease tensions, not to create them. To sum up these paragraphs, we would use again the often repeated comment found in many nursing texts, "The modern pediatric nurse is mother's friend and helper—not mother's substitute."

ORIENTATION

If the circumstances of hospital admission and the patient's age and condition permit, the child and his parents should be shown briefly around his unit and be introduced to other children. The parents should be introduced to key personnel and shown where such conveniences as the public telephone, rest rooms, the public dining area, and waiting rooms are located. Many children receive a simple toy such as a hand puppet or coloring book at the time of admission, which helps to entertain and to pass the difficult periods of waiting for examination or surgery. The nurse should be sure the child has something appropriate at the bedside for diversion. A specially beloved toy or blanket may be brought from home. The nurse should make sure that any personal toys or clothing left at the hospital are carefully labeled. In most cases the use of the child's own clothes, with the exception of bathrobes and slippers, is discouraged because of the high incidence of loss in the hospital laundry, despite attempts to avoid such confusion.

When speaking to children, it is psychologically good technique to bend or crouch down to their eye level for special introductions, serious talks, or mutual enjoyment. No one likes to talk to knees or stretch his neck to look up all the time!

NURSING PROCEDURES

The patient is usually admitted directly to his own unit. During the admission, it

359

is customary to secure the following:

1. Pertinent information regarding his habits, vocabulary, possible allergies, normal diet, preparation for hospitalization, and family structure. This type of information may be obtained on a form filled out by the parent while the admission is in progress if it was not secured before the actual hospitalization.
2. His height, weight, and age.
   a. Babies are routinely weighed without clothes.
   b. Be sure that the scale is covered with a diaper or technique paper and is balanced before weighing!
   c. This information is used to:
      (1) Determine dosages of medications.
      (2) Determine general condition and progress.
      (3) *Note:* All children with diarrhea and vomiting or intake-output problems are routinely weighed every morning before breakfast.
3. His temperature.
   a. A rectal temperature is usually routine for all children 5 years old and under. The age when a child's temperature is taken orally differs in various hospitals.
   b. Never leave a child alone while taking his temperature (oral, rectal, or axillary). When rectal temperatures are secured, always have one hand on the thermometer and another on the child to assure safety and accuracy.
   c. Rectal temperatures should always be taken when:
      (1) The child has seizures or poor muscular control. (There is danger that the child may bite the thermometer, causing self-injury.)
      (2) The child has difficulty keeping his mouth closed because of oral surgery, general condition, or breathing difficulties.

(3) The child is receiving oxygen by mask, nasal catheter, or cannulae.
   d. Remember, rectal temperatures are one degree Fahrenheit higher than oral temperatures, whereas axillary temperatures are one degree lower, on the average. All rectal temperatures of 100.4° F. or over and all oral temperatures of 99.4° F. and over should be reported orally to the head nurse or team leader as soon as determined.
   e. In a few instances, rectal temperatures may be contraindicated (rectal surgery or ulceration).
4. His pulse.
   a. For infants, an apical pulse rate is secured by placing a stethoscope between the left nipple and the sternum. It is too difficult to secure an accurate radial pulse.
   b. Other pulse points may be used in the older child (the temple, the neck) if there is difficulty keeping the wrist still.
   c. Pulse determinations may be made in most cases by timing for 30 seconds and multiplying by 2 on the very young child.
   d. Irregularity and quality as well as rate should be noted.
   e. The activity of the child should be taken into account. (For example, the pulse of a sleeping child should be so labeled.)
   f. For rate ranges, see Table 28-1.

TABLE 28-1. Approximate pulse and respiration rates at rest based on age*

Age	Pulse	Respiration
Birth-1 mo.	110–150	30–50
1 mo.-1 yr.	100–140	26–34
1-2 yr.	90–120	20–30
2-6 yr.	90–110	20–30
6-10 yr.	80–100	18–26
Over 10 yr.	76– 90	16–24

*Pulse and respiration rates become slower with age.

5. His respirations.
   a. The rate and the character of respirations are important. The nurse should be alert to detect sternal retractions and Cheyne-Stokes respirations.
   b. For rate ranges, see Table 28-1.
6. His blood pressure.
   a. Blood pressure is usually not determined in children under 3 years of age.
   b. The correct-sized cuff is very important. The cuff should cover two thirds of the upper arm measured from the shoulder to the elbow.
   c. If no sound can be detected on auscultation, the twitching of the needle on the aneroid dial or the bouncing of the mercury column may be recorded, but a note must be made that this was the method used to determine the systolic reading. Auscultation or palpation of the pulse, when possible, is more accurate.
   d. Note must be made of any unusual activity of the child just prior to or during the blood pressure determination.
   e. Blood pressures are often taken to determine the onset of shock or buildup of intracranial pressure.
   f. For some average readings, see Table 28-2.
7. His general appearance and behavior as evaluated through observation.
   a. Overall clinical *appearance.*
      (1) In no acute distress.

TABLE 28-2. Some average blood pressure readings based on age*

Age	Systolic	Diastolic
4- 6 yr.	90	60
7-10 yr.	100	64
11-14 yr.	110	70
15-20 yr.	114	74

*Blood pressure increases with age.

      (2) Mildly ill.
      (3) Severely ill.
   b. Growth and development.
      (1) Appropriate for age and sex of child.
      (2) Special physical considerations such as orthopedic problems, imperfect vision, deafness, speech or language barriers, malnutrition, obesity, cosmetic defects, prostheses (dentures, glasses, contact lenses, artificial eyes, limbs), history of seizures, and general vigor.
      (3) Cultural intellectual, and emotional considerations, such as cultural heritage (for example, Mexican-American), mentally retarded or gifted, parent-child-nurse interaction, and initial response to hospitalization.
   c. Skin manifestations.
      (1) Unusual color, flushed, pale, cyanotic, or jaundiced.
      (2) Unusual birthmarks.
      (3) Rashes, bruises, possible boils, blisters, possible infestations (body or head lice, scabies).
      (4) State of cleanliness.
   d. Nervous system manifestations.
      (1) Level of consciousness.
      (2) Abnormally dilated or unequally dilated pupils.
      (3) Tremor, twitching, or periods of blank staring.
      (4) Limp, flaccid extremities.
      (5) Bulging fontanels.
      (6) One-sided or lower extremity weakness or paralysis.
   e. Other signs and symptoms important to note on admission.
      (1) Diarrhea, nausea, vomiting, abdominal distention (type of stool or emesis).
      (2) Nasal drainage, coughing. (Signs of respiratory infection noted in a child scheduled for surgery should be reported

immediately. Surgery may be cancelled.)

(3) Difficulty in voiding.

All these observations do not make the nurse a diagnostician. She simply observes as accurately as possible and reports.

Collection of specimens

In addition to the preceding measurements and observations, the patient routinely is scheduled for urinalysis and blood examinations.

Urine specimens. The collection of a urine specimen in a child over 2½ years old is not usually difficult. The collection of a specimen from an infant or young toddler poses real problems. Various methods have been recommended. Some pediatric areas use small adhesive-backed plastic bags that adhere to the perineal region or base of the penis (Fig. 28-2). These are usually satisfactory except when the child has a rash or perineal excoriations. Other hospitals use various appliances that are strapped or tied into place. A birdseed cup fitted into a perineal strap secured by a waistband has been used to collect speci-

mens from little girls. A test tube, enclosing the penis and held in place by a similar strap and waistband or adhesive tape, has been used for boys. With these types of arrangements, restraints may be necessary to stop the child from removing the apparatus. All these bags and containers must be checked frequently to avoid losing the precious commodity!

Blood samples. A blood specimen is not secured by the nurse, but she may help restrain the child in preparation for the taking of the specimen by the physician or laboratory technician. The specimen may be obtained by a toe, heel, or finger prick or a venous puncture in the arm, groin, or neck. If the child must be restrained and if he is old enough to understand, he should be told that the hands, sheets, or other appliances that may be employed are used to help him hold still so that the physician can help him get well. He should not think of the restraints as a means of punishment. Various types of restraints are used during a child's hospitalization. These are discussed in Chapter 29. Common procedures or diagnostic tests that may be

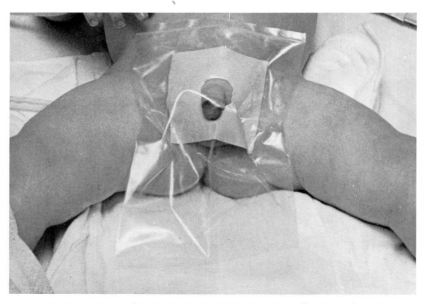

Fig. 28-2. Application of an adhesive-backed plastic bag for collection of a urine specimen. Be sure it isn't upside down!

ordered at the time of admission (spinal puncture, Clinitest, sweat test) are also discussed in a separate chapter.

Diet and fluid orders

The diet of a newly admitted child depends, of course, on the reason for the hospitalization, his age, and his general condition. Patients scheduled for pending surgery may be allowed nothing to eat or drink. The diet is ordered by the attending physician. Children may have many allergies often involving not only pollens, animal furs, fibers, and dust but also common foods. Chocolate, milk and wheat products, tomatoes, oranges, and strawberries are among the frequent offenders. Nurses should be alerted to these problems and the allergic manifestations they usually cause. The cultural patterns of some patients may cause feeding problems and poor acceptance of the routine hospital diet.

ADMISSION RESPONSIBILITY

The member of the nursing team who has the responsibility of actually admitting a patient will depend on the condition and needs of the child. In certain situations the admission may be made in its entirety by a registered nurse. At other times it may be a joint or delegated responsibility carried out by both the registered nurse and the licensed vocational nurse. A sample admittance record made in the nurse's notes is shown in Fig. 28-3.

Time	Intake in c.c. Total each 8 hours		B.P.	Diet	T.	P.	R.	Treatments	Remarks	Output in c.c. Total each 8 hours		
	Paren-teral	Oral								Defeca-tion	Urine	Emesi drain

Date of first entry on page ___ 8/22/65

| P39AM | | | 11°/80 | N.P.O. | 98⁴ | 100 | 30 | | Admission of 6 year old Caucasian female, in no distress, ambulatory c̄ mother to Rm 20, for T+A this AM. No signs of URI noted. No allergies known. Upper left central incisor loose. Upper right central incisor missing. Skin clean and clear except old bruise on left knee. Urine specimen obtained, sent to lab. Clear yellow voiding.
J. Smith, LVN. | | ✓ | |

GROSSMONT HOSPITAL

La Mesa, Calif.

NURSE'S BEDSIDE RECORD

FIG. 28-3. Sample admission record. (Courtesy Grossmont Hospital, La Mesa, Calif.)

Discharge

PLANS FOR DISMISSAL

The discharge day is usually extremely busy for the parent. Arrangements must be made for transportation (after all, Mary, in a hip spica cast, won't fit in the family Volkswagen). A baby-sitter for the other children in the family may be necessary while mother takes her home. Maybe father will have to take time from work to provide transportation. Unless special arrangements are made, the child usually must be dismissed in the morning to avoid a hospital charge for an additional day. If mother will have little help after her child comes home, she will be busy trying to shop and run errands not immediately possible when the child first returns home. If possible, the nurse should write out any instructions for home care for the parents, whether observations to be made or medications and procedures prescribed, rather than rely on oral instructions. The arrangements for the next follow-up visit to the physician should be clear.

PREPARATION FOR HOME CARE
Helps in convalescence

If convalescence at home is expected to be prolonged, more preplanning is necessary. The location of the sleeping quarters of the child may need to be changed to save steps and provide greater opportunity for observation. Special equipment may need to be improvised, rented, or purchased. Provisions for help by a visiting nurse may be desirable. A tentative schedule providing the needed care and rest for the convalescent but still allowing the other members of the household opportunity to pursue a fairly normal range of activity and relaxation is desirable.

Possible behavior changes

Parents should be alerted that hospitalization affects children differently. Occasionally, children will have a period of difficulty readjusting to life at home. They may regress developmentally, and activities that they had already mastered previous to their illness may not be attempted. Irri-

FIG. 28-4. Sample dismissal record. (Courtesy Grossmont Hospital, La Mesa, Calif.)

tability and wetting by a previously toilet-trained child are quite common.

ACTUAL LEAVE-TAKING

At the time of discharge, every attempt should be made to give all the belongings of the child that can be sent home (the isolation department may recommend some restrictions) to the parent. Return trips to the hospital to pick up articles left behind are annoying. Bedside stands, closets, cupboards, bedclothes, and flooring must be carefully scrutinized.

In most hospitals, after the physician's dismissal is written, the parent is sent to the hospital business office to complete any financial arrangements necessary and notify the administration of the departure.

Before actually leaving the hospital premises, a form must be signed indicating who is taking the child. Great care must be taken that the person given responsibility for the child at the time of discharge has the legal right to assume that responsibility. At this time a final check is made regarding any medications to be taken home or special instructions to be given.

If at all possible, the child should be taken to the point of actual transfer to the car in a wheelchair, a rolling bassinette, or on a gurney. He must always be accompanied by a nurse or hospital employee.

A sample record of the dismissal, which is a part of the nurse's notes, is shown in Fig. 28-4.

Admissions and discharges are part of the everyday pattern of hospital routine. The nurse must remember that they are far from routine for most of the patients and parents who find themselves within the sound of her voice and influence of her actions.

29
Basic patient needs and daily planning

Every patient has individual needs that, by their unique combination or background setting, are particularly personal and special. At the same time, these needs may be said to represent the needs of all people because they usually fall into broader, more basic categories of care. For this presentation, the patient's needs have been grouped to form seven areas of discussion.

Basic patient needs

The nursing staff is responsible for helping to provide the following:
1. Safety
2. Observation
3. Diagnostic tests
4. Supportive procedures
   a. Aiding respiration and oxygenation
   b. Regulating body temperature
   c. Positioning
   d. Adequate nourishment and fluid balance
   e. Cleanliness
   f. Rest
   g. Diversion and self-expression
5. Medications and special treatments
6. Rehabilitation
7. Recording of events

SAFETY

The problem of safety is constant in any hospital. In a pediatric hospital it seems to be constant and compounded. The environment must be continually evaluated to prevent accidents. The patients are often too small to regulate their own surroundings and lack the judgment to evaluate their environments properly. Unrestrained or un-attended children in high beds or cribs should always have the bed or crib sides securely raised. No nurse should turn her back on an unrestrained child in a crib with the side lowered. Children who have climbing urges should have crib nets properly applied to form a tightly fitting net roof unless supervision is constant (Fig. 29-1). Beds of inquisitive boys and girls should be at a "no touch" distance from wall electricity, suction, and oxygen outlets. Toys should be checked for sharp edges, points, or potential danger. Plastic bags should not be used for storage of toys or playthings. Notices of known allergies should be clearly posted in the child's unit. All equipment should be in good working order and used properly. Special precautions should be observed when administering oxygen and working with warm humidification units. When a child is transported in a wheelchair, in most instances a waist or jacket restraint should be used to avoid the possibility of his tipping forward or sliding down (Fig. 29-2). Unnecessary traffic and congestion in the halls should be avoided.

An important component of safety is firm but kindly discipline. Explaining to the child who is old enough to understand the reason for some rules often works wonders. Good discipline also means realistic expectations and prompt follow-through by the nurse responsible for supervising behavior. It means that nurses must not give choices when no alternatives are possible. It also means offering a choice when the ability to choose would bring pleasure, importance, and a sense of self-direction or

FIG. 29-1. This little boy was a climber at night. A crib net was applied over the top of his bed before lights out. (Courtesy Children's Health Center, San Diego, Calif.)

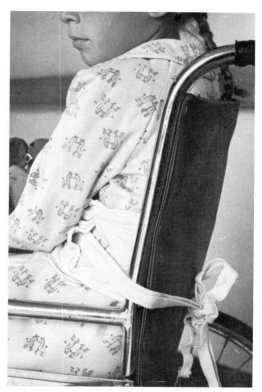

FIG. 29-2. One type of wheelchair restraint. A muslin band equipped with ties is brought from behind the child, crosses in front (one end threaded through an opening in the other), and then is tied behind the chair. (Courtesy Childern's Health Center, San Diego, Calif.)

achievement to the child. Promises kept, a "yes" that means "yes" and a "no" that means "no," and a loving regard for the ultimate welfare of the child are extremely significant in maintaining good discipline.

Sometimes the child must be restrained during a treatment to protect him from himself. Such restraint should never be presented as a punishment but as one way to help the child hold himself still for a little while. An example of such a restraint is the "mummy wrap," which can either cover or expose the chest area (Figs. 29-3 and 29-4). A commercial "mummy restraint" used in many emergency rooms is the Olympic papoose board shown in Fig. 29-5. Another type of control used to prevent a child from touching his face or pulling on

a gavage tube is elbow restraints, which are usually fastened to the child's hospital gown (Fig. 29-6). However, elbow restraints are not effective if the child can reach his face with a toy or an implement without bending his arms. To control leg motion in cases of urine specimen collection, specially constructed ankle restraints (Fig. 29-8) or the time-proved clove hitch tie (Fig. 29-9) may be used. A pediatric Posey belt may sometimes be employed to allow some movement in bed and yet prevent the patient from getting up. A jacket restraint is pictured in Fig. 29-7.

Restraints must be removed periodically to check circulation and exercise the body part involved. They should be so constructed that they will not become tighter

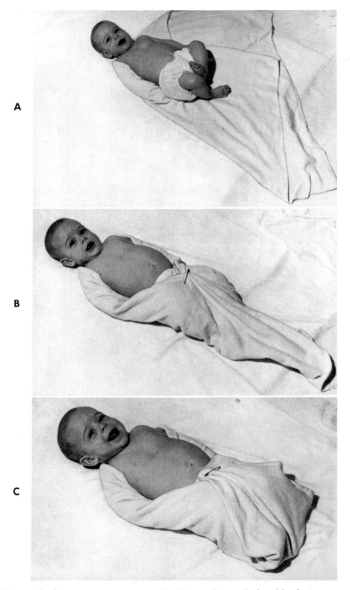

FIG. 29-3. Exposed chest mummy wrap. **A,** Use a large baby blanket or small sheet. Fold down one corner, positioning the folded edge slightly above the baby's shoulder level. Place one arm at his side and pull one side corner of the blanket over the arm and under the baby's body. **B,** Enclose other arm in the same way. Pull out the remaining "skirt" of the blanket slightly to obtain enough material to bring over the legs and pin. **C,** Bring up the "tail" of the blanket and pin it to the rest of the blanket or diaper.

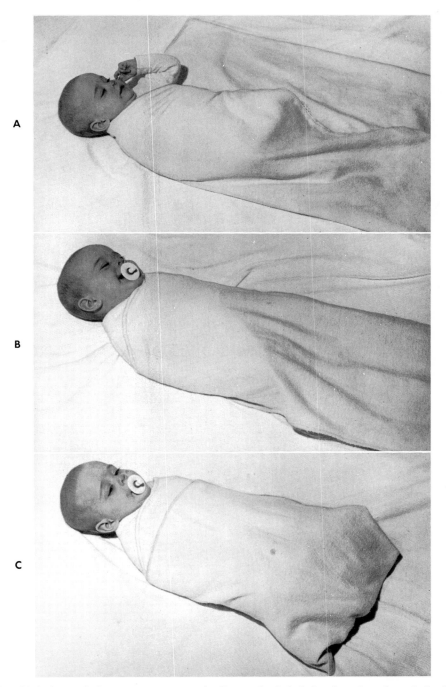

FIG. 29-4. Covered chest mummy wrap. **A,** Center the baby's head at the edge of the "short side" of an open baby blanket or sheet. Place one arm at his side and pull the blanket snugly over his shoulder, arm, and chest and tuck the blanket under the baby. **B,** Position the opposite arm similarly and pull the opposite corner over and around the baby. **C,** Open out the loose end of the blanket and bring it up and around the baby snugly. (We do not generally advocate pacifiers but believe they have a place in certain situations.)

with increased tension and impair circulation or endanger respiration.

OBSERVATION

Provision for observation is crucial to the welfare of the patient. To plan and pursue the therapy of a patient intelligently, enlightened observation must become an inseparable part of the patient's care. Observation of the patient should be made especially in the light of his diagnosis. If the diagnosis is pneumonia, for example, the fact that the child is pale and has a frequent, loose cough producing thick, white mucus is significant. Sometimes negative observations are important to make. It is important to record that a child admitted because of convulsions has had no seizures for a certain period. The observation that a child hospitalized for vomiting and diar-

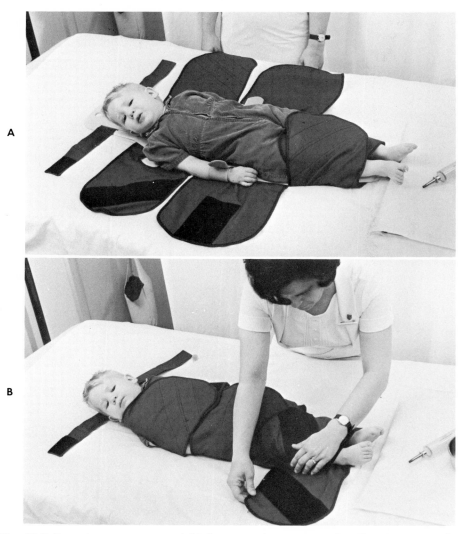

Fig. 29-5. Preparing to restrain a child for gastric lavage using the Olympic papoose board. Various wraps are possible with the velco-lined restraining folds. (Courtesy Olympic Surgical Co., Inc., Seattle, Wash.)

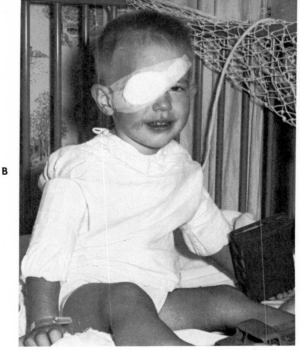

FIG. 29-6. Elbow restraint. **A,** In addition to this equipment a long-sleeved gown or shirt that cannot be easily removed by the child is needed. The tongue blades are inserted into the cloth pockets of the restraint and the top flap folded over. The enclosed tongue blades are then positioned over the elbow on top of the sleeve. The cuff of the sleeve is turned up over the tongue blades and fastened with adhesive tape. In addition, the top of the restraint may be held in position by a safety pin. **B,** This young man has had a "squint" operation. Elbow restraints allow him to play but protect his dressing from "busy" fingers. (Courtesy Children's Health Center, San Diego, Calif.)

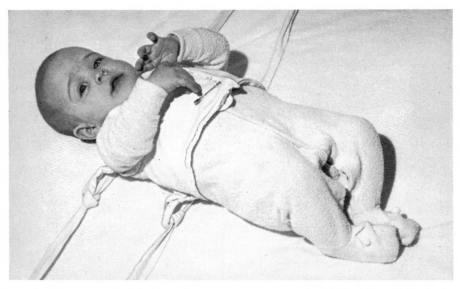

Fig. 29-7. Restraining jacket. The ties are fastened to the bedspring frame, and the pins are placed in front. It may also be used as a wheelchair restraint for small children.

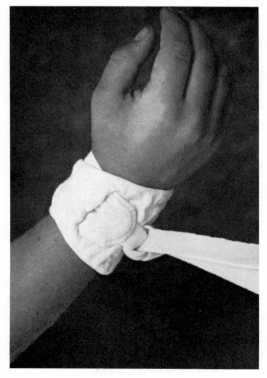

Fig. 29-8. Wrist restraint. It is applied in basically the same way as the wheelchair restraint in Fig. 29-2. It may also be employed to restrain an ankle.

rhea retained a feeding and had no stools for a specific interval may be significant. When observing the patient and recording his appearance, activity, and treatment, refer back to his diagnosis. What would be especially important for the physician or supervising nurse to know? A change in a child's bed placement may sometimes be needed to observe him more closely.

DIAGNOSTIC PROCEDURES

The diagnostic procedures ordered must be understood so that adequate preparation, execution, and follow-up may be provided. It would be impossible to describe all the diagnostic procedures encountered by the nurse in a pediatric setting within this brief text. Only a few of the most common are described in this chapter. For more details the student or graduate is referred to the procedure manual of the school or hospital in which she is working. However, the following principles may be emphasized.

1. Collection of specimens.
   a. All collection of specimens for analysis should be made in clean

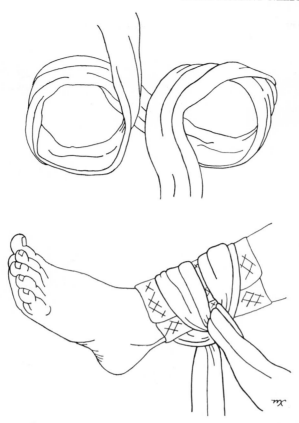

FIG. 29-9. Application of the clove hitch restraint. The formed loops are placed one on top of the other and the body part put through the opening. The body part should always be previously padded.

containers. In addition, specimens to be obtained for culture studies should be collected in as sterile a manner as possible into a sterile container.

b. All culture material, cerebral spinal fluid, and stools to be examined for ova (eggs) and parasites should be sent immediately to the examining laboratory.

c. All other specimens should be taken to the laboratory for analysis and study as soon as possible. If for some reason they must be detained, they should be refrigerated.

d. All timed urine collections, in which urine is to be collected for a definite interval, should start and stop with an emptied bladder. Therefore the first specimen obtained is discarded and the time noted. All urine is then saved until the time period is complete. At the end of the interval the patient empties his bladder, and this last specimen is added to the rest to close the collection. When test results are crucial and involve infants and very young children, a specially designed "urine collection bed" or catheter may be used.

e. No talking should be allowed while the actual collection of a specimen for culture studies is being made.

f. Sputum specimens must come from

373

deep in the respiratory tree and are usually obtained after a period of postural drainage.

g. Some common blood tests (chemistries) must be performed on specimens secured after periods of fasting. Check for early morning orders that a patient be NPO.

h. All specimens must be plainly and correctly labeled and sent with appropriate instructions to the laboratory.

2. Diagnostic x-ray procedures.

a. The patient must be adequately prepared physically and, as much as possible, psychologically for the procedure. Some x-ray studies (for example, barium enemas, intravenous pyelograms) will require extensive potentially fatiguing preparations of the patient.

b. Relatively simple x-ray films of the chest or bone may often be explained to a child as "like having your picture taken."

c. The nurse helping to position and hold the child for the film should be protected by a lead apron during the x-ray procedure.

d. Orders regarding the need for further films in a series or the resumption of food and fluid should be clearly understood on the patient's return to the unit.

SUPPORTIVE PROCEDURES

Various types of supportive procedures and techniques are used to maintain or improve the physical and emotional resources of the patient. These may include special provisions for aiding respiration or oxygenation, regulating body temperature, positioning, maintaining fluid balance or nutrition, relieving pain, or improving body function. They also include the interest and love expressed by parents, family, friends, and nurses and the physical and spiritual serenity promoted by the development of trust. The use of oxygen and humidification equipment will be discussed in a separate chapter as will the methods of regulating body temperature. Positioning of the bed patient, however, will be described in the following paragraphs.

Positioning the patient

Even the child who is ambulatory and active needs to be supervised so that he does not develop poor posture habits that will interfere with the optimum function of his body and cause him to look less than his best. The child in bed, particularly if he must remain fairly quiet for long periods, must be especially helped to maintain good alignment, functional positions, range of motion, and good tissue health for all body parts. Barring special treatments involving traction, casting, or specifically ordered body placement, the child in bed should have a posture, when in supine position (on his back) or in prone position (on his abdomen), similar to that which would be considered in good alignment if he were standing. Included in this section are some illustrations showing some of the do's and don't's of positioning.

In Fig. 29-10, *A,* the feet are not supported in a functional position. A patient who remains in bed for an extended period without adequate foot support or with tight covers pressing down on his feet will develop a tightening of the Achilles tendon, or heel cord, causing *foot drop,* which results in difficulty walking. One leg has been allowed to fall outward toward the side *(external rotation),* and the knee is in a flexed position, which, if not changed often, can result in fixation and *contracture* in a relatively short period. The position of the arms across the chest and the partially flexed head position decrease respiratory capacity. The arm and hand positions (very typical of the arthritic patient), if maintained, cause flexion contractures of the shoulder and elbow and *wristdrop,* with loss of function in the hand.

Fig. 29-10, *B,* illustrates how good alignment may be achieved with the help of a footboard, pillows, and hand rolls. Incapacitated teen-age patients usually need

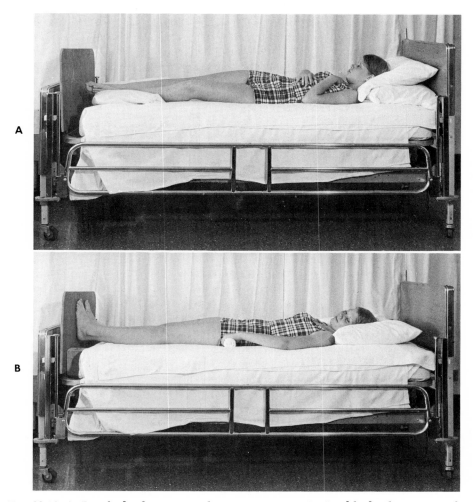

FIG. 29-10. **A,** *Poor* body alignment in the supine position. **B,** *Good* body alignment in the supine position. (Courtesy Children's Health Center, San Diego, Calif.)

considerable help. It should be noted that a type of foot support is being employed. The knees are straight up, rotated neither to the inside nor outside. Sometimes this correct position is maintained in part by a rectangularly folded blanket that has been partially slipped under the buttocks of the patient. The long protruding end is then rolled under tightly toward the thigh to stabilize the leg in neutral position. A rolled towel or *small* pillow placed under the calves may help relax the knee joints and lift the heels off the bed just enough to relieve pressure. Some patients appreciate

a small pillow placed in the small of the back. The arms are alternately rotated for comfort. Soft hand rolls help maintain functional finger-thumb relationships.

The prone, or abdominal, position pictured in Fig. 29-11, *A,* looks and is very uncomfortable. The toes should be either over the end of the mattress pointing down between the foot of the bed and the mattress or positioned over the edge of a pillow. A thin pillow support under the abdomen takes pressure off the chest and reduces the lumbar curve. The arms are usually comfortable abducted and flexed.

375

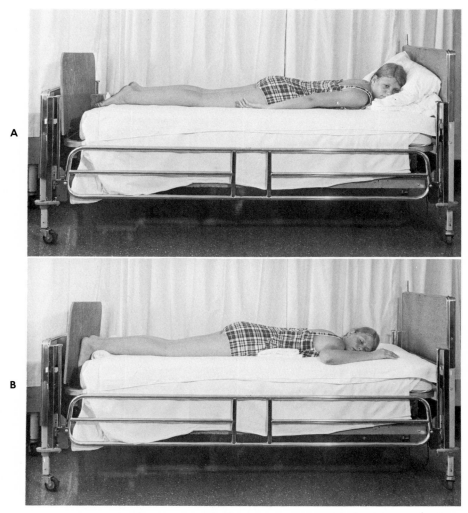

FIG. 29-11. A, *Poor* body alignment in the prone position. B, *Good* body alignment in the prone position. (Courtesy Children's Health Center, San Diego, Calif.)

No pillow may be required under the head.

The side-lying position is often preferred. The main problem illustrated in Fig. 29-12, A, is the strain placed on the hip joint and lower back by the upper leg, which has been allowed to fall forward. For a patient with no back or hip problems who is able to move freely, this is no great difficulty. However, if these problems or conditions exist, this leg position should be avoided by the addition of a pillow supporting the upper leg. Sometimes a pillow tucked lengthwise against the back is com-

forting. A support for the upper hand relieves the chest.

Good positioning and frequent turning (every 2 hours or less) will do much to comfort the patient; avoid respiratory, circulatory, and urinary complications; reduce deformity; and speed rehabilitation. Infants and toddlers do not require such elaborate supports to maintain alignment and prevent deformity, but they do need to be frequently turned and positioned if they do not move themselves. An older infant or young toddler often sleeps with his head

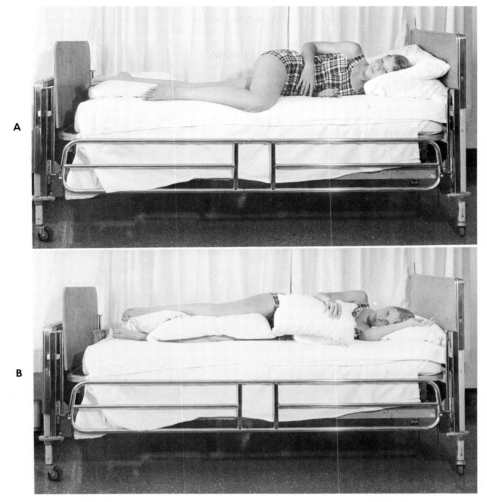

FIG. 29-12. A, *Poor* body alignment in the side-lying position. B, *Good* body alignment in the side-lying position. (Courtesy Children's Health Center, San Diego, Calif.)

and chest down on the mattress, face turned to the side, while his knees are pulled under his abdomen to make his buttocks form the highest point of his sleeping silhouette. This is a perfectly normal and characteristic posture for this age. A young infant should not be left unattended flat on his back because of the danger of aspiration. A rolled blanket should be placed at his back to maintain a side position.

Nourishment and fluid balance

Diet. The diet of a patient does not consist of the type of diet order that the physi- cian writes on the patient's chart. It is not that easy. The diet of a patient consists of what he eats, drinks, and retains of that which has been sent from the kitchen or prepared by the nursing staff in response to the physician's order. Some diets look beautiful on paper but, unfortunately, are not eaten by the person for whom they have been prepared.

Before a tray is served to a patient it should be carefully checked to see that it is compatible with his diet order, food allergies, abilities, and cultural or religious background. Nuts, raw carrots, and celery should not be served to toddlers who do not know how to handle such "chewy" foods. They sometimes suffer from aspiration. Common diets served in the pediatric area are clear liquid, full liquid, soft, high protein, high carbohydrate, low residue, diabetic, and salt or sodium restricted. Students should review these diets in a diet manual.

A child must often be helped at mealtime. A nurse cannot simply put a tray on a bed or crib table and expect even an older child to automatically eat. His utensils should be appropriate. The food must be easily available and attractive. Toddlers often do well if placed in a high chair for feedings. Some young children prefer to try to feed themselves, but very young children enjoy being held during meals. Bibs and nurse's feeding gowns again ease laundry problems.

Infants often drink better if they have a "breathing space" between the time they finish their solids and are offered their formula. Infants and toddlers who need a greater fluid intake may be offered fluids before solid foods when appetites are sharpest to encourage fluid acceptance. Plastic bottles should be used with older infants who enjoy "holding their own." Young children may sometimes be fooled into eating unwelcome vegetables if they are disguised with pureed fruit, etc.

Whether it is necessary to record every bit of food eaten by a child depends on his diagnosis and condition. A diabetic child would require very close observation and recording of food intake. Any food left on his tray must be reported in detail so that a replacement may be calculated and prepared by the diet kitchen. Usually, the dietitian wishes all the trays of diabetic patients to be returned separately to the kitchen for evaluation after meals. The true diet of a patient with any metabolic, growth and development, digestive, or feeding problems should certainly be carefully recorded. This would include most medical patients and some surgical patients. The intakes of children who are

long-term patients with fairly stabilized conditions could be adequately described as "ate well," "ate fairly well," or "ate poorly." *All* pediatric patients are routinely on measured fluid intake, expressed in cubic centimeters (cc.) or milliliters (ml.). Many are on measured fluid output.

Hydration. Fluid intake is really of greater immediate importance than solid feeding. The hydration of a child is extremely important. A young child may become dehydrated more rapidly than an adult. An infant is especially vulnerable, having a greater surface area and higher metabolic rate per unit of weight than an adult. Maintaining an adequate fluid intake is one of the very important responsibilities of the bedside nurse. The amount of fluid that is urged depends on the size and condition of the child. An infant needs at least 2¼ ounces per pound (150 ml./kg.) of body weight per day to maintain hydration and more if he must combat preexisting dehydration.

An older child will probably do well on fluid intakes of 1,500 to 2,000 ml. per *day,* depending on his individual needs. Students are reminded that patients who are immobilized in casts or traction apparatus and all those with indwelling urinary catheters must have special attention to assure an abundant fluid intake.

Encouragement. Assuring oral intake often calls on a nurse's ingenuity, patience, and persistence. Small amounts taken frequently are tolerated better by the ill child than copious amounts taken rapidly, no matter how willingly. Fluids taken rapidly often are not retained by children who are ill, upset, or excited.

The kinds of fluids that may be offered a child depend on his diet order and any allergies he may have. Clear fluids include any liquid through which one may see the bottom of its container—water, bouillon, strained fruit juices, Popsicles, gelatin, and soft drinks. A full liquid diet would include milk products such as ice cream, sherbet, milk shakes, and creamed soups and unstrained fruit juices.

Learning which fluids the child has accepted well in the past may save time. Offering a choice is often helpful. Sometimes the manner in which fluids are offered is significant. Some older babies seem insulted by a bottle and drink well from a cup. Others regress and will only take fluids well from a bottle with a certain kind of nipple. Some small children are accustomed to warm milk, others like it cold. Older children often reject milk unless it is ice cold. A nurse who is able to sit down with the child beside her or in her lap and offer fluid as part of good companionship is more likely to be successful than the nurse who expresses her frustration in constant verbal harassment. In some cases the use of straws, doll tea-party dishes, colored ice cubes, or a paper star on Johnnie's fluid intake record may help. Popsicles are usually very acceptable. Just plain water should not be forgotten in the search for fluids. With older children, the factual knowledge that other steps (intravenous feedings) will be necessary to assure hydration if oral fluid intake is too low may encourage drinking. For most children, a carton of milk and a glass of fruit juice at breakfast, a glass of some other fluid or dish of ice cream or gelatin equalling approximately 200 ml. during midmorning, soup and beverage at lunch, and a midafternoon liquid snack fulfill the responsibilities of the day nursing shift.

Restriction. Patients scheduled for operative procedures are usually not allowed any oral intake for several hours before their surgeries. After the procedures the amount and type of fluids offered may be restricted. After heart surgery oral liquid intake may be limited to 300 ml. during the morning and only offered in small quantities for an extended period. Some postsurgical patients will be allowed nothing by mouth for a considerable period after their procedures, receiving their fluids parenterally (by other routes than oral, such as by vein) until the physician believes that oral administration could be profitably attempted. The child who has had stomach or intestinal surgery will be offered very small amounts at a time initially to ascertain his tolerance and to decrease stress on the surgical site. Infants with severe cases of diarrhea and vomiting are usually allowed nothing by mouth or placed on a limited oral intake to rest the gastrointestinal tract. Fluids in these cases are also administered *parenterally.*

Fluid and electrolyte balance. It has become increasingly apparent in recent years that the content and volume of the body fluid is a key consideration in the maintenance of cellular health and therefore the health of the total individual. The body organs and systems function to maintain the proper internal and external cellular environments and enable the survival of the person. The following brief simplified discussion of fluid and electrolyte balance is included in the belief that an understanding of this area of biology will become more and more necessary for the general public as well as the bedside nurse. The body functions in sensitive equilibrium. One of the most delicate balances maintained by the body is demonstrated by the composition of body fluid. Major ingredients of this fluid are water and certain chemicals termed *electrolytes.* Electrolytes are so called because they develop electrical charges when they are dissolved in water. Some electrolytes carry a positive charge and are called *cations.* Negatively charged electrolytes are called *anions.* In either case, the electrolytes may be referred to as *ions.* There are also a small number of chemical compounds found in body fluid that do not ionize or carry electrical charges. Organic compounds such as glucose and urea are the main nonelectrolytes of body fluid.

Body fluid occupies three permeable compartments (Fig. 29-13): blood vessels, tissue spaces (interstitial areas outside of tissue cells), and the areas inside the cells. *Extracellular* fluid (ECF) is located within the blood vessels and between the tissue cells, and *intracellular* fluid (ICF) lies inside the cells.

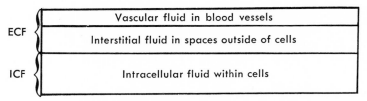

ECF	Vascular fluid in blood vessels
	Interstitial fluid in spaces outside of cells
ICF	Intracellular fluid within cells

FIG. 29-13. Body fluid compartments.

Every tissue cell is surrounded by a semipermeable membrane that permits selective passage of certain substances and free passage of water molecules in both directions. Water always passes from the more dilute to the more concentrated solution. This transfer of water and ions between the intracellular and extracellular compartments is called *osmosis*. In health a dynamic equilibrium of electrolytes and water is maintained between the two areas. Therefore, although each of the fluid compartments of the body contains electrolytes, the concentration and composition of electrolytes in the water of each compartment varies. The electrolytes found in the fluid inside the cells differ greatly from those found in the fluid outside the cells. Interstitial fluid in the tissue spaces is similar to plasma (the fluid portion of the blood), except that it contains very little protein. In interstitial fluid the principal cation in sodium, and the main anions are chlorides and bicarbonates. Intracellular cations are mostly potassium and magnesium, whereas the anions are chiefly phosphates and bicarbonates. Thus chemical differences exist between the extracellular and the intracellular fluids.

Acid-base balance. The acidity or alkalinity of a solution depends on the concentration of hydrogen, or the "H" ions present. An acid may be defined as a compound that has enough H ions to give some away. A base or alkali is a compound possessing few H ions. An increase in H ions makes a solution more acid, and a decrease makes a solution more alkaline. The concentration of hydrogen ions is expressed by pH. A neutral fluid has a pH of 7.0 (a lower pH means higher hydrogen ion concentra-

tion). An acid solution has a pH value below 7; an alkaline solution has a pH value above 7. The acid-base balance of the blood is maintained in an extremely narrow pH range, normally 7.35 to 7.45. Any slight deviation from this range causes pronounced changes in the cellular functions. This in turn may threaten life. Blood is normally slightly alkaline (pH 7.4). The acid-base balance is maintained by the action of the lungs, kidneys, and buffer systems. The lungs assist in maintaining this equilibrium by varying the rate at which CO_2 is blown off, retaining this slightly acid substance when blood plasma is getting too alkaline, or increasing the respiratory rate when the plasma is becoming too acid. The kidneys assist in maintaining the normal pH of blood by regulating the rates of excretion of acids and bases in the urine. Excessive retention of base, or loss of acids, results in metabolic alkalosis; excessive retention of acids, or loss of base, produces metabolic acidosis.

Buffer systems protect the acid-base balance of a solution by rapidly offsetting changes in its ionized H concentration. Buffer systems defend and maintain the pH of body fluids by protecting against added acid or base.

Fluid volume. The volume of blood plasma, interstitial fluid, and intracellular fluid normally remains relatively constant. Any blood plasma changes that take place during illness usually reflect changes in all the body fluids. Since plasma is relatively easy to obtain from the body and the other fluids are not, it is the chosen fluid for analysis.

Fluid balance. Fluid balance is maintained chiefly by the kidneys, which are in-

TABLE 29-1. Major electrolytes and imbalances

Electrolyte	Deficit	Excess
Sodium (Na$^+$)—normal value 136-143 mEq./L.*	*Hyponatremia* Na$^+$ below 135 mEq./L. Muscular weakness; abdominal cramps; clammy skin; weak, rapid pulse; hypertension; drowsiness; confusion; coma Predisposing factors—excessive sweating and water intake; gastrointestinal suction and excessive oral water intake; glucose water infusion without sodium; diarrhea	*Hypernatremia* Na$^+$ above 150 mEq./L. Thirst; dry skin; loss of skin elasticity ("doughy" tissue turgor); fever; weight loss; scanty urine formation; confusion; stupor; seizures; circulatory embarrassment Predisposing factors—sodium chloride infusion; inadequate water intake; watery diarrhea; renal concentrating disease; anorexia; nausea; vomiting; high fever Additional feeding factors—undiluted cow's milk‡; boiled skim milk; powdered electrolyte mixtures; salt and sugar mixtures; bouillon soup, etc.
Potassium (K$^+$)—normal value 4.1-5.6 mEq./L.	*Hypokalemia†* K$^+$ below 4.0 mEq./L. Weak pulse; hypotension; muscular weakness; diminished reflexes; cardiac arrest Predisposing factors—diuretics; diarrhea; vomiting; gastric suctioning	*Hyperkalemia* K$^+$ above 5.7 mEq./L. Nausea; apprehension; muscular weakness; confusion; hypotension; cardiac arrest Predisposing factors—burns, excessive tissue damage; excessive infusion of potassium; kidney disease; severe dehydration with scanty urine formation
Calcium (Ca^{++})—normal value 10-12 mg./100 ml. (5-6 mEq./L.)	*Hypocalcemia* Ca^{++} below 9 mg./100 ml. Tetany; tingling around mouth and fingers; muscular cramps; convulsions Predisposing factors—hypoactive parathyroid; malabsorption syndromes; chronic renal disease; distressed newborns	*Hypercalcemia (rare)* Ca^{++} above 12 mg./100 ml. Vomiting; constipation; polyuria; abdominal pains Predisposing factors—prolonged bed rest; overactive parathyroid; overdose of vitamin D
Bicarbonate (HCO$_3$)$^-$—normal value 19-26 mEq./L.	*Metabolic acidosis* (HCO$_3$)$^-$ below 12 mEq./L. Apathy, drowsiness or lethargy; deep, rapid breathing (Kussmaul type) disorientation; stupor; weakness; coma Predisposing factors—diabetes mellitus; starvation; kidney insufficiency; excessive parenteral NaCl; severe diarrhea; salicylate intoxication	*Metabolic alkalosis* (HCO$_3$)$^-$ above 30 mEq./L. Depressed, shallow respirations; hypertonic muscles; tetany; disorientation Predisposing factors—vomiting (pyloric stenosis); ingestion of alkalies; gastric suction; diuretics

*Milliequivalents per liter (mEq./L.).
†Potassium may be given intravenously only after urinary output is well established.
‡Hill, L. F.: Infant feeding: Historical and current, Pediat. Clin. N. Amer. **14:**265, 1967.

TABLE 29-2. Approximate daily intake and output of water in children whose body surface equals 1 square meter

	Intake	Output
1,500 ml.	liquids food metabolism (oxidation of food)	900 ml. kidney 500 ml. lungs and skin (insensible loss) 100 ml. intestine
1,500 ml.		1,500 ml.

fluenced by various hormones. A cardinal principle of fluid balance is that fluid intake must equal fluid output (Table 29-2). The store of water in the body comes from ingested liquids and foods. Water leaves the body via the kidneys, lungs, skin, and intestine. Water loss through the skin and lungs always increases when respirations are increased, fever is present, the environment is very warm, or the skin is injured or burned. Any condition that interferes with an adequate intake of fluid or produces excessive fluid loss threatens the life of the young child.

Fluid imbalance. Fig. 29-14 illustrates that plasma is the only portion of body water in contact with the external environment. It is the first fluid storage supply to be tapped in gastrointestinal disturbances (vomiting, diarrhea, rapid respirations, or deficient fluid intake). Interstitial fluid is the reservoir that responds most easily to the shifting fluid conditions present in disease (e.g., overhydration causes edema, and dehydration causes the skin to lose its turgor and become wrinkled). The intracellular compartment represents the largest reservoir and is the least accessible. Here water is lost or gained over a period of days. Without water, a well infant in a temperate environment can live about 3 days, and an adult can survive about 10 days.

Electrolyte disturbances in children. With regard to fluid and electrolyte balance, several differences between the infant and older child must be considered.

A newborn infant's weight is approximately 80% water, the older child's is 70% water, and the adult's is 60% water. This percentage varies with the amount of fat. Since fat is essentially water free, a lean individual has a greater proportion of water to total body weight. The proportion of intracellular fluid to body weight remains comparatively constant at all ages. Extracellular fluid constitutes about 40% of the infant's weight as compared to 20% of the adult's body weight. An infant, then, may approach a fluid loss of 10% of his body weight before a severe fluid deficit occurs. A weight loss of 5% represents a severe fluid volume deficit in the adult. However, remember, 10% of a baby's body weight is not very much!

Although the infant's body has a relatively greater fluid content per pound, he is *more vulnerable* to fluid volume deficit than is the adult. He ingests and excretes a relatively greater daily water volume because of several factors peculiar to his age group. The infant's body surface in relation to his body weight is three times that of the older child. Therefore he loses a relatively greater amount of fluid through the skin and gastrointestinal tract. His high metabolic rate produces more waste products, which must be diluted for excretion. His immature kidneys are less able to concentrate urine, adding to the volume of urine. Accumulation of acidic wastes (because of the high metabolic rate and immature kidneys) stimulates respiration, causing greater evaporation through his lungs. Infants react to infections with higher temperatures, which also result in a higher evaporation water loss. As the nurse reviews these facts about the infant's body fluid balance, she can more readily understand why the infant, at one twentieth the adult's weight, requires one third as much water. He requires five times as much water per kilogram of body weight (150 ml./kg./24 hr., as compared with 30 ml./kg./24 hr. in the adult). The infant may exchange half his extracellular fluid volume daily. The adult may exchange only

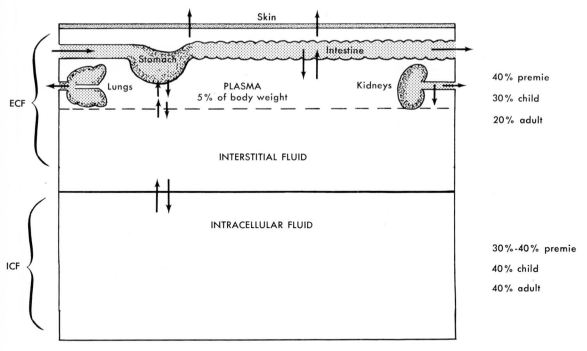

FIG. 29-14. Relative fluid balance in children and adults as expressed in percentage of body weight.

one sixth his extracellular fluid volume. Infants and young children may become severely dehydrated in a short time.

Dehydration. Inadequate fluid intake and/or excessive fluid loss causes dehydration. It is almost always associated with fever, burns, vomiting, diarrhea, hyperventilation, or hemorrhage. Dehydration seldom denotes water loss alone but rather loss of fluid volume, electrolytes, and water. During periods of dehydration, plasma volume is usually maintained at the expense of interstitial volume.

Early signs of dehydration in a patient are dry lips and mucous membranes, diminished urinary output, reduced weight, and lethargy. Moderate dehydration is further characterized by depressed fontanels, sunken eyeballs, loss of skin turgor, and a 5% to 10% loss of weight. As dehydration increases, the child becomes acutely ill, bordering circulatory failure. His skin is grayish, his pulse rapid and weak. Temperature elevation and low blood pressure are characteristic. Recorded output is scant, and weight loss is obvious, 10% or higher. Apathy, restlessness, and even convulsions may occur.

Intravenous therapy. Because many times it is difficult to perform and maintain a conventional intravenous infusion for prolonged periods in the small child, a *cut-down* may be performed (Fig. 29-15). This is a minor but important surgical procedure that is usually completed in the treatment room. The physician "cuts down" to a vein, directly exposing it. A small plastic tubing is inserted into a minute nick in the vein and sutured in place. The tubing is then attached to a needle adaptor, which, in turn, is joined to the intravenous tubing.

Whether fluids are administered through a cut-down or a needle puncture through the skin into a vein of the scalp or extremity, it is very important that the amount of fluid being given the child be gauged very carefully to avoid overloading the circulatory system. The rate of flow ordered

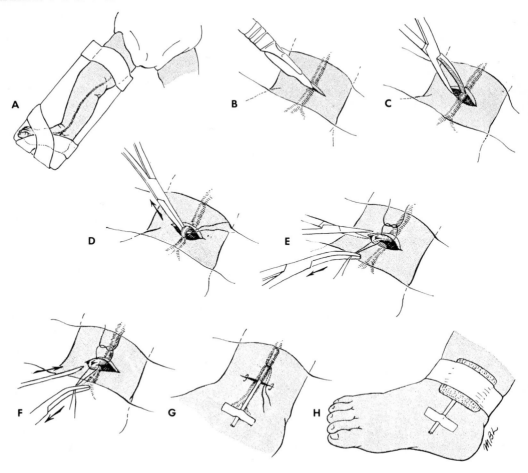

FIG. 29-15. A cut-down procedure. Great care is necessary in immobilizing the leg to prevent impairment of circulation and pressure areas. A cut-down may be used for a number of days to help maintain fluid balance or administer medication.

should be known, marked on the bottle, and meticulously observed. The use of special pediatric intravenous counting chambers or bags that simplify calculation is to be commended. Although a number of semiautomatic infusion sets (Fig. 29-16) have added a special margin of safety to administering fluids, the nurse must continue to keep a close watch on the flow rate, as well as the child's response to the fluid therapy. The infant and small child must be appropriately restrained to avoid dislodging the infusion. The nurse should be aware that changes in the child's position may slow or speed the infusion, and she should frequently observe the rate of flow in the drip chamber (Fig. 29-17). Extreme care should be exercised in moving the patient. The vocational nurse shares responsibility for observation of the intravenous apparatus with the supervising registered nurse. If a vocational nurse observes an infusion running more rapidly than ordered, she may slow it to the known ordered rate, but she must immediately contact the supervising nurse regarding her action, since there may have been a change in orders or some reason for the increased infusion rate. The insertion point of the needle must be checked frequently to detect infiltration or inflammation. Pain and swelling are signs of possible dislocation of the needle.

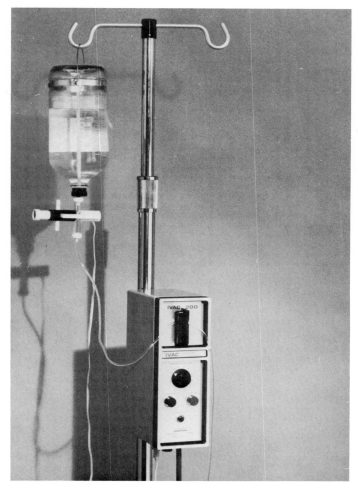

FIG. 29-16. One example of an infusion pump, which may be set for a specific amount of fluid delivery. (Courtesy IVAC Corp., San Diego, Calif.)

The responsibility for observation is even greater if the child is receiving blood or plasma. There is more danger of circulatory overload, tissue damage, and untoward reactions. Patients receiving blood should be carefully watched and, when necessary and possible, questioned regarding back or chest pain or chills. The temperature, pulse, and respiratory rate should be frequently determined to detect any possible incompatibility. Hives may occur.

Cleanliness

Satisfying the need for cleanliness is almost entirely the responsibility of the nursing staff. The way in which it is met depends on the condition of the individual patient and the facilities of the pediatric unit.

Bed bath. A bath is usually administered each day to prevent skin irritation and provide refreshment, stimulation, and comfort. It also serves as an excellent period for patient observation and evaluation. Patients who are quite ill, are especially susceptible to chilling and respiratory infections, have dressings or incisions to be protected, or are in traction or casting routinely have bed baths. Most children with elevated temperatures usually have bed

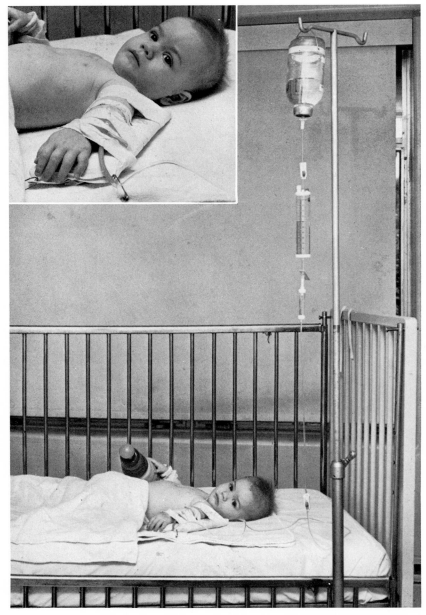

FIG. 29-17. Intravenous feedings for a young patient with prolonged vomiting and diarrhea. Side rail down for illustration only. The arm board is pinned to the bedding. Inset shows arm immobilization. (Courtesy Children's Health Center, San Diego, Calif.)

baths, although occasionally a tepid tub bath may be ordered to reduce fever, a treatment that may also be a period of cleansing. Bed baths are carried out in essentially the same manner for children as for adults. A bath blanket or towel should be used for a covering, and, except in the case of an infant, the area should be curtained or screened. Unless contraindicated, a good light should be available for the bath area to aid in the detection of any special changes in skin color, rashes, or other abnormalities.

Perineal care. The child should be helped with the care of his genitalia if he is too young to cleanse the area properly. Any irritation of the penis or labia should be reported. If the little boy is uncircumcised, no extraordinary force should be exerted to retract the foreskin, nor once retracted should it remain so, but observation of the area for cleanliness and possible inflammation should be made. Occasionally, more formal perineal care using an irrigation technique will be desirable to encourage cleanliness, especially in the case of older girls having their menses.

Nails. The nails of young children often need attention. Cleaning and cutting the nails when necessary should be part of the daily care. Usually, the nails may be cut or filed without an order except when the patient is a diabetic.

Oral hygiene. Oral hygiene should also be carried out routinely. However, remember that a child with a recent cleft lip, cleft palate, or dental repair usually is not allowed to have a brush or anything hard in his mouth. For those too young to have more than two or three teeth, oral hygiene may be a simple drink of water, but for older children the essentials of good care of the teeth should be taught. A small toothbrush that can easily fit into the mouth is needed. Massage of the gums and correct up-and-down brushing of the teeth are important health habits and often make food and fluid intake more pleasant. Cracked or dry lips may be lubricated with petrolatum.

Bed patients are usually dressed in pajamas or gowns, but sometimes if the child is convalescent, a bright dress or striped tee shirt may be a big lift to the morale of the child and parents.

Unit care. Part of the daily care of the patient is the care of his unit. The bath is not technically complete until the unit is clean and orderly. Whether a complete linen change is necessary depends on its condition. Most children's beds need frequent changes, but do not use linen needlessly!

The patient's bedside stand should be neat (inside and out), and the unit furniture wiped down with a moist paper towel. The aim is not to have each little bed "just so" with a neat and clean but unhappy occupant but to cut down on confusion and reduce safety hazards. A child *needs* to have toys and a certain amount of freedom in his bed activities. But he is not aided by mounds of equipment taking over his bed or crib. In some hospitals, special bags are available for toy storage. The patient's room should be comfortably warm and well ventilated but free from drafts.

Tub bath. When tub baths are allowed, the amount of supervision required depends on the age and condition of the child. Young children should never be left alone because of danger of burning from the hot water faucet, drowning, or falling while trying to climb out. Teen-agers usually resent much observation in the tub room and many times need only a minimum of supervision. For many children the addition of a bubble bath preparation makes a tub bath a pleasantly anticipated event. Unless a prolonged tub bath is ordered for treatment purposes, the bath should not be too extended. There is greater possibility of chilling, and others may be waiting in line. When facilities are available, there is a greater tendency than formerly to give hospitalized children tub baths. Be sure to clean the tub well after each child is finished.

Prolonged tub bath. A prolonged tub bath lasts at least 20 minutes. It may be ordered to relax the muscles before physical therapy, to help remove dressings or crusts, or to apply a certain soothing medication to the skin, such as oatmeal and Alpha-Keri. To help the patient relax in the bath and get his whole body in contact with the water, a pillow may be constructed from a rolled bath blanket to raise the head out of the water while the child lies flat in the tub. If a rubber headrest is available, it may be used for this purpose.

Table tub bath. The infant who may have a tub bath is placed in a smaller basin for greater security and easier handling. The following procedure could be used for a newborn infant whose umbilicus has healed or, with modification, for an older infant. It may be carried out at the bedside or at a special table or counter. The instructions are written to help the new mother at home bathe her newborn infant, but the principles are the same. Only the organization of equipment may be different. The older child, who enjoys the bath and is able to sit steadily, may have more freedom in the tub and could be soaped while he is in the water. (See Fig. 29-19.)

FIG. 29-18. I guess everybody likes bubbles!

TABLE TUB BATH
Materials needed:
1. Baby bathtub, large basin, or bathinette
2. Tray with
   a. Mild soap, dish
   b. Jar of cotton balls and twists
   c. Jar of safety pins
   d. Bottle of baby oil or lotion
   e. Capped 4-ounce baby bottle of sterile water.
   f. Small box of tissues
3. Large heavy towel or mat (possibly placed on several thicknesses of newspaper on the surface used for drying and dressing)
4. Newspaper or hamper for dirty clothes discard

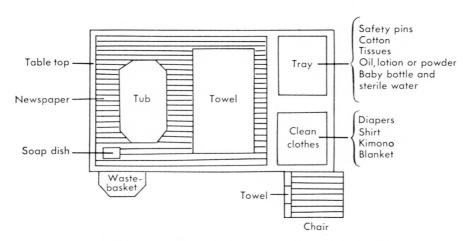

FIG. 29-19. Diagram of possible home setup for a table tub bath.

5. Paper bag or handy wastebasket to receive waste
6. Two soft towels
   a. One on which to undress and inspect baby
   b. One for drying baby
7. Two soft washcloths
8. Baby clothes (clean)
   a. Diaper
   b. Shirt
   c. Kimono
   d. Receiving blanket
9. Apron

Procedure:

1. Check the temperature of the room (72° to 75° F. and free from drafts).
2. Wash hands thoroughly, put on apron.
3. Assemble equipment (the kitchen table is a good place).
   a. Tray of baby supplies
   b. Tub on newspapers on table
   c. Mat or heavy towel for undressing and drying (next to tub)
   d. Wastebasket slightly under table
   e. Newspaper on seat of chair to receive dirty clothes; clean towel for drying on back of chair
   f. Clean clothes and blanket stacked in order of use
   g. Tub one-third full of water comfortable to your elbow

Note: You may want to put a bottle of formula in warm water to be ready to give to the infant.

4. Place the infant on the mat.
   a. Inspect the eyes, and wash the lids with sterile cotton and water if any discharge is present, proceeding from the inner corner of the eye outward. With older infants, a fresh washcloth or cotton dipped in clear water is sufficient. Inspect the ears.
   b. Wash his face with the washcloth and clear water from the tub. Dry.
   c. Soap the scalp; support the infant using the football hold, if possible. The infant's head should be over the tub, and his ears should be covered with the nurse's fingers. Rinse the scalp carefully. Dry.
5. Remove his shirt and diaper. If the buttocks are grossly soiled with stool, discard the washcloth used for the cleanup and use another to continue the bath or use tissues for initial cleanup.
6. Quickly soap the infant's entire body, except the head, paying special attention to body creases and the area under the chin.

7. Lift the child carefully into the tub, feet first, using appropriate holds.
8. Rinse the soap off the infant quickly.
9. Lift the infant back to the clean towel on the mat. Pat him dry. Oil or lotion may be used sparingly on the body creases.
10. Inspect and clean the genitalia with cotton balls. Dress the child quickly in clean clothes and wrap him in a receiving blanket.
11. Offer drinking water and inspect his mouth. Feed the child his formula.

Shampoo. The state of the patient's scalp, his general condition, and the length of his hair will determine the need for a shampoo.

Whether a shampoo for an older child must be ordered by the physician depends on hospital policy, the condition of the child, and the type of shampoo contemplated. Many children can easily have their hair shampooed by lying on a gurney with their head extended over the end next to a sink or tub. A trough to guide the water may be constructed of plastic or rubber sheeting. If a wall spray hose is used, great care should be taken in regulating the water temperature before the water touches the child.

If the child is bedfast, a simple head basin and trough may be constructed from two bath blankets rolled together lengthwise (like a snake) and curved into a horseshoe shape with the open end pointing toward the side of the bed. This form is draped by a plastic or rubber sheeting to make a waterproof basin that leads off the side of the bed into a large bath basin or baby tub. Some hospitals use inflated Kelly pads. A few have bed shampoo basins available, similar to those found in beauty salons. The hair must be rinsed of suds until squeaky clean. Some patients like a vinegar or lemon rinse. Hair should be dried quickly to avoid chilling.

Rest

Personal and environmental cleanliness and order should promote rest, but rest is not automatic. Nap times must be provided and promoted. Most children do best with a rest period after lunch lasting at least an hour. Other nap times should be encouraged, depending on the needs of the child. Shades should be drawn, the television set turned off, the area straightened up, and the child covered comfortably. A reminder of something pleasant that can happen when the child has rested is often helpful in making the nap more acceptable.

Diversion and self-expression

A convalescing child should not be expected to sit or lie quietly all day long without diversion and opportunities for self-expression. Although rest is very important, a child may rest better when allowed moderate activity during the day. To stay perfectly still is impossible and the attempt may be fatiguing in itself. The nurse can help by supplying appropriate toys, providing suitable television programs, setting up controlled group play for patients in the same room when possible, playing with the child herself, or asking for the help of the "play lady" or auxiliary worker. She may enlist the aid of the occupational therapy department if one is available. A hospital library may supply interesting books for pleasure or help with schoolwork.

MEDICATION

The administration of medication to young children entails special skills and knowledge. It is a particularly heavy responsibility because dosages vary so greatly from child to child, as the result of weight, body area, and metabolic differences.

General principles

Pediatric dosages may be calculated in different ways by physicians. Young's rule uses age as a basis for determination.

Young's rule:

Child's dose =

$$\frac{\text{Age of child in years} \times \text{Average adult dose}}{\text{Age of child in years} + 12}$$

More helpful, since the size of children the same age may differ, is Clark's rule

based on weight:

Clark's rule:

Child's dose =

$$\frac{\text{Weight of child in pounds}}{150} \times \text{Average adult dose}$$

A newer concept in computing pediatric dosage is based on the surface area of a child. Some dosages must be individualized for the specific child by his physician.

Giving medication is sometimes difficult because the child often does not recognize the need for the medicine and may, despite the kindliest approach, resist its administration. However, although the licensed vocational nurse is not given major responsibility in the administration of medicines in the pediatric area, she should know the principles involved and receive practice in giving selected medications to children during her pediatric experience.

As with the administration of medication anytime, the following factors must be identified:

1. The right patient
2. The right medication in the right form
3. The right dosage
4. The right method of administration
5. The right time of administration

Before any medication is given, it should be identified on a medicine card and checked against the physician's order. In some hospitals, orders for certain medications must be renewed after a certain time. Common medications that are often automatically stopped unless reordered are broad-spectrum antibiotics and narcotics. Medications that are ordered on an "as necessary," or p.r.n., basis must be checked to see when they were last given to avoid too frequent administrations. It also must be determined whether the need for the medication truly exists. The nurse should look up any unfamiliar medication before assuming the responsibility of its administration. She should know its common usages, contraindications, side effects, common dosages, and peculiarities of administration.

Common measurements

Before giving medications, the nurse should review the common measurements used in the metric and apothecary systems and frequently used conversions. There should be an easily read table available for her reference. Some of the most common conversions follow:

1 dram or ʒ	=	4 ml.
1 teaspoon or tsp.	=	5 ml.
1 tablespoon or tbsp.	=	15 ml.
1 ounce or ʒ	=	30 ml.
15 or 16 minims or		
℥xv or ℥xvi	=	1 ml.
gr. xv	=	1 Gm.
gr. i	=	0.06 Gm. or 60 to 65 mg.

Oral medication

Preparation. A minim glass (Fig. 29-20) may often be used in measuring oral dosages. If possible, medications for children are prepared as solutions for greater ease in administration. Suspensions must always be shaken well before being poured. Most may be diluted, although it is not wise to dilute medicines more than a few cubic centimeters to wash out the measuring container. The child may not take the increased volume easily. Placing a medication in a baby's formula is also precarious. If he refuses to take all the formula, how much has he taken? Was the medication evenly distributed throughout? These are difficult questions to answer.

Administration. Before giving any type of medication, check the patient's identification. Many hospitals now do not rely on bed tags; patients may change beds. Most have a system of banding or identification bracelets. Very young children cannot identify themselves. It is imperative that the nurse be positive of her identification. If the child is old enough he should be asked in addition, "What is your name?"

Always place a bib on a small child before administering oral medications. Such a simple maneuver will save many extra changes and important minutes of the

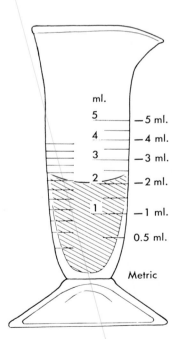

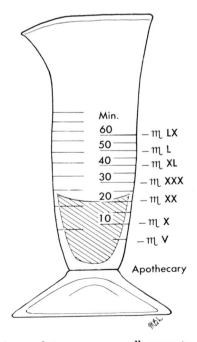

Fig. 29-20. A minim glass or a standard syringe may be used to measure small amounts. Remember, 1 ml. = 1 cc.; ℥vx or ℥xvi = 1 ml.

nurse's time, best used in other ways. Remember, if a child is given water or other fluid to wash down a pill, this liquid must be recorded on his intake.

Fluid medications may be given fairly easily to infants when placed in a nipple fitted in a standard ring (used on ring-and-disc–type baby bottles). The baby sucks out the medication while the nurse supports his head to prevent aspiration. Small medication cups are also employed. Syringes may also be used to administer oral fluids, thus increasing the accuracy of the dose. The medicine is poured slowly with the baby in sitting position or with his head elevated. Rubber-tipped medicine droppers may be helpful too. Pills and capsules must be crushed or opened for small children under 5 years of age. The medication may be placed in a cherry syrup, honey, or jelly and given from a spoon. Many of these medications are bitter so that a good disguise must be used.

The child who takes his medicine well should be praised for being such a "big boy or girl." If a child finds it difficult to take medicine, he should be made to feel that his nurse understands some of his distaste and fear and wants to help him during this brief but difficult period. Although a young child may be helped by gentle restraint in the administration of medicines (the nurse may hold the child on her lap with one of his hands wedged behind her and the other controlled by her encircling arm and hand), pouring medication down the throat of a struggling, crying youngster is an invitation to aspiration, early emesis of the medication, and subsequent trying periods when medicine time comes again. At times a child will respond much better if he is allowed to hold the cup and drink at his own rate. Many of the small, disposable medicine cups are safe play objects for successful medicine takers, who, in turn, medicate dolls and stuffed toys. A child must never be told that he is taking candy when he is receiving a medication. The two ideas seem to become easily confused, and many toddlers have raided medicine chests in search of something more appetizing but have settled for orange-flavored aspirin.

Intramuscular injections

When the nurse gives an intramuscular injection to a child she usually needs a second person to help support, distract, restrain, or comfort the child receiving such an injection. If the child is old enough to understand, the nurse should explain the procedure just before administering the injection. The resistant, tearful child might be told that the medicine will help him get better so that he can go home sooner. The infant or younger child needs to be restrained adequately to assure safe and correct administration of the drug. For most infants and children, an injection means simply "hurt" and may establish a lasting fear. To lessen his fear and to maintain a degree of trust, the nurse should always comfort the child by holding him afterward. When dealing with an older child, she should indicate that she understands why he reacts the way he does.

In final preparation for intramuscular injection, 0.2 to 0.3 ml. of air is drawn into the syringe. When the syringe is inverted, the bubble rises and serves to clear all the solution from the needle into the tissues and prevent backflow.

Equipment
Damp antiseptic sponge
1 or 2 ml. syringe
22-gauge, 1-inch needle for infants and children
23-gauge, ¾-inch needle for tiny infants

Because the gluteal muscle is not well developed in the infant or young child, and permanent sciatic nerve damage is possible, the buttocks are never used for an intramuscular injection. The most desirable sites for pediatric injections are the lateral and anterior aspects of the thighs, the deltoid areas, and the soft tissue inferior to the iliac crests. The medicine and syringe should be completely prepared and ready for use before the nurse enters the child's room.

Method. The site is cleansed with the

antiseptic damp sponge, using a circular motion. The skin is pulled taut. In young children who have minimal muscle, the needle is inserted at a slightly oblique angle; if the child is large and well developed, it is inserted perpendicularly. The plunger is pulled back to assure that the needle is not in a blood vessel, and the medicine is injected slowly. When the air bubble leaves the syringe, the sponge is placed over the needle, the needle is quickly withdrawn, and the area is gently wiped with the sponge. A bandage is placed over the site. Many older children seem to be helped a great deal if they can grasp the crib sides with their hands and count during an injection. Some gain satisfaction in helping to put on a Band-Aid after the procedure. Afterward, a child should be comforted by the nurse administering the injection, if possible. After all, she is not his enemy but a special friend, and everything should be done to help him recognize this.

Suppositories

Aspirin, sedative drugs, and bowel stimulants are often given to children in the form of rectal suppositories. Most of these suppositories may be lubricated with a jellylike material before insertion. Since they are kept refrigerated to preserve their shape, warming them, unwrapped, in a clean hand for about a minute may be helpful. The nurse should wear a clean glove or finger cot for the insertion of the suppository. The child should be asked to take a deep breath, if possible, and the medication should be pushed about 2 inches past the rectal sphincter. After insertion, pressure should be exerted on the buttocks, holding them together for more than a minute, or the suppository may be ejected and its effect lost.

Nose drops

Nose drops are ordered fairly often for infants and children. They are primarily used to combat nasal congestion and make breathing, eating, and drinking easier. In the case of an infant, nose drops may be ordered 20 minutes before meals to improve sucking and formula intake. If the nose is very congested, gentle suctioning of the nasal passageway may be indicated before the drops are administered. It will do no good if the drops only roll in and out again or do not remain in the nose! Young children do not understand the reason for nose drops and may need to be gently restrained by a second person or a modified mummy restraint. The child should be lying down with the head tilted back over a folded towel or small pillow. The dropper should be pointed slightly toward the top of the nasal cavity. The child should remain positioned for several seconds after the instillation. Oily nose drops should be avoided because of the possibility of aspiration and lipoid pneumonia.

Eardrops

Eardrops are still used occasionally in the pediatric area. They should not be cold but close to body temperature or warm. Cold eardrops are painful. The child's head should be resting comfortably on the bed, turned with the ear to be treated exposed. The child's ear should be pulled down and back to straighten the external auditory canal. After instillation, cotton should not be routinely inserted because it may interfere with drainage of discharge to the exterior or serve to soak up the recently instilled medication.

Eyedrops

Eyedrops, when ordered, should not be dropped on the cornea but instilled in the lower conjunctival sac while the child, lying flat, tries to look at the hair on top of his head! After instillation of the eyedrops, the eyes should be lightly closed, not squeezed shut, since this may force out the medication. It is a good practice with some toxic medications such as atropine to put a little pressure at the inner angle of the eye after the drop has been placed to prevent drainage into the nose through the tear duct.

Topical medication

Ointments or creams may be applied to the skin with a finger cot or buttered on gauze with a sterile tongue blade if the area is to be covered with a sterile compress. Liniments and lotions are often applied with clean hands or cotton balls, depending on their contents and the condition of the area to be treated.

SPECIAL TREATMENTS

Special treatments related to the particular physical problem that the child may be facing will be discussed in separate chapters describing procedures involving the various body functions, systems, or diseases.

PROVISIONS FOR REHABILITATION

As convalescence progresses, provisions for rehabilitation may be necessary to recapture skills lost during illness. This usually begins during hospitalization and continues after discharge. In some cases the problem involved is not so much rehabilitation as *habilitation,* or the formation of skills not previously mastered. This is particularly true of patients suffering from neuromusculoskeletal problems. Emphasis is placed on the development of function with the least cosmetic defect and maximum appearance of normalcy. Priority is placed on skills needed for daily tasks.

Physical therapy

Those engaged in the specialty of physical therapy concern themselves primarily with the treatment of disease and injury by physical agents such as heat, cold, electricity, and water. The most common techniques used involve therapeutic exercises in and out of water. These specially prescribed exercises are fundamental to the treatment of delayed motor development and respiratory, orthopedic, and neuromuscular disease. They are designed to prevent and correct deformities, increase muscle strength and function, and establish normal postural reflexes. The physical therapist institutes normal patterns of motion

and teaches coordination, balance, walking, and stair-climbing (with and without orthopedic appliances), as well as other activities of daily living. Thus, through the careful selection of techniques, he or she prevents deformity, relieves pain, and promotes functional capacity.

Occupational therapy

Occupational therapy is more often concerned with the maintenance or stimulation of small muscle control necessary for the accomplishment of more refined but equally important skills involving finger and wrist manipulation. Occupational therapy uses many crafts to motivate and involve the patient in activities that strengthen muscles or are psychologically stimulating. Weaving, ceramics, shell jew-

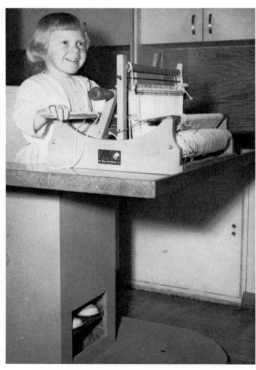

FIG. 29-21. Susan enjoys her weaving in occupational therapy. The stand-up table with a little gate at the back helps her maintain balance. The finger exercise encourages the joint movement that is so necessary for rheumatoid arthritis patients like Susan. (Courtesy Children's Health Center, San Diego, Calif.)

elry manufacturing, woodworking, and painting are usually just means to an end —a better functioning patient. Often the occupational therapy department can help by locating or fashioning equipment to aid the patient in carrying out necessary activities for daily living: appliances that help malfunctioning hands to hold combs and toothbrushes, special cups, plate guards, angled spoons and forks to help with eating, and elastic shoestrings and long-handled gadget sticks to help with dressing are just a few of many possible examples (p. 561).

Other specialties

Speech therapists and hearing specialists may be part of the efforts to better fit the child or youth for life and meet his needs for communication and participation. A bedside teacher provided by the public school system may help to make the return transition from hospital to regular school less difficult. Greater provision for socialization, according to the developmental needs of the child, may need to be considered to provide for optimum personality development for children undergoing long-term hospitalization. A sense of individual worth, importance, and purposefulness should be fostered.

• • •

An appreciation of the importance of each individual and the contribution he may make to his world should be part of the nursing perspective of the staff. If the child or youth is personally incapable of making a constructive contribution, then society's reaction to the sad situation may itself become a source of growth and hope by channeling efforts toward rewarding research and increasing compassion and understanding. A nurse should have a faith that will recognize the tragic realities of life without destroying its sweetness, a philosophy that will allow her to give without becoming empty and brittle, and an outlook that carefully measures minutes in the light of an eternity.

RECORDING

Although the recording of nursing observations and care may seem to be of minor importance when compared to the proper execution of these responsibilities, clear, concise, and appropriate record keeping is a nursing necessity. It serves as a permanent record of the patient's treatments, medications, and changing condition. It is especially important to have a clear record of the pediatric patient who often, because of his age, lacks communication skills. The nurse's notes may help influence therapy, may be important in research studies, and may become of specific legal importance.

The notes should be hand printed in ink. Errors in charting should never be erased. A line should be drawn neatly through the error in such a way that the entry may still be read and the portion labeled "error." All notes should be signed with the first initial, last name, and title of the person making them. Some comment or an appropriate summary statement should be made concerning the pediatric patient's condition or activity at least every hour. In recording, one should always ask oneself, "What is the reason for this child's hospital entry? What signs and symptoms would be significant to record? Is there any change in his condition? Is the intake and output record accurate?" If the child has had any bowel movements, they should be described in terms of amount, consistency, and color. Of course, treatments and medications and patient reactions also form part of the record and are recorded after they are completed or administered. The visits of physicians and parents and relatives should be noted.

The nurse should not be too wordy, but she should give an accurate description of the condition of her patient. Good charting for most nurses is not automatic. If it develops, it is the result of concentrated effort and experience. Each hospital will probably have a different form to use, but the principles of charting will remain the same.

Daily planning for patient care

After the basic needs of patients have been identified, learning to plan nursing care to meet the needs of patients takes time, ingenuity, and experience. The student requires guidance in executing care so that priorities in need are recognized and work progresses safely and efficiently, benefiting all the patients and staff.

NURSING STAFF ORGANIZATION AND UTILIZATION

The planning of the nurse's tasks will depend in part on the organization and work patterns of the ward or nursing area to which she is assigned. The several ways in which care may be rendered are as follows:

1. A nurse may have the responsibility for the total care of a patient under the direction of the supervising head nurse. She would watch for changes in his condition and concern herself with his safety, general hygiene, nutrition, special medications, and treatments. Licensed vocational nurses (LVN) may function in such a manner with patients having relatively stabilized conditions and/or when complex nursing care is not indicated. They may work as private duty or staff nurses.

2. A nurse's responsibility may be for a specific group of patients but involve only certain types of functions. One nurse may observe a patient and render hygienic care and simple treatments. Another may provide supervision, observation, medications, and special treatments. Usually, a nursing aide, orderly, or LVN would have the former responsibilities, and a registered nurse would perform the latter, although in hospitals for the chronically ill and in convalescent settings the LVN may be given more responsibility for medications and treatments. This has been a common nursing pattern.

3. A nurse may be assigned to a nursing team, which is responsible for all patients in a specific area. The team may consist of registered nurses, LVN's, nurse's aides, and orderlies. The team leader, a registered nurse working under the head nurse, gives specific detailed patient assignments to each of her team members. In addition, she acquaints all team members with the general condition and primary needs of all the patients in their total area of responsibility. Some functions are literally performed at the same time, for example, taking temperature, pulse, and respiration and passing trays. Others are performed by the assigned team nurse or the supervising registered nurse as the need of the patient involved dictates. The LVN may be assigned observation responsibility, general hygiene, treatments, and medications, depending on her patients and the medications involved. Periodic conferences involving the entire team are held to report and discuss patient needs and ways in which they can best be met. When well-planned and understood, the team concept, which is gaining support in various parts of the United States, has the advantage of bringing the registered nurse back closer to the bedside to help the patient and her staff. It can provide better utilization of nursing personnel and better analysis and coverage of the patients' needs.

In a pediatric setting, nursing patterns involving LVN's are usually either 2 or 3 in the preceding list. Pediatrics is a specialty that deals with many variables. Because of the young ages and immature development of many of the patients, some procedures that would not be considered complex in certain settings become more difficult when their performance involves a pediatric patient. Medication dosages must be calculated often and closely scrutinized. When making nursing assignments, a supervisor must consider not only the level of nursing preparation represented by the personnel but also the experience and individual capabilities of the nurses involved.

INDIVIDUAL PLANNING AND ORGANIZATION

When given her morning assignment and report, a nurse must plan her individual care in order to accomplish her goals in the best way possible. The head nurse, team leader, or student instructor (if she is a student) may assist in this planning.

Usually, the best beginning is a *quick* tour of all the patients assigned to check on any immediate needs. The following things could be done during the tour:

1. Introduce the nurse to the child and/or parent, when appropriate.
2. Check the general safety of the patient's environment.
   a. Restraints and side rails, crib nets.
   b. When necessary, intravenous apparatus for rate of flow and possible infiltration.
   c. Humidification devices for function.
   d. Oxygen equipment.
   e. Inappropriate toys.
3. Help set up and supervise breakfast, when appropriate, checking diet for accuracy.
4. Evaluate the need for supplies.
   a. Linen.
   b. Sizes of underwear, dresses, trousers, shirts, hospital gowns, or pajamas.
   c. Procedural supplies.
      (1) Dressing supplies.
      (2) Solutions—irrigating sets, etc.

After this brief "grand tour" the patient's needs must be evaluated again. In deciding which patient should receive basic care first, one must consider the following:

1. Any prior appointments that have been scheduled for the patients.
   a. X-ray examination or therapy.
   b. Physical therapy.
   c. Speech therapy.
   d. Bedside tutoring.
   e. Scheduled dressing changes.
2. General condition of the patient.
   a. As a general rule, the patient who is least comfortable has the priority.
   b. Presurgical patients who have had their preoperative medications are usually not disturbed.

c. Patients who are sleeping and need the rest may, at the discretion of the supervising nurse, be left temporarily undisturbed. Sleep may be their most pressing need.
3. Types of treatment that are ordered and when they are to be given.
   a. Enemas would ordinarily be given before the bath and bed change.
   b. Shampoos would ordinarily be given after the bath but before the bed change.
   c. A patient's care would preferably be completed before a blood transfusion or other infusions are started.
   d. Ideally, sterile dressings are best changed when local movement, bed making, mopping, etc. is at a minimum.
4. Hospital routine.
   a. Taking the temperature, pulse, and respiration is routine on most patients. The time at which it is done depends on the hospital policy and the type of nursing organization pattern followed. Many team patterns say that all TPR's should be taken before or immediately after the breakfast period and the results recorded on a special sheet handy for quick perusal by nurses and physicians.
   b. Meal schedules. Children usually need more supervision and aid than adults. Babies are usually fed their ordered solids, bathed, and then given their formula.

A good rule to follow that saves steps and time during the morning is, if possible, never go anywhere empty-handed. There is usually something that needs to be carried to or from a patient's unit.

May an active brain, gentle skill, and good humor accompany your many steps.

30
Common diagnostic tests

A day does not pass in a busy hospital without many diagnostic tests being performed. The tests may entail the services of the clinical laboratory, the x-ray department, the operating room suite, or other specialized areas. They may be performed in the nursing unit. Although the nurse does not need to know the details of all these procedures, she should know the purpose of the test, whether patient preparation is necessary, the general procedure followed during the test, its effect on the patient, and the follow-up care needed.

For convenience the tests described in this chapter are arranged in table form and grouped as follows: tests of blood specimens, tests of urine specimens, tests of stool specimens, miscellaneous specialized tests, and x-ray tests. Only those tests commonly performed and of special interest in obstetrical or pediatric areas are described. The details of each test frequently differ from hospital to hospital. The nurse is advised to consult the procedure manual of the institution where she is employed before participating in any test.

Tests of blood specimens
General considerations

1. Blood specimens are secured by the physician, the laboratory technician, or, occasionally, the registered nurse.
2. Blood specimens for chemical analysis must be collected after a period of fasting, unless otherwise specified. Water, however, may be allowed in *small amounts.*
3. Blood specimens are obtained by the following methods:

a. Prick of the great toe, heel, or finger. The drops of blood are collected by pipette or capillary tube; equipment is supplied by the laboratory.
b. Venipuncture.
   (1) Various sites may be used in children (Fig. 30-1).
      (a) Infants—jugular, femoral, or scalp vein or sometimes veins of the arm
      (b) Children 2 or 3 years old or more—usually veins of the arm
   (2) Necessary equipment includes the following:
      (a) Tourniquet or blood pressure cuff
      (b) Antiseptic and sponges
      (c) Needles, Nos. 19 to 22 (depends on vessel size), 1 to 1½ inches
      (d) Syringes, sterile and dry (size depends on amount of specimen)
      (e) Collecting containers or tubes, with or without oxalate (to prevent coagulation), special tubes as needed, and rack
      (f) Glass slides
      (g) Band-Aids
4. Nursing care during the collection of blood specimens usually consists of explaining the procedure to the young child and helping support or restrain him.
5. Blood specimens must be collected, labeled, transported, and checked into

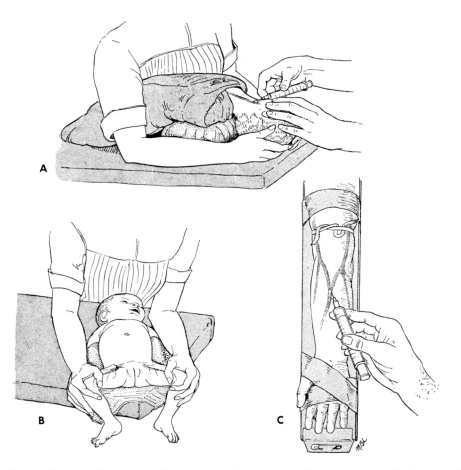

FIG. 30-1. **A,** Suggested restraint and positioning for puncture of a jugular vein. **B,** Suggested positioning for a femoral puncture. **C,** Suggested arm restraint in preparation for venipuncture for blood samples, intravenous medication, or infusion. The arm board should be well padded.

the laboratory properly. Before transporting specimens, invert oxalated specimens slowly six to eight times to assure mixture—do not shake. If an addressing machine is available, stamping the paper tape with the patient's charge-a-plate will easily assure the inclusion of the patient's name, unit, physician's name, and date on the label. A laboratory requisition form should accompany each specimen. The fact that the specimen has been sent should be recorded.

Tests of urine specimens
General considerations

1. Urine specimens are secured by the nurse.
2. Urine specimens may be obtained in various ways, depending on the physician's orders. Specimens may be ordered regulating the preparation of the patient or the timing of the specimen collection.
   a. Routine voided specimen. No special preparation usually needed. The patient is asked to void into

Text continued on p. 405.

TABLE 30-1. Tests of blood specimens

Test	Purpose and rationale	Preparation of patient and/or specimen	Special considerations	Normal value
Albumin, globulin, total protein, and A/G ratio (usually performed together)	To aid in diagnosis or in evaluating treatments of many diseases, including those of liver and kidney Blood may produce excessive globulin when albumin is abnormally displaced or lost, causing change in blood plasma ratio	Fasting patient Specimen—6 ml. venous blood in unoxalated tube		A/G ratio—1.5:1-2.5:1 Total protein—6-8 gm./100 ml. serum (lower level for newborn infant)
Antistrepto-lysin O titer	To aid in diagnosis of suspected rheumatic fever (not specific for this disease) Indicates presence of antibodies formed to combat recent streptococcal infection	Fasting patient Specimen—5 ml. venous blood in unoxalated tube		Up to 200 units/ml. serum
Bleeding time	To determine time needed for small cut to stop bleeding (involves constriction of small blood vessels) Prolonged bleeding time in thrombocytopenic purpura and other blood disorders	Nonfasting patient Basic procedure—standardized puncture wound made in fingertip, earlobe, or forearm, drops of blood produced removed with filter paper every 30 sec., and the time bleeding ceases noted		1-6 min., depending on details of procedure
Blood counts Platelet count (thrombocytes)	To aid in diagnosis of bleeding tendencies, thrombocytopenic purpura, aplastic anemia, etc. Platelets necessary for coagulation	Nonfasting patient Specimen—drops of capillary or oxalated venous blood (if automated procedures used, larger sample may be necessary)		200,000-500,000/mm.^{3}
Red blood count (erythrocytes)	To aid in determination of primary blood disease or effects of secondary disease on blood Red blood cells carry oxygen and carbon dioxide	Nonfasting patient Specimen—drops of capillary or oxalated venous blood (if automated procedures used, larger sample may be necessary)	Newborn infant has higher red blood count than adult	Adult: 4.5-5 million/mm.^{3}

TABLE 30-1. Tests of blood specimens—cont'd

Test	Purpose and rationale	Preparation of patient and/or specimen	Special considerations	Normal value
	Elevated counts may indicate dehydration or polycythemia; low counts hemorrhage, red blood cell destruction, or failure in red blood cell formation			
White cell count (leukocytes)	White blood cells help combat infectious organisms Blood levels usually elevated in infections, may be elevated in blood diseases (leukemia) Depressed levels may result from blood disease and toxic drugs or chemicals	Nonfasting patient Specimen—drops of capillary or oxalated venous blood (if automated procedures used, larger sample may be necessary)	White blood count averages 20,000/mm.^{3} at birth; however, counts as high as 38,000/mm.^{3} may be considered normal White blood count gradually falls with age; approaches that of adult by 3 yr. of age	Adult: 5,000-10,000/mm.^{3}
White blood cell differential	To aid in diagnosis of certain diseases by study of white blood cell percentages Five main types of white blood cells; certain diseases cause alterations in proportions of different cells found in circulating blood	Nonfasting patient Specimen—drop of fresh or oxalated blood spread on glass slide, stained, and examined under microscope	Usual percentage pattern of type of white blood cells for adults: Neutrophils—50%-65%, increased during infections; eosinophils–0%-6%, increased in allergic conditions and parasitic infections; basophils–0%-1%, increased in some blood disorders; lymphocytes—25%-40%, increased in some viral and bacterial infections and leukemia; monocytes—0%-10%, increased during some infections	
Blood culture	To identify microorganisms that may be circulating in bloodstream Drug sensitivity test usually performed subsequently if organisms found	Nonfasting patient Special venous blood container with culture media Often ordered when high temperature spikes present	Culture must be made at bedside because microorganisms do not survive prolonged standing or temperature change without special media Operators should not speak during collection of specimen to avoid contamination	Normal blood is sterile

Continued.

TABLE 30-1. Tests of blood specimens—cont'd

Test	Purpose and rationale	Preparation of patient and/or specimen	Special considerations	Normal value
			Inside of container lid or stopper should not become contaminated; specimen to laboratory immediately Preliminary reports may be available in 36 hr.	
Blood sugar	To aid in determination of abnormal glucose metabolism Disorders of blood sugar include hyperglycemia, caused by diabetes mellitus, liver diseases, or other endocrine overactivity; hypoglycemia, caused by tumor of islets of Langerhans (in pancreas) or other endocrine disturbances; insulin-glucose imbalance, caused by diabetic treatment	Fasting patients unless otherwise ordered Specimen—3-5 ml. venous blood in oxalated tube (or in tube with sodium fluoride and thymol if blood cannot be examined immediately)		80-120 mg./100 ml. (Folin-Wu method)
Blood types Major groups	To determine blood type for possible transfusion or maternal-newborn blood studies	Nonfasting patient Both oxalated and clotted blood desired for transfusion cross matching		Four main blood types found in general population: A—38% B—12% AB—5% O—45%
Rh factor	To determine blood type for possible transfusion or maternal-newborn blood studies	Nonfasting patient Both oxalated and clotted blood desired for transfusion cross matching		85% of Americans, Rh + (positive); 15% of Americans, Rh − (negative)
Blood urea nitrogen (BUN)	To determine kidney disease or urinary obstruction Urea, a waste product of protein metabolism, normally excreted by kidney; if urinary system fails, blood urea levels will be elevated	Fasting patient Specimen—5 ml. venous blood in oxalated tube		7-20 mg./100 ml. blood

TABLE 30-1. Tests of blood specimens—cont'd

Test	Purpose and rationale	Preparation of patient and/or specimen	Special considerations	Normal value
Carbon dioxide combining power (carbon dioxide capacity)	To aid in determination of acidity or alkalinity of blood High carbon dioxide combining power may be result of persistent vomiting, hypoventilation, or excessive administration of ACTH or cortisone Low carbon dioxide combining power may be found in diabetic acidosis, severe diarrhea, certain kidney diseases, and hyperventilation	Nonfasting patient, unless otherwise ordered Specimen—8 ml. venous blood, completely fill test tube to avoid air contact		Adult: 55 vol. %, 24-32 mEq./L. Child (under 2 yr.): 40-60 vol.%; 18-28 mEq./L.
Clotting (coagulation time)	To determine time needed for blood to clot outside body Many factors necessary for normal clotting; clotting may be slow in hemophilia, anticoagulant therapy, etc.	Nonfasting patient Several methods, using fresh venous or capillary blood		Wide range, depending on method used
Coombs	To detect weak or incomplete type of antibody reactions Used especially to diagnose erythroblastosis fetalis, caused by Rh incompatibility	Nonfasting patient Specimen—2-5 ml. clotted or oxalated blood, depending on laboratory methods and type of test ordered	Direct or indirect Coombs' tests may be ordered	Direct Coombs' test negative
C-reactive protein (CRP)	To aid detection of inflammation and tissue breakdown Nonspecific test, often used to aid diagnosis of rheumatic fever and infarctions	Clotted capillary blood or clotted venous blood may be used, depending on technique employed		Normally, no C-reactive protein present
Glucose tolerance	To aid in determination of abnormal glucose metabolism More sensitive than fasting blood sugar determination	Fasting patient, except for glucose; oral or intravenous glucose tolerance tests may be ordered Fasting blood and urine specimen	Patient's current weight determined to calculate amount of glucose to be given; unsweetened lemonade or carbonated	Normal range: Oral—peak of not more than 150 mg./100 ml. serum, return to fasting level within 2 hr.— Intravenous—re-

Continued.

TABLE 30-1. Tests of blood specimens—cont'd

Test	Purpose and rationale	Preparation of patient and/or specimen	Special considerations	Normal value
		secured; calculated oral or intravenous dose of glucose given fasting patient Concurrent periodic blood and urine specimens may be ordered during 2-5 hr. period	drinks, commercially prepared for this purpose, may be used to dilute glucose Testing procedures differ according to basic reason for test (possible hypoglycemia or hyperglycemia); procedure manual of individual hospital should be consulted	turn to fasting level within 1 hr.
Hematocrit (hct.)	To determine relative proportion of cells and plasma in blood Most reliable screentest for anemia—low in anemia, high in polycythemia and dehydration	Nonfasting patient Specimen—4 ml. of venous blood in oxalated tube Specimen measured into a special centrifuge tube and spun; height of resulting column of packed red blood cells checked	Newborn infants have higher norman values than older children or adults; a low of 35 may be seen at about 2-6 mo. of age	Adult: Male—40-50 mm. red blood cells/ 100 mm. of column height Female—35-45 mm. red blood cells/100 mm. column of height
Hemoglobin (hgb.)	To determine amount of hemoglobin in blood available for transport of oxygen Hemoglobin levels help determine color of blood; amount of red blood cells and level of hemoglobin in blood are not always parallel	Nonfasting patient Specimen—capillary or venous blood in oxalated tube	Newborn infants have higher normal levels than older children or adults (14-19 gm.); low of 11 gm. may be seen at 3-6 mo. of age	Adults—12-16 gm./ 100 ml. of blood
Protein-bound iodine (PBI)	To aid in determination of thyroid function Increased concentration of protein-bound iodine in blood may indicate hyperthyroidism; a decrease, hypothyroidism	Fasting patient Specimen—8 ml. venous blood in unoxalated tube	Patient must not have had any previous iodine-containing substances (for example, intravenous pyelogram or gallbladder visualization) during preceding 6 mo.; administration of thyroid hormone may be discontinued for preceding 14 days	Adults: 3-8 μg./100 ml. serum

TABLE 30-1. Tests of blood specimens—cont'd

Test	Purpose and rationale	Preparation of patient and/or specimen	Special considerations	Normal value
Sedimentation rate	To aid in detection of inflammation and tissue breakdown Nonspecific test, which, when elevated, may point to rheumatic fever activity, arthritic infections, and infarctions	Nonfasting patient Specimen—4 ml. venous blood in oxalated tube Blood measured into a calibrated thin tube, and level of the formed elements settled in a certain time noted	If patient anemic, "corrected sedimentation rates" may be reported	Depends on equipment—0-20 mm./hr. (Wintrobe), 10-13 mm./hr. (Westergren)
Serology test for syphilis (Wassermann, Kahn, VDRL, etc.)	To aid in detection of syphilis Legally required before marriage in some states; routine at prenatal examination; some hospitals require on all admissions	Nonfasting patient Specimen—5 ml. venous blood in unoxalated tube	Nonspecific tests— false positive and false negative results may be obtained Handle report of positive results discreetly	Negative

a clean container. (*Note:* Children and some adults do not understand the word "void"; select terminology in accord with the age and education of the patient. Little children may say "peepee," "tinkle," "number 1," "pass water," or "urinate.") The patient should be told not to put toilet paper in with the specimen. If the patient is menstruating, a routine voided specimen will be of no diagnostic value. A "clean catch" or catheterized specimen may be ordered, or the test deferred until later.

b. Voided "clean catch specimen." Special preparations are made before the specimen is collected.
  (1) Necessary equipment includes the following:
    (a) Five or six sterile cotton balls
    (b) Aqueous benzalkonium chloride (Zephiran), 1:750, or pHisoHex and warm water solution in squeeze bottle or bowl
    (c) Paper bag or other waste receptacle
    (d) Sterile or clean collecting bottle, depending on situation; specimens for culture always collected in a sterile container
    (e) Clean gloves
  (2) For female patients the perineum is carefully cleansed with cotton balls, usually saturated with pHisoHex solution. The labia are retracted, and each cotton ball is used only once, moving from front to back. When the urinary stream begins, the collecting bottle is positioned to collect an adequate specimen. Older patients may be able to carry out the procedure alone if properly instructed. Younger patients may find it difficult

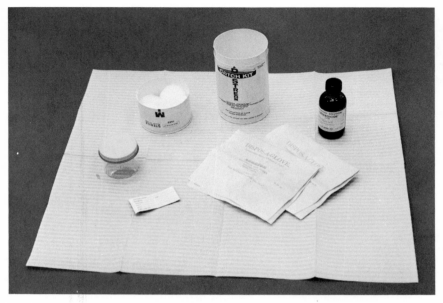

FIG. 30-2. One type of midstream clean catch kit, which includes everything necessary for the collection of sterile specimens. (Courtesy Grossmont Hospital, La Mesa, Calif.)

to void when directed. Little girls may be washed off and placed directly on a sterile bedpan if unable to void with the labia retracted. If the patient is well hydrated, the request for a specimen is more easily fulfilled. A midstream collection kit is pictured in Fig. 30-2.

(3) For male patients the glans penis is carefully washed with pHisoHex solution, and the foreskin, if present, is retracted to assure proper cleansing. When the patient begins to void, the container is positioned to collect an adequate specimen. Older boys and young men often carry out this procedure alone or with the assistance of an orderly.

c. Three-glass specimen (for male patients). The glans penis is cleansed. Three sterile urine specimen bottles are labeled No. 1, No. 2, and No. 3. The patient begins the urine stream, voiding approximately 20 ml. in bottle No. 1. Without interrupting the urine stream he voids about 100 ml. into bottle No. 2. Without interrupting the urine stream he continues to collect the specimen in No. 3 until his bladder is empty. The assistance of the orderly or a male nurse may be needed.

d. Catheterized specimen. Male catheterizations are performed by a male nurse or orderly; female catheterization technique has been described in Chapter 15. The urethra of the female infant curves downward; therefore, the catheter should be inserted in a slightly downward direction. Urine specimens for culture are always collected in a sterile container.

e. Timed specimen. This specimen (Fig. 30-3) usually consists of voided urine, although it may involve drainage from a urinary catheter. To begin the specimen collection,

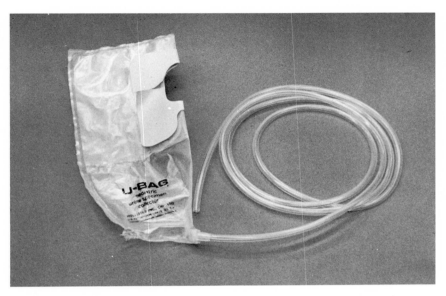

Fig. 30-3. One type of 24-hour collection bag and tubing, which may be inserted into a sterile bottle. (Courtesy Grossmont Hospital, La Mesa, Calif.)

have the patient empty his bladder. Note the time. Discard this first urine specimen. Label a large collection bottle with the patient's name, his physician's name, and the time the discarded urine specimen was voided. This is the start of the test. Collect all voided specimens for the ordered period in this single large collection bottle. If a special preservative is not used, keep the bottle in the refrigerator. At the end of the period have the patient empty his bladder again and add this specmien to the total collection. Send the total specimen to the laboratory. Since this represents the total urine output of a patient within a known period, the collection *must* begin with an empty bladder. Twenty-four-hour urine specimens are notoriously difficult to obtain in pediatrics, especially from little girls. One of the newer methods employs a modified incubator, crib, or bed in which a nylon screening device is placed above a drainage unit. The child is positioned on the screen. As she voids, the urine is "filtered" through the screen.

3. Urine specimens should be properly collected, labeled, transported, and checked into the laboratory with proper requisitions. Urine specimens should be sent promptly to the laboratory unless protected from deterioration by a preservative or refrigeration.

Tests of stool specimens
General considerations

1. Stool specimens are obtained by the nurse.
2. Stool specimens are obtained by collection from a bedpan or diaper or, occasionally, by rectal swab. They are placed, with tongue blades, into a clean cardboard receptacle. The entire specimen need not be sent to the laboratory unless a timed specimen is ordered or the reason for the stool collection is the detection of a tapeworm head. Specimens for ova and

TABLE 30-2. Tests of urine specimens

Test	Purpose and rationale	Preparation of patient and/or specimen	Special considerations	Normal value
Addis count	To aid in diagnosis of type of kidney disease present (acute, latent, or chronic nephritis, etc.) Cells and casts in urine sediment secured from 12 hr. specimen counted, and amount of each compared	Patient usually dehydrated—no fluids after breakfast until next morning and dry lunch and dinner At 8 P.M. patient begins 12-hr. urine collection After genitalia cleansed, saved specimens are voided directly into special container At 8 A.M. specimen closed and pretest diet resumed	Not performed on patients with severe kidney disease Special preservative must be placed in container	Results variable, depending on disease present
Phenolsulfonphthalein (PSP)	To determine ability of kidney tubules to excrete dye Dye excretion decreased in chronic nephritis and urinary tract obstructions, increased in certain liver diseases	Procedure differs in various hospitals; consult laboratory manual for details Equipment—venipuncture equipment, 1 ml. dye solution, and urine specimen bottles Principles—patient empties bladder, and specimen discarded; patient is hydrated (no coffee or tea); physician injects 1 ml. of dye solution; specimens collected in separate bottles at various intervals, usually 15, 30, 60, and 120 min. after injection	Warn patient that urine may be pink or red after injection of dye because of pH of urine	Elimination of 63%-84% of injected dye in 2 hr.
Routine urinalysis				
Acetone	To determine presence of ketones in urine, a possible sign of developing acidosis	Usually done by nurse for diabetic patients; 1 drop of urine placed on Acetest tablet, and color change after 30 sec. compared with scale	Diabetic patients may have urine specimen free from sugar but containing acetone, although this is not common	No acetone present normally
Albumin	To detect loss of plasma albumin through kidney	Amount needed depends on method used		Usually no albumin present; however, orthostatic or pos-

TABLE 30-2. Tests of urine specimens—cont'd

Test	Purpose and rationale	Preparation of patient and/or specimen	Special considerations	Normal value
	May indicate kidney disease, heart failure, drug poisoning, or toxemia of pregnancy			tural albuminuria sometimes occurs in absence of disease Albuminuria is common finding in newborn infant
Glucose	To detect presence and amount of glucose in urine, possibly caused by diabetes mellitus	Less than 1 ml. urine needed Clinitest—follow directions issued with Clinitest tablets Benedict's test—place 5 ml. of Benedict's solution in test tube with 8 drops of urine, shake, and place tube in boiling water bath for 5 min.; compare color change to Benedict scale Clinistix—simple to use but most expensive; follow directions	When performing the Clinitest, observe reaction—rapid passage through green, tan, orange, and finally to dark shade of greenish brown indicates amount of sugar is over 2% May be orders to further dilute specimen and test again Do not touch tablets; store away from heat and sun; watch for deterioration	No glucose usually present
Gross appearance (color, clarity)	To aid in estimation of degree of hydration and ability of kidneys to concentrate urine			Color depends on amount of hydration—may change markedly from one time to next Smoky urine may indicate hematuria; cloudy urine, abnormal sediment
Microscopic studies Cells	Red blood cells and white blood cells found in urine in kidney disease	Specimen of urine placed in centrifuge and sediment examined microscopically	Presence of red blood cells or white blood cells in voided specimen of mature female has little significance, since these results may be caused by contamination Recheck of catheterized specimen indicated	No red blood cells May be a few white blood cells May be a few epithelial cells

Continued.

TABLE 30-2. Tests of urine specimens—cont'd

Test	Purpose and rationale	Preparation of patient and/or specimen	Special considerations	Normal value
Casts	Casts, representing abnormal sediment in urine, may be formed of many substances passing relatively slowly through tubules; presence usually indicates kidney disease	Specimen of urine placed in centrifuge and sediment examined microscopically		None found normally
Specific gravity	To measure density of urine Detects presence of many abnormal substances, but does not identify them High specific gravity may occur in albuminuria, glycosuria, and dehydration Test also indicates patient's ability to concentrate urine	Tested with a urinometer (calibrated float)		1.003-1.030
pH	To determine acidity or alkalinity of urine	Strip of Nitrazine paper is dipped into urine or placed in a baby's diaper; color change compared to scale	pH should be measured quickly because urine becomes alkaline on standing Sometimes alkaline urine is needed to keep excreted substances soluble (during sulfadiazine therapy or blood or tissue destruction), and therapy is directed to this end	4.5-7.5 (urine is usually acid, but pH may vary to maintain pH of blood)

parasites or culture should be sent to to the laboratory immediately.

3. Stool specimens should be collected, labeled, transported, and checked into the laboratory immediately and properly.

Tests of cerebrospinal fluid (C.S.F.)
General considerations

1. Cerebrospinal fluid specimens are secured by the physician.

2. Cerebrospinal fluid specimens are obtained by spinal tap (lumbar puncture), cisternal puncture, or ventricular tap.

   a. Necessary equipment includes the following:

   (1) Sterile tray containing:
       (a) 5 ml. syringe
       (b) Needles, Nos. 22 and 26
       (c) Spinal needles, Nos. 20 and 22 (1½ inches for

TABLE 30-3. Tests of stool specimens

Test	Purpose and rationale	Preparation of patient and/or specimen	Special considerations	Normal value
Fat determination	To confirm diagnosis of steatorrhea (excess fat in stools), signs of celiac syndrome	Patient on normal diet 2 or 3 days before test Timed specimen usually ordered		Between 15% and 25% of weight of fecal sample
Occult blood	To detect presence of fecal blood, which is changed by process of digestion	Usually random specimen used If positive, patient is on meat-free diet for 3 days and another specimen obtained	Diet containing meat may sometimes cause positive result	No occult blood
Timed stool specimen	To determine amount of certain substances excreted in feces in given time	Patient should not void or place tissues in bedpan with stool Determine date and approximate time of previous defecations; this will be start of test collection; refrigerate total specimen until complete and then take to laboratory		

small infant, 2 inches for older infant or small child, and 3 inches for older child)

(d) Cotton applicators or sponge forceps and cotton balls or gauze cherries (to cleanse area)

(e) Medicine cup (for antiseptic)

(f) Three hand towels (or one towel and small drape sheet)

(g) Three-way stopcock

(h) Spinal fluid pressure manometer (water manometer)

(i) Three test tubes with stoppers labeled No. 1, No. 2, and No. 3 for specimen collection

(j) Four 4 × 4-inch gauze compresses

(2) Sterile gloves (sized for physician)

(3) Antiseptic, for example, benzalkonium chloride (Zephiran), 1:750, tincture of iodine, alcohol, 70%

(4) Desired local anesthetic, for example, procaine hydrochloride, 1%

(5) Good lighting, stool, firm table, and supply surface

(6) Band-Aid

b. Position of patient.

(1) Lumbar puncture (Fig. 30-4)

(a) Patient on his side or sitting up with his spine curled forward to increase the spaces between the vertebrae for needle insertion.

(b) Patient must be supported by an assistant on

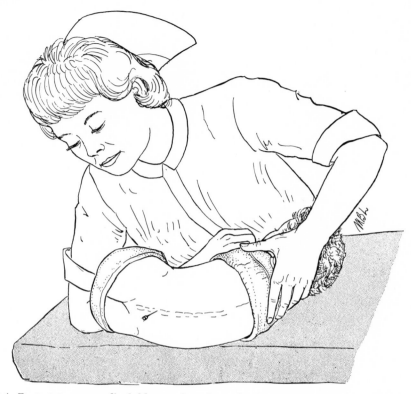

Fig. 30-4. Restraining a small child or infant for a lumbar puncture. When older children (2 to 3 years old) are positioned, the child's head may be tucked under an elbow, and the nurse may have to lean over her charge in a gentle but firm fashion to maintain positioning.

a firm table. Suggest that he arch his back like a kitty or cat. This position must be maintained to assure a proper spinal tap.

(2) Cisternal and ventricular punctures are less often attempted. The needle is introduced at the base of the skull, the fontanel, or the coronal suture.

c. Procedure.

(1) Supplies are assembled and opened, and the local anesthetic is withdrawn. (The nurse disinfects the stopper of the bottle, shows the label to the gloved physician, and holds the bottle in such a way that he may easily withdraw the amount desired with a needle and syringe.)

(2) Patient is positioned.

(3) Selected skin surface is identified and prepared in a sterile manner. (Usually the puncture site is at the level of the iliac crests between the third and fourth lumbar vertebrae.)

(4) Anesthetic is infiltrated.

(5) Physician inserts the spinal needle.

(6) If the child is not too upset, measurement of spinal fluid pressure may be done before and after the fluid is withdrawn by attaching the three-way stopcock and water manometer.

(7) Three specimens of fluid are obtained. The first specimen

TABLE 30-4. Miscellaneous specialized tests

Test	Purpose and rationale	Preparation of patient and/or specimen	Special considerations
Electrocardiogram (ECG or EKG)	To aid in determination of irregularities in electrical impulses controlling heart action and to help diagnose heart damage	Usually no special preparation except simple explanation; no pain involved Leads positioned on various parts of trunk by technician	
Electroencephalogram (EEG)	To aid in determination of abnormalities in brain waves Useful in diagnosing convulsive disorders, brain tumors; estimating cerebral activity	Simple explanation Young children need to be sedated before test Testing takes approximately 1 hr.; no pain involved Electrodes placed on scalp with adhesive substance by special technician in quiet atmosphere	
Nose, throat, or wound culture	To detect presence of pathogenic organisms in active diseases and carrier states	Extreme care needed to prevent spread of pathogenic organisms Area to be checked carefully swabbed with sterile applicator; swabbed material suspended in sterile test tube and capped aseptically	While sterile applicator exposed, operator should not speak or should wear mask In some cases, because of suspected organism, special media necessary Sensitivity tests routine if cultures positive
Sweat test	To help detect presence or carrier state of cystic fibrosis. Abnormal amount of sodium chloride present in perspiration of affected persons	Hand impression technique (used for screening purposes)—hands washed, rinsed, and dried, and then pressed against test medium, which is observed for color change Plastic bag technique—extremity to be used is washed, dried, and enclosed in clean plastic bag (heating pad may be applied); when adequate perspiration evident, bag is carefully removed without touching the inside, and perspiration allowed to collect in bottom of bag; bag closed and transported in upright position to laboratory Iontophoresis technique—perspiration stimulated by use of special electrodes and pilocarpine; collecting pads weighed and analyzed	

TABLE 30-5. X-ray tests

Test	Purpose and rationale	Preparation of patient and/or specimen	Special considerations
Barium enema	To aid in diagnosis of lower bowel pathology by outlining colon with radiopaque material May be part of treatment for intussusception	Cathartics or cleansing enemas may be ordered on previous day or morning of test Clear liquid diet may be given 1 day before test until test completion Barium enema given in x-ray department when patient is under fluoroscope; examination takes 1 to 2 hr. Enema or cathartic may be ordered after roentgenograms completed	Carefully note and record patient's bowel movements after procedure
Cystogram	To aid in diagnosis of urinary obstruction or other abnormality by visualization of bladder, ureter, and urethra with radiopaque material during filling and emptying of bladder	Urethral catheter inserted prior to procedure Bladder emptied Radiopaque material injected into bladder and x-ray film taken Catheter removed	
Voiding cystourethrogram		Roentgenograms taken during voiding process	
Ciné cystourethrogram	To determine whether reflux appears or increases at voiding pressure	Continuous fluoroscopic pictures taken during voiding process	
Gastrointestinal series (G. I. series)	To aid in diagnosis of stomach and small bowel pathology by outlining areas with radiopaque material	Night before test, patient may have light supper No food, fluids, or medications after midnight until 6 hr. x-ray studies completed X-ray department gives barium under fluoroscope Patient remains NPO until x-ray department gives release after 6 hr. studies If 24 hr. studies ordered, no enema or cathartic given until studies completed Check for enema or cathartic orders when test completed	

TABLE 30-5. X-ray tests—contd

Test	Purpose and rationale	Preparation of patient and/or specimen	Special considerations
Intravenous pyelogram (IVP)	To detect kidney or urinary disease by intravenous dye injection followed by abdominal roentgenograms	Cathartic or enema ordered to clear bowel on day before test Patient may eat light dinner with little fluid Fluids, food, and medications withheld after midnight Roentgenograms of abdomen taken before and after intravenous injection of dye by physician Fluids usually forced after completion of test	Allergy to iodine is contraindication to routine technique
Pneumoencephalogram	To detect abnormalities of brain by injection of air or oxygen into spinal canal Lumbar puncture done, and and some spinal fluid withdrawn and replaced by air, which rises to ventricles of brain, forming characteristic outlines	Patient NPO 6 hr. before test; given preoperative sedative and analgesic; may be done under local or general anesthetic in x-ray department After procedure, patient kept flat and observed carefully; headache, nausea, and vomiting fairly common; signs of increasing intracranial pressure should be reported; treated as postoperative patient	
Ventriculogram			Similar to pneumoencephalogram, except air introduced directly into ventricles through burr holes in skull Performed in operating room

goes into tube No. 1, the second into tube No. 2, etc.

(8) The needle is removed and a Band-Aid placed over the site.

(9) The child is allowed to rest (preferably kept flat in a prone position).

3. Cerebrospinal fluid specimens should be collected, labeled, transported, and checked into the laboratory immediately and properly.

4. Tests commonly performed involve chemical analysis, culture, and cell count. Spinal fluid sugar is lowered in cases of meningitis. Spinal fluid protein is elevated in meningitis or subarachnoid hemorrhage. White blood cell count is moderately increased in encephalitis and poliomyelitis. It is greatly elevated in most cases of meningitis.

31
The child surgical patient

Not too many years ago the child was considered, in many ways, to be a miniature adult. Old photographs reveal that he was dressed like an adult, and at times he received similar treatment. However, age does make a difference. Anatomical relationships, physiological activity, and psychological responses are greatly influenced by the phenomena of normal growth.

This chapter discusses some of the differences that set the child apart from the adult and reviews a few routines and procedures encountered fairly commonly when nursing the pediatric surgical patient.

Child-adult distinctions

The following list of child-adult distinctions is not complete, but it may prove helpful in the evaluation of the needs of children.

1. The metabolic rate of infants and young children is much greater proportionately than that of adults. Children are growing and need to be fed more frequently.

2. Abnormal fluid loss is more serious in the infant and young child than in the adult. Fluid intake and output must be calculated very carefully, including fluid loss from diaphoresis or wound drainage. A 7-pound infant who sustains a blood loss of 1 ounce (30 ml.) has been compared to a 150-pound man who has lost 600 ml. of blood.[*]

[*]Stanley-Brown, E. G.: Pediatric surgery for nurses, Philadelphia, 1961, W. B. Saunders Co.

3. The child lacks the reserve physical resources that are available to the adult. His general condition may change very rapidly, almost without warning.

4. The body tissues of the child heal quickly because of his rapid rate of metabolism and growth.

5. The child usually needs less analgesic proportionately than an adult patient to obtain relative comfort after surgical procedures.

6. The young child lives more in the present than an adult does. This may be both to his advantage and disadvantage. "Now" is understood and very important, but he has difficulty understanding "later." On the other hand, he usually does not become upset by anticipating unpleasant future procedures or prospects or worrying about finances or loss of a job!

Preparation for surgery

The child entering the hospital for surgery may have had considerable preparation for the event, or he may have had none. The condition for which he is admitted may be relatively simple to correct, or it may entail an operation of considerable complexity and risk. He may have had numerous previous admissions and know many of the staff by name, or he may never have seen a blood pressure cuff, call light, or bedpan.

Psychological preparation

The nurse should remember that in all contacts with patients, regardless of age, there should be explanation and emotional

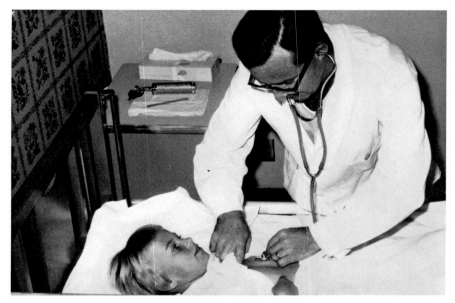

FIG. 31-1. Before surgery each child is examined by an anesthetist. (Courtesy Children's Health Center, San Diego, Calif.)

support adapted to the individual's ability to understand and his personal needs. She should also remember that as parents are reassured, the confidence they gain in turn helps support the child.

Physical preparation

Patients being admitted for surgery should be especially evaluated for the presence of respiratory infection and signs of malnutrition. Occasionally, surgery may be delayed until the general condition of the child improves.

Physical preparation for surgery usually (except in emergency situations) begins the night before the procedure. Although some children may be admitted to the hospital early in the morning of the day of minor surgery, most come into the hospital the previous afternoon.

If orthopedic surgery is planned, the child is usually given a pHisoHex tub bath in the evening. The body part to be involved in the surgery is carefully washed and inspected. The fingernails or toenails of any extremity involved are cleansed and trimmed. In many cases the ordered shave of the operative area is delayed until the morning of surgery, unless the surgery is scheduled very early. For some types of surgery, preparatory enemas may be ordered.

Food, fluids, and oral medications are withheld as ordered, depending on the type of surgery planned, the age of the child, and the time of the procedure. The fact that the child must not receive anything by mouth should be conspicuously posted. The child should be told of the fact so that he does not think that he has been forgotten when the breakfast trays are passed. Any loose or missing teeth should be noted and recorded on the chart.

Sedative and analgesic drugs are given, usually in two stages. Preliminary sedation is usually ordered approximately 2 hours before surgery. Analgesic and atropine compounds, which prepare the patient for general anesthesia, are routinely given "on call." Every effort should be made to see that the child is allowed to rest after receiving his preoperative medications. The room should be dimmed and quiet and television sets or radios turned off.

417

After the child is taken to surgery on a cart, his unit is prepared for his return. His bed is made up according to his postoperative needs, and any special equipment desired is placed conveniently. An orthopedic patient may need bed boards under the mattress, an overbed frame and trapeze, and extra plastic-covered pillows. Other equipment that may be required, depending on the individual, includes a suction machine, intravenous standard, oxygen mask, mist tent, bed lift, and properly sized restraints.

Postoperative care
Immediate observation

When the patient returns to the nursing unit from the recovery room, his general condition must be noted. Periodically, his pulse, respirations, and, possibly, his blood pressure are determined and recorded. Until the patient is responsive and alert, he should be kept on his abdomen or side unless the surgery performed contraindicates these positions. The nurse should note the condition and placement of any dressing and describe any apparent drainage. The presence of a plaster cast or mold should be noted. Casted extremities should be elevated, and frequent checks for circulatory disturbances should be made. Intravenous infusions should be checked for possible infiltration and correct rate of flow. The child should be protected from harming himself (pulling out needles or tubes or tampering with suture lines) by the use of an appropriate restraint, as necessary. Urinary catheters should be connected to dependent drainage and stabilized properly to the bed with a safety pin and rubber band to prevent the formation of a dependent loop of tubing, which obstructs drainage. The type and amount of urinary drainage should be observed. The patient's skin color and temperature are checked. The nurse must always watch for and quickly report signs of shock—low blood pressure; cold, moist, pale, or cyanotic skin; rapid pulse; dilated pupils; and restlessness.

Diet

Whether the child will be allowed oral fluids after he is responsive will depend on the physicians orders and the child's general condition. Sometimes surgical patients are not allowed oral fluids for a considerable period; instead, they are fed intravenously. When oral feedings are introduced, they are begun gradually, and the patient's tolerance is observed. The routine postsurgical diet follows this sequence with modifications for different ages—clear liquid, full liquid, soft, and regular. Rich, spicy, highly seasoned, or gas-forming foods should be avoided.

Ambulation

Early progressive ambulation for the general surgery patient is the rule in the modern care of patients. In only a few cases and situations will the physician delay ambulation beyond the second postoperative day. The general surgery patient usually has orders to stand at the bedside and take a few steps the day after surgery. The nurse should be sure to follow these orders because judicious ambulation strengthens the patient, aids in the restoration of gastrointestinal function, and helps prevent such complications as pneumonia and the formation of blood clots and pressure areas.

When the patient's condition or young age makes it impossible or inadvisable for him to get out of bed, the nurse must be sure that he is turned frequently, receives good skin care, and breathes deeply at intervals. The physician may order intermittent positive pressure treatments to aid lung expansion.

After surgery, toddlers and preschool-aged youngsters usually move about quite spontaneously in their cribs or beds; ambulation presents few problems for them. However, older children may express the same timidity and fear of pain that most adult patients exhibit when asked to move or get up and may need a great deal of initial support and encouragement from their parents and the nursing staff.

Fortunately, in most cases it is not long

before these same youngsters are enjoying the freedom of the playroom. Most will recover quickly and gather together their little hoard of treasures and say their "good-byes" in a few days. At times some possessions are overlooked; one nursing staff fondly remembers Bobby, who left his turtle in the linen closet!

Common procedures

A few of the common procedures encountered when nursing pediatric surgical patients are described in the following pages. Some of these treatments may also frequently involve medical patients. They will include skin preparation for surgery, cleansing enema, dressing change, gavage feeding, gastrostomy feeding, urinary catheter irrigation, and irrigation of nasogastric or intestinal tubes.

SKIN PREPARATION FOR SURGERY

Purposes: To cleanse the area of prospective surgery to help prevent infection, provide a clearly visible operative field, and carefully inspect the skin for possible pustules, lesions, or signs of poor circulation.

Materials:

1. Sharp, sterile razor
2. Clean bowl for warm water
3. Prescribed soap or antibacterial solution
4. Waterproof pad or sheeting
5. Towels (2)
6. Washcloth or gauze sponge
7. Clean cotton applicators, if the areas to be "prepared" involve the umbilicus or toes
8. Nail clippers, if extremities are involved
9. Bath blanket or drawsheet
10. Gooseneck lamp

Procedure:

1. Check the order, the operative permit, and the time preoperative medications will be given. The preparation should be finished before the medications must be given.
2. Identify the patient.
3. Explain the procedure to the patient according to his level of understanding. Small children usually respond to the explanation, "We're going to wash your tummy to make it very clean." When you are ready, begin by doing just that. Explain as you work. As the child gains confidence, you may show him the tiny hairs on his arm and talk about how adults shave. Run your finger

along his skin to show him how the razor feels. Suggest that it may tickle a little but that he will help by being very still.
4. Position the lamp and raise the bed to a convenient working level.
5. Wash your hands.
6. Place the waterproof pad and towel under the patient to protect the bed.
7. Prepare and place the warm water and ordered antibacterial agent conveniently. (Some physicians may order a dry shave.)
8. Apply tension to the skin with the washcloth or a gauze sponge as you shave. (If the feet or fingernails are very dirty, they may be soaking in a basin of warm water while the adjacent areas are being shaved.)
9. Crouch down frequently to look *across* the surface of the skin to check for remaining hairs.
10. Retain your "prep setup" until the skin preparation has been checked by the team leader, head nurse, or instructor.
11. Record the procedure. Any skin lesions (for example, pustules) must be reported. Pustules are *not* to be opened. Razor nicks should be treated with direct pressure with a sterile sponge and reported. Great care must be used in shaving, especially in areas of old scars, insect bites, or bony prominences, where nicking may easily occur.
12. In some cases a pHisoHex or povidone-iodine (Betadine) scrub of 10 minutes may be ordered after the shave is complete. The physician may order the prepared area wrapped in sterile towels until surgery.

CLEANSING ENEMA

Purposes: To cleanse the lower bowel prior to surgery, relieve constipation or flatulence, and aid in the expulsion of parasites.

Materials:

1. Rectal catheter or tubing and clamps, appropriately sized
   a. For infants, size 12 to 16 French
   b. For young child, size 12 to 20 French
   c. For older child, size 16 to 22 French
2. Container of ordered solution
3. Lubricant and wipes
4. Asepto syringe barrel or enema can or bag, depending on the amount of fluid to be given and the size of the child
5. Ordered solution (kind and amount) at 105° F. when given

Procedure:

1. Identify the patient.
2. Explain to the child what will be done as you do it according to his level of understanding. In the case of the very young

child, understanding will not be complete, of course, but the tone of voice and the socialization such explanation offers can be helpful. Telling a small child that you are "going to put a little water in where we take your temperature to help you go to the bathroom," sometimes helps.

3. Screen the unit and position the child. A number of positions are advocated when giving an infant or toddler an enema.

   a. For most children the side position with the upper leg flexed seems to be the most comfortable. The left side is preferred because this placement puts the descending colon lowest. However, a left-sided position is not absolutely mandatory. In fact, some investigators question the supposed advantages of left-sided placement. Infants and small toddlers often do well if placed on a firm pillow, which has been draped with a lightweight plastic sheet and covered with an absorbent towel, with their hips pulled to the edge. The plastic extends over the side of the pillow into or beside a curved basin or small bedpan, which is placed snugly against the buttocks just below the rectum. For warmth, the child is covered by a bath blanket or towel.

   b. If the infant is very active and a nurse has no one to help maintain him in a side position, the infant may be gently restrained in supine position over a small bedpan. His back and head are supported by a small pillow or folded bath blanket. His buttocks are placed over the bedpan and his legs gently drawn to either side and secured by a diaper placed under the bedpan and drawn up and over the lower extremities and pinned to itself as illustrated in Fig. 34-5, p. 481.

   c. Older children with sphincter control are usually positioned on their sides and given enemas in basically the same way as any adult.

4. Place the ordered amount and type of solution in a can or Asepto syringe attached to a rectal tube. Expel the air from the tube and lubricate the tip. Do not occlude the eyes of the catheter.

5. Gently insert the tubing approximately 2 to 3 inches into the rectum and observe the flow. Hold the container of solution no higher than 12 to 18 inches above the patient's hips.

6. Observe the patient closely during the procedure for an increase in respiratory and pulse rates and exhaustion.

7. As needed, put the child on a bedpan or potty chair or allow him to go to the bathroom.

8. Remove equipment and tidy up the area.

9. Record the procedure and the results obtained.

STERILE DRESSING CHANGE

Purposes: To protect the incision or wound from contamination by replacing wet dressings, allow direct observation of the incision or wound to evaluate the healing process, increase the cleanliness and comfort of the patient, and, in some instances, apply local medications or carry out irrigations that assist in treatment.

Materials: (Materials vary according to the area to be dressed, whether sutures are to be removed or local debridement attempted, and the wishes of the physician. Generally, the following supplies are needed, although not all the supplies listed are needed every time. Simple dressings may require only sterile compresses, handling forceps, adhesive tape, and a discard bag.)

1. Dressing tray containing the following (Figs. 31-2 and 31-3):

   a. Basic instrument kit with sterile
      (1) Suture-remover scissors
      (2) Clip removers
      (3) Sharp-pointed suture scissors
      (4) Tissue forceps
      (5) Smooth forceps
      (6) Small hemostat
      (7) Probe

   b. Wrapped, sterile cotton applicators

   c. Wrapped, sterile dressings of various thicknesses and sizes
      (1) Thick, absorbent pads (ABD pads)
      (2) 4 × 4-inch and 2 × 2-inch gauze squares (flats)
      (3) Nonadherent dressings (Telfa)
      (4) Soft gauze dressings that have been fluffed out (fluffs)

   d. Various sizes of gauze roller bandage and Ace tensor bandage

   e. Various sizes and kinds of adhesive tape

2. Sterile gloves (used when the area to be dressed is large or difficult to manage)

3. Large paper bag to receive old dressings

4. Clean kidney basin for antiseptic pour-off overflow

5. Bandage scissors

6. Appropriate antiseptic, irrigating solution, or medication

7. Clean paper towels

Procedure:

1. Select a time when there is little bedmaking or mopping activity in the area. These

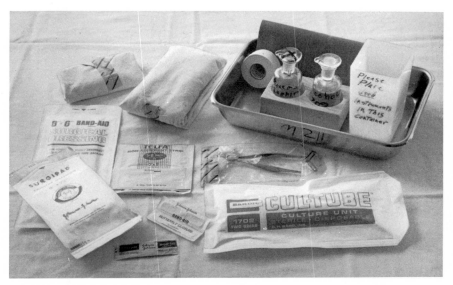

FIG. 31-2. Sample dressing tray. The wrapped packages at the back contain commonly needed instruments. (Courtesy Grossmont Hospital, La Mesa, Calif.)

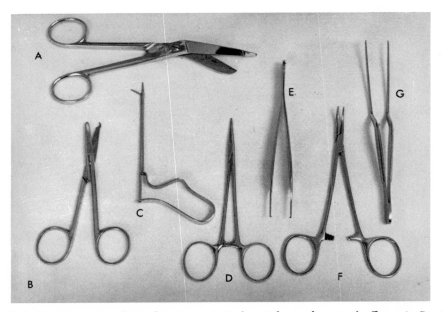

FIG. 31-3. Various commonly used instruments in hospitals or physicians' offices. **A,** Bandage scissors; **B,** suture-remover scissors; **C,** alligator forceps (for removing foreign bodies); **D,** mosquito forceps (small hemostat); **E,** tissue forceps; **F,** curved mosquito forceps (small hemostat); **G,** bayonet forceps.

activities increase the bacteria count in the air.

2. Identify and screen the patient and explain the purpose of the dressing change according to his level of understanding. At times positioning assistance may be needed.
3. Drape the patient appropriately.
4. Adjust the lamp, if needed; position and open discard bag and kidney basin, if needed.
5. Wash your hands.
6. Open only those supplies needed.
7. Place sterile handling forceps on the edge of a sterile wrapper—points on the sterile surface, handles over the edge.
8. Remove bandages or adhesive tape. (Always pull tape toward the incision or wound to prevent undue strain or pain.)
9. Lift off the top dressing, your hand protected by a clean, folded paper towel. Contact only the side of the dressing that was exposed to the exterior. Drop dressing and towel into open paper bag. (*Note:* Two handling forceps would be ideal for the procedure. However, they are not always provided. This technique is thought to be a safe compromise.)
10. Lift off any remaining inner dressing with the handling forceps. Be careful not to pull drains, if present. Dressings that stick to the skin may usually be moistened with a small amount of sterile saline solution to facilitate their removal.
11. Cleanse the area gently of any old drainage present with mild antiseptic or ordered solution and sterile gauze sponges mounted on handling forceps. Pour the solution onto the sponge over the discard kidney basin. Dry the area with a sterile compress.
12. Place a dressing, appropriate for size of the incision and amount of drainage present, using handling forceps.
13. Secure with adhesive tape, Elastoplast, or Montgomery tapes.
14. Discard used dressings, wash your hands, and tidy up the area.
15. Record the procedure and the condition of the wound or incision. Describe the type and amount of any drainage present and report any unusual odor. Note any skin irritation caused by adhesive.

GAVAGE FEEDING

Note: Vocational nurses do not usually pass feeding tubes. However, they are frequently asked to administer a feeding per indwelling tube.

Purposes: To avoid mouth and lip motion when it may endanger surgical repair (cleft lip or cleft palate procedures), nourish a child who is too weak to be fed orally in the normal fash- ion, and supplement oral feedings when nutritional buildup is imperative and sufficient intake by normal means is impossible.

Materials:
1. Sterile Asepto or piston-type syringe. (If the child is receiving sterilized formula, a sterile syringe will be secured for each feeding. If he is not receiving sterilized formula, the nurse may wash and store the syringe in a clean manner for use next time.)
2. Container of formula (infants who receive sterilized formula will have the tube feeding sterilized)
3. Basin of warm water to heat formula
4. Glass of water (bottle of sterile water for infants)
5. Towel or napkin
6. Perhaps bib and infant seat

Procedure:
1. Identify the patient and explain the procedure according to his needs and level of understanding.
2. Warm the formula and water if necessary so that it will be tepid at the time of the feeding. (Feeding cold formula can be very upsetting to the patient and may initiate vomiting.) Evaluate the consistency of the feeding: Is it too thick? Will it clog the tube? Volume must also be considered. Many times one cannot dilute a feeding and administer the entire amount to maintain the caloric count ordered. Such a feeding would overload the stomach.
3. Unless contraindicated, raise the backrest of the bed or put a baby in an infant seat. This position lets gravity aid the flow of the formula.
4. Protect the area next to the tube opening with a towel. Put a bib on an infant.
5. Test the position of the end of the tube by each of the following methods:
   a. Observe the length of the tube exposed.
   b. Place the open end of the tube under water and watch for a flow of bubbles on expiration. Some gas in the stomach may cause an occasional bubble, but it will not cause a flow of bubbles synchronized with expiration.
   c. Attach the Asepto syringe barrel to the gavage tube. Depress the rubber bulb and place it in the top of the barrel to aspirate stomach contents (Fig. 31-4). Observe the portion of the tube nearest the nose for returning gastric contents.
   d. Ask the patient to hum, if possible. If the tube is in the trachea, the patient cannot hum.

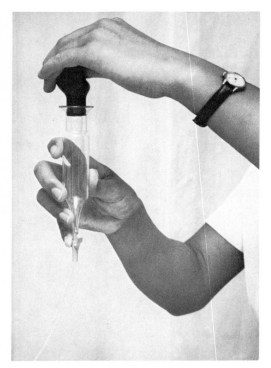

FIG. 31-4. Be sure to check the position of the feeding tube. Hold on to the tube-barrel connection with your finger to prevent separation.

e. Pour in approximately 15 ml. of water, stopping the flow before the barrel is empty to check the patency of the tube and observe the reaction of the patient. Watch for cyanosis and respiratory distress.

6. Continue with the administration of the formula. Allow the formula to flow by gravity. Exerting additional pressure may be dangerous. If the flow is sluggish, raise the barrel. If it is too fast, lower the barrel or pinch the tube. If the flow has stopped, change position of the patient slightly. If the flow still does not continue, *gentle* pressure with a syringe bulb or piston may be made to *start* the flow. If no response is forthcoming, the tube must be removed and another inserted. If the infant is crying, flow will be slower than when he is quiet.

7. Add more formula before the barrel is empty to avoid introducing additional air into the stomach. When the formula is finished, just before the last few drops leave the barrel add approximately 15 ml. of water to rinse the tube. (Failure to include this step will cause a clogged tube.)

8. Any infant must be bubbled after gavage just as he would be bubbled after routine oral feeding.
9. Record the amount and type of feeding and the tolerance of the patient.

GASTROSTOMY FEEDING

Purpose: To provide nourishment via a tube that has been surgically inserted through the abdominal wall into the stomach because of obstruction or surgical repair of the normal oroesophageal tract.

Materials:
1. Tray containing the following:
   a. Syringe barrel (sterile for small infants receiving sterilized formula)
   b. Container of formula (sterile for small infants)
   c. Container of water (sterile for small infants)
   d. Basin of warm water to heat formula if necessary
2. Towel or napkin

Procedure:
1. Identify patient and explain the procedure according to his needs and level of understanding.
2. Warm the formula and water so that it will be tepid at the time of the feeding. (Feeding cold formula can be very upsetting to the patient and initiate vomiting.) Evaluate the consistency of the feeding: Is it too thick? Will it clog the tube? Volume must also be considered. Many times you cannot dilute a feeding and administer the entire amount to maintain the caloric count ordered. Such a feeding would overload the stomach.
3. Keep the patient flat, if possible, during the gastrostomy feeding.
4. Attach the syringe barrel to the tube and fill with formula before unclamping the tube. (*Note:* There may be orders to aspirate the contents of the stomach into the barrel. The amount aspirated is noted, and it is allowed to return to the stomach. The feeding to be given is decreased accordingly to prevent overloading.)
5. Unclamp the tube and allow the fluid to flow slowly by gravity. Never use pressure of any kind to start the flow of formula into the gastrostomy tube. This may cause unwanted backflow into the esophagus.
6. Continue to add formula to the barrel before it completely empties to avoid introducing air into the stomach.
7. Finish the feeding by adding 15 to 30 ml. of water to rinse the tube. Clamp off the

tube before all the water leaves the barrel to avoid introducing air into the stomach. (*Note:* In some cases involving infants the physician may order that the tube not be clamped but be left opened with the barrel attached and elevated above the baby's body. The formula is allowed to return to the barrel as the child cries or changes position.)

8. Record the amount and type of feeding and the tolerance of the patient.

URETHRAL CATHETER IRRIGATION

Purposes: To prevent the clogging of the catheter by blood clots, salts, or cellular debris and instill medication into the bladder.

Materials:

1. Tray containing the following:
   a. Sterile syringe
   b. Sterile solution basin
   c. Sterile drainage basin
   d. Sterile 4 × 4-inch gauze squares, towel, or catheter cap
2. Ordered solution (e.g., physiological saline)
3. Basin of warm water to heat solution to tepid temperature.

Procedure:

1. Check the order and identify the patient.
2. Explain the procedure to the patient according to his needs and level of understanding.
3. Place the solution bottle in warm water.
4. Disconnect the catheter drainage tubing from the catheter proper. Let the catheter drain into the drainage basin. After allowing the contents of the drainage tubing to flow into the collecting bottle, place the sterile end in a sterile 4 × 4-inch gauze square, towel, or cap.
5. Pour the ordered solution into the basin and draw the ordered amount into the syringe.
6. Inject the ordered amount of solution slowly into the catheter. Momentarily pinch off the catheter and disconnect the syringe. Allow the flow to return by gravity.
7. Evaluate the amount and the character of the returned drainage.
8. Reconnect the catheter and drainage tubing.
9. If any difficulty is experienced with the irrigation, report it to the team leader or supervising nurse.
10. Record the procedure, the kind and amount of injected solution, and the character and amount of the return flow. Note the reaction of the patient.

IRRIGATION OF A NASOGASTRIC OR INTESTINAL TUBE

Purposes: To prevent the clogging and assure the patency of an indwelling nasogastric or intestinal tube. The tube may have been inserted for the following reasons:

1. To prevent vomiting
2. To relieve postoperative abdominal distention, discomfort, and pressure on surgical repairs

When the tube has been inserted for the reasons cited, it is attached to some type of suction or drainage device. Usually the suction ordered is intermittent, occasionally it may be continuous. High or low negative pressure may be prescribed. Sometimes only gravity drainage is ordered. Most children are placed on low intermittent suction. Irrigation is only carried out when the wishes of the physician concerning the individual case are known.

Materials: Unless the type of surgery would make it necessary to employ sterile technique, the materials used to irrigate a tube must be kept meticulously clean but need not be sterile. The type and amount of irrigating fluid to be used is ordered by the physician. Physiological saline is frequently requested. The amount to be used will depend on the size of the child and the type of surgery performed.

A setup would usually include the following:

1. Syringe (10 to 30 ml., depending on amount to be used)
2. Basin or solution reservoir
3. Clamp
4. Towel and emesis basin
5. Ordered solution

Procedure:

1. Identify the patient.
2. Explain to the child according to his level of understanding. For young children it is usually sufficient to say that you are putting a little "water" in the tube.
3. Draw up the amount and kind of solution ordered in the syringe.
4. Place a folded towel and emesis basin under the junction of the tube leading to the suction apparatus or gravity drainage.
5. Turn off any mechanical suction device.
6. Clamp the tubing leading to the suction or drainage bag and disconnect the two parts of the tubing, wrapping the end of the tubing leading to the suction machine in a towel or covering it with some type of cap.
7. Fit the syringe of irrigating fluid into the patient's tube and gently instill the ordered amount. Whether the nurse will be allowed to withdraw any of the irrigating solution

with the attached syringe will depend on the preferences of the physician.

8. Detach the syringe, and reconnect the tube either to the suction machine (removing the clamp and restarting the suction) or to the gravity drainage.

9. Remember, this patient is usually not allowed oral fluids except perhaps *small* amounts of ice chips. However, lubrication of the nares, renewal of the tape maintaining the tube's position, and oral hygiene are fairly frequent patient needs.

10. Record in the patient's output record the amount of irrigating fluid used. (*Note:* If a tube is not draining and resistance is encountered during an attempted ordered irrigation, the nurse should notify her supervisor immediately.)

32
Aiding respiration and oxygenation

The process of respiration brings oxygen into the body for circulation to the individual cells via the bloodstream and removes waste products, carbon dioxide, and water from the body. In some diseases the transfer of oxygen to the tissue cells is made very difficult by a breakdown in the anatomy or physiology concerned. To aid the handicapped processes, various procedures, apparatus, and medications have been developed to help clear the airway, enrich the oxygen content of inspired air, stimulate or maintain adequate respiratory effort, or achieve the proper circulation of blood.

Within the last few years a technical specialty, inhalation therapy, has developed that is devoted to the maintenance of optimal respiratory exchange and prevention of respiratory disease. In many hospitals an inhalation therapist will supervise gaseous therapy (intermittent positive pressure, special tents) and initiate resuscitation measures.

Hindrances to oxygenation of the blood

To understand the rationale of many of the treatments ordered the student should review the structure and function of the respiratory system. The passageways from the exterior of the body to the microscopic air sacs, or alveoli, which make up the functional tissue of the lungs, must remain open to assure proper oxygenation. Any obstruction, whether caused by the position of the tongue, aspiration of a foreign body, edema, a tumor, the presence of tenacious secre-

tions in the laryngotracheobronchial "tree," or spasm of the bronchioles, will lead to respiratory difficulty. Any condition such as pneumonia, emphysema, tuberculosis, or a malignancy that causes a depletion in the ability of the lung tissue to receive air and transfer oxygen and carbon dioxide may cause respiratory distress. Any interruption of the mechanisms of breathing involving the creation of an intermittent suction (negative pressure) in the thoracic cavity through contraction of the diaphragm and intercostal muscles because of nervous system stimulation caused by carbon dioxide buildup in the bloodstream will also affect respiration and therefore oxygenation. Of course, in the final analysis the circulatory system must also be adequate to deliver the oxygen to the final destination, the individual microscopic body cells.

The most accurate way of determining the extent of oxygenation present in a patient's blood is by chemical analysis of the oxygen and carbon dioxide level in a blood sample.

The airway
Securing and maintaining an airway

The first concern in aiding breathing always involves the airway. Occasionally it may be obstructed because of the position of the tongue. This may be true in the case of the unconscious patient; the tongue is not actually swallowed, but it may fall backward and obstruct the pharynx. An open airway may be obtained by placing the patient on his back with his head in "sniffing" position and his lower jaw held

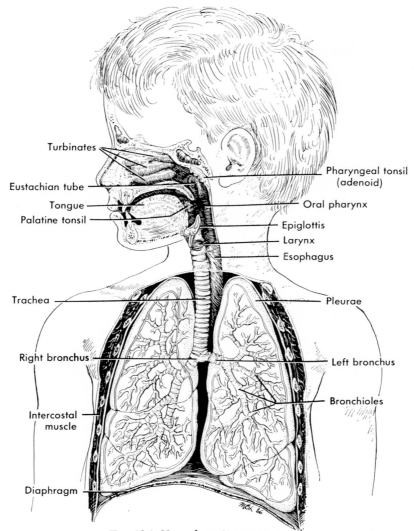

FIG. 32-1. Normal respiratory tract.

up. This returns the tongue to normal position. At times the insertion of a plastic oropharyngeal airway will be helpful.

If the airway is obstructed by a foreign body or secretions, the emergency relief usually attempted *first* involves gravity drainage. Occasionally the bronchi may need to be visualized with a special instrument called a bronchoscope for removal of the foreign body.

To prevent aspiration, a child in danger of vomiting or regurgitating should be maintained on his side or abdomen. If this is impossible because of other more impor-

tant considerations (type of surgery, administration of an anesthetic, etc.), the head should be lowered and turned to the side during episodes of nausea and vomiting.

Suction. Suction of the naso-oropharyngeal passages or even deeper suction may be necessary to clear the airway. Suction may be accomplished by using a bulb syringe, a simple manual suction catheter (DeLee trap), or a catheter setup attached to wall or portable suction. The following points should be remembered regarding the procedure when a catheter is used:

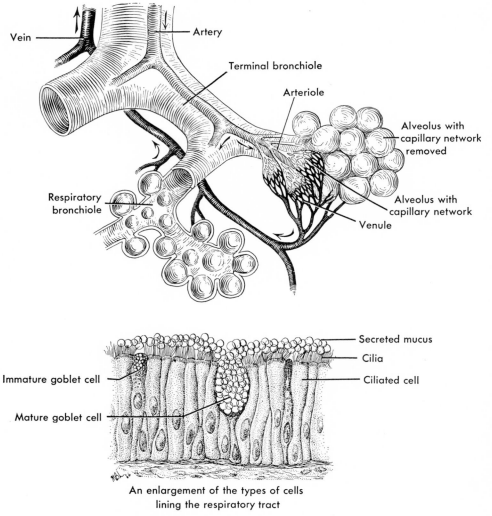

An enlargement of the types of cells
lining the respiratory tract

FIG. 32-2. Microscopic anatomy of the lower respiratory tract.

1. The suction apparatus should be personal for each patient and kept free from contamination. Some hospitals now employ a "use-once-only-and-throw-away" catheter technique.

2. The drainage bottle should contain about 1 inch of disinfectant solution at the outset to thin out the secretions, ease its cleaning, and reduce the number of bacteria in the bottle. It should be opaque or covered with a small pillowcase.

3. The catheters should be lubricated with water before use to assure greater ease of insertion.

4. During catheter insertion the suction should be temporarily discontinued by pinching the catheter or uncovering the Y-tube control to avoid depleting the patient's supply of oxygen or injuring the mucous membranes.

5. The lowest amount of suction necessary should be applied. Suction should not be prolonged; suction administered too frequently may aggravate congestion instead of relieve it.

6. The catheter and tubing should be immediately rinsed after use to prevent clogging and stored conveniently in an aseptic manner, unless the catheters are not reused.
7. The child usually will need to be restrained during the procedure.

Sometimes secretions are so thick that they are difficult to drain by gravity or suction, and various procedures and agents may be used to thin out the secretions. These may take the form of simple steam inhalations provided by a convenient vaporizer or unheated ultrasonic mist obtained from a specially constructed unit under a canopy or in a tent.

Steam tent. A steam tent, also called a "croup tent" because it is frequently used as therapy for croup, is sometimes used to provide steam inhalation. It may be employed for patients with bronchitis or sinusitis or in situations in which increased warm humidification will aid breathing.

Prefitted canopies, which fit over the top of a large crib, are available in many hospitals. Before the actual canopy is constructed it is advisable to stretch and secure a doubled bath blanket over the top of the crib to provide an additional layer of material for absorbency so that large drops of moisture do not collect on the inside of the roof of the tent and fall on the child. Great care must be taken in the home or hospital that the tent, however constructed, is stable and secure so that it will not fall and frighten or injure the child. There must also be protection against accidental burns. Not only must the patient himself be protected but also the treatment area must be carefully selected and observation provided so that members of the family in the home or other patients in the hospital will not be burned by the steam or vaporizer. (Indeed, some physicians prefer to always order cool mist for humidification because of the very real danger of accidental burns.) A board or large piece of heavy cardboard wrapped in a small blanket may be wedged between the crib rungs and secured with safety pins to serve as a

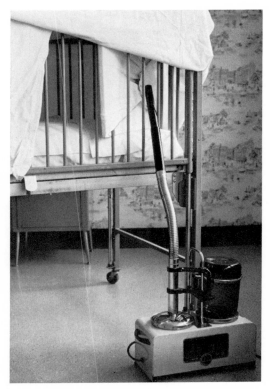

FIG. 32-3. One type of steam tent construction. Note how the guard board between the vaporizer and patient is secured to the crib. In practice the vaporizer would be in a corner away from the "traffic pattern." (Courtesy Children's Health Center, San Diego, Calif.)

barrier between the vaporizer and the child. If a space of only 1 inch is left between the top of the board and the tent roof, sufficient steam will reach the child because steam rises to the top of the tent. When setting up such a canopy and protective board, attention must be paid to the position of the electrical outlet and the side of the crib that would be most convenient to open. (See Fig. 32-3.)

Of course, if the child is too big for the crib available, the problem of providing a high concentration of warm, humid air may call for a different type of tent construction. In the hospital a canopy suspended from an overhead bar may be used. Some hospital services prefer to use a plastic canopy, such as provided by the Misto-

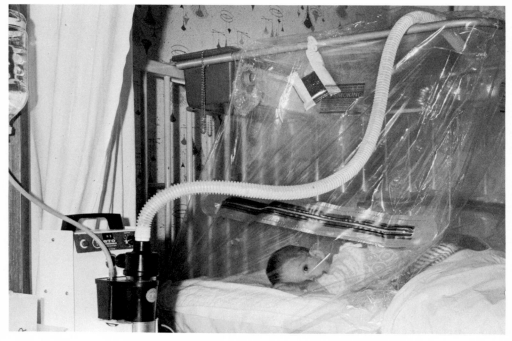

Fig. 32-4. Ultrasonic mist has gained favor because its small particle size penetrates the respiratory passages better than former misting techniques. The equipment is compact and relatively easy to handle. In real therapeutic situations the mist may be so dense that the child is obscured.

gen tent, for all patients and increase the interior temperature by omitting the ice.

Occasionally, a medication such as tincture of benzoin, oil of eucalyptus, or some other commercial preparation may be added to a cup or special reservoir in a vaporizer. Hospital personnel find that humidification equipment lasts much longer if distilled water is used to prevent the deposit of hard-water salts in the appliance.

Ultrasonic mist. Another form of aerosol therapy that has been found to be especially effective in liquefying thick respiratory secretions is that provided by the ultrasonic nebulizer (Fig. 32-4). This unit, although generally used with a tent, is not dependent on a gas source for mist formation, produces fine penetrating water particles, is quiet, and occupies little space. It employs sterile distilled water. It has been used with exceptional success by cystic fibrosis patients. However, the small infant in such a dense water-aerosol environment

must be observed carefully for overhydration, since relatively large amounts of water can be absorbed from the lung into the circulation. Infants may be weighed frequently to assess the amount of such absorption, and fluid intake modifications may be necessary in certain cases. Patients should be removed from the mist tent at intervals.

Medications. Medications are frequently ordered to aid in providing an airway.

Nose drops. Nose drops, such as phenylephrine hydrochloride (Neo-Synephrine), may be ordered to shrink mucous membranes and ease nasal congestion.

Expectorants. Oral expectorants, which increase the bronchial secretions and may help thin mucus, are occasionally ordered. Common medications of this type are potassium iodide and ammonium chloride.

Aerosols. Acetylcysteine (Mucomyst) reduces the thickness and tenacity of mucus. If a vial of acetylcysteine is opened and not completely used, it should be stored in the refrigerator and used within 48 hours. In tents a 20% volume solution is usually ordered.

Isoproterenol hydrochloride (Isuprel), administered in *drops* or aerosol form, helps dilate or relax the bronchioles to relieve spasms, shrinks swollen mucous membranes, and reduces the secretion of thick mucus. When isoproterenol hydrochloride is used, the heart rate must be carefully watched, since this medication may cause an abnormally rapid pulse (tachycardia).

• • •

If the airway is impaired because of spasm of the bronchi or bronchioles, as is often the case in asthmatic attacks, the addition of other medications to relax the bronchioles may be needed to relieve wheezing and respiratory distress. Chief among such medications used is the very powerful epinephrine (Adrenalin).

Some anatomical alterations of the respiratory system are difficult to treat and may be of long duration. However, some of the swelling and/or distortion of lung tissue and bronchioles may respond to the use of antibacterial drugs or medications used for specific chest diseases such as tuberculosis. Abnormal dilatation of the air sacs, or emphysema, may be particularly persistent and troublesome in the asthmatic child. Air is typically breathed in and depleted of its oxygen content. The air sacs have lost their normal elasticity and cannot force the "old air" out of the lungs properly. Another full breath of well-oxygenated air cannot be taken, since the "old air" still occupies some space in the air sacs. Real distress may develop, especially on expiration. Medication such as epinephrine and a calm, reassuring manner on the part of the nurse help, but structural changes may be enduring.

Postural drainage and percussion techniques. Some respiratory diseases (e.g., cystic fibrosis, emphysema) produce such exaggerated amounts of tenacious secretions deep in the lungs that it may be difficult for the patient to expel them even with the aid of medications, humidification, and suction techniques. These secretions interfere with proper pulmonary ventilation and set the stage for frequent respiratory infections that further endanger the patient. Another way of promoting drainage of a clogged or potentially obstructed respiratory tree is through the use of breathing exercises and selective postural drainage consisting of positioning, cupping, and vibration, followed by purposeful coughing.

When physical therapists are available, they usually perform these maneuvers and instruct the family if continued treatment is necessary at home. In the event that physical therapists are not available, nurses may be asked to learn the techniques. Anyone responsible for performing them should be specially instructed and initially supervised in their use. The following is a brief explanation, which is not intended to take the place of such instruction.

The treatment is most effective when preceded by aerosol therapy and is enhanced by diaphragmatic breathing. It may be prescribed as a prophylactic as well as a therapeutic measure.

Various postures assumed by the patient help drain different parts of the lungs. Therefore the position or positions in which the patient is placed depend on the site of his congestion and the general aims of his therapeutic program. In general, the placement of the patient enlists the forces of gravity and the sweeping action of the respiratory cilia in clearing the lungs. Any constrictive clothing should be removed. The patient's knees and/or hips should be flexed in the various positions necessary, so that relaxation will be promoted, and there will be less strain on the abdominal muscles when coughing is encouraged. When the patient's head must be lowered, usually all that is needed for an infant or young child is a well-positioned, firm pillow (Fig. 32-5). An older child may have to assume a modified jackknife position, lying over an elevated knee-gatch. A teen-ager may be able to hold his head and chest down crosswise over the side of the bed, while helping

431

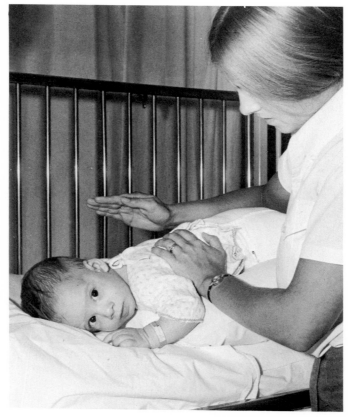

FIG. 32-5. The physical therapist is performing the early morning, before breakfast ritual on a small patient with congenital structural weakness of the bronchi. Scheduled cupping and vibrating have proved particularly helpful. (Courtesy Children's Health Center, San Diego, Calif.)

to support himself by grasping a low stool. However, he should not be left alone in this predicament! Needless to say, this therapy should be done before meals or at least an hour after eating. It is never initiated if the patient is hemorrhaging or in pain. When the desired positions are secured, the percussion is begun.

Two basic maneuvers are used: (1) cupping, also known as clapping or tapping, and (2) vibrating. The first is performed with the palm of the hand raised, the fingers and thumb forming the sides of a firm cup. When the cupped hands are gently but abruptly applied to the patient's chest wall, the wrist is alternately flexed and extended. A characteristic hollow sound is produced. The technique is continued

about 30 seconds over the affected area while the patient both inhales and exhales. It is then followed by the vibrating motion done only while the patient is exhaling slowly. This second maneuver is accomplished by tensing the hands, arms, and shoulders and producing gentle and fine vibratory movements on the chest wall. It is continued only during expiration. The two maneuvers are then repeated several times, depending on the tolerance of the patient.

Percussion techniques should not be used over the spine, kidney area, abdomen, sternum, or developed breast tissue. Coughing should be encouraged as needed.

Laryngoscope. If a patent airway cannot be maintained through positioning,

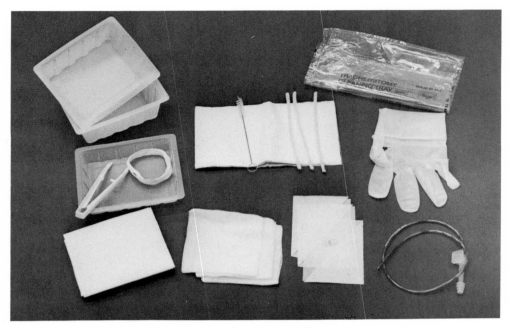

FIG. 32-6. These sterile materials are found in a disposable tracheostomy cleaning tray now available. Note the thumb control on the suction catheter. (Courtesy Grossmont Hospital, La Mesa, Calif.)

simple suction, insertion of an oropharyngeal airway, humidification, percussion, or administration of appropriate mucus-thinning or bronchodilatory medications, the larynx may be visualized with a laryngoscope and an endotracheal tube inserted for suction and ventilation. The laryngoscope blades and endotracheal tubes must be of an appropriate size, or they are useless.

Tracheostomy. If continued airway obstruction is observed or contemplated, a surgical opening of the trachea (tracheostomy) may be created to provide an artificial airway and allow easier access to the trachea for suction. Care of a patient with a tracheostomy is a very serious responsibility.

The adult or child who has had a tracheostomy usually cannot speak or make any vocal noise unless the opening of the tracheostomy tube, which retracts the surgical incision, is temporarily covered. For any person who has previously been able to comunicate well orally and for the young child who lets his wants be known by crying, failure of oral communication, accompanied by respiratory problems, is extremely frightening.

Children with tracheostomies should be placed in areas where they will be under constant observation. When appropriate, signal cords or handbells should always be available. For those able to write, a magic slate or paper and pencil should be near at hand. The method of temporarily closing off the tracheostomy opening with the fingers to speak should be taught to the older child during his convalescence. Temporarily obstructing the tube in this way will also aid defecation. A calm, efficient nurse does wonders in alleviating the anxiety of tracheostomy patients.

A double-walled tube is generally used in the tracheal opening. A second tube, or inner cannula, fits directly inside the outer tube, providing a means of quickly clearing the larger, outer tube if the inner tube becomes blocked. Periodically, the interval depending on the needs of the patient, the inner cannula is suctioned or removed and

433

cleaned. When the inner cannula has been removed, the outer cannula is also suctioned. The nurse may suction as deeply as necessary to remove secretions. Occasionally, orders are left that small amounts (3 to 5 drops) of sterile physiological saline solution be dropped into the tracheostomy tube to help thin out any secretions before suctioning. If oxygen is being administered, a small humidification unit may be fitted directly over the tube, or a vaporizer may be placed in the patient's room to instill the necessary moisture.

To provide the equipment necessary for the care of a patient with a tracheostomy, a special tray is available at the bedside. Materials necessary for cleaning the inner cannula and maintaining the suction equipment should be on the tray (Fig. 32-6). When caring for a new tracheostomy, use a new sterile catheter and glove each time the patient is suctioned. Complete equipment should include the following items:

1. Sterile gloves
2. Sterile basin of detergent or hydrogen peroxide for soaking the tube and removing mucus and crusts
3. Sterile pipe cleaners to thread through the tube and ensure patency
4. Sterile basin of sterile water for rinsing the tube
5. Antiseptic solution for storage of the catheter in use (if catheter is reused)

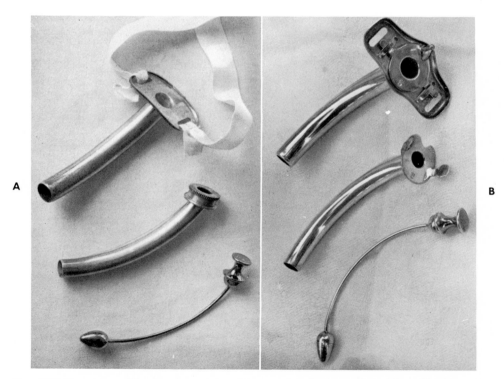

FIG. 32-7. Four types of tracheostomy tubes (shown when in descending order, the outer tube, inner tube, and obturator). **A,** The Hollinger, the head or knob on the inner tube rotates to fit under the small lip at the back of the outer tube. **B,** The Jackson, the small metal flap on the back of the outer tube rotates to hold the inner tube securely. **C,** The plastic Portex, with a pop-in-and-out inner cannula that fits under two opposing flanges. This set comes with two inner cannulae. **D,** A single cannula, double-cuffed tracheostomy tube. The smaller attached tubes are alternately used to inflate two "balloons" around the lower end of the larger tube. This device is used when ventilation is assisted by mechanical means.

6. Extra tracheostomy tube of the same size as the one being used
7. Tracheal dilator or curved hemostat for emergency use to hold a temporary tracheostomy open in the event that the outer tube is accidentally expelled
8. Supply of *lint-free* tissues for wiping away expelled mucus
9. Bottle of physiological saline solution
10. Supply of sterile, lint-free precut gauze tracheostomy dressings
11. Medicine dropper, if instillations are ordered
12. Paper bag taped conveniently to the supporting table to receive waste

Tracheostomy tubes may be made of silver, plastic, or rubber. They are especially manufactured to be used together and cannot be interchanged. There are actually three parts to most tracheostomy tubes: the inner cannula, the outer cannula, and the obturator, a small, curved rod ending in an olive-shaped tip. The obturator is placed within the outer cannula at the time of insertion to help keep the tube clear, protect the mucous lining from injury, and help direct the cannula placement. As soon as placement is secured, the obturator is removed. It is then stored in an obvious spot (on the tracheostomy tray or in a clear bag taped to the head of the bed) for use during reinsertion of the outer cannula in case of

C

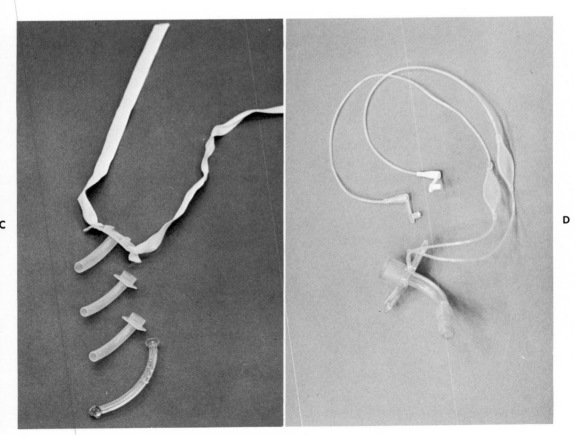

D

FIG. 32-7, cont'd. For legend see opposite page.

an emergency. The inner cannula is inserted and locked into place after the withdrawal of the obturator. There are three main types of locks available—a metal flap that turns down over the inner cannula, a knob-turn lock, and an interlocking lateral plastic flange. Tracheostomy tubes are now available with a single cannula—no inner tube. They are manufactured with or without cuffs. A cuffed tracheostomy tube is used principally with ventilators. The inflatable cuff (or cuffs) around the inserted tube blocks the escape of air around the tube and increases the efficiency of the machine. The cuff must be periodically deflated to prevent pressure injury to the mucous membrane. Fig. 32-7 shows a double-cuffed tracheostomy tube. First one cuff and then the other are inflated and deflated, easing pressure on the tracheal lining.

All the equipment used in the maintenance of a new tracheostomy should be handled in a sterile manner. However, when the tracheostomy is "old," clean technique is usually followed. All equipment is presterilized before being used on a patient, and the suction catheters, tray, bowls, and solutions are frequently renewed or changed. The suction catheter in use is often stored in an antiseptic solution to reduce the possibility of contamination. Therefore tracheostomy care of a long-term convalescent patient becomes, in the final analysis, a clean procedure; to insist on throw-away catheter technique would appear to be financially and practically unfeasible. Nevertheless, the nurse must be careful in her technique and wash her hands conscientiously.

A Y-tube connection is recommended on the suction catheter to facilitate its use. Suction is obtained by covering the open end of the Y-tube with the thumb. It is more gentle to the mucous membranes than a catheter, which has been pinched to stop suction during insertion. Insertion of the catheter is made with no suction applied. Suction is applied periodically as the tube is rotated on withdrawal. It has been suggested that the nurse hold her breath during suctioning so that she will not suction for too long an interval and inadvertently interfere with respiration. (The catheter may partially block the passage of air or remove necessary air.) If bronchial suction is desired, the patient's head should be turned first to one side and then the other during the suctioning process, if possible. This assists the catheter to enter both bronchi instead of following the easiest pathway to the less angled entrance of the right bronchus. Too frequent aspiration should be avoided. Very young children usually resist suctioning. Often better results are obtained if they are positioned on their backs with the shoulders raised on a folded bath blanket and the head dropped back. Assistance or a modified mummy restraint may be needed.

Enriched oxygen environments
Oxygen concentration

Various methods and devices are used to make inspired air richer in oxygen. The oxygen content of air in a well-ventilated room is about 21%. Therefore any device used to elevate the oxygen content must be capable of administering oxygen of a higher percentage. However, in the care of premature or very small infants, oxygen levels should routinely be kept below 40% to guard against retrolental fibroplasia, which causes blindness. When oxygen therapy is used, frequent oxygen concentration checks should be made to determine whether the desired concentration is actually being attained. When concentrations are determined, the air at the same level as the patient's nose should be analyzed, since oxygen is heavier than air and will pool at the bottom of any container. (See Fig. 32-8.)

Safety factors

When oxygen is being used, the safety factors involved must be clearly understood to avoid fire. Oxygen readily supports combustion, and all sources of possible ignition of flammable materials should be removed

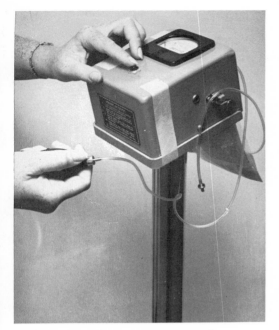

FIG. 32-8. This nurse is measuring the amount of oxygen in an open room to test the analyzer. What percentage reading should she get? (Courtesy Children's Health Center, San Diego, Calif.)

from the environment. Also, safe storage and maintenance of oxygen cylinders, if used, must be carried out to avoid fire and explosion hazards.

Rules for oxygen administration. The following rules should be observed during oxygen adminstration:

1. No open flames, cigarettes, cigars, matches, cigarette lighters, or candles should be allowed in a room in which oxygen is being used. Signs that read "Oxygen In Use—No Smoking" should be clearly posted.

2. No device that is capable of producing a spark should be operated in the oxygen-enriched environment. Any electrical equipment used must be especially grounded to be safe. Therefore most electrical equipment is prohibited; no standard television sets, radios, vaporizers, heat lamps, or electrical call bells should be used.

3. No oil or alcohol rubs should be

given in oxygen tents or other closed units.

4. No wool blankets should be used on the bed of a patient receiving oxygen.

5. At no time should an oxygen outlet, tank, regulator, or administering apparatus be oiled, greased, or handled with greasy hands or gloves.

6. All enclosed oxygen units (e.g., incubators, tent) should be "flushed" with oxygen before the patient is enclosed within them.

7. Because of the potential danger of excess carbon dioxide accumulation, all tents or enclosures should provide some method of ventilation or chemical control that will prevent this problem.

*Rules for use of oxygen tanks.** The following rules are related to the use of oxygen tanks or any cylinder containing gas under pressure:

1. All cylinders contain gas under pressure unless truly empty. If a cylinder falls and the valves are damaged, oxygen may escape with tremendous force. All cylinders must be stabilized with proper supports to guard against falling (for example, strapped to the bed or positioned in an oxygen tank carrier or a heavy metal baseplate).

2. An oxygen regulator must always be used when administering oxygen from a cylinder to reduce the pressure of the oxygen to safe levels before it reaches the patient. The regulator includes a dial, which measures the amount of oxygen remaining in the cylinder, and a flowmeter, which measures, in liters per minute, the amount of oxygen being administered. The particular type of regulator employed must be thoroughly understood before it is put into use. There are several types, and the details of their op-

---

*Many hospitals now have piped-in wall oxygen, but the nurse should also be acquainted with the use of oxygen stored in cylinders.

FIG. 32-9. Starting and stopping oxygen therapy when tank oxygen must be used. *Note:* Be sure the tank cylinder valve and the flowmeter valve on the regulator are at *off* positions. Attach the regulator to the tank with a wrench. **A,** Open the cylinder valve slowly, standing out of the way. **B,** Open the flowmeter to the approved amount. **C,** When discontinuing cylinder oxygen for more than half an hour, first turn off the cylinder valve; when the flowmeter registers 0, close the flowmeter valve. **D,** Detach the regulator if a change of tank is desired. (From Oxygen therapy handbook, ed. 5, New York, 1962, Linde Co., Division of Union Carbide Corp.)

eration differ. Fig. 32-9 shows only one type of regulator. However, the following principles hold true for all types, although the way in which they are fulfilled will depend on the individual apparatus.

a. All cylinders should be momentarily opened by loosening the cylinder valve (out of earshot of the patient) before the regulator is attached. This is called "cracking the cylinder," which produces a sharp, noisy blast. It is done to dislodge any particles of dust from the cylinder valve and prevent injury to the equipment and leakage. The nurse should stand to the side of the cylinder when it is "cracked," out of the way of the brief stream.

b. Regulators should be attached with a hand wrench to assure a tight connection.

c. Before the oxygen flow is started:
   (1) The flowmeter must be closed.
   (2) The operator must step to the side of the regulator-tank connection, out of the way in case the regulator should be dislodged when the flow is begun as the result of some defect.

d. The cylinder valve is opened slowly. When the cylinder valve is opened and the needle registering the contents of the tank comes to rest, the flowmeter may be adjusted to the approved amount.

3. When discontinuing cylinder oxygen for periods of half an hour or less, simply close the flowmeter. When longer periods without therapy are desired or when one wishes to replace the tank or regulator, proceed in the following manner:

   a. Close the cylinder valve. When the pressure registered on the dial is 0, continue to wait until all the oxygen is exhausted in the flowmeter and the flowmeter indicator also rests at 0. Then close the flowmeter, and detach the regulator if a cylinder change is desired.

Methods of oxygen enrichment

Oxygen tent. A large oxygen tent may be ordered for an older child. Such a tent is usually a plastic canopy suspended from an overhead rod and attached to a cabinet containing a machine, which, when properly adjusted, regulates the tent's ventilation and temperature and may also provide facilities for increased humidity along with a proper entrance for the appropriate oxygen flow (Fig. 32-10). An oxygen tent may be set up in the following manner:

1. If time and the patient's condition permit, place a bath blanket between the bed mattress and the bedspring to prevent snagging the plastic canopy, which can be easily torn. A plastic or rubberized sheet under the sheet covering the mattress will cut down on oxygen loss if the mattress is permeable.

2. The tent canopy and control cabinet are brought to the bedside. The overhead bar extension, designed to support the tent during use, is extended, and the tent folds are expanded slightly along the bar.

3. The electrical cord leading to the

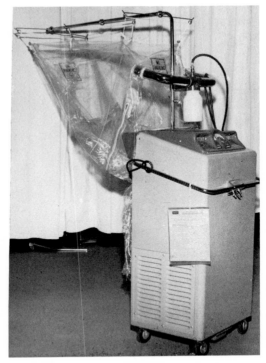

Fig. 32-10. One type of oxygen tent with a temperature control and ventilating humidification units. (Courtesy Children's Health Center, San Diego, Calif.)

control cabinet is plugged in, and the motor is turned on.

4. The air circulation or ventilation control on the cabinet, if available, is set halfway between low and high.

5. The temperature control on the cabinet is usually placed at 70° F. However, even in extremely hot weather the temperature setting should not be more than 10° to 15° F. below the room temperature to prevent shocking the patient when the canopy is lifted and decreasing the working efficiency of the tent.

6. If ventilation deflectors are present in the tent, they should be arranged so that the cool air entering the tent does not blow directly on the patient.

7. The oxygen inlet tube is connected to the wall flowmeter or oxygen cyl-

439

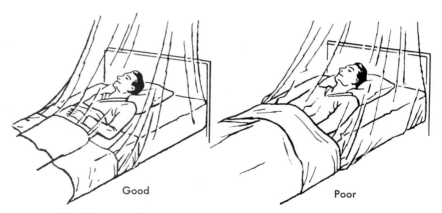

FIG. 32-11. Good and poor methods of draping the tent canopy to assure proper oxygen concentrations with minimum waste. (From Oxygen therapy handbook, ed. 5, New York, 1962, Linde Co., Division of Union Carbide Corp.)

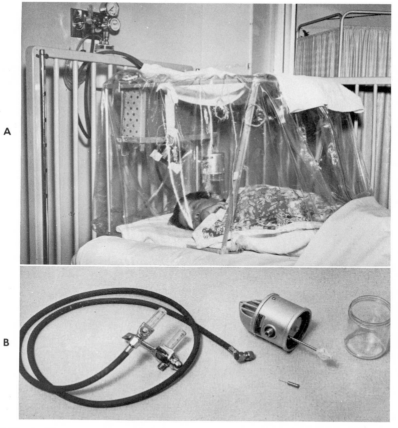

FIG. 32-12. **A,** Tony, a congenital heart patient, is in a Mistogen tent. The side rail was lowered for the photograph only. **B,** Parts of the humidifier and hose attachment. From left to right: double flowmeter (used if two tents must operate from one wall oxygen outlet), oxygen hose, needle valve, humidifier head with nylon filter attached, and fluid reservoir. (Courtesy Children's Health Center, San Diego, Calif.)

inder regulator and the flow started at 15 liters per minute. This rate is maintained for 30 minutes, and then an analysis of the oxygen concentration should be made. If the ordered concentration is attained, the flow is usually reduced to 10 to 12 liters per minute—the minimum flow required to wash out and dilute exhaled carbon dioxide. Instead of increasing the oxygen flow to 15 liters per minute for 30 minutes, many times the same concentration can be achieved by holding a flush valve open for at least 2 minutes after the tent has been placed around the patient. The patient should be warned that such a valve opening causes a rushing noise as the tent floods with oxygen.

8. The canopy should be gently placed over the patient in such a way that its sides (skirts) do not touch his face.

9. Many tents of this type seem drafty to the patients. How much protection from cold is necessary depends on the patient's own body temperature. Little girls may wear scarfs and bed jackets, if desired. Boys like hoods and cotton jackets.

10. The tent canopy should be molded around the child's body to prevent unnecessary oxygen loss (Fig. 32-11). A folded sheet may be placed at the end of the tent, molded around the child's body, and tucked under the mattress with the tent. If the tent is not tucked in properly, much leakage will occur.

11. When lowering or raising the head of the bed, care should be taken so that the tent canopy is not caught in the mechanism or put under undue tension. Many times the patient in an oxygen tent will feel better with the head of the bed moderately raised, if orders permit.

12. The patient's nursing care should be planned so that the tent is opened as little as possible and many of his needs met during one interval. The

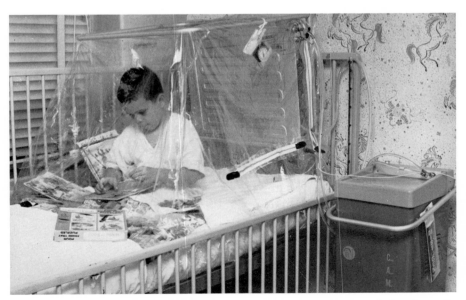

Fig. 32-13. The C.A.M. tent, a newer version of the Mistogen tent, is cooled and ventilated electrically. The working apparatus is not near the patient, and more room is available for activity. This boy has asthma; the side rail was lowered for photograph only. (Courtesy Children's Health Center, San Diego, Calif.)

motor blower may be shut off before opening the tent to reduce oxygen waste. Be sure to restart the motor after the nursing care has been completed.

13. High humidity concentrations may be achieved with the addition of jet humidifiers on many of the units. Sterile distilled water alone or additional ordered medications may be used.

High-humidity oxygen units. A tent that provides both high humidification and oxygen and rests on top of the bed is often used for younger children. Various models are available. The one shown in Fig. 32-12 is the Mistogen tent. Fig. 32-13 is a photograph of the Child-Adult Mistogen tent,

a newer model that is electrically refrigerated. Fig. 32-14 shows another manufacturer's tent cooled by ice and water placed in an outside reservoir not available to busy fingers. The tent hangs from a bar.

Most of these tents do not include an electric ventilator to circulate the air as do the larger oxygen tents and have a real tendency to overheat. To prevent overheating the patient, ice is added to the environment, with or without water, depending on the individual style of the oxygen tent. The Mistogen tent makes use of a perforated metal chest (suspended from the tent frame), which is filled with ice cubes. Tubing constantly drains off the water into a drainage collection bottle hanging from the bed, as the ice melts. The Hudson tent

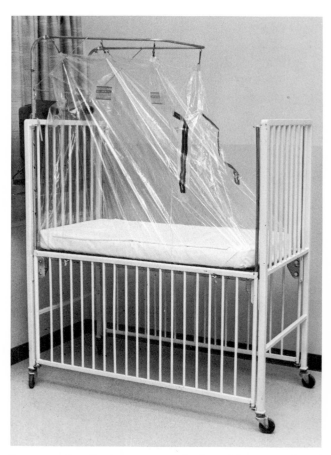

FIG. 32-14. Another type of pediatric mist tent. The humidification and cooling units are located outside the tent. (Courtesy Grossmont Hospital, La Mesa, Calif.)

uses an ice reservoir in which both ice and water are placed. The metal tubing, which carries the mist from the humidifier, runs through this melting ice to cool the mist. The chamber is emptied periodically by lifting a plug in the reservoir and allowing drainage to flow down a tube to a collecting bottle. Routinely, ice or ice and water are added to maintain a tent temperature in the range of 68° to 72° F. The temperature of the tent must be frequently checked because it may quickly rise. However, the factor that actually determines whether more ice will be added to help cool the tent is the body temperature of the patient. If, for instance, the child has a subnormal temperature, a minimal amount of ice may be used. If the child has an abnormally elevated temperature, a cooler tent temperature will usually be sought and more ice added.

The humidifier used in such tents also differs with the manufacturer. Fig. 32-12, B, shows the different parts of the Mistogen humidifier. If this particular humidifier does not produce mist, the following factors should be checked:

1. Is the filter dirty?
2. Is the needle valve clogged?
3. Is the oxygen flow sufficient?
4. Is the fluid level sufficient?
5. Has lint collected inside the metal humidifier head?
6. Is the oxygen hose connection correct?

Sterile water is now being used in most hospitals to try to reduce bacterial growth.

The oxygen liter flow necessary for such tents depends primarily on the size of the tent and the oxygen concentration desired. Flow rates of 4 to 10 liters per minute may be ordered. If the tent has an open top like the Mistogen model, a small blanket may be secured over most of the opening to help increase the humidity and oxygen concentration.

Patients placed in the cool, high-humidity environments produced by such tents must be checked *frequently* to see if their hair and clothing are damp. If the child does not have an excessively elevated temperature, he should have an undershirt under his light cotton gown. Infants seem to do best when dressed in long-sleeved, foot-in sleepers.

Nasal cannula. Oxygen may also be administered by nasal catheter or nasal cannula. However, the catheter is rarely used because it is unnecessarily irritating and confining for children. The cannulae used are usually short, paired, open tubes made of plastic or metal that are attached to a larger tube leading to the oxygen supply. These tubes are placed just inside the nostrils. A nasal cannula should be used when only low concentrations of oxygen, less than 35%, are desired. Oxygen administered by cannula should be passed through a humidifier to prevent uncomfortable drying of the mucous membranes (Fig. 35-7, A). The cannula should not obstruct the nostrils, and the patient should not breathe through his mouth.

Oxygen mask. Oxygen by mask is usually administered through a tube leading from the oxygen supply to a light plastic face mask. Some of the units available are disposable. Masks are capable of administering high-oxygen concentrations quickly and are ideal for emergency use. A rather wide variety of oxygen masks is available; some masks allow rebreathing of the first one third of the air expelled with each expiration (the fraction of an expiration richest in oxygen content) along with oxygen from the tank or wall supply. A well-known partial rebreathing face mask is the BLB, named for the initials of its inventors, Boothby, Lovelace, and Bulbulian. A partial rebreathing mask must fit tightly to the face, but a simple face mask that does not provide for rebreathing and is used for emergency or short-term use should not be applied tightly unless an escape valve or opening for carbon dioxide release is present. Nurses should be well acquainted with the particular oxygen equipment used in their setting and should study the manufacturer's instructions.

Incubators with increased oxygen. Incubators are often used in the treatment of newborn infants and small infants. Basically, they are glass or plastic boxes that provide warmth, oxygen, humidity, and easy observation of the infant. They are sometimes used only to provide additional heat, controlled electrically by presetting the temperature control and watching the thermometer inside. In some cases the temperature of the incubator is regulated by the body heat of the baby as determined by a temperature probe taped to the baby's trunk. The interior temperature of the incubator desired is usually about 80° to 85° F., but higher levels are sometimes ordered, depending on the infant's temperature response. Often, oxygen is added to the environment to ease respiration and relieve cyanosis.

Incubators are available in two basic styles—those that have lift-up lids at the top, which open for nursing care, and those that also provide special entries through the sides for nursing care, such as the Isolette shown in Fig. 32-15. The roof of the Isolette rocks back to provide space for special procedures, but if oxygen is being used, as much infant care as possible should be accomplished through the side sleeved portholes without lifting the lid and disturbing oxygen concentrations. The incubator is made up with a pillowcase folded over the mattress; diapers are placed under the infant's head and buttocks to catch drainage. Many times, to aid observations, the infant wears no clothes or only a diaper. The mattress platform may be slanted to aid oral drainage or help prevent regurgitation.

The desired humidity is usually controlled by a dial setting and sterile, distilled water placed in a reservoir under the incubator deck. The sterile water is often rendered less hospitable to bacterial growth by the addition of antiseptics. The amount of relative humidity desired by different physicians may be quite variable. High humidity supplied by jet humidifiers may be ordered with appropriate aerosol medications.

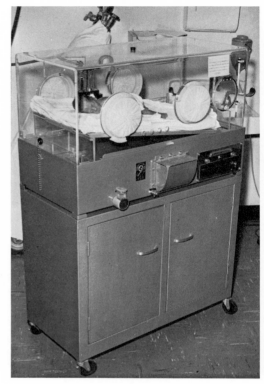

Fig. 32-15. An Isolette. No added oxygen was being given this premature infant when the photograph was taken, although low concentrations of less than 40% were ordered in case of cyanosis. The porthole sleeves are closed to provide additional warmth. Note the air vents at the lower front of the plastic enclosure. (Courtesy Grossmont Hospital, La Mesa, Calif.)

A small infant may be weighed while in an Isolette by suspending him in a muslin hammock attached to a hook, which protrudes through a hole in the Isolette roof, secured to a small scale.

Some patients who use an incubator for a temporary home are cared for using so-called "newborn technique." All linens have been sterilized and the nurse wears a special gown.

Stimulation and maintenance of respiratory effort

If respiratory effort is absent or precarious, various methods may be employed to stimulate or maintain respiration. They all presuppose an *adequate airway*.

Fig. 32-16. Positioning for mouth-to-mouth resuscitation.

In the nursery if a newborn is not breathing well because of the lingering effects of maternal sedative and analgesic drugs, the infant is often stimulated to more effective respirations by the nurse rubbing his back or perhaps snapping the soles of his feet.

Mouth-to-mouth resuscitation

However, if respiration has actually ceased, mouth-to-mouth resuscitation is a very practical prompt source of aid, since it requires no additional equipment and can be instituted while other methods are being prepared for use. The following is a description of mouth-to-mouth resuscitation:

1. The airway is cleared of any foreign material.
2. The child is positioned on his back with the head in "sniffing" position and the jaw elevated to jut out, clearing the airway of the tongue (Fig. 32-16).
3. The operator places her mouth tightly over the child's mouth and obstructs the child's nose with her cheek. (In the case of infants, both the mouth and nose may be covered by the operator's mouth.)

4. One hand is placed on the child's abdomen to check for distention.
5. Controlled, small puffs of air from the operator's cheeks are blown into the mouth of the infant or young child so that the chest is seen to rise at the rate of 20 times per minute or more.
6. Resuscitation of some kind is continued until the child responds spontaneously or is pronounced dead.
7. *Note:* If the heartbeat cannot be heard, external heart massage may be attempted. The patient should be placed on a firm surface—a table, counter, or the floor, if necessary. Some hospitals have cardiac resuscitation boards, which can be slipped under the thorax of the patient. Respiratory ventilation should precede external cardiac massage. In the case of an infant, massage is accomplished by depressing the midsternum firmly with two fingers at the rate of three depressions to one inhalation. In the case of an older child the heel of one hand is abruptly pushed against the lower sternum by an overlying hand at the rate of about five depressions to one inhalation. Such emergency resuscitation usually requires two oper-

445

ators. External heart massage is not without danger. However, the danger of injury (broken ribs, traumatized liver) is probably less than the danger of circulatory collapse. It is usually not attempted in cases in which such dramatic efforts would only delay a death that will take place minutes or hours after the treatment is terminated (e.g., a child dying of a malignancy or advanced leukemia).

A nurse should make use of every opportunity to secure practice and instruction regarding resuscitation measures during nonemergency situations. She should know where emergency resuscitation and oxygenation equipment is stored in the area in which she works. This would include knowledge of the location of the following items:

1. Resuscitation apparatus
2. Suction setup
3. Oxygen mask and cylinder
4. Emergency stimulant tray

Ambu resuscitator

A common type of resuscitation apparatus available is the Ambu resuscitator (Fig.

32-17). Use of this resuscitator is much less fatiguing for the operator than mouth-to-mouth resuscitation. The operator may stand or sit behind the supine patient's head with the top of the patient's head stabilized against her body. One hand of the operator holds the mask firmly against the patient's mouth and nose, while tilting the head back and maintaining the forward position of the jaw to clear the airway. With her other hand the operator periodically compresses the air bag in a rhythm of *1, 2, 3, 4, 1, 2, 3, 4,* taking her hand completely off the bag when not on the count of *1.* Too rapid, excited compression of the bag will cause greater respiratory distress. The operator should be sure to allow the patient time to exhale adequately. When the patient makes an effort to breathe spontaneously, the treatment may be discontinued while the patient's respiratory attempts are evaluated.

Positive pressure apparatus

Several positive pressure appliances are available that may, when appropriately "set," sustain respiration artificially for prolonged periods while administering oxy-

FIG. 32-17. The Ambu resuscitator. Various sized masks and plastic airways. (Courtesy Children's Health Center, San Diego, Calif.)

gen at predetermined percentages. These are intermittent positive pressure machines, which usually force air into the lungs through endotracheal or tracheostomy tubes. They may be regulated to automatically cycle at a certain rate and depth of respiration. These positive pressure ventilators allow an ease of nursing care not possible with the old tank respirators or iron lungs used formerly.

Intermittent positive pressure breathing devices are also used periodically on patients to prevent or reduce respiratory complications by expanding the lungs, administering aerosol medication, and helping to thin respiratory secretions. They are especially helpful in the postoperative period. Orders directing their use should include the number of treatments to be given per day, the length of the treatment, the pressure to be used, the oxygen concentration to be employed, and the type

and strength of solution to be used in the nebulizer. A face mask or mouthpiece is utilized for this type of therapy.

Although an inhalation therapist usually has the responsibility for these treatments, the nurse should familiarize herself with the equipment in use in the hospital in which she works.

Gases other than oxygen

At times gases other than oxygen or compressed air are employed to aid respiration. A patient may breathe briefly in and out with a paper bag over his face, which supplies about a 4% concentration of carbon dioxide, or he may be given intermittent breaths of carbogen (an oxygen–carbon dioxide mixture), which helps increase the rate and depth of respiration. Carbon dioxide is a potentially dangerous gas and may elevate respirations and blood pressure seriously. It should be administered

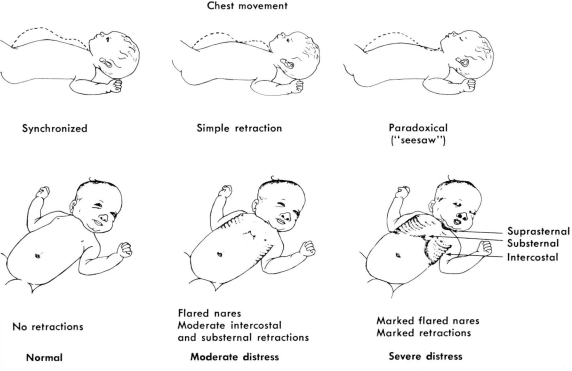

Chest movement

Synchronized   Simple retraction   Paradoxical ("seesaw")

No retractions   Flared nares / Moderate intercostal and substernal retractions   Marked flared nares / Marked retractions

Suprasternal / Substernal / Intercostal

Normal   **Moderate distress**   **Severe distress**

FIG. 32-18. Types of respiration—visible signs of respiratory distress.

only by people who are thoroughly familiar with the equipment and the possible dangers to the patient.

Helium is sometimes used at the bedside in combination with oxygen instead of the normal mixture of nitrogen and oxygen found in air. Such a combination of helium and oxygen is only one third as heavy as air. Use of this combination of gases some-times eases the respiratory effort necessary for selected patients.

Evaluation of respiratory difficulties

If the signals of respiratory distress are unknown, unobserved, or ignored so that proper methods of instituting aid are not begun promptly, the patient will not benefit. A child may be suffering from lack of

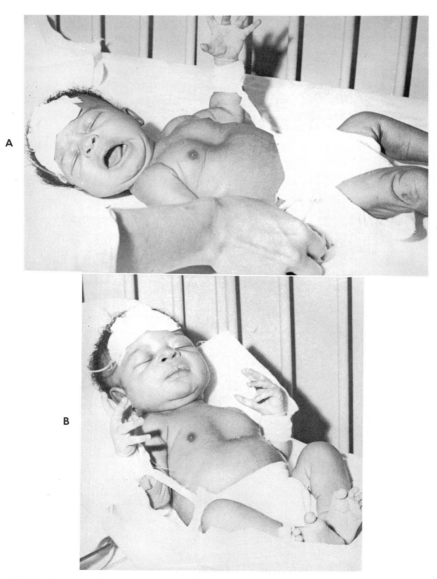

FIG. 32-19. A, Deep substernal retractions caused by pneumonia (note hollow in chest area). B, Note improvement in breathing when baby is quiet and in a more upright position in the infant seat. (Courtesy U.S. Naval Hospital, San Diego, Calif.)

ventilation; he may have proper equipment for his aid nearby. But unless aid is given properly, no improvement will result. A nurse should be thoroughly familiar with signs of respiratory difficulty or potential difficulty. Such signs and symptoms of respiratory difficulty may include the following (Fig. 32-18):

1. Depressed or elevated respiratory rate at rest for the age of the child considered (see p. 360 for a pulse and respiration table)
2. Sternal or costal retractions
3. Noisy, labored breathing
4. Flaring nostrils and the use of facial and neck muscles in attempts to aid respirations
5. Pallor or cyanosis (gray to purple skin coloring) may be localized or generalized and associated with circulatory problems
6. Restlessness, apprehension, and disorientation
7. Inflamed respiratory tree with thick nasal discharge and intermittent blockage of the nasal passageways
8. Frequent productive or nonproductive coughing

Note: The absence of coughing is not in itself necessarily a sign of respiratory improvement.

The observation of any of the preceding signs and symptoms deserves prompt report and evaluation. If a child becomes cyanotic and a bedside oxygen unit is available, first make sure that the child's airway is open, then start the oxygen and signal the supervising nurse for assistance and further evaluation of the patient. The pulse rate and respirations should be counted. Many children with circulatory and respiratory problems in which fluid tends to collect in the chest or the abdomen breathe more easily when propped in a semi-Fowler's position or supported in an infant seat (Fig. 32-19).

A breath is such a small thing, but so necessary. One who watches and records respirations is a guardian of life.

33
Traction, casting, and braces

This chapter presents, for initial consideration or review, basic nursing procedures and responsibilities involved in the care of patients receiving therapy in traction, casts, or braces. These patients may be hospitalized for various reasons; fractures, musculoskeletal diseases, and neurological disorders account for most of their diagnoses. For more information regarding specific illnesses in this grouping, the student is referred to Chapter 37, which discusses, in greater detail, some of these problems and the nursing care they require. However, to avoid needless repetition, the orthopedic nursing entailed in the care of such patients is discussed separately in this section.

Traction

Traction, or methods of exerting pull, is discussed first because, at times, it must precede casting. Traction is used for the following reasons:

1. To bring a broken bone back into alignment (reduce a fracture) and provide immobilization for correct union
2. To secure a corrected position to treat a congenital or acquired deformity not involving a fracture (reduce a dislocated hip, scoliosis)
3. To prevent or treat contracture deformities
4. To relieve muscle spasm and pain (back injury)

BASIC TYPES

Traction may be exerted manually or by the use of certain appliances. There are two main types of traction—skin and skeletal.

Skin traction

Skin traction helps position the bone indirectly by pulling on the skin and muscles. It is relatively simple to apply and involves no surgical operation. However, only a limited amount of weight may be added with this type of traction, and occasionally the amount of pull possible is not sufficient to produce the desired results. Also, the skin may show signs of irritation—allergic reactions, circulation difficulties, or friction—caused by the supportive wrapping. The attachment of the weight to the skin is usually secured by running strips of adhesive-type material, cotton or perforated plastic-backed adhesive tape, or foam rubber up both sides of the extremity and securing the strips with Ace bandage. The ends of the strips are then attached to a foot spreader, which, in turn, is connected to the desired weight.

Skeletal traction

Skeletal traction is secured by inserting some mechanical device directly into or through the bone and attaching the prescribed weight. Wires, pins, or tongs may be used to obtain the bone contact. Considerable weight may be attached to such an arrangement, and no bulky or irritating skin wrappings are necessary. Nevertheless, skeletal traction, too, has its drawbacks. Since the bone is actually pierced there is always danger of infection, and a surgical procedure is involved in both the insertion and the removal of the mechanical attachment. The areas where the holding devices are inserted through the skin must be frequently inspected for signs of inflammation, infection, and drainage.

NURSING CONSIDERATIONS

The beginning student often expresses a feeling of perplexity after viewing her first traction patient. Often there seems to be a surplus of weights, ropes, pulleys, and bars, and she wonders how they all fit in to produce a desired result. The mechanical apparatus used may seem quite complex at times, but the basic principles of traction that guide their use are neither numerous nor obscure.

Maintenance of proper traction

The maintenance of proper traction depends on the direction and amount of pull exerted through the use of ropes, pulleys, and weights and the positioning or alignment of the patient. Therefore it is very important that the nurse understands the orders concerning the care of each individual patient in traction and maintains the correct relationship of the various parts of the traction apparatus to the patient. The following points should be noted:

1. Pulleys increase the amount and change the direction of pull on a body part by a weight. A rope should ride properly on a pulley to exert the ordered weight.

2. Weights should not be added or subtracted by the nurse. Too much weight may cause the nonunion of a break; too little weight may cause unwanted overriding and an extremity of unequal length. Weights should always hang freely. They should be frequently observed so that they do not "come to rest" on a rung of the bed, a poorly placed chair, or the floor.

3. The amount of time that traction is to be applied should be clearly understood. Skin traction may occasionally be removed (but such removal is always dependent on the physician's order). Skeletal traction is usually continuous at all times.

4. Ropes should be in good condition and frequently inspected for signs of wear. Knots should be taped for additional safety. Multiple weights attached to the same rope should be taped together so that they cannot easily fall or be removed. Some pediatric-orthopedic areas place the foot of the beds over which weights hang next to the wall to discourage tampering by the small fingers of ambulatory patients.

Countertraction

Pull in one direction must be balanced by pull in the opposite direction for traction to remain effective. This opposing pull is called *countertraction.*

Countertraction may be exerted in various ways. If the weights used to create the initial pull are not extremely heavy, it may only be necessary to keep the patient in a certain placement in bed, checking periodically to see that he has not slipped past the desired place. The patient's body provides the countertraction. The friction of the patient's body against the bedding may also help prevent him from slipping out of position.

If the pull is stronger, the end of the bed where the initial traction is applied may need to be elevated to allow gravity to increase the countertraction created by the patient's body weight. Elevation may be achieved through the use of grooved blocks under two legs of the bed or a mechanical bed lift.

If it is very difficult to maintain the child in proper position in bed, sometimes some type of restraint may be used (a restraining jacket or waist restraint). However, the use of such devices may cause other problems—pressure areas, hypostatic pneumonia, and constipation. The use of restraints must be carefully evaluated.

Sometimes the body part being treated is placed in a type of frame or splint that is lifted off the surface of the bed. When this arrangement is used, a counterweight may often be connected to this frame, exerting force in the opposing direction.

In review, countertraction may be created in four basic ways:

1. Maintenance of body placement in bed by constant observation and correction, if needed
2. Elevation of the part of the bed next to the weights
3. Use of restraints
4. Application of a counterweight

The method employed depends on the desires of the physician and the responses of the patient. Failure to maintain correct placement in bed while the patient is in traction may (1) cause the weights, which are supposed to create initial pull, to rest on the floor or some other surface and temporarily stop traction altogether, in some cases allowing possible displacement or (2) change the angle of pull and distort the result desired.

Both situations are potentially harmful. When a nurse is told "Keep Susie's hips at the level of the tape markers on the bed," or "Be sure that Roger is kept pulled up in bed," the staff is trying to avoid the situations just described.

Activity and body position

The amount of movement and activity allowed the patient in traction should be understood and promoted, and good body alignment and support should be maintained. Bed boards should be placed under the mattress to prevent sagging.

Some patients are allowed relatively little movement or position change because of their individual musculoskeletal problems or traction arrangements. If the nurse allows these patients to sit up or turn on their sides, the traction may be lost or altered so that no treatment or, perhaps, even real damage may result. A patient who has a leg in a Thomas splint support raised off the surface of the mattress is allowed considerable movement because such a traction maintains proper alignment when the patient's trunk is raised. Even a slight amount of turning toward the splinted leg is usually possible. Such an arrangement is termed "balanced traction." When balanced traction is used in conjunction with an overhead bar and trapeze, the patient enjoys considerably more activity, and nursing care is greatly simplified (Fig. 33-9).

Although it is important that the patient not be moved in a way that will disrupt his traction, it is also important that he be moved to the extent permitted to encourage proper body function, elimination, respiration, and circulation and avoid pressure areas. Exercise and correct positioning of the uninvolved extremities are very necessary to prevent other problems (stiffness or deformity) from occurring in some patients. As in all cases of prolonged immobilization, a high fluid intake should be encouraged. A diet well supplied with roughage and natural laxatives such as prunes helps avoid constipation. Special attention should be given to the prevention of foot drop or undesired internal or external rotation of the lower extremities.

Circulation and skin condition

The circulation and skin condition of a patient in traction or other immobilization devices such as casts should be frequently evaluated.

The skin of any patient who is bedfast for long periods with only limited movement permitted must be meticulously observed and protected. Pressure areas are most likely to develop over bony prominences such as the hips, sacrum, ankles, elbows, scapulae, and shoulders. Areas exposed to continuous friction are also likely spots for skin breakdown. If a Thomas splint is being utilized, the skin area under the padded ring must be frequently inspected. The heels of both the affected and nonaffected leg should be carefully observed. Often the foot that is not being treated may develop a sore heel because the patient helps himself move up in bed by digging his good heel into the mattress to obtain leverage. To prevent unnecessary pressures the bed linen must be kept smooth and tight, and crumbs and other irritating small objects must be eliminated from the bed. Skin traction wrappings may cause circulation and nerve interference similar to that occasionally encountered with the casted patient (p. 465). Inability to dorsiflex the exposed big toe of a wrapped affected lower extremity should be reported to the physician promptly.

Pressure areas are much easier to prevent than to treat. Frequent inspection, cleansing, and massage of susceptible areas and encouragement of as much movement as is allowed and consistent with the patient's well-being will greatly reduce, if not entirely eliminate, pressure areas. Every complaint of skin tenderness, a burning sensation, or aching should be investigated. It does not take long for a small red area to become an enlarged open sore, particularly in areas where circulation may be already impaired. Rubber rings, padded doughnuts, or foam-rubber supports, which lift a pressure area off a surface, must be used with caution and frequently evaluated, since such devices may sometimes cause circulatory disturbances. Patients who are paralyzed or suffer from sensory loss must receive special care and observation. A child in traction should routinely receive back and skin care during his bath and at least twice more during the day shift. The use of an overhead bar and trapeze can greatly facilitate back and skin care when such aids are feasible. If no such arrangement is possible, a nurse may press down on the mattress with one hand to allow her other hand to massage, or two nurses may work together to lift the child *slightly* to facilitate skin care, depending on the type of traction used.

Sometimes the use of imitation or genuine lamb's-wool mats under the patient is helpful. Tincture of benzoin applications on closed areas of pressure or potential pressure are sometimes prescribed. The benzoin serves to toughen the areas but may stain the sheets.

Bedmaking

Some hospitals are supplied with special traction linen designed to fit under or around different traction appliances such as the Thomas splint. A special "split" top sheet may be available to use on either side of the splint. More commonly, a large sheet is simply pulled to one side over the good leg and a light baby blanket draped over the splinted leg at night. Another satisfactory and modest arrangement uses two blankets, each contained within a separate folded sheet. One such blanket-sheet combination is placed over the chest and abdomen of the patient, open edges under the chin; the other is placed on top of the good leg and below the suspended leg, open edges toward the foot of the bed where they are tucked in. The upper and lower blanket-sheet combinations are then pinned together around the thigh of the leg in traction. This makes a very neat bed. Traction patients may have special snap-on pajamas (tops and bottoms) to facilitate dressing, or perineal draps or G-strings may be used.

TYPES OF TRACTION EQUIPMENT

Traction equipment may be quite varied, depending on the individual needs of the patient.

Progressive abduction traction

Figs. 33-1 and 33-2 show types of traction used to achieve progressive reduction of congenital dislocation of the hips. Fig. 33-1 shows an infant who is almost ready for casting. When this child was first placed in the skin traction, her legs were suspended at right angles to the bed. Gradually her legs have been abducted until they are almost flat on the bed. When her legs are properly abducted, she will be placed in a plaster cast for further treatment. Such a patient must be carefully observed for developing circulation problems because the leg wrappings may interfere with blood flow. Swollen, cool, or "blotchy" looking toes, slow blanching on pressure, or delayed return of skin color after pressure is released from a toenail bed are all signs that should be promptly reported. The pulse at the ankle may also be checked to detect circulatory problems. This type of patient should be raised slightly during

FIG. 33-1. This baby is almost ready for a hip spica cast. Frequent back care is essential. (Courtesy Children's Health Center, San Diego, Calif.)

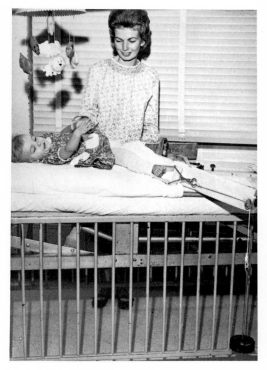

FIG. 33-2. A-frame traction, or a Putti board. Mother stays as much as she can to cheer her toddler. (Courtesy Children's Health Center, San Diego, Calif.)

feedings to prevent aspiration. The jacket restraint may be loosened or removed if a responsible party is *at* the bedside, but it should be in place when the child is alone. To make the bed, one nurse may lift the baby's body just enough to allow another nurse to slide the bed sheets under her hips and back. The weights should not be removed. Frequent back care and diaper changes are a necessity.

Fig. 33-2 shows another traction device used to treat dislocation of the hip by progressive abduction. It is known as an A-frame, or Putti board. The angle of a padded wedge is progressively widened to produce increased abduction. This type of traction is advantageous because the child may be placed in either prone or supine position and, depending on his physician's

orders and the setup, he may be carefully turned. Turning helps prevent respiratory problems and pressure areas and encourages appetite.

Bryant's traction

Bryant's traction is often used for the treatment of fractured legs in young children (Fig. 33-3). Nursing care of the child in Bryant's traction is similar to that described for children in the traction pictured in Fig. 33-1.

Russell's traction

Russell's traction, a skin traction using a sling and single rope arrangement attached to one weight supported by multiple pulleys, is used to treat fractures in older children (Fig. 33-4). Because the ex-

454

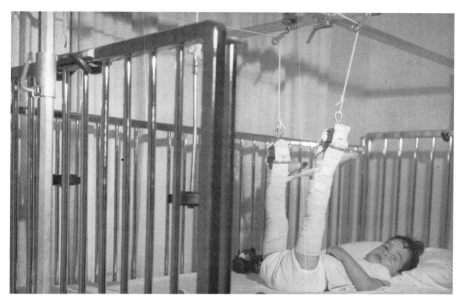

FIG. 33-3. Bryant's, or vertical, traction is often used when infants or young children sustain leg fractures. (Courtesy Mercy Hospital, San Diego, Calif.)

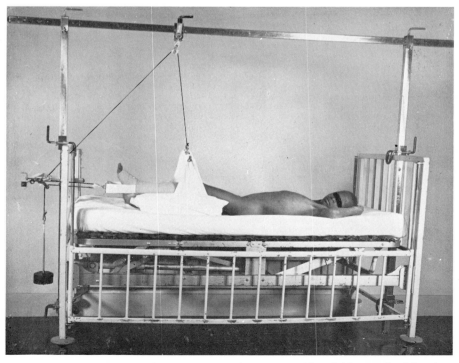

FIG. 33-4. Russell's traction may be used to treat fractures in older children and adults. (From Shands, A. R., and Raney, R. B.: Handbook of orthopaedic surgery, ed. 7, St. Louis, 1967, The C. V. Mosby Co.)

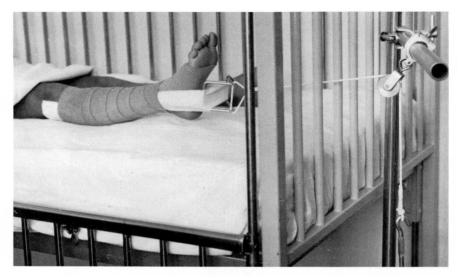

Fɪɢ. 33-5. Buck's extension. Note that the heel clears the mattress. Some physicians use a small flat pillow under the leg to provide clearance. (Courtesy Children's Health Center, San Diego, Calif.)

tremity is suspended, more patient movement is allowed, and nursing care is considerably easier.

Buck's extension

A rather simple, frequently used skin traction for treatment of the lower extremities or lower back is called Buck's extension (Fig. 33-5). Note the adhesive strips on the sides, the elastic bandage wrapping, the foot spreader (to prevent pressure of the adhesive strips against the ankle), the pulley, and the freely hanging weight. Some physicians order a small flattened pillow under the leg just above the Achilles tendon to protect the heel from pressure.

Cervical traction

The patient in cervical traction may have a sling or halter arrangement around the chin and occiput (Fig. 33-6), or he may be placed in skeletal traction, which involves the placement of some type of tongs into (but not through!) the cranium (Fig. 33-7). Orders regarding the placement of the patient, the movement allowed, and whether any elevation of the backrest is permitted should be clearly understood.

Patients in skeletal-cervical traction are often positioned in slight hyperextension, and flexion of the cervical spine is not permitted. If cervical skin traction is used, foam-rubber padding may be necessary in the chin area to prevent skin irritation. Gum-chewing may help relieve aching jaw joints.

Pelvic traction

Occasionally pelvic traction may be ordered to relieve lower back pain. Pelvic traction is exerted by use of a pelvic band or girdle attached to a weight or weights. Sometimes a thoracic belt may be used for countertraction. Such an arrangement is designed to relieve muscle spasm and lessen pressure on nerve roots. Pelvic traction may be ordered continuously or intermittently. Many patients are given bathroom privileges.

Balanced traction

As previously mentioned, *balanced traction*, involving the suspension of the affected limb above the surface of the bed, provides the opportunity for more movement or activity on the part of the patient.

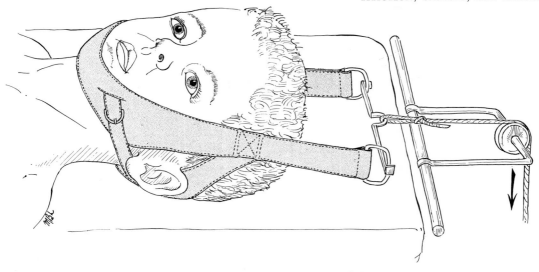

FIG. 33-6. Cervical skin traction with halter.

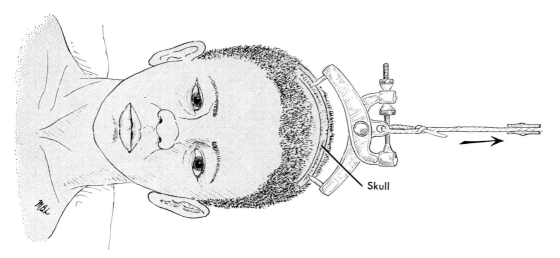

FIG. 33-7. Crutchfield tongs, cervical-skeletal traction.

The patient may raise his hips, have his backrest elevated, or turn slightly toward the side of his splinted lower extremity. An overhead bar and trapeze greatly facilitates lifting. The suspension device takes up the slack created and maintains the line of traction. It is well to remember that these patients should rest flat intermittently without the elevation of the backrest to prevent hip contractures—no matter how much they want to stay up!

Although suspended traction gives greater liberty of movement and effectively relieves heel pressure, the area where the ring of the Thomas splint rests must be frequently inspected for the development of skin problems. Each day the skin may be gently pulled up or down from under the ring and washed, dried, and massaged. The ring itself may be polished with saddle soap. Fig. 33-8 shows a Thomas splint with a complete ring and a Thomas half-ring splint with a Pearson attachment, which is used to actually support the extremity. Fig. 33-9 shows a young girl with a balanced skeletal traction, including an extra support

457

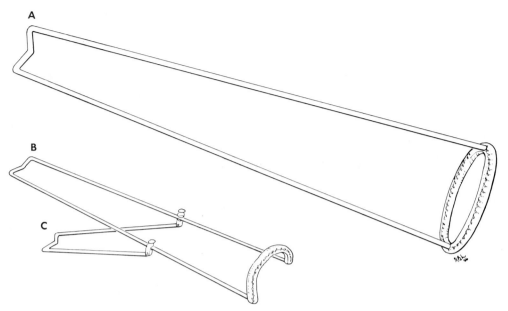

FIG. 33-8. **A,** Thomas splint with complete ring; **B,** half-ring Thomas splint; **C,** Pearson attachment.

to prevent foot drop and an additional weight to correct a tendency toward pronounced internal rotation of the leg. Not long after this photograph was taken the girl was sent home in a long leg plaster cast.

Casts

Casts are often applied subsequent to treatment by traction, supplying a form of external immobilization of a body part. Occasionally, a cast may be applied over a skeletal pin, thus helping to continue traction as well as contributing immobilization. Such a procedure may be called plaster traction. The ends of the protruding pins should be covered with plaster or some sort of protective device to avoid the snagging of clothing or bed coverings or injury to others. Plaster traction allows greater mobility for the patient (when feasible). In addition to immobilization and possible traction, casts may also be a means of aiding proper positioning or resting a body part.

The most common kind of cast consists of plaster-of-Paris–impregnated crinoline bandages that have been applied and molded while moist over some type of soft, protective layer and allowed to dry to a hard, resistant shell. Dry plaster of Paris is a form of calcium sulfate; when mixed with water, it forms the substance known as gypsum. Plastic materials have also occasionally been used to form casts.

APPLICATION OF THE CAST

Because of the "orderly disorder" that invariably accompanies plaster applications, it is preferable to schedule cast work in a room especially designed for such procedures—a room that is easily cleaned and contains all the equipment and supplies usually needed.

Commonly needed supplies are as follows:

1. Materials to protect the skin from the harsh plaster (to wrap around the body part before application of the plaster)
   a. Sheet wadding (Webril)
   b. Tubular stockinette

2. Various widths of plaster-of-Paris bandages and strips (splints)
3. Materials to reinforce or protect areas of the cast or body that are under special pressure or strain
   a. Felt
   b. Yucca board
   c. Wire netting
   d. Rubber heels (for leg casts of ambulatory patients)
4. Special tools
   a. Various types of cast knives
   b. Plaster shears
   c. Cast spreaders and cast benders
   d. Manual and electrical cast cutters
   e. A bucket for tepid water to moisten the plaster
5. Other possible needs
   a. Sterile and nonsterile cover gowns
   b. Gloves, caps, and masks

The furnishings of a cast room need not be elaborate. Usually, an examining table, some benches, good lighting, an x-ray view box, and a sink are sufficient. A sink with a plaster trap is convenient because water used to soak the plaster-of-Paris rolls may be discarded into the drain without too much danger of plugging the plumbing. If large body casts or scoliosis jackets are applied, additional supportive frames, tables, or slings will be needed. Newspapers placed on the floor under the working area will aid cleanup.

Preparation of the patient

Some patients undergoing casting procedures are anesthetized to aid muscle relaxation, relieve pain, and facilitate the entire procedure. Patients who have open reductions of fractures or other operative procedures just prior to casting are, of course, always anesthetized. Small children are many times anesthetized for closed reduction procedures. Such patients are given nothing by mouth for several hours before the procedure and usually receive preoperative sedation. When a general anesthetic is used, all precautions against explosions should be taken. The staff must be dressed appropriately and all equipment properly grounded. Even if no use of anesthetics is contemplated and a closed manipulation prior to casting is the only maneuver scheduled, a preoperative analgesic drug may be ordered and oral feedings temporarily withheld.

Duties of the nurse

The nurse helping the physician in the cast room is responsible for making available all the necessary equipment and supplies. She may also help by preparing the plaster rolls for use. The desired width of plaster-of-Paris bandage is removed from its wax-paper wrapper and immersed on end in water (approximately 105° F.). When air bubbles no longer rise from the roll, the bandage should be lifted from the water. The sides of the closed bandage may be gently squeezed to help remove water and retain plaster. The loose end of the bandage is unrolled slightly, and the roll and its end are handed to the physician for application. The bandage should not be dripping at the time of the transfer. The nurse may also assist by helping to hold the extremity being casted. She may be asked to support part of the newly formed cast. If she does, she should remember to use only the palms of her hands in rendering such support to prevent the formation of pressure areas.

CAST CHANGES AND REMOVAL
(Fig. 33-10)

Sometimes a patient must have one cast removed and another applied. The frequency with which a child must have his cast changed depends on his rate of growth, the condition of the cast, and the progress of the desired correction. The cast may be cut manually with a cast knife, which may be shaped like a short kitchen paring knife, and a hand cast cutter. The cut is made along a predetermined line, which may have been dampened by a vinegar solution, hydrogen peroxide, or water from a syringe. A metal strip may be inserted just below the cutting line to protect the body part. An electrical vibrating-blade cast cutter may be used instead. The electrical saw is safe but makes a great deal of noise, which sometimes frightens the patient. When the cast has been cut, the sections are separated by a cast spreader, and the padding underneath is released with a large bandage scissors. The body part that has had the support of the cast must be gently supported and handled and not forced into new, unfamiliar positions. Sudden lack of support or movement will often cause considerable pain and distress.

Professional opinion differs regarding the care of the skin of a patient who has been in a cast for a considerable time and will

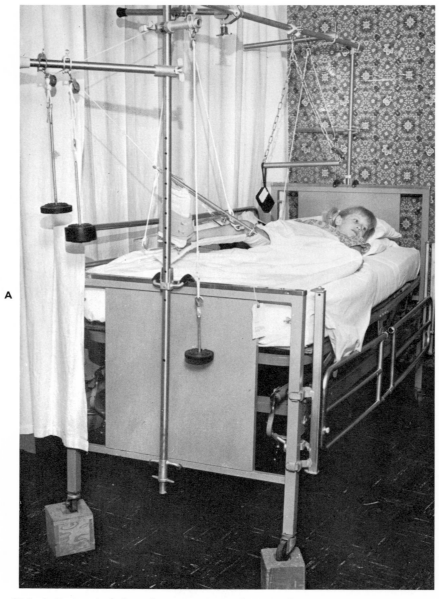

Fig. 33-9. **A,** Patient in balanced traction. **B,** Explanatory drawing. **C,** Close-up view of leg. (Courtesy Children's Health Center, San Diego, Calif.)

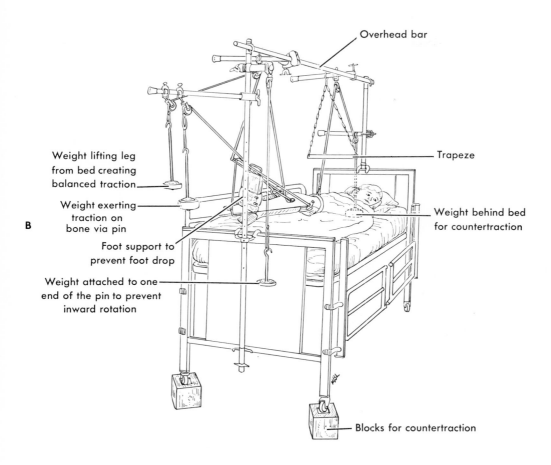

Overhead bar

Weight lifting leg
from bed creating
balanced traction

Weight exerting
traction on
bone via pin

B

Foot support to
prevent foot drop

Weight attached to one
end of the pin to prevent
inward rotation

Trapeze

Weight behind bed
for countertraction

Blocks for countertraction

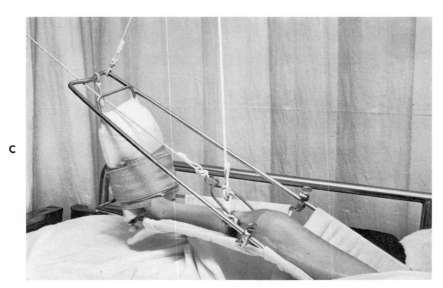

C

FIG. 33-9, cont'd. For legend see opposite page.

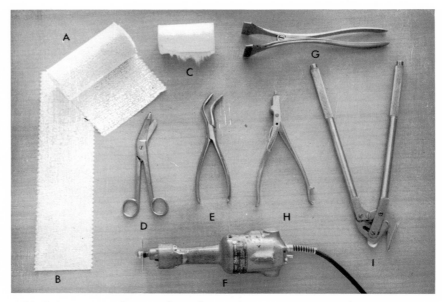

Fig. 33-10. Instruments and materials used in preparing or removing plaster casts. **A**, Plaster roll; **B**, plaster splint; **C**, Webril (sheet wadding); **D**, plaster shears (large bandage scissors); **E**, cast bender; **F**, cast cutter or saw (electrical); **G** and **H**, cast spreaders; **I**, cast cutter (manual). (Courtesy Children's Health Center, San Diego, Calif.)

almost immediately be enclosed in a cast again. Some physicians wish their patients to have pHisoHex baths. Others believe that the least amount of handling possible is the best choice. All wish to avoid trauma to the skin, which would lead to trouble during the subsequent period of casting. If the use of a cast will be discontinued permanently or for a considerable time, the physician may order a combination of gentle pHisoHex baths and the application of baby oil to help loosen the crust of old skin and sebaceous material that has collected on the surface of the body part that was under the cast. With patience and time this crust may be removed with no injury to the underlying epidermis.

CARE OF THE NEWLY CASTED PATIENT AND HIS CAST

A newly casted patient may complain of the heat generated by the plaster as it undergoes its physical reaction with the water. This heat of crystallization is transitory; however, in the case of body casts it may cause considerable annoyance.

Newly applied casts are soft, damp, and grayish white and have a slightly musty smell. They must be handled carefully.

Transfer of the patient

When transferring a newly casted patient, lift the cast with the palms of the hands, do not grasp it by the fingers. Finger pressure may cause indentations, tissue injury, and disturbances in circulation. If the patient is in a body cast covering the trunk or hips and legs (hip spica), many hands may be necessary to make an efficient, smooth transfer from cart to bed.

Preparation of the unit

The unit of a patient who is having a new body cast applied requires special preparation. Bed boards should be placed under the mattress to prevent sagging. Numerous plastic-covered firm pillows should be available to support the contours of the soft cast.

If the child is old enough and able to benefit, an overhead bar and trapeze should be attached to the bed. The room

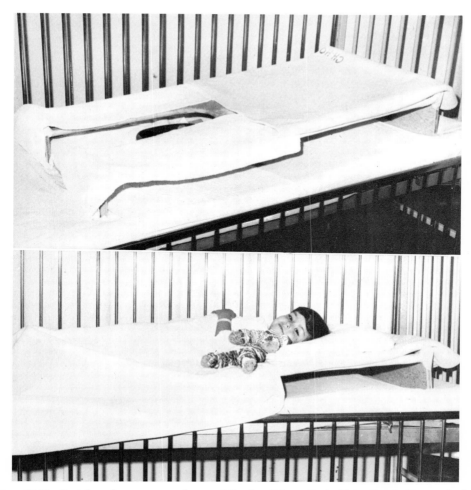

Fig. 33-11. Cast board, premeasured especially for this patient. Note the incline and the positioned bedpan. (Courtesy Children's Health Center, San Diego, Calif.)

should be well ventilated to assist in the drying of the cast. Occasionally special cast driers may be available or an undraped heat cradle may be utilized to help speed drying. A new cast should be exposed to the air. However, for modesty's sake a G-string or diaper may be positioned over the perineal area. A fracture pan should be available in the bedside stand. In many hospitals infants and small children in body casts are measured for so-called "cast boards," which hold the child at a slight incline, elevated from the bed mattress (Fig. 33-11). A bedpan is kept positioned under the child at all times, and plastic strips tucked into the perineal area of the cast guide waste material into the pan below. Very young children who are incontinent may be "taped" as for a urine specimen until the cast is dry enough to be protected against accidental soiling with some type of waterproof material.

In cases of newly casted extremities often all that is necessary for the nurse to have ready in the patient's unit is a supply of firm, waterproof pillows to aid in the elevation of the body part to help prevent swelling. Sometimes elevation is best maintained through the use of a Gatch bed or the placement of pillows under the end of

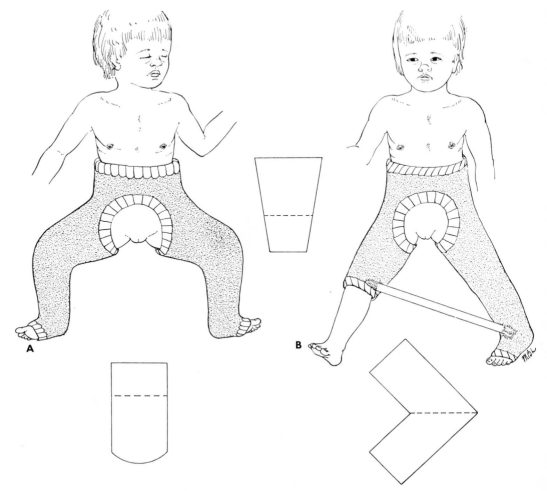

FIG. 33-12. Different types of petalling. **A,** Bilateral hip spica cast. **B,** Unilateral hip spica cast with an abductor bar.

the mattress. The cast, again, should be left exposed to the air to facilitate drying. Most casts dry in approximately 24 hours.

Care of the cast

When the cast is dry, as indicated by a chalky white finish and a hard, nonmoist surface, it should be protected against accidental wetting in the perineal region. This may be done in several ways. Various types of plastic material may be cut to fit under the perineal edge of the cast and to protect the curved band of the cast just adjacent. It may be held in place by pieces of water-repellent adhesive tape. Some pe-

diatric departments use a plastic adhesive tape, which may be cut into wedge-shaped pieces and positioned around and under the perineal rim and on the outer surface (Fig. 33-12). Regardless of the method selected to protect the cast, the waterproof material should not be applied until the cast is dry because the cast may become moldy. In many such cases the strips do not adhere anyway, and all the time spent in applying the plastic is time lost! When the cast is dry, all rough or potentially rough edges of the cast should be covered. This process is called "petalling" because the pieces of adhesive tape first used for this purpose were cut in the shape of flower petals. However, nurses today may use adhesive tape cut like chevrons, circles, or wedges as well as the traditional "petal" to protect cast edges (Fig. 33-12). Petalling keeps small bits of plaster from the cast edges from falling into the cast, helps prevent skin irritation around the cast, and usually improves the overall appearance of the cast. If tubular stockinette is applied before the plaster bandage during the construction of the cast, it may be neatly trimmed and brought up over the cast edge and secured with adhesive or plaster splints to make a smooth, attractive edging when the cast is dry.

Various methods have been employed to enhance the appearance of a cast and help protect it from damage and soil. Some physicians finish a cast by dusting on plaster powder and rubbing it in. Some apply shellac, varnish, or plastic spray to a dry cast to increase its longevity and help keep it clean. It is best not to get a cast dirty or stained in the first place, but if it does become soiled, the nurse may clean the area with a damp, not wet, cloth and a small amount of white cleanser (Bon Ami, etc.) or fast-drying white shoe polish. Some dry, dirty areas may be covered by adhesive tape or additional plaster-of-Paris strips. Children should be cautioned against getting their casts damp. Swimming is definitely out!

The preceding paragraphs have been concerned primarily with the cast itself; however, the most important consideration in orthopedic care is not the cast but the patient it encloses. Casts are a great help in correcting various musculoskeletal problems, but they may also cause or accentuate problems. The casted patient must be carefully observed to detect the development of any of these difficulties.

Observation for circulatory complications

A newly casted extremity may suffer impaired circulation. Sometimes circulatory problems compound themselves. Because of injury, operative procedure, or a tight cast application, there may be swelling under the cast. The increasingly tight cast impedes circulation further, and tissue damage may take place. There are certain signs and symptoms of abnormal pressure and swelling that should be reported long before significant tissue damage occurs. They should be sought frequently after casting and daily thereafter. They include the following:

1. Swelling of the toes or fingers
2. Cold toes or fingers (they should be pink and warm)
3. Pale, cyanotic, or mottled toes or fingers or an absent or delayed blanching sign (Pressure is made on the nail beds to blanch the area. When the pressure is removed, the normal nail color should return immediately. If the area does not blanch, this is also significant because it indicates local congestion and lack of good circulation.)
4. Inability to find a pulse in an extremity (when the area to be palpated is accessible)
5. Inability to move exposed toes or fingers
6. Complaints of the following:
   a. Tingling
   b. Numbness
   c. Burning sensation
   d. Pain
   (Of course, very small children are unable to verbalize these subjective symptoms. They are watched for "fussiness.")
7. Excessive bleeding after surgery, as estimated by bloody drainage seeping through the cast layers (This is rather difficult to evaluate. One should consider the type of surgical procedure involved. Physicians seem to differ in opinion concerning the advisability of circling with pencil the drainage stains on a cast and marking them with the time noted. One orthopedist was heard to say that he thought that such a practice alarmed patients un-

duly. Perhaps the nurse could make a few guide dots instead of the more obvious circle and mark the time in her written notes if she thought the amount of seepage needed closer observation.)

When possible, the corresponding unaffected extremity should be compared with the casted arm or leg. Some people have cold hands most of the time, with or without casts! Any complaint of a burning sensation or pain should be promptly reported and investigated. Considerable damage may occur in a relatively short period. If such complaints are neglected, the body part may become numb and no additional complaints may be heard for some time, until tissue damage is significant.

A casted extremity that is swelling must be relieved soon. In a hospital situation it would be rare not to be able to call a physician who could take appropriate measures to relieve the pressure. A nurse should not hesitate to call a physician if circulation is impaired even though the hour may be inconvenient. In the unusual situation in which no physician can be contacted, the nurse should be prepared to cut the cast herself. Certainly such a situation would be extraordinary, but if no help will be available for a considerable period, it is better to have a damaged cast than a gangrenous extremity. The usual emergency procedure involves cutting the cast in half and forming an upper and lower or anterior and posterior shell. The inner wrappings should also be cut, since they may cause considerable pressure. The extremity may be maintained in the shell with the halves held opposite one another by elastic bandage. Such a cast is said to be *bivalved*. Occasionally physicians intentionally plan to bivalve casts; such casts provide support but also allow some movement and exposure and facilitate the skin care of an area. Bivalved casts are occasionally used as splints in conjunction with elastic bandage.

Even when the cast is dry and relatively old, the daily care of the patient in a body cast or a hip spica cast should continue to include observation for disturbance in circulation and possible areas of pressure and skin breakdown. The skin next to the cast edges must be carefully inspected and massaged. Alcohol or lotion may be used. The heel and heel cord and the perineum should be especially watched for signs of irritation.

Turning the patient

The patient in a dry body cast is routinely turned at least every 2 to 3 hours in an attempt to prevent pressure sores and promote respiration and elimination. The number of people needed to turn a patient in a body cast depends on the size and general condition of the patient and the age of his cast. Remember the following when turning a patient in a large body cast:

1. If there is a choice, plan to turn the patient toward the nonoperative side.
2. Before turning the patient, pull or lift him to the side of the bed, placing his "turning side" toward the center of the bed. Have the patient lift his hands above his head or, if this is not feasible, have them held against his sides with a towel or diaper placed between the hands and the cast just before turning to prevent injury. *Do not* use the abductor bar to turn the patient. It is held in place with only a few turns of plaster bandage. It helps support the cast, but it is not a handle.
3. If possible, place the protective pillows needed under the cast in the new position before the patient is turned.
   a. If the patient is placed *on his abdomen,* a flat pillow just below the chest area sometimes helps chest expansion and respiration. A small pillow for the head increases comfort. Legs need to be supported to prevent the toes from digging into the bedding and the problem of foot drop. Curved up-and-

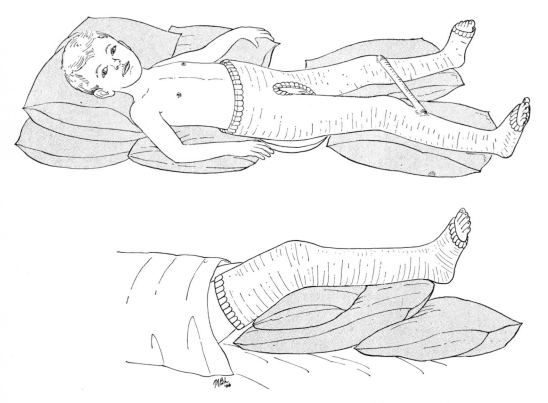

FIG. 33-13. Methods of using pillows to support a cast. The child shown at the top is on a bedpan.

down contours of the cast also should be protected from strain. The abdominal position is preferred for older children at mealtime to aid in swallowing and self-help.

b. If the patient is placed *on his back,* a small pillow is needed under his head. Curved up-and-down contours of the cast should be protected from strain and the heels lifted from the pressure of the mattress.

c. When positioning the patient, be sure that the edges of the cast do not press against the skin. The patient should be made as comfortable as possible.

d. A young child who is not continent and does not have a cast board may be placed on a sort of horseshoe-shaped pillow arrangement, and a small bedpan or large kidney-shaped basin may be positioned under the patient with a plastic strip tucked under the cast leading to the pan or basin (Fig. 33-13). Such a pillow support should elevate the child on a slight incline, the head higher than the feet, to prevent urine backflow into the cast.

Safety factors

Children in casts of any type must be carefully observed and taught not to put *anything* down into the cast. Small objects such as crayons, bobby pins, etc. can cause pressure areas, pain, infection, and a delay in recuperation. The nurse must also be vigilant regarding the use of so-called scratchers, employed to relieve itching. If scratchers are allowed at all, they must be relatively soft, such as a strip of gauze that has been strategically placed before the cast application is begun. Bent coat hangers and even pipe cleaners may cause excoriation, and we do not recommend them for such purposes. Gently blowing air from a syringe under the rim of the cast may be soothing at times. One must be sure that the child is not scratching a healing surgical incision.

General nursing considerations

Bathing. Parts of the body that might be overlooked during the daily bath are the fingers and the areas between the toes. Plaster crumbs may collect between the digits and cause pressure areas. Cotton-tipped applicators dipped in baby oil help clean these areas satisfactorily. Fingernails and toenails should be kept trimmed and neat.

Diet and fluids. The child who is immobilized not only needs meticulous skin care but also special attention to his diet and fluid intake to promote healing and avoid constipation and urinary stasis. A liberal fluid intake should be maintained, and a high-protein diet is often encouraged. At times prune juice or some mild laxative may be indicated to avoid a less agreeable enema.

Support of a casted extremity. When a child with a casted extremity is allowed to be up in a chair, the cast should be elevated and not allowed to become dependent. The physician may order that a casted arm be supported in a sling. There are several types of slings available. Fig. 33-14 shows the classic sling, formed from a triangular bandage. Note that the fingers are exposed but the wrist is supported and that the hand is higher than the elbow. The knot should not rest over the cervical

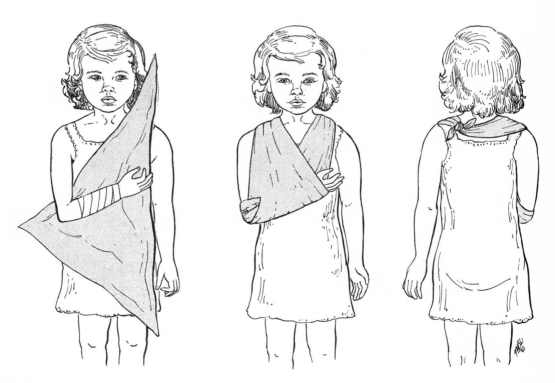

Fig. 33-14. Classic triangle bandage sling. Note that the fingers are exposed and elevated higher than the elbow. The knot does not rest on the spine.

spine; this is uncomfortable and may cause a pressure area. Fig. 33-15 shows a commercially prepared hammock-type sling. It is available in several sizes.

When local swelling of an extremity is present, some physicians order that the arm be elevated with pillows. Such elevation, to be effective, requires that the child's wrist be higher than his elbow and his elbow be higher than his shoulder. Occasionally, an extremity may be suspended from a sling attached to an overhead bar or an intravenous standard.

Diversion and intellectual stimulation. A person may be clean, free from pain, on the mend physically, but not particularly happy. The nurse who is interested in the total patient, not just the body in the cast, should help provide proper diversion, intellectual stimulation, and interpersonal con-

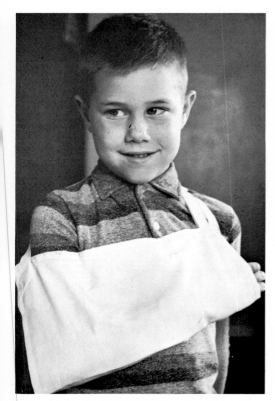

FIG. 33-15. A commercial hammock-type sling. Note that the arm enters the sling from the top, not from the side.

tacts for her patients. This is a time when older children can develop constructive hobbies and lasting interests.

Discharge. Of course, many of the casted patients do not remain in the hospital very long. Often, the cast is applied, dried, protected, and petalled, and the patient's discharge is written within 48 hours or less. The family must be instructed in detail concerning skin care, observation for circulatory problems, cast protection, and cleansing if they are not already familiar with cast care. Appropriate transportation must be arranged. Patients in long leg casts or hip spica casts cannot be comfortably placed in all automobiles!

Braces

A removable, external support used to maintain position or provide strength to a body part is called a brace. A brace may be made of numerous kinds of material but characteristically is constructed of metal, leather, felt, and lacings. Braces are expensive pieces of equipment. They are individually fitted and produced and demand the respect of both patient and nurse. They furnish support by exerting pressure on at least three points of the body. There are many different types of braces. The Milwaukee brace for the treatment of scoliosis is one example of a body brace. There are short, below-the-knee braces for ankle or foot support or full-length leg braces for both knee and ankle stabilization. Some patients (postpoliomyelitis victims) must have combined body and long leg braces because of extensive residual muscle paralysis. Many braces include movable joints, which may be locked, using various mechanisms to provide greater stability for weight bearing.

MAINTENANCE OF THE BRACE

The routine care of a brace includes protecting it from rust, carefully cleaning and oiling any hinges with a fine-grade oil, and removing any excess oil to prevent staining of leather supports or clothing. It also includes the care of any leather parts by

469

the periodic application of saddle soap, followed by polishing or the use of cleaning fluids such as benzene. Cleaning fluids may also be used on felt pads. Laces should be maintained intact and free from pressure-causing knots. Shoes incorporated in any leg brace should be frequently inspected for abnormal wear. Any missing part (felt kneepads, screws, etc.) should be promptly reported because the loss may seriously jeopardize the ability of the brace to fulfill its purpose.

NURSING RESPONSIBILITIES

The nurse and patient should be familiar with the purpose of each brace, the way in which it should be applied and positioned, when it should be worn, the length of time it should be worn, and its mechanism and maintenance. Patients wearing braces should be frequently inspected for bruises and pressure areas. Those wearing leg braces should have well-fitted, "no-hole" stockings. A body brace is usually worn over a cotton shirt. It should be applied with the patient lying flat in bed. Back braces are buckled or laced from the bottom up. They are then adjusted as necessary with the patient in standing position.

The use of braces enables many patients who would otherwise be confined to bed or wheelchair to maintain locomotion and varied activity. Sometimes braces may be ungainly, heavy, and uncomfortable, but they are often a blessing in disguise.

Crutches

Often, a patient is required to use crutches, with or without braces, to be ambulatory. The physical therapist is usually responsible for teaching crutch walking and the particular gait best suited to the individual patient. However, the nurse may be asked to measure the patient for crutches and assist him in developing good habits involving their use.

One method of measuring patients for standard-type crutches is to measure the distance from the patient's axilla to the sole of his foot when he is lying flat in bed; then add from 6 to 8 inches to allow for the slant of the crutches away from the body during walking. The nurse should be sure that the rubber guards on the crutch ends are not worn smooth. The patient should not lean on the "armpit rests." The weight of the body should be borne by the hands. It is easier for a patient using crutches to rise from a firm, rather than an overstuffed, chair. When walking with a patient who is learning to use crutches, the nurse should walk behind her patient. In case of difficulty she may grasp the patient by his belt, trousers, or waist.

• • •

Orthopedic nursing can be extremely satisfying. A straightened back and a corrected foot may take much skill, patience, determination, and time to achieve, but they are well worth all the effort involved.

34

Methods of temperature control and therapeutic uses of heat and cold

The regulation of body heat and the effects of localized temperature change on body parts are significant considerations in the medical and nursing care of many patients. The regulation of body temperature through the use of therapy may not only bring greater comfort to the patient but may also avoid complications that occur in the presence of high fever or abnormal loss of body heat.

Occasionally extremes of body temperature have been induced for therapeutic reasons. Local hot and cold applications are commonly used for treatment. Both the regulation of general body temperature and local reactions to temperature extremes will be discussed in the following paragraphs.

Regulation of body temperature
(Figs. 34-1 and 34-2)

Although the normal oral temperature is usually cited as 37° C., or 98.6° F., these figures indicate only the average normal temperature. Oral temperatures ranging from 36.4° to 37.2° C. (97.6° to 99° F.) are not considered abnormal. Rectal temperatures *average* 1° F. higher than oral readings, whereas axillary temperatures register 1° F. lower, *on the average*. Normal body temperature in a human being represents a balance between heat production and heat loss in the body. The main source of body heat is inadvertently created in the process of carrying out normal body functions. Production of body heat is the result of the activity of all cells, made possible by the oxidation, or burning, of food-

stuffs within those cells. Blood, flowing through the various parts of the body, helps distribute heat, and although measured body temperature differs depending on the method by which it is determined (oral, rectal, axillary, or skin probe), the remarkable fact is that these various measurements record temperatures so similar. Body heat is conserved by the involuntary constriction of the blood vessels of the skin, forcing more blood into the warm interior of the body and cutting it off from cooler areas near the skin's surface; it is also conserved by the automatic reduction of perspiration. Of course, the maintenance of body heat is also aided by the voluntary activity of the person. Adding a sweater or coat to provide better insulation or exercising to increase metabolism and circulation increases the tolerance of cold environmental conditions. Much heat is produced through the activity of the skeletal muscles. When additional warmth is necessary, these muscles will even contract involuntarily to produce heat, a process we call shivering. Conversely, removing insulation, increasing surface evaporation, and reducing muscular activity decrease body heat.

Body heat is lost primarily through the dilatation of the capillaries in the skin, the evaporation of increased perspiration on the skin's surface, and the process of warming inspired air, which is subsequently exhaled.

The part of the body that ultimately controls the unconscious processes necessary for the regulation of heat production, heat

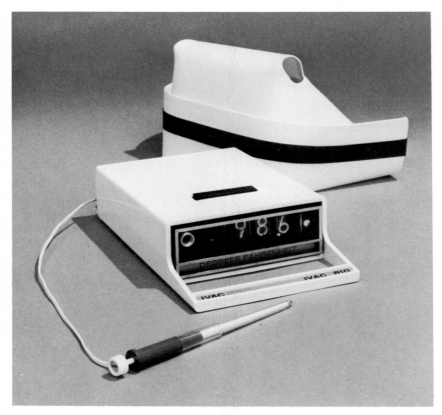

FIG. 34-1. One type of electric thermometer able to register temperatures in seconds. (Courtesy IVAC Corp., San Diego, Calif.)

maintenance, and heat loss is thought to be located deep in the brain. The part of the brain considered most responsible for heat regulation is the hypothalamus, often dubbed the "thermostat" of the body. It probably controls the processes of vasoconstriction and vasodilation, the associated activity of the sweat glands, and the involuntary skeletal muscle motion. Perhaps indirectly it influences the appetite and digestive and metabolic regulation through glandular stimulation or control.

In infants and young children temperature regulation is not perfected, and rather wide swings in body temperature occur readily. During the first days of life an infant is more likely to be influenced by the temperature of his environment, hence the frequent use of incubators. Toddlers and young school-age children often react to the common infectious diseases of child-

hood by running temperatures of 104° F. or more. A child may initiate a temperature elevation during a hard crying spell.

Causes and effects of elevated body temperature

At times a temperature elevation may produce a beneficial effect. In fact, fever is often looked on as a protective mechanism, since it helps kill certain heat-susceptible microorganisms and warns the individual of the possible presence of a pathological process. In the past fever has even been artificially induced in the treatment of certain infectious diseases.

Fever has been described as a resetting of the body's thermostat in response to the presence of toxins produced by infection. Sometimes a fever is dramatically announced by violent chills and shivering. This phenomenon has been explained on

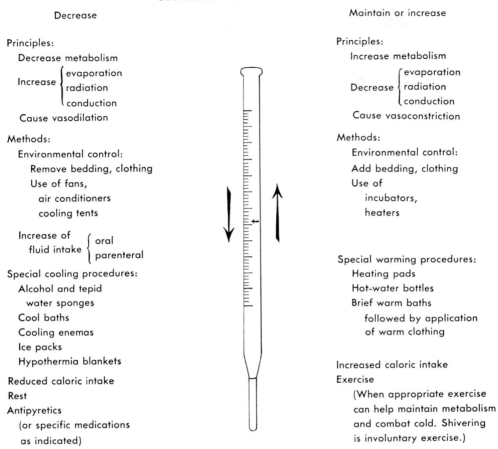

CONTROL OF BODY TEMPERATURE

Decrease

Principles:
Decrease metabolism
Increase { evaporation / radiation / conduction
Cause vasodilation

Methods:
Environmental control:
Remove bedding, clothing
Use of fans,
air conditioners
cooling tents

Increase of fluid intake { oral / parenteral

Special cooling procedures:
Alcohol and tepid
water sponges
Cool baths
Cooling enemas
Ice packs
Hypothermia blankets

Reduced caloric intake
Rest
Antipyretics
(or specific medications
as indicated)

Maintain or increase

Principles:
Increase metabolism
Decrease { evaporation / radiation / conduction
Cause vasoconstriction

Methods:
Environmental control:
Add bedding, clothing
Use of
incubators,
heaters

Special warming procedures:
Heating pads
Hot-water bottles
Brief warm baths
followed by application
of warm clothing

Increased caloric intake
Exercise
(When appropriate exercise
can help maintain metabolism
and combat cold. Shivering
is involuntary exercise.)

FIG. 34-2. In health, the body keeps its temperature within safe ranges. However, during unusual conditions or illness, normal temperature controls may be disturbed, and special regulating measures may be needed.

the basis that the resetting of the body's thermostat interrupts normal heat-dissipating mechanisms. The capillaries at the skin's surface contract, causing the patient to feel cold, and he shivers to reduce the feeling of cold. The muscular activity of shivering further elevates the body temperature. The skin of chilling patients should be kept sufficiently warm to halt shivering while other means of combating excessive internal temperatures or eliminating the initial cause are instituted.

An exaggerated elevated systemic temperature, whether initiated by infectious processes, certain chemicals, or elevated environmental temperatures (heat exhaustion, sunstroke), can cause serious injury, especially if it is prolonged. It can be the cause of dehydration if adequate fluid intake is not maintained. On the other hand, one sign of dehydration from any cause (vomiting, diarrhea, or poor fluid intake) is an abnormal rise in body temperature. A frequent companion to high fever in children is a convulsion. A common phrase in a pediatric setting is "febrile convulsions." The word "febrile" refers to the state of being feverish. A person who has no abnormal temperature elevation may be called "afebrile."

Causes and effects of depressed body temperature

A depressed body temperature may simply reflect inactivity. The early morning temperature reading may be quite low, only because body processes are at a naturally low ebb. However, an abnormally low systemic temperature may also indicate circulatory collapse or the tiring of basic body processes prior to death.

In cases of cardiac and thoracic surgery it may be particularly desirable to slow down metabolism during surgery and postoperative care by cooling the body to extremely low temperatures to rest the heart and respiratory system. The narrowing of the blood vessels in the skin that results from surface cooling forces the blood into the interior of the body, thickens the blood (increases viscosity), slows the blood flow, and necessitates less oxygen intake. Uncompensated by muscle activity, the drop in temperature is of therapeutic importance. At times during chest surgery the surgeon may elect to actually stop the heart and lungs through the combined use of a heart-lung machine and profound hypothermia, which is cooling the bloodstream through the use of a special temperature-regulating attachment. The use of such techniques has been extremely helpful to the surgeon.

Local application of heat

Local application of heat and cold for the treatment of disease may be ancient therapy, but it is also very contemporary. Local heat is frequently ordered to prevent chilling, relieve pain, hasten superficial abscess formation or the drainage of an infected wound, or relieve congestion in one body part by increasing the blood supply to another.

Effects

The primary effect of locally applied heat is vasodilation of the treated area (the skin becomes warm and pink). Locally applied heat also speeds up metabolism; enhances associated muscle relaxation; increases the temperature of the underlying skin, subcutaneous tissue, and muscle; and even raises the skin temperature of remote body areas. Studies have shown that immersion of an arm in a hot soak will raise the temperature of the big toe. There is controversy regarding the degree of reflex vasodilation achieved in *deep* tissues through the application of surface heat. When the effects of heat are desired in the deep-lying organs of the body, diathermy treatments, using high-frequency currents or ultrasound, are often ordered. These treatments are administered using special equipment and are not usually part of the nurse's responsibility. They more properly lie within the sphere of the physical therapist.

Dangers

The surface application of heat is not without danger. The nurse should never apply heat (other than in the form of extra blankets) without a physician's order.

When an internal abscess or localized infection is suspected (such as appendicitis), local heat should never be applied because of danger of rupture, subsequent spread of infection, and peritonitis.

Skin temperatures surpassing 110° F. cause tissue damage. However, compresses or soaks that are prepared with solution above 110° F. do not necessarily raise skin temperatures to 110° F. Skin temperatures depend on the extent of the exposure to heat, considering body area, time, method employed, and temperature of the solution.

Water temperatures have been placed by several authors in the following descriptive classifications:

Neutral (warm)	93° to 98° F.
Hot	98° to 105° F.
Very hot	105° to 115° F.

The area receiving heat treatments should be frequently observed for signs of congestion and tissue damage. The fact that the nerve endings that detect the presence of hot and cold have the capacity to adjust when temperatures are not extreme, becoming less sensitive to variations, should be recognized. Temperatures may be increased to an injurious level unless this loss of sensitivity is recognized. Fair-skinned individuals are more likely to be burned than darkly pigmented individuals and should be observed especially closely. Special precautions should be observed when the area to be treated reveals poor circulation or sensory loss. Patients may sustain tissue damage from burning and not realize that they are being burned because of the lack of feeling in the area. Before the prolonged application of warm, moist compresses, the skin area involved should be protected by a thin coat of petrolatum.

The time interval ordered for heat application should be carefully observed because if significant warmth is applied to a local area longer than approximately an hour (some say 30 to 45 minutes), a reflex vaso-constriction may reduce the blood supply to the area, and a reverse effect may occur.*

Methods

Dry heat. Dry heat may be administered by an electric heating pad, a hot-water bottle, or a unit that circulates warm water through a plastic pad. An electric heating pad is rarely used in a hospital setting because of the danger of electrical malfunction and the problems of maintenance and disinfection. Hot-water bottles are not recommended because of the many instances of accidental burning that have resulted from their use. If hot-water bottles are employed for infants and young children, they should never contain water hotter than 115° F., although temperatures up to 120° F. are permitted for older children and adults. They should be emptied of excess air, tightly stoppered, and turned upside down to check for leaks. A dry, warm cloth cover should be placed on the bottle to provide proper insulation. Hot-water bottles should not be placed between skin surfaces or under the back.

---

*Jensen, J. T.: Introduction to medical physics, Philadelphia, 1960, J. B. Lippincott Co.

The plastic pad containing tubing, through which warm water may be circulated at a preset temperature from a bedside heating unit, has become popular. A well-known appliance of this type is the K-pad (Fig. 34-3). Such an apparatus uses distilled water, which is periodically added to a reservoir at the top of the heating and circulating unit. Warm water is pushed out of the unit, flows through the continuous pattern of tubes embedded in the plastic pad, and returns to the heating unit. No pins should be used in stabilizing the position of the various sized pads available. Pads may be tied or taped in place if they do not become bent, interfering with the circulation of the warm water. Ideally, a pad should be neatly wrapped in a pillowcase or towel and the tubing covered with stockinette. Detailed operating instructions accompany the unit. Another method of applying heat in a small area is the activation of a chemical mixture contained within a waterproof envelope by abruptly striking a premarked spot. These units are convenient, disposable, efficient, but somewhat expensive. (See Fig. 34-4.)

Moist heat. Moist heat therapy is more penetrating and faster acting than dry heat therapy. Moist heat may be applied locally in the form of hot soaks, packs, or compresses.

Hot soaks. If the condition of the young child permits such treatment, soaks of body parts when no open skin areas are involved may be carried out as part of a general bath, depending on the reason for the order. If this is not feasible, basins of water or other ordered solution may be provided at the bedside. If the area to be soaked involves an open lesion or wound that is not too extensive, a sterile container is provided. Sterile water, tap water, or pHiso-Hex and tap water may be ordered. (Tap water from an approved water system is generally accepted as free from disease-producing microorganisms.) However, normal saline solution (properly called physiological saline solution or sodium chloride, 0.9%) is often preferred because it contains

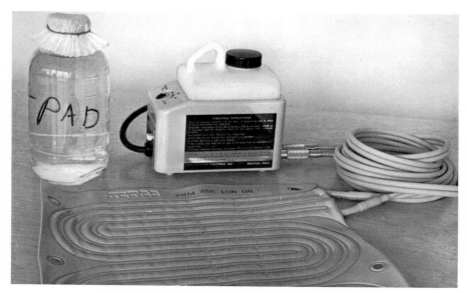

Fig. 34-3. The K-pad circulates distilled water through tubing in a plastic pad at a preset temperature. (Courtesy Grossmont Hospital, La Mesa, Calif.)

Fig. 34-4. New methods of applying heat or cold. The Curity heat lamp warms foil-wrapped sterile compresses. The instant cold and warm packs are activated by striking the dark circles. (Courtesy Grossmont Hospital, La Mesa, Calif.)

approximately the same salt concentration as normal tissue fluid and therefore will not cause abnormal drying or bogginess in the body tissues. Because sterile physiological saline solution is usually readily available in the hospital setting, it is often used for soaks involving small body areas. (Physiological saline may be prepared in the home by adding 2 teaspoons of salt to 1 quart of water.) The temperature of hot soaks for children, unless ordered otherwise, is 105° F. (41° C.). The duration of the soak may vary according to orders, but the treatment is usually prescribed for 20 minutes. When the soak is terminated, any open skin area is dried and dressed as ordered.

Soaks involving large body areas are usuallly carried out in a bathtub. The tub is disinfected before and after use, but the procedure is not really sterile, just clean. Tepid (about 98° F.) body soaks are often ordered for severely burned patients. The soak, in these cases, is not administered as a heat treatment but for the cleansing and debriding action that occurs when the patient's inner dressings are removed in the water and the tub solution agitated. Frequently such soaks, followed by the application of sterile dressings, are performed in a physical therapy department using a whirlpool bath.

Hot packs. Heat applied to the body in the form of packs involves the use of relatively heavy, moist pieces of flannel, which, when properly insulated, hold heat for considerable periods. Since the dramatic decrease in poliomyelitis, hot packs are seldom ordered. In the past they were quite commonly used to relieve muscle spasm.

Hot compresses. Hot or warm compresses, however, are commonly part of a nurse's responsibilities. They may be applied to speed superficial abscess formation, promote wound drainage, or improve circulation. If the skin in the area to be compressed is broken, sterile gauze is used. The following are general suggestions for warm compress application (usually several alternatives in procedure are available):

1. The procedure should be explained to

the patient according to his ability to understand and cooperate.
2. The area under the body part to be compressed should be protected by a clean, waterproof material overlaid by an absorbent towel or bath blanket.
3. The sterile gauze pads may be placed in a hot (110° to 115° F.) sterile solution as ordered (usually physiological saline) and wrung with two sterile forceps until dripping stops. The pads may be placed on the designated area and replaced with new compresses about every 2 minutes.
4. In areas where the additional weight will not cause pain or injury, two or three warm compresses may be quickly covered by sterile, lightweight waterproof plastic and the body part wrapped or covered by an insulating towel warmed by an overlying K-pad, a hot-water bottle, or a low-set electric pad.
5. In another method of preparing hot, moist compresses the dry compresses are placed over the area and irrigated with warm solution using a sterile syringe. The compresses are either changed periodically or wrapped as previously described.

Clean warm compresses are applied in much the same manner, except that sterile precautions need not be observed. Wriggly toddlers usually need to have the compresses gently tied in place and fairly constant nursing attendance to prevent the dismantling of the nurse's handiwork. Great care should be taken not to burn the child. When no open skin area is involved, petrolatum may be ordered applied to the skin prior to the compresses to avoid injury. The child should not be left in a position in which he may come into direct contact with the hot water used for heating the compresses.

Local application of cold
Effects

The local application of cold may also be therapeutic. Cold applied to the skin

477

surface for brief periods (30 to 45 minutes) produces vasoconstriction of the area treated, which helps in the prevention (but not treatment) of swelling, the control of hemorrhage, and the retardation of any inflammatory process. Cold applied for a sufficient period will significantly cool muscles and other underlying organs, either directly or by reflex action. Cold also has an anesthetic quality that may sometimes become of primary importance. The use of ice cubes in the treatment of minor burns illustrates both the anesthetic and vasoconstrictive effects of cold. If applied to the skin for longer periods, cold may trigger a reverse reflex mechanism that results in vasodilation. A corresponding reverse reflex mechanism was noted in the discussion of the effects of the local application of heat.

Dangers

The local use of cold applications, like that of heat, is not without hazard. The skin surface must be frequently observed for mottling and tissue damage. Cold applied to areas in which circulation is inadequate may produce injury (frostbite) and lead to gangrene. The anesthetic quality of cold may make the patient unaware of injury inadvertently produced by other factors.

Methods

Like heat, cold may be used therapeutically in dry or moist form. Moist cold is more penetrating than dry cold.

Dry cold. An example of the application of dry cold would be the typical ice bag or ice collar. Some of these, like the Freez-A-Bag, are prefilled and sealed. Others must be filled. Using small cubes and a small amount of cold water, fill the bag two-thirds full, press out any air (it delays the transfer of cold), and cap the bag. The bag should be wrapped in a cover to prevent condensation from wetting the patient or bedding. For effective local reaction an ice cap or ice bag should be removed approximately every 30 to 45 minutes to observe and allow the skin to return to nor-

mal and enable the cold to continue its process of vasoconstriction when reapplied.

Moist cold. Moist cold may be applied in the form of cold, damp compresses, cold soaks, or sponge baths.

Cold compresses. One may remember the Sunday comic strips, picturing moist cold in the form of raw steak being applied to black eyes to prevent swelling. Steak is a rather expensive compress, however!

If the body part compressed can tolerate weight, clean cold compresses are best made from washcloths or towels. If a delicate organ like an eye or an extremely tender body part is to be treated, gauze compresses may be used. The adjoining area is protected by a waterproof plastic or rubber sheet lined with an absorbent layer. A basin of water and ice, large enough to accommodate the compresses, should be at hand. The compresses should be wrung out well to avoid dripping. A cold compress is left exposed. Covering it would soon make it only tepid as a result of the heating capability of the body. The compresses have to be changed frequently, depending on their size and density and the temperature of the body part to which they are applied.

It is difficult to apply sterile cold compresses because ice is not sterile. However, if sterile technique is necessary, sterile cold solutions may be maintained in a refrigerator and the sterile container packed in ice at the bedside during the treatment. Sterile compresses may be handled in an aseptic manner with forceps or gloves. We do not recommend the use of forceps around the eyes and faces of young children in the usual bedside setting. Their movements are too unpredictable. Wearing gloves is much less cumbersome and is safer.

Light gauze compresses must usually be changed about every minute to maintain their temperature. If any drainage or open skin area is present, the compress should not be reused but discarded.

Cold soaks. Cold soaks, often recommended to prevent the swelling of a twisted or sprained ankle, usually consist of cold water in a basin into which an extremity is placed for about 20-minute intervals. Occasionally alternating cold and hot soaks are ordered to stimulate circulation.

Sponge baths. Alcohol solution sponge baths and tepid water sponge baths are fairly frequent procedures in a pediatric setting. Sponge baths use the following four basic techniques in reducing systemic body heat:

1. Friction before or during the cool sponging produces greater vasodilation that, when combined with the heat loss caused by evaporation, increases cooling.

2. Strategic positioning of cool cloths over areas where large blood vessels approach the surface of the body (e.g., in the axilla and groin) hastens cooling of the blood.

3. Placement of an ice cap to the head reduces cerebral temperature and lessens the danger of convulsion.

4. Light covering of the part of the body not being sponged and the use of solutions that are not excessively cold protect the patient from chilling. If the patient shivers for a prolonged period as the result of his abrupt exposure to cold, the shivering may actually maintain or raise his temperature. Some texts recommend the application of a warm-water bottle or other dry heat source to the feet of the patient to prevent excessive chilling.

An alcohol sponge bath is ordered in response to an elevated temperature; therefore checks of temperature, pulse, and respiration would normally precede it.

ALCOHOL OR TEPID WATER SPONGE BATH

Purposes: To reduce body temperature and relieve discomfort.

Materials:
1. Waterproof sheet
2. Absorbent bath blanket or towels, depending on the size of the child
3. Light bath blanket to place over the patient
4. Basin of solution

a. Tepid or cool water at approximately 70° to 80° F. or solution of alcohol, 25% to 50%, and water at approximately 80° F. (Alcohol evaporates rapidly and promotes cooling more rapidly than tepid water alone.)
b. Small supply of ice to add to the sponging solution, if necessary
5. Four washcloths
6. Wrapped Freez-A-Bag or ice cap for the head (Some hospitals do not include this as part of the procedure.)

Procedure:
1. Explain the procedure to the patient as much as possible.
2. Place the child on top of a waterproof sheeting and absorbent blanket (unless this is already part of the base of his bed) fairly close to the side of the bed so that he may be easily reached. Remove any pillows.
3. Undress the child except for diaper or loincloth and cover him with the light bath blanket.
4. Place the ice cap or Freez-A-Bag under the child's head.
5. Rub the skin of the anterior trunk and extremities briefly with a dry washcloth to bring the blood to the surface, decreasing the sensation of chilling and aiding in heat reduction when the cool moist washcloths are applied.
6. Place cool, moist, but not dripping, folded washcloths on the axilla and groin on the side of the child that you will sponge last.
7. Wash the patient's face and neck with the solution.
8. Expose only the area being sponged. Use firm, long strokes in sponging the upper extremity, thorax, abdomen, and lower extremity on the side farthest from you. Place the washcloths on the groin and axilla of the opposite side. Continue sponging the patient, first the upper extremity, then the thorax, abdomen, and lower extremity.
9. During the sponge bath, periodically evaluate the patient's reaction. How are his color, pulse, and respiration? If he seems to be chilling or shivering excessively or other untoward reactions occur, stop the treatment and cover the patient. Report reactions to the supervising nurse.
10. Turn the patient on his side. Rub and sponge his back firmly.
11. Gently pat the skin dry at the end of the sponge bath with a towel and dress the child in a light gown. The sponge bath should take about 20 to 25 minutes.
12. Cover the child with a light sheet or blanket. Remove the bed protectors and encourage rest.

13. Take the patient's temperature, pulse, and respiration 30 minutes after the sponge bath and report them to the supervising nurse or physician.
14. Record the procedure, the patient's reaction, and the results.

Reduction of body temperature

A sponge bath is only one method of reducing temperature, and it is usually not the first or only method employed. There are approximately seven basic ways in which one may try to reduce fever or lower body temperature.

Fluid intake

The first method of body temperature reduction involves encouraging fluid intake. It has already been noted that fever may result from dehydration. If oral fluids are impractical because of the state of the gastrointestinal tract or exaggerated body need, many times fluids must be administered intravenously.

Environmental control

Body temperature may be lowered and the patient made more comfortable by attention to the immediate environment. The removal of extra blankets and heavy clothing (unless the patient is complaining of chills and shivering) is often helpful. A well-ventilated, draft-free room may also be an aid. In warm weather well-placed fans, which circulate the air without blowing on the patient directly, may be used.

Medication

Medication may be ordered to help reduce fever; such medications are called *antipyretics*. The most frequently prescribed medication is, of course, acetylsalicylic acid, commonly known as aspirin. Aspirin is also used for its analgesic effect. It seems to reduce temperature chiefly by producing greater amounts of perspiration and, therefore, greater cooling by evaporation. Adult dosage of aspirin is usually 10 grains every 4 hours, although for certain conditions the dosage may be raised considerably, usually without the appearance of toxic symptoms.

Aspirin dosage for children is considerably less. It may be ordered in suppository form or crushed and given with small amounts of syrup or jelly. Flavored aspirin designed specifically for children has been on the market for a considerable time. It is usually available in the form of small, orange-flavored tablets of 1¼ grains per tablet. Most children who can chew and swallow well have no objection to aspirin in this form. In fact, they may like it too well. Despite tight capping, many little hands have gotten into the supply of household aspirin with disastrous results. Salicylate poisoning is an extremely common diagnosis in a hospital emergency room. Every safety precaution must be taken to teach childen what medicines are and to keep medicines out of reach in a safe place—preferably locked. Children's aspirin must be packaged with not more than thirty-six tablets to each bottle. (For aspirin dosage and treatment of salicylate poisoning, see pp. 327 and 574.)

Sponge bath and tepid bath

Tepid water or alcohol sponge baths are also administered to reduce fever; these have already been described. Sometimes the child will be placed in a tepid tub bath, especially if the child is not sufficiently responsive to other therapy. The child should never be left alone while undergoing such treatment.

Cooling enema

Another method that has been used to reduce fever is the cooling enema. This procedure usually consists of the intermittent administration of cool tap water per rectum. The infant and toddler has little or no sphincter control, and the solution usually returns fairly quickly even before the entire amount to be given is administered. When treating children of this age group, it is usually unrealistic to speak of clamping the tube for several minutes and then siphoning out the remainder of the fluid before repeating the process. However, even the brief introduction of cool fluid into the lower gastrointestinal tract may prove helpful if the child does not become too upset. Infants under 6 months of age usually do not tolerate more than 100 ml. of fluid administered at one time. Infants 6 months and older or toddlers usually are not given more than 250 ml. at one time. Physicians should be encouraged to write enema orders for young children that include the amount of solution to be given.

COOLING ENEMA

Purpose: To reduce fever.

Materials:

1. Rectal catheter or tubing and clamps, appropriately sized
   a. For infant, size 12 to 16 French
   b. For young child, size 12 to 20 French
   c. For older child, size 16 to 22 French
2. Container of ordered solution (for cooling enemas usually tepid or cool tap water)
3. Lubricant and wipes
4. Asepto syringe barrel or enema can or bag, depending on the amount of fluid to be given and the size of the child

Procedure:

1. Explain to the child, if possible, what will be done. Understanding will not be complete, of course, but the tone of voice employed and the socialization such explana-

tion offers can be helpful. Telling a small child that you are "going to put a little water in where we take your temperature to make you cooler" sometimes helps.

2. Assemble the correct equipment and type and amount of solution.

3. Prepare the unit and position the child. A number of positions are advocated when giving an infant or toddler an enema. The following suggestions may be helpful:

   a. For most children the side position with the upper leg flexed seems to be the most comfortable. The left side is preferred because this placement puts the descending colon lowest. However, a left-sided position is not absolutely mandatory. In fact, investigators question the supposed advantage of left-sided placement. Infants and small toddlers often do well if placed on a firm pillow, draped with lightweight plastic and covered by an absorbent towel, with their hips pulled to the edge. The plastic extends over the side of the pillow into or beside a curved basin or small bedpan, which is placed snugly against the buttocks just below the rectum. For warmth the child is covered by a bath blanket or towel.

   b. If the infant is very active and a nurse has no one to help maintain the side position of the child, he may be gently restrained in supine position over a small bedpan. His back and head are supported by a small pillow or folded bath blanket.

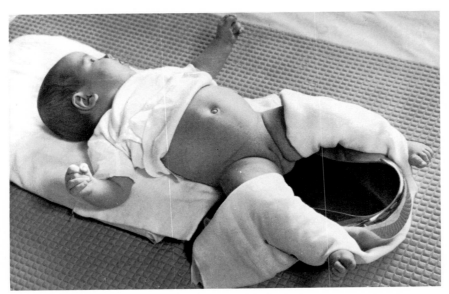

Fig. 34-5. One way of positioning an infant for an enema. The restraining diaper is centered under the tip of the pan and then brought up and over the infant's legs and pinned to itself.

His buttocks are placed over the bedpan, and his legs gently drawn to either side and secured by a diaper placed under the bedpan and drawn up and over the lower extremities and pinned to itself as illustrated in Fig. 34-5.

c. Older children with sphincter control are usually positioned on their sides and given enemas basically the same way as any adult.

4. Expel the air from the rectal tube and lubricate the tip of the catheter. Do not occlude the eyes of the catheter.

5. Gently insert the tubing 2 to 3 inches into the rectum and observe the flow. Hold the container of solution no higher than 12 to 18 inches above the patient's hips.

6. Infants and young toddlers usually do not have repeated instillations of fluid. However, older children who have sphincter control may have repeated instillations. When multiple small enemas are desired, a type of intermittent enema setup may be constructed using a Y tube for administration of clear fluid and disposal of the evacuated fluid. Another technique is to lower the can and, after several minutes, clamp the tube close to the can. The can is then emptied and refilled with cool solution, which is administered to the child. The patient must be closely observed during the procedure for an increase in respiratory and pulse rates and exhaustion.

7. Check the efficiency of the enema(s) by taking the child's temperature 30 minutes after the termination of the treatment.

Hypothermia blankets

Patients with temperature elevations that are exaggerated or fail to respond to other methods of treatment may be placed on so-called hypothermia blankets—a sort of K-pad in reverse (Fig. 34-6).

There are several hypothermia blankets manufactured. Although the operating instructions on each may differ, the principles involved are similar. Cold, distilled water or alcohol and distilled water (depending on the model) are circulated through tubes embedded in a plastic mat or mats. The water is cooled and circulated by a refrigeration pump unit to which the pads are attached. With some units, adjustment of the pad temperature is accomplished manually by the nurse, depending on the temperature of the patient. With others, a rectal probe is inserted, which enables the patient's temperature to be continually monitored. The temperature of the patient revealed by the probe may regulate the temperature of the pads au-

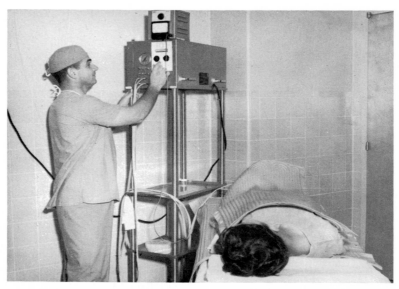

Fig. 34-6. This photograph illustrates one type of hypothermia blanket and control unit. The bath blankets, which usually cover the pads, have been removed to permit a better view. (Courtesy Children's Health Center, San Diego, Calif.)

tomatically, according to predetermined temperature settings. Several pads of various sizes may be used, both under and over the patient according to his needs. There is always a light bath blanket or sheet between the patient and the plastic pad. The pad should not be folded or creased, and no pins should be used to secure them. The temperature desired and the time it should be maintained should be ordered by the attending physician.

Ice packs

If a hypothermia blanket is unavailable and there is a sufficient quantity of ice, patients may be placed in a bathtub, one-fourth full of ice. The use of two bath blankets is recommended. The bed of ice is covered by one half the width of the bath blanket. The other half is rolled to the side to cover the patient when he is placed in the tub. The patient himself is wrapped in a second bath blanket before he is placed in the tub. He is lowered onto the bath blanket covering the ice. The upper layer of bath blanket is adjusted over the supine patient, and the blanket covered with approximately 2 inches of crushed ice. Water is added to make the whole ice pack wet. The temperature of the patient must be taken frequently. Checks for excessive shivering and deviations in pulse and respiration are made often. When the desired temperature reduction is secured, the patient may be returned to bed with ice packs. The length of such a procedure depends on the physician's order and the reaction of the patient.

Raising of body temperature

At times it becomes the duty of the nurse to carry out techniques to maintain or raise body temperature. This may be done to provide comfort, regulate metabolism, or combat exposure. It may be accomplished most simply by increasing room temperatures, applying more blankets, adding clothing, and offering warm but not hot drinks. In the home situation, placing a child who has been chilled in a *brief* warm bath, dressing him warmly, and tucking him in bed is a time-honored technique.

An infant is most easily warmed by the use of an incubator—a cozy box supplied with a built-in heating unit, a thermometer, and a humidity source—or one of the radiant heat infant warmers. In an emergency situation in which no incubator is available the warmest place for a newborn infant would be directly next to his mother, who could share her own body heat.

The application of local heat is helpful in raising total body temperature. We have previously described the use of hot-water bottles and various heating pads. Some hypothermia blankets may be regulated to function like giant heating blankets.

• • •

The local use of heat or cold applications can be of strategic importance in patient care. It may involve old principles, but they have proved worthy of our study and application.

UNIT X

SUGGESTED SELECTED READINGS AND REFERENCES

Aufhauser, T. R.: Parent participation in the hospital care of children, Nurs. Outlook 15:40+, Jan., 1967.

Barness, L. A., and Young, L. N.: A simplified view of fluid therapy, Pediat. Clin. N. Amer. 11:3-15, 1964.

Blake, F. G., Wright, F. H., and Waechter, E. H.: Nursing care of children, Philadelphia, 1970, J. B. Lippincott Co.

Brunell, P. A., editor: Symposium on laboratory diagnosis, Pediat. Clin. N. Amer. 18:entire volume, 1971.

Clifton, J.: Collecting 24 hour urine specimens from infants, Amer. J. Nurs. 69:1660+, Aug., 1969.

Egan, D. F.: Fundamentals of inhalation therapy, St. Louis, 1969, The C. V. Mosby Co.

Flatter, P. A.: Hazards of oxygen therapy, Amer. J. Nurs. 68:80+, Jan., 1968.

Flitter, H. H., and Rowe, H. R.: An introduction to physics in nursing, ed. 5, St. Louis, 1967, The C. V. Mosby Co.

French, R. M.: Nurse's guide to diagnostic procedures, ed. 2, New York, 1966, McGraw-Hill Book Co.

Fuerst, E. V., and Wolff, L.: Fundamentals of nursing, ed. 4, Philadelphia, 1969, J. B. Lippincott Co.

Garb, S.: Laboratory tests in common use, ed. 4, New York, 1967, Springer Publishing Co., Inc.

Geis, D. P., and Lombertz, S. E.: Acute respiratory infections in young children, Amer. J. Nurs. 68:294+, Feb., 1968.

Gross, R. E.: An atlas of children's surgery, Philadelphia, 1970, W. B. Saunders Co.

Hughes, W. T.: Pediatric procedures, Philadelphia, 1964, W. B. Saunders Co.

Hymovich, D. P.: ABC's of pediatric safety, Amer. J. Nurs. 66:1768-1769, Aug., 1966.

Kelly, A. E.: Current cardiovascular diagnostic measures and associated nursing care, J. Nurs. Education 5:13+, Nov., 1966.

Kelly, A. E.: Mist therapy, Pediatrics 39:160+, 1967.

Kerr, A.: Orthopedic nursing procedures, ed. 2, New York, 1969, Springer Publishing Co., Inc.

Kurihara, M.: Postural drainage, clapping and vibrating, Amer. J. Nurs. 65:76-79, Nov., 1965.

Larson, C. B., and Gould, M.: Orthopedic nursing, ed. 7, St. Louis, 1970, The C. V. Mosby Co.

Leifer, G.: Principles and techniques in pediatric nursing, Philadelphia, 1965, W. B. Saunders Co.

Madore, E. C., and Deutsch, Y. B.: Talking with parents, Amer. J. Nurs. 62:108-111, Nov., 1962.

Petrillo, M.: Respiratory tract aspiration: Programmed instruction, Amer. J. Nurs. 66:2483+, Nov., 1966.

Petrillo, M.: Preventing hospital trauma in pediatric patients, Amer. J. Nurs. 68:1468+, July, 1968.

Pringle, J. A.: Respiratory distress unit, Amer. J. Nurs. 68:2370-2373, Nov., 1968.

Raffensperger, J. G., and Primrose, R. B., editors: Pediatric surgery for nurses, Boston, 1968, Little, Brown & Co.

Sacharin, R. M., and Hunter, M. H. S.: Pediatric nursing procedures, Baltimore, 1969, The Williams & Wilkins Co.

Sato, F.: New devices for continuous urine collection in pediatrics, Amer. J. Nurs. 69:805+, April, 1969.

Secor, J.: Patient care in respiratory problems, Philadelphia, 1969, W. B. Saunders Co.

Silver, H. K., Kempe, C. H., and Bruyn, H. B.: Handbook of pediatrics, ed. 8, Los Altos, Calif., 1969, Lange Medical Publications.

Sutton, A.: Bedside nursing techniques in medicine and surgery, ed. 2, Philadelphia, 1969, W. B. Saunders Co.

Tate, G., Gohrke, C., and Mansfield, L. W.: Correct use of electric thermometers, Amer. J. Nurs. 70:1898+, Sept., 1970.

Tepe, P.: A physiological approach to pediatric medicines, Nurs. Clin. N. Amer. 1:111+, March, 1966.

Totman, L. E., and Lehman, R. H.: Tracheostomy care, Amer. J. Nurs. 64:96+, March, 1964.

Webb, C.: Tactics to reduce a child's fear of pain, Amer. J. Nurs. 66:2698, Dec., 1966.

Wu, R.: Explaining treatments to young children, Amer. J. Nurs. 65:71+, July, 1965.

UNIT XI

COMMON PEDIATRIC PROBLEMS AND THEIR NURSING CARE

35

Conditions involving the integumentary system

The integumentary system consists of more than just the skin; it also includes the hair, nails, sweat and oil glands, and superficial sensory nerve endings. These organs form the first line of defense against body injury. The integumentary system prevents both excessive loss of fluid from the body and the entry of certain poisons and microbes into the body. It is of special importance in the regulation of body temperature, principally through capillary dilatation and constriction and the formation of cooling perspiration. It is of considerable aid in the evaluation of environmetal conditions and therefore in the determination of individual safety. Embedded within the tissues of the integumentary system are nerve endings, which relay to the brain sensations of pressure, touch, hot, cold, and pain. The skin can be an important avenue of fluid loss. However, it has only limited powers of absorption.

The health of the skin is often a reflection of the health of the individual. Skin color, hydration, and the presence of detectable surface irregularities and disturbances in sensation may reveal significant information about an individual's health habits and status. The skin may also give clues to a patient's emotional reactions. Involuntarily, we may blush with embarrassment or pale with fright.

The epidermis is paper thin, and it consists of several microscopic layers. The uppermost layer consists of dead cells ready to be shed from the body's surface. They are constantly being replaced by new cells, which are formed in the lower layers. The lower layers of the epidermis secure their nourishment from the dermis, or true skin, over which they lie.

The dermis, also called the *corium,* is a dense layer of connective tissue well supplied with blood vessels and nerves. It also contains sweat and oil glands and hair follicles, some of which may extend into the deeper subcutaneous tissue. Small muscle fibers may be attached to the hair follicles.

The subcutaneous tissue is noted for the presence of fatty tissue in a framework of elastic and fibrous tissue. It serves to connect the skin to the superficial muscles. (See Fig. 35-1.)

The observation of the skin and the description of its condition is often the responsibility of the nurse. Her patients may not be hospitalized primarily because of skin problems. Skin difficulties may be, at times, of secondary importance in the diagnostic picture. However, the condition of the skin is always of significance as the nurse views her patient's total needs.

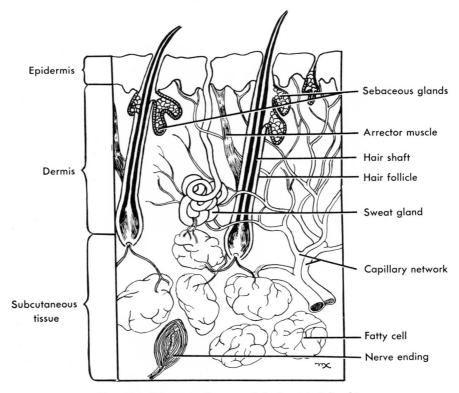

Epidermis

Dermis

Subcutaneous
tissue

Sebaceous glands

Arrector muscle

Hair shaft

Hair follicle

Sweat gland

Capillary network

Fatty cell

Nerve ending

FIG. 35-1. Schematic drawing of the layers of the skin.

Key vocabulary

Certain terminology to aid in the description of the condition of the skin is used commonly by physicians. Some of the words the nurse may wish to use in her own recording. Others she may not choose to employ, but she should be able to interpret their meaning. Some of these commonly used terms, simply defined, are as follows:

abrasion (adj., abraded) loss of superficial tissue by friction (chafing).

contusion (adj., contused) a bruise; a black-and-blue mark.

crust (adj., crusted) the temporary covering of a lesion formed primarily by dried blood or serum (scab).

ecchymosis (adj., ecchymotic) a black-and-blue mark.

erythema (adj., erythematous) a reddened area of the skin.

excoriation (adj., excoriated) a superficial laceration; a scratch.

jaundice or *icterus* (adj., jaundiced or icteric) a yellow tinge to the skin or sclerae.

laceration (adj., lacerated) a jagged cut or tear.

lesion any change or irregularity in tissue caused by disease or injury.

macule (adj., macular) a flat spot or stain; the typical measles rash is macular.

papule (adj., papular) a small, solid elevation on the skin; the typical early stage of a pimple is papular.

petechia (adj., petechial) a small bluish purple dot caused by capillary hemorrhage.

pruritus (adj., pruritic) itching.

pustule (adj., pustular) a pus-filled papule; a superficial cutaneous abscess.

ulcer (adj., ulcerated) a raw area often depressed or forming a cavity, caused by loss of normal covering tissue.

urticaria (wheals and hives) (adj., urticarial) large, slightly raised reddened or blanched areas, often accompanied by intense itching.

vesicle (adj., vesicular) a small elevation of the skin obviously containing fluid such as a blister.

A skin lesion should be described in such a way that the following information is included:

1. Size of the lesion(s) (pinpoint, dime

sized, approximately ¼ inch in diameter, etc.)

2. Elevation (raised, flat, depressed)
3. Quality (smooth, rough, scaly, moist)
4. Color
5. Distribution (localized, scattered, etc.)
6. Associated sensory disturbances (numbness, itching, pain, burning, etc.)
7. Type of any drainage or exudate noted

Common skin problems of the infant and toddler

Miliaria rubra (prickly heat, or heat rash)

Miliaria rubra is a common problem caused by blockage of the sweat pores. The exits of the sweat ducts are plugged, causing sweat to seep into the dermis or epidermis. This produces a red, pinhead-sized vesicular-papular rash associated with underlying erythema, especially in areas where perspiration is common or friction is frequent. It may be accompanied by considerable itching. Occasionally the rash may include pustular lesions. Prevention is easier than treatment; avoid overdressing children. Any procedure that will reduce the need for perspiration will help improve the condition. Light dusting of the skin with a fine cornstarch or baby powder may be beneficial. Some dermatologists may recommend the use of a skin lotion containing menthol and camphor. In the event of secondary infection an antibiotic drug may be prescribed.

Intertrigo

Intertrigo is often simply called *chafing*. It is commonly found in the folds of the skin where friction is frequent and hygiene may be lacking; examples of problem areas include the creases in the neck and in the folds of the groin and gluteus muscles, where the skin may become quite inflamed. As in miliaria rubra, prevention is more simple than cure. Meticulous hygiene and keeping the area dry and lightly powdered is of great importance.

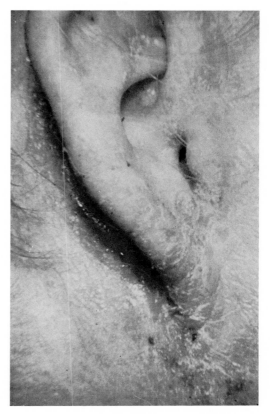

FIG. 35-2. Seborrheic dermatitis. (Courtesy W. W. Duemling, M.D., San Diego, Calif.)

Seborrheic dermatitis (Fig. 35-2)

Seborrheic dermatitis is characterized by a chronic scaling eruption, most often found in hairy areas or in areas bordering hair growth. When the condition involves the scalp, the common name is *dandruff*. It commonly is found in areas well supplied with oil glands. In older children it often creates scaling behind the ears, in the eyebrows, and on the chest and shoulders. In adolescents it is often associated with acne. In infants seborrheic dermatitis is seen most commonly as "milk crust" or "cradle cap," yellowish, slightly adherent large scales found principally on the top of the head. It sometimes is related to a reluctance on the part of the mother to wash the soft spot on the baby's scalp for fear of causing injury. It also develops fairly often in the groin and may become secondarily infected with yeast (*Candida* or *Monilia*) or bacteria. Frequent shampooing and the use of mild medications containing sulfur, salicylic acid, or coal tar are often prescribed for seborrheic dermatitis.

Diaper rash

Infants who have diaper rash are quite often victims of seborrhea. The rash may take multiple forms from simple erythema to blisters and ulceration, depending on the causes. As a group, children with irritation of the diaper area usually have sensitive skins—a predisposition said to be inherited. Unfavorable conditions quickly trigger an unfavorable response. Situations that often set the scene for skin problems are poorly washed and rinsed diapers, infrequent diaper changes aggravated by prolonged use of plastic diaper covers, and incomplete or infrequent washing and drying of the diaper area. Careful attention to cleanliness is necessary. However, overzealous ministrations can cause problems, too!

To reduce the formation of irritating ammonia produced by the action of bacteria on urine, every effort is made to cut down the bacterial population on the diaper area. The use of a gentle antiseptic final rinse, like methylbenzethonium chloride (Diaparene), is often recommended. The use of antiseptic rinses by diaper laundries is standard practice.

The cautious application of heat to diaper rash often improves the skin condition. A gooseneck lamp with a 25-watt bulb may be positioned over the prone infant. Precautions against burning should be observed. The lamp should be out of the child's reach and away from the bed linens. The bulb should be at least 12 inches from the child's buttocks. During heat treatments the diaper area should be free of ointments. If the application of heat is difficult, simply exposing the area to the air is frequently helpful. Sunshine, if present, can be used for brief periods, but an infant should be carefully watched for overexposure.

A fine baby powder to decrease area moisture is usually an aid. Certain antibacterial and vitamin-enriched topical medications may be ordered. Often prescribed are A and D ointment, Polysporin, nystatin, and hexachlorophene-containing products, depending on the needs of the particular patient.

Infantile eczema (atopic dermatitis) (Fig. 35-3)

Infantile eczema most often appears between the first and the sixth month. In most cases it has subsided considerably by 2 years of age. It is characterized by skin lesions, which first present themselves as localized, swollen, red areas usually on the head, neck, wrists, elbows, and knees, although involvement may become progressively more extensive. Fairly rapidly, small vesicles, which break and weep a yellow, sticky fluid, develop in these reddened areas. The fluid dries, forming crusts or scales on the skin. The skin may become thickened and fissured. Since itching is in-

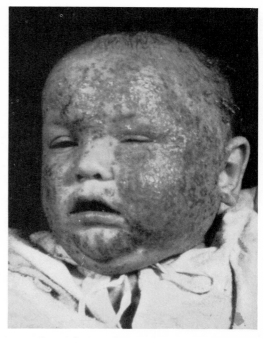

Fig. 35-3. Infant with severe eczema. (Courtesy R. B. Pappenfort, M.D., San Diego, Calif.)

tense, the child invariably scratches the lesions, and thus secondary infection is usually present. Lesions on various parts of the body may be in different stages of development—some quite moist, others dried and scaling. For this reason different types of topical medications may be applied to the parts of the body, depending on the aims of the treatment. Seborrheic dermatitis and fungal infections may be associated with atopic dermatitis. Permanent scarring does not occur.

Infantile eczema is considered to be an essentially allergic response. It is, more properly, a symptom of a disorder rather than the disorder itself. Infantile eczema has been called the most frequent manifestation of the allergic state in infancy. It is not always clear, however, just what agents, or *allergens*, cause the dermatitis. Allergens may be contacted in the following ways:

1. Eaten (common foods causing difficulties in infancy are cow's milk, egg whites, wheat products, and citrus juices)
2. Inhaled (dust, pollen, animal dander)
3. Touched (wool, nylon, plastic)

Many investigators believe that child-parent relationships and emotional stress play a significant role in the initiation and course of the disease. There is often a family history of allergy manifested by eczema, asthma, or hay fever. Eczema usually improves during the summer months and worsens during the winter. The infants affected usually appear well nourished, and some tend to be overweight.

Many factors must be considered in the treatment of eczema. If possible, the offending allergens should be identified and eliminated from the infant's environment. Secondary infection, if present, should be treated, and itching, scratching and exposure to known infections should be avoided. Treatment of the lesions to clear scaling, minimize discomfort, and improve appearance is continued. Psychologically, supportive care for the child and his family is of great importance.

To identify those substances that help to initiate the dermatitis, a careful history is taken by the physician. Usually an elimination diet is prescribed in which the foods that are allowed are listed in detail. If the baby is not breast-fed, evaporated milk, goat's milk, or soybean milk may be prescribed. The importance of rigidly following the diet must be impressed on the parents. As time goes on more foods are added, one by one, to the diet. The child is carefully observed for changes in his skin condition and general health after each addition.

The home environment of the infant must be carefully controlled also. Since many of these little patients show sensitivity to dust, their nurseries are stripped of all drapes, rugs, and fuzzy toys. The crib mattress is encased in a nonallergenic cover, and wool blankets or clothing are eliminated. Although infants do not usually have pets, the presence of a dog or cat in the household may cause significant problems, and so, sad to relate, pets must sometimes find new homes. However, fish and turtles generally do not cause allergies. The house should be frequently vacuumed with special attention to the child's sleeping quarters. Skin testing, with special patches and scratch techniques, in an effort to determine allergens is usually reserved for older children.

A child with eczema should *not* be vaccinated against smallpox because of the great danger of the virus spreading to the open lesions and causing a serious complication called *generalized vaccinia*. For the same reason he should not be allowed to be with children who have themselves been recently vaccinated. Other immunizations are recommended, however. The eczema patient should also be protected against deliberate contact with people who have staphylococcal, streptococcal, or viral infections such as herpes simplex (the cause of the common fever blister). In many hospitals the child with eczema is placed on isolation precautions; however, routine isolation creates problems of its own—psychological stress and financial strain!

To help reduce the possibility of secondary infection by scratching, various methods are used. Efforts are made to decrease the itching by the use of a minimum of clothing, all softly textured. Diapers are changed frequently. Fingernails and toenails are trimmed short.

Different types of medications are used. Systemic antihistaminic drugs may be tried. Sedation may be ordered to allow the infant to sleep. Oral penicillin may be useful in combating secondary infection. Bacitracin and neomycin are recommended for local application for the same reason. Various topical ointments containing hydrocortisone may be used to reduce inflammatory response if infection is not present.

Coal tar and zinc oxide combinations are popular agents to help clear the affected areas. If coal tar preparations are used, care should be taken that the areas not be exposed to sunshine because a chemical reaction, which in itself is irritating to the skin, may take place. Jars containing coal tar ointments should be tightly closed to prevent deterioration. Coal tar ointment should be removed in special baths or with liquid petrolatum before a new application is made.

Ointments are applied with clean hands or a finger cot or glove. They are generally used on a small area on a trial basis to test skin reaction. Many of these medications are expensive. Do not be wasteful.

Mattresses are often covered by a smooth plastic, such as clear x-ray film, to prevent scratching by rubbing against the sheeting. Parents should be cautioned not to use lightweight plastic bags, such as those used by dry cleaning establishments, because of the danger of accidental suffocation. Of course, if the baby is also allergic to plastic, forget about this method!

Usually the baby's arms and, perhaps, feet will have to be restrained in some way. Elbow restraints are preferable if they are sufficient, since some motion is still possible with their use. However, many times they do not provide enough protection; the child may quickly learn to rub his chin with his shoulder. Wrist restraints may be necessary. The child should be closely supervised to see that the restraints accomplish the intended purpose. Periodic supervised exercise of an extremity that has been restrained is necessary to prevent circulatory problems, pressure areas, and stiffness. The child needs to be picked up during the day and cuddled and loved. Rooming-in for the mother should be seriously considered. It must be very trying, both physically and emotionally, to have an itch and not be able to scratch it!

Sometimes special baths or soaks are prescribed for the infant to help remove crusts and reduce pruritus. Common ingredients are cornstarch or oatmeal preparations such as Aveeno or bicarbonate of soda solutions. The water should be tepid, about 95° F. If possible, a small baby bathtub should be used. Sometimes the skin of the infant is so dry that the physician restricts bathing. In routine bathing a soap substitute is regularly used. pHisoHex may be ordered for shampoos.

Continuous, tepid, wet, medicated compresses are sometimes employed. These must be *kept wet* to accomplish the aim of the treatment. This type of compress or gauze bandage is not covered by waterproof material but is left exposed to cool the area by evaporation.

Older children may undergo so-called desensitization procedures. Through the injection of small but gradually increasing amounts of allergen, the body is sometimes able to eventually tolerate the substance without untoward reaction.

The course of infantile eczema is usually not one of steady improvement. The child will improve, have a relapse, and improve again. The parents should be told to prepare themselves for a rather long seige of skin difficulty. However, after 2 years of age a respite can usually be expected. Unfortunately, as eczema disappears other allergy-type manifestations such as asthma or hay fever may develop. The child with eczema is infrequently hospitalized because of (despite precautions) the

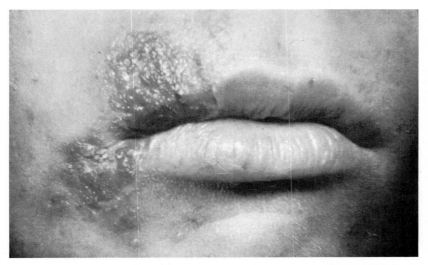

FIG. 35-4. Impetigo. (Courtesy W. W. Duemling, M.D., San Diego, Calif.)

increased exposure to infection, the emotional upset that may occur in the child as a result of the change of environment, and the need for the "maternal figure." However, exhaustion and tension on the part of the mother or father may also be a factor in obtaining an admission to the pediatric unit of a hospital.

Common skin problems of the preschool-age and young school-age child

Impetigo (Fig. 35-4)

Impetigo is a skin infection caused by either coagulase-positive staphylococci or beta-hemolytic streptococci. It is very contagious and serious in newborn infants and fairly contagious but less serious among children and adults. It is often associated with poor hygiene. Inflammation begins with the appearance of reddish spots on the skin, which develop into small blisters. These blisters become pus filled and break, causing thick yellow-red crusts on older children but few crusts on infants. When the crusts are removed, small superficial ulcers are seen. The face and hands are the areas most frequently affected, but other body areas may become involved. In the hospital, isolation is indicated.

Treatment includes careful cleansing with pHisoHex and removal of the crusts, with compresses if necessary, and the use of neomycin-bacitracin ointment. A course of systemic penicillin is recommended because of the demonstrated association between certain strains of beta-hemolytic streptococci and nephritis. Also, a more rapid improvement of the lesions is seen when systemic therapy is used. Erythromycin is the second drug of choice. The nurse should be especially cautious in the care of the lesions and disposal of infected material because the infection spreads easily. The child's fingernails should be clipped short. Restraints may be necessary to prevent scratching. The dermatitis usually responds well to treatment.

Erythema multiforme and the Stevens-Johnson syndrome

Erythema multiforme is a skin condition characterized by the sudden appearance of a macular erythematous rash on the skin and mucous membranes, which may progress to papules and vesicles of exaggerated size in the next stage. It usually is associated with the appearance of respiratory symptoms, fever, and chills. It is more common in male children of school age. Ery-

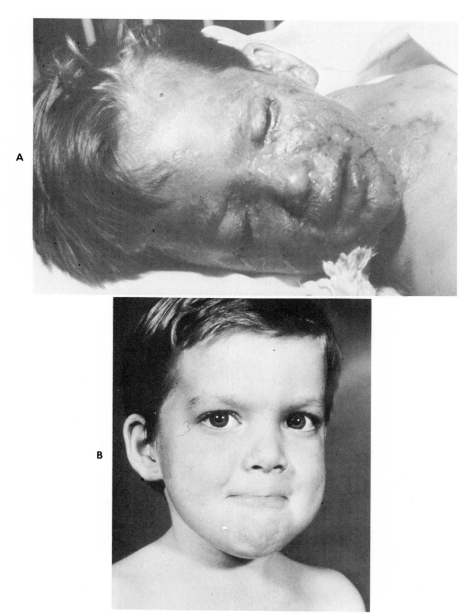

FIG. 35-5. Stevens-Johnson syndrome. **A,** 5-year-old boy at admission. **B,** 5 days after therapy. (Courtesy U. S. Naval Hospital, San Diego, Calif.)

thema multiforme has been linked with a type of hypersensitivity reaction to infection or drugs, but the exact cause remains unknown. A rare explosive form of this condition involving the conjunctivae of the eyes is called *Stevens-Johnson syndrome*. This type may be fatal. Treatment consists of symptomatic supportive measures and, in severe cases, short-term, high-dosage steroid therapy and intravenous fluids. Although the child may be seriously ill, he may respond quite rapidly to medication (Fig. 35-5).

Furuncles and carbuncles

Furuncles and carbuncles are deep infections of the hair follicles. They may occur singly or in groups. If the furuncles run together, forming one sore with several draining points, the resulting lesion is called a carbuncle. Carbuncles are not common in small children but are seen with greater frequency among adolescent boys. A furuncle begins as a single papule associated with a hair. The papule becomes a pustule, which enlarges and points.

At this time the physician incises and drains the "boil." Warm compresses or soaks may be ordered to prepare the lesion for lancing. If multiple furuncles are present, systemic antibiotic therapy may be prescribed.

Sty, or hordeolum

A sty, an infection involving an eyelash follicle, is usually lanced. Recurrent sties suggest the possibility of eyestrain.

Ringworm of the scalp, skin, and feet (Fig. 35-6)

Ringworm of the scalp, or *tinea capitis*, used to be fairly common among school-aged children and is still seen from time to time, particularly in urban areas. It can be caused by several kinds of fungus. Some types of fungus are contracted from human beings, whereas others are contracted from animals. The fungus attacks hairs at their bases, causing them to break off close to the skin and leave circular balding areas. The scalp in the area of the hair loss may become red and scaly. Mild itching may be present. Diagnosis is usually made on

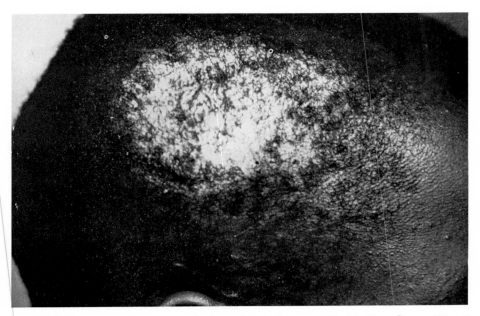

Fig. 35-6. Tinea capitis (ringworm of the scalp). (Courtesy W. W. Duemling, M.D., San Diego, Calif.)

the basis of the clinical history, an ultraviolet light called *Wood's lamp,* or a microscopic examination of the affected hairs. Most types of fungi that commonly cause ringworm of the scalp fluoresce brightly when exposed to the rays of Wood's lamp. In the past, treatment of ringworm was quite difficult, and the disease had a tendency to become chronic, usually healing spontaneously at puberty. Treatment included shaving the head. Boys and girls wore little stocking caps in an effort to cover the hair loss and prevent the spread of the disease. X-ray treatment was sometimes prescribed. The oral administration of the antibiotic griseofulvin has been quite successful. The drug does not kill the fungus but prevents its spread into uninfected cells. As the infected cells are shed or removed they are replaced by healthy cells. The use of a cotton skullcap that is washed and boiled daily is still recommended by some physicians. Clipping of the affected hair after a few weeks of treatment is also desirable. In addition, a local antifungal ointment may be ordered.

Ringworm of the skin is of two main types. One type, *tinea cruris,* involves the groin, and the other, *tinea corporis,* characteristically involves the face, neck, arms, and hands. Although there are exceptions, the classic lesion of ringworm of the skin is rounded or circular with a gradually extending, small, raised vesicular border with central healing. The lesion may vary considerably in size, but it is usually about the size of a quarter. Treatment consists of prevention of scratching and application of one of several topical remedies—ointments containing sulfur and salicylic acid, solutions of gentian violet, or tincture of iodine, to mention a few. Local treatment is combined with systemic use of griseofulvin in some cases.

Ringworm of the feet, *tinea pedis,* or so-called athlete's foot, is more common in the adolescent than in the younger school-aged child. However, it is discussed here with the other types of ringworm. Ringworm of the feet is most often character-ized by itching or burning of the feet, blisters, and painful cracks between the toes. At times it may extend to involve other areas and become quite serious. It is caused by several kinds of fungi. Treatment consists of the use of griseofulvin. Better ventilation of the feet and the reduction of sweating in the area are helpful. Frequent changing of socks (white socks are recommended because they may be boiled or treated with strong bleach) is a necessity. If the infection has been intense and tends to recur, the advisability of discarding shoes worn during the infection should be considered. Antifungal preparations such as Desenex or Whitfield's ointment are often used locally. The feet should be carefully dried. A prophylactic antifungal dusting powder is often advised for susceptible persons. For the protection of other people, victims should not use public showers or swimming pools.

Pediculosis, or louse infestations

Although there are three types of lice—head lice, body lice, and pubic lice—only one type is of significant importance to children, *pediculosis capitis,* or infestation of the hair of the head by lice. This condition is often seen in neglected children of lower socioeconomic levels. However, children who are well cared for may inadvertently become exposed and contract the infestation, much to their parents' shock!

The parasitic head louse travels on the scalp, causing itching. Small, grayish, oval eggs called *nits* are laid and attached to the base of the hair shafts with a type of mucilage produced by the louse (Fig. 35-7). As the hair grows, the nits become more visible; they resemble tiny flakes of dandruff except that they do not brush out. New lice hatch in 3 or 4 days, and the cycle repeats. Pediculosis is often accompanied by excoriation and secondary infection caused by scratching.

Old-style treatment involved the local use of crude oil or kerosene. More acceptable and very effective are shampoos with gamma benzene hexachloride (Kwell or

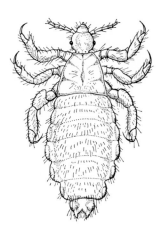

Fig. 35-7. Top, the female head louse; center, an enlargement of nits on hair shafts; bottom, life-sized louse.

Gexane). DDT (chlorophenothane) preparations may be ordered. After the end of the treatment the hair should be combed with a fine-tooth comb to remove the devitalized nits. Warm vinegar solution also aids in the mechanical detachment of nits. The entire family of an affected person should be treated, if possible.

Scabies

Scabies is a superficial infestation by the itch mite (*Acarus scabiei*, or *Sarcoptes scabiei*). The female mite burrows under the skin, making a tunnel about half an inch long, which is visible as an elevated line from the skin's surface. The insect is so small that it is rarely visible to the naked eye. Scabies usually involves those body areas where the skin is moist and thin—between the fingers and toes, in the axillae, and on the groin and abdominal areas. The itch mite causes itching, as the name indicates. Various treatments are now available. Gamma benzene hexachloride (Kwell) may be applied in cream form, or applications of benzyl benzoate emulsion or sulfur may be ordered. Prolonged soap and water baths are usually prescribed before and after the therapy. Again, the entire family of an affected person should receive therapy, if possible.

Common skin problems of the adolescent
Acne vulgaris

Vulgar means "common," and acne vulgaris is a skin inflammation that is exceedingly common among teen-age boys and girls. It may exist in a very mild form, or it may be extremely severe. The exact cause of acne is unknown. Probably there are several causes that, appearing together, produce the problem. When acne is present it first appears, almost without exception, at the time of puberty. Therefore hormone levels in the body are believed to play a role. Recent data reveal that *Corynebacterium acnes*, an inhabitant of normal hair follicles, plays an important role in the pathogenesis of acne. Many times the parents of the affected child also experienced similar difficulty; therefore hereditary factors are not discounted.

The oil or sebum secreted by the sebaceous glands is altered by hormones or the *Corynebacterium acnes* organism, producing irritation in the surrounding tissue. Clogging of the pores occurs, and blackheads (plugs of keratin, sebum, and microorganisms, also called *comedones*, the primary lesions of acne) form. The pores may also be clogged with dirt, but commonly blackheads are not caused by dirt particles

495

but by oxidation of the top of the plug, a process that may occur no matter how carefully the youngster washes. Plugging of the oil ducts may lead to papules, pustules, and, at times, cyst formation and permanent scarring. Since acne most often occurs on the face, shoulders, and back, it is of great cosmetic and psychological concern. The teen-ager should be given professional help during this distressing period so that it is as short and free from complications as possible. Acne fosters a sense of inferiority and social insecurity at a difficult period in life.

Treatment includes a review of general health habits. The patient is advised to avoid an excess of carbohydrates and fatty foods such as chocolate, nuts, and peanut butter. His diet should be well balanced. Increased intake of vitamin A may be helpful. Lack of sleep, nervous tension, and menstrual problems may lead to a flare-up. Mild cases are treated with topical measures such as antibacterial detergent soaps or skin cleansers (pHisoHex, Fostex, Acne-Aid) and lotions containing *keratolytic* compounds (salicylic acid, resorcin) and sulfur (Komed, Kummerfeld's) lotion. There are numerous tinted antibacterial creams or lotions available that help heal and mask the lesions, a very important psychological consideration. Frequent shampooing is often very helpful. Patients should be instructed not to press or scratch the lesions because this may break down tissue walls and spread infection. However, despite this advice, most patients find it extremely difficult not to tamper with the lesions they see in the mirror. The physician may remove comedones in his office with a special extractor, or he may give careful instructions to the patient's family regarding the removal of comedones. The drug treatment of choice in advanced cases is either tetracycline to kill the bacteria or hormones to alter the sebum-producing activity of the sebaceous glands.

Usually, acne is self-limiting and subsides in 1 or 2 years. However, severe cases may persist into middle age. The partial removal of scarred tissue may be accomplished, in selected cases, by superficial abrasion, a technique called *dermabrasion*. X-ray treatment is no longer recommended by many dermatologists because of the possibility of causing skin changes later in life and the availability of other therapeutic alternatives.

Herpes simplex

Herpes simplex is a viral infection that often causes an irregular vesicular lesion on the margin of the lip (fever blister) or gums. The blister breaks, a crust develops and eventually clears. These lesions have a tendency to recur in the same area, causing considerable annoyance, discomfort, and cosmetic concern. Occasionally herpes simplex will take on a more important aspect. It is serious when a newborn infant or very young child is involved because the lesions have a tendency to multiply, and it is serious when the eye is involved because an impairment of vision may result. Local treatment may involve the application of alcohol. Control of nervous tension and gastrointestinal upsets may be helpful. Repeated smallpox vaccination has been used therapeutically, although the way in which this treatment aids the situation is unknown. Some believe it is of "suggestive value."

Dermatitis venenata

Dermatitis venenata may be seen at any age; it is an inflammatory skin response resulting from external contact with some irritating substance such as fibers, plants, synthetics, adhesive tape, etc. However, it is most often observed in those groups who go hiking in the midst of some poison oak or poison ivy. Signs of skin irritation usually occur several hours after exposure and consist of redness, swelling, and small blisters at the point of contact. Itching is intense. If the patient knows that he has been exposed, the best immediate treatment before the appearance of symptoms is washing the area with a laundry soap and rinsing and drying the area well. Of course, the best course of action is proper identification of the offending plants in the first place and a prudent detour. After the blisters have developed, the urge to scratch must be resisted to prevent spreading. Calamine lotion and cortisone preparations applied locally may help relieve itching.

Burns

Another problem, which primarily involves the skin but may finally affect many organs and processes of the body, is burns. Burns may be caused by exposure to hot liquids, strong chemicals, direct flame, radiation, sunlight, or electrical current. Toddlers and young children are most often scalded by hot coffee, grease from frying pans, or hot water from unguarded bathroom faucets. Older children are frequently burned when their clothes catch fire while they are playing with matches, using kerosene, or standing too close to household heaters. In the United States approximately 5,000 children are hospitalized because of burns on a given day.

Classification

Burns are classified into four categories, depending on the depth of penetration of the body's surface. A *first-degree* burn involves only the epidermis. It is very superficial; a tender, slightly swollen redness results. A common illustration of a first-degree burn is the typical summer sunburn. A *second-degree* burn involves the dermis, or corium. Some authors divide this category into superficial secondary burns and deep secondary burns. A secondary burn is characterized by blister formation or a reddened, discolored region with a moist, weeping surface. A *third-degree* burn involves the entire dermis and portions of the subcutaneous tissue. It is often called a full-thickness burn. The region affected has a brown, leathery appearance with little surface moisture. A *fourth-degree* burn involves tissue under the skin—fascia, underlying muscle, and perhaps bone. The tissue appears blackened and contracted. It is not always easy to evaluate the depth of a burn immediately after the injury.

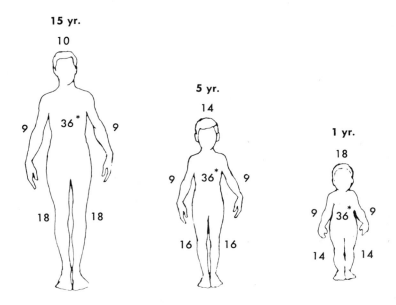

*18 anterior, 18 posterior

Fig. 35-8. Modification of the "rule of nines." (Courtesy Burns Institute, Galveston Unit, Shriners Hospitals for Crippled Children.)

Not only is the degree of burn important but also the amount of body surface affected is significant. A person usually can survive a rather extensive superficial burn, but he may tolerate only a small area involvement if the burn is deep. In evaluating the extent of a burn on an adult the so-called "rule of nines" may be applied; it gives a certain percentage value to each part of the body—a percentage that is almost always nine or a multiple of nine. This method of calculation, unless modified, is not helpful when working with children because of the relatively large size of a baby's or young child's head and the reduced length of his legs. (One example of modification based on size differences is illustrated in Fig. 35-8.)

Therapeutic management and nursing responsibility

Initial considerations. Any person who is at the scene when someone is burned should first extinguish the fire if the victim's clothes are aflame. If an abundant source of water from a hose or bucket is readily available, it should be used; if not, handy blankets or throw rugs may be employed to smother the flames, since fire cannot continue in the absence of oxygen. If neither water nor blankets are available, the victim should be rolled on the ground or floor to help smother the flames. When the fire has been extinguished, the burned area should be rinsed with cold water. The victim should be taken immediately to a physician's office or, preferably, a hospital for evaluation and care. He should be transported wrapped in a clean sheet and blanket. Time should not be lost in trying to remove the child's clothes. No medication of any type should be administered.

When a burned child is admitted to an emergency room or other hospital receiving area, his clothes should be removed gently, cutting along the seams of the garments if necessary. He should be placed on and covered by sterile sheets in a room with good lighting. The extent of his burns will be estimated by the attending physician, and the need for hospitalization will be determined. All those in attendance should wear face masks. Those in contact with the patient should be provided with sterile gowns and gloves.

Care of first-degree burns does not routinely entail hospitalization unless other complications occur. Care usually consists of keeping the area clean and covering it with a mild anesthetic ointment. The technique of immediately immersing the area briefly in cold water or holding an ice cube on the injured surface to reduce pain and edema has become quite popular. As previously indicated, cold water immersion is helpful in first-aid treatment of burns of greater depth as well.

The first phase of therapy when serious burns are present is the maintenance of an *airway* and the prevention of *shock*. The airway is not a problem in all cases but occasionally because of the location of the external burn, the inhalation of fumes, or internal burning of the respiratory tract, it is of great importance. A tracheostomy may be necessary. The administration of oxygen may be required.

Intravenous fluid therapy is usually initiated. In young children cut-downs are performed. With second- and third-degree burns there is danger of great fluid loss and an upset in electrolyte balance. A urinary catheter is usually inserted because the amount and type of urine formation per hour is important in determining the rate of intravenous therapy and providing an index of the patient's general condition. A dwindling urinary output may serve as a warning of developing toxicity. A urinary output of 20 to 30 ml. per hour for a 5-year-old child is desirable. An adult's output would approximate 50 to 60 ml. per hour. Signs of overhydration revealed by excessive output should also be reported. The urinary catheter output should be observed frequently and recorded hourly. Specific gravity determinations are frequently ordered. It is extremely important to report irregularities in the urinary output, the loss of a urine specimen, or an error in the measurement of a urine specimen because of the danger of miscalculating the need for and amount of intravenous therapy. Many blood tests also help determine the kind of fluids that are needed. Frequent hemoglobin and hematocrit studies are carried out. Blood gas studies may be ordered. Overloading the circulatory system is a real possibility unless great care is exercised. Blood typing and cross matching are performed in the event transfusions may be necessary. The patient is weighed to provide a base line for subsequent weight loss or gain. Vital signs are checked frequently, although meaningful blood pressure readings may be difficult to secure because of the age of the child and the location of the burn area. Some hospital services make use of venous pressure determinations.

There is lack of agreement among physicians concerning the immediate need for antibiotics. The wound is frequently cultured. All authorities consulted recommended tetanus immunization. Pain medication administered parenterally will help control shock. There is more pain accompanying a second-degree burn than a third-degree burn because in the second-degree burn some nerve endings are still intact. Most hospitals routinely isolate their burn patients in an effort to prevent or reduce infection. Burn patients are often considered to be contaminated patients. However, if silver nitrate therapy is selected as the method of treatment, there is evidence to indicate that routine isolation is not uniformly necessary. This would certainly be a great boon for the patient and his family psychologically. Immediate care of second- and third-degree burns usually consists of washing the involved areas with a physiological saline solution or distilled water rinse, depending on the type of treatment to follow. Loose skin and blisters are surgically removed by the physician at the time of admission in a procedure called debridement. The child may be placed on a Stryker turning frame or a CircOlectric bed to facilitate positioning and nursing care. The shock phase of the body's response to

extensive burns is usually considered to last from 48 to 72 hours.

The vocational nurse should not have the total assigned bedside responsibility of a severely burned child during this critical period, although she may skillfully assist the registered nurse in important aspects of the care. The vocational nurse must understand the principles of the patient's treatment, and as the patient's condition becomes more stable she will participate more fully in his care.

Types of treatment. Second-, third-, and fourth-degree burns may be treated in several ways—the closed method, the open or exposure method, and the modified exposure, or silver nitrate regimen. More than one technique may be used with one patient, depending on his needs.

Closed method. If the burned area is relatively small and hospitalization is not indicated, the closed method is usually preferred. In certain cases in which a burn extends completely around the body this method may also be preferred in areas where the body would bear weight. The closed method of treatment involves covering the burned area with various dressings and bandages: first a sterile gauze impregnated with ointment, next sterile compresses or fluffs, followed by sterile gauze bandage, Kerlix, or abdominal pads and a snug covering of elastic bandages. Depending on the condition of the dressing, the condition of the patient, and the physician's preference, this dressing may be left on without disturbance for more than a week, or orders may be written for the inner dressing to be soaked and removed at specific intervals to help in the cleaning of the wound and separation of dead tissue from the burned area. This may be done in the form of tub baths, whirlpool treatments, or local soaks. Dilute chlorine, Dreft, or PVP-I (Betadine) solutions are currently being used. An experimental innovation designed to ease the difficulty and pain often experienced by the patient required to take frequent therapeutic tub baths is the Stryker burn-bed (Fig. 35-9). The patient

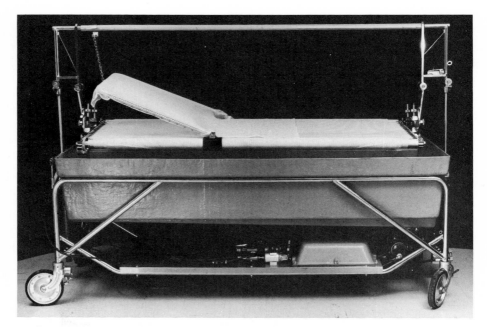

FIG. 35-9. An experimental burn-bed now being evaluated at the Shriners Burns Institute, Galveston Unit. The patient is positioned on the bed frame. This frame may be lowered into the therapeutic bath as ordered. (Courtesy Burns Institute and the Stryker Corp., Kalamazoo, Mich.)

rests on a bedlike support that is periodically lowered into the bath and then raised for continued care. All dressing materials should be ready to reapply in a sterile manner after the soak. Through soaks and redressing and/or intermittent surgical debridements, the burned areas are cleaned and the developing granulation tissue is prepared for grafting. Granulation tissue is a deep pink, fragile tissue that bleeds easily. When the tissue is sufficiently prepared, the child will undergo grafting. Donor sites are selected on the patient himself. (Skin donations from other individuals [other than an identical twin] do not "take" and eventually slough away. Such grafts are used only as stopgap treatment in emergency situations.) The donor site is usually covered with fine gauze and a pressure dressing. Later, when bleeding has been controlled, the outer pressure dressing may be removed. Donor sites heal in about 2 weeks. The newly grafted area is kept covered. The dressing should be

observed for amount and type of drainage and odor. Exposed adjacent areas should be observed for edema and circulatory problems. Grafts are usually firmly attached by the twelfth day after the grafting procedure.

Open method. The open method is particularly helpful in treating burns of the face and perineum and thermal injuries involving only one side of the trunk or extremities. This method of burn therapy necessitates rigid isolation technique because no dressings are used in the initial period of burn care. It has the advantages of allowing greater motion, reducing the incidence of contractures and thereby speeding rehabilitation, allowing direct observation of the involved areas for complications, and reducing odor. The child is placed on sterile linen. A sterile bed mat should be placed under the sheets forming the base of the bed, since wound seepage may extend to the mattress. A metal frame or cradle, from which sterile sheets covered by a blanket or

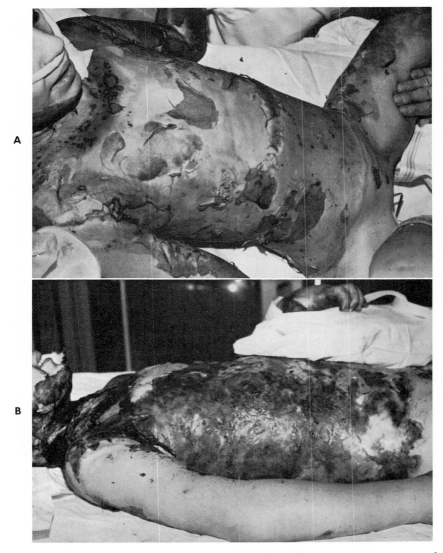

FIG. 35-10. A, This 6-year-old child has just been admitted into an emergency room because of second- and third-degree burns. She is receiving oxygen by nasal cannula. B, *Open therapy* was the treatment used. A heavy eschar formed over the trunk. (Courtesy Matthew Gleason, M.D., San Diego, Calif.)

canopy are draped, is placed over the child. Specially protected electric light bulbs may be incorporated in the frame to provide warmth, since the patient often feels cold without some additional source of heat. In some hospitals special burn cribs or tents may be available. The interior temperature of such a bed unit should be maintained between 85° and 95° F.

As the hours pass, a thick black crust called *eschar,* composed of the drying wound secretions, will form over the burned area—a protection against infection (Fig. 35-10). During this period the nurse may be ordered to gently wash the burned areas with an antibacterial solution and rinse with physiological saline solution. Days later the eschar will begin to separate, and the physician will cut away portions of the dried crust, revealing new granulation tissue. When the granulation tissue is exposed by removal of the eschar, antibiotic-impregnated gauze is usually laid over the open granulation areas. Debridements may continue daily in the nursing unit, or less often, in the operating room. Some physicians preface grafting procedures by saturating the gauze that covers the granulation tissue with solutions containing benzalkonium chloride (Zephiran), acetic acid, or antibiotics: such a technique is said to reduce the possibility of infection by staphylococci or pseudomonas-type organisms.

Modified exposure method. With the advent of various ointments and creams that have proved useful in combating common wound contaminants, a kind of modified open therapy has evolved. The patient is usually placed on sterile precautions as well as routine isolation. No occlusive dressings are used. A thin layer of the medication may be applied directly to the injured area using a sterile glove or tongue blade, or the medication may be embedded in sterile gauze strips that are positioned as needed. A spray form may also be available. Some drugs currently employed are as follows:

1. Mafenide acetate (Sulfamylon acetate cream), 10%: This water-soluble medication is particularly helpful in preventing pseudomonal infections. It should be removed completely each day for wound inspection by irrigations or baths. It is reapplied every 12 hours or more frequently as necessary. It causes an intense burning sensation when first applied, which is diminished if the cream can be applied directly after the irrigation or bath while the wound is still damp. Allergic reactions (itching and hives) may occur. Reports of occasional acid-base imbalance (acidosis) associated with its use have been published.

2. Gentamicin sulfate ointment or cream (Garamycin): This antibiotic is applied directly to the wound or embedded in fine mesh gauze. It decreases bacteria but does not combat *Pseudomonas* effectively.

3. Silver sulfadiazine ointment: This drug is designed to combine the best features of mafenide acetate and silver nitrate therapy. It is active against *Pseudomonas*, painless on application, stainless, and not associated with acid-base imbalance.

4. Triclobisonium chloride (Triburon) ointment: This is a water-soluble, semi-transparent ointment that acts as a broad-spectrum topical microbicide. It has been useful in combating many types of infections.

Silver nitrate therapy. The old method of treating burns with silver nitrate solution has undergone modification and a dramatic revival. After an initial pHisoHex wash and distilled water rinse, the burned area is flooded with 0.5% silver nitrate solution. The use of this antiseptic is continued by the application of thick saturated compresses directly against the burned surfaces. The dressings must not be allowed to dry out. Saturation may often be maintained with greatest ease by the incorporation of multieyed catheters within the gauze layers. A syringe is used to inject tepid silver nitrate into the exposed end of the catheters to moisten the dressing. To reduce the heat loss that may occur with this treatment, the area compressed should be covered with a dry, but *not* water-tight, sheet or blanket. A clean rather than a rigid sterile technique is sufficient during these treatments. The constant compressing is interrupted only for special salt solution baths (to help maintain the body's fluid balance) and intermittent debridements. Careful, frequent blood studies must be carried out to be certain that electrolyte imbalance does not occur because of the possibility of excessive sodium and chloride loss through the burn site. The use of the silver nitrate therapy has greatly reduced the incidence of infection. It reduces or prevents odor, decreases the need for skin grafting, and usually allows earlier placement of grafts. It also permits greater mobility and therefore seems less likely to be associated with lasting functional loss.

However, this treatment also presents certain peculiar problems. Silver nitrate, although colorless when poured from the opaque storage container, rapidly forms a black stain on almost everything it touches. Unfortunately, it seems to touch almost everything, even when care is used. Bed linen, floors, shoes, uniforms, and woodwork are not exempt! Nurses and physicians participating in silver nitrate treatment usually adopt rather unprofessional-appearing dress in an effort to be more protected against the black stains. Plastic sacks may be cut to allow the head and arms to protrude in a workable manner. Plastic aprons, if availble, may be used. Footwear is protected with smaller plastic sacks, or old shoes are worn. Cotton cover gowns that have already been worn during silver nitrate treatment are also worn over the plastic gowns. They may be stained, but they are clean. One burn service reports that they have dyed the linen used on their area a deep chocolate brown. The theory must be, "if one can't beat it, join it!" Rubber gloves are included to protect the hands, particularly the nails. Many stains on fabric can be removed with a solution of iodophor (Wescodyne), 1 ounce to 1 gallon of water, followed by a bleach or exposure to sunshine. Wescodyne is also used to help clean the room. The floor should be covered with plastic. Only old and necessary furnishings should be used.

With this treatment, the patient's skin will become dark and scaly. The film can be gradually washed or peeled off, depending on the areas involved and the physician's wishes. Participating in silver nitrate therapy is a fascinating and unforgettable experience.

Continuing concerns. No matter what methods of burn therapy are selected, all treatment is done to accomplish the following aims:
1. Preserve life
2. Promote healing
3. Prevent infection
4. Prevent deformity
5. Provide emotional and physical rehabilitation

An important part of the nurse's responsibility is the provision of a good nutritional intake. Initially the child will probably not be allowed oral feedings, but fairly soon he may be fed orally with or without a nasogastric tube, depending on his progress. It is very important for the nurse to keep an accurate record of all nourishment and fluids taken. Many physicians will want a detailed daily intake record kept to be analyzed by the dietitian for caloric and foodstuff (protein, fat, carbohydrate, and mineral) content. Protein consumption is particularly important. Usually supplemental vitamins and iron will be ordered. Vitamin C and zinc are substances believed to be particularly helpful in aiding tissue healing. A stress lesion called *Curling's ulcer* sometimes develops in burn patients. Nurses should be alert for signs of blood in the stool or nasogastric tube. The child's appetite should not be discouraged with servings that are too large. Feedings should be judiciously planned. The patient should not be expected to eat directly after an exhausting dressing change. A different schedule for the kitchen on some days or better planning of ward procedures on other days may be necessary, but the patient should receive his meals when he can best *eat*. Likes and dislikes should be noted. Sometimes permission to bring food in from home brings forth happy cooperation on the part of both parents and child. The child must be weighed periodically to help determine his nutritional status.

The immediate and long-term positioning of a seriously burned patient is critical in preventing extensive deformity. Although the position of flexion may be the position of greatest comfort to the patient, it will also become the cause of crippling contractures. The posture of extension recommended (Fig. 35-11, *A*) may at first appear "heartless" but, in the final analysis, such placement of the head and extremities may save the patient weeks, if not months, of needless hospitalization and additional pain. The hand brace in Fig. 35-11, *B*, is designed to prevent the development of a claw-type deformity. Note the forced extension of the fingers. This splint and the neck splint pictured in Fig. 35-11, *C*, are made of a type of plastic, "Orthoplast" Isoprene, that, when

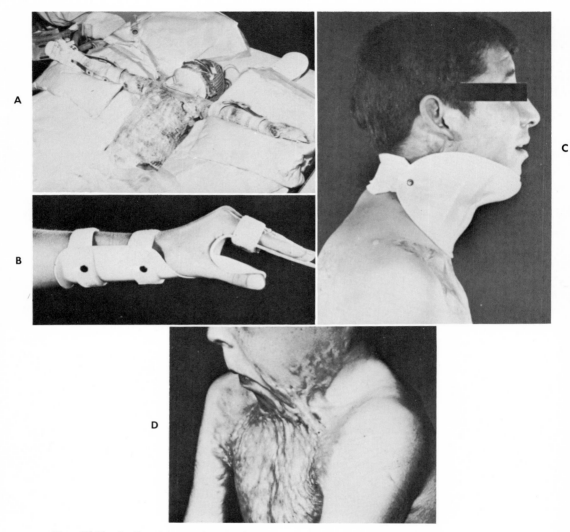

FIG. 35-11. **A,** Routine positioning for severely burned patient with lesions involving the trunk, arms, neck, and face. Neck, arm, and hand splints have been applied. Oxygen and mist are being administered. **B,** An "Orthoplast" Isoprene hand splint. Note the extended fingers. **C,** An "Orthoplast" Isoprene neck splint. **D,** An example of the condition the neck splint is designed to help prevent—severe contractures of the chin and neck. (From Willis, Barbara: Amer. J. Occup. Ther. 24:187-191, 1970 [A, C, and D]; 23:57-61, 1969 [B].)

molded and fitted to the individual patient, has been quite successful in preventing deformities (Fig. 35-11, *D*) that had previously been difficult to avoid. They are applied over a mafenide acetate gauze dressing almost immediately after the patient is admitted. These helpful devices have been developed at the Shriners Burns Institute, Galveston Unit, under the direction of the charge occupational therapist, Barbara Willis.*

*Willis, B.: The use of orthoplast isoprene splints in the treatment of the acutely burned child: preliminary report, Amer. J. Occup. Ther. 23:57-61, 1969. Willis, B.: The use of orthoplast isoprene splints in the treatment of the acutely burned child: a follow-up, Amer. J. Occup. Ther. 24:187-191, 1970.

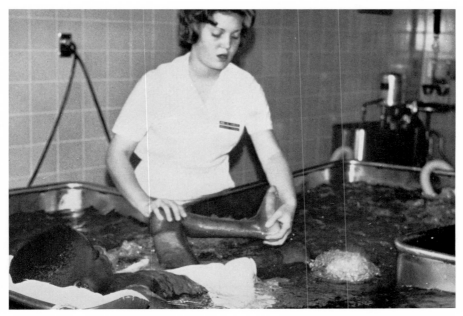

Fig. 35-12. Bobby exercises in the Hubbard tank as part of his therapy after extensive burns. (Courtesy Children's Health Center, San Diego, Calif.)

Active and passive exercises of the affected body parts, if neglected when ordered, may retard convalescence significantly. It is the nurse's responsibility (along with the physical therapy staff) to see that these important movements, which are often resisted, are carried out. Appropriate exercises plus good positioning to avoid flexion contractures can make a big contribution to the early rehabilitation of the patient. (See Fig. 35-12.)

During the entire period of treatment and observation of the extensively burned patient, the morale of the parents and their child is of tremendous importance. Often the parents feel guilty concerning their child's accident. They may be appalled at the condition of the child and his appearance. Some will be overly protective; others may hardly be able to make themselves approach the child. All will be extremely upset whether they appear so or not. The child may have serious guilt feedings if he considers himself responsible for his injury. Some of these children have had a history of emotional disturbance before their ac-

cident. Good communication between the physician, the nursing staff, the parents, and the burned patient is essential. A feeling of acceptance and freedom to talk and not feel criticized for talking are important for both the child and his parents. Simple explanations of treatments take time at the beginning, but they save much time and anguish later on. For an excellent presentation of the emotional needs of a child with a burn, we recommend Maxine Rubin's article, "Balm for Burned Children," which appeared in the February, 1966, *American Journal of Nursing*. Nursing personnel, as well as the patient and his parents, may need psychiatric support in carrying out their roles.

Rehabilitation. The rehabilitation of a burned child may be long and exhausting, but despite the pain and fatigue, the end result is well worth the continuing effort. Fortunately, with the use of new techniques the time needed for rehabilitation promises to become much shorter. Splinting, traction, and frequent visits to the physical therapy department's pool or exercise room may be necessary. Plastic surgery may be needed in some cases to relieve contractures or remove keloid formation (exaggerated scar tissue). Special tutoring or educational provisions may be required to prevent educational loss. Social contacts must be maintained, particularly in the case of older children. A positive, constructive attitude toward therapy should be encouraged.

•   •   •

Patients who have been seriously burned will probably be among the nurse's most challenging and difficult responsibilities. They will also be among her most rewarding.

36

Isolation technique and communicable childhood diseases

The student nurse often contemplates her experience with patients suffering from contagious disease with a fascinating mixture of eager anticipation and fear. Under control, both these emotions work to her advantage. There is much to learn in this nursing area about the needs of the patients and about safe methods of meeting these needs. There are new words, new techniques, and a new awareness of the unseen. The student must be impressed with the importance of carrying out the isolation, or barrier, techniques recognized in the area where she is working. Any lapse in technique by *anyone* jeopardizes other patients, the entire staff, and, indeed, perhaps the entire hospital.

However, the student nurse should also appreciate that in a number of ways she is probably working in the safest part of the hospital. In the isolation area, precautions are taken that are not observed elsewhere. Nurses in other hospital areas may inadvertently be exposed to contagious conditions without precautions because the conditions, although present, may be undetected.

Key vocabulary

The following list includes some of the new words the nurse may encounter when working in an isolation area:

communicable or *contagious diseases* disorders caused by small living forms (organisms) or their toxins, which may be passed directly from person to person or indirectly from person to inanimate object, airborne particles, or other living creatures to other persons to continue the spread of disease.

infectious diseases disorders caused by small living forms (organisms) that invade tissue and cause symptoms of illness. (Most infectious diseases are also communicable, but there are exceptions. A person suffering from tetanus but with no draining wound would not have to be on isolation precautions; neither would a person with a disease caused by an organism that is present everywhere but causes disease only when introduced unnaturally into the body, for example, an *Escherichia coli* urinary infection.)

contaminated in isolation technique, or medical asepsis, this adjective is applied to any person or thing that has touched a patient with a contagious disease, has touched anything the patient has touched, or has undergone prolonged exposure to such a patient before proper disinfection has occurred. (The student may remember that the word "contaminated" used in a surgical setting means "touched by anything not sterile." In isolation technique it means "touched directly or indirectly by the patient or his excretions or discharges.")

portal of entry the way that infections gain entrance into a person's body, for example, respiratory tract, digestive tract, skin, and mucous membranes, with or without the aid of living creatures (insects, mites, etc.).

incubation period time that must elapse between the infection of an individual at a time of exposure until the appearance of signs or symptoms of the disease.

carrier person or animal capable of transmitting a contagious disease although the person or animal shows no outward sign of the disease.

isolation prevention of direct or indirect contact with a person with a contagious disease during its period of communicability by the observance of certain barrier techniques designed to stop the spread of illness.

quarantine confinement of a person or group of persons who have been exposed to a contagious disease to a specific place without outside contacts for the duration of the longest usual incubation period of the disease in question.

immunity ability to protect oneself against the development of an infectious disease. Immunity may be natural or acquired. *Natural immunity* may be hereditary—related to racial strengths and the individual capacity for protective antibody formation. It is stimulated by exposure to disease-producing organisms. *Acquired immunity* may be *active,* with formation of protective antibodies as a result of having actually contracted the disease or of having been exposed to milder or related forms of the organism that causes the disease. Acquired immunity may also be *passive,* with protection gained through the introduction of antibodies already manufactured by some other living creature against a certain disease-producing organism (immune serum globulin [ISG]). Active immunity is relatively long lasting and more desirable than passive immunity. Passive protection is immediate but relatively brief, and there are unfavorable reactions experienced because of the use of sera from animals.

vaccine preparation containing killed or weakened living microorganisms, which, when introduced into the body, cause the formation of antibodies against that type of organism, thereby protecting the individual from the disease.

toxoid preparation containing a toxin or poison produced by pathogenic organisms that is capable of producing active immunity against a disease but too weak to produce the disease itself.

antitoxin preparation containing antibodies designed to produce passive immunization; often administered by the injection of *horse serum* rich in specific antibodies. (To produce the antitoxins, a horse is often injected by a toxoid, and after a period of time antibodies are manufactured and identified in the horse's blood serum; this serum is modified for injection. Some people are allergic to the serum containing the antibodies. Extreme caution must be taken in administering antitoxin.)

Isolation technique
TYPES OF ISOLATION

Various barrier techniques may be ordered for the patient, depending on the diagnosis. Routine isolation usually implies that gowning technique must be carried out, but the gown may be reused, if prop-

erly handled, and no mask is necessary. Strict isolation, however, usually implies that the gown must be discarded in the laundry after use and a mask and perhaps gloves must be worn.

Strict isolation is generally ordered in cases in which the infection is airborne and of a particularly serious nature, for example, during the early stages of treatment for meningococcal meningitis and pulmonary tuberculosis.

Isolation techniques are designed to accomplish two main objectives: to prevent the spread of any communicable disease that the isolated patient may have and to protect the isolated patient from any outside source of infection.

The first objective is accomplished by erecting barriers between the patient, his environment, and his bodily excretions or discharges and the rest of the hospital and hospital staff. Special protective coverings are worn by the nursing staff, and special hand-washing instructions are observed. Anything *coming out* of the unit that has been exposed to the patient for a prolonged period or that has directly contacted his person or his unit must undergo some type of disinfection. This technique also helps cut down on the introduction of secondary infection from outside the unit, since the attendants must wear gowns, which are worn nowhere else in the hospital, over their uniforms while performing direct patient care.

When the second objective is paramount, as is the case in the care of a noninfectious newborn infant, a type of reverse isolation is practiced. As much as practicable only sterilized linens and clothing and sterile attendant's gowns are used, and masks are worn in the room. Good hand washing before and after patient care is stressed. No special precautions are followed in removing objects and materials from the room, only in the kind of things going into the room for use. This type of reverse isolation is called *newborn technique* and is essentially the same as that practiced in the newborn nursery. This same type of technique may be employed with certain burn cases. In fact, burn cases may have both types of isolation techniques being observed concurrently, which makes nursing doubly interesting and the laundry problem tremendous! With modification, reverse isolation technique may be used with children suffering from heart or urinary complications who must be protected against upper respiratory infections. It is also employed often with leukemic children. However, patients who are placed on these reverse isolation procedures are not treated routinely on a nursing area that serves patients with contagious diseases. Students working on the regular isolation wing or area usually will not have both types of isolation to deal with unless a burn patient is ordered on the double type technique previously described or a child with leukemia develops a contagious complication.

PERSONAL PRECAUTIONS

The nurse working with isolation patients must take certain personal precautions for her own safety and for the safety of her co-workers and patients. Some of these are essential for every nurse to follow, regardless of the area in which she finds herself; others are particularly important when dealing with known infectious conditions. The following precautions should be noted:

1. Fingernails should be short and clean.
2. The nurse should be free from symptoms of contagious illness (upper respiratory infections, skin infections, diarrhea).
3. Any open lesion on the hands or face should be reported and evaluated before going on duty. Perhaps a change of assignment would be prudent to protect the nurse.
4. No rings should be worn. A watch, although used, should not be kept on the wrist.
5. A nurse's cap should not be worn while performing bedside care in this area.

6. Eyeglasses, if worn, should be periodically disinfected.
7. Shoes should be kept off chairs and other clean areas. Think where they have been!
8. The nurse's hands should not touch her face.

There are certain areas in a hospital that are always considered contaminated. All floors are contaminated regardless of the location. In most hospitals the entire room of a patient with a communicable disease is considered contaminated *with the exception* of the supply of paper towels inside a dispenser near the sink. This supply is located as far from the patient as possible. At times there is an adjoining anteroom where such supplies are kept and washing and laundry discard facilities are available.

THE ISOLATION GOWN
Occasions for use

An isolation gown should be worn in a unit whenever there is a possibility of contact with the patient or any contaminated equipment in the room. When strict isolation is ordered, anyone going into the room, whether or not she will be touching anything, should wear a gown and mask. However, in the case of routine isolation the attendant may enter several times to bring in supplies and equipment without touching anything already in the room and not be required to gown or wash her hands —if she is *careful*. If the nurse touches something contaminated with her hands, she should, of course, follow the hand-washing technique before leaving the room. A gown should not be worn outside a patient's room once it has been worn inside the room, with the following exceptions only:

1. When transporting a patient for an ordered procedure in a separate tub room
2. When transporting a patient to the x-ray department or some other distant therapy
3. When changing the location of a patient to a different room and assisting

with the movement of contaminated furniture.

When a contaminated gown must be used outside the patient's room, it should be as fresh as possible. The nurse should be very discreet about what she touches and where she goes. When the transportation of a child with a communicable disease through the hospital corridors is necessary, his wheelchair or gurney should be draped with clean linen. The nurse pushing the wheelchair or gurney should have a clean supply of towels or tissues, which she can use to open doors or push buttons when her hands are contaminated. She should also have a bag in which to discard these tissues after use. The child should be properly restrained to prevent falling; he should be covered to prevent chilling. If the trip will be long or the wait protracted, an appropriate fluid, if allowed, may be taken along in the case of an infant. The child's chart should be placed in a bag

for protection. The chart itself should be handled only by people with clean hands.

Gown techniques

Gowning. When a clean gown is used for the first time, it preferably is put on before entering the patient's unit or room. Since the gown and the nurse are "clean," any part of the gown may be touched by the nurse as she puts it on. It should be tied at the back of the neck and then the rest of the back of the gown adjusted in such a way that no part of the nurse's uniform is exposed. If gowns are reused, agreement should be reached concerning the method by which coverage is to be achieved so that all staff members can use the same technique. If gowns must be reused, it is preferable that the same nurse use the same gown during her tour of duty for the day. Following are two ways in which a gown may be closed:

1. Pull the left-hand side of the back of

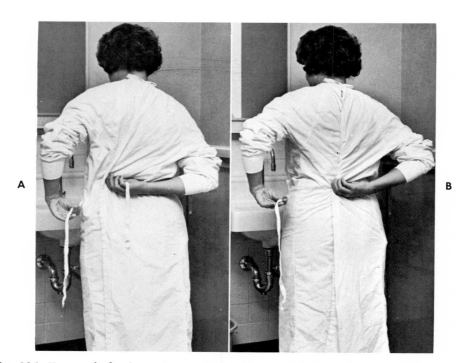

Fig. 36-1. Two methods of gowning. **A,** Right side over left. **B,** Back inside edges together; then roll until snug. (Courtesy Children's Health Center, San Diego, Calif.)

the gown as far to the right as possible and lap the right-hand side over the left. Pull the belt around, cross it at the back, and tie it in the front. Push up the sleeves above the wrists (Fig. 36-1, *A*).

2. Hold the right and left inner edges of the gown together and fold over the back part of the gown until it is snugly closed against the wearer's back. Pull around the belt. Cross it in the back, and tie it in the front, pushing the sleeves above the wrists (Fig. 36-1, *B*).

Note: The entire inside and all surfaces of the neckband of a previously used gown are considered clean. When a previously used gown is put on, observe the following steps:

1. Grasp the neckband of the gown with clean hands and open up the gown with the inside toward you.
2. Hold on to the neckband or the inside of the top of the gown with one hand and slip one hand and arm into an empty sleeve.
3. When one hand is through the sleeve, reach up and grasp the neckband with the clean hand protruding from the sleeve to allow the other arm and hand to be placed in the second sleeve and help pull the sleeve into place. When both hands are through the sleeves, reach up and tie the neckband.
4. Continue gowning by closing the back as has been agreed.
5. Push up the sleeves from the outside to expose the lower forearm. (This is done to avoid getting the sleeves wet during nursing care. A wet gown must be replaced because its effectiveness as a barrier is lost.) Sleeves must be pushed up—never rolled up!

Removing a gown. The steps for removing an isolation gown are basically the same whether the gown is to be discarded or saved for further use. The procedure is as follows:

1. Untie the belt, letting the ends drop to the side.
2. Turn on the running water.
   a. If faucets are used, they are opened with unwashed hands and closed with clean hands protected by a paper towel.
   b. If a knee lever is used, it is turned on and off with a knee covered by the isolation gown.
   c. If foot pedals (the most preferable device) are used to control the water flow, one does not need to consider the possibility of contaminating clean hands. Shoes are always considered contaminated.
3. Carefully wash the hands and exposed portion of the arms for one minute with an antibacterial detergent, using considerable friction (Fig. 36-2, *A*). However, we believe that the use of a brush is overly irritating and unnecessary. The areas are rinsed and patted dry with paper towels. The hands should be kept lower than the elbow when washing, as part of isolation technique, to avoid wetting the sleeves or later increasing the area of possible contamination.
4. Untie the neckband with newly washed hands and drop the ties toward the back (Fig. 36-2, *B*).
5. Reach under the cuff of one sleeve with the clean fingers of one hand, pulling it down past the other hand completely (Fig. 36-2, *C*).
6. Reach over to the other sleeve with the covered hand and, through the gown, pull down on the opposite sleeve (Fig. 36-2, *D*). Care must be taken to prevent the contaminated sleeve from brushing against the clean arm and hand in the process. If necessary, hands protected by covering sleeves may continue to help remove the gown from the outside. When hands and arms clear the inside of the sleeves, the neckband is grasped and folded once to close the gown.

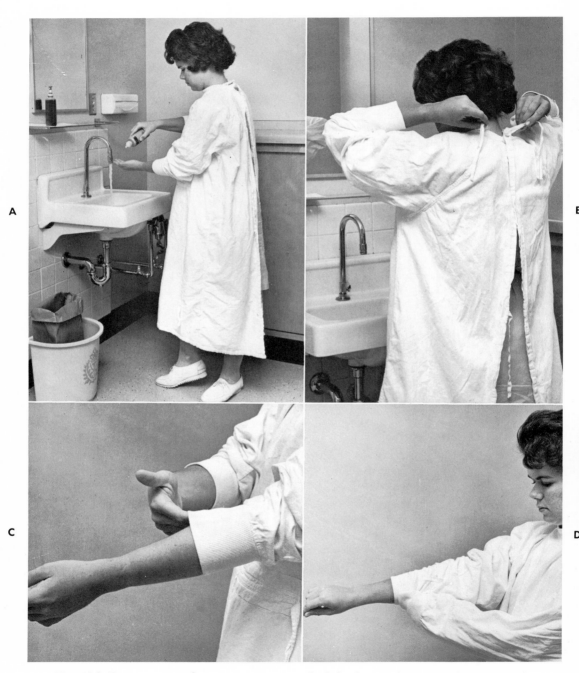

FIG. 36-2. Removing an isolation gown. **A,** Untie the belt, then wash your hands. **B,** Untie the neck strings. **C,** Reach under one cuff and pull the sleeve over the hand. **D,** With the one hand covered, grasp the opposite sleeve. (Courtesy Children's Health Center, San Diego, Calif.)

Hanging or discarding the gown. If the gown will be hung *in the patient's room,* it must be hung contaminated side, that is, *right side,* out. If it is hung *outside the patient's room,* it should be hung inside out (without reversing the sleeves). The procedure includes the following steps:

1. Fold the neckband once and hold it closed with two hands. Hang the gown from the pole in such a manner that the neckband stands up and the gown is firmly held by the hook at the top of the sleeves (Fig. 36-3, *A*). If necessary, the edges of the gown may be adjusted so that the surface to be protected is completely covered.

2. If the gown is to be discarded after it is removed, hold it carefully away from your uniform and drop it into the laundry hamper.

3. After hanging or discarding the gown, rewash your hands and arms using the same technique described previously, *except,* if a knee lever is used to control the water flow, open it with a hand before washing. If the lever is opened with knee action at this point, the nurse's uniform becomes contaminated. After the hands are washed, close the faucet or knee control with a hand protected by a paper towel (Fig. 36-3, *B*).

Leaving the patient's room. The following precautions are taken when leaving the room of an isolation patient:

1. Open the door with the paper towel

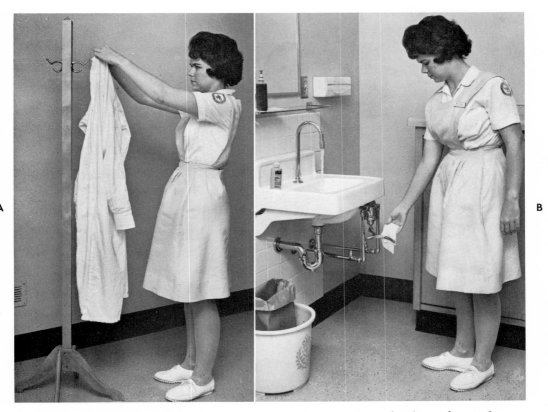

A   **B**

Fig. 36-3. **A,** When hanging the gown, do not contaminate your uniform! **B,** After washing your hands, if a knee control is used, turn it off with a paper towel. (Courtesy Children's Health Center, San Diego, Calif.)

used to turn off the water. Walk through.

2. Turn around before letting the door close and discard the paper in the wastebasket.

3. All doors to isolation rooms should be routinely kept closed.

USE OF MASKS

There are two drawbacks to the use of face masks. Masks are likely to give a false sense of security to the wearer, and masks, in themselves, may serve as a source of infection unless changed often (approximately every 30 to 60 minutes and always as soon as damp).

However, masks may help filter out some bacteria, thus protecting the wearer or the patient. It is the only practical method we now have, except good and discreet housekeeping, to protect against airborne organisms. Masks also keep the attendant's hands away from her face!

The following techniques are important in the use of masks:

1. Store masks conveniently outside the patient's unit. Many times they are placed in a paper bag taped on the outside of the patient's room where they are required to be worn.

2. Tie the mask in place before entering the room.

3. Remove a mask after your hands are washed by touching only the supporting ties and dropping it directly into the laundry receptacle.

4. Never leave a patient's room with a mask dangling around your neck!

USE OF TECHNIQUE PAPERS

A technique paper enables a nurse to carry out a procedure with greater skill and observance of asepsis by providing a temporary barrier between contaminated and clean objects. A clean paper towel usually serves as a technique paper. Taken directly from the dispenser, it is folded to form at least two layers of paper. It may be placed on a dry contaminated surface with clean hands, serving as a temporary island of cleanliness on which to place articles like watches, pencils, and perhaps specimen bottles. The underside of the paper touching the bedside table is contaminated; the upper side is not considered contaminated.

A watch is not worn on the nurse's wrist in an isolation situation because of the many times that the hands and lower arms must be washed and the danger that it would come in contact with the patient during his care. A watch cannot be sprayed or soaked with Amphyl or other disinfectants—both procedures seem to do something to its insides! Nevertheless, a watch is necessary to the nurse. The situation is bettered by enclosing the watch in a clear, small, waterproof plastic bag or box and using technique papers. A watch may be placed on a technique paper for a brief period in such a position that the dial may be easily seen to enable the nurse to observe a patient's pulse or respirations.

Neither the chart nor the nursing assignment sheet should be taken into the isolation patient's room. Because of memory problems, some student nurses have found it helpful to initially backfold a border of approximately an inch on a technique paper before placing it on a contaminated surface. This space is used to temporarily write the temperature, pulse, and respiration of the patient with a contaminated pencil, which is left in the unit. When the nurse is ready to leave the unit and has removed her gown, she picks up her watch with clean hands and, using the technique paper, opens the door, reviews the temperature, pulse, and respiration, and throws the paper in the wastebasket. Of course, if parents are in the room, it is not a good idea to have a slip of paper with the vital statistics of their child's condition in full view. If many observations must be remembered over a period and the nurse cannot leave the patient's room, it would be permissible for her to jot down the bare essentials on a contaminated paper towel and take it with her in one hand as she leaves the room. She could briefly place this paper on another clean technique paper on a well-marked spot until she is able to wash her hands and record the information in the patient's chart. The contaminated papers are then discarded in the trash, which will be double bagged. She could also create a small, clean writing space in the patient's room using clean technique paper, notepaper, pencil, and freshly washed hands. In this way she could carry out the uncontaminated "prompting sheet" to her charting area. However, this situation is an exception. Usually, the nurse should be able to remember such information unless it becomes quite complex or voluminous.

SERVICE OF MEALS

1. All food prepared for isolation patients in the hospital should be served on disposable dishes. (If special precautions must be taken at home because disposable dishes are not practical, dishes should be scraped in the patient's room and then placed directly in cool water to be boiled at least 10 minutes and then washed.)
2. No serving tray should enter the patient's room. Food in the serving dishes should be lifted from the tray and taken into the room without the tray.
3. Serve the food as soon as possible. No one enjoys cold meals. Prepare the setting for the children who can feed themselves and then go help feed others who need assistance.
4. Knives, forks, and spoons may be stored in the patient's room. After the meal they are washed and dried at the sink in the room and wrapped in a clean napkin until needed again.
5. Uneaten solid food should be scraped into a paper dish or cup and placed in a refuse sack in the wastebasket. Unfinished liquids may be poured into the toilet.
6. If intake-output records must be kept, the record is posted outside the isolation room, usually on the outside of the patient's door.

CARE OF LINEN, TRASH, AND DIAPERS

1. Soiled linen, usually with the exception of diapers, should be placed in a laundry hamper in the patient's unit. Handle soiled linen carefully. Do not "wave it in the breeze." Remember, careless handling of linen increases the organism count in the air.
2. At the end of each tour of duty or when the hamper in the room is two-thirds full, close the top of the bag and place it upside down in a clean hamper or a clean bag held by another nurse just outside the door.

Note: A "contaminated nurse" may touch only that part of the outer laundry bag that will be on the inside of the bag when it is closed.

3. Contaminated trash is collected in a

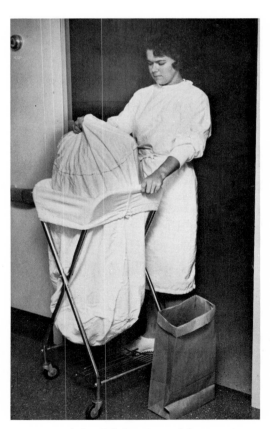

FIG. 36-4. She's glad her bag of linen isn't any bigger! (Courtesy Children's Health Center, San Diego, Calif.)

paper bag, which stands in the waste-basket. At the end of a tour of duty or when appropriate, the bag is carefully closed and placed in a clean outer bag just outside the door for disposal.

4. Double-bagged linen or bags of trash should be completely closed as soon as the nurse is able to remove her gown and wash her hands so that contaminated material does not remain unattended in the corridors. Sometimes it is possible for two or more nurses to work together to facilitate the removal of contaminated linen and trash. One will work in the patient's room, and the other(s) will close all the clean outer bags and place them in the approved areas for removal. The outer bags should be identified in some way (color, tagging) as containing isolation linen.

5. The handling of contaminated diapers depends on the facilities and services available. Many hospitals use professional diaper services. The instructions of these companies regarding the pretreatment of diapers (if necessary) and collection should be followed. Any diaper pails used for collections should be closed with lids that ideally are operated by a foot-pedal control.

DISPOSAL OF URINE, FECES, EMESIS, AND OTHER BODY DISCHARGES

1. Bedpans and emesis basins are usually emptied directly into the toilet in areas where urban sewage facilities are available. The hospital staff should know the sewage precautions needed in its own community. It is strongly recommended that each isolation unit have its own toilet facilities. In certain situations special precautions may have to be taken in the event of the occurrence of typhoid-related illnesses.

2. Any patient with nasal discharge should have a small paper sack attached to his bedside in which to put used cellulose wipes. When this bag is almost full, it is closed and added to the trash in the large paper bag in the wastebasket.

DISINFECTION OF EQUIPMENT

1. Disposable equipment is used in an isolation unit as much as possible.

2. Only essential equipment should be taken into an isolation room.

3. Large, nondisposable items (basins, bedpans, etc.) may be washed in the patient's room, sprayed with a disinfectant, and then transported directly to a dishwasher with a prewash cycle that disinfects the utensils. If this is impossible, they may be boiled in water or soaked in disinfectant. If no other means of disinfection are available, such items may be sprayed with a disinfectant such as Septisol or Amphyl.

4. Small items such as baby bottles, spoons, and hemostats are washed in the patient's room and taken to the utility room to be boiled or soaked in disinfectant for the appropriate time and then rewashed, dried, and stored appropriately.

5. Stethoscopes, percussion hammers, and flashlights are usually sprayed with disinfectant. Sphygmomanometers are wiped off with disinfectant. Blood pressure cuffs should have plasticized washable surfaces.

6. All needles used, whether disposable or not, should be soaked in disinfectant before leaving the patient's room and then carefully discarded in a pierce-proof box or sterilized for reuse.

THE HOSPITAL ADMISSION
Parental needs and fears

Almost without exception, admission to the hospital is a period of strain for the parents and child. The anxiety and feeling of helplessness often experienced by parents is increased considerably when the admission necessitates the use of certain barrier techniques or entry into a special nursing unit labeled "Isolation." The sight of the medical and nursing staff wearing gowns and perhaps masks and the sound of such potentially alarming terms as "contaminated" and "contagious" does not tend to reassure parents. Everything seems so strange. Disquieting and not always accurate deductions often disturb their peace of mind. "If Johnny has to be here, he must be terribly ill. I wonder what the other children here have. Couldn't Johnny catch something else from them?" Parents need a lot of support and instruction at such a time, and both physicians and nurses must contribute the necessary time and effort to provide it.

Unit preparation

Usually the admission of a new patient is anticipated, and an individual isolation unit is set up before his arrival. Patients are not placed in the same room unless it is confirmed that their diagnoses are the same and the attending physicians involved grant permission. The room should be comfortably warm and well ventilated. In addition to a correctly sized bed or crib, bedside stand, and overbed table found in all standard patient units, an isolation unit should include the following items:

1. Laundry hamper and two laundry bags
2. Clothes tree or rack on which gowns may be hung in a special way (unless a throw-away technique is possible)
3. Paper bags, used to line the wastebasket, wrap or collect objects for transport home, or collect and prepare trash for discard.
4. Disinfectant, used to soak needles before safe disposal and wipe down the room after the patient's basic care
5. Antibacterial detergent (such as pHisoHex or Betadine) for hand and arm care of the attendants
6. Access to a sink, running water, and a toilet
7. Paper towels in a dispenser

8. Knife, fork, spoon, as needed
9. Clean masks, gowns, and gloves readily available

The following articles, usually necessary for an admission, should also be at hand:

1. Appropriately sized gown or pajamas and diapers and pins, if appropriate
2. Bath towel set
3. Washbasin and emesis basin
4. Bedpan and/or urinal, toilet paper, or wipes
5. Coloplast bag or other means to help obtain a urine specimen from an infant or young child, if appropriate
6. Correctly sized blood pressure cuff (plastic coated if possible) and sphygmomanometer (for child 3 years old or over)
7. Thermometer, petrolatum, and cellulose wipes
8. Scales, properly draped and balanced
9. Soap, lotion or powder, toothbrush and toothpaste, and comb (To cut down on waste, dispensable supplies in small sample sizes are often used.)
10. Emergency equipment, oxygen, and suction machines, as indicated.

It is important that all equipment be in readiness because much time is lost if the nurse must leave the patient to obtain equipment. However, unnecessary equipment should not be brought into the unit, since it would be needlessly exposed to contamination and could not be used with other patients without the completion of certain procedures to render it noninfectious. A safe individual patient's unit also necessitates adequate, well-planned utility and laundry rooms.

Admission modifications in isolation

Unless a special order is written, usually only parents or legal guardians are allowed to visit a patient in isolation. In some cases, when strict isolation is followed, even these visitors are limited.

In our opinion, the mother should be allowed to put on a gown and be with and assist the child during the admission in most instances. After all, she has already been exposed to the infection, and the reassurance the child gains by her presence is usually significant.

The child's clothes are usually placed in a clean bag and returned to the parents.

Questions are often asked. "What do we do with Johnny's clothes when we get them home?" "What about all the things that Johnny used at home while he was sick?" In most cases it is sufficient to tell the parents to wash his clothes separately, using a hot setting on an automatic washer or to boil the clothes in soap solution and let them hang out in the sun for at least a day. The utensils or machine used may also be disinfected with the use of a chlorine solution rinse.

The former sickroom or sickrooms should be carefully cleaned (preferably vacuumed), damp dusted, and well aired. Objects that the child had handled should, whenever possible, be washed and exposed to sunshine for at least a day. Objects difficult to clean and relatively unimportant probably are best discarded. If the disease is of a serious nature, the discard of some types of objects, for example, stuffed animals, would be preferable. After all, stuffed animals, or their reasonable facsimiles, are usually replaceable. People are not!

The parents should be shown where they may store their coats and purses outside the patient's room when visiting. They should be shown where the supply of clean gowns are kept and how to put them on. They should be taught simply to take the gowns off, place them in the laundry hamper, and wash their hands just before leaving, and open the door with a paper towel. They should be told to always check at the nurses' desk before taking anything in to the child, since all objects cannot be adequately disinfected, and in the case of a serious disease, the article may have to be destroyed when the child goes home. This might cause considerable unnecessary distress! Expendable toys are encouraged. Television sets may be available for enter-

tainment; check on this for older children.

When weighing an isolated patient, the scales must be draped and balanced and then brought into the patient's room. The child is weighed and the drape discarded in the laundry hamper. The scale is then wiped down or sprayed with disinfectant.

A urine specimen is collected in the usual way, except that when the specimen has been obtained in the Coloplast bag, bedpan, or urinal, the specimen container to be sent to the laboratory is held by a "clean nurse" while the "contaminated nurse" pours the specimen. The clean nurse is responsible for capping and labeling the specimen. Stool specimens may be collected in a similar manner, using tongue blades to lift the specimen to the cardboard container. If only one nurse is available, the open specimen container may be set on a clean technique paper. The stool is then transferred and the nurse ungowns, washes her hands, covers the specimen, and labels it outside the patient's room. The outside of any specimen container to be sent to the laboratory must always be clean.

SUGGESTIONS FOR NURSING ORGANIZATION

Suggestions for organizing and completing your work when working in isolation are as follows:

1. Try to have *everything* you need in the room or just outside the room before gowning, including the following:
   a. Linen for the bed
   b. Clean clothes for the patient
   c. Hygienic supplies
   d. Supplies for early morning treatments
   e. Liquids to encourage fluid intake, if appropriate
   f. Paper sacks, to replace those you will remove when emptying trash or removing diapers
   g. Clean laundry bag, to replace the one you will be taking out later in the day
2. Before ungowning, always ask your

patient (if he talks!) if there is any-thing more he wishes.

3. Use the intercom for assistance, if one is available.
4. Remember, charting and clearing your units of contaminated linen and waste takes time. Plan your working schedule with this in mind. Be sure you have taken any unnecessary equipment, bottles, etc. from the room before you report off duty. At the completion of your morning care, the table tops, bed, and counters in the isolation room should be wiped down with a paper towel moistened with disinfectant.

Note: When only routine isolation is ob-served, it is permissible to go into a room without gowning and check for the sup-plies that will be needed. Carefully open up cupboards and drawers in a way such that *only* your hands are contaminated. At the same time you can be making friends with your patient and discovering any spe-cial thing he may desire. Wash your hands carefully at the end of your brief tour and leave, opening the door with a paper towel.

DISCONTINUING ISOLATION TECHNIQUE

If isolation precautions are discontinued before the patient is discharged from the hospital, a "termination of isolation" bath is given. If the child's condition is satis-factory and the physician is agreeable, a shampoo followed by a tub bath is ideal. After the tub bath, the child is dressed in clean clothes and returned to a new bed and unit, or he is kept on a clean gurney in another room until his old room can be wiped down and aired or fogged with a special disinfectant. However, if the tub room is used, it too must be fogged or wiped down, which is a disadvantage.

If the child's condition or the physical setup of the isolation area precludes a tub bath, another type of bath must be given in his bed. The child is placed on top and under a clean bath blanket. He is given a bed bath using a fresh clean washcloth, basin, and towel. The nurse giving the bath

is dressed in a fresh clean gown. The child is then lifted to a draped uncontaminated gurney, dressed in fresh bedclothes, and covered with a fresh bath blanket. The nurse removes her gown, washes her hands, and takes the child to a new "clean" unit.

Everything transferred from the patient's old isolation unit to his new uncontami-nated unit must undergo some type of dis-infection. The former isolation room is stripped of everything easily moveable that can be best disinfected in the utility room (including any wall oxygen and suction equipment). The linen is double bagged. All paper goods are discarded in the trash (special papers may be exposed to the sun if it is very important to save them and the disease was not serious). Potted plants may be sprinkled with water and exposed to the sun and air outside for several hours. The stripped room is then either wiped down with a disinfectant or fogged, and the room is completely cleaned.

When a child is discharged from the hos-pital before termination of isolation is of-ficially completed, the child is placed in a draped wheelchair for the trip to his par-ents' car. His belongings that are saved are washed or sprayed and placed in a clean bag. His room is then stripped.

Parents should be told of the precautions, if any, that must be observed at home. If isolation precautions are still necessary, de-tails of ways these precautions may be ob-served should be discussed so that the parents will feel confident regarding their use. These procedures must be simple and effective. Better to have a few rules under-stood and followed wisely than many rules confused and finally disregarded.

Significant childhood communicable diseases and their nursing care

Descriptions of some of the communica-ble diseases seen or mentioned most often in pediatrics are included in Table 36-1. Briefly summarized, also, are nursing points to remember in each case. Fortunately, not all the diseases described will be encoun-

Text continued on p. 529.

TABLE 36-1. Communicable childhood diseases

Disease	Infectious agent and general description	Importance	Mode of transmission	Communicable period	Incubation period	Symptoms	Treatment and nursing care	Prevention
Bacillary dysentery (shigellosis)	Shigella dysenteriae and Shigella paradysenteriae Acute inflammation of colon	Extremely widespread in areas with poor sanitary facilities and hygiene practices Disease often severe in infancy but often mild after age 3 yr.	Direct or indirect contact with feces of infected patients or carriers Contaminated food, water, and flies play important role	As long as patients or carriers harbor organisms (as determined by stool or rectal swab cultures) Healthy carriers common; they should not become food handlers In areas where sanitary treatment of sewage is not routine, stools should be disinfected	1-7 days (usually 3-4 days)	Mild to severe diarrhea; in severe cases blood, mucus, and pus may be seen in stool Abdominal pain, fever, and prostration may be present	Treatment depends on severity of infection Ampicillin drug of choice; chloramphenicol; tetracycline (used after age 8 yr.); furazolidone Paregoric and bismuth may help control diarrhea Keep patient warm; oral fluids may be restricted; intravenous therapy may be necessary to prevent dehydration	Attack appears to confer limited immunity No preventive known other than improved individual and community hygiene
Chicken pox (varicella)	Virus capable of causing varicella or herpes zoster Mild, chiefly cutaneous infectious disease Varicella—response to primary infection Herpes zoster—reactivation (in debilitated persons or persons receiving immunosuppressive therapy)	Very common, highly contagious, usually mild disease Complications other than secondary infection from scratching rare; however, encephalitis possible Overwhelming severe infection seen in children receiving immunosuppressive therapy CAUTION: Contact!	Direct or indirect contact with secretions from mouth or moist skin lesions of varicella or herpes zoster	Approximately 24 hr. before rash appears until 7 days after its onset; dried crusts not contagious	10-21 days (usually 14 days)	Slight fever; malaise; rapidly progressing papulovesiculopustular skin eruption in all stages of development, first appearing on trunk and scalp	Keep fingernails short and clean to minimize secondary infections caused by scratching Calamine lotion, oral antihistaminics reduce pruritus	None; immune after one attack Immune serum globulin (ISG) or hyperimmune zoster globulin for the corticosteroid-treated child or others at increased risk

Disease		Mode of transmission	Period of communicability	Incubation	Symptoms	Treatment	Immunity
Diphtheria	*Corynebacterium diphtheriae* (Klebs-Löffler bacillus) Severe, acute infectious disease of upper respiratory tract and perhaps skin Toxins produced may affect nervous system and heart	Rarely seen because of routine childhood immunization, more comprehensive public health regulations, and enforcement of milk standards and carrier control 5%–10% mortality Serious complications include neuritis, paralysis, and myocarditis	Direct or indirect contact with secretions from respiratory tract or skin lesions of patient or carrier	As long as virulent organisms are present in discharges and lesions Isolation until satisfactory nose and throat cultures obtained; contacts may be isolated	2-6 days	Depend on type and part of upper respiratory area inflamed Formation of fibrinous false membrane, which may or may not be visible in throat or nose Nausea, possible muscle paralysis, and heart complications	Administration of analgesics, antitoxin, erythromycin (preferred), and penicillin Absolute bed rest; gentle throat irrigations; bland, soft diet; humidification Possible need for tracheotomy Watch for muscle weakness	Immunity after one attack, but person may be immune without history of disease Immunity determined by Schick test Routine primary schedule–DTP booster injection on exposure
German measles (rubella, 3-day measles)	Virus Acute infectious disease characterized chiefly by rose-colored macular rash and lymph node enlargement	Very common, frequently occurring in epidemic form Complications rare for victim but may cause deformities of fetus if contracted by pregnant woman during first trimester	Usually direct contact with secretions from mouth and nose May be acquired in utero	From 1 wk. before rash appears until approximately 5 days after its onset	14-21 days (usually 18 days)	Rose-colored macular rash occurring first on face, then on all body parts; enlargement and tenderness of lymph nodes; mild fever	Supportive nursing care with good personal hygiene	Rubella vaccine Immune after one attack
Gonorrhea (see pp. 142 and 143)							
Herpes zoster (shingles)	Virus Same virus causes both chicken pox (varicella) and herpes zoster	Overwhelming severe infection seen in children receiving immunosuppressive therapy *CAUTION: Contact!*	Direct or indirect contact with secretions from mouth or moist skin lesions Zoster less contagious, but susceptible children exposed to zoster lesions may develop chicken pox	Approximately 24 hr. before rash appears until 7 days after its onset	10-21 days (usually 14 days)	Zoster lesions confined to skin over sensory nerves and preceded by local pain, itching, and burning Meningismus associated with cranial nerve involvement	Cut fingernails to prevent scratching Analgesics, sedation, thiamine; prednisone in severe cases; wet compresses to lesions	Usually immune after first attack Rarely, second attack seen in some individuals

Continued.

TABLE 36-1. Communicable childhood diseases—cont'd

Disease	Infectious agent and general description	Importance	Mode of transmission	Communicable period	Incubation period	Symptoms	Treatment and nursing care	Prevention
Measles (rubeola, or 2-week, or red, measles)	Virus. Acute infection characterized by moderately high fever, inflammation of mucous membranes of respiratory tract, and macular rash	Very common, highly infectious disease frequently occurring in epidemic form. Possible serious complications include pneumonia, otitis media, conjunctivitis, and encephalitis	Direct or indirect contact with secretions from nose and throat, perhaps airborne. May be acquired in utero	From time of "cold symptoms" until about 5 days after rash appears	About 10 days	Catarrhal symptoms, like a common cold; conjunctivitis; photophobia. Fever followed by macular, blotchy rash involving entire body. Koplik's spots (eruption on mucous membrane of mouth) diagnostic	Antibiotics (to prevent complications). Aspirin and tepid sponge baths for severe cases; various soothing lotions. Boric acid eye irrigations; protection from bright lights—eyeshade. Observation for onset of pneumonia or ear infection	Live measles vaccine, immune serum globulin (ISG) lessens disease. Usually immune after first attack
Meningococcal meningitis (cerebrospinal fever)	*Neisseria meningitidis* (*N. intracellularis*). Meningococcus. Serious, acute disease caused by bacteria that invade bloodstream and eventually meninges, causing fever and central nervous system inflammation	Occurs fairly often where concentrations of people are found (army bases, schools) because of healthy carriers. Very severe or relatively mild. Mortality depends on early diagnosis and treatment. Complications include hydrocephalus, arthritis,	Direct contact with patient or carrier by droplet spread. Organism may be found in urine	As long as meningococci are found in nose and mouth. Usually not infectious after 24 hr. of appropriate therapy	1-7 days (usually 4 days)	Sudden onset of fever, chills, headache, and vomiting (convulsions fairly common in children). Cutaneous petechial hemorrhages; stiffness of neck; opisthotonus; joint pain; possibly delirium; convulsions	Spinal tap and culture needed to confirm diagnosis. Temperature control; penicillin G, ampicillin, analgesics, and sedatives. Watch for clinical signs of increasing intracranial pressure or meningeal irritation and eye and ear involvement	Extent of immunity after attack unknown. Sulfonamides have been used prophylactically during epidemics

Continued.

Disease	Cause/Characteristics	Complications	Transmission	Communicability	Incubation	Symptoms	Treatment/Nursing care	Immunization
(continued from previous page)		blindness, deafness, impairment of intellect, and cerebral palsy					Maintain dim, quiet atmosphere; turn gently; watch for constipation and urinary retention; attention to fluid balance	
Mononucleosis, infectious (glandular fever)	Virus? Mildly contagious disease characterized by increase in monocyte-type white cell in blood, lymph node enlargement, fever, and fatigue. Heterophil agglutinin studies positive fairly late in course of disease. Isolation not recommended*	Typically, disease of teen-agers or young adults. Trauma may rarely cause ruptured spleen; hepatitis in 8%-10% of cases. May involve prolonged convalescence	Probably droplets from nose and throat, saliva, or intimate contact	Not known. Probably only during acute stage	Unknown (probably 2-6 wk.)	Sore throat, malaise, depression, enlarged spleen, liver, and lymph nodes. Possible jaundice with liver damage	Symptomatic, no specific therapy known. Bed rest, high carbohydrate, protein intake. Possible use of corticosteroids with severe throat involvement and airway obstruction	No immunization available
Mumps (infectious parotitis)	Virus. Acute infectious disease causing inflammation of salivary glands and, at times, testes and ovaries	Possible serious consequences for male after puberty, when an attack is more severe; sterility can be complication. Meningitis or encephalitis occur infrequently. Mild pancreatitis may be encountered	Direct or indirect contact with patient by droplet spread	From several days before apparent infection until swelling disappears	14-21 days (usually 18 days)	Tender swelling chiefly of parotid glands in front of and below ear. Headache; moderate fever; pain on swallowing	Bed rest; bland, soft diet; analgesics; warm or cold applications to swollen glands. Watch for tenderness of testes—scrotal support may be necessary. Observe for abdominal pain and signs of complications	Mumps vaccine. Usually immune after first attack. Immune serum globulin (ISG) may help those exposed to have milder cases or avoid symptoms

*Report of the Committee on Infectious Diseases, ed. 16, Evanston, Ill., 1970, American Academy of Pediatrics.

Table 36-1. Communicable childhood diseases—cont'd

Disease	Infectious agent and general description	Importance	Mode of transmission	Communicable period	Incubation period	Symptoms	Treatment and nursing care	Prevention
Poliomyelitis (infantile paralysis)	Virus Acute infectious disease, may occur in many forms and degrees of severity Attacks primarily gastrointestinal and nervous systems; may cause muscular paralysis	New cases uncommon since vaccine When paralysis takes place, many complications may occur involving respiratory, musculoskeletal, urinary, and digestive systems	Direct or indirect contact with pharyngeal secretions and feces of infected persons (many infected persons have no symptoms)	Communicable for indefinite period before onset of symptoms Usually isolated for 7 days after onset or until fever subsides Virus may persist in stool for weeks; local sewage facilities should be evaluated Careful personal hygiene needed	7-12 days?	Variable; may include diarrhea, constipation, emesis, painful stiff neck, rigid back, tender skeletal muscles, and respiratory distress Cranial nerve involvement Three main types 1. Inapparent infection, 2. Nonparalytic, and 3. Paralytic a. Spinal, affecting skeletal muscles and diaphragm, b. Bulbar, affecting swallowing, facial muscles, and respiration, c. Mixed	No specific treatment known Supportive treatment depends on patient needs; bed rest, hot packs to relieve muscle spasms, observation for respiratory or bulbar involvement Possible tracheotomy and respirator support; observation for constipation and urinary retention Gentle positioning; physical and occupational therapy	Routine primary schedule and boosters; OPV (Sabin-oral) optimum immunization schedule; IPV (Salk-injections) primary schedule plus repeated biennial booster doses
Rabies (hydrophobia)	Virus Only one nonfatal case reported, acute infectious encephalitis, causing convulsions and muscle paralysis	Exceedingly dangerous Household pets may acquire rabies through bite of rabid wild animals All dogs should	Bite of rabid animals or entry of infected saliva through previous break in skin or mucous membrane	During clinical course of disease plus 3-5 days before appearance of symptoms	Usually 2-6 wk.	Mental depression, headaches, restlessness, and fever Progresses to painful spasms of throat muscles, especially when	No effective treatment known Supportive nursing care to help prevent convulsions; analgesics; death usually occurs in about 7 days	Vaccination of dogs; 10-day confinement of any dog who has bitten human Laboratory investigation of brain of dog that

Disease	Infectious agent and description	Occurrence	Method of transmission	Period of communicability	Incubation period	Symptoms	Treatment and nursing care	Immunization and prevention
(Rabies, continued)						attempting to drink Delirium, convulsions, and coma	dies during this period; if rabies is diagnosed, person bitten must receive rabies vaccine	be immunized periodically; cats may also be carriers, but impractical to insist on immunization
Smallpox (variola)	Virus Highly contagious infection involving constitutional symptoms—fever and characteristic scarring rash; may occur in severe or mild forms	There should be no cases of smallpox in United States; preventive vaccine has been known and available over 100 yr., but not everyone maintains protection, every year cases occur Mortality 20%-50% Complications include secondary infection, bronchitis, and bronchopneumonia	Direct or indirect contact with secretions from skin lesions or mouth; airborne for short distances	From first appearance of illness until all crusts disappear	10-14 days (usually 12 days)	Sudden onset of high fever with flulike symptoms; rash appears in 3-4 days, involving normally exposed parts of body, face, arms, and upper chest Rash progresses to deeply seated pustules, all at same stage of development, leaving typical scars Photophobia	No specific treatment Antibiotics used to avoid secondary infection Procedures to relieve fever and itching Possible blood transfusions Shield eyes from light; special oral hygiene; encourage nutritious fluids; attention to fluid balance Deodorizing procedures for patient and room	Routine primary immunization smallpox vaccination Booster at school age and every 10 yr. Permanent immunity usually follows first attack
Staphylococcal infections	Coagulase-positive staphylococci (Micrococcus pyogenes, var., aureus) pus-producing coccus Descriptions variable	Found almost everywhere; causes many hospital infections; does not respond well to usual antibiotic therapy; extremely difficult to control; anyone may be carrier at intervals	Depends on body area infected Asymptomatic nasal carriers common May be airborne Direct or indirect contact with infected secretions	As long as lesions drain or carrier state persists	Variable; 1-2 days to several weeks	Depend on area infected Fever and characteristic signs of inflammation typical	Antibiotics according to drug sensitivity pattern of organism: methicillin, oxacillin Topical antibiotics: bacitracin, neomycin, polymyxin	No immunization able and effective generally available Good hygiene and aseptic technique best preventive

Continued.

TABLE 36-1. Communicable childhood diseases—cont'd

Disease	Infectious agent and general description	Importance	Mode of transmission	Communicable period	Incubation period	Symptoms	Treatment and nursing care	Prevention
Staphylococcal infections—cont'd		Complications include skin lesions, pneumonia, wound infections, arthritis, osteomyelitis, meningitis, and food poisoning						
Streptococcal infections	Strains of hemolytic streptococci. Diseases include septic sore throat, scarlet fever (scarlatina), erysipelas, impetigo, puerperal fever	Interrelated group of infections; septic sore throat probably most common. Early complications include otitis media. May cause serious complications not contagious in themselves—nephritis and rheumatic fever, with possible arthritis and carditis	In septic sore throat and scarlet fever, direct or indirect contact with nasopharyngeal secretions from infected patient; probably airborne. In erysipelas, impetigo, and puerperal fever, direct or indirect contact with discharges from skin or reproductive tract	Variable. Carrier state possible	2-5 days	Depend on manifestations. Septic sore throat, severe pharyngitis and fever. Scarlet fever, pharyngitis, fever, and fine reddish rash and strawberry tongue. Erysipelas, tender, red skin lesions and fever often recurrent. Puerperal fever, refer to pp. 177 and 178	Depends on manifestation. Penicillin for at least 10 days	No artificial immunization available. Penicillin prophylaxis may be used with special groups. Good asepsis important
Syphilis (see pp. 141 and 142)								
Tetanus (lockjaw)	Bacillus *Clostridium tetani*. Acute infectious disease attacking chiefly nervous system	Always considered in event of burns, automobile accidents, or puncture wounds. Mortality rate of about 35%	Entrance of spores into wounds through contaminated soil. Person-to-person transmission	Infectious, but only potentially communicable if draining wound present	3-21 days (usually 8 days)	Irritability, rigidity, painful muscle spasms, and inability to open mouth. Exhaustion and	Antitoxin and sedation plus muscle relaxant. Quiet, dim room. Possible suction and tracheotomy	Routine primary immunization; booster at school age and Td every 10 yr.

Disease	Causative agent and nature	Mode of transmission	Period of communicability	Incubation period	Symptoms and diagnosis	Treatment and nursing care	Prevention and control
	Wounds deprived of good oxygen supply especially vulnerable	unlikely unless discharges from infected wound contaminate open lesion			respiratory difficulty	Observation of fluid balance; watch for constipation and respiratory distress; protect from self-injury during convulsions	
Tuberculosis	*Mycobacterium tuberculosis* (tubercle bacillus) Typically chronic infection that may affect many body organs Human type most often causes pulmonary infection Bovine type causes much of tuberculosis affecting areas outside lungs Serious world health problem, particularly in economically deprived areas Infants and young children very susceptible Pulmonary complications, hemoptysis, spontaneous pneumothorax, or spread to other organs with varied symptoms; possible orthopedic problems	Direct or indirect contact with infected patients; body excretions or droplet spread (depending on type) Respiratory tuberculosis often airborne; bovine type may result from drinking milk from infected cows (now rare in U.S.)	As long as organism is discharged in sputum or other body excretions Communicability may be reduced by medication, therapy, and teaching cough control and asepsis to patients Body often walls off a primary infection, controlling spread and preventing active disease	From infection to primary lesion, 2-10 wk. Time of appearance of active symptoms variable	Active pulmonary tuberculosis: anorexia, weight loss, night sweats, afternoon fever, cough and dyspnea, fatigue, and hemoptysis; in children dyspnea and cough often absent Diagnosis based on symptoms and microscopic studies of sputum, gastric washings, and chest x-ray examination	Several drugs may prevent growth of organism, including streptomycin (STM), para-aminosalicylic acid (PAS), and isoniazid (INH) Nursing care includes provision for mental and physical rest; nutritious diet; observation for toxic drug reactions and increasing respiratory distress; provision for and instructions in personal hygiene; moral support	BCG vaccine to build up immunity in high-risk populations advised by some Early detection and control of known cases through periodic x-ray examination, possible skin tests, and close medical supervision
Typhoid fever (enteric fever)	*Salmonella typhosa*, a bacillus (many types have been identified) Relatively severe febrile systemic infection with symptoms Always of potential public health importance when community hygiene breaks down Carrier states may persist Complications in-	Direct or indirect contact with urine and feces of infected patients and carriers Food and water supplies may be infected by con-	As long as typhoid organism appears in feces or urine 2%-5% of those affected become permanent carriers	1-3 wk. (usually 2 wk.)	In children symptoms may be atypical, may at first resemble upper respiratory infection; intestinal tract becomes inflamed and even ulcerated;	Chloramphenicol and supportive nursing care; liquid to bland, soft diet as tolerated; bed rest Watch for abdominal distention and hemorrhage;	Immunity usually acquired after one attack Triple vaccine against forms of paratyphoid as well as typhoid available

Continued.

TABLE 36-1. Communicable childhood diseases—cont'd

Disease	Infectious agent and general description	Importance	Mode of transmission	Communicable period	Incubation period	Symptoms	Treatment and nursing care	Prevention
	toms involving lymphoid tissues, intestine, and spleen, which may be accompanied by complete prostration and delirium Condition has prolonged course and convalescence	clude intestinal hemorrhage and perforation, thrombosis, cardiac failure, and cholecystitis	taminated *flies* or unsuspected *carriers*; community sewage facilities should be evaluated; excreta may have to be disinfected before being added to local system			spleen enlarges; fever mounts; pulse relatively slow; rash, "rose spots" may be present	small enemas may be ordered; observation of fluid balance	
Whooping cough (pertussis)	*Bordetella pertussis* (pertussis bacillus) Acute infection of respiratory tract, characterized by paroxysmal cough ending in "whoop," often accompanied by vomiting	Severe disease in infants, may terminate fatally Complications include bronchopneumonia and convulsions, widespread hemorrhages, hernia, and possible activation of pulmonary tuberculosis	Direct or indirect contact with nasopharyngeal secretions of infected patients (droplet infection)	From 7 days after exposure to 3 wk. after onset of typical cough Greatest in catarrhal stage before onset of paroxysms	5-21 days (usually within 10 days)	Early symptoms resemble typical common cold Cough worsens and may become violent and paroxysmal Vomiting may be caused by coughing or nervous system irritation; cough may linger after convalescence	Diagnosis confirmed with bacterial studies of exposed cough plates and presence of leukocytosis Immune serum globulin; erythromycin antibiotic of choice; provision for rest and quiet; sedatives Light nutritious diet; judicious fluid intake to prevent dehydration; weight determinations Observation for onset of respiratory distress or other complications	Immunity produced after one attack Routine primary schedule plus boosters

tered by nurses today. However, all those described, and some not included, pose a potential threat to our communities. Diseases such as diphtheria, typhoid, tetanus, polio, and smallpox, for which we have proved preventives, could again ravage our population if public health standards decline and public education and support for immunization programs are not constantly maintained.

37

Conditions involving the neuromuscular and skeletal systems

All the systems of the body are intimately related. If a difficulty in one part of the body is severe enough or sufficiently prolonged, many body systems, in fact, the entire person, will react. The interdependence of the neuromuscular and skeletal systems is especially noteworthy.

Traumatic, infectious, or toxic injury to the nerve centers or nerve fibers that control the skeletal muscles often leads to wasting of those muscles and an inability to control or perhaps even initiate motion in related parts of the body. Poorly developed, abnormal, or damaged muscles may cause orthopedic deformities. Broken bones frequently cause muscle spasm and pain. This chapter will attempt to present or review some of the more common neuromuscular and skeletal problems found in children, the methods of treatment, and, of course, the nursing care involved.

A number of the problems affecting these interrelated systems are present at birth, or congenital in nature. The more common of these congenital defects were discussed in the chapter treating abnormalities of the newborn infant. For a brief description of hydrocephalus, cranial stenosis (craniosynostosis), microcephaly, spina bifida, clubfoot, congenital dislocated hip, syndactyly, and polydactylism, refer to Chapter 18.

Fractures

A very common problem in childhood is a broken bone, or fracture. Roller skates, skate boards, bicycles, and the rather rough-and-tumble life of youngsters (especially boys) contribute to the high incidence of fractures. Probably even more broken bones would occur in childhood if it were not for the relatively plastic condition of the child's skeletal system. The bones of children in this age group tend to bend rather than break. Frequently, if a break does happen, it does not completely sever the bone. A portion of the bone remains intact. This type of fracture is called an incomplete, or a *greenstick*, fracture (Fig. 37-1).

Classifications

Other common types of fractures described according to the course of the break sustained include *transverse, spiral,* and *oblique.* A *comminuted* fracture is especially difficult to repair because the bone is typically broken into several pieces. A *depressed* fracture is particularly important when the fractured bony area is the skull and abnormal pressure is exerted on sensitive brain tissue.

Fractures may result from excessive or sudden direct pressure, exaggerated muscular contractions, or a basically unsound bony structure. If an unsound bony structure is the cause, the fracture is termed "pathological." Some of the causes of pathological fractures are osteomyelitis (inflammation of the bone marrow and surrounding bone cells), primary bone tumors or metastases, and osteogenesis imperfecta congenita (congenital brittle bones, a disease of unknown origin in which bones may fracture even before birth, causing characteristic skeletal malformations occa-

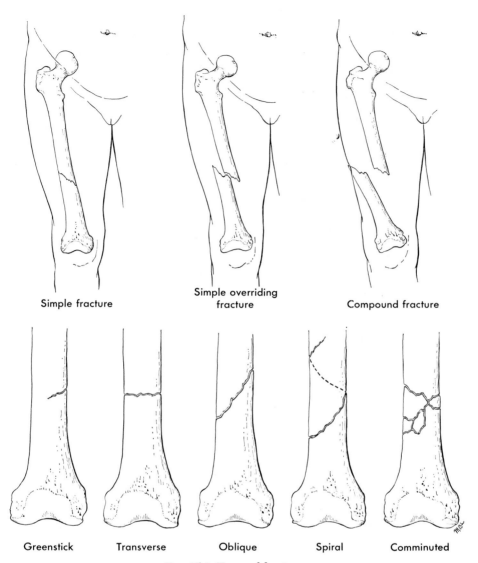

Simple fracture   Simple overriding fracture   Compound fracture

Greenstick   Transverse   Oblique   Spiral   Comminuted

FIG. 37-1. Types of fractures.

sionally accompanied by deafness). If it is known that a patient has an underlying bone disease, great care and gentleness must be practiced in his turning and positioning. (See Fig. 37-2.)

A careful note must be made of the general condition of a child who enters the hospital with a fracture of unknown origin, multiple fractures, or a repeated fracture. Sometimes these little patients are the victims of abuse from their own parents, who are unable to meet the daily frustrations

of parenthood in a mature manner or who have deep-seated psychological problems. Such children usually exhibit multiple bruises and suffer from malnutrition (battered child syndrome). (See Fig. 37-3 and p. 332.)

Every fracture, irrespective of the course or extent of the break or its basic cause, may be placed in one of two main categories. If a bone is broken but the skin overlying the fracture has not been pierced by the end of the broken bone and there

531

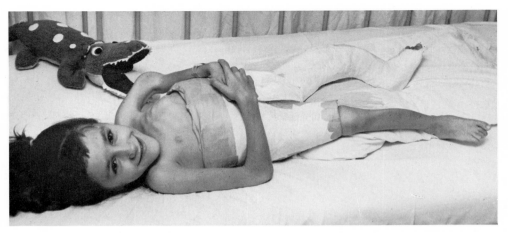

FIG. 37-2. This alert young lady is a victim of osteogenesis imperfecta congenita. She was hospitalized for corrective surgery involving previous fractures. (Courtesy Children's Health Center, San Diego, Calif.)

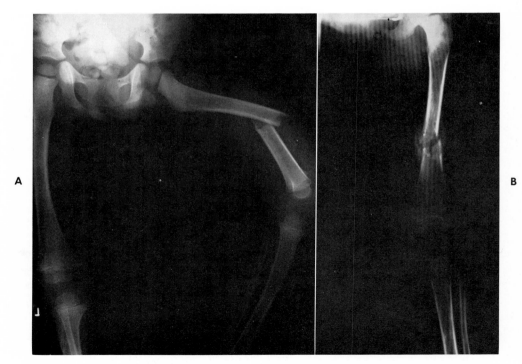

FIG. 37-3. A, X-ray film of the left femur of a 19-pound, 2½-year-old child who entered the hospital with multiple body bruises. Provisional diagnosis was "battered child syndrome." B, X-ray film showing the same leg after the reduction of the fractured femur. The shadowy outline around the break is callus. (Courtesy U. S. Naval Hospital, San Diego, Calif.)

is no opening in the skin that may serve to introduce organisms from the exterior to the bone, the result is called a *simple,* or *closed,* fracture. If, however, the skin has been broken, exposing the bone to infection, the resulting trauma is called a *compound,* or *open,* fracture. Compound fractures are surgical emergencies because of the increased danger of infection and extensive soft tissue damage usually involved.

First-aid considerations

A nurse encountering an accident victim with unknown injuries should take the following action:

1. Evaluate the safety of the immediate environment. (Turn off ignition of car, set out warning flares if on the highway, etc.) Send someone for help, if possible.
2. Establish an airway if respirations are not present.
3. Control hemorrhage, if present.
4. Restore and maintain breathing, if necessary.
5. Evaluate for spinal injury and fracture. Do not move victim until proper help is available.
6. Keep the patient warm and quiet to prevent and treat shock.

If a victim with spinal injury is moved improperly, the injury may be increased and permanent paralysis or even death may occur. If the victim is conscious but cannot move any extremity, the nurse must consider the possibility of a *broken neck* or cervical fracture. A patient with a possible broken neck should be moved by a team of persons so that no twisting or injurious movement of the spine will take place. He should be transported on a rigid support on his back, *chin up.* The victim with a suspected *broken back* may be unable to move his legs (lower extremity paralysis). He should be moved, log fashion, with considerable help to a *prone* position and also carried on a rigid support. The prone, or abdominal, position is maintained to prevent flexion of the middle and lower portions of the spine. Persons with suspected spinal injuries should be moved as little as possible. They should be frequently observed to detect the onset of respiratory difficulty and abdominal distention. The higher the injury occurs on the spinal cord, the more body functions will be affected. Nonspinal fractures are less serious but still necessitate careful attention and first aid.

Indications of fracture. Fracture of an extremity may reveal itself early through the presence of the following:

1. Deformity in alignment and swelling
2. Pain or tenderness at the fracture site
3. Loss of function or abnormal mobility of the part
4. A "grating sensation" heard or felt at the suspected point of fracture (crepitus)
5. Black-and-blue areas caused by subcutaneous hemorrhage

However, the real proof of the presence of fracture must be detected by x-ray examination. Sometimes clinical symptoms are virtually lacking or very inconclusive, but the x-ray film reveals a break. Every suspected skeletal injury should be treated as a fracture until proved otherwise.

Use of splints. First-aid treatment of a possible fracture includes limitation of the movement of the injured part by stabilizing the part and the joint above and below the break to relieve muscle spasm and pain and prevent further injury. Splint the arm or leg without attempting to correct any deformity. Do not attempt to straighten it because this may cause still further damage. Do not attempt to push back a broken bone protruding from the skin in the case of a compound, or open, fracture. Just cover the area. If bleeding is present, use direct manual pressure to obtain control. A tourniquet is a potential hazard because it can cause gangrene and loss of a limb. It should be used only as a last resort. If a tourniquet is used, its presence should be clearly indicated by obvious signs or skin markings. Splints may be made from rolled magazines, blankets, or pillows. They should be applied in a position comfortable for the patient. Rings and bracelets on a fractured arm should be removed to avoid difficulty in the event of swelling. The application of ice bags may decrease the possibility of swelling. Do not apply heat. In case of bleeding from an arm or leg, elevate the part if possible.

When a fracture involving the bones of an extremity occurs, usually the muscles attached to the broken bone, which have been under a certain amount of tension, contract as a result of loss of proper skeletal support. The pain associated with the fracture causes the muscles to go into spasm in an effort to splint the injured part. If this spasm is exaggerated, the severed ends of the broken bone may be pulled further out of alignment or may override, causing abnormal shortening of the limb.

Hospital care

Observation. When a patient with a possible bone fracture is first admitted to the hospital, his general condition is evaluated in detail. Vital signs (temperature, pulse, respiration, and blood pressure recordings) are obtained. Elevated blood pressure is important to report because of the possibility of skull fracture. Low blood pressure is equally important because of the possibility of shock. The patient's level of consciousness should be evaluated and the pupils of the eyes checked for abnormal pupil dilatation or inequality of pupil size (other signs of possible skull fracture and brain injury). Depending on the patient's condition, he may be given intravenous solutions or blood. He should not be given any food or fluid by mouth because corrective surgery may be indicated. An x-ray examination of possible fracture sites should be made.

Reduction and casting. If overriding or angulation of a fractured bone has occurred, the displaced bone will be pulled into alignment through some form of traction until the broken fragments are in proper position. The process of bringing the fragments into proper relationship is termed "reducing," or "setting," the fracture. If the fractured bone can be set without performing a surgical operation that actually exposes the involved bone, the procedure is called a *closed* reduction. If it is necessary to expose the site of the fracture to direct view to secure proper alignment and optimum healing or use some method of internal immobilization such as the installation of a nail, pin, or screws, the procedure is called an *open* reduction. Most children's fractures may be treated by closed reduction.

At times alignment may not be disturbed. The x-ray examination reveals a break, but the bony segments are still in proper relationship. If this is happily the case, no mechanical traction apparatus is needed. A plaster cast or protective splint is applied to maintain correct positioning to assure proper healing. Occasionally there is only a relatively minor disturbance in alignment that can be reduced easily at the time the patient is first seen or may not even require reduction. In children a fracture often stimulates the formation of bone, and, curiously enough, at times the physician may desire a certain amount of overriding to avoid excessive growth of the fractured extremity.

If sufficient initial alignment is difficult or impossible to achieve and maintain, some form of constant pull, or traction, must be exerted to reduce the fracture and bring the ends of the broken bone into proper apposition. The position of the bone and progress of the healing process are intermittently checked by x-ray studies. When a sufficient amount of new bone (callus) is formed at the fracture site to help hold the broken segment in position, traction is discontinued and a protective cast is applied, allowing the patient more mobility. For a discussion of the basic nursing care involved in the care of a patient in traction or a cast, please refer to Chapter 33.

Fractures involving the legs of infants and young children often are treated by suspending both legs, wrapped in bandages, from a frame hanging directly above the bed. The infant's trunk almost entirely rests on the crib mattress, only the pelvis is raised slightly from the surface of the bed. His legs are suspended at right angles to the mattress. Such an arrangement is called *Bryant's,* or *vertical,* traction (see Fig. 33-3). It is useful in treating lower extremity fractures of children weighing under 40 pounds in the infant or toddler age groups. Even though only one leg may be fractured, both are customarily placed in traction to help stabilize the position and prevent undue twisting on the part of the child. Older children will usually be placed in types of traction similar to those used for adult fracture patients, only smaller.

The healing of a broken bone is referred to as the *union* of a fracture, accomplished through the deposit of new bone cells. In children, union is usually achieved in a relatively short time. Union is seldom delayed, and it is rare indeed to see a case in which union never takes place.

Rehabilitation. After the bone has united, the weakened muscles attached to the bone may have to be gradually strengthened through a program of exercise as prescribed by the physician. This part of therapy is not so necessary with young children, however, since they start using the part immediately and often do not need the encouragement required by many adults. The resources of the physical therapy department may be used on an inpatient or outpatient basis. The aims of treatment are a return of function, freedom from pain, and a normal appearance.

Other skeletal problems

The skeletal system may become distorted for reasons other than fracture. Various developmental, nutritional, and metabolic diseases may soften or distort the bones.

Coxa plana (Legg-Calvé-Perthes disease)

Legg-Calvé-Perthes disease, a developmental problem occasionally seen in children, involves the head of the femur, which undergoes degenerative changes that are primarily the result of disturbances in blood supply. Its occurrence may be secondary to other disease conditions or trauma. In some cases no specific cause may be identifiable. It has several names, some of which are more descriptive and helpful than others—coxa plana (flat hip), osteochondritis deformans juvenilis, aseptic necrosis of the upper femoral epiphysis, or Legg-Calvé-Perthes disease!

The condition occurs more often in boys than in girls and usually affects only one hip. It begins as an inflammation of the joint capsule; this phase is followed by a prolonged period of bony degeneration in which the softened femoral head may reveal a mushroomlike appearance on x-ray examination. The child may complain of pain in the hip or knee and walk with a limp. Unless the joint is kept at rest, with no weight bearing until spontaneous healing finally occurs, a significant progressive and lasting deformity may result. Unfortunately, even with prolonged enforced rest there may be hip problems in later life. Trying to keep a child from placing weight on a leg over a period of 2 to 3 years presents many problems. Traction may be used intermittently to reduce muscle spasm and pain. Casts may be ordered for relatively brief periods. A sling arrangement (Fort harness) may be used to keep the involved leg off the floor if the child is allowed up on crutches. Sometimes braces are helpful. In any case this condition calls for much patience on the part of the parents, physician, and child.

Childhood rickets

One disease resulting from nutritional disturbance is common childhood rickets. The name is misleading, however, because nowadays a classic example of this disease is sometimes difficult to find in the United States. Rickets is always a potential health hazard in communities where there is little sunshine or little exposure of the children to outdoors and a diet deficient in vitamin D and/or calcium or phosphorus. Vitamin D is crucial because it regulates the absorption and deposit of calcium and phosphorus. Most evaporated milks are now specially irradiated or fortified to provide adequate levels of vitamin D to infants and children. Other rich sources are the fish-liver oils. Sunshine, if it is not screened by window glass and clothing or rendered unavailable by air pollution, is the most inexpensive source of vitamin D. Of course, vitamin preparations are also obtainable for a price. Cases of rickets may be mild and pass undetected or may be very severe and remarkable. Classic manifestations are knock-knees or bowlegs, kyphosis (hump-back) or scoliosis (an abnormal lateral spinal curvature), delayed closure of fontanels and protruding forehead (bossing), thickened wrists and ankles, and enlargement of the cartilaginous area of attachment of the ribs to the sternum, forming the famous *rachitic rosary*, pigeon breast, and contracture of the pelvis. Treatment consists of greater intake of vitamin D, calcium, and phosphorus. It is possible, but not probable, to have an excessive vitamin D intake so discretion should be used in the selection and dosage of therapeutic vitamins.

Other forms of rickets may be caused by poor absorption or utilization of vitamin D, phosphorus, or calcium. In some cases such softening does not respond to normal dosages of vitamin D. This type of rickets is said to be vitamin D resistant. At times rickets may appear as a secondary problem in disease conditions affecting assimilation of foodstuffs (celiac disease, cystic fibrosis, endocrine disorders, or renal disease). Adult rickets, or osteomalacia, refers to softening of the bone, usually the result of limited calcium intake and withdrawal of normal calcium deposits from the bone. You may recall that this form of rickets may occur during pregnancy.

Spinal curvature

Spinal deformities such as scoliosis (S-shaped lateral curvature), kyphosis (hump-back), and lordosis (exaggerated lumbar curvature) may be the products of many different conditions, including the following:

1. Nutritional deficiencies (common childhood rickets [discussed in the preceding paragraphs])
2. Inflammation of the bony spine (osteomyelitis, tuberculosis, arthritis, or dislocation of the hips)
3. Nerve injury resulting in paralytic conditions and unequal muscle pull (myelomeningocele, poliomyelitis)
4. Primary muscle weakness or dystrophy

Of the three kinds of abnormal spinal curvatures, scoliosis is the most common. Scoliosis is often idiopathic in origin, that is, no one knows the precise cause of the condition. Idiopathic scoliosis frequently occurs in young adolescent girls at the time of a sudden growth spurt. If the scoliosis can be voluntarily corrected by the patient and no abnormality in spinal vertebrae has

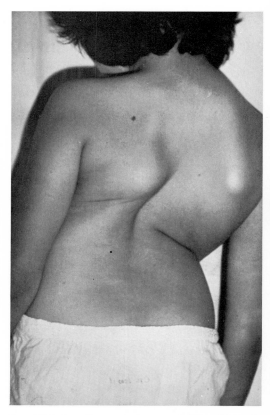

FIG. 37-4. A rather typical case of idiopathic scoliosis in a teen-age girl. (Courtesy Children's Health Center, San Diego, Calif.)

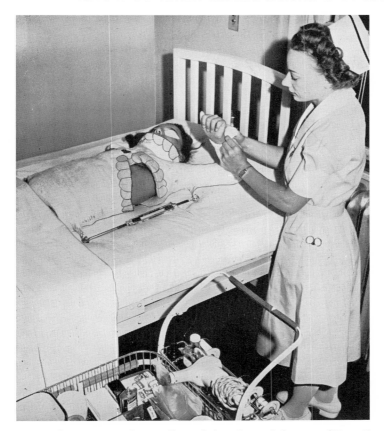

FIG. 37-5. Turnbuckle cast. Note the petalling of the edges of the cast. (From Larson, C. B., and Gould, M.: Orthopedic nursing, ed. 7, 1970, St. Louis, The C. V. Mosby Co.)

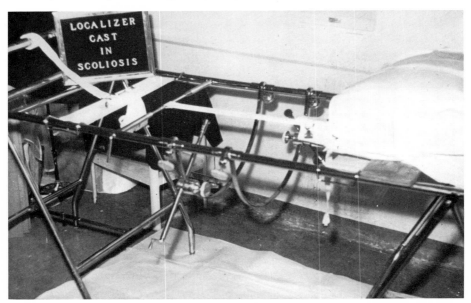

FIG. 37-6. Risser frame, used to apply localizer casts for the treatment of scoliosis. (Courtesy Paul E. Woodward, M.D., San Diego, Calif.)

taken place, it is called *functional*. If the scoliosis cannot be voluntarily corrected and is associated with vertebral deformity, it is *structural* in character. Scoliosis is usually painless until far advanced. However, it causes deformities in posture. One hip may be lower or more prominent than the other. The chest may be abnormally rotated and the shoulders uneven. Advanced scoliosis may cause significant problems in weight bearing and respiration. (See Fig. 37-4.)

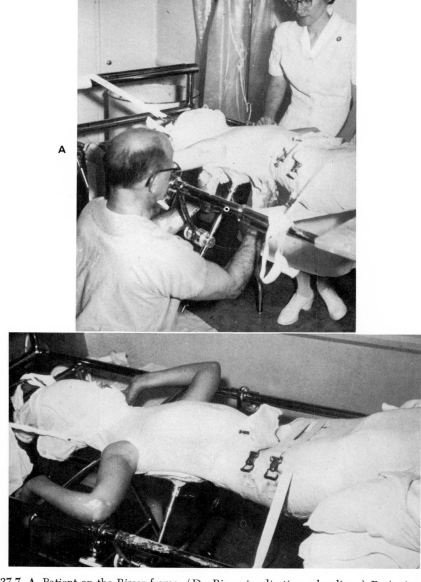

FIG. 37-7. **A,** Patient on the Risser frame. (Dr. Risser is adjusting a localizer.) **B,** A view of the neck halter and pelvic band in place for traction and the positioned localizer. **C,** Diagram of the push and pull involved. (Courtesy Paul E. Woodward, M.D., San Diego, Calif.)

Treatment. Various types of treatment are prescribed for scoliosis, depending on the cause (if known) and extent of the abnormality. In all types adequate nutrition with a high-protein content, correct positioning, and avoidance of fatigue are emphasized. For mild cases an awareness of posture and persistent, correct exercise as prescribed by the orthopedist and physical therapist may be all that is necessary. In moderately advanced to severe cases progressive bracing or corrective casting followed by a spinal fusion operation may be necessary.

Braces. A fairly common type of body support used for the correction of scoliosis and the maintenance of a position after a spinal fusion is the *Milwaukee brace.* This brace may be adjusted by the physician, exerting pressure on the chin, pelvis, and convex side of the spinal curve to achieve correction. Orders regarding the use of the brace and the length of time it may remain off will depend on the stage in the

child's treatment and the individual physician's desires.

Turnbuckle cast (Fig. 37-5). Application, subsequent wedging, and positioning of parts of a plaster cast with a turnbuckle has been used for scoliosis treatment. First, a heavy body cast, usually reaching from the chin and occiput of the head to the hip on one side and the knee on the other, is applied. After a few days a pie-shaped piece of plaster (wedge), extending to the midline on both the front and the back of the cast, is cut out of the cast on the convex side of the scoliosis curve. A transverse cut is also made on the concave side of the curve, allowing movement of the top portion of the cast. Hinges and a turnbuckle (a metal connector, capable of being rotated to increase tension on the movable parts of the cast) are attached to the cast to control the amount of lateral angulation of the top portion of the cast to the lower portion. Progressive tightening of the turnbuckle by the physician gradually forces the deformed spine into a correct position. When the desired position is attained, the open parts of the cast are usually plastered shut and a window cut in the cast over the spine in the area of the proposed spinal fusion. The child is then taken to surgery, and the operative procedure is performed through the cast window. This usually involves the use of bone grafts from the patient's own iliac or tibial bones or a bone bank to achieve stability of the fusion.

Risser localizer cast. More common now than the use of the so-called turnbuckle cast is the application of successive scoliosis jackets using the Risser table or frame. This table, devised by Dr. Risser in the early 1950's, helps straighten the spine by both pulling and pushing the patient. It also is designed to provide increased ease in the subsequent application of the corrective cast. The patient is supported on the frame after being protected by layers of tubular stockinette and/or cellulose padding, and plaster casts are applied to the pelvis and head in two separate sections. Traction is applied to the head by a halter

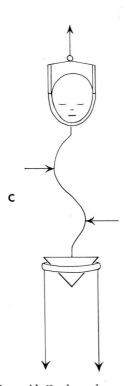

C

FIG. 37-7, cont'd. For legend see opposite page.

and to the pelvis by a special band. At the same time pressure is exerted on the convex sides of the spinal curves by means of padded plaster-backed jacks or localizers attached to the sides of the table that are pressed against the patient. When maximum correction at the time of this procedure is achieved, the casting is then completed by joining the head and pelvic areas with a plaster cast of the trunk, which includes localizer pads. Successive castings are usually followed by spinal fusion. (See Figs. 37-6 to 37-8.)

Halo traction. The halo traction is used in the treatment of a rigid spinal curvature associated with weakness or paralysis of the neck and trunk muscles. It also may be employed in the care of cervical fractures and fusions (Fig. 37-9). The halo

consists of a metal ring that is attached to the skull by two posterior pins in the occipital bone and two anterior pins inserted into the temporal bones. It is attached to a weight while countertraction is exerted by weights connected to two Steinmann pins inserted into the distal ends of both femurs. The weights are increased daily as tolerated by the child until maximum correction is obtained.

When maximum correction of the curve is evidenced by x-ray examination, a spinal fusion is usually done. Weighted halo traction may be continued to prevent loss of the correction, or a body cast or jacket is applied, incorporating the halo by means of an extended frame, to maintain the gains accomplished by the original traction and fusion.

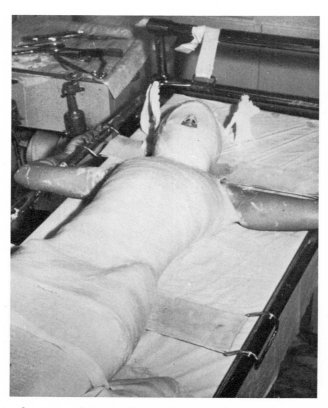

Fig. 37-8. The trunk portion of the localizer scoliosis cast has just been completed; now the head cast will be partially removed and the face exposed. (Courtesy Paul E. Woodward, M.D., San Diego, Calif.)

NURSING CARE. The procedure should be explained step-by-step to the child, in words that he can understand. His questions should be answered carefully. He may complain that the pins hurt. This usually indicates that they need to be tightened to make the child more comfortable. The pins are cleaned daily with hydrogen peroxide, and the skin around each pin is painted with an antiseptic.

Proper alignment of all equipment, especially the ropes, is necessary for effective traction. The little patient may prefer to remain in the supine position, but he should

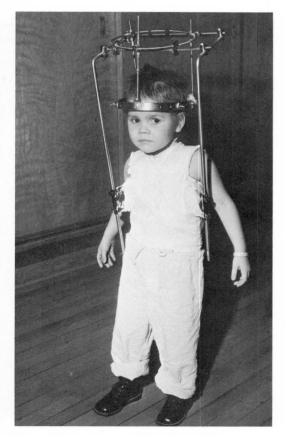

FIG. 37-9. This 4-year-old youngster has congenital deformities of the vertebrae and ribs that caused a severe scoliosis. A spinal fusion was performed. The halo frame and plaster cast combination maintains correction while allowing Ross to move about with relative ease. (Courtesy Children's Health Center, San Diego, Calif.)

be turned at least every 2 hours, from back to side and side to back. The patient is encouraged to breathe deeply for a few minutes each time he is turned. Adequate ventilation of the lungs is extremely important because a respiratory deficit often accompanies advanced scoliosis. Treatment includes promotion of pulmonary function, which is accomplished by specific breathing exercises.

Active and passive range of motion helps maintain muscular strength. Careful attention is given to the skin, especially bony prominences and the heels. Neurological and cardiac complications are not uncommon. Appropriate notice should be given to these important considerations without frightening the child. Bowel and bladder difficulties are frequent. They may be lessened by adequate intake of fluids, foods rich in bulk, and occasional laxatives. Remember that immobilization decreases appetite. The child should be given every opportunity to help select his diet when a choice is possible. His psychological growth is just as important as his physical well-being.

Spinal fusion. Casts may be worn for an extended period after the fusion procedure, which makes the turning of the patient much simpler and safer. However, casting is not always present after a spinal fusion, and if it is not, care must be exercised so that the spinal column is not twisted during changes in position. The patient's bed should be kept flat unless specific permission has been granted to allow the patient to be on a slight incline while in *supine* position (on his back). A noncasted patient who is allowed to be turned should be gently logrolled from back to side with the use of a turning sheet and at least two nurses (more if the size of the patient indicates that more hands are needed). Such a patient, casted or not, who is turned from his back to a side-lying position should have a pillow between his thighs to prevent the adduction of the top leg and pull on the small of the back. Just how much motion will be allowed a patient will depend on his physician's wishes. Sometimes during the operative procedure just before the actual spinal fusion metal rods are inserted on either side of the spinal column that by their attachments help force the vertebrae into a closer to normal alignment. This procedure is called the Harrington operation.

Spinal fusion patients need the same basic preoperative and postoperative care required for all surgical patients. In addition, they may need the special attention necessary for all casted patients (see Chapter 33). Constipation may be a particular problem; therefore special attention to the type of diet, fluid intake, and habit-times are important.

Therapy for marked scoliosis is usually long. It characteristically will involve innumerable visits to the physician for evaluation, hospitalization at intervals for cast changes, brace adjustments, or surgical interventions, and physical therapy. The parents and child (young lady or man) need to be constantly encouraged to continue treatment faithfully until optimum, lasting results are achieved.

Joint and extremity diseases

Congenital deformities and intervening paralytic or inflammatory diseases of the skeletal system may also, of course, affect parts of the skeleton other than the spine. Some diseases cause muscular weakness or bone destruction, producing joint instability, which prevents normal weight bearing. Some disorders reduce joint mobility so that the usefulness of a body part is greatly reduced. Other conditions may affect the growth patterns of individual extremities. Various surgical procedures have been devised to increase the effectiveness of various body joints either by increasing their ability to bear weight or by permitting greater motion. If a choice between motion and stability must be made, the decision is made in favor of stability.

The following are a few of the basic procedures used in some cases to promote healing or gain greater usefulness for a body part or increase its contribution to the individual's total welfare:

1. *Arthrodesis* is a fusion of a joint performed to gain stability for weight bearing. It may be accomplished by removing the cartilage from the opposing ends of the bones forming a joint and/or grafting bone into the area followed by a prolonged period of immobilization in a cast to promote fusion. A *triple-arthrodesis* is occasionally performed on a foot; as the name implies, it involves fusion of three joints. It prohibits some lateral movements of the foot itself but preserves ankle motion. Considerable bleeding may be expected after this type of surgery, and considerable pain may be involved. Application of weight to the newly fused part is delayed until fusion is secure, in approximately 2 to 3 months.

2. *Arthroplasty* is the reconstruction of a joint to provide greater movement when it may be an asset. The joints usually involved in the procedure are those at the elbow, hip, or knee. Sometimes synthetic materials, such as the metal Vitallium, are used in the process of reconstruction of a joint socket (cup arthroplasty).

3. *Osteotomy* is an opening into or a controlled fracture of a bone performed to correct a congenital or acquired skeletal deformity. A *rotational osteotomy* involves a turning of the distal fragment of bone to secure the desired correction.

4. *Bone block* is a type of operative procedure that incorporates a piece of bone into a joint to limit motion and help produce increased joint stability. It may precede an arthrodesis.

5. *Tendon transplant* is a procedure in which tendon from one part of the body is transplanted to another. It may be performed for various reasons—to substitute the action of neighboring strong muscles for paralyzed or weak muscles, to replace badly damaged tendons, or to decrease a deformity caused by exaggerated muscle pull.

6. *Epiphyseal arrest* may be performed to slow up the growth of one extremity in the case of inequality in length. Properly

handled, it may also aid in the correction of such deformities as knock-knees or bow-legs. It may be accomplished by the placement of stainless steel staples into the epiphyseal area where bone growth takes place. This procedure stops normal growth. The staples are removed when the desired results are obtained.

Osteomyelitis

Inflammatory bone conditions caused by disease-producing organisms have been more common in the past than at present. With the increase in the availability of different types of antibiotics and other helpful medications, osteomyelitis, or inflammation of the bone resulting from infectious agents, has decreased remarkably. If the term "osteomyelitis" is used without a qualifying phrase, it is assumed to mean infection of the bone by either pathogenic staphylococcal or streptococcal organisms. However, broadly speaking, osteomyelitis may also be caused by the tuberculosis bacillus, the gonococcus, or a wide variety of lesser known bacteria. The form of osteomyelitis caused by staphylococci or streptococci is often preceded by some type of local injury to the bone, which either introduces the organism directly or weakens the bone so that it is more susceptible to any offending organisms brought to the area by the bloodstream from some distant source of infection. Boys are more frequently affected than girls. Osteomyelitis reveals itself by local pain and temperature elevation. Diagnosis is substantiated by laboratory findings of leukocytosis and a positive blood culture or a telltale culture from the local lesion. Treatment consists of the administration of appropriate antibiotics, possibly excision and drainage of the localized infection, removal of the layers of bone destroyed by the infection (sequestra), and provision for rest of the affected body part, usually by cast application. The affected body part must be handled with great gentleness because the bone destruction may be extensive, and pathological fractures may be associated with this condition.

Bone tumors

Some of the symptoms of infectious osteomyelitis are duplicated when the problem is not that of pathogenic organisms but concerns the development of new abnormal cells within the bone itself, producing a tumor or tumors. Some of these masses of abnormal tissue are benign and of purely local importance. They may cause pain and deformity, at times accompanied by fever. They may weaken the structure of the bone, but they do not spread (or metastasize) to distant parts of the body. Other types of bone tumors have an exceptional ability to send tissue to other parts of the body where destructive colonies of cells eventually may interfere in vital body processes. These colonizing tumors are termed "malignant." A malignant tumor originating in connective tissue (of which bone is one example) is called a *sarcoma*. Sarcomas usually metastasize fairly rapidly, frequently to the lungs.

If x-ray studies and the clinical history and examination point to bone tumor, it is necessary to determine the type of tumor by biopsy and pathological study of the tissue. Occasionally tumors of the bone may be metastases from a tumor located elsewhere. If a tissue of bony origin is malignant, radical methods of treatment, including amputation, are often endorsed in an effort to save the patient. The recorded number of 5-year cures is relatively low.

Juvenile rheumatoid arthritis (Still's disease)

Arthritis, or inflammation of the joints, may be caused by a wide variety of factors, including infection, trauma, and the wear and tear of aging. However, the most common form of arthritis encountered in pediatrics—juvenile rheumatoid arthritis, or Still's disease—is of unknown etiology.

This disease affects the entire body's health. In studies it is often grouped with the collagen diseases, which affect all the connective tissues of the body. It does not confine itself to symptoms of joint pain, although this is the most remarkable manifestation of the disease. The joints swell and become stiff, slightly warm, and painful with movement. Almost all the joints may eventually become involved, but the knees, ankles, and fingers are most frequently affected. The fingers often assume a spindle shape as a result of the swelling of their middle joints (Fig. 37-10). Unless joint activity is maintained, a joint will become permanently stiffened or immovable, a condition known as *ankylosis* of the joint. For this reason it is important to maintain reasonable joint activity by reducing pain and providing specific tasks or play goals designed to exercise the involved joints.

The rheumatoid patient, unless very careful, is likely to assume positions of comfort, which if maintained for prolonged periods will cause deformities that will interfere with motions necessary to meet the needs of daily living. Mobility should be encouraged as much as tolerated, even during periods of active disease and inflammation. When pain and inflammation are suppressed by salicylates most children are encouraged to ambulate. The most effective,

continuous, therapeutic exercise program is provided through the child's own play activities. Play activities should be directed to provide the maximum exercise for the joints most involved. Planned activity and formal exercises will help prevent the stiffness and deformity that result from inactivity. The physical therapist will teach the child and his parents exercises designed to give complete range of motion in each joint.

Fever is a significant manifestation of the disease. It may swing daily as high as 105° F. in the evening and return to normal by morning. The pattern on the temperature chart is usually characteristic and of great value in the differential diagnosis of a patient with acute rheumatic arthritis.

Other signs and symptoms of rheumatoid arthritis include enlargement of the liver, spleen, and lymph nodes, anemia, anorexia, pallor, and possibly a salmon-colored, blotchy rash. Infrequently, heart murmurs or carditis is encountered. The relationship (if any) of rheumatoid arthritis to rheumatic heart disease is not clear. The two are

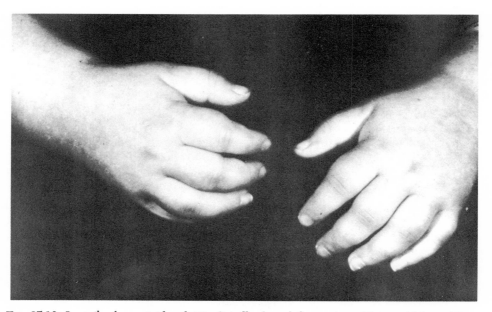

Fig. 37-10. Juvenile rheumatoid arthritis. Spindle-shaped fingers in a 2½-year-old boy. (Courtesy U. S. Naval Hospital, San Diego, Calif.)

usually discussed as separate disorders. Rheumatoid arthritis is aggravated by emotional stress and fatigue.

Kind and understanding parental support, promotion of general health, and physical therapy will achieve most of the therapeutic goals. No specific treatment is known. Although many medications have been tried, aspirin is the drug of choice to relieve pain, reduce swelling, and increase range of motion. It is prescribed four times daily, and the dosage is often increased to toxic levels and then reduced for best results. The children are carefully observed in the clinic and the patients cautioned about early signs of toxicity (p. 327). Indomethacin (Indocin) is a new drug that has been found to be effective in the treatment of rheumatoid arthritis. It is presently being used in the larger clinics but is still considered experimental.

Prednisone and other corticosteroid derivatives will help alleviate symptoms of inflammation, but these drugs taken over a prolonged period of time are toxic, and rheumatoid symptoms recur when they are discontinued. So they are prescribed prudently during periods when joint inflammation does not respond to more conservative therapy. Toxic manifestations of such hormone therapy may include decalcification of the skeleton, altered tissue response to infections and other injuries, personality changes, moon face, abnormal growth of the clitoris in girls, and the appearance of excessive body hair (Fig. 37-11).

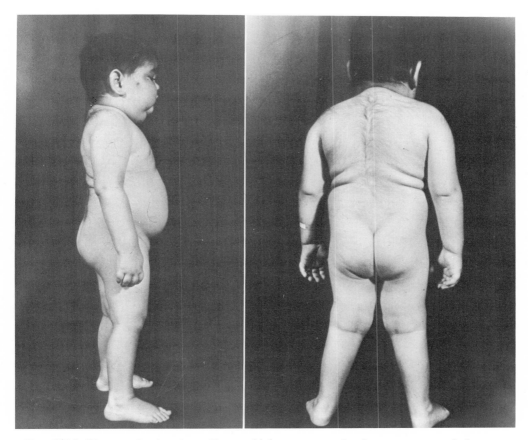

FIG. 37-11. Hypercortisonism in a 2½-year-old boy as a result of intensive steroid therapy. Note moon facies, excessive growth of hair (hirsutism), prominent fat pads, buffalo hump, and marked weight gain. (Courtesy U. S. Naval Hospital, San Diego, Calif.)

Although juvenile rheumatoid arthritis may improve and then worsen over a period of years, usually it gradually subsides as puberty approaches. However, in some cases it may persist actively into adulthood and may leave difficult deformities.

Orthopedic complications of hemophilia

The problem of damaged joints should not be completely closed without at least mentioning another interesting cause of joint difficulty. The child with hemophilia, the classic bleeder, may sustain considerable joint destruction because of "insignificant initiating injuries" followed by hemorrhages into the joints of the knees and elbows. These patients must be placed in traction and protective casts fairly frequently.

Muscular problems

Orthopedic disorders resulting from primary muscle disease are quite rare. Nevertheless, perhaps the two conditions included in the following paragraphs could be placed in this category. The first is muscular dystrophy; the second is torticollis, or wryneck.

The "muscular dystrophies"

Muscular dystrophy probably should be spelled using the plural form of the noun because there are a number of conditions that are characterized by a progressively developing musculoskeletal weakness and eventual wasting of muscle tissue. They differ in the main muscles affected, the course of the disability, and the usual age of onset. Pseudohypertrophic muscular dystrophy is the commonest form of the progressive types of muscle weakness. The onset of this form of the disease usually occurs between 2 and 10 years of age. It is a hereditary sex-linked, recessive condition that is said to affect males almost exclusively. In this type of dystrophy a fatty infiltration of the muscle cells may produce a deceptively large muscle, lacking strength, hence its title "pseudohypertrophic" muscular dystrophy. This is especially true of the calf muscles. The affected young child has difficulty in walking and falls easily as the muscular weakness attacks, in sequence, the muscles of the legs, pelvis, and abdomen. A pronounced lordosis develops as he struggles to remain upright. The child who attempts to rise to his feet from a seated posture on the floor displays a characteristic method of supporting himself during the change in position. He rises to his knees, then extends both legs and arms, and, grasping the lower part of his legs with his hands, gradually pushes himself upward in a sort of "self-climbing procedure." Observation of this method of rising to an upright position (Gowers' sign, Fig. 37-12), a history revealing the progressive nature of the problem, the physical examination, and the muscle biopsy report help determine the diagnosis. Muscular dystrophy is not a pleasant diagnosis for a parent to receive, no matter what type of the disease is suggested. In the case of this most common type, life expectancy is usually limited to the teen-age period. Death often results from respiratory weakness and intervening infection. The course of the disease is downhill all the way and particularly disheartening to parents who first see their child confined to a wheelchair and then eventually bedridden to the extent that he needs help to turn over. Many times much can be gained if the parents of such victims can meet together to share their common burdens and learn from one another how certain problems can be met. The local Muscular Dystrophy Associations often sponsor such groups. The nurse sees the child with muscular dystrophy in the hospital setting chiefly at the time of diagnosis, when orthopedic appliances such as braces and splints are being evaluated, or when the presence of other health problems makes it especially difficult to nurse the child at home.

Torticollis (Fig. 37-13)

Torticollis, or wryneck, may occur in infancy or later childhood. It is an involuntary tilting of the head sideways because of a shortening of either sternocleidomastoid muscle. The child seems to have a perpetual "look of inquiry" because of this head tilt. The shortening of the muscle may be the result of its injury during birth and subsequent benign tumor formation or the result of various infections or inflammatory processes indirectly causing muscular imbalance, from either weakness or spasm. The probable cause must be considered in

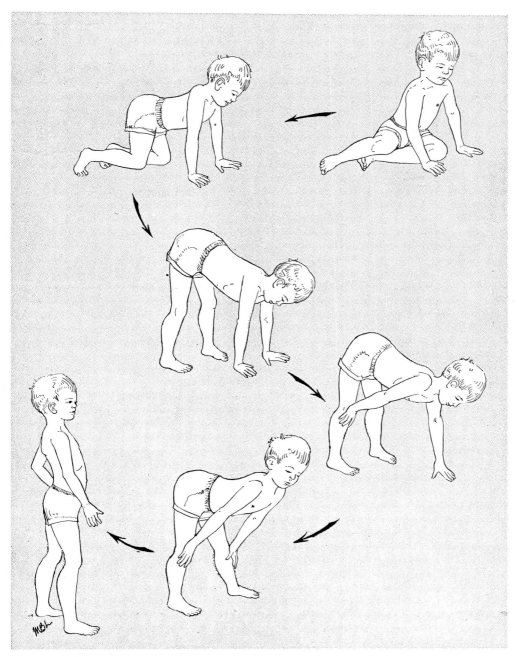

FIG. 37-12. Gowers' sign, the "self-climbing procedure" characteristic of pseudohypertrophic muscular dystrophy.

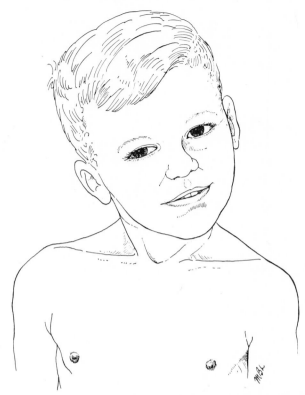

Fig. 37-13. Torticollis, or wryneck, in this case a shortening of the right sternocleidomastoid muscle.

instituting treatment. Sometimes manipulation or exercise is the only therapy needed; sometimes traction or casting may be prescribed. In some instances a surgical procedure involving a partial clipping of the involved muscle may be advised.

Nervous system diseases that may affect the musculoskeletal system

Meningitis

Meningitis, simply stated, is inflammation of the meninges. Not all types of meningitis are infectious, but the infectious types are by far the most common. The hemophilus influenza bacillus, meningococcus and pneumococcus are common etiological agents responsible for acute bacterial meningitis in children past 1 month of age. Meningitis is most commonly seen in children under 2 years of age and the *Haemo-*

philus influenzae is by far the most common type. Whatever the causative agent or age of onset, the treatment of meningitis is always considered a medical emergency! Early recognition and prompt treatment are essential for a favorable recovery. The severity and duration of the infection affects not only mortality rates but also the incidence of lingering neurological damage.

Typically the child is irritable and restless or drowsy. Previous upper respiratory infections, especially ear infections, are associated with *Haemophilus influenzae* meningitis. (For this reason, the nurse should impress on parents the importance of continuing medications for otitis media, etc., and all antibiotics prescribed for as long as ordered.) Fever, vomiting, chills, headache, rigidity of the neck and back, and convulsions are common. In more severe cases the child may be in shock or exhibit an invol-

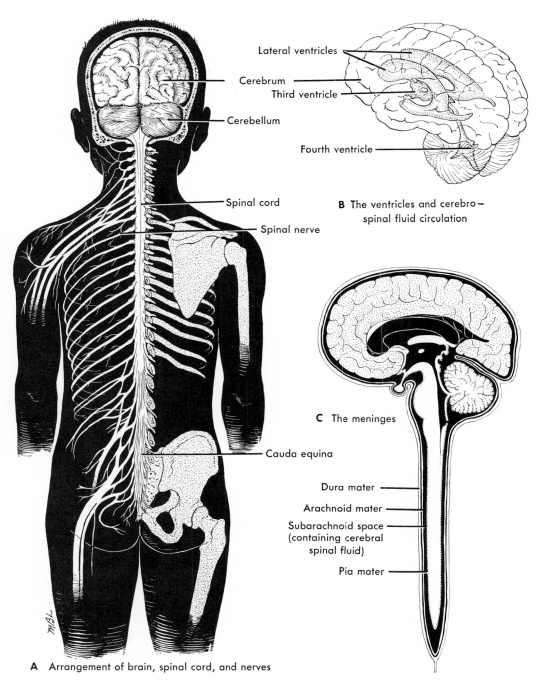

Lateral ventricles

Cerebrum

Third ventricle

Fourth ventricle

B The ventricles and cerebro—
spinal fluid circulation

Cerebellum

Spinal cord

Spinal nerve

C The meninges

Cauda equina

Dura mater

Arachnoid mater

Subarachnoid space
(containing cerebral
spinal fluid)

Pia mater

A Arrangement of brain, spinal cord, and nerves

FIG. 37-14. Simplified central nervous system anatomy and peripheral nerve relationships.

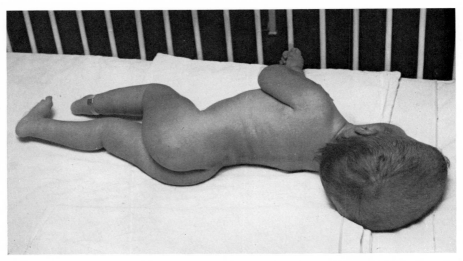

FIG. 37-15. This child with hydrocephalus is also suffering from meningitis. Her entire body is rigid and her back is arched, or opisthotorric. (Courtesy U. S. Naval Hospital, San Diego, Calif.)

untary arching of his back known as opisthotonos (Fig. 37-15). A high-pitched cry is characteristic. Meningococcal meningitis is usually accompanied by petechiae, a hemorrhagic skin rash caused by meningococcal invasion of the bloodstream. However, meningococcemia may occur without central nervous system involvement.

A lumbar puncture is done at the slightest suspicion of meningitis, even a convulsion. Parents and children fear a lumbar puncture. Parents should be reassured of the importance and necessity of this procedure. The child, if conscious and old enough to understand, should be mentally prepared just before the procedure. He should be told what is going to happen and why and what he is likely to feel. Reminding him that it is important to lie still during the procedure may provide a sense of control and thereby reduce feelings of helplessness. The assisting nurse must understand the importance of maintaining the position of the child during this procedure. Several holds are possible, depending on the size of the child. A side position is usually preferred. The back of the patient is arched "like a kitten's" to provide greater room for the insertion of

the needle between the vertebrae at the level of the iliac crest. The skin is usually prepared with an antiseptic by the gloved physician. At the time of the lumbar puncture the pressure of the fluid within the meninges may be measured by attaching a measuring tube or manometer to the spinal needle. Three specimens of spinal fluid are usually collected consecutively in specially numbered sterile specimen containers. All three containers are sent to the laboratory where they should be immediately examined for cellular and chemical content. A Gram stain or culture is done to identify any organisms that may be present. A Gram stain can often identify an organism at once, before the return of the culture report. At the conclusion of the puncture procedure a Band-Aid is placed over the site of the needle insertion.

The child is isolated for 24 hours after the start of antibiotic therapy. The meaning of this isolation and why the nurse wears a gown should be explained to parents. If they are not allowed to enter the room, the child's crib should be turned so they might at least see his face.

An intravenous infusion is started as soon as the lumbar puncture is completed. Large doses of ampicillin are given intravenously with fluid and electrolyte replacement. Ampicillin is currently the drug of choice for undiagnosed meningitis. Good supportive care requires that dehydration be corrected promptly, but the alert nurse will guard against overhydration. Symptoms of water intoxication are headache, confusion, sudden weight gain, edema, convulsions, and coma.

Effective restraints must be used to safeguard the infusion. The nurse should carefully position the restrained child on his side during intravenous therapy lest he convulse or aspirate vomitus. Constant nursing care and frequent observation of the child are necessary during the acute phase. Monitoring the vital signs is especially important when increased intracranial pressure is suspected. Slowed pulse, irregular respirations, and elevated blood pressure are signs of increased intracranial pressure and should be called to the physician's attention at once. Cerebral pressure may be lessened either by drugs such as an infusion of mannitol or by surgical intervention. Such methods are often life-saving.

The infant may be placed in an oxygen-enriched environment in an incubator. The older child may be placed in an oxygen tent. Other nursing responsibilities include control of temperature by sponging and a cool environment. Antipyretics are usually not recommended because they interfere with monitoring the temperature response, which determines the length of ampicillin therapy. Accurately recording the intravenous intake and the urinary output is important (urinary retention and fecal impactions are real possibilities). As the child progresses favorably, the nurse may safely encourage the parents to hold their infant or toddler during intravenous therapy, allowing for body contact and love, as well as position change. Granting as much freedom from restraint and provision for psychological comforts (such as thumb-sucking), as is consistent with therapy and safety is very important.

The convalescent period should be long enough to permit the child to regain his previous physical status. The young child should be carefully reevaluated at intervals during his convalescence. Residual complications may include hydrocephalus, subdural effusion, incoordination, sensory loss, mental deterioration, or behavior problems.

Aseptic meningitis syndrome. This term includes a number of meningeal disorders caused by viruses, which have in common an acute onset and usually a self-limited course with varying meningeal manifestations. Meningismus or meningeal irritation such as nuchal (neck) or spinal rigidity is present. Lumbar puncture reveals a sterile culture. To rule out other diseases, hospitalization is necessary for at least 48 hours for observation. Treatment is supportive and symptomatic.

Neonatal meningitis. Newborns are frequent victims of meningitis. Most often the organisms attacking these babies are *Escherichia coli* and staphylococci. About 1 in every 1,000 to 2,000 newborns is affected. These infections are often associated with low birth weight. Maternal infection, premature rupture of membranes, and complicated deliveries are often part of the obstetrical history. Signs of meningeal irritation are minimal. The infant characteristically is lethargic and irritable and refuses to suck. Vomiting, respiratory distress, and convulsions are common. Penicillin and kanamycin are specific, and medications are given intravenously, usually by scalp vein. The hair should always be shaved in advance. Intensive supportive nursing care is essential. Because of the difficulty in recognizing the disease early and the inability of the debilitated small infant to respond to treatment, prognosis remains very poor, and the children who do survive have a high incidence of cerebral damage.

Encephalitis

Encephalitis is inflammation of the brain, also called the encephalon. Sometimes a disease involves both the meninges and brain tissue; then the condition is labeled meningoencephalitis. One of the meanings of the word element "myelitis" is inflammation of the spinal cord. It is possible to have a widespread inflammation of the central nervous system involving the meninges, brain, and spinal cord, but the terminology that describes the situation is almost as foreboding as the condition itself. Imagine seeing "meningoencephalomyelitis" listed as a tentative diagnosis in a patient's records!

Encephalitis cases may be infectious, postinfectious, or toxic in origin. Some types of encephalitis are caused by viruses that may be carried by infected mosquitoes, ticks, or mites. Encephalitis following rubeola (2-week measles) is relatively common, occurring once in every 600 to 1,000 cases of measles.

Noninfectious forms of encephalitis may be caused by toxins contacted by ingestion or inhalation. Lead poisoning in children, although not as common as formerly, is still reported every year. All furniture and toys used by a young child (who considers tasting at least equally as important as feeling or smelling) should be protected by nontoxic, lead-free paint.

Encephalitis is often characterized by personality change, headache, drowsiness, convulsion, and fever. Cranial nerves may become paralyzed, affecting speech, muscle strength, and reflex response. Double vision may be reported. Like meningitis, encephalitis may cause mental retardation and residual paralysis.

The nursing care of a child with encephalitis is very much like that of a child with meningitis. Lumbar punctures may be frequently performed to relieve intracranial pressure. The difference between encephalitis and meningitis may not be detected clinically on the basis of demonstrated symptoms. The differentiation is made on the basis of the results of the laboratory examinations.

Poliomyelitis

Poliomyelitis, a disease caused by the invasion of the spinal cord or medulla (bulb) by strains of a particular virus, is fortunately now uncommon in the United States in its acute form because of the development of effective vaccines. The virus primarily attacks the anterior horn of the gray matter

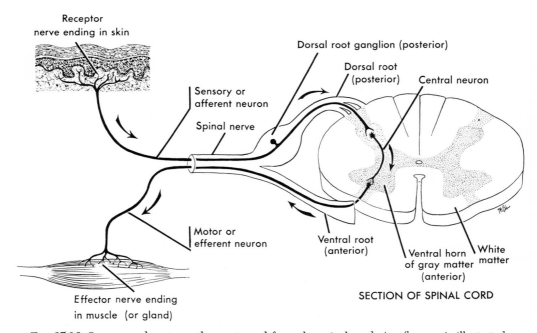

Fig. 37-16. Sensory and motor pathways to and from the spinal cord. A reflex arc is illustrated.

in the spinal cord containing the motor neurons. However, the gastrointestinal, circulatory, and respiratory systems are also involved to some degree. Typically no diminishment of sensation in the muscles involved occurs. The skin and muscles may be very tender and require very gentle handling. Paralysis of varying duration and extent occurs in a relatively small but significant number of cases involving the skeletal muscles and/or centers controlling respiration and swallowing. The type of poliomyelitis that involves the spinal cord and nerves is called "spinal." If the cranial nerves and medulla are affected, it is termed "bulbar." A mixed bulbospinal type is also possible. Spinal poliomyelitis involving the diaphragm or intercostal muscles or bulbar type poliomyelitis is especially dreaded because of the respiratory embarrassment that may occur and the need for mechanical aids to maintain an open airway or adequate breathing. A nurse should be constantly alert for signs of medullary involvement and developing respiratory difficulty in a patient with acute polio. Signs of bulbar involvement include difficulty in swallowing and talking, a nasal voice, increased mucus pooling in the mouth and throat, intensified apprehension, and personality change. For a brief outline of the characteristics of the infection and the nursing care involved, the student is referred to Chapter 36 for the discussion of communicable diseases.

The nurse still sees and treats a considerable number of postpoliomyelitis patients who may suffer from loss of muscle function and subsequent skeletal distortion caused by their contact with the disease. These patients often exhibit scoliosis and/or flail or unequal extremities. Various joint stabilization procedures or tendon transplants have been devised to aid rehabilitation. Braces or splints may be indicated. The needs of each patient must be evaluated and positioning, nursing procedures, and self-help skills developed and executed according to the best interests of the patient as determined by the attending physicians, physical therapists, and occupational therapists.

Convulsive seizures

The term "convulsive seizure" is really not a diagnosis but simply a description of recent episodes of behavior. As you have already noted, convulsive seizures may be caused by a number of conditions. An exaggerated body temperature may be the precipitating cause. Seizures may originate from increased intracranial pressure caused by congenital brain deformities, tumor or abscess formation, or edema of the brain. Cerebral irritation resulting from toxic or infectious agents may be implicated. A chronic or recurrent convulsive disorder also may be called *epilepsy*. Some writers reserve the term "epilepsy" to signify only recurrent convulsions of the idiopathic variety (cases of unknown cause). There are differences of opinion regarding the role of heredity in cases of idiopathic seizures. Some authorities believe that it may be a significant cause; others deny this. Because some states and communities may have laws limiting the activities of those persons who have been diagnosed as epileptic and because the public does not always understand what the word may mean in a specific case, many physicians hesitate to use this particular term when describing the patient's problem. The nurse would also do well to use the word very discreetly. It has been estimated that approximately 1% of the population has some type of convulsive disorder.

There are two main types of seizures: grand mal (great pain or evil) and petit mal (small pain or evil). Grand mal seizures affect the large muscle groups of the body. Usually the entire body becomes involved in dramatic, involuntary muscular contractions of considerable force. Petit mal seizures, on the other hand, are characterized by minor tremors or brief losses of consciousness revealed perhaps only by a prolonged blank stare or the dropping of an object held in the hand. The frequency of either type of seizure may be extremely variable. A child may experience a seizure rarely or multiple times during a 24-hour period. Diagnosis is aided by a study of the child's brain waves or an electroencephalogram.

Children who have grand mal seizures may experience a subjective warning of an impending episode. Such a warning is called an aura. It may occur a few minutes, hours, or, rarely, even days before the attack. It may come in the form of a vague feeling of uneasiness or as some type of sensory cue. For example, the patient may hear, see, or smell things in a particular manner. Such auras are useful to patients because they may seek out places of safety and privacy if they are forewarned of an attack.

The grand mal seizure usually begins with a period of rigidity and temporary respiratory arrest. The first sign of an attack may be involuntary movements of the eyeball (the eyes rolling upward or to the side) and a stiffening of body parts. The patient temporarily suspends respirations and may become cyanotic. Saliva is not swallowed, and the patient may drool. A high-pitched cry may be heard. This first period, called the *tonic* phase, is usually followed by intermittent contractions of the muscles. This secondary period is the so-called *clonic* phase. During this time the tongue and lips may be bitten and saliva, as a result, may be blood tinged.

The nursing care of a patient having a convulsion emphasizes the need to protect the patient from accidental injury and the importance of close observation and report. If possible, a patient should be placed on his side or lie with his face turned to one side to avoid aspiration. He should be placed in an area where the possibility of personal injury as a result of uncontrolled muscular contractions would be minimal: on the floor on a rug, if possible, or in bed. The beds or cribs of patients who experience fairly frequent convulsions of the gand mal type should be equipped with side rails padded with folded blankets or pillows. In the hospital setting nurses are taught to have a well-padded tongue blade readily accessible at the bedside for insertion into the mouth between the back teeth before the onset of the clonic phase of the seizure to prevent mouth injury. If a tongue blade is not available, a rolled washcloth may be helpful. However, discrimination must be practiced; do not put just any old thing in the mouth. It may cause more problems than failure to use anything at all. Nurses should not pry open a patient's mouth to insert a tongue blade. Such a maneuver may cause considerable injury and serves no real practical purpose because the damage to the mouth in most cases has already occurred. The Epilepsy Society does not advise the general public to place anything into the victim's mouth. There have been too many incidents of mouth injury or aspiration due, not to the convulsion, but to the insertion of an improper tongue protector.

After first securing a safe position for the convulsing patient, the nurse should focus her powers of observation in order to be able to describe the circumstances and sequence of the attack. She should note the following information:

1. When the seizure began and what type of activity immediately preceded its occurrence.
2. What the first signs of difficulty noted were. What part of the body was affected first. How the convulsion progressed.
3. How long the attack lasted.
4. Whether the patient was incontinent.
5. Whether prolonged cyanosis or profuse saliva appeared (may signal the need for the use of oxygen or possible suctioning).

In the great majority of cases the seizure subsides and the child falls into a deep sleep. When finally awake again, he may not remember the seizure but feel tired and sore. He should be reassured regarding the episode and be gently questioned to determine if he had any warning, or aura, of the attack.

Almost all patients who suffer from idiopathic seizures and many with organically initiated seizures are on some type of anticonvulsant therapy. There are a number of medications available. They are prescribed according to the individual needs of the patient. Some commonly used drugs are

diphenylhydantoin sodium (Dilantin sodium) and phenobarbital. The time schedule established for taking anticonvulsants should be faithfully followed to avoid any interruption in treatment and the possible appearance of a seizure. Other ways to

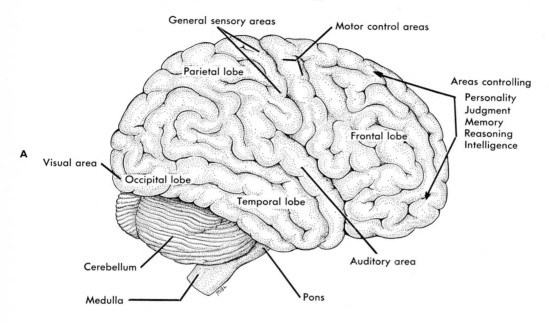

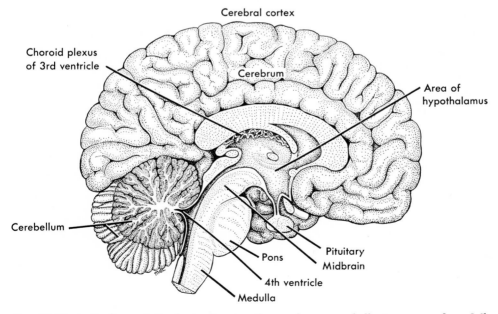

FIG. 37-17. A, Surfaces of the brain showing the cerebrum, cerebellum, pons, and medulla with identification of specialized areas of cerebral function. B, Simplified sagittal section of the brain showing internal relationships. Brain tumors in children often involve the cerebellum.

help prevent seizures that are sometimes employed involve the limitation of fluids and a high-fat–low-carbohydrate (ketogenic) diet. Complete or almost complete control can be obtained in approximately half the cases. Many patients can be very well regulated with medical therapy and are able to live fairly normal lives. Some types of epilepsy (usually types of petit mal) tend to disappear after puberty; others, unfortunately, persist throughout life. The nurse should realize that fatigue, excitement, hyperventilation, or blinking lights may help bring on certain seizures.

The patient and his family need continuous, good medical supervision and counsel. The patient should be encouraged to live life to the fullest within the limits of his disease as imposed by the community and his own sense of responsibility. The intelligence levels of people with epilepsy are very similar to those found in the population as a whole.

The Epilepsy Societies have done considerable work in the area of public education regarding the disorder, attempting to remove false ideas and any legislation that unjustly limits the activities of its victims.

Brain tumors (Fig. 37-17)

Although brain tumors are not found as frequently in children as in adults, they are not uncommon in childhood. Most of these brain tumors are situated rather deeply within the brain structure, making it difficult to assure complete removal of the abnormal cells. About three fourths of the brain tumors occurring in childhood involve the supportive connective tissue of the brain, called *glial* cells. The two most common gliomas are astrocytomas and medulloblastomas. Nelson states that complete cure is almost restricted to the cystic cerebellar astrocytoma.* It is relatively slow growing and usually encapsulated, making

it easier to remove. Symptoms of developing brain tumor may appear very slowly in the case of a slowly progressing lesion. However, some tumors (for example, medulloblastomas) grow rapidly and cause remarkable signs and symptoms rather soon. The signs and symptoms are those caused by the increased intracranial pressure. They may include headache, dizziness, lethargy, indifference, or irritability. Emesis often occurs (many times unassociated with nausea and not always projectile in character, although projectile vomiting is significant). Double or blurring vision and speech problems are reported fairly often. The pupils may be abnormally or unequally dilated or slow to react to changes in light intensity. Balance and gait may be affected because a large number of childhood brain tumors involve the cerebellum, a part of the brain that plays a significant role in the maintenance of equilibrium. Rigidity, tremors, or convulsions occasionally occur. Local muscle weakness may be present. (Periodic testing of the handgrip is sometimes ordered.) If the child is under 4 years of age, considerable enlargement of the head may still take place because the suture lines are not completely knit, and there may be interference in the ventricular drainage of the cerebrospinal fluid, as well as direct pressure from the enlarging tumor itself. The blood pressure may be elevated and the pulse may be slowed when compared to the normal values for the age group represented by the patient. Respirations may be of the Cheyne-Stokes variety. Fever or wide swings in temperature occasionally occur. Diagnosis may be confirmed through various procedures: spinal taps, skull roentgenograms (x-ray films), brain scans, electroencephalograms, ventriculograms, and arteriograms, as well as clinical observation.

Naturally, if a nurse has the responsibility of the care of a child with a possible brain tumor, she will be careful to assess his capabilities before attempting to ambulate the patient when allowed and to be sure she has sufficient help to avoid falls.

---

*Nelson, W. E., Vaughan, V. C., III, and McKay, R. J., editors: Textbook of pediatrics, ed. 9, Philadelphia, 1969, W. B. Saunders Co., p. 1286.

Some of these patients have very poor balance. The patient should be observed for any of the signs and symptoms previously described. Observation of vital signs, including blood pressure and eye reactions, should always be part of the nursing care. If intracranial pressure is elevated or mounting, a padded tongue blade should be available at the bedside. Side rails should always be in place.

Surgery and x-ray or cobalt radiation are the treatments currently available. Surgery, of course, is preferred. The complete removal of a well-confined tumor almost always produces a more optimistic prognosis.

Nursing care in the days immediately after a craniotomy, or surgical opening of the skull, is usually a complex affair. The vocational nurse may assist the registered nurse, but she should not have the responsibility of the child's complete bedside care. His condition is too unstable. The patient must be turned slowly and gently to prevent dizziness, nausea, vomiting, and a rise in blood pressure. Since crying elevates the blood pressure, all measures designed to prevent fear or distress are especially important. The head dressings may become damp from cerebrospinal fluid drainage and require reinforcing until they can be changed by the physician. The face, especially the eyes, may be bruised and swollen. Special eye irrigations may be necessary to avoid infection or ulceration resulting from disturbances in tear formation and drainage because of trauma. Frequent suctioning may be necessary. Although the child may appear unconscious, he may be able to hear quite well. Conversations at the bedside should be prudent.

As improvement occurs, efforts to rehabilitate the child should be made. Although the patient may finally succumb to his disease, many months may be left in which he may be able to live a relatively satisfying life. Both patient and parents need much physical and emotional support to make the most of this indeterminate and occasionally prolonged period.

Subdural hematoma

Another cause of increased intracranial pressure is bleeding into the potential space just under the dura of the brain. This condition (really a blood tumor) is most frequently encountered in infants as the result of injury at birth, falls, other trauma, or abnormal bleeding tendencies. It is rather frequently found in cases of "battered" children. The brain becomes compressed under the developing collection of bloody fluid. The onset of symptoms may be rapid or slow, depending on the extent of bleeding and the area affected. Diagnosis is made possible through subdural taps, usually performed in infants by insertion of a needle through one side of the anterior fontanel or in the suture line. The area is shaved and cleaned with antiseptic. The child must be carefully restrained (mummy fashion) and the head gently stabilized during the procedure. Withdrawal of abnormal fluid indicates the diagnosis. Successive aspirations and craniotomy may be necessary to relieve pressure and evacuate any membrane that surrounded the hematoma to prevent permanent injury to the brain. Such injury can be manifested by mental retardation and loss of normal motor function. Careful observation and report of vital signs, the tension of the fontanel, eye signs, and any emesis are necessary to prevent such unfortunate complications.

Cerebral palsy (Fig. 37-18)

In reality cerebral palsy is not in itself a disease but a condition that may result from numerous diseases, which may cause damage to those parts of the brain that are responsible for voluntary muscular coordination. Such causes may include pressure on the brain or oxygen deprivation to the brain before or during birth, direct injury, tumor, embolus or hemorrhage, hydrocephalus, cerebral anoxia, and infection or toxicity occurring any time after birth. Although one may develop cerebral palsy at anytime, it is most often caused by events associated with the prenatal or perinatal

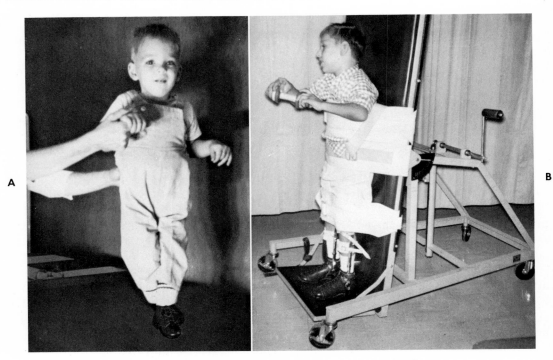

FIG. 37-18. This little fellow cannot walk at all without support. **A,** With support, a scissors gait is present (one foot crossing the other caused by adductor spasticity). **B,** Many hours on the tilt-table and the consistent work and concern of therapists and parents have markedly strengthened this young child's legs. (Courtesy Crippled Children Services, Department of Public Health, San Diego, Calif.)

period. It may be limited and mild or severe and far-reaching, involving many body functions. It is said that there are approximately from 100 to 600 cases of cerebral palsy per 100,000 persons in the general population.

Since more than the motor areas of the brain may be involved in such injuries and conditions, it is fairly common for children with cerebral palsy to have other symptoms as well. Many have disorders in visual perception. Some are blind, others may be able to see, but they may not see objects in the normal way. Written words may seem reversed. Spatial relationships may appear distorted, leading to additional problems in judgment, reading, writing, balance, and coordination. The muscles of the mouth, tongue, and throat may be affected, influencing the ability to receive, chew, and swallow food as well as to speak. A significant percentage of children suffer

from hearing loss, a condition that also affects speech. Occasionally the sense of touch may be impaired. Mental retardation is a fairly common complication, although not all children with cerebral palsy are mentally retarded and a few have above average intelligence. The amount of motor difficulty the child experiences is not necessarily indicative of his mental capacity. Some patients are victims of seizures and must receive appropriate medication.

Therapists usually speak of the following three main types of cerebral palsy:

1. Spastic, characterized by increased muscle stiffness or tone, exaggerated contraction of affected muscle groups when stimulated (stretch reflex), jerky motions, and a tendency to have contractures. The lower extremities are more often involved. A scissors gait is common.

2. Athetoid, characterized by involun-

tary, uncoordinated, purposeless movements involving joint motion rather than single muscle action. The upper extremities are more often involved.

3. Ataxic, characterized by loss of a sense of balance, problems in evaluating spatial relationships, and the relative positions of body parts.

Subgroupings and combinations of these types of cerebral palsy also occur.

It can readily be appreciated that the care of a cerebral palsied child and his family cannot be the responsibility of just one practitioner. Their problems are usually too extensive. A team approach is necessary. The team includes the pediatrician, orthopedist, physical therapist, occupational therapist, speech therapist, psychologist, medical-social worker, public health workers, office and hospital nurses, and schoolteachers.

These children and their families often have considerable emotional problems. These may relate to methods of treating the child and the aspirations that the parents may have concerning his future. The parents may be overprotective and do too much for the child, making it difficult for him to master the skills of which he is capable. On the other hand, they may need help in establishing realistic goals and in providing an environment conducive to good mental health as well as good physical health. They may expect too much of their child and cause painful frustrations. Parents often have guilt feelings regarding the child's handicap.

Association with other parents with similar problems and psychiatric assistance are often very rewarding. One hopeful aspect of cerebral palsy is that if the initiating cause is not progressive in character, the neuromuscular involvement will not worsen. Cerebral palsy is not a degenerative disease as are, for example, the muscular dystrophies. Usually considerable improvement can be gained through physical and occupational therapy (Fig. 37-19), surgical techniques, and medication to assist

these youngsters to meet their own daily personal needs and, in some cases, to prepare them for self-supporting occupations. Special public school programs may be available in the community that are especially geared to meet the needs of such handicapped children. They may attend some regular public school classes as well as special sessions designed to meet their individual needs during the school day.

When a child with cerebral palsy is hospitalized, it is very important that the hospital staff know his capabilities as an individual. Information regarding successful feeding and dressing techniques, toileting practices, communication aids, and special problems may save hours of frustration and distress. The care of some patients will require little modification, since their total neuromuscular involvement is slight. The care of others will require considerable study and adjustment.

A child who has a history of seizures or upper extremity or head involvement should not have his temperature taken orally regardless of age. Each child's diet must be evaluated to make sure that it is appropriate for his age, nutritional needs, and ability to handle and swallow. As much as possible the child should feed himself using techniques he has been taught, although self-feeding may take considerably more time and cause more disorder. Aids such as swivel spoons, plate guards, training cups, and rocker knives may be invaluable (Fig. 37-20). Occasionally special weights may be attached to the child's arms to help control involuntary motion. Children who because of their condition must be fed should be assisted with patience. Severely involved children may require the occasional use of suction. An apparatus should be available. When feeding the child, the nurse should hold him in such a way that the child's arm closest to her extends behind her. This often causes the child's head to rotate comfortably to the same side (tonic neck reflex). Gentle support of the chin or stroking of the cheeks may help lip closure and swallowing. Some

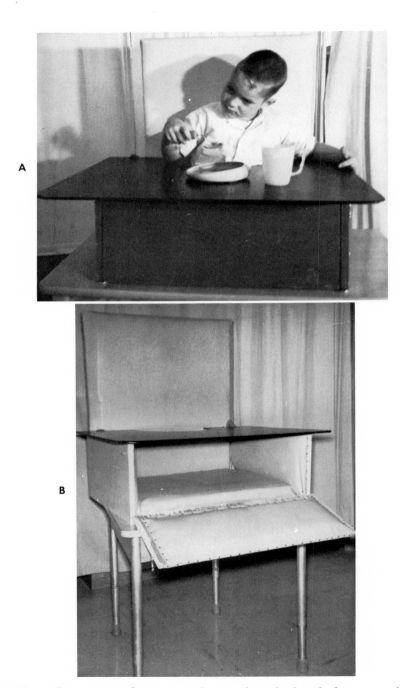

FIG. 37-19. **A,** This youngster demonstrates the use of a tailor box, built-up spoon handle, and rimmed plate, stabilized by base suction, so often helpful to patients. **B,** An open tailor box, a padded chair that supports a child while he sits cross-legged to help "loosen" spastic adductor muscles. (Courtesy Crippled Children Services, Department of Public Health, San Diego, Calif.)

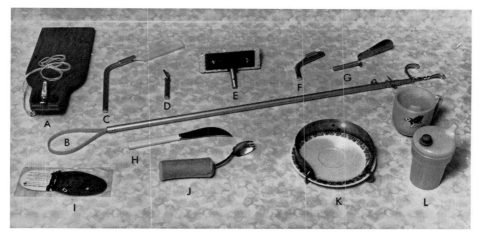

Fig. 37-20. Various aids for everyday activities for the handicapped. **A,** Nail clippers on wooden base, operated by string and foot action; **B,** gadget stick with hook attachment; **C,** comb attachment; **D,** clip attachment; **E,** mop or sponge attachment; **F,** magnet attachment; **G,** shoehorn attachment; **H,** rocker knife; **I,** elastic shoelaces; **J,** built-up handle on swivel fork (Spork); **K,** plate and plate guard; **L,** two types of weighted "trainer cups." (Courtesy Children's Health Center, San Diego, Calif.)

children who have difficulty swallowing may find carbonated drinks a problem. Waiting until the carbonation is minimal or serving other types of liquids is helpful.

The child with this condition should receive gentle, deliberate care. Excessive stimulation, sudden jarring movements, and the pressure of "having to hurry" induces greater tenseness and makes performance of relatively simple tasks extremely difficult. These children find it very difficult to relax, and they become fatigued easily. The simplest kind of controlled movement may require a tremendous amount of concentration and energy.

As much as possible the cerebral palsied child should benefit from contact with other boys and girls and should not be socially deprived. Contact with other youngsters has frequently been limited. Even those who have moderately severe muscular involvement often enjoy working with Play Dough or modeling clay, finger paints, large blocks, and hand puppets. Music, television, and reading can be enjoyed by many. The occupational therapist may work with the children to perfect certain skills needed to meet everyday needs. These are presented to the young child in the form of games or special projects. His progress, although at times seemingly small, is always recognized and praised. The child responds to this recognition and continues his efforts to improve.

Although it may seem to some critics that a tremendous amount of time, effort, and financial outlay is represented in a community program to help cerebral palsied youngsters, such programs are rewarding from many points of view. In the long run it is less expensive to educate the individual to achieve his potential than to provide the type of state-supported custodial care offered in the past. It often brings a measure of independence and a feeling of self-respect and personal worth to the individual patient. It brings hope and aid to concerned and burdened parents and inspiration to those who observe and help when they can.

Vision and hearing defects

This discussion of problems involving the nervous system should not close before some common problems affecting sight and hearing are at least mentioned.

Visual problems

The gift of sight is indeed precious. Proper care of the eyes should be taught to the growing child. It is always better to prevent eye damage rather than be required to treat it. Children should be observed for the following signs of possible visual difficulty:

1. Complaints of poor or blurred vision; inability to see the blackboard well
2. Frequent headaches, dizziness, nausea, or fatigue
3. Burning or "scratchy" eyes
4. Recurrent styes, swollen or red-rimmed eyelids, inflammation and tearing, unequal pupils, or crossed eyes
5. Frequent frowning, squinting, blinking, or grimacing; tilting the head to one side or shutting one eye while inspecting objects; rubbing the eyes often; irritability
6. Difficulty in reading, holding the book too close, or avoiding all "close work"

Blindness. It is estimated that out of every 100,000 schoolchildren in the United States more than 34 have been classified legally blind. Causes include hereditary factors, intrauterine or postnatal infections, retrolental fibroplasia (as a result of the use of prolonged high concentrations of oxygen in the care of premature infants), malignant tumors (retinoblastoma), and trauma.

The child who is blind from birth or infancy usually makes a satisfactory adjustment to his lack of visual perception. Special classes or schools may teach him to perform necessary tasks and concentrate on skills that bring special reward—music, reading (through the study of Braille techniques), writing (using Braille typewriters), and learning through the use of tape-recorded instruction.

The emotional and physical adjustment of the child who becomes blind after having been sighted is more difficult. Both types of blind children need to be treated as much like a sighted child as possible. Parents require special instruction to be able to help their children in the best way possible and avoid the pitfalls of overprotection or unrealistic demands.

Myopia and hyperopia. Myopia, or nearsightedness, is hereditary and fairly common in children. Hyperopia, or farsightedness, is less common. Children who must wear glasses to achieve clear vision must be carefully taught to keep their glasses in a case when they are not on their noses. The proper methods of handling and cleaning the lenses should also be demonstrated. When a young patient wearing glasses or contact lenses is admitted to the hospital, a note concerning his aid should be included in his admission record.

Amblyopia. An eye examination should be routinely made before any child reaches school age (preferably at 3 years of age) to detect problems that may affect normal usage and development of the eyes. If the child has an undetected strabismus (crossed

Fig. 37-21. This industrious boy, reading from his Braille Bible, was blinded because of retrolental fibroplasia.

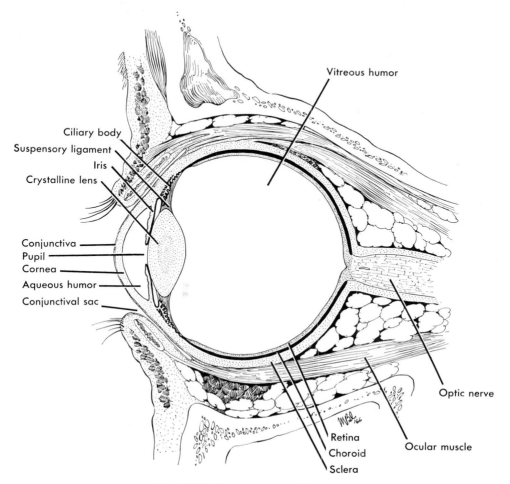

FIG. 37-22. Basic anatomy of the eye.

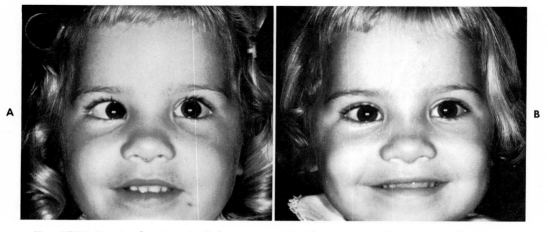

FIG. 37-23. Repair of squint. **A,** Before surgery. **B,** After surgery. (Courtesy Orville Graves, M.D., La Jolla, Calif.)

or crooked eyes) or some other visual problem that may cause him to use one eye and not the other, his unused eye may not develop proper vision. This condition has been called *amblyopia*. Its frequency has created considerable concern. It is estimated that 1 in every 20 schoolchildren in the United States suffer from this problem!

Strabismus. Strabismus, or squint, as it is often called, may be treated in several ways, depending on its extent (Fig. 37-23). Some eyes are severely crossed or crooked. Other cases may be difficult to detect. Strabismus is common during early infancy but should not persist. About 1% to 2% of all children continue to have the disorder. It is important because it may eventually cause blindness in the "lazy" eye, and a cosmetic defect may initiate adjustment problems with playmates. For mild conditions, eye exercises may be prescribed. Placing a patch over the unaffected eye to force the use of the weak eye may be all that is necessary. Glasses may be recommended. However, many times a surgical repair of the condition is necessary. This involves the lengthening or shortening of the muscles controlling the position of the eyeball.

The child who has had a squint repair may return to his unit postoperatively with or without eye dressings, according to his physician's preference and his individual needs. He may or may not have restraints, depending on his age, level of consciousness, and ability to cooperate. Many physicians request elbow restraints. If no dressings are in place, the parents should be advised to expect their child to have "bloodshot" eyes. If restraints and dressings are used, it is very important that the child be oriented well to the hospital before his surgery and that he be told that his eyes will be covered after surgery. Some children may benefit from having their eyes bandaged before surgery in order to know what to expect. It is difficult to adequately prepare very young children. Mother's presence at the bedside is the best security. There is usually no postoperative limitation

of head movement in the case of squint repair.

Cataracts. Congenital cataracts are occasionally seen. The student should recall that a cataract is an abnormal opacity of the crystalline lens, located just in back of the pupil. By obstructing the pathway of light to the retina, cataracts can cause partial or total blindness. Congenital cataracts may be caused by infectious agents during the mother's pregnancy (for example, rubella), metabolic disorders in the child, or hereditary factors. Whether corrective surgery is recommended for a child with congenital cataracts will depend on many factors, since surgery may not always produce the desired results.

The amount of movement a child is allowed after the surgical removal of cataracts will depend on the type of procedure performed and the preferences of the attending physician. Some physicians may insist on jacket and elbow restraints as well as sandbags placed at the sides of the head and maintenance of a supine position. Others are more liberal and believe that the agitation that full restraint may cause is more dangerous to the child than most movements he may make. Every effort should be made to reduce crying and prevent vomiting, since this increases intraocular pressure, strain on the sutures, and bleeding. Aspiration is a real danger when the child is maintained on his back and great care should be taken at feeding time. The child's eyes will be bandaged. His food and surroundings should be described when appropriate. Before touching a child who cannot see, the nurse should speak to be sure that the child is not startled by her care. Again, orientation to the hospital setting, preparation for the postoperative period, and parental support are very important.

Hearing problems

Approximately 5% of preschool-age children have appreciable hearing loss. Almost 3 per 1,000 children are totally or nearly totally deaf. The earlier that hearing loss is

FIG. 37-24. Child with hearing aids during therapy. (Courtesy San Diego Speech and Hearing Center, San Diego, Calif.)

detected in the child the more possibility there is of a good corrective result and reduced problems involving speech and personality formation.

It is now advocated that even infants exhibiting hearing loss be fitted with hearing aids so that they may be "tuned in" to the world about them and not suffer from the problems that isolation resulting from deafness creates. Early use of hearing aids may even prevent further hearing loss. Most children can be successfully fitted with one or two aids and learn to talk. (See Fig. 37-24.)

The nurse should be alert for signs of possible deafness. Before 7 to 8 months of age the normal infant attempts to localize sound. At 9 months or more he should be able to localize sources of sound with little difficulty. Older children who have speech that is unclear, problems with consonant formation, or flat or excessively loud voices may be victims of auditory impairment. A child who consistently turns or tips his head or insists that the television be turned up beyond the normal needs of his playmates may also be suffering from hearing

loss as may the child who pulls or pokes at his ears.

Loss of hearing can result from many causes. Either conduction or nerve deafness may occur. Common causes of hearing difficulty are chronic otitis media (middle ear infection), obstruction caused by the presence of a foreign body or excessive wax (cerumen) in the ear canal, congenital malformations involving the external canal or interior of the ear, damage to the auditory nerve caused by prenatal or postnatal infections or toxins, anoxia, or, occasionally, the prolonged use of certain antibiotics such as streptomycin or kanamycin (Kantrex). Many children are left with defective hearing because of the effects of prenatal rubella, or German measles. (Review anatomy of the ear, Fig. 38-3.)

When speaking to a deaf child, it is courteous to face him directly, if at all possible, so that he may supplement his limited sound perception with visual cues from your lips. Parents and nurses should take every opportunity to expose the young child to auditory stimulation to help in the improvement of hearing. He cannot hear or learn to listen if there are no sound waves present!

The fact that a child has a hearing defect or wears a hearing aid on admission to the hospital is an important nursing observation. If the child is scheduled for surgery, permission should be sought to allow him to wear the aid until he is anesthetized in the operating room. The aid should be reapplied as soon as he has reacted from surgery. Such permission will greatly reduce the fear of the little patient and facilitate the entire procedure.

• • •

This chapter has covered a great deal of information—perhaps too much! It has treated no subject in depth. However, it is hoped that the student has been challenged to attempt further studies in the area of the needs of the child with neuromuscular and skeletal problems.

38

Conditions involving the respiratory and circulatory systems

If one speaks of the respiratory system without mentioning the circulatory system, only part of an important story is told because these two body systems are intimately related. One might say that the respiratory system begins and ends a story but the circulatory system contributes the bulky middle chapters! For this reason pediatric disorders of the respiratory and circulatory systems are considered here in the same general section, although for convenience they may also be studied as separate units. To put it another way, the respiratory system is responsible for so-called *external respiration,* whereas the circulatory apparatus includes in its duties the responsibility for *internal respiration.*

Key vocabulary

A brief reexamination of some following basic terminology used in describing respiratory and circulatory action and problems may also be helpful:

anemia condition in which there is a reduction of hemoglobin in the blood.

apnea absence of breathing.

atelectasis airless segment of lung.

bronchiectasis abnormal dilatation of the bronchi in response to inflammation, which, if prolonged, will lead to associated structural changes and a chronic productive cough.

Cheyne-Stokes respiration irregular, cyclic-type breathing characterized by a period of increasing respiratory action followed by an interval of apnea.

dyspnea difficult breathing.

edema abnormal, excessive amount of fluid within the body tissues.

emphysema abnormal dilatation and loss of elasticity of the microscopic air sacs, or alveoli, of the lung.

empyema collection of pus in a body cavity, especially the pleural cavity.

eupnea normal breathing.

leukocytosis excessive increase in the number of white blood cells circulating in the blood.

orthopnea condition in which breathing is possible by the patient only when he is in a standing or sitting position.

pneumothorax abnormal collection of air or gas in the pleural cavity between the lung coverings.

remission lessening of severity or abatement of symptoms.

stenosis abnormal narrowing of a passage or opening.

Disorders affecting the respiratory passages

In conjunction with the study of disorders of the respiratory system, the student should review Chapter 32, which briefly outlines the basic anatomy and physiology of the respiratory system and discusses methods of aiding respiration and oxygenation.

Respiratory difficulties that are particulary associated with the newborn period, such as respiratory distress syndrome, tracheoesophageal fistula, and diaphragmatic hernia, are discussed in Chapter 19. In this presentation of respiratory pathology we will begin with a consideration of those common problems affecting the upper respiratory system (generally considered to be those respiratory passages down to and including the trachea).

THE NOSE

Function

The nose is an extremely interesting structure; although for some people it may not be a cosmetic asset, it performs certain important functions. First of all, it prepares air for entry into the interior of the body. It filters, warms, and moistens the air. Human beings may also breathe through their open mouths and, except during the period of infancy, do so fairly often. However, if large amounts of air enter the throat through the mouth, there is a tendency for the posterior pharynx to feel dry and uncomfortable. The nose is also involved in the identification of different odors because the olfactory nerve endings are located within the nasal cavity. Many of the finer perceptions of the palate are influenced by the sensitivity of these nerves. Consider how uninteresting food seems when one has a cold and the proper ventilation of the nose is disturbed. A normal nose is also necessary for proper vocal resonance.

Common problems

Epistaxis. In childhood probably the most common disorder involving the nose per se, exclusive of the general inflammatory conditions that accompany the so-called common cold, is *epistaxis*, or nosebleed. Bleeding from the nose may develop because of numerous problems, but the usual cause is injury or trauma. Some children seem to have an especially fragile network of capillaries in the lower anterior portion of the nasal cavity. Recurrent nosebleeds unassociated with injury should be evaluated by a physician. At times such nosebleeds may be a symptom of underlying blood diseases such as purpura, leukemia, or conditions associated with an abnormal rise in blood pressure. Occasionally they may herald the onset of febrile diseases such as typhoid fever or rheumatic fever.

If possible, a child with a nosebleed should be kept quiet, supported comfortably in a sitting position to elevate the part, discourage bleeding, and prevent the blood from dripping down into the throat and possibly causing aspiration. Manual pressure exerted for a prolonged period (5 minutes) by the thumb and forefinger is often sufficient to stop the bleeding. The application of ice or ice-cold compresses to the nose may be helpful. The child should be cautioned not to blow his nose during this period. If none of these measures help, it may be necessary for a physician to insert a pack or Gelfoam strips into the nose, apply solutions of epinephrine (Adrenalin) locally, or use a cautery.

Foreign bodies. Children frequently push objects other than their fingers into the nasal cavity. This is probably the result of natural curiosity. If the object does not spontaneously drop out or is not dislodged by sneezing and the episode is not reported by the child, it may be indicated by a bloody or purulent, foul nasal discharge originating from one nostril only. Such a discharge should make one suspect the presence of a foreign body. Removal of such an object should be attempted only by a physician who has the necessary instruments.

Deviation of the septum. In some instances the cartilaginous wall, or septum, that divides the nose into two lateral chambers does not occupy the midline. It may deviate toward one side or another as the result of natural development or, more commonly, as an aftermath of trauma. This may indirectly cause occlusion of a nostril and difficult breathing, particularly when the nose is inflamed. This structural anomaly may be corrected surgically by an operation called a *submucous resection.* It is not usually performed until adolescence is reached to prevent external nasal deformity resulting from the surgery.

THE PHARYNX

The pharynx is a passageway shared by both the respiratory and digestive systems. It extends from the back of the nasal cavity down past the posterior portion of the oral cavity to the level of the larynx and esophagus. Consequently, it is divided descriptively into three parts: nasal, oral, and laryngeal.

Adenoids and tonsils

The pharynx is the location of several structures of particular interest to the pediatric nurse. Situated in the nasal pharynx are the pharyngeal tonsils, more often called the *adenoids.* Farther down on the lateral walls of the oral pharynx are found the palatine, or faucial, tonsils, which are the structures indicated when one whispers, "I've just had my tonsils out." These two kinds of tonsils are composed mainly of lymphoid tissue, and like all structures composed of such tissue, they are supposedly helpful in preventing infections in neighboring areas. However, they themselves may become chronically inflamed,

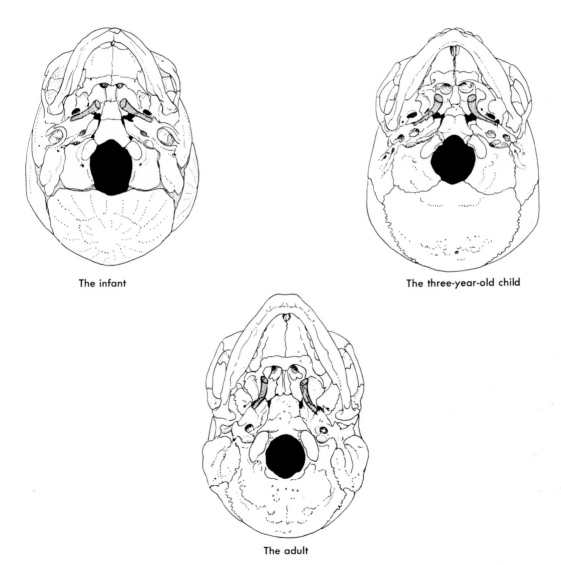

The infant

The three-year-old child

The adult

Fig. 38-1. Progressive changes in the contour of the eustachian tube as a result of aging. The short, broad, horizontal tube of the infant makes him a more frequent victim of middle ear infection.

infected, and enlarged (tonsillitis) and may be the cause of recurrent pharyngitis. Enlarged adenoids may necessitate mouth breathing and cause persistent rhinitis and snoring. The child with overly large adenoids often has nasalized speech and may appear intellectually dull because of his almost constant mouth breathing.

Indications for removal. Because the adenoids are located close to the opening of the eustachian, or auditory, tube, enlarged adenoids may also be an underlying cause of frequent middle ear infections, or *otitis media*. The eustachian tube in infants and young children is more horizontal, broader, and shorter than in adults; thus ascending ear infections are fairly common (Fig. 38-1). Recurrent otitis media and respiratory obstruction are accepted reasons for removal of the adenoids. Chronic throat infection and abnormal enlargment of the palatine tonsils are considered to be an indication for tonsillectomy. Occasionally a history of rheumatic fever or nephritis may lead a physician to decide to extract the tonsils and adenoids of a certain child in the hopes of eradicating possible sites of future infection. All decisions to perform a tonsilloadenoidectomy (T and A) should be made on the basis of the individual child's need for the procedure and not simply because they are there. Young children occasionally undergo only an adenoidectomy.

Tonsilloadenoidectomies are delayed as long as possible so that very young children will not have to be admitted to the hospital and subjected to the psychological stresses that this experience places on boys and girls of preschool age. Preparation of the child for hospitalization for any reason is extremely important and is discussed in Chapter 24. It is preferable that the child have no evidence of upper respiratory infection at the time of the operation. However, occasionally it seems impossible to find a period when the child is free from infection. Then the physician may elect to go ahead after ordering the administration of preoperative and postoperative antibiotics.

Complications of removal. Although there are numerous tonsilloadenoidectomies performed daily and the incidence of complication is relatively low, important complications do occasionally occur. The student should review general preoperative considerations, Chapter 31. The child undergoing a tonsilloadenoidectomy should be carefully observed and attended (and so should his parents, who intermittently may have even more pressing needs than those of their child). Because of the numerous blood vessels in the operative area and the character of the procedure, the most frequent complication of a tonsilloadenoidectomy is hemorrhage. For this reason the nurse should be especially vigilant in watching for symptoms of excessive bleeding and shock. Since the advent and use of recovery rooms the burden of the immediate postoperative care of the surgical patient carried by the "floor staff nurse" has been lightened. However, it has not been eliminated.

Postoperative care. When the postoperative tonsilloadenoidectomy patient returns from the recovery room to his unit after having been gently suctioned and observed for immediate signs of cardiorespiratory distress, he is positioned on his abdomen or side to facilitate oronasal drainage and prevent aspiration. His nurse frequently checks his pulse and respirations. She notes the child's level of consciousness and any pronounced restlessness. She observes his skin for color and moisture. She carefully evaluates the amount and kind of oronasal drainage, always asking herself: "Is it profuse? Is it a constant drip or ooze? Is the child swallowing frequently, perhaps swallowing the blood? Does he need suctioning? Approximately how many tissues have been used? What is the color of the discharge?" Persistently forming, bright red drainage indicates active bleeding. It is many times difficult for a student to evaluate the amount of bleeding considered normal after tonsilloadenoidectomy. She should never feel apologetic for asking a more experienced nurse to help her judge the condition

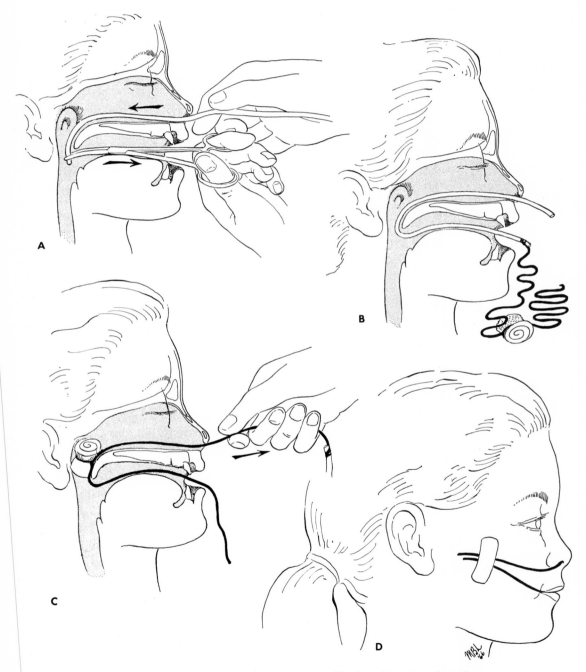

FIG. 38-2. Insertion of a postnasal pack to stop bleeding from the adenoid area.

of her patient. Unless special indications develop, blood pressure is not routinely determined on a young child after a tonsilloadenoidectomy.

If the patient is bleeding excessively, the attending physician should be called. Occasionally postnasal packs may be inserted (Fig. 38-2), or a bleeding blood vessel may have to be tied off. Infrequently, blood transfusions may be needed.

As soon as the child is conscious and responding, he should be given frequent sips of water to ascertain his tolerance of oral fluids. The early introduction of clear, bland fluids helps prevent dehydration and elevated temperature. It also eventually helps to ease the sore throat always present. By the next day the child is ready for a soft, bland diet. The incidence of postoperative nausea has been greatly reduced through the use of anesthetics other than ether.

The pediatric tonsillectomy patient is usually returned home the day after surgery. Parents should be told to continue with a soft, bland diet for approximately 1 week and to encourage fluids. The child should be kept quiet and resting and guarded from sources of infection. Aspirin may be prescribed for discomfort. Signs and symptoms that should be reported promptly by the parents to the physician include signs of fresh bleeding, earache, fever, chest pain, or cough. As already stated, the most common postoperative complication is hemorrhage; however, other possible difficulties that have been reported are otitis media, lung abscess, pneumonia, and, in rare cases, even meningitis and septicemia.

Associated myringotomy. When infection of the middle ear has been a preoperative consideration or represents a postoperative possibility, many physicians perform a surgical incision of the eardrum, called a *myringotomy,* at the time of the tonsilloadenoidectomy. To maintain this small opening, promote drainage, and avoid otitis media, it is now standard procedure for some physicians to insert a small polyethylene tube about ¾ inch in length through the eardrum into the middle ear. These little tubes usually fall out spontaneously in a few days.

Otitis media and hygiene of the ear

Otitis media has been mentioned as a possible complication of upper respiratory infections several times in this chapter. It may also be associated with measles (rubeola) and scarlet fever. The common signs, symptoms, and treatment of this fairly common disorder of the middle ear will now be described. The causative agents of the inflammation may differ. Hemolytic streptococcal or pneumococcal bacteria are often identified when the drainage is cultured. Bacteria usually gain access to the middle ear through the eustachian tube or a perforated eardrum. When the eustachian tube becomes inflamed, it may swell shut, and the purulent material produced by the infection builds up within the middle ear, causing symptoms. Earache or pain, ringing of the ears, elevated temperature, occasional vomiting, and perhaps spontaneous rupture of the eardrum resulting in a "running ear" may be experienced. Infants are especially susceptible and may announce their discomfort by crying, fussy behavior, or pulling at the affected ear. Rupture of the eardrum should be avoided by the use of a planned incision of the eardrum (myringotomy). Such a procedure helps prevent the increasing buildup of pressure in the middle ear and the possibility of an extension of the infection into the porous mastoid bone. It also saves the eardrum from an uncontrolled laceration and the hearing loss that sometimes may follow. In the past if the mastoid bone became involved, a mastoidectomy was performed. This left a large depression behind the child's ear. Today, with the availability of increasing numbers and types of antibiotics with which to combat middle ear infections, mastoiditis is much less frequent. In an effort to reduce the incidence of middle ear infection the child should be taught to blow his nose gently while his mouth is open with no compression of either nostril. This

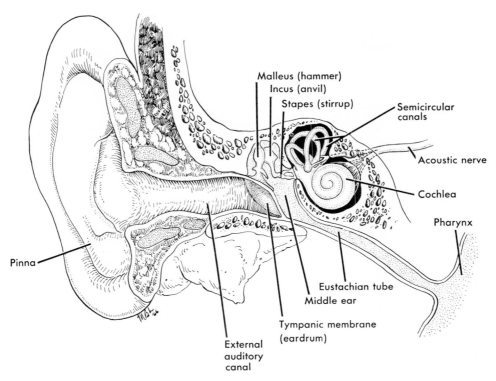

FIG. 38-3. Basic anatomy of the ear.

will diminish the possibility of forcing infective material up into the eustachian tube.

In some instances damage to the ear may follow ill-advised probing of the external auditory canal with such implements as hairpins and matchsticks. The old saying, "Never put anything in your ear except your elbow," contains considerable wisdom. The outer canal should be cleaned only by a washcloth or a tightly rolled piece of cotton. If the presence of a collection of hardened wax, or *cerumen,* is suspected, the ear should be examined, and a physician or nurse trained in the technique of irrigating the ears should carry out the procedure.

Any body opening seems to offer a challenge to some children. Boys and girls will occasionally push foreign bodies into the external ear canal. When foreign bodies are detected, they should be removed by a physician because the general public has neither the knowledge, skill, nor instru-ments necessary to perform such a task. An irrigation should never be attempted before the child is taken to a physician. If the object is made of vegetable matter, it will swell with the liquid and become more difficult to extract.

Acute nasopharyngitis (acute coryza, or the common cold)

The so-called common cold has plagued humanity for countless years, and since no specific preventive or treatment has yet been discovered, it will probably be present among us to cause consternation for at least several more. Young school-age children average from three to six colds per year. The common cold is probably caused by several viral organisms. The structures they attack are primarily the nose and throat. Symptoms include a dry, scratchy, sore, inflamed pharynx and an inflamed nasal mucosa, first producing a clear mucoid nasal discharge, which later becomes thick and purulent. These local symptoms are often accompanied by headache, muscular pains, general malaise, and fever. As the viral infection continues it often is complicated by the intrusion of pathogenic bacteria, which may prolong the respiratory congestion and promote the extension of the inflammation to the middle ear, sinuses, larynx, trachea, and even bronchi and lungs. It is mainly the possibility of extension that makes the common cold a potentially dangerous condition.

A common cold is probably contagious for a number of hours before symptoms are observed by the patient. It is believed that the cold sufferer remains contagious at least 48 hours after the onset of visible signs. Spread by droplet contamination is most common. It is very important to protect infants from exposure to colds because they are affected more seriously than older children. An infant may have a high temperature of 104° F. and the possibility of febrile convulsions. His ears are almost always affected. His smaller nasal passages are relatively easily blocked, causing difficulties in breathing, nursing, and eating. It is impossible to prevent a child from ever having a cold, but everything possible should be done to protect a baby.

Supportive treatment consists of rest, relative isolation, encouraged fluid intake, a bland, soft diet as desired, maintenance of an airway through the use of nonoily nose drops and humidification procedures, and the relief of associated pain and fever through the use of proper dosages of aspirin or the nonsalicylate acetaminophen (Tempra, Tylenol). Remember, both the amount of aspirin given and the interval and duration of treatment must always be considered. Many children suffer from salicylate poisoning every year! A rule of thumb a nurse may want to remember is that a child of average weight should be given only 1 grain (60 mg.) of aspirin per year of age up to 5 grains and should not be given aspirin more than five times at 4-hour intervals without medical consultation. Dosages for babies under 1 year of age must be very carefully determined. Chil-

dren over 5 years of age but less than 12 years of age may usually be given 5 grains at a time if administration is not repeated more often than every 4 to 6 hours for a brief period. To protect the nares or upper lip from excoriation caused by the fairly constant nasal discharge, cold cream or petrolatum may be applied. Antibiotics are usually not indicated in the event of viral infections unless secondary bacterial invaders become a problem.

"Strep throat"

Occasionally a severe pharyngitis develops because of an infection caused by the group A beta-hemolytic streptococcus. Such a condition is commonly called a "strep throat." Classically it is accompanied by a high fever and swollen lymph nodes in the neck. It is only one form of streptococcal infection, and in the early stages it may be difficult to differentiate from its close relative, scarlet fever, which is set apart primarily by the development of a yellowish red rash. Streptococcal infections may initiate abnormal immune mechanisms that cause rheumatic fever or glomerulonephritis. For this reason it is important to seek medical advice when any severe sore throat accompanied by prolonged significant fever manifests itself. Definite diagnosis is made on the results of throat cultures. A number of antibiotics can usually be prescribed, based on drug sensitivity tests. Children who have a history of glomerulonephritis or rheumatic fever are often placed on a regimen of prophylactic antibiotics to reduce the possibility of streptococcal reinfection and a reactivation or worsening of their conditions.

THE LARYNX AND TRACHEA
Spasmodic laryngitis (croup)

Laryngitis, or inflammation of the larynx, may be the result of an extension of an obvious nasopharyngeal infection or may occur spontaneously without any previous symptomatology. The condition called *spasmodic laryngitis* or *croup*, is particularly common in early childhood. Croup usually attacks children 2 to 4 years of age. It is characterized by a harsh, barklike cough and difficult, noisy inspirations caused by intermittent spasms of the larynx that usually commence in the early hours of the morning. These episodes are very frightening to the child as well as to the uninitiated parent. The patient's pulse is usually rapid, and his skin may be clammy. His face may be congested and his lips and nails cyanotic as he struggles for breath. Respiratory distress is often relieved by procedures that supply warm, humidified air and reassurance (see p. 529). Sometimes an expectorant or emetic drug like syrup of ipecac is prescribed. Whether ipecac acts as an expectorant or emetic depends on the dosage ordered. It is used to relieve, by reflex stimulation, the laryngeal spasm. After vomiting occurs a sedative is often administered. There is little or no fever associated with croup, and in most cases the attack subsides after a few hours, leaving the patient with only a residual hoarseness and occasional harsh cough. However, nightly attacks may recur, and the parents may become exhausted from nervous tension if not loss of sleep. Hospitalization may be recommended to rule out other possible diagnoses (for example, the laryngitis of diphtheria or streptococcal infections) or because of the particularly severe or protracted nature of the laryngeal spasms. The nurse caring for a patient with croup should observe the rate and quality of the child's respirations and the amount of cyanosis, apprehension, and restlessness present. She should keep the environment at an even, warm temperature (unless a warm atmosphere is contraindicated by the presence of an excessive body temperature). Sudden drops in temperature and cold rooms often foster laryngeal spasm. The patient with croup rarely needs a tracheostomy because of the development of laryngeal obstruction.

Aspiration of foreign objects

Aspiration of foreign objects into the trachea and bronchi occasionally occurs. Most often the victim is the older infant or the unsuspecting adventurous toddler. It is remarkable what kinds of objects have been retrieved from small bronchi: beads, pins, parts of toys, and pieces of misguided food. It is very important to teach young children not to put objects other than eating utensils or food into their mouths and to supervise the play of young children to provide a safe environment for those too young to understand or follow such instructions. Toddlers should not be given nuts, celery, carrot sticks, or chewing gum. They do not know enough about chewing, talking, laughing, swallowing, and breathing. All small objects should be put out of reach.

If a child is discovered choking, he should be turned upside down. If this simple procedure is not effective alone, a short, controlled blow on the back with the hand may dislodge the object; however, children who are choking should not be "pounded on the back," especially if they are in an upright position, since this may cause a sudden intake of breath and greater aspiration. If respiratory distress continues, the child should be seen immediately by a physician, who may have to schedule a chest x-ray examination and perform a bronchoscopy. Such objects may cause respiratory obstruction, inflammation, infection, and possible atelectasis or emphysema. Sometimes the actual aspiration of an object is not noted because it is small enough not to cause immediate spasmodic choking. Then noisy, dyspneic respirations, cough, and fever may be among the signs reported.

THE LOWER RESPIRATORY TRACT

The lower respiratory tract is usually considered to include the bronchi, bronchioles, alveoli, which form the tissues of the lungs, and pleurae, or coverings of the lungs. Infectious conditions involving these structures are, for the most part, more difficult to cure and more threatening to general health than those involving the passages of the upper respiratory system.

Laryngotracheobronchitis (LTB)

Laryngotracheobronchitis, a serious, acute respiratory disease involving inflammation of the larynx, trachea, and bronchi, is often called LTB. It may be caused by one of several viral or bacterial agents. Commonly implicated are *Haemophilus influenzae* bacilli, pneumococci, or hemolytic streptococci. LTB usually attacks infants or very young children. Symptoms usually consist of a rather high temperature and respiratory difficulty, caused by the thick nature of the abnormal secretions in the bronchi and edema of the involved tissues, particularly the larynx. Partial obstruction of the respiratory passages causes very noisy breathing called *stridor*. Extreme dyspnea and cyanosis are characteristic. A cough may not always be present. A tracheostomy may be indicated to help remove the secretions. The child must be continually observed to detect a worsening of his condition. Oral fluids and food may be curtailed or omitted and intravenous therapy instituted, depending on the vitality of the child. Some children may actually lose their lives because of respiratory obstruction, exhaustion, secondary pneumonia, or septicemia. However, the use of appropriate drug therapy has greatly reduced the former alarming mortality of this disease.

Treatment may include antibiotics, humidification techniques, oxygen administration, and tracheotomy. Provision for rest is very important. The need for meticulous observation cannot be overemphasized. Sedatives are usually avoided, since they may depress the cough reflex and partially counteract the effects of humidification by decreasing secretions and thereby thickening mucus in the respiratory tract.

Acute bronchitis

Bronchitis may occur alone without any other symptoms related to other portions of the respiratory tract, it may be an extension of inflammatory problems involving neighboring respiratory anatomy, or it may be associated with infectious diseases such as measles, pertussis (whooping cough), scarlet fever, and diphtheria. It is a rather common problem for toddlers. It may remain quite mild or progressively become more severe, leading to pneumonia. In infants, emphysema (abnormal dilatation of the alveoli) may develop, greatly interfering with the normal carbon dioxide–oxygen exchange in the lungs. A productive cough, which may be quite disturbing, appears as the disease develops. Paroxysms may occur, particularly when the position of the child is altered, for example, in the morning on rising or when he is first placed in bed after sitting for a period. This is caused by the movement of the secretions in the bronchi that stimulate coughing. Chest pain may be present, and dyspnea, wheezing, and cyanosis may appear in more severe cases. Infants with bronchitis may also suffer from diarrhea and vomiting.

However, unless the condition worsens, acute bronchitis usually subsides in a little more than a week. Treatment consists of antibacterial or expectorant drugs, warm humidification, and increased oxygenation, if needed.

The pneumonias

Any inflammation of the lung tissue may be called pneumonia. It is characterized by the presence of fever, chest pain, productive cough, and abnormal physical findings. The diagnosis is aided by x-ray films and sputum culture studies. A discussion of pneumonia can be very confusing. Many descriptive terms may be used, and many are applied simultaneously to the same patient. One may wonder how to sort them out so that they are meaningful. In describing a case of pneumonia four basic perspectives may be used: (1) One may consider the disease from the perspective of etiology, or the kind of organism or agent causing the inflammation. Some examples of adjectives used in this case are viral, bacterial, or fungal. These terms suggest the causative agent. (2) One may describe pneumonia from the perspective of the anatomy attacked. The words lobar pneumonia (involving one or more lobes of a lung), double pneumonia (involving both lungs), bronchopneumonia (involving particularly the terminal bronchioles) point out the structures involved. (3) One may classify a case of pneumonia according to the method by which the inflammation was primarily contracted. Frequently the modifying terms "aspiration" or "hypostatic" are used. When newborn infants contract pneumonia, it is often an aspiration type. Bedfast patients must be guarded against hypostatic pneumonia, which results from too little respiratory activity. (4) One may describe pneumonia according to the symptoms created in the patient and the response to therapy. Examples of the use of such descriptive terminology are the so-called atypical, or walking, pneumonias.

Certain types of pneumonia are more common in certain age groups. Disseminated types (that is, pneumonias not confined to one part of the lung) are more often diagnosed in infants. Some writers include bronchiolitis as an example of disseminated pneumonia. Aspiration pneumonas, whether caused by the introduction of oily materials (lipoids) or other irritants into the lower respiratory tract, are also more characteristic of infants. Lobar pneumonia is usually more common in older children.

Although more organisms may be implicated as causative agents of pneumonia, this discussion will briefly describe the effects of only three: the pneumococcus, staphylococcus, and virus.

Pneumococcal pneumonia. The pneumococcus (*Diplococcus pneumoniae*) is a frequent cause of pediatric pneumonia. It enters the body through the respiratory passages and brings about a succession of changes in the affected portions of the lungs, causing cough, chest pain, and fever. Breathing is usually rapid and shallow, and the pulse is elevated. The type of onset may be influenced by the age of the patient. The first sign in an infant or young child may be the appearance of a convulsion. An older child may first complain of a chill. The pneumococcus usually causes lobar pneumonia in children beyond infancy. Symptoms related to the gastrointestinal tract are not uncommon, and vomiting and diarrhea may be present, especially in the toddler. Abdominal distention

is still occasionally a complication. Stiff neck may also be noted, adding to the problem of diagnosis. X-ray examination, nose and throat cultures, and careful auscultation of the chest are the most important methods of determining the cause of the multiple complaints.

Treatment has been highly successful in recent years because of the sensitivity of the pneumococcus to various antibiotics and sulfonamides.

The high temperature usually responds dramatically to the administration of drug therapy. Early proper treatment has reduced the mortality to less than 1% in infants and children. Oxygen and humidification therapy along with the administration of aspirin and mild sedatives are also still important.

Nursing care involves careful observation of respiratory patterns, pulse, color, and the general condition of the patient. Fluid intake, particularly, must be maintained to assure proper excretion of toxic products. Observance of the positioning orders of the attending physician, with frequent modification of body position within the limits prescribed, is also important. Patients often breathe better with their heads and chests elevated; babies are often placed in infant seats. Isolation techniques are observed. Convalescence should not be rushed; adequate time for recuperation is very important to regain strength and weight.

Staphylococcal pneumonia. The incidence and importance of staphylococcal pneumonia has increased in recent years with the emergence of a strain of staphylococci that is resistant to standard drug therapy (although some more effective drugs have been developed). The disease may result from an extension of an infection involving another part of the body. Abscesses form in the lungs. The possibility of pneumothorax must be considered. Nursing care parallels that of pneumococcal pneumonia.

Viral pneumonia. A viral pneumonia is often termed "interstitial pneumonitis," or "acute bronchiolitis." Viral agents do not respond to antibiotics or sulfonamides. Treatment is symptomatic, including the nursing measures previously described.

• • •

Although the diagnosis of pneumonia does not cause the same alarm today that it once produced in the hearts and minds of parents, it is still a potential threat to the life and future health of the child. Patients suffering from this disease must be frequently evaluated and expertly nursed.

RESPIRATORY DISEASE INVOLVING ALLERGY

The word "allergy" describes an unfavorable body reaction resulting from the presence of certain substances in food or the environment for which an individual may have little tolerance. The tendency to develop allergies appears to be strongly hereditary. Allergies often affect the skin, causing hives or eczema. They may upset the digestion. They frequently initiate some type of respiratory disease. Pollens, feathers, animal hairs and dander, dust, certain drugs, or certain foods (often wheat, eggs, cow's milk, chocolate, tomatoes, or citrus fruit) may trigger respiratory problems. The inciting substances of allergic reactions are termed "allergens."

The mechanism of allergic responses is still obscure. It has been described as an abnormal antigen-antibody reaction. However, more recent investigation emphasizes the role of possible inborn metabolic errors that interfere with the normal breakdown, formation, and use of chemicals in the body.

The most common respiratory problems with a strong allergic basis are allergic rhinitis (hay fever) and asthma. Some types of bronchiolitis also seem to have an allergic foundation.

Allergic rhinitis (hay fever)

The typical patient with hay fever has an annoying nasal discharge, itching, watery eyes, and a tendency to suffer from recurrent bouts of sneezing. This is a trouble-some, but usually not a serious, condition. It is helped by removal of the allergen, when possible, antihistaminic medication, or desensitization techniques involving multiple injections over a long period. The condition, in itself, is usually not serious. However, persons who suffer from hay fever may in time develop asthma, a more debilitating and critical type of respiratory disorder.

Asthma

Asthma is the most common major allergic manifestation in childhood. It involves from 1% to 2% of all children. It is characterized by difficulty in breathing as the result of spasm of the small bronchi, obstructive edema of the bronchial mucosa, and the production of tenacious secretions, which also tend to obstruct air exchange. There is more difficulty in exhaling than inhaling because of the frequent development of emphysema secondary to the respiratory obstruction. A pronounced expiratory wheeze is usually present. Rapid, shallow inspirations are characteristic.

A number of factors may cause these anatomical changes. An inherited tendency to react in an allergic manner is usually found. The child often has a history of eczema, hives, gastrointestinal upset, hay fever, or recurrent respiratory infection. Other members of his family may be troubled by such symptoms. Asthmatic attacks are often associated with emotional episodes and family tensions. Psychiatric counseling is sometimes necessary and very helpful.

The diagnosis of asthma is based on careful history of the patient's health problems and the health problems of his family, observation or description of the actual attack, blood and sputum studies to discover evidence of elevated eosinophil count, and evaluation of the patient's response to epinephrine (Adrenalin) given for treatment.

Asthmatic attacks may occur at any time and are related to multiple factors. There is no single cause. The child becomes symptomatic when he reaches a certain level or threshold of exposure to certain offenders. Upper respiratory infections, changes in temperature, and physical exertion are all known to precipitate attacks. Difficulty in breathing always produces anxiety, and the patient's anxiety and that of his parents tend to compound his respiratory problems.

Treatment of acute attacks of asthma usually includes the administration of epinephrine (Adrenalin) by injection or inhalation to produce relatively quick relief. Epinephrine hydrochloride (Sus-Phrine) or aminophylline may be used to achieve more lasting effects. Humidification with or without additional oxygen is helpful in thinning the secretions. Adequate fluid intake is very important. After the acute phase, postural drainage after intermittent positive pressure breathing (IPPB) is very effective in the removal of bronchial secretions or mucous plugs.

A life-threatening situation, *status asthmaticus,* exists when the patient does not improve after three consecutive doses of Adrenalin, 1:1,000, given at 20- to 30-minute intervals. These children are critically ill and must be hospitalized.

Isoproterenol (Isuprel) with IPPB is frequently effective for patients who do not respond to Adrenalin. It is administered promptly to all cooperative children. Dehydration is quickly corrected by the administrations of intravenous fluids. Aminophylline, a potent bronchodilator, may be added to the intravenous drip chamber and given over a period of 15 to 30 minutes every 6 to 8 hours. Children who do not respond to these measures are given hydrocortisone 21–sodium succinate (Solu-Cortef). However, steroids are used sparingly except with chronic asthmatics who are in "status." In these, steroids are usually given first.

Every attempt should be made to discover the precipitating causes of the attacks and to eliminate them, if possible, from the environment. Medication or desensitization through the injection of slowly increasing concentrations of materials to which

the child has been sensitive when exposed to greater quantity may be recommended.

The use of special breathing exercises and the amount of physical activity allowed asthma patients between attacks varies according to their individual conditions and the concepts of the attending physicians. The psychological aspects of the disorder must not be overlooked. The nursing staff and parents must realize that the child suffering from asthma needs a great deal of reassurance and support during his distress. Both parents and staff may need counseling regarding the need to provide consistent and loving discipline in such a setting and ways in which it may be applied.

CYSTIC FIBROSIS (CYSTIC FIBROSIS OF THE PANCREAS, OR MUCOVISCIDOSIS) (Fig. 38-4)

It is always difficult to decide just where to place the discussion of cystic fibrosis in a pediatric nursing curriculum. When the disease was first described, the pancreatic pathology and digestive difficulties of the patient received the most attention. Later, when the constitutional nature of the disease became more apparent, the changes in the activity of the exocrine glands (sweat, salivary, mucus-producing, etc.) were emphasized. Currently, because respiratory failure is most frequently the eventual cause of death, cystic fibrosis has been included with those diseases primarily involving the respiratory tract.

Cystic fibrosis is probably inherited as a recessive characteristic; that is, if both parents carry the gene of the disease but do not have the disease, approximately 25% of their children (by the law of inheritance) would be expected to develop the problem. Evidently the condition may exist in mild or severe forms. Some persons who in the past were believed to have very poor resistance to respiratory diseases, such as bronchitis and pneumonia, were actually suffering from complications of cystic fibrosis. Some victims of cystic fibrosis appear to have only respiratory complications, whereas others may be troubled mainly by

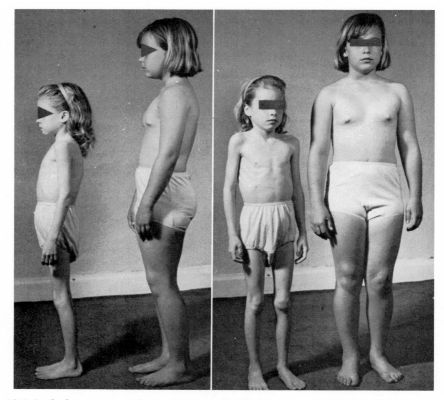

Fig. 38-4. Both these young girls are 10 years old. The youngster on the left demonstrates the effects of severe cystic fibrosis.

the digestive disturbances. A number will have both digestive and respiratory problems. Cystic fibrosis occurs once in every 1,000 to 2,000 live births. It is much more important than generally recognized because of its chronic character and the incapacity and fatality it causes.

Symptoms

Cystic fibrosis affects the exocrine glands, causing changes in many of the secretions. In a small percentage of cases the disease is diagnosed in the newborn infant nursery because of the detection of meconium ileus. In this condition the meconium, or stool formed by the newborn infant, is even more thick and sticky than usual (certainly normal meconium is sticky enough!) because of the absence or reduction of normal pancreatic digestive enzymes. The abnormal stool sticks to the walls of the ileum like paste and obstructs the lower digestive

tract. The intestine becomes distended, and abdominal distention, or bloating, is noted. No passage of stool occurs. Vomiting and dehydration may ensue. Meconium ileus is a surgical emergency. Any newborn infant who does not pass stool within 24 hours after birth should be especially evaluated and examined for possible obstruction.

Since the pancreatic digestive enzymes may be reduced or absent, foodstuffs (fats and proteins especially) may be poorly digested and assimilated. If much of the food eaten does not leave the digestive tract by the normal processes of assimilation, the child will pass large amounts of feces and develop a protuberant abdomen. During infancy the stools may not be especially bulky or offensive. However, if the child is not treated, the stools may assume these characteristics as he becomes older. The strong odor is caused by the impaired digestion of fats. The child is hungry and usually has an eager appetite. However, because he is unable to use much of the food he eats (and respiratory complications may interfere with development), his arms and legs are characteristically spindly, his buttocks are emaciated, and his growth is retarded. Fortunately the digestive problems usually improve with the addition of commercial preparations of pancreatic enzymes to the diet. Medical opinion differs on the advisability of restricting the normal intake of fat. Most physicians recommend diets high in protein content to offset the amount of protein lost in the stool. Simple carbohydrates are easily digested, and banana products are especially favored. Special formulas reinforced with glucose, skimmed, powdered milk, or banana powder may be utilized. Diets should be supplemented by vitamins prepared in such a way that they can be combined with water (since oil-based vitamins are poorly absorbed). Extra salt intake is necessary because of the large amounts lost in the perspiration. Heat prostration is a real danger to these children when excessive sweating occurs.

The secretions of the mucus-producing glands of the bronchi may become extremely thick and tenacious and block the bronchioles, causing cough, wheezing, respiratory obstruction, emphysema, and frequently infection (usually staphylococcic). The lungs are virtually defenseless against microbes. In severe cases the chronic respiratory disease causes a deformed, barrel-type chest, cyanosis, and even clubbing of the fingers and toes as a result of secondary disturbances in heart action and circulation. Because of the difficulty the heart may encounter in pumping blood through the scarred lung tissue, abnormal dilatation of the right heart and thickening of the right ventricular wall may occur. Death may be the result of heart failure that developed because of the severe respiratory difficulty. Cardiac stress secondary to problems in the action of the lungs is termed "cor pulmonale."

Diagnosis

Diagnosis of cystic fibrosis is based on laboratory analysis of several features of the disease as well as clinical observation. The excessive loss of sodium and chloride in the body perspiration has led to the so-called sweat test, one type of diagnostic aid. The analysis of perspiration has been of considerable benefit in detecting the disease. This feature is so pronounced that mothers have noted that their affected children have a "salty taste" when they are kissed. One screening device consists of placing the child's hands on a special gelatin preparation impregnated with silver nitrate. A high sodium chloride level on the skin results in the formation of a hand print. However, carriers of this disease, who have no other demonstrable signs or symptoms, also have elevated sodium chloride levels in their perspiration or saliva. This sign in itself is not conclusive.

Another diagnostic finding is the determination of a reduction or absence of the pancreatic enzyme *trypsin* in material aspirated from the duodenum of the patient or in dilutions of fecal material. Still another test involves finding an excessive amount of fat in the child's stool.

Treatment

Treatment is designed to meet the needs of the individual patient, depending on his symptoms. Diet modifications and enzyme administration have already been discussed. To help alleviate respiratory complications and distress, the child may be placed on oral prophylactic antibiotic therapy and antibiotic aerosol administration. In some cases he may sleep in a mist tent, even at home. Oxygen therapy, with or without intermittent positive pressure and medicated mist, may be ordered. The fine mist particles of ultrasonic nebulizers have been especially helpful. A combination of chest vibration or percussion (cupping) followed by coughing and postural drainage is sometimes prescribed with beneficial results. The manual percussion techniques are usually executed and taught by physical therapists.

Nursing care

Good nursing care entails a careful observation of the dietary intake and its effect on the child and his elimination. Every effort should be made to offer a variety in the meals within the limitations imposed and to make eating a pleasant experience.

Provision for frequent changes in position to prevent pneumonia and reduce skin problems should be an important consideration. Some of these children are very emaciated, and the skin over bony prominences is in special need of care. The rectal area must be meticulously cleaned. Rectal prolapse may occasionally be a complication. A soothing, local ointment may prevent irritation from the bulky stools. Any material soiled by feces should be removed immediately from the child's room. Appropriate air fresheners may be useful. Stools should always be described regarding their size, color, consistency, and odor.

The observation and report of any respiratory symptoms or distress is, of course, of paramount importance. Every effort should be made to protect the child from persons with any type of respiratory infection.

Because of the chronic nature of the disease, the severe strain it may place on the family finances, and the psychological needs of the child, home care is recommended except when the child's condition indicates that he or his family need the relief that can be provided through hospitalization. Parents must receive much counseling and practical assistance to help meet their child's social and emotional requirements, as well as his physical needs. They also must be cautioned against becoming so preoccupied with the sick child that the needs of other family members are continually neglected. Although some children with diagnosed cystic fibrosis have reached adulthood, usually those little patients with manifest symptoms and pronounced difficulty fall far short of attaining this age. The nurse caring for the child with cystic fibrosis must realize the strain under which the parents may be operating and their feelings of fatigue and frustration. Many families have lost other children because of this disease and have traveled almost the same road to final farewells before. Such a journey is not any easier just because some of the scenery may be familiar.

Disorders affecting the heart, heart vessels, and blood

This section will introduce the student to some of the more common pediatric problems involving the heart and its vessels and circulating blood. Although some of the frequently encountered congenital heart defects were briefly described in Chapter 18, no mention was made of the surgical possibilities of repair of such defects or the nursing care of the cardiac patient. These next paragraphs will supply these omissions.

Varied abnormalities of the heart and large blood vessels may occur. Some cause little inconvenience. Others are incompatible with life or produce severe problems in their victims. Such defects account for 50% of all deaths caused by all types of congenital malformations in the first year of life. Congenital cardiac defects form early in embryonic life, usually between the second and tenth week of gestation. The causes are not always known, but maternal nutrition, infections, heredity, and drugs are possible factors.

DIAGNOSTIC PROCEDURES

To evaluate heart function and detect possible cardiac abnormality, an accurate history of the patient's complaints is sought, a complete physical examination is carried out, and various tests and specialized procedures may be ordered.

Commonly used tests include direct observation of the shape and action of the heart and great blood vessels by *fluoroscopy*, permanent recording of the size and shape of the heart by *x-ray examination*, external pulse and heart sound recordings

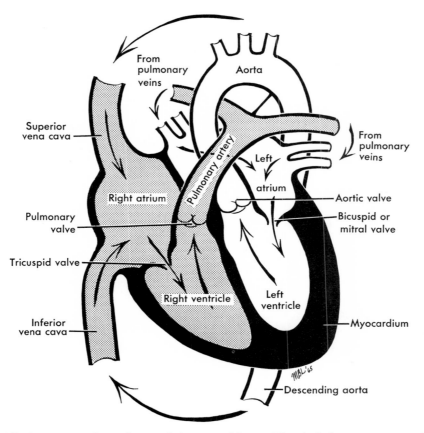

FIG. 38-5. Structure and circulation of the normal heart. The shaded area represents blood with low-oxygen content.

by *phonocardiography,* and measurements of the electrical activity of the heart by *electrocardiography.*

Laboratory tests of special significance include a complete blood count and hematocrit and hemoglobin determinations. Patients with cyanotic-type heart disease may have either an excessive amount of circulating red blood cells (polycythemia) manufactured in an attempt to deliver more oxygen to the deprived body cells or may suffer from anemia. If polycythemia is present, thickening and slowing of the circulating blood occurs, which may occasionally cause the development of abnormal clots in the bloodstream, always a dangerous situation.

Specialized procedures occasionally arranged may involve the injection of a con-

trast medium into the circulation and observation of its flow by x-ray examination or fluoroscopy. This is termed "angiography." When a contrast medium is injected directly into a heart chamber, it is termed "angiocardiography." Such visualization of the aorta is termed "aortography." Special procedures may also include the performance of right or left *heart catheterizations,* which are concerned with the introduction of a small catheter seen by x-ray examination into a vein or artery and its gentle manipulation into various chambers of the heart as well as large associated vessels. This procedure is done on an anesthetized or sedated patient and, although it is not without risk, yields considerable information. If possible, the children are sedated, not anesthetized, so that they may be able to cooperate consciously during the procedure. It reveals the pressure in various areas of the cardiocirculatory system and the percentage of oxygen at different sites. The presence of abnormal openings may be demonstrated by direct passage of the small catheter through the defects or by evaluation of oxygenation patterns.

Children returning to the nursing unit after cardiac catheterization should be treated as postoperative patients. Vital signs—pulse, respirations, and blood pressure—should be noted every 20 minutes until stable. Children should have blood pressure determinations on the arm not used for the catheter insertion. A mist tent or oxygen mask should be in readiness as ordered or indicated. Any dressing applied should be noted and observed. It is important to note skin color and temperature and character of the pulse in the extremity catheterized because this may detect arterial occlusion due to thrombus formation.

COMMON CONGENITAL DEFECTS OF THE HEART AND GREAT VESSELS (Fig. 38-6)
Patent ductus arteriosus

Patent means "open." The condition called patent ductus arteriosus refers to a holdover from the fetal circulation pattern. Review Fig. 7-6. You will remember that the ductus arteriosus is a short blood vessel that connects the pulmonary artery with the aorta, making it unnecessary for the blood circulating through the pulmonary artery to continue on to the nonfunctioning lungs of the fetus. Normally this arterial duct closes soon after birth and within a few weeks becomes a ligament.

If the ductus arteriosus does not close, the higher blood pressure in the aorta, which results after birth, forces well-oxygenated blood from the aorta back into the pulmonary circulation for a return trip to the lungs. This puts an abnormal work load on the left ventricle and may cause a significant elevation of the blood pressure in the pulmonary circulation. The growth of children suffering from this defect may be impaired if the duct remains

large. They may suffer from dyspnea when they are active, and without appropriate treatment their life expectancy is often reduced. The defect does not characteristically produce cyanosis unless pressures in the aorta and pulmonary artery are changed as the result of excessive pulmonary blood flow, which may increase pulmonary vascular resistance.

Diagnosis is usually made on the basis of several findings. The detection of a continuous murmur or an abnormal sound accompanying heart action is only one. A "thrill" may be noted; the word "thrill" in this case refers to a vibration felt over the cardiac area. Blood pressure determinations may reveal a wide range between the systolic and diastolic readings—termed a "wide pulse pressure." The appearance and stamina of the patient are noted. The patent duct may be visualized by aortography or by direct passage of the small catheter through the duct during fluoroscopy.

This condition may be treated surgically, usually with excellent results. The duct is tied off (ligated) or divided.

Coarctation of the aorta

The aorta is the largest blood vessel in the body. As it leaves the heart it normally arches to the left. Three major vessels sprout from the aortic arch before it starts its descent into the lower thorax and abdomen. These are the innominate, left carotid, and left subclavian arteries, which supply the head and upper extremities with oxygenated blood. The ductus arteriosus also joins the aorta in this general area before the change from the fetal to the newborn infant circulation pattern. Sometimes the aorta is abnormally narrowed in the area of the arch, usually involving the segment just past the subclavian artery. Many times smaller "collateral" vessels (usually branches of the subclavian and intercostal arteries) develop and bypass the narrowed portion to help supply circulation to the lower extremities. The narrowing of the aorta is often called "coarctation," since a narrowed figure results when two arcs

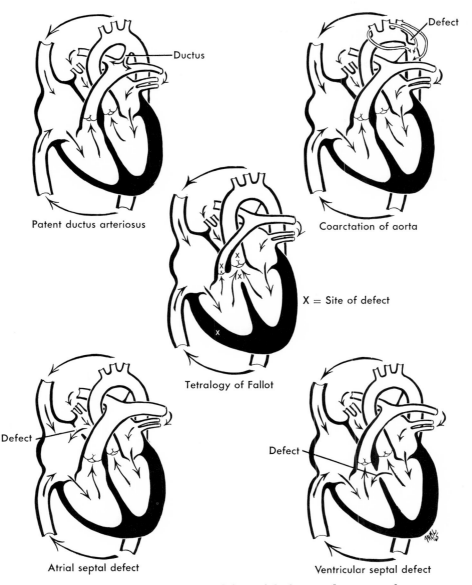

Ductus

Defect

Patent ductus arteriosus

Coarctation of aorta

X = Site of defect

Tetralogy of Fallot

Defect

Defect

Atrial septal defect

Ventricular septal defect

FIG. 38-6. Common congenital defects of the heart and great vessels.

are drawn side by side, like two C's back to back. The symptoms resulting depend on the location of the coarctation and whether any other blood vessel abnormalities exist.

The presence of coarctation is suspected when there are forceful arterial pulses in the upper extremities but weak or absent pulses in the lower extremities and a systolic murmur is heard. The patient may have few complaints, although occasionally

headache, leg cramps, excessive fatigue, and frequent nosebleeds may be reported. Diagnosis is confirmed by x-ray examination, electrocardiogram, and aortogram.

Without appropriate treatment the lifespan is often shortened because of the onset of such complications as cerebral hemorrhage, subacute bacterial endocarditis, or heart failure.

Definitive treatment is surgical. The narrowed portion may be cut out and the adjoining normal-sized segments sewed together. Occasionally the repair involves the insertion of a prosthesis to take the place of a large segment that has to be removed.

Atrial septal defect

An abnormal opening in the wall separating the right and left atria may be the result of the persistence of the foramen ovale, which during fetal life shunts some of the blood from the right to left heart. It may also be caused by the presence of a septal opening unassociated with normal fetal circulation. Cyanosis does not characteristically occur, since the blood pressure is higher in the left heart and unoxygenated blood does not enter the general circulation. However, if some other abnormality is present (for example, pulmonary artery valve stenosis), right to left flow may occur, and cyanosis may result. Children with atrial septal defects usually have an overworked right heart and congested pulmonary circulation because of the backflow through the defect to the right atrium. They may demonstrate cardiac enlargement, a systolic murmur, decreased resistance to respiratory infections, lowered exercise tolerance, and physical underdevelopment. When surgery is attempted depends on the condition of the individual child, since some do quite well without operative intervention. Surgery itself presents a small risk. During surgery the defect is either repaired by direct closure by sutures only or by the incorporation of a plastic patch into the repair. The patch is eventually penetrated by growing heart fibers and becomes part of the septum.

Ventricular septal defect

The presence of an opening between the two ventricles is always an abnormality whether it occurs in the fetus or newborn infant. How seriously such an opening may disturb normal heart function depends on the position and size of the defect and the presence of any other abnormalities in the cardiac–large-vessel anatomy. If a large defect is found in the membranous portion of the septum, symptoms are usually severe. The blood usually travels through the opening from the left to the right ventricle. However, in some cases the shunt may reverse as resistance in the pulmonary capillary bed increases and the pressure in the right side of the heart mounts. Diagnosis is made on the basis of clinical symptoms, a characteristic heart murmur, and the results of x-ray examination, electrocardiograms, and cardiac catheterization. Specific treatment may be recommended for the individual child and consists of surgical repair by open heart surgery similar to that employed for atrial septal defects. Surgical risk is somewhat increased with ventricular septal defect repair.

Tetralogy of Fallot

The word element "tetra" refers to "four." Tetralogy of Fallot is a heart condition that is characterized by the presence of four heart malformations: an interventricular septal defect, a narrowing of the opening of the pulmonary artery (pulmonary stenosis), an aorta situated very near the septal defect (overriding aorta), and an enlarged, thickened right ventricular wall (right ventricular hypertrophy). Because the narrowed pulmonary artery causes the pressure to rise in the right ventricle, hypertrophy of the right heart wall results, and the shunt of blood through the septal defect goes from right to left, usually causing considerable cyanosis. In fact, the child suffering from tetralogy of Fallot has been termed the typical "blue baby." The moderately to severely affected young child with this diagnosis typically has blue lips and nails beds and a dusky tinted skin, which becomes more cyanotic on exertion. Clubbing of the fingers and toes is often a feature (Fig. 38-7). Thrill and chest deformity may also be noted. The child may have "spells" of respiratory distress, deep cyanosis, loss of consciousness, and even convulsions. He is small for his age. When the

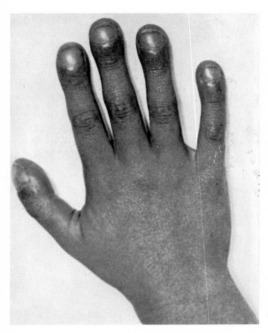

FIG. 38-7. When the ends of the fingers become wide and thick, they are termed "clubbed." These fingers are also very cyanotic. (Courtesy U. S. Naval Hospital, San Diego, Calif.)

FIG. 38-8. The squatting position improves the cardiac output of some children with congenital heart defects.

young child with cyanotic heart disease is fatigued, he often squats (Fig. 38-8). This position improves return of blood to the heart, traps desaturated blood in the lower extremities, and improves cardiac output.

Diagnosis depends on clinical manifestations, x-ray examinations, electrocardiograms, angiocardiograms, and cardiac catheterizations. Treatment may be medical or surgical, depending on the condition of the patient. Before open heart surgery was available, surgical techniques were devised to improve the pulmonary circulation by creating an artificial ductus arteriosus, which would recirculate poorly oxygenated blood to the lungs for oxygen enrichment. The Blalock-Taussig operation and the Potts operation are such techniques. This type of palliative surgery is still useful when the child is considered too small for total correction but is having life-threatening "hypoxic spells." Now open heart

surgery with total correction is preferred because the sources of difficulty may be viewed and repaired under direct vision.

Without surgical intervention the typical patient with tetralogy of Fallot faces a brief future.

Complete transposition of the great vessels

Transposition of the great vessels is a very serious cyanotic congenital heart defect. In this condition the pulmonary artery originates from the left ventricle, whereas the aorta arises from the right ventricle. Life is possible as long as the foramen ovale or ductus arteriosus remains open or an interventricular septal defect exists. Prominent features are extreme cyanosis and congestive heart failure. Diagnosis is made on the basis of electrocardiogram, x-ray examination, angiocardiogram, and/or cardiac catheterization. A palliative surgical procedure to create or enlarge an atrial septal defect may be helpful in prolonging life (Blalock-Hanon operation). A special balloon catheter is often used to create or enlarge an atrial septal defect without the high risk of surgery. Total correction is now possible by utilizing a pericardial patch to deflect blood to the proper chambers. Success of this operation depends on the condition, size, and age of the child.

CARDIAC SURGERY

Assuming that facilities and skilled physicians are available, surgical treatment of large blood vessel or heart defects depends on the extent of incapacity suffered by the patient, the possibility of a satisfactory repair, and the risk involved. Surgery on the aorta, pulmonary artery, or other associated blood vessels is similar in some respects to chest surgery. However, when the malformations exist in the interior of the heart and cardiac circulation must be interrupted, the difficulty of the procedure and the risk to the patient increase significantly. A heart-lung machine was perfected in 1955. Prior to that time it was impossible to discontinue the beating of the heart long enough to make a lengthy repair without seriously depriving some vital structure (for example, brain or kidneys) of vital carbon dioxide–oxygen exchange and causing tissue damage.

The heart-lung machine receives blood from the patient's venous circulation through tubes inserted into the inferior and superior venae cavae. It removes the carbon dioxide, instills oxygen, regulates blood temperature, and pumps the blood back into the systemic circulation by way of the iliac, femoral, or subclavian arteries. Needless to say, this is a highly complex procedure, requiring a team of skilled physicians, nurses, and technicians.

Any child who is to have any type of surgery must be carefully prepared for the event. This is especially true in the case of scheduled chest or heart surgery because of the seriousness of the operation and the many procedures that must be carried out that require the trust and cooperation of the child to achieve optimum results.

A prepared child presupposes prepared parents. This does not mean that the parents must feel totally calm and serene or that they and their child must know all the details of the procedure. The former would be unnatural, the latter would be both impossible and undesirable, probably causing many more anxieties than it would ease. How much the child is told will depend on his age, expressed concerns, and intellect. How much the parents are told will depend on their expressed concerns, intellects, and familiarity with the sciences involved. Whatever information is given, however simple, should be truthful.

Children who are scheduled for heart surgery are usually admitted to the hospital several days in advance of the procedure to enable them to learn about the hospital, to become acquainted with some of the nurses who will be caring for them, and to be introduced to some of the equipment and techniques that will be used after surgery. This preliminary period is also used as a period of evaluation of the child. It is a time when his general condition may be observed and nutritional needs noted and, as far as possible, met. His weight is recorded each morning, and scheduled blood pressure, respiration, and pulse checks are particularly important. The nurses should be alert for and report any signs of respiratory infection or rash, which may indicate the presence of other diseases. Such signs may necessitate a postponement of surgery.

It is usually very helpful to demonstrate some of the equipment that will be used with the child before its use under more stressful conditions is needed. The child may be shown an oxygen tent with humidifier and may get inside to see how the "small house" feels. He may "practice" taking his breathing exercises with the intermittent positive pressure machine or learn how to cough with the nurse holding his chest. Explanations should be calm, factual, and geared to the child's understanding.

TREATMENT AND NURSING CARE OF THE CHILD CARDIAC PATIENT
Postoperative nursing care

The nursing care of postoperative open heart surgery patients is a nursing specialty in itself. A patient usually remains in the intensive care unit for several days. While the child is in the intensive care unit, his condition is usually monitored by machines that record heart action graphically. In some cases heartbeat may be stimulated by the use of a mechanical pacemaker. Both the arterial and venous blood pressures are frequently determined. The rate and quality of respirations are evaluated, the color and feel of the skin are noted. Chest suction is maintained to prevent a buildup of secretion or gas in the thorax, causing respiratory distress and atelectasis. Humidified oxygen is often administered by an oxygen tent. The indwelling catheter is checked frequently to determine kidney output. Intravenous fluids and blood transfusions are calculated and maintained according to order. Wound drainage and dressings must be checked. Turning and encouraging the patient to cough are extremely important. Intermittent positive pressure may be prescribed. Tracheal as well as nasopharyngeal suctioning may be ordered. Some patients may have temporary tracheostomies. Initially the patient's temperature may be subnormal, but later temperature-reducing procedures may be necessary, including the use of the hypothermia blanket. A relatively high temperature after open heart surgery is fairly common, in some cases believed to be caused by a reaction to the massive blood transfusion received. However, the possibility of infection must not be discounted when a patient's temperature rises abnormally.

Continuing care

The child needs constant, expert nursing observation and care. Many important nursing evaluations must be made during this critical postoperative interval. Caring for this type of patient in the immediate postoperative period is not within the scope of the vocational nurse. However, at times she may be called on to help "lend a careful hand," with supervision, during a treatment or in changing a position, depending on the needs and condition of the patient. The vocational nurse should know how important it is that the chest tubes remain intact and the drainage bottles and suction machine not be disturbed. The bottles containing drainage from the chest should always be maintained lower than the lowest level of the child's chest to prevent backflow. To avoid backflow the bottles should be fastened to the floor or to a correctly positioned holder. In the event a chest bottle should break or the tube should become disconnected, the part of the tube coming from the patient's chest must be immediately clamped off near the chest wall to prevent pneumothorax. Symptoms of pneumothorax include cyanosis, dyspnea, and chest pain.

As the patient's condition improves, his chest suction will be discontinued and the tubes removed. As his condition becomes stable, he may be assigned to the care of a licensed vocational nurse under the supervision of a registered nurse. The nurse should know that the child is usually weighed while undressed each morning before breakfast to determine fluid retention. He may be on a diet that limits sodium and carefully spaces a certain maximum oral fluid intake. The patient's pulse and respirations should be noted and recorded before and after any new activity. During periods of ambulation he should be carefully evaluated for fatigue and given periods of rest as his respirations, pulse, and color dictate. The pulse of these young children and infants is always taken over the heart with a stethoscope, that is, apically, for 1 minute. This technique requires training, since there are normally two sounds to each cardiac cycle. Older children may have radial pulse determinations for 1 minute. The quality as well as the rate should be noted.

Occasionally apical-radial pulse determinations will be ordered. These pulse rates are taken simultaneously and then compared; they may be written 110A/100R. There may be more apical beats than radial beats (pulse deficit), but there is never an excess of radial beats! Blood pressure determinations are routinely made with the patient's pulse and respiration at scheduled intervals. Care must be taken in the selection of the size of cuff—it should cover two thirds of the distance from the shoulder to the elbow, or be 20% wider than the diameter of the patient's arm. Ambulation and activity privileges will be gradually increased. Many times conferences must be arranged with physician-nurse-parent participation to help parents adjust to the new capabilities of their children and avoid the hazards of overprotection. Help regarding school responsibilities to be assumed and even vocational planning may be sought.

Nonsurgical treatment and care

Sometimes a patient's cardiac problem cannot be helped by surgery, or he has to wait until he is in better condition or older before surgery is attempted. In these cases the child is treated by medicines, planned diet, and general health supervision. The nurse should be aware of the types of medications the child is receiving and the expected accomplishments, side effects, and toxic reactions of these medications. Sodium restriction is common. Often cardiac patients must be weighed daily, and accurate intake and output records are maintained. Signs of developing heart failure, cardiac irregularities, or possible respiratory infection should be promptly reported. Limitations of activity may be necessary, although many pediatric patients with congenital type cardiac defects automatically limit themselves to only the activity they can best tolerate. Quiet play is often more restful than enforced, resented "complete bed rest." The child who must be in an oxygen tent or who demonstrates susceptibility to fatigue should be disturbed as little as possible, and when he is disturbed, several procedures should be carried out at the same time to allow relatively long uninterrupted periods of sleep or rest (for example, TPR and B/P determinations, offering fluids, changing the child's gown or diapers, and shifting his position). Changes of position are important in preventing hypostatic pneumonia and skin breakdown. However, no *vigorous* back rubs should be performed on a cardiac patient. Proper positioning helps ward off contractures and other deformities and assists proper body function.

POSSIBLE COMPLICATIONS OF CONGENITAL CARDIAC DEFECTS
Cardiac decompensation

Certain complications that may develop with congenital heart patients prior to, during, or after surgery should be mentioned. Probably the most common is the failure of the heart to continue the circulation of the blood in sufficient volume to meet body needs and prevent abnormal congestion of the blood in certain areas. Sometimes the heart can maintain an adequate blood flow by gradually increasing its size or altering its rate. If this occurs, the heart is said to be in *compensation*. If the heart cannot maintain the necessary blood flow, it is said to be in *decompensation*, or failure.

Pulmonary congestion resulting from the inability of the left ventricle to pump effectively is characterized by pooling of blood in the lung capillaries, causing coughing and dyspnea—symptoms not unlike bronchitis. Blood-tinged sputum may be expectorated. Acute pulmonary edema may occasionally occur, sometimes necessitating rather drastic measures such as the removal of from 5% to 10% of the circulating blood (phlebotomy) or rotating tourniquets on the extremities to reduce the amount of blood returning to the heart at one time.

Congestion of blood in the systemic venous system as the result of inefficient right ventricular contraction may cause nausea and vomiting, enlargement of the liver, edema of the tissue spaces, and possible accumulation of fluid in the abdominal cavity (ascites). In infants, edema is often seen around the orbit of the eye. However, edema in infants is best detected by rapid weight gain. Any marked failure of the circulation of the blood in the body may cause cyanosis and dyspnea.

Treatment always involves rest (decreasing the cardiac work load). Sedatives or analgesics such as morphine may be used to promote mental and physical rest and relieve respiratory distress. Digitalis preparations are employed to increase cardiac efficiency. Digitalis slows and strengthens the heartbeat and may help in the removal of sodium by the kidneys. A patient may receive high doses of digitalis initially. The administration of this high dosage to produce sufficient cardiac response is called *digitalization*. The child must be watched for signs and symptoms of excessive dosage. Some of these indications would be anorexia, nausea, vomiting, and excessive slowing or irregularity of the pulse. In toxic doses, digitalis has been known to cause heart block, revealed by an extremely low pulse rate (considering the age of the individual involved). A low-sodium diet is also often prescribed to relieve or prevent edema. If insufficient response to rest, sedation, the use of digitalis, and dietary restriction occurs, diuretics may be ordered. Rarely, artificial withdrawal of fluid from the abdominal cavity (paracentesis) or thorax (thoracentesis) is required.

Subacute bacterial endocarditis

Any damage to cardiac tissue or slowdown in the flow of blood through the heart may set the stage for inflammation of the lining of the heart (endocarditis) and arteries (endarteritis). The inflammation usually results from a blood-borne infection, originating at some other body site. It may have its onset after surgical procedures such as dental extraction, tonsillectomy, or adenoidectomy, or it may be spread from an abscess or infection elsewhere in the body. Signs and symptoms include temperature elevation, weight loss, fatigue, anemia, leukocytosis, the presence of petechiae, an enlarged spleen, and perhaps even partial paralysis or other central

nervous system symptoms caused by the presence of emboli in the brain that originated in the inflamed heart tissue. Prophylactic antibiotics may be prescribed prior to and during certain procedures such as dental surgery.

Cerebral thrombosis

Cerebral thrombosis may develop when an excess of circulating red blood cells is called into action to increase the oxygen-carrying capacity of the blood. The presence of dehydration may result in a thicker, slower-moving fluid in the blood vessels. Clots, or thrombi, may form, and a cerebral vascular accident may take place. Maintenance of adequate fluid intake, the use of oxygen to relieve episodes of cyanosis, and possibly the cautious use of anticoagulants in patients likely to develop such a complication are suggested means of reducing the risk.

RHEUMATIC FEVER (Fig. 38-9)

Rheumatic fever, in itself, would probably not be a disease to be considerd in this chapter. More properly, it is classed as a collagen disease because it affects the connective tissues in the entire body. However, because its most important complication is extensive cardiac damage, it will be discussed here. Although rheumatic fever may be decreasing in incidence, it is still a chief cause of acquired heart disease.

The mechanism of the disease is not completely known, but it is fairly certain that the symptoms constitute an allergic-type reaction to the prior presence of group A beta-hemolytic streptococcus, which causes the so-called "strep throat," erysipelas, and scarlet fever. However, rheumatic fever itself is not communicable. It is not understood why some people develop rheumatic fever after beta-hemolytic streptococcus infections, whereas others do not. Rheumatic fever is most commonly found in the school-age child.

Signs and symptoms

The symptoms of rheumatic fever vary. It is a rare case that exhibits all the possi-

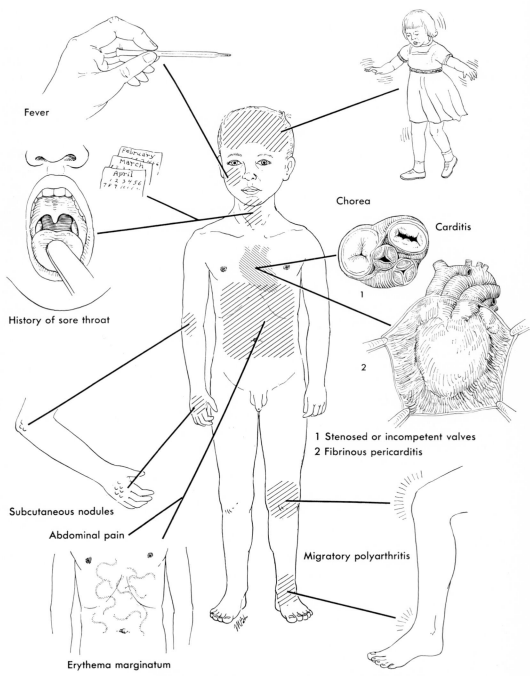

Fever

History of sore throat

Subcutaneous nodules

Abdominal pain

Erythema marginatum

Chorea

Carditis

1 Stenosed or incompetent valves
2 Fibrinous pericarditis

Migratory polyarthritis

Fig. 38-9. Possible signs and symptoms of rheumatic fever.

ble signs and symptoms listed in a text-book. The onset of the condition usually occurs about 2 weeks after the streptococcal infection. However, the infection may have been unapparent at the time. The child may complain of leg aches and joint tenderness, which migrates from joint to joint—one time involving a knee, next an ankle, later a wrist, etc. (polyarthralgia). These pains occur during the day as well as the night. When the child presents with migratory, hot, swollen, tender enlarged joints (polyarthritis), the diagnosis is quickly suggested. Salicylates relieve the symptoms and there is no permanent joint damage. The child may fatigue easily and have a fever. The extent of the fever varies considerably, depending on the severity of the disease. He may also report abdominal pain, believed to be caused by lymph node enlargement. Epistaxis (nosebleed) may occur.

Carditis, or inflammation of the heart, happens in about 40% to 50% of cases during the initial attack of rheumatic fever. Constant observation for rapid or irregular pulse, heart murmurs, increased heart size, and signs and symptoms of cardiac failure must be carried out. Small inflammatory nodules or growths may form in the heart. Often they interfere with the action of the mitral or aortic valves, making it difficult for the valves to close properly or open sufficiently. Carditis is the most important feature of rheumatic fever. The prognosis of the patient largely rests on the severity of carditis.

Another sign that may occasionally accompany rheumatic fever is the development of painless *subcutaneous nodules* near the occiput, knuckles, knees, elbows, and spine. These nodules appear late in the course of the attack and are usually associated with severe carditis.

Another feature that may be seen at times, especially in preadolescent girls, is Sydenham's *chorea* (known in earlier times as St. Vitus' dance). Chorea may be described as involuntary muscular twitching or movement. It sometimes manifests itself

as grimacing. The child may seem exceptionally clumsy and may fail to accomplish muscle tasks involving concentration or fine control. The disorder is characterized by jerky, uncoordinated movements. It may be preceded by a period of emotional instability and behavior problems. It may be so mild as to escape the notice of the casual observer or so severe that it makes normal, daily activities dangerous or impossible. Speech may become slurred and handwriting difficult to decipher.

Still another diagnostic sign of acute rheumatic fever is the appearance of a highly distinctive rash known as *erythema marginatum*. This red-line eruption forms irregular patterns on the trunk and extremities but not the face. However, it is rarely seen.

Diagnosis is made on the evaluation of the signs and symptoms present plus the reports of several laboratory tests. None of the laboratory tests are specific for rheumatic fever, but when made in conjunction with a clinical evaluation of the patient, they are valuable aids. An increased blood *sedimentation rate* and *antistreptolysin O titer* and determination of *C-reactive protein* in the blood indicate the presence of an inflammatory process in the body that may be rheumatic fever. It is also possible to detect, with suitable tests, the presence of antibodies in the blood, formed in response to the invasion of streptococci. But as previously stated, not all beta-hemolytic streptococcal infections cause rheumatic fever. Sometimes a nose and throat culture will return a positive result. Other members of the patient's family should be checked for the presence of a streptococcal infection or the carrier state. Rheumatic fever, because of factors not yet completely determined, has a tendency to run in families.

Treatment

Treatment of rheumatic fever includes the prescription of penicillin to eliminate any lingering residual streptococci and prevent a reinfection. Penicillin does not cure the symptoms of rheumatic fever; it only helps prevent further attacks. If the patient is allergic to penicillin, erythromycin may be used to eradicate the streptococcus. Sulfonamides or penicillin are equally useful in preventing reinfections. Aspirin is helpful in controlling the pain of arthritis and lowering the fever. Prednisone is often used in acute cases of carditis, with the hope of decreasing the possibility of permanent heart valve damage. Prednisone is often lifesaving in overwhelming inflammation involving all the structures of the heart.

Nursing care

The nursing care of the child with rheumatic fever depends on the severity of his disease and the symptoms present. When laboratory tests and clinical features indicate that the disease is active and perhaps progressive, every effort should be made to reduce the work load of the heart by providing emotional and physical rest. However, "doing nothing" is not very restful for most children, especially if they do not really feel very sick. The nurse and the patient's family need a great deal of ingenuity to provide rest that is acceptable and therefore therapeutic for the child. Good observation is essential. The pulse rate is taken for a full minute to determine quality and rhythm. Often the determination of the pulse while the patient is sleeping is requested. The nurse should review the signs and symptoms of rheumatic fever and check her charge for indications of these during her care. Possible signs of cardiac failure are extremely important to report (see pp. 590 and 591). Careful positioning and skin care are necessary. The child with symptoms of chorea needs special supportive care; careful explanation of the condition to the parents is a necessity. Chorea may appear as the sole symptom of rheumatic disease. In the event of moderate to severe disability, rest, prolonged warm baths under supervision, and tranquilizers may help. Patient nursing care is a must. The condition usually subsides spontaneously in from 2 to 3 months.

When the signs of inflammatory activity subside, the electrocardiogram results are favorable, and the pulse rate is within normal limits, the child may be allowed more freedom. However, he must continue to be carefully evaluated to discover his tolerance for increased exercise. Because recurrences of the disease are fairly common and the possibility of permanent heart damage increases with each attack, it is imperative that the parent understand the importance of continued medical supervision. To prevent recurrences the patient should avoid exposure to infections and receive either daily oral or monthly intramuscular penicillin therapy.

DISORDERS OF THE BLOOD AND BLOOD-FORMING ORGANS

The entire cardiovascular apparatus (heart and blood vessels) is designed so that nutrients, hormones, and oxygen reach the individual body tissue cells and waste products from those cells are properly transported for elimination by the kidneys, lungs, or skin. To do this efficiently the circulating fluid within the cardiovascular system—the blood—contains many substances. Of particular interest are the three types of structures called the "formed elements." The red blood cells, or *erythrocytes,* help transport oxygen and carbon dioxide in the blood to and from the lungs. The white blood cells, or *leukocytes,* and antibodies of various types help protect the bloodstream and surrounding body tissues from the intrusion of disease-producing microorganisms and foreign proteins. The platelets, or *thrombocytes,* assist in the formation of clots to repair any leak in a damaged blood vessel. However, any lack or defect in the normal makeup of the blood is likely to cause symptoms of disease. It is impossible and of little practical nursing value to describe within the pages of this text all the various problems that may occur when the blood is abnormal. However, four kinds of disorders that are seen with some frequency on the pediatric service will be briefly discussed. They are the *anemias, leukemias, hemophilias,* and *purpuras.*

The anemias

Types. When the term "anemia" is used, it indicates a condition in which the total hemoglobin content of the blood is abnormally reduced, either because of lack of sufficient hemoglobin in the red blood cells or lack of red blood cells. Hemoglobin is the substance in the red blood cells so necessary for the normal transport of oxygen to the body cells. Anemia may develop because of (1) dietary deficiency or absorption difficulties affecting principally iron, vitamin B_{12}, vitamin C, or folic acid, causing a lack of sufficient building materials to produce satisfactory hemoglobin; (2) problems in red blood cell production usually occurring within the bone marrow as a result of the use of toxic drugs or radiation; (3) abnormal destruction of normal circulating red blood cells as the result of disease processes; and (4) loss of circulating blood as a result of hemorrhage.

Signs and symptoms of anemia include fatigue, pallor, irritability, growth retardation, and possible enlargement of the liver and spleen.

The most common cause of anemia in the infant is iron-intake deficiency, the so-called *milk anemia.* This condition occurs when milk has been almost the sole source of infant nutrition. The child characteristically has a "waxy pallor." Treatment consists of administration of oral iron preparations, a revision of diet to include iron-rich foods (egg yolks, liver) and, if the condition is particularly severe or oral therapy is contraindicated, intramuscular injections of iron compound. Transfusions are rarely ordered for this kind of anemia. The premature infant or a twin is likely to suffer from insufficient iron reserves.

So-called *pernicious anemia,* caused by the inability of the body to absorb the vitamin B_{12} needed for normal erythrocyte production, is rarely diagnosed in children. In *megaloblastic anemia,* folic acid and perhaps vitamin C administration is needed.

An anemia of particular interest, related to defective hemoglobin manufacture and subsequent abnormal red blood cell destruction, is *sickle cell anemia.* It is found almost exclusively in the Negro population and is inherited as a recessive characteristic. Both parents must contribute a gene for so-called hemoglobin-S before a child exhibits symptoms. Under certain conditions the red blood cells change their shape, assuming the shape of the blade of a sickle or crescent. This change in shape makes passage through the small capillaries difficult, causing exceptional red blood cell destruction manifested in jaundice as well as anemia. The pileup of sickled cells in the capillaries may also cause thrombosis and even infarction of tissues. Pain from these circulatory disturbances will depend on the organs primarily affected by the blood destruction or thrombi. There may even be symptoms of circulatory shock, convulsions, or coma. Fever is common during a hemolytic crisis.

Treatment of this type of anemia depends on the severity of the difficulties encountered. Oxygen and increased low electrolyte fluid intake are usually recommended. Transfusions may be required in certain cases. Prednisone may be prescribed. The prognosis is generally poor.

Another type of hereditary anemia, which may be particularly severe in certain individuals, is found characteristically in those people whose ancestry may be traced back to the Mediterranean area. For this reason it is called *Mediterranean anemia.* It is also termed "Cooley's anemia," or "thalassemia." Blood cell formation is congenitally defective, and excessive erythrocyte destruction results. Large numbers of immature red blood cells are found in the circulating blood. The liver and spleen are outsized, and the long bones are characteristically thin. Removal of the spleen may be helpful in some cases. Transfusions are usually required at regular intervals.

The anemias often occur secondary to diseases characterized by chronic or hemorrhagic blood loss. Chronic ulcerative colitis, bleeding ulcers, and leukemia are but a few examples.

Nursing care. The nursing care of children with anemia, whatever its basic cause, must take into account the excessive fatigue experienced by most of these boys and girls. Their energy must be conserved. They especially need help and inspiration to eat and build good habits in nutrition. Frequent, small feedings are more successful than large, infrequent meals. The enlarged liver and spleen and tender muscles of some of these patients all demand gentle care. Attention to signs of bleeding (external or internal) is important. Signs of jaundice, increased pallor, increased lethargy, or irritability should be reported. Patients receiving blood transfusions should be carefully observed and protected against possible infiltration of the blood (a potentially serious event). Signs of toxic reactions, complaints of chest or back pain, itching hives, or elevated temperature with or without chills should be noted and reported early. The rate of administration should be closely watched to be sure that the circulatory system is not overloaded.

The leukemias

Leukemia has often been called "cancer of the blood." It is a fatal disease characterized by the overproduction by the body of abnormal, immature, white blood cells (blast forms), which cannot function properly. Since this kind of leukoctye, even when present in tremendous numbers is incapable of protecting the body from pathogenic microorganisms, intercurrent infections are common. These abnormal white blood cells invade the various tissues of the body, causing pressure symptoms (e.g., infiltration of the bone marrow produces severe pain in bones and joints; mediastinal nodes may cause tracheal compression that in turn causes respiratory difficulty and cough). The predominating symptoms depend on the area of the body primarily invaded by the leukemic cells. Diagnosis is suspected on the basis of discovery of immature white blood cell forms in the circu-

lating blood. The diagnosis is confirmed by microscopic examination of the bone marrow, usually obtained from the posterior iliac crest. Anemia and a lowered platelet count often complicate the patient's problems. At times the number of circulating white blood cells is extremely elevated. Some cases may demonstrate total white blood cell counts of above 100,000/mm.[3] At other periods the total white blood cell count may appear depressed. In the course of the disease when the number of white blood cells in the blood is high and when a large percentage of "blasts" are seen, the blood picture is said to be leukemic. When the number of white blood cells in the peripheral circulation is relatively low and proportionately few immature forms are seen, it is said to be *aleukemic*. However, at this time the bone marrow may be packed with abnormal cells.

Incidence. Leukemia is the most common form of cancer in children. There is a slightly increased incidence in boys, and the peak age of onset in children is 3 to 4 years of age. Leukemia accounts for almost 50% of deaths from malignant diseases in children under 15 years of age.

Types. There are a number of different types of leukemia classified according to the kind of white cells principally involved and the relative speed of the disease process. The most common leukemic cell observed in pediatric practice is the undifferentiated form called a "blast," or stem cell, a very immature form of white blood cell, usually of the lymphocytic cell line. Acute lymphoblastic leukemia accounts for the majority of cases. Acute granulocytic or myelogenous leukemia accounts for about 15% of cases. This form, however, does not respond favorably to the antileukemic agents presently available. The cause of the disease is unknown at present, although intensive research is now being carried out in an attempt to discover this elusive feature.

Signs and symptoms. The signs and symptoms of leukemia may be rather slow and insidious in onset or rapid in their de-

TABLE 38-1. Current drugs used in the treatment of leukemia

Agent	Route	Toxicity
6-mercaptopurine (6MP)	Oral	Bone marrow depression*; nausea, vomiting
Methotrexate (MTX)	Oral; intravenous; intrathecal	Oral and gastrointestinal tract ulceration; bone marrow depression*; (hair loss rare)
Prednisone	Oral	Fluid retention; hypertension; ulcers; increased susceptibility to infection; personality changes
Vincristine (Oncovin)	Intravenous	Peripheral neuropathy; hair loss, constipation
Cyclophosphamide (Cytoxan)	Oral; intravenous	Bone marrow depression*; skin rashes; hair loss; hemorrhagic cystitis; oral ulceration; diarrhea
Daunomycin (Daunorubicin)	Intravenous	Bone marrow depression*; nausea, vomiting; oral ulceration; myocarditis
Cytosine arabinoside (Cytarabine, Cytosar)	Intravenous	Bone marrow depression*; nausea, vomiting
L-Asparaginase	Intravenous	Chills, fever, nausea, vomiting, hypersensitivity reactions

*Bone marrow depression is characterized by leukopenia, thrombocytopenia, and anemia.

velopment. The child may complain of fatigue, weakness, and weight loss. He may be pale and bruise easily. Fever, with a persistent respiratory infection, is a common complaint. Swollen lymph nodes may be the first symptom that the parent notes. His liver and spleen, infiltrated with abnormal cells, may be enlarged. One out of four children affected suffer leukemic infiltration of the meninges. Increased intracranial pressure occurs and is typically manifested by headache, nausea and vomiting, slowed pulse, and elevated blood pressure. The child is very irritable and tired. Central nervous system involvement is most likely to arise late in the course of the disease but is rarely present at the onset. Spinal fluid examination confirms the physician's sad suspicions of the nature of the problem. The course of the disease usually involves several hospitalizations and remissions.

Treatment. At this writing no curative treatment for leukemia exists. However, complete remissions of the disease for extended periods have been induced with drugs.° The major objectives of chemother-

apy are the induction of a complete remission and the maintenance of patients in a state of remission for the longest possible time. A complete remission is defined as "restoration to normal health and clinical well-being." Physical and laboratory examinations are negative, blood and bone marrow are considered normal, and all evidence of disease is absent. Best results to date have been achieved with intensive courses of drug combinations and with optimal supportive care, including transfusion of platelets and antibiotic therapy.

Since 1947 when the first brief, temporary remission was induced with aminopterin, antileukemic drug therapy has been greatly improved. Previously the drugs were used singly, with a progression in sequence to another agent as each successive one became ineffective. Then, any one of the drugs was administered coincidently with prednisone. Later the drugs were rotated at regular intervals to avoid development of tolerance while each was still effective. More recently, periodic but massive parenteral treatment with one drug supplemented by oral administration of another has been advocated.

Dosage schedules as well as the effects of different routes of administration continue to be compared and reevaluated.

° A report by the National Advisory Cancer Council: Progress against cancer, 1970, Washington, D. C., U. S. Department of Health, Education, and Welfare.

Today, modern treatment consists of intermittent administration of high doses of several drugs in combination. Early recognition of signs of relapse and an immediate change of therapy may reestablish the remission state without psychological trauma to the child or his parents. Complete remissions for long periods of time have been induced in almost all patients with acute lymphoblastic leukemia. A patient in remission must have regular medical supervision, usually involving outpatient evaluation, every 4 to 6 weeks. While intensive research continues toward complete control of leukemic cells, a real effort is being made to extend the complex treatments now available to patients at the major research centers to those in community hospitals.

Supportive care. Platelet transfusions have reduced the number of deaths caused by hemorrhage and increased the opportunity to use effective drugs that depress platelet production.

Infection poses the greatest threat to the life of the leukemic child. Antibiotic therapy administered intravenously with the most up-to-date drugs has diminished effect in the absence of competent white cells. Two methods are effective in the control of infection: white blood cell transfusions (particularly granulocytes) and germ-free rooms (laminar-flow rooms). These methods of controlling infections are costly and not readily available.

Antileukemic drugs may cause a rapid breakdown in the malignant cells, which in turn raises the uric acid load that must be handled by the kidneys. This increased load, especially coupled with a state of dehydration caused by poor fluid intake and vomiting, causes renal injury. Allopurinol helps accelerate the excretion of uric acid and reduces the risk of kidney stone formation. Parenteral fluid therapy also lessens this risk.

Another side effect of some of the antileukemic drugs is that of alopecia, or hair loss, a nondangerous but distressing development. It has recently been found that if a scalp tourniquet (rubber band around the head above the ears) is in place immediately before and for 5 minutes after the injection of vincristine, the amount of hair loss induced by the drug will be reduced. The superficial blood vessels in the scalp can be temporarily occluded. This minimizes contact of the drug with the hair follicles and reduces the amount of hair loss.[*]

The nursing care of the leukemia patient is emotionally taxing. Both the parents and the child need emotional support; a philosophy that recognizes that we can live only one moment at a time and that we are not called on to face all our yesterdays or tomorrows all at once is helpful. For a discussion of the needs of the dying child, his parents, and his nurses, see Chapter 27.

The child with leukemia who is admitted to the hospital because of a recurrence of symptoms is usually very uncomfortable and irritable. Pressure from the large number of white blood cells infiltrating the various body organs makes him sore. He usually does not like to be moved, although changes in position are necessary to avoid respiratory infection and skin breakdown. His lowered platelet count leads to easy bruising and spontaneous hemorrhages in many parts of the body. His anemia contributes to his fatigue and pallor. Because of the frequent ulceration of his mucous membranes, oral hygiene must be gentle. Only soft toothbrushes, gauze, or applicators should be used. Mouthwashes of equal amounts of hydrogen peroxide and saline and the application of viscous lidocaine (Xylocaine) before meals are helpful local measures that often provide comfort. (See Fig. 38-10.)

Fever is often present, and measures to reduce temperature elevation (see Chapter 34) must be frequently employed. Because the rectal mucosa may be bleeding, an axillary temperature may be ordered. The presence of a member of the family at

---

[*]O'Brien, R., et al.: Scalp tourniquet to lessen alopecia after vincristine, New Eng. J. Med. **283:** 1469, 1970.

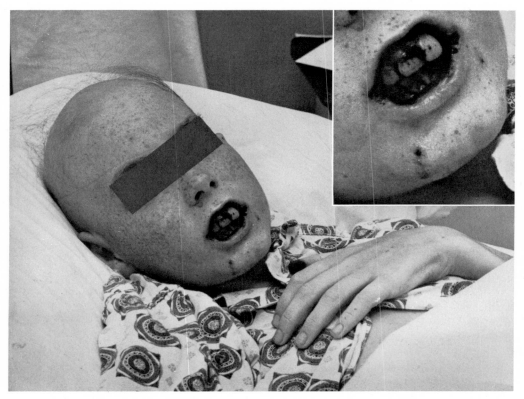

FIG. 38-10. This young boy with leukemia demonstrates the typical mouth lesions. Loss of hair resulted from therapy. (Courtesy U. S. Naval Hospital, San Diego, Calif.)

the bedside at frequent intervals is a great help to the little patient, and often he will respond by taking fluids offered by the parent when he will refuse all other overtures. The ability to administer to the needs of their child in these trying days is almost always a source of strength to the parents who feel a need to do something for him. Little routines and special ways of doing things that comfort the child are important to the parent and patient. As much as possible, they should be followed. We the nursing staff should not withdraw from the parents, thinking that there is little we can do. We must continue to provide support throughout the illness.

Prognosis. In childhood, approximately 97% of the leukemias are acute rather than chronic. Before current methods of treatment were available, the survival time for children with acute leukemia from the time

of diagnosis until death was sometimes as brief as 3 to 4 weeks and rarely spanned 6 months. Current methods of therapy can induce complete remissions in almost all patients, and the median survival in some specialized centers is at least 2½ years. There are a few patients on record who have had extended remissions. A registry established by the Acute Leukemia Task Force of the National Cancer Institute lists patients surviving 5 years or more after diagnosis of their disease. Information from hematologists all over the world revealed that 157 children had survived 5 years, and 87 were reported alive and well without evidence of disease. A small number of these patients have lived 7 years from the time of diagnosis and have had no evidence of leukemia for 4 years. Such fortunate cases are extremely rare, however, and it is not known why these few have reacted so fa-

599

vorably, whereas other patients receiving the same therapy have not responded in like manner. Until further progress is made, leukemia must still be considered a fatal disease. Death usually comes in the form of massive hemorrhage or infection.

The hemophilias

Hemophilia A–factor VIII deficiency. Classic hemophilia, antihemophilic globulin (AHG), or factor VIII, deficiency, is a very interesting and disturbing disease, involving a defect in the clotting mechanism of the blood. Because of its hereditary feature, it has figured prominently in the history of royal families and has been called the disease of kings. It is passed from one generation to another from the affected father to his daughters, who, although they carry the gene, exhibit no symptoms of the disease. The daughters, however, pass the gene on to their sons, who become victims of hemophilia. The son of a hemophiliac does not ordinarily pass on the disease although his sons will be hemophiliacs if he marries a female carrier of the disease. In this rare case, it is said that even female children may have this type of coagulation problem.

This coagulation difficulty is caused by the lack of antihemophilic globulin, or factor VIII, in the blood plasma. A wide range of factor VIII values (50% to 200%) exists, but in most healthy individuals the average is 100%. A severe hemophiliac has less than 1% of factor VIII. These patients are prone to spontaneous, unprovoked hemorrhage. Mild hemophiliacs have from 2% to 35% of factor VIII and may bleed excessively on minor trauma. Surgical procedures, dental extractions, and even the normal rough-and-tumble existence of young boys are especially hazardous for a hemophilic patient.

Current treatment consists of administration of factor VIII concentrate in any amount necessary to control hemorrhage. However, protection afforded from one infusion rapidly disappears because the concentration of factor VIII falls to half its original level in 8 to 10 hours. Because of this, it is necessary to administer factor VIII as quickly as possible to obtain optimum benefits. The precise level of factor VIII needed to control bleeding is not known exactly, but serious bleeding has been controlled by levels as low as 30%. The combination of immobilization and a level of 10% to 20% is usually adequate to control soft tissue bleeding (provided by 1 to 4 doses of factor VIII plasma concentrate). When desired, a maintenance level is achieved by administering factor VIII at 12-hour intervals. Small children with severe hemophilia may be given daily doses in the hope that they might have fewer spontaneous hemorrhages. Efforts to control bleeding, using local measures (pressure, cold, or applications of thrombin) should be attempted, if possible. Some cities have hemophilia centers that are prepared to render intravenous therapy to these victims on an outpatient basis. Some patients are being taught to administer the concentrate to themselves.

Factor VIII inhibitors. A small number (about 5%) of patients with classic hemophilia develop inhibitors (antibodies that destroy factor VIII). The presence of a circulating inhibitor is usually detected by the lack of response to a dose of factor VIII that normally would control the bleeding. Inhibitors may develop in young children after a few exposures to factor VIII, but there is no evidence that the inhibitors are related to the number of transfusions a patient receives. Without exposure to plasma products, the amount of inhibitor gradually decreases, and factor VIII can be given again with full benefit. There is no particular method for effective control of bleeding in patients when the inhibitor is circulating.

Hemophilia B–factor IX deficiency (Christmas disease). Factor IX plasma thromboplastic component (PTC) deficiency accounts for about 15% of patients with hemophilia. Causation and symptomatology are similar to hemophilia A. A factor IX concentrate has recently become available for treatment and is used in the same manner as factor VIII.

Hemophilia C—factor XI deficiency. Factor XI plasma thromboplastin antecedent (PTA) deficiency differs from hemophilia A and B. It is usually a mild disorder and may appear in ether boys or girls as the result of an inherited dominant trait. Normal plasma corrects the defect during bleeding episodes. The nursing care of all patients with bleeding problems is similar except that the type of intravenous therapy ordered will differ, depending on the kind of replacement needed.

The mother of a patient with hemophilia is under considerable strain. She must constantly observe the environment of her adventuresome toddler or growing boy. She, with the help of her husband and attending physician, must progressively educate the child to make choices in activity with consideration for the degree of hazard it may entail. She does not want to make her son a psychological cripple, unable to live an interesting, creative life, or a reckless rebel.

Supervision and nursing care. The nursing care of children with hemophilia must emphasize prevention. The sides of infants' cribs should be padded. Toddlers should be denied toys and objects with sharp edges or objects that are easily broken. Rubber toys are very satisfactory for play. Sharp pencils and forks must not be given these youngsters until they are old enough to understand their use and potential hazard. Little people learning to walk may be fitted with kneepads. Bleeding into the joints may produce considerable pain and deformity. Every effort should be made to prevent stiffening of the joint and loss of function. The nurse must provide her charge with interesting but safe diversion and watch for any signs of increasing bruises or internal or external blood loss. She must observe the child for untoward reaction during transfusion and check whether the intravenous infusion is flowing as ordered. Her care must be gentle and thoughtful. The nurse caring for the child

with hemophilia has a heavy responsibility. At the end of the day she may appreciate, to some degree, the underlying anxiety of the family.

The purpuras

Purpura is the purple discoloration that occurs as a result of spontaneous bleeding into the skin or mucous membranes. Sometimes the bleeding is minute, causing very small, purplish "dots" called *petechiae*. At other times rather large areas of bleeding into the tissues may cause outright black-and-blue spots. Bleeding may also occur internally. Purpura may be a feature of many different diseases. In the case of meningococcal meningitis or bacterial endocarditis, the infecting organisms may lodge in the capillaries and cause increased fragility of these tiny blood vessels. Sometimes, however, purpura may result from an abnormal decrease in platelets, the formed element in the blood so necessary to normal coagulation. This is the case in leukemia. In some instances the reason for the decrease of platelets in the body is not known. Then the resulting disorder is labeled *idiopathic thrombocytopenic purpura.*

Purpura resulting from an unexplained reduction in platelets may be mild or severe in nature. In severe cases, fever and prostration may be present and hemorrhage from the mucous membranes of the mouth and nose may be significant. Internal bleeding is often present. In a few instances the severe form of idiopathic purpura may even cause death. It necessitates blood transfusions, and hormone therapy with prednisone may be helpful. If the disease is not sufficiently responsive to this therapy, splenectomy may be advised. Removal of the spleen may reduce the number of platelets being destroyed. However, the exact way that this surgery aids the condition has not been clarified.

Nursing care involves gentle oral hygiene as indicated, observation of the progress of the skin lesions, protection from increased injury, and alertness for signs of internal bleeding. As usual, transfusions must be carefully watched and the patient evaluated for untoward symptoms.

. . .

The lungs, heart, blood vessels, and blood are separate anatomical entities. However, if one of these entities is dis-turbed, the others will invariably respond to the change in the one to meet the physiological needs of the individual. The nurse who recognizes this interdependence is better able to serve the person to whom that deformed heart, inflamed respiratory tract, or abnormal blood belongs.

39

Conditions involving digestion and associated metabolism

A well-behaved digestive system can be a source of great pleasure. The digestive system can also initiate considerable distress, depending on its general condition and the amount of dietary discretion its owner employs. This discussion will present briefly the malformations, infestations, infections, and foreign body problems commonly found in children that involve the digestive tract (Fig. 39-1). Also, although it is not considered to be basically a digestive problem, a review of diabetes mellitus will be included, since it influences the metabolism of digested glucose and dietary regulation is required. The presentation will follow the path of digestion itself, starting with the mouth and ending at the anus.

Anatomy and physiology

The digestive system is formed by the mouth, esophagus, gastrointestinal tract, and related organs such as the liver, gallbladder, and pancreas. The adult alimentary canal is an unsterile tract of many shapes and turns, which, if stretched out its entire length, would reach about 30 feet. Although in children the size of the alimentary canal may be greatly abbreviated, its importance is not. Hunger is a primary drive, and appetite, its educated twin, is soon acquired. The child may not know all about his digestive tract, but he knows that it represents a real need. Parents, rather desparingly, have often called it the "bottomless pit." The digestive tract and its accessory organs serve to reduce foodstuffs (carbohydrates, proteins, and fats) to their smallest working chemical units. These chemical units are then absorbed through the mucous membrane of the intestinal walls and eventually reach the bloodstream to be distributed to the individual cells, providing the body with building materials, heat, and energy. To accomplish this, the digestive system works on the food both *mechanically* (through the action of the teeth, tongue, cheeks and muscular contractions of the tract, called *peristalsis*) and *chemically* (through the activity of various enzymes, emulsifiers, acids, and bacteria, which are normally active in different portions of the tract). The student is invited to review Chapter 23 if more details of the digestive process are desired. Substances not absorbed into the rest of the body via the bloodstream or lymphatic system are removed normally by periodic defecation, or bowel movement.

Disorders of the digestive system manifest themselves in several predictable ways. Anorexia, nausea, vomiting, constipation, abdominal distention and pain, diarrhea, and weight loss are common manifestations. The observation of a child's stool is of great importance in pediatrics. The amount, color, consistency, general appearance, and odor of a child's bowel movements can be of real diagnostic significance and aid in evaluating the condition of the digestive tract.

Key vocabulary

digestion process by which food is broken down mechanically and chemically in the gastroin-

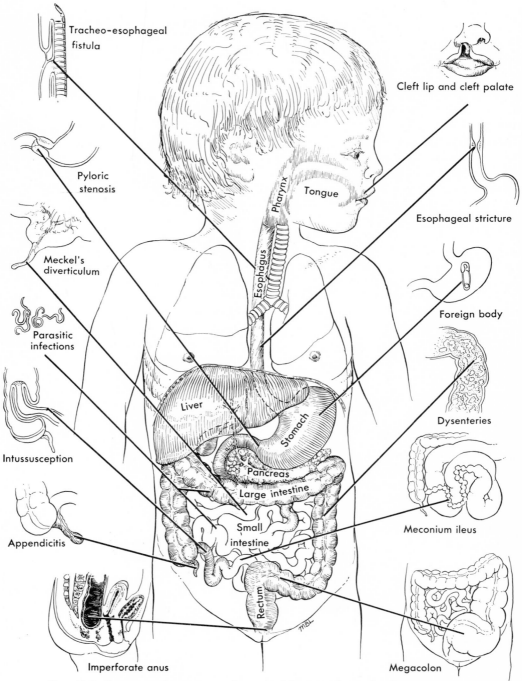

Tracheo-esophageal fistula

Cleft lip and cleft palate

Pyloric stenosis

Pharynx

Tongue

Esophagus

Esophageal stricture

Meckel's diverticulum

Foreign body

Parasitic infections

Liver

Stomach

Dysenteries

Intussusception

Pancreas

Large intestine

Small intestine

Meconium ileus

Appendicitis

Rectum

Imperforate anus

Megacolon

FIG. 39-1. Summary of common pediatric problems involving the digestive system.

testinal tract and converted into absorbable forms.

endocrine gland structure producing a hormone that is discharged into the bloodstream.

exocrine gland structure that produces a secretion that is deposited in a particular area of the body via a duct.

glycosuria presence of glucose in the urine.

hypoglycemia deficiency of glucose in the blood.

ileus obstruction or paralysis of small intestine.

metabolism all energy and material transformations that occur within living cells.

Pediatric digestive problems

PROBLEMS AFFECTING THE MOUTH

Tooth decay

The most common problem affecting the mouth is that of dental decay, or *caries*. The care of decayed teeth is within the province of the dentist, not the nurse. However, the nurse can help in the prevention of caries by teaching proper techniques of dental and gum hygiene and the value of good nutrition and fluoridation programs and by advising periodic professional examinations of the teeth and mouth.

Vincent's angina

Any type of inflammation involving an opening of the body may be called a *stomatitis*. The most common type of stomatitis involves the mucous membrane of the mouth. One of the more common types of oral inflammation is Vincent's angina, or trench mouth, so-called because of its prevalence among the ground troops of World War I. Vincent's angina principally involves the gums. It may be caused by two types of organisms working together, spirochetes and bacilli. Their presence is characteristic. The gums become swollen, tender, and bleeding; the cheeks and oral pharynx may become involved and ulcerate. Even gangrene may develop in severe cases. Treatment may involve hydrogen peroxide or perborate of soda mouthwashes, antibiotics, vitamins, and meticulous but gentle oral hygiene. The disease is likely to attack those people whose general hygiene, nutrition, and habits of living need revision, and efforts should be made to correct such underlying deficiencies.

Oral moniliasis

Thrush, or oral moniliasis, has been mentioned as a possible complication during the newborn period as the result of contamination of the child's oral cavity with infected vaginal secretion at the time of birth or improper hygiene and feeding techniques after delivery. Thrush is also a fairly common condition among children receiving long-term, broad-spectrum antibiotic therapy. The antibiotics destroy the normal flora of the alimentary canal and allow the fungus *Candida*, or *Monilia*, *albicans* to multiply without competition. White, curdlike plaques appear on the tongue and cheeks and adhere to the surface of the mucous membrane (see p. 196). The mouth may be tender, and the desire to eat may be decreased. Thrush and other manifestations of *Candida albicans* may be prevented in high-risk patients by the regular use of a bacterial culture, such as is found in Lactinex granules or tablets, at mealtime. It may be treated by the oral application of nystatin or even the old standby, gentian violet, 1%. Adequate sterilization of all objects that have entered the infected infant's mouth should be completed. The condition usually responds well to therapy.

Cleft lip and cleft palate

Cleft lip and cleft palate are malformations that may occur singly or in combination. The student is referred to Chapter 19, p. 247, for a discussion of the problems encountered and the nursing involved.

PROBLEMS AFFECTING THE ESOPHAGUS, STOMACH, AND SMALL INTESTINE

Esophageal atresia with tracheo-esophageal fistula

Esophageal atresia with tracheo-esophageal fistula is also mentioned in Chapter 19, p. 251.

Esophageal stenosis

The narrowing of a child's esophagus, esophageal stenosis, may be congenital in origin; however, more often it is posttraumatic. The most common cause is probably the ingestion of some corrosive substance such as lye, which burns the tissues and produces scarring, leading to stenosis.

The patient usually must undergo periodic esophageal dilatations by catheters. He may need a gastrostomy, or artificial opening into the stomach, because of difficulty in maintaining nutrition. Surgical excision of the narrowed area and joining together of the remaining parts (anastomosis), replacement of the area by a bowel transplant, or esophageal reconstruction using tissue from the greater curvature of the stomach may be undertaken.

Foreign body ingestion

Children do not limit their experimental tasting and swallowing to articles that are meant to tempt an appetite or even to indigestible items that might appear delicious. All kinds of objects have gone down the "little red lane." Fortunately most complete the entire journey without incident. Small round objects are simply watched for by careful stool examination. However, sharp or long, angled objects may pose the threat of perforation. If the object is detectable by x-ray examination, it is viewed and periodically watched. If the object seems to threaten trauma, an operation to retrieve it may be necessary. The abdomen of a child who has swallowed a foreign object should not be palpated. One physician even suggests placing a small sign on the child, cautioning would-be investigators to avoid such maneuvers.

Giving a child large amounts of bread or potato after ingestion of a foreign object is of doubtful value. A laxative should never be given in such circumstances.

Congenital pyloric stenosis

Abnormal narrowing of the pyloric sphincter, which forms the exit of the stomach, may cause progressive vomiting and nutritional disorders in the infant (Fig. 39-2). This narrowing is caused by spasm of the sphincter, local edema, and an overgrowth of the circular muscle fibers of the

pylorus. The symptoms do not usually begin until the child is approximately 2 weeks old and rarely have their onset after 2 months of age. This disorder seems to have a slight hereditary tendency and occurs more often in male than female infants.

At first the vomiting is only occasional. However, if the stenosis is unrelieved, it becomes more frequent and forceful, even projectile in character. If this situation persists, the child will lose weight and begin to show signs of dehydration, electrolyte imbalance, and malnutrition. The emesis contains no bile, since the opening to the duodenum is too small to allow such staining. Despite the frequent vomiting, the baby continues to have a good appetite and will take fluids when they are offered. The physician makes his diagnosis on the basis of the history, the clinical examination, and x-ray studies that use a contrast medium. A hard, olive-shaped tumor (the hypertrophied pylorus) may be palpated, and visible, left-to-right peristalsis may be noted as the stomach tries to force the swallowed formula into the duodenum. When this effort proves ineffective, the peristaltic waves reverse themselves and emesis results.

In the United States, treatment of pyloric stenosis is usually surgical. The procedure is called the Fredet-Ramstedt operation. The surgeon cuts down through the enlarged muscle of the pylorus to the mucous membrane. This relieves the constriction. This operation, when performed on infants well prepared for the procedure, is highly successful in relieving the cause of the persistent vomiting. Postoperative care consists of observation of the surgical site or dressing and careful introduction of weak fluids in small amounts as ordered at fairly frequent intervals. The infant should be held at a steep incline while being fed, bubbled well before, during, and after his feeding, and placed in an infant seat or propped on his right side after his feedings. When he is in the infant seat, gravity aids the drainage of the offered fluid. Placing the infant on his right side also aids

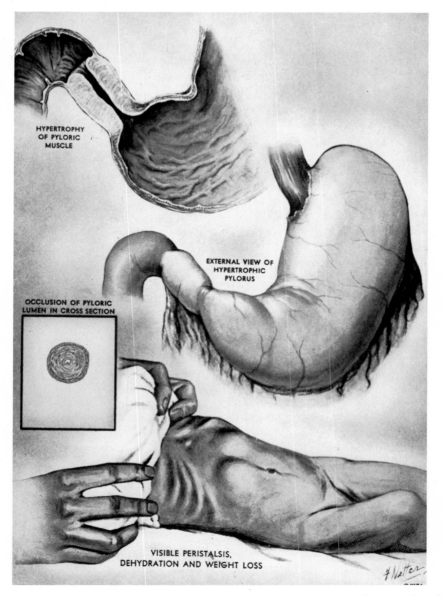

HYPERTROPHY
OF PYLORIC
MUSCLE

EXTERNAL VIEW OF
HYPERTROPHIC
PYLORUS

OCCLUSION OF PYLORIC
LUMEN IN CROSS SECTION

VISIBLE PERISTALSIS,
DEHYDRATION AND WEIGHT LOSS

FIG. 39-2. Congenital hypertrophied pyloric stenosis. (From the CIBA collection of medical illustrations, by Frank H. Netter, M.D., Copyright CIBA.)

drainage and helps bubbles come to the top of the stomach where they can be expelled with less formula loss. A side or upright position also helps prevent aspiration. After drinking, the infant should be disturbed as little as possible. It is very important that the child not be overfed. Such a situation leads to possible vomiting and strain on suture lines. Gradually the amount of formula given at one time is increased, and the formula is strengthened. Any postoperative vomiting should be immediately reported. Parenteral fluids may be ordered for the immediate postoperative period, depending on the condition and oral intake of the child.

Occasionally a medical regimen is tried for infants with mild pyloric stenosis. It usually consists of thickened feedings, using a cereal nipple, and antispasmodic drugs. The child is usually refed after emesis to replace the amount lost. Although occasionally this form of treatment may be successful and the child may outgrow his difficulty, surgery is considered by many authorities to be less risky for most children.

Meckel's diverticulum

A structural leftover from embyronic life is the persistence of a pouch on the ileum called Meckel's diverticulum. At one time a duct joined the umbilicus with the intestine and led to the yolk sac, which gave temporary nourishment to the developing fetus. In the course of normal development this duct closes. However, remnants persist in a small percentage of people. Sometimes they cause difficulty. An open tract, capable of discharging the contents of the small bowel onto the abdominal wall, may endure. More often a blind pouch with no connection or only a cord attachment to the umbilicus remains. Occasionally gastric mucosa is found within the pouch. Meckel's diverticulum may cause ulceration and hemorrhage with symptoms similar to appendicitis or intestinal obstruction. Many times its presence is undiagnosed until exploratory surgery reveals the problem. Nursing care is similar to that involving any condition that necessitates exploration of the abdominal cavity.

Meconium ileus

Obstruction of the small intestine in the newborn infant caused by the presence of exceptionally thick, sticky meconium is called meconium ileus. The meconium is so gummy that it cannot pass normally through the bowel. Obstruction often occurs near the ileocecal junction. This condition is always indicative of the exocrine disorder, cystic fibrosis of the pancreas, although it is not present in all cases of cystic fibrosis.

Meconium ileus results because enzymes normally produced by the pancreas, which help liquefy the meconium, are unavailable. See p. 579 for a discussion of cystic fibrosis.

Symptoms include bile-stained emesis, abdominal distention, and absence of the normal meconial stool. This is a difficult pediatric problem because of the type of malfunction, the age of the patient, and other aspects of the total disease process. In mild cases the treatment may be medical, with reliance on special enemas of substances that help dissolve or mechanically clear the impaction and oral administration of pancreatic enzymes. Many cases, however, require surgery to try to clear the obstruction. Resection of the intestine and a temporary enterostomy may be necessary. The child is usually very ill, and the prognosis is guarded.

Celiac syndrome

The word "celiac" refers to the abdomen. All children with conditions having celiac manifestations have large, protuberant abdomens because of poor absorption of certain foodstuffs from the gastrointestinal tract. The stools are characteristically bulky, pale, greasy, and foul smelling. The arms, legs, and buttocks of these children are emaciated as a result of nutritional deficiency. Although the symptoms may be similar, the underlying causes of the indigestion may be quite varied. The most common pediatric disorders that manifest the celiac syndrome are cystic fibrosis of the pancreas and gluten-induced enteropathy (commonly referred to as *celiac disease,* or chronic intestinal indigestion). Today, celiac disease in its severe, classic form is not as frequent as formerly. However, milder degrees of such difficulty are not rare. The problem usually affects children from 2 to 5 years of age.

Children suffer from celiac disease probably because of an inborn metabolic or enzyme defect or an allergic-type reaction. They are especially sensitive to the ingestion of gluten, a protein commonly found in wheat, rye, and oats. This sensitivity, combined with emotional stress, concurrent infections, and general malnutrition, adds up to a particularly unhappy child. Starches and fats are poorly absorbed.

However, simple sugars and nongluten proteins are tolerated. Diagnosis is based on clinical observation, studies of fat content in the stools, and response to a gluten-free diet. The little patients are often fretful and moody. They frequently have poor appetites. When admitted into the hospital, they may be in *celiac crisis*. A crisis may be precipitated by an upper respiratory infection. The child suffers from copious diarrhea and vomiting. He rapidly becomes dehydrated and may have signs and symptoms of acidosis. Immediate attention to electrolyte balance must be given. Until vomiting and diarrhea subside, parenteral therapy is indicated.

An important part of the treatment of celiac disease consists of careful dietary restriction that excludes the many sources of gluten from the diet. This means meticulous reading of all labels on prepared food, since wheat flour is a frequent additive. The infant or young child is given a high-protein, low-fat, starch-free diet. Simple sugars such as dextrose and sucrose are well received, and banana powder has long been favored. Large amounts of supplementary water-based preparations of vitamins A and D should be given. As the condition of the child improves and weeks pass by, foods may be gradually added to the diet and his response measured by the resulting type of stool, amount of abdominal distention, weight gain, appetite, and behavior of the patient.

The child with celiac disease requires much patient nursing to deal with his irritability, regressive behavior, and appetite problems. The nurse should understand the child and the reasons why the process of eating has become so burdensome and unrewarding for him. Accurate daily calculation of weight should be made. Detailed charting of the type and amount of intake, as well as accurate stool descriptions, is a necessity.

The patient suffering from celiac disease perspires a great deal and because of his ungainly shape may not move frequently. He should be periodically turned

if this is the case. Skin care is a never-ending responsibility.

With good general hygiene and extended dietary management, the tolerance of these children for other types of foods gradually increases, and although upsets may continue irregularly even into adult life, the prognosis as a whole is good. This knowledge usually encourages the parents to continue supervision. A conference with the hospital dietitian before the child's discharge is often very helpful. She has access to special recipes that may make the limited diet prescribed more interesting to the child. She will be able to explain to the mother in more detail the practical implications of the dietary restrictions imposed.

PROBLEMS AFFECTING THE LOWER DIGESTIVE TRACT
Intussusception

A telescoping of adjacent parts of the bowel is called intussusception (Fig. 39-3). When intussusception occurs, it commonly involves the area of the ileocecal valve. Such an abnormal relationship of parts of the intestine may disturb circulation to the involved portions and result in gangrene and perforation of the bowel as well as obstruction. This condition most often affects infants and toddlers. The onset is usually sudden. At first the child may draw up his legs and cry out intermittently. Later his discomfort is intensified by progressive vomiting of bile-stained and even fecal emesis. His stools, at first loose, become scanty and characteristically assume the color and consistency of currant jelly because they are formed at this time largely of mucus and blood. If the condition is unrelieved, the child rapidly becomes prostrate. A high temperature develops, and his life is endangered. A favorable prognosis depends on early detection and treatment of the condition.

Diagnosis is made by considering the history, the physical examination, and the results of a barium enema, which often may reveal a typical pattern. Sometimes the pressure of the inflowing enema may

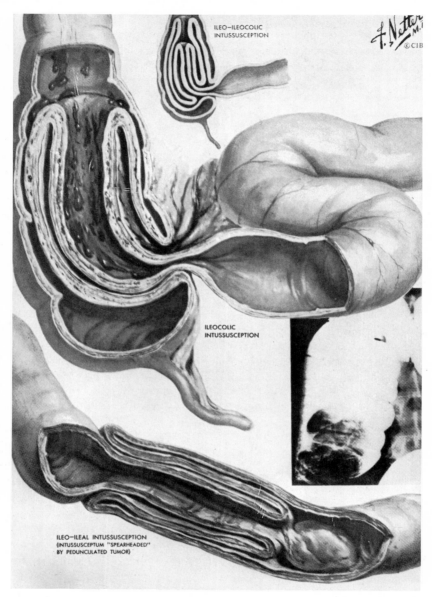

ILEO–ILEOCOLIC
INTUSSUSCEPTION

ILEOCOLIC
INTUSSUSCEPTION

ILEO–ILEAL INTUSSUSCEPTION
(INTUSSUSCEPTUM "SPEARHEADED"
BY PEDUNCULATED TUMOR)

FIG. 39-3. Different types of intussusception. (From the CIBA collection of medical illustrations, by Frank H. Netter, M.D., Copyright CIBA.)

cause the reduction of the intussusception! Then, the diagnostic procedure may become the treatment. However, there is controversy concerning the long-term effectiveness of such a method of "cure." Surgery is preferred by some physicians. The intussusception is identified and usually gently "milked backward" until the telescoping is completely relieved. Nursing care after the surgical procedure parallels that after most abdominal operations.

Appendicitis

Inflammation caused by local obstruction or infection of the vermiform appendix, located at the base of the cecum, is a common indication for abdominal surgery. However, it is not always easy to diagnose appendicitis in young children. Other problems may mimic the condition, and the young child is not often very descriptive regarding his general discomfort. Pain may first be felt in the umbilical area. Later it may be localized in the lower right-hand abdominal quadrant. Restlessness, mild constipation or diarrhea, and repeated vomiting are often reported. A low-grade fever is characteristic. The white blood cell count is usually elevated. If the inflamed appendix is removed before it has ruptured, recovery is usually prompt and uneventful. However, delay or the use of ill-advised laxatives may result in the rupture of the appendix. Peritonitis may complicate the condition. Recovery in this case is slower, and the risk to the patient is multiplied considerably. The campaign to educate the public not to give laxatives or enemas to persons complaining of abdominal pain has not yet been won.

The patient with a ruptured appendix, related abscess, and/or peritonitis is very ill. He usually cannot be sent to surgery immediately but must wait until the administration of antibiotics, intravenous fluids, and possible cooling measures are completed in order that he be in the best condition possible for the appendectomy. A nasogastric tube is often passed to relieve flatus and prevent vomiting. At the time of the surgery, a drain is usually placed in the abdominal wound, and drainage may be significant. Intravenous feedings are continued for several days postoperatively, and only ice chips or sips of water are allowed by mouth. Intake and output determinations are important observations because a number of appendicitis patients may have difficulty voiding. Fortunately, more and more of these patients are recuperating satisfactorily, and the phrase "ruptured appy" is no longer as dreaded as formerly.

Congenital megacolon (Hirschsprung's disease)

Classic congenital megacolon, or Hirschsprung's disease, is characterized by lack of normal peristaltic activity in the distal segment of the colon, usually the sigmoid, because of improper nervous control (lack of the necessary nerve ganglia in the musculature of the affected bowel or lack of coordination between the parasympathetic and sympathetic divisions of the nervous system). It is seen more often in males than in females. Signs and symptoms of congenital megacolon appear early in infancy. Constipation, sometimes interrupted by small amounts of stool; progressive abdominal distention, which may be sufficiently marked to cause respiratory embarrassment; anorexia; and occasional vomiting are all indications of the disorder. Pronounced abdominal distention may grossly distort the apearance of the child. Diagnosis is made after a review of the patient's history, palpation and auscultation of the abdomen, rectal examination, x-ray examination, and perhaps a rectal biopsy for microscopic investigation of the tissue.

The condition may be treated medically or surgically, depending on its severity and its response to conservative measures.

Medical management includes almost daily enemas (usually physiological saline solution, 2 teaspoons salt per 1 quart water). Tap water enemas are not given because of frequent difficulty in expelling the fluid and the real danger of water intoxication. The amount of fluid given at one time is larger than that given nonaffected children the same age because of the gross distention of the bowel. Digital removal of fecal material from the rectum may be necessary. Stool softeners such as Zymenol or mineral oil may be ordered. The use of drugs that affect the activity of the parasympathetic and sympathetic nervous systems may help obtain more regular bowel movements. A low-residue diet may be helpful in reducing the amount of feces and in keeping the stool soft.

If the condition of the child does not improve sufficiently with medical management, surgical treatment may be elected. The type of procedure done will depend on the age and individual needs of the child. The most satisfactory treatment appears to be an abdominoperineal removal of the abnormal section of bowel with an anastomosis of the remaining normal colon to the anal canal. This operation has been called Swenson's pull-through procedure. Postoperatively, the child is fed parenterally. Gastric suction and an indwelling urinary catheter are continued for an indefinite period. The anal sphincter may be dilated daily. The presence of bowel sounds and normal stool are eagerly awaited. At times this procedure is inadvisable, and a colostomy is performed.

More common than classic aganglionic megacolon is pseudo-Hirschsprung's disease, which has a psychogenic basis. It does not have an onset in the newborn period; x-ray studies and biopsy studies are negative. Investigation of family living patterns and stresses by qualified personnel is necessary.

Colic

Although colic is often spoken of as a disease entity, it is not a disease but a symptom. In the dictionary it is defined as "acute abdominal pain." However, when parents and nurses speak of "the colic," they are usually referring to the intermittent abdominal distress in the newborn infant that is fairly common in the early months of life. Fortunately, the problem does not always last 3 months, in spite of the frequent use of the phrase "3-month colic." The child and his parents seem to be troubled most in the early evening and night. The baby suddenly draws up his legs on his abdomen, clenches his fists, becomes red in the face, and starts to cry. This goes on intermittently as though he were troubled with periodic intestinal cramping. During these episodes he may pass gas by mouth or rectum.

Various explanations for the abdominal discomfort have been advanced. Probably there are multiple causes. Babies troubled with colic tend to have a low birth weight (5 to 7 pounds). It may be caused basically by an immaturity of the gastrointestinal system. Most explanations of the pain experienced involve the presence of excessive gas in the digestive tract. Excessive air may result from the following:

1. Poor feeding techniques, including failure to tip the bottle sufficiently to assure a full nipple at all times, too rapid feeding, the use of nipples with very small holes, which necessitates considerable suction (and air swallowing) to obtain the formula, and failure to bubble the baby often enough.

2. Excessive use of carbohydrate in the formula, which may cause increased fermentation and gas formation.

3. A tense, nervous baby fostered by a tense, nervous mother.

Attempts to remedy colic consider these possible causes. Various types of bottles and nipples have been marketed as anti-colic devices, some of which may merit a try if the baby does not respond to other techniques. The Playtex Nurser with presterilized plastic-bag bottles is one such device. The physician may recommend a change in formula. Occasionally antispasmodics, tranquilizers, or phenobarbital may be prescribed for both baby and mother! An infant will not be hospitalized because of colic alone, but the nurse may care for colicky babies and must realize why feeding techniques are so important. A baby who is not well bubbled will usually not feed well and is more prone to regurgitation, vomiting, and colic.

Parasitic infestations

All bacteria are parasites; however, when one speaks of *parasitic infestations*, he is usually referring to organisms that as adult forms are multicellular and large enough to be seen with the naked eye. There are many kinds of parasites in this category that trouble mankind. Many of them are found in abundance in tropical areas of the world and represent tremendous public health problems. This text will mention only those found fairly frequently in the United States: pinworm and ascaris.

Oxyuriasis (pinworm, threadworm, or seatworm infection). The official name of the pinworm is *Enterobius vermicularis.* The name of the disease this small, white, threadlike worm causes is known as oxyuriasis, or enterobiasis, an extremely common infestation. It does not always produce symptoms and often goes undiagnosed.

The pinworm eggs are ingested or possibly inhaled. Most often the child introduces the eggs into his own mouth by his contaminated fingers. His fingers become contaminated by touching objects used by infected children who have not carried out proper toilet hygiene. When the infestation has become established, the child may easily reinfect himself. The eggs are swallowed and hatch in the intestine. They mature in and near the cecum. When the adult female worms are ready to lay their eggs, they migrate down the intestinal tract to the anus. During the night the female worms leave the anus and lay their eggs in the folds of the anal sphincter and the perineum. Occasionally the worms may migrate to the vagina and cause a vaginitis in a little girl. All this activity usually causes considerable local irritation and itching. The child usually scratches the area, contaminating his fingers with the eggs layed in the region. In the course of time, fingers travel to the mouth again, and the cycle repeats (Fig. 39-4). The interval between the ingestion of an egg and the appearance of the female pinworm at the anus is approximately 6 to 8 weeks.

Usually mild pinworm infestations cause few symptoms other than anal itching and secondary complications caused by scratching. However, in some cases pinworms may cause anorexia, restlessness, and irritability. In cases of large infestations, inflammation of the appendix may occur.

Diagnosis is made on the basis of viewing the worms as they emerge from the anus or are inadvertently expelled on the surface of a stool or by the microscopic detection of the eggs. Since the female lays her eggs in the skin folds outside the body of the child, ova are rarely found in the stool. Usually a so-called Scotch tape test

is ordered. The night nurse goes to the bedside of the child before he wakes and shines a light on the rectal region. Sometimes the gravid worms may be seen. She then takes a piece of Scotch tape, which has been fastened "sticky side out" to a tongue blade, and presses it against the rectal area. Some microscopic eggs will adhere to the tape. The tape is then carefully secured to a glass slide "sticky side down" and sent to the laboratory for examination.

Treatment, to be carried out effectively, must involve the entire family. In the past, gentian violet tablets were used extensively. Nowadays two other more pleasant forms of therapy are available. Doses of piperazine citrate (Antepar), a fruit-flavored syrup, may be ordered for a total of 14 days, or pyrvinium pamoate (Povan) may be given in one or two doses. The nurse and parents should know that pyrvinium pamoate colors the stools red and if the child has an emesis while the medication is still present in the gastrointestinal tract, the emesis may also be reddish.

Other measures must be followed to help assure a cure. Personal toilet hygiene should be stressed. The necessity for hand washing after using the toilet is not grasped by children unless it is taught. Frequent cleansing of the rectogenital area is required. The toilet seat must be cleansed often. Because of the intense itching that may occur at night, an infected child should have very short fingernails, and his hands may be placed in mittens or socks to try to prevent scratching. Snug panties or diapers may also help. Bed linens, towels, underwear, and nightclothes of the infected patient should be washed separately in very hot water, preferably boiled. In the hospital setting the linen is bagged separately and labeled for the benefit of the laundry. Because many children are infested without the nurse's knowledge, it is always good technique to refrain from shaking used bed linen. Instead, it should always be rolled. Waving the child's linens only helps scatter the eggs. Hands must be

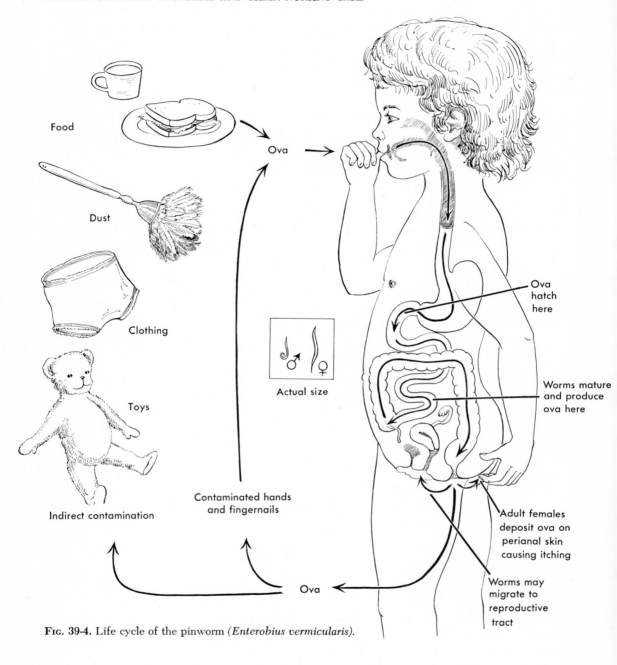

Food

Dust

Clothing

Toys

Indirect contamination

Actual size

Contaminated hands
and fingernails

Ova

Ova

Ova
hatch
here

Worms mature
and produce
ova here

Adult females
deposit ova on
perianal skin
causing itching

Worms may
migrate to
reproductive
tract

FIG. 39-4. Life cycle of the pinworm *(Enterobius vermicularis)*.

washed frequently, and a protective cover gown may be worn when intimate care of the patient is required.

Ascariasis (roundworm infestation). Ascaris lumbricoides, the worm that causes ascariasis, looks like a pink or white earthworm. It is usually 6 to 15 inches long. The eggs are found in the soil or on objects contaminated by soil containing infected feces. The disease is perpetuated by poor sanitary facilities and poor hygiene practices.

The infective egg is swallowed and hatches in the duodenum. The small inter-

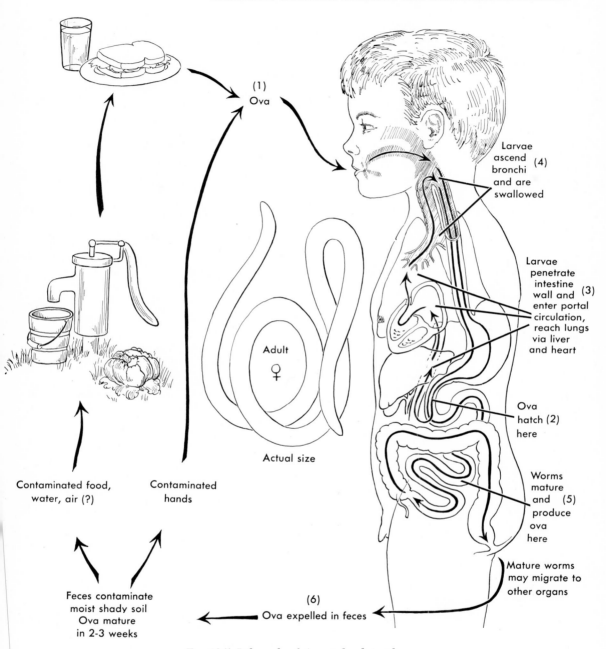

(1) Ova

Larvae ascend bronchi and are swallowed (4)

Larvae penetrate intestine wall and (3) enter portal circulation, reach lungs via liver and heart

Ova hatch (2) here

Adult
♀

Actual size

Worms mature and (5) produce ova here

Contaminated food, water, air (?)

Contaminated hands

Mature worms may migrate to other organs

Feces contaminate moist shady soil Ova mature in 2-3 weeks

(6) Ova expelled in feces

FIG. 39-5. Life cycle of *Ascaris lumbricoides*.

mediate stages of the worm (larvae) pass through the wall of the intestine to penetrate the venules and/or lymphatics. They commonly migrate to the liver, right side of the heart, and lungs. The small larvae then penetrate the alveoli and ascend the bronchioles, bronchi, and trachea. On reaching the glottis they are swallowed. These same larvae develop into adult male and female forms in the small intestine. The adult male may be approximately 6 to 10 inches long. The female may be about 8 to 15 inches long and about the diameter of a pencil. The adult worms subsist on the

615

semidigested food in the intestinal canal. Fertilized eggs expelled in feces must undergo a period of maturation in the soil before becoming infective. (See Fig. 39-5.)

This parasite, because of its migratory habits (even the adult worm may travel up and down the digestive tract, occasionally making an alarming appearance at either end), may cause a variety of symptoms if the infestation is of some intensity. The larval migrations may cause nausea and vomiting or initiate symptoms of pneumonitis or intestinal obstruction. They even may produce perforation. Allergic reactions, skin rash, nervousness, and irritability are not uncommon.

Positive diagnosis is made on the basis of finding the ova in the stool or seeing the worms emerge from the gastrointestinal tract. Treatment by piperazine citrate (Antepar) is effective for ascaris infestation, provided that reinfection caused by poor hygiene practices does not occur. All infected persons must be treated to have successful control of the disease. Public education programs teaching general hygiene are a must. Turning infested topsoil under has also been believed helpful. The prognosis is very good unless secondary complications such as pneumonia, intestinal obstruction, or perforation have developed. The outlook then becomes more guarded.

The diarrheas

Any diarrheal disease causing profuse fluid loss is a particular threat to the very young person, the very old person, or the debilitated person, regardless of the initiating cause of the diarrhea. Subsequent dehydration and electrolyte imbalance is a very real danger. Fortunately, with the improvement in community sanitation and hygiene, the increased availability of refrigeration, and the adoption of the disinfection techniques used in infant formula preparation, infectious-type diarrheas are not now so common in the United States as they were 50 years ago.

Children who become dehydrated because of diarrhea or diarrhea and vomiting are admitted to the hospital. The child should be weighed and a stool culture obtained immediately.

Diarrheal disease of early childhood is a syndrome, the course of which varies with age, severity, nutritional status, and etiology. Some of the common causes of diarrhea include infection, anatomical abnormalities, malabsorption syndromes, and disease outside the gastrointestinal tract. Most acute diarrheas appear to have a viral etiology and frequently accompany acute upper respiratory infections. Other causes of infectious diarrheas include staphylococci, pathogenic *Escherichia coli,* and *Salmonella* and *Shigella* microorganisms. Diarrheal disturbances may also be initiated by injudicious diets or emotional upset.

General nursing care. Whatever the cause, acute diarrheal disorders need immediate treatment. The disturbance in intestinal motility and consequent malabsorption causes dehydration and fluid and electrolyte imbalances. Usually diarrhea subsides when fluid and electrolyte therapy is administered intravenously and oral intake is briefly reduced. Oral intake is restricted to rest the gastrointestinal tract and make it less irritable. Antibiotic therapy is indicated for treating diarrheas caused by pathogenic *Escherichia coli,* staphylococci, and salmonella and shigella-type organisms. The child's fluid intake and output will be carefully calculated. Daily weights must be accurate! Because of the frequency of stools, a special medicated ointment may be prescribed to apply after each cleansing of the perirectal area. A diarrheal stool should be promptly reported, since the physician may have written an order for the administration of a constipating medication after each liquid stool. Of course, the color, consistency, general appearance, and amount of the stool should be faithfully noted and recorded. (See p. 383.)

The dysenteries. The term "dysentery" may refer to a number of disorders. Strictly defined, it means "difficult intestines" and refers to those diseases characterized by abdominal cramping and frequent loose stools (especially those that may contain mucus or blood). The two main types of dysentery will be mentioned—amebic dysentery and bacillary dysentery.

Amebic dysentery (intestinal amebiasis). Intestinal amebiasis is caused by the ingestion of the cysts of a microscopic, one-celled organism known as *Entamoeba histolytica* in contaminated food or drink. It is found more frequently in tropical climates but is not limited to those areas. The cysts break open and expel the motile, or vegetative, form of the ameba in the lower small intestine. These microscopic motile forms, or *trophozoites,* invade the wall of the intestine and engulf and destroy red blood cells. Small bleeding points, ulcers, or abscesses may develop at the places where the amebae penetrate the mucous membrane of the gastrointestinal tract. The symptoms these areas of trauma produce depend on the extent of the amebic infection. Some persons have few or no complaints. Others may be troubled by abdominal tenderness or pain, bouts of constipation followed by diarrhea, nausea, malaise, and flatulence. More severe symptoms include bloody, mucoid bowel movements, fever, vomiting, and dehydration.

Some of the amebae are expelled in the feces in the motile form; others have formed cysts, which carry on the life cycle of the organism. Carriers of amebic dysentery are an important source of the disease. Complications, such as liver abscess, may develop when the motile forms migrate to other parts of the body.

Diagnosis depends on finding the cysts or trophozoites in the warm stool. Sigmoidoscopy may reveal lesions of the colon, and microscopic examination of scrapings from the lesions may disclose the organisms.

Treatment will vary, depending on the patient's needs and the severity of the disease. Drugs often used include glycobiarsol (Milibis), oxytetracycline (Terramycin), and emetine. Emetine is toxic. It is recommended that the patient receiving emetine have complete bed rest and fre-

quent blood pressure and pulse determinations. All family members should be treated, since they usually are affected. Treatment and observation may be prolonged, but the prognosis is usually favorable.

Bacillary dysentery. Bacillary dysentery is caused by several groups of bacteria of the genus *Shigella.* Since the causative agents are bacilli this infectious disease is described in Table 36-1, p. 520.

ABDOMINAL HERNIAS

A hernia is an abnormal protrusion of a portion of the contents of a body cavity through a defect in its surrounding wall, commonly causing an abnormal swelling or pressure symptoms. The general public calls the condition a "rupture." Common in infancy and childhood are inguinal and umbilical hernias. They are usually congenital.

Inguinal hernia

Hernia repair (herniorrhaphy) in the inguinal region is a common surgical procedure. Such hernias are found most often in males. They may be unilateral or bilateral. When the testes originally descend into the scrotum from the abdominal cavity, they are surrounded by a small sac or tube of peritoneum continuous with the abdominal lining. Usually this sac soon closes off, making any further communication with the abdominal cavity impossible. However, occasionally the closure is incomplete or does not take place, and the intestine slips down the open inguinal canal, causing a swelling in the area. This prolapse of the intestine is not important in itself. However, there is a possibility that the misplaced loop of intestine could become trapped (incarcerated) in the inguinal canal or scrotum and the circulation to the trapped segment could become impaired (strangulation), causing intestinal obstruction and gangrene of the bowel.

Inguinal hernia may also develop in girls. The anatomy is different but parallel. The inguinal canals, which are occupied by the round ligaments, may allow loops of intestine to enter the area of the groin. Only 10% of inguinal hernias involve females.

Various mechanical braces or trusses have been devised to maintain the intestine in its correct position within the abdomen. Sometimes their use has allowed the defect to close without surgery. Most popular has been the yarn truss, formed by two loops

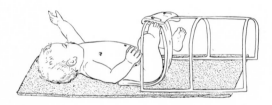

FIG. 39-6. Steps in constructing Stile's dressing. (Be sure that the gown is pulled tightly when attached to the cradle. At times the cradle must be tied to the crib.)

of a skein of yarn encircling the hips and groin and exerting gentle pressure. However, in recent years the success of surgical intervention and the slight amount of "inconvenience" suffered by the healthy infant undergoing the brief procedure have greatly decreased the use of the truss.

The surgical incision is usually performed in a natural skin crease where it will be difficult to see the scar. The hernia sac is carefully tied off. In the case of boys, an abnormal collection of fluid may be found in the scrotal area surrounding the testes (hydrocele). This fluid is aspirated, and the abnormal peritoneal sac is excised. The infant or young child usually tolerates the entire procedure very well, and in most cases little postoperative analgesia is required.

The tendency is to omit all gauze dressings over the new incision and use a protective spray dressing. This allows direct observation of the area and prevents a urine-soaked dressing from remaining over the incision. Diapers are usually not applied in a routine fashion until 24 hours after surgery.

Another approach to the diaper problem is the use of Stile's dressing (Fig. 39-6). A small bed cradle is placed over the legs of the infant. His diaper is brought upward between his legs and fastened to the frame of the cradle. A long infant gown, securely tied in back, is drawn tightly upward over the frame and also fastened with pins. The cradle is then draped with a small blanket. With the physician's permission, the child's position may be altered slightly for care, but the extent of movement allowed should be understood.

Umbilical hernias

Umbilical hernias often close spontaneously after the abdominal muscles strengthen with usage, when the child learns to stand and walk. Sometimes an elastic bandage is prescribed to help support proper positioning. Nowadays the placement of coins over the area is thought to delay rather than aid closure. Umbilical hernias are particularly common in Negro children. If there appears to be no progressive decrease in the size of the hernia, if the skin covering is exceptionally thin, if incarceration develops (rare), or if parents insist on correction, umbilical repair may be carried out. In any event the umbilicus is retained in place. The absence of an umbilicus in these days of bikini beach wear might prove distressing!

IMPERFORATE ANUS

The problem of imperforate anus has already been mentioned in Chapter 19. Fig. 19-15 depicts the common types of the malformation encountered. In most cases, surgery for correction must be performed very early to avoid complications and assure a better possibility of success. If a male newborn infant has a rectourethral fistula, surgery must be prompt to avoid intestinal obstruction and ascending urinary tract infection. For infant girls with an associated posterior vaginal anus, corrective surgery may be delayed until the child is 4 to 6 months of age.

Whether an abdominal and/or perineal surgical approach will be necessary depends on the type of defect and the distance of the terminal end of the colon from the perineum. A temporary colostomy may be necessary. After creation or repair of the anorectal area, frequent dilatation of the canal may be ordered.

Metabolic disorders associated with food intake

DIABETES MELLITUS

Diabetes mellitus is a common metabolic disorder. It is not a true digestive problem, since carbohydrates are reduced to glucose by the digestive system and the glucose is absorbed into the bloodstream. Difficulty arises because the glucose in the bloodstream is not subsequently converted and stored or burned properly by the body in the absence of effective insulin, a hormone produced by the islands of Langerhans in the pancreas.

Diabetes mellitus may manifest itself any time during a person's lifetime. In the United States there are approximately 67,000 known diabetic persons under 25 years of age. This group represents about 5% of all known diabetic persons. The earlier the disease appears the more severe it is likely to be. This disorder in glucose metabolism is a recessive hereditary trait.

Mechanism

Glucose is absorbed from the digestive tract, but in diabetes mellitus sufficient functional insulin is not available to convert it to glycogen and store it in the liver and muscles or burn it properly. It remains at a high level in the bloodstream (hyperglycemia). The large amount of sugar in the blood going to the kidneys cannot be entirely reabsorbed by the tubules of the nephron; therefore glucose spills over into the urine (glycosuria). To excrete the sugar, more water must also be excreted to dilute the sugar. Excessive urine production results.

When the amount of glucose available is insufficient to provide heat and energy to meet the body's needs, protein and fats may be used to help furnish these necessities. However, the metabolism of fat is not complete without the concurrent metabolism of carbohydrate. This incomplete fat metabolism produces ketone bodies (acetone, diacetic acid, and oxybutyric acid) that accumulate abnormally in the blood. Diacetic acid and oxybutyric acid must be neutralized in the body by bases, or alkalies. As the ketones are excreted, the neutralizing bases are also excreted. The body's supply of base is depleted, the sensitive electrolyte balance is upset, and acidosis gradually develops.

Symptoms

In children the first symptoms of diabetes mellitus noted may be excessive thirst and fluid intake (polydipsia). This ties in with the increased urinary output (polyuria), which may be so excessive that enuresis, or bedwetting, results. Exceptional appetite (polyphagia) may or may not be present in diabetic children. The affected child demonstrates a slow weight gain or a definite weight loss. He is easily fatigued.

Acidosis, the outcome of untreated diabetes or upsets in the glucose-insulin balance of the treated patient, usually develops over a period of days. At first its progressive increase usually causes general malaise, nausea, and vomiting. Abdominal pain may be present. As acidosis becomes more pronounced, symptoms of dehydration develop. The skin is warm, dry, and often flushed, and the eyeballs are soft and sunken. The body, using every method available to get rid of the abnormal ketones present, expels acetone from the respiratory system as well as the urinary tract. The typical fruity "apple-pie" breath results. Respirations become long, deep, and labored (Kussmaul's respirations). The patient becomes irritable, drowsy, and then unconscious or comatose. His blood pressure is typically low and his pulse rapid and thready.

Treatment of diabetic coma must be intensive. Intravenous therapy to restore the electrolyte balance and provide suitable dosages of insulin is routine. Frequent blood chemistries and urine testing for glucose and acetone levels are mandatory.

Diagnosis

Of course, the primary diagnosis of diabetes mellitus is confirmed with the help of laboratory tests. The presence of sugar in the urine points to the possibility of this disease, but in itself is not conclusive, since some children have a low renal threshold for glucose but no other problem. However, detection of glycosuria coupled with the finding of an elevated blood sugar level is diagnostic. Children are more likely to have a more abrupt onset of the disease than adults, who tend to develop diabetes gradually.

The oral glucose tolerance test is usually employed to determine the presence of hyperglycemia. After the child has fasted during the night, blood and urine samples are obtained. A calculated amount of glu-

cose based on the child's age and weight is then given (usually in unsweetened lemonade or an especially prepared carbonated beverage). Specimens of blood and urine are secured at intervals for a period of 2 hours or more. Sometimes continued urine specimens are not ordered. It is not always easy to have little people void on cue. Diagnosis of diabetes mellitus is made when the blood sugar level becomes abnormally elevated or does not fall to normal limits within 3 hours. Occasionally a physician will order a blood sugar determination 2 hours after a meal to evaluate glucose metabolism. This is termed a "postprandial specimen."

Treatment

The treatment of childhood diabetes mellitus always involves the injection of insulin. Although the insulin dosage of some children may be reduced by the concurrent administration of oral hypoglycemic agents such as tolbutamide (Orinase), the oral medication is unable to stimulate sufficient insulin production to meet the total needs of the young patient. Children with diabetes mellitus usually require a much higher insulin dosage than adults.

The amount and type of insulin prescribed will depend on the patient's caloric requirements (based on his weight, growth rate, and activity) and his individual response to therapy. Some children may be insulin resistant and require exceptionally large doses. In calculating a diabetic diet and the amount of insulin required, not only must the total amount of caloric intake derived from carbohydrates, fats, and proteins be considered, but also one must assure the patient an adequate intake of protein and sufficient minerals and vitamins for normal growth.

Basic philosophies. There are basically two different philosophies regarding the diet and management of the child diabetic patient. The traditional, or strict, approach recommends the prescription of a dietary formula based on the child's needs, which is followed closely. The formula outlines the total daily caloric count, the daily percentages of carbohydrate, fat, and protein to be included, and the intervals at which certain amounts are to be eaten. Sometimes these diets are ordered using the concept of total available glucose (TAG). The physician will stipulate the daily TAG allowed and the intervals and proportions of intake that should be observed. When the dietitian calculates such a diet order, she counts carbohydrate as 100% glucose, protein as 58% glucose, and fat as 10% glucose. It may seem strange to consider protein and fat as glucose, but it must be remembered that these foodstuffs may be stored in part as glycogen, a form of glucose. Thus they serve as a source of glucose. After the diets are calculated the foods are carefully weighed, or in some cases, converted to common volume or serving exchanges. This latter device greatly eases the planning of meals. Advocates of this type of dietary supervision often believe that the best way for the diabetic patient to avoid complications is to strive toward a sugar-free urine at all times, that is, to be *aglycosuric*.

In recent years a more relaxed system of control has found favor with some physicians. It is usually called the *free,* or *glycosuric,* diet. It allows the patient more freedom of dietary choice and does not strive for sugar-free urine, only ketone-free urine. It counsels moderation in food intake with avoidance of rich carbohydrate or fatty foods. Advocates of this system believe that the frequency of complications is not any greater than when the stricter regimen is followed. It is true that some responsible teen-agers do much better psychologically with the free-type diet.

Insulin-food relationships. In the hospital the patient is almost always on a strict type of diet. No food or liquids should be given with the exception of water or black coffee without the physician's authorization. The patient should be encouraged to eat all the food served on his tray on time. (Before serving his tray the nursing staff should determine whether he has received any ordered insulin. The type of insulin he

receives will dictate when his meal should be served.) The diabetic patient's tray is returned by his nurse directly to the kitchen. The glucose content of any uneaten portion is calculated, and a replacement (usually a drink) that he must finish is sent to the patient. Any inability to eat or emesis should be promptly reported. The way in which the young patient is adhering to his diet should be carefully reported and recorded. Diet conferences in which the physician and dietitian work along with the older child may be arranged and are often profitable. Sometimes when a youngster feels that he has "made some of the rules," they are easier to keep.

Insulin dosage and administration. There are approximately seven types of insulin now available on the market. Fig. 39-7 describes their administration and activity. They may be grouped as rapid, intermediate, or long acting.

The addition of crystalline zinc to regular insulin aids in preventing reaction at the injection sites but does not alter the basic activity of the medication. Regular or crystalline zinc insulin is used to combat acidosis. It has a rapid but relatively brief action. Many times both short-acting and long-acting insulin will be prescribed.

When a diabetic child is being regulated in the hospital, he is often placed on "regular insulin coverage." The amount of insulin he receives will depend on the amount of sugar found in his urine at specific times during the day. The sites of injection should be changed each day to prevent the atrophy of subcutaneous fat. The child should be taught to keep a record of the daily placement of his insulin. Children 7 and 8 years old often express curiosity about the process of preparing the dosage, and some (those intelligent and composed) may even be capable of injecting themselves. Children must have considerable practice in preparing dosages with adequate supervision. Insulin is a powerful medication, and in most hospitals any nurse giving insulin must show to another nurse the physician's order, insulin bottle,

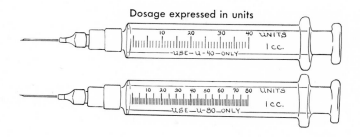

Dosage expressed in units

Type	Time of injection	Onset	Peak action hours after injection	Duration in hours
Regular or crystalline zinc	20 min. before meals; in emergencies as needed	Rapid, within hour	2-4	5-8
*Semilente	½ - ¾ hr. before breakfast; deep subcutaneous injection	Rapid, within hour	6-10	12-16
Globin zinc	½ - 1 hr. before breakfast	Intermediate, within 2-4 hrs.	6-10	18-24
NPH (neutral protamine Hagedorn)	1 hr. before breakfast	Intermediate, within 2-4 hrs.	8-12	28-30
*Lente	1 hr. before breakfast; deep subcutaneous injection	Intermediate, within 2-4 hrs.	8-12	28-32
PZI (protamine zinc insulin)	1 hr. before breakfast	Slow, within 4-6 hrs.	16-24	24-36+
*Ultralente	1 hr. before breakfast; deep subcutaneous injection	Very slow, 8 hrs.	16-24	36+

*Lente insulins are used when children are allergic to other types or difficult to control.

FIG. 39-7. Types of insulin and their span of effect. (Adapted from Bergersen, B. S., and Krug, E. E.: Pharmacology in nursing, ed. 10, St. Louis, 1966, The C. V. Mosby Co.)

and dose drawn up in the syringe before it can be administered.

Insulin shock

Insulin itself may cause problems. Too much insulin may be just as disastrous as too little insulin. A balance between insulin need and insulin available must be maintained to avoid either diabetic acidosis or the other extreme known as insulin shock.

Unlike acidosis, insulin shock may develop quite rapidly, within minutes or hours. The rapidity with which the symptoms appear is greatly influenced by the type of insulin the patient is receiving be-

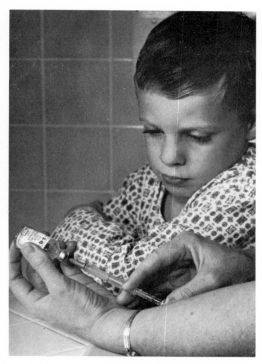

FIG. 39-8. "Be sure to get the bubble out, Mom."

cause peaks of maximum effect differ, depending on the kind of insulin used.

One of the first signs of surplus insulin is a change in personality. This change will take various forms, depending on the patient, but each individual usually reacts in a way that is particularly characteristic for him. One may become irritable and edgy. Another may become excited. Some appear sluggish. Fatigue is a common complaint. If the student will recall the way she feels just before a needed lunch, she may be able to remember some of the signs and symptoms of insulin excess more easily. As the reaction increases, sudden, exaggerated hunger pangs, weakness, dizziness, blurred or double vision, dilated pupils, pallor, and rather profuse perspiration are noted. The patient may stagger. Adults suffering from reactions have been falsely accused of being drunk! If the condition is not relieved, the patient will develop deep shock, become unconscious, suffer from possible

tremors or convulsions, and, if no treatment becomes available, eventually die.

Nurses and patients should be familiar with the early signs of insulin reaction so that it may be easily counteracted. Children usually learn to recognize their symptoms well. All diabetic persons should carry some rapidly available source of glucose with them in the event that they should feel the beginning of an insulin reaction. Usually a sugar lump or small piece of candy is recommended. In the hospital a small glass of orange juice or crackers are usually given. If no improvement is obtained in 15 minutes, additional food should be given. If it is difficult to get the child to take the necessary oral glucose, an intramuscular or subcutaneous injection of glucagon is many times ordered on an "as needed" basis for insulin reactions. Sometimes intravenous administration by the physician of a 20% to 50% solution of glucose may be required. If the patient has been given a slow-acting, long-duration insulin, response to therapy for hypoglycemia may be slow and treatment more complex. The physician should always be notified of the occurrence of insulin reactions. When a patient complains of symptoms of possible reaction or the nurse is suspicious that such a process is occurring, the nurse should secure and test a current sample of urine if possible. If symptoms of shock are present, the specimen will prove negative for glucose and acetone. At times it may be difficult to determine clinically whether the complaints and appearance of the patient are caused by the lack of sugar or too much sugar in the blood. If no laboratory test is feasible, glucagon or intravenous glucose is often ordered. If the difficulty is caused by insulin reaction, the patient responds. If it is not, no real harm will have been done. Insulin shock should be treated promptly. Prolonged, severe hypoglycemia may cause brain damage and subsequent mental deterioration, motor incoordination, and, of course, even death.

As you can see from Fig. 39-9, there are a number of causes of insulin surplus and

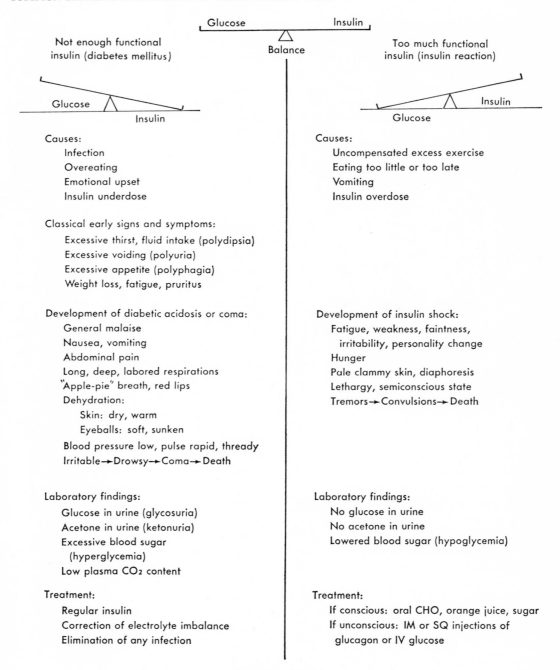

FIG. 39-9. Glucose-insulin balance chart.

resulting reaction. Probably the most common cause is uncompensated excessive exercise. Exercise causes sugar to be metabolized more effectively and reduces blood sugar levels. Unless insulin dosage is reduced or glucose intake is increased, insulin reaction is very likely in the presence of unplanned exercise. For this reason it is important for the diabetic child to have periods of regular exercise suitably spaced *after* meals and to recognize the possibility of needed adjustment to compensate for special activites.

Another cause of insulin reaction or shock is failure to eat the planned diet as prescribed (failure to eat enough or to space the food intake conscientiously). Diabetic patients often have ordered interval feedings in the midafternoon and at bedtime. The nurse should be sure that they are given to the patient and that they are consumed. If the child is nauseated or has an emesis, this should be immediately reported because this condition may also cause an insulin surplus. Meals must be served on time; a long delay after the injection of regular insulin also sets the stage for an episode of hypoglycemia.

Difficulties in determining the regulated doses of insulin may also be a source of glucose-insulin imbalance. The patient may not respond to the dosage as expected. Errors in insulin administration resulting in an overdose are also a real possibility. Great care must be taken in reading the orders and in preparing the injection. One must be certain that the scale on the syringe and the number of units per cubic centimeter in the bottle of insulin agree. If the nurse has been given medical permission to mix two types of insulin in the same syringe, she must be sure of her technique.

1. Inject just enough replacement air into the bottle of cloudy insulin without dipping the injecting needle into the insulin. Remove the needle from the bottle.
2. Withdraw the clear, regular insulin into the syringe, using the proper scale.
3. Withdraw the cloudy insulin into the syringe, using the proper scale.
4. Put an air bubble into the syringe and rock the syringe back and forth to mix the two types.

Because diabetic patients may develop important complications if infection occurs, the technique of preparation and injection should be particularly meticulous.

Acidosis

Acidosis, the opposite body condition from insulin shock, occurs when the insulin available in the blood is insufficient to metabolize the glucose present. We have already discussed the development of acidosis in untreated diabetic persons. Treated diabetic patients may occasionally have problems with acidosis.

The most frequent cause for the development of acidosis in a treated diabetic patient is the onset of infection, any infection. Infection greatly intensifies the body's need for insulin, and unless insulin dosage is increased, acidosis may result. Infections of the skin are quite common in diabetic patients. Pruritus is a fairly frequent complaint. At times a vulvitis is the problem that brings the patient to the physician, and diabetes mellitus is subsequently diagnosed. Close attention must be paid to preventing infection and treating vigorously any infection present. Special care of the toenails and feet is encouraged. Nurses do not cut the toenails of diabetic patients.

Failing to follow the prescribed diet or "snitching sweets" may be a possible problem. It takes a great deal of self-understanding and self-discipline to refrain from eating some of the tempting but forbidden food combinations available, especially if one feels hungry. The development of self-direction and self-control is paramount for the young diabetic person, particularly the young adolescent. Dietary discipline should be encouraged by allowing the youngster to express his frustrations, providing as much variety in the diet as possible, allowing him to participate in its planning, and possibly making provision for a *rare* special treat. With the advent of so many 1-calorie soft drinks, the social life of the teen-ager with diabetes mellitus is a bit less strained. However, he should be cautioned that the label "dietetic foods" does not necessarily mean "foods for the diabetic." The child should be made to believe that ultimately, the only person he cheats is himself when he knowingly chooses unwisely or tries to falsify urine tests.

Emotional upset also increases the possibility of acidosis. The insulin requirement rises in periods of stress. The emotionally stable child is much easier to regulate with insulin than a child with many emotional problems.

The difficulty determining the proper dosage of insulin has already been described. Possible errors in the administration of insulin that can result in an underdose as well as an overdose have also been discussed.

Urine tests

Long before the child is ready to give his own insulin injection he will be able to test his urine for the presence of glucose and acetone. Several types of tests for glycosuria are available. They are of varying convenience and expense. In the hospital, Clinitest tablets are usually employed (Fig. 39-10). However, at home, with the availability of kitchen facilities, the patient or his parents may prefer to use the less ex-

pensive Benedict test. When traveling, the family may prefer to use the newer urine-sugar analysis paper, Clinistix. Urine analysis for the presence of acetone is also routine. The mechanics of these various tests are described on pp. 408 and 409.

The nurse should be sure that she is not only performing the individual test correctly but also that she is collecting the urine specimens as ordered. Urine specimens are usually secured and tested half an hour before scheduled meals (that is, 7:30 A.M., 11:30 A.M., 4:30 P.M., and bedtime). The physician may wish either spot or fractional specimens. A spot specimen theoretically tells the sugar-insulin balance currently. The patient is asked to void (emptying his bladder) at 7 A.M. Then he is given a glass of water. A portion of this 7 A.M. specimen is saved but will be discarded later if it is not needed. At 7:30 A.M. the patient is asked to void again, and a portion of this specimen is tested and reported. The procedure is repeated before lunch, before dinner, and before bedtime. However, practically speaking, it is some-

FIG. 39-10. "You're not supposed to touch the tablet with your fingers." Clinitest analysis of urine.

times difficult for a little patient to produce the needed urine specimen on schedule. If the second specimen is not forthcoming, the first specimen secured (which has not been thrown away) will be tested and appropriately reported and recorded.

When the physician orders fractional specimens, the total urine output between testings is saved, and at the time of the scheduled urine examination the entire collected volume is mixed, and tests are made on a specimen from the total volume; for example, Johnny is asked to void at 7:30 A.M. This voiding is added to the urine collection started the previous night for the period from 8 P.M. bedtime until 7:30 A.M. The collection is mixed and a small amount of the mixture tested. Then the collection is discarded. The next time Johnny voids, the total voiding is placed in the large, empty, clean collection bottle. If he voids again, this voiding too is put in the collection bottle. At 11:30 A.M. he is asked to void, and the complete voiding is added to the collection. The urine is mixed and a specimen tested, etc. The results of urine examinations should be promptly reported to the team leader or head nurse.

It is very helpful for patients with diabetes mellitus to be able to room together. They usually are mutually supportive and learn from one another. (Most of the time such learning is positive and beneficial!) Children with this disorder should be encouraged to participate in school, church, and community activities and not look on their metabolic problem as an excuse for difficult behavior or special privileges. The fact that they have diabetes mellitus should not be hidden. Teachers, schoolmates, and employers should be aware of the presence of the condition. In many states there are special summer camping experiences set up for children with this disorder. These 2-week sessions have been of great help to many youngsters.

Review of nursing responsibility

The nursing care of the diabetic patient has been discussed throughout this section;

however, the following questions should be of assistance in aiding the nurse to organize and evaluate her care:

1. Insulin requirement. Do you know the type of insulin your patient is receiving and when he receives his injections? Do you know how his injections are being rotated?

2. Diet. Do you know what type of diet the physician has prescribed? If a strict diet is ordered (usually the case), have you made sure that your patient has eaten everything or has received a replacement? Do you evaluate his meals for variety and interest? Do you watch for and limit the possibility of the patient obtaining food not calculated in his diet? Does he have a scheduled interval nourishment?

3. Urine testing. Do you know the method to be used? Are you collecting the specimens properly?

4. General hygiene. Is the patient getting as much exercise as possible so that his insulin requirement (because of differences in amounts of exercise taken) will not change greatly on discharge? Is his skin in good condition? Are there any signs of infection anywhere in the body?

5. Glucose-insulin imbalance. Do you know the signs and symptoms of developing insulin shock and acidosis?

6. Patient-parent education and participation. Are you assisting the patient and his parents in learning more about the disease and its treatment and control, depending on their level of understanding? Are you helping the patient to develop attitudes of self-control and feelings of achievement and well-being? Does the child keep records of his insulin intake, urine tests, and general health? How much is he able to participate in his care?

7. What special interests and aspirations does this patient have?

8. What has this patient taught you?

For a diabetic patient to become a contributing citizen in the community and enjoy life to its maximum, he must understand his disease, accept the limitations it imposes, and learn to function in a relatively independent setting. The alert, intelligent, warm-hearted nurse can do much to help him meet these goals.

OTHER METABOLIC DEFECTS THAT INFLUENCE DIET

As research continues in the fields of genetics, metabolism, and biochemistry, more and more genetically determined defects in body metabolism have been identified. Some of these defects (for example, diabetes mellitus, cystic fibrosis of the pancreas, celiac disease, and phenylketonuria) have been previously mentioned. Nelson, in his *Textbook of Pediatrics,*° lists thirteen separate categories of inborn errors of metabolism. Obviously, the problems are very complex.

Galactosemia

One metabolic defect that has dietary significance and has received considerable attention in the literature recently is *galactosemia*. If this congenital error in the metabolism of the sugar galactose is untreated, it may cause physical and mental retardation, cataracts, enlargement of the liver and spleen, and cirrhosis. The body is unable

---
°Nelson, W. E., Vaughan, V. C., III, and McKay, R. J., editors: Textbook of pediatrics, ed. 9, Philadelphia, 1969, W. B. Saunders Co.

to change galactose to glucose, a chemical reaction that normally takes place primarily in the liver. An enzyme needed to accomplish the task is deficient or missing. Galactose builds up in the bloodstream and spills over into the urine, where it may be identified by appropriate tests.

Early signs of galactosemia in the infant are vomiting, listlessness, and failure to thrive. These signs are not apparent until at least a week or two after birth. Since galactose is present in milk sugar, it is very important that the defect be diagnosed early and that a milk substitute such as Nutramigen or a meat-base formula be used. Like those of children with phenylketonuria (PKU), the diets of galactosemia patients must be very closely supervised to avoid the ingestion of the offending food. Also like the little patient with PKU, the small victim of galactosemia may be able to gradually expand his dietary horizons after a period of several years on a rigid, restricted regimen.

* * *

A source of much pleasure and occasional pain, the digestive system continually struggles to meet the challenges of unskilled cooks, individual abuse, and emotional stress. Nurses should be able to help prevent or ease some of the difficulties faced by this sensitive body servant. In so doing, they fulfill part of their obligation to the individual whose total well-being is their concern.

40
Conditions involving the genitourinary system

Urinary system

The urinary system consists of two kidneys, two ureters, the bladder, and the urethra (Fig. 40-1). The primary function of these organs is to excrete metabolic waste products and other substances not necessary in the blood.

To regulate the composition of blood, the kidneys perform the complex task of secreting urine. The ureters, bladder, and urethra are involved in the transportation, storage, and elimination of the urine.

Kidneys

The kidneys are paired organs located on either side of the vertebral column, just above the waistline. They lie outside the peritoneal cavity against the posterior abdominal wall.

In the adult the kidneys are about 4½ inches long and 2½ inches wide; they are somewhat bean shaped. On the medial border of each kidney is a concave notch called the *hilus*. The renal artery, renal vein, nerves, and ureter join the kidney at the hilus.

When describing the internal structure of the organ, one may speak of two areas: the functioning portion, the *parenchyma*, and the collecting portion, the *pelvis*. A longitudinal section of the kidney reveals that the parenchyma in turn is composed of two parts: an outer portion called the *cortex* and an inner portion called the *medulla*. The pelvis is formed by the expansion of the upper end of the ureter. The pelvis subdivides to form the major and minor *calyces*.

The physiological structural unit of the kidney is called the *nephron*. The nephron consists of the renal corpuscle plus its tubule. The renal corpuscle consists of the glomerulus (a cluster of connecting capillaries) and Bowman's capsule, into which the capillaries protrude. The convoluted tubules, the loop of Henle, and the renal corpuscle constitute the nephron. The blood supply of the nephron comes from microscopic branches of the renal artery. The renal corpuscle and the convoluting tubules are located in the cortex of the kidney; the loop of Henle and the collecting tubules are located in the medulla. Each kidney contains more than 1 million nephrons.

The kidneys perform the complex task of removing toxic metabolic wastes, such as urea and uric acid, and excessive nontoxic substances, such as water and electrolytes, from the blood. In this way the kidneys regulate the composition and volume of blood. The kidneys also influence blood pressure, but the way in which this is accomplished is not completely clear.

Three processes are involved in the production of urine: filtration, reabsorption, and secretion.

1. *Filtration* takes place under the influence of blood pressure in the renal corpuscle. A single arteriole forms each glomerulus. Water and nonprotein solutes filter out of the glomerulus through Bowman's capsule. Blood cells, platelets, and plasma proteins are normally retained in the glomerulus.

2. *Reabsorption* takes place through the walls of the convoluted tubules and Henle's loop. By means of a highly selective and discriminating process, the cells of the tubule efficiently re- absorb certain amounts of water, glucose, and electrolytes. This rec- clamation process is vital to the main- tenance of the fluid and electrolyte balance of the body.

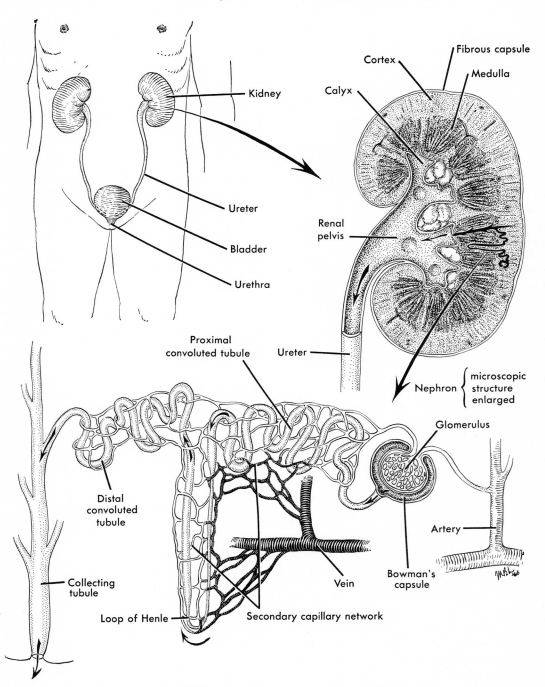

FIG. 40-1. Gross and microscopic structures of the urinary system.

3. *Secretion* takes place in the convoluting tubules. A number of substances are secreted directly into the tubule from the secondary capillary network. In the proximal convoluting tubules, penicillin, iodopyracet (Diodrast), phenolsulfonphthalein, hippuric acid, and creatinine are among the substances secreted and excreted. In the distal convoluting tubule, hydrogen ions and ammonia are secreted in the varying amounts necessary to control and maintain the acid-base balance of the body.

The final filtrate, urine, passes from the distal convoluting tubule into the straight collecting tubule and into the renal pelvis.

In the normal adult approximately 190 liters of blood are filtered through the glomeruli daily. The tubules reclaim about 188.5 liters of filtrate. The remaining filtrate is excreted as urine. The average daily urinary output is about 1,500 ml. In children the daily output of urine varies greatly with the age of the child and his fluid intake.

Ureters

In the adult the ureters are small tubes about $\frac{1}{5}$ inch in diameter and 12 inches in length. (The size varies with age.) The expanded upper end of the ureter collects the urine as it forms, and peristaltic waves convey the urine down the ureters and into the bladder. The ureters lie behind the peritoneum and descend from the kidney to the posterior bladder wall. They enter the bladder in an oblique manner, which prevents reflux, or the backflow of urine.

Bladder

The bladder is a dome-shaped, hollow, muscular sac that stores urine. It is located directly behind the symphysis pubis. Three layers of smooth muscle form the bladder wall. These three unique muscular layers are collectively called the *detrusor muscle*. The outlet of the bladder is surrounded by a band of smooth muscle known as the internal sphincter. The bladder outlet and the two ureteral openings outline a triangular area called the *trigone*.

The detrusor muscle is usually relaxed, allowing the bladder to expand as needed to accommodate urine storage. After a certain volume of urine is collected, the urge to void is felt. In the child this urge is usually recognized when the bladder contains approximately 200 ml. The desire to void is recorded by the sensory parasympathetic endings in the detrusor muscle. If the child decides to void, the detrusor muscle contracts, the internal sphincter opens, and urine enters the posterior urethra. Voiding may be postponed, but when the bladder becomes very full, a point is reached at which even the most desperate efforts can no longer retain the urine.

Urethra

The urethra is a small tube that serves as a passageway for the elimination of urine from the bladder. The external opening of the urethra is called the *urinary meatus*.

The urethra is a comparatively short tube in the adult female; it is about 1½ inches long. In the midportion of the female urethra is a circular striated muscle that forms the external sphincter.

The male urethra is about 8 inches long and also serves as part of the reproductive tract. It is divided into three sections: prostatic, membranous, and anterior. The prostatic urethra is about 1 inch long and extends from the internal sphincter of the bladder through the prostate gland to the pelvic floor. The membranous urethra is about ½ inch long and lies between the prostatic and anterior sections of the urethra; it is surrounded by the external sphincter. The anterior urethra is about 6 inches long and extends through the penis, terminating at the urethral meatus.

Urine

Urine is a transparent, amber-colored liquid with a characteristic odor. It is usually acid in reaction. The specific gravity of urine ranges from 1.003 to 1.030. Approximately 95% of urine is water. The remaining 5% consists of wastes from protein metabolism and inorganic components such as sodium and potassium chloride.

The examination of urine is the keystone in diagnosing disorders of the urinary system. A properly collected specimen can yield a wealth of information about renal function and the nature of kidney disorders. Urinalysis also reveals much information about infections and toxic and metabolic disorders.

Key vocabulary

anuria failure of kidney function; lack of urine formation.

albuminuria presence of albumin in the urine.

enuresis bed-wetting at an age when urinary control should be present.

frequency number of repetitions of a periodic process in a unit of time; when speaking of urinary function, the term implies an abnormal increase in the number of voidings.

hematuria presence of blood in the urine.

nocturia excessive urination during the night.

oliguria diminished amount of urine production with subsequent scanty urination.

polyuria abnormally increased urinary output.

proteinuria finding of protein, usually albumin, in the urine.

reflux return or backward flow (e.g., regurgitation of urine from the bladder into the ureter).

uremia toxic condition associated with renal insufficiency and the retention in the blood of nitrogenous substances normally excreted by the kidney.

Anomalies of the urinary tract

The embryological development of the urinary system is closely related to the development of the genital organs in both sexes. Because of this factor, genital and urinary tract deformities will be discussed together. Genitourinary deformities comprise 30% to 40% of all congenital anomalies. Often a deformity of the genitalia is accompanied by a deformity of the upper urinary tract. Deformities are multiple in approximately 20% of cases and often accompany anomalies in other systems, for example, imperforate anus.

Malformations of the genitourinary tract may lead to death. When the anomaly can be recognized early, surgical correction or treatment is lifesaving. This is true because most anomalies are obstructive and lead to hydronephrosis, which ultimately results in renal failure.

External deformities are obvious and readily detected. However, there is little evidence of internal disease unless it is far advanced. The nurse should be aware of this and know the few signals demanding close observation. It is important to note the number and amount of voidings in the newborn infant. Failure to void within the first 24 hours after birth is always a danger sign and should be reported to the physician immediately. Abdominal enlargement or swelling in the area of a kidney also warrants immediate attention.

The signs and symptoms of urinary problems in older children are more easily detected. Crying on urination, urgent and frequent urination, straining to void, and dribbling all may point to genitourinary system difficulties. Unexplained fever, lassitude, weight loss, and failure to thrive are nondescript symptoms but may relate to advanced disease. Serious kidney infections often run a silent course. It is always wise to investigate any of the above signals, since renal failure is often the result of a hidden anomaly.

Renal agenesis

Bilateral renal agenesis is incompatible with life. Autopsy has revealed that it is more common in males than females and not as rare as once believed. *Unilateral renal agenesis* is compatible with life, but the single kidney is more apt to be diseased, since it is often located in the pelvis and associated with other malformations, especially of the ureter.

Double kidney

Duplication of the kidney and ureter is more common in girls than in boys. The ureters from each double kidney may enter the bladder at different points or may unite to enter the bladder as one ureter. Sometimes the ureter from the upper kidney enters the genitourinary tract ectopically, and may cause incontinence. Duplication of the kidney and ureter is clinically significant only when other anomalies causing obstruction or infection exist.

Horseshoe kidney

A horseshoe kidney results when the lower ends of both kidneys fuse, forming a single mass shaped like a horseshoe. The kidneys lie closer to the spine and usually lower than separate kidneys do. Horseshoe kidney may be asymptomatic, but complications, especially infection, are common.

Polycystic kidney

True polycystic disease is always congenital and always bilateral. Polycystic kidneys are larger than the normal kidneys and sometimes are huge, filling the entire abdomen. They contain innumerable cysts, compressing the parenchyma. Such kidneys are constantly prone to infection, obstruction, and stone formation. Treatment can only be palliative. Some children live many years with the condition. Others develop uremia within the first year of life.

Ureterocele

A ureterocele may be described as a ballooning of the lower end of the ureter because of an abnormally narrow ureteral orifice. Ureteroceles are usually unilateral. Double ureters are commonly associated with the anomaly. When there is an extra ureter, the one that enters the bladder normally is often distorted by the enormous ureterocele. As a result, it becomes obstructed, and kidney infection may ensue. Treatment consists of excising the redundant portion and reconstructing the orifice so that obstruction is eliminated. If an obstruction does not exist, treatment is symptomatic.

Exstrophy of the bladder

Exstrophy of the bladder, fortunately, is a rare condition. It ranks with the most severe anomalies of mankind. Because of a defect in midline closure associated with incomplete development of the pubic arch, the interior of the bladder lies completely exposed through an opening in the lower abdominal wall. A number of genital anomalies may accompany the defect.

The child becomes foul smelling because he is constantly soaked in urine. Often the surrounding skin becomes excoriated, causing great pain. Early in life, the exposed bladder mucosa becomes inflamed, bleeds readily, and is acutely sensitive. Infection is frequent but can usually be controlled by antibiotic therapy.

Treatment is surgical. An anatomical reconstruction of the bladder is the operation of choice. The most desired time for this operation is when the child is between 12 and 18 months old, when he is old enough and strong enough to tolerate a long operative procedure. After this operation, the child is totally incontinent for a period of years; during this time the bladder grows sufficiently to make antireflux operations possible. When the bladder (vesicle) sphincters are made more complete and function somewhat normally, efforts can be directed to make the child continent. Dilatation of the ureter, reflux, and chronic infection often occur when the child is rendered continent too early.

When the ureters are enlarged or the kidney damaged by infection, anatomical reconstruction of the bladder is contraindicated. Other methods of diverting urine are employed, especially ileal bladder or conduit procedures.

Exstrophy of the bladder is compatible with life, and the prognosis depends in great measure on the extent of renal damage resulting from defective drainage and infection.

Hypospadias

Hypospadias is a common deformity in which the urethra terminates at some point on the ventral (under) surface of the penis (Fig. 40-2). The position of the urethra on the penis or perineum will determine the type of treatment. When the urethra terminates near the glans, a high circumcision is performed so that the child can learn to

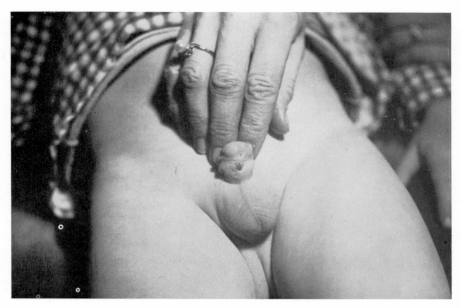

FIG. 40-2. Hypospadias (meatus located on undersurface of penis.) (Courtesy Matthew Gleason, M.D., San Diego, Calif.)

direct his urine stream. Because the prostatic urethra is never involved in hypospadias, the sphincters function normally and the child has good urinary control. Often a meatal stricture is associated with varying degrees of hypospadias. When such a stricture is recognized, it is easily corrected by dilatation or meatotomy.

In the more severe types a cordlike anomaly may arc the penis downward (chordee). These more extensive deformities all require surgical repair to establish normal control of voiding and make normal reproduction possible later in life. Boys with severe types of hypospadias should not be circumcised, since the foreskin is needed in the repair.

Treatment. Operative repair is usually done in two stages before the child enters school. In this way the child avoids severe ridicule and lasting psychological problems.

The chordee is released early to straighten the penis and allow for normal growth. This is accomplished in the first-stage operation when the child is 2 years of age. When the child is 4 years old or when-

ever the amount of local tissue permits, a second-stage operation (urethroplasty) is performed. Various plastic techniques have been employed to correct hypospadias, but the Denis Browne technique seems to be most successful.

The difficulties encountered in achieving a successful result in the correction of hypospadias are considerable. The parents should be well aware that more than one operation is usually required. They should also know that after a successful urethroplasty the penis will show scars and that some penile bowing may remain even though the child is able to urinate normally.

Postoperative care. When surgery is completed, the penis is wrapped in petroleum gauze and then covered with a dry gauze bandage. This helps to prevent postoperative swelling, pain, and bleeding. Unless this precaution is taken, necrosis of the glans may occur. A catheter drains the bladder while the incision is healing. The nurse must observe the patient carefully for signs of swelling and bleeding.

After the operations the child is kept on

his back. A bed cradle helps to prevent pressure on the operative area. Many times, Stile's dressing will be used (Fig. 39-6).

On the second postoperative day the child may be allowed freedom of movement in his crib, provided the nurse can take time to sit, talk, and play with him. She should attempt to keep his little hands busy lest he busy them with his dressing. Parents should be encouraged to stay with their children for they are usually best able to keep them constructively occupied.

Epispadias

When the urethra opens on the dorsal (upper) surface of the penis, the condition is called epispadias. Various degrees of epispadias may occur. However, the deformity is uncommon except when associated with exstrophy of the bladder. Treatment is the same as that for hypospadias and/or exstrophy.

Intersexual anomalies

A semiemergency exists when simple inspection of the newborn infant's genitalia does not reveal the sex of the child. Skin biopsy or buccal smears with chromosome studies are sometimes helpful in these cases. Exploratory abdominal surgery for gonadal biopsy may be undertaken to identify the sex of the sexually indeterminate child.

Pseudohermaphroditism. When an individual possesses external genitalia resembling those of one sex and the gonads of the opposing sex, the condition resulting is termed "pseudohermaphroditism." Sometimes a severe hypospadias with undescended testicles or a hypertrophied clitoris and malformed labia cause problems in sex identification. Female pseudohermaphrodites possess ovaries but their external genitalia mimic those of the male. Such masculinization of the female infant is due to an overdeveloped adrenal cortex (congenital adrenal hyperplasia) and subsequent increased production of male sex hormones (androgens). Male pseudohermaphrodites are chromosomal males, but

due to testicular dysfunction and/or other problems, sexual ambiguity is present.

Whatever the condition, it should be corrected as soon as possible, but only after the true sex has been determined. Treatment usually consists of corrective plastic procedures on the external genitalia and/or the administration of appropriate missing hormones.

Hermaphroditism. An extremely rare condition exists when a child possesses gonads and genitalia of both sexes. Prompt attention to this problem lessens the possibilities of serious emotional sequelae. Treatment consists of removing the gonads of one sex. Acceptable female genitalia may often be formed by relatively simple procedures. For this practical reason, when a choice can be made, the male gonad tissues are removed and the child is made female. Conversion of sex should be done as soon as possible so that the individual may have an opportunity for a normal, happy, and successful life.

Undescended testicle (cryptorchidism)

Failure of the testes to descend into the scrotum affects about 2% of the male population. The condition is usually unilateral. Frequently an inguinal hernia is present.

There are usually no symptoms associated with undescended testicles except for some tenderness in the inguinal canal. Injury to the testicle is more likely to occur if it is confined to the inguinal canal than if it is in normal scrotal position. Torsion of the undescended testicle may take place, necessitating prompt surgical relief. Development of testicular malignancy is more common in cases of cryptorchidism. Lack of correction may also lead to severe psychological difficulties.

Treatment is usually surgical, although spontaneous descent may occur. Spontaneous descent, if forthcoming, is usually completed by the first year. Almost all undescended testes can be satisfactorily positioned in the scrotum by surgical means. However, the optimum time for the procedure (orchiopexy) is disputed. Some physicians advocate waiting until puberty with the hope that the testicle will descend spontaneously. However, the little child with an undescended testicle is often the subject of ridicule and may develop feelings of inferiority. Since normal location of the testicle assures fewer possible complications, it is best that orchiopexy be done before school age. Results of treatment are usually good.

Renal disturbances
Infections of the urinary tract

Whenever a significant number of bacteria (colony counts above 100,000 per milliliter) are found in a urine specimen, one knows that a significant infection of the urinary tract is present. Urinary tract infections are always considered serious and are often difficult to eradicate. Such infections are thought to rank second in frequency only to infections of the respiratory tract.

Ascending infection via the urethra and lower urinary tract is by far the most common way in which urinary tract infections occur. Other routes of infection are the bloodstream and lymphatics. A wide variety of organisms may produce urinary tract infection, but the colon bacilli are responsible for the majority of infections. Repeated infections necessitate a complete evaluation of the urinary tract. An intravenous urogram and a voiding cystourethrogram are necessary to assess renal impairment and the presence of reflux.

Reflux

The incidence of reflux (regurgitation of urine from the bladder into the ureter) detected by cystourethrography during investigation of persistent lower urinary tract infection is significant. It is thought that inflammatory changes in the bladder caused by infection may render the junction of the ureters and bladder temporarily incompetent. Most of these children do well when they receive intensive and specific antimicrobial therapy. There is no progression of renal damage, and reflux frequently disappears.

The diagnosis of primary reflux is considered if infection and reflux persists with renal impairment. Primary reflux seems to be most common in girls with congenitally deficient ureterobladder junction mechanisms. An extensive evaluation of the lower urinary tract reveals an increased reflux but a normal urethra and no significant residual urine or bladder abnormalities. If children with primary reflux continually harbor infection while on medication, have persistent recurrence of infection after adequate medical management, or show evidence of continuous renal impairment, they usually require surgical intervention to eliminate reflux and prevent progressive renal damage. The defect is then corrected by reimplanting the ureter into the bladder.

Nursing care. The general postoperative care of this patient is much the same as any surgical patient. The nurse should recognize the importance of changing surgical dressings that have become saturated with urine. Urine is an excellent medium for the growth of bacteria. However, she should be aware that some surgical drains may be purposely attached to the dressings and special care is therefore required. Some physicians wish to change the dressings themselves for this reason. Drainage tubes must be carefully checked for patency. These postoperative patients may return to the nursing area with as many as five urinary catheters, depending on the extent of the surgery (two nephrostomy tubes inserted into the left and right flanks, draining each kidney pelvis, one suprapubic cystotomy tube that empties the bladder of any urine not drained via the nephrostomy tubes, and two ureteral catheters acting as splints for the newly implanted ureters). Drainage from each of the tubes present should be closely observed and recorded separately. These catheters are never clamped. When the patient is able to be up in a wheelchair the catheters should be arranged so that they do not kink. The collection bottles must hang below the level of the kidneys, draining freely. Water intake is always encouraged and recorded, particularly in young children who quickly dehydrate. Dehydration promotes the growth of bacteria.

Pain is commonly associated with this type of surgery. Narcotics should be given as ordered on time! Antispasmodic drugs such as propantheline bromide (Pro-Banthine) or methantheline bromide (Banthine bromide) are also ordered. These drugs usually relieve the immediate postoperative colicky pain.

Reflux associated with renal involvement may also be caused by lower tract congenital obstructions. Unless the obstruction is corrected by reconstructive surgery when indicated, pyelonephritis may progress, leading to severe renal impairment.

Pyelonephritis

Pyelonephritis is an infectious process involving the renal pelvis and the working units of the kidney, the nephrons. Infection of the ureter and bladder often coexists. Pyelonephritis is recurrent in nature and characterized by repetitive exacerbations of one underlying and continuous infection.

Etiology. Ascending infection is the usual cause of pyelonephritis.

Some type of obstructive process may be the causative factor. Infection itself frequently causes inflammation, which leads to scarring and obstruction. Obstruction leads to urinary stasis and persistent infection. Thus infection and obstruction may both assist in perpetuating a chronic infection that proceeds to progressive renal destruction.

Incidence. Pyelonephritis is the most common renal disease of childhood. Because of the relatively short female urethra and the ease with which fecal contamination of the urethral orifice may occur, girls are affected at least ten times more frequently than boys. In the obstruction group, boys are affected two times more frequently than girls and usually present symptoms before 3 years of age.

Clinical symptoms. Symptomatology varies considerably in pyelonephritis. In children under 3 years of age the onset is likely to be abrupt and severe, accompanied by a high temperature, which may reach 104° F. Pallor, anorexia, vomiting, diarrhea, and convulsions may occur. These *acute* symptoms usually disappear in a few days even without treatment.

Older children complain of localized discomfort. Sharp or dull pain in the flank or abdominal tenderness is described. Bladder symptoms such as frequent, urgent, and burning urination are also common complaints. In addition to these problems, chills and fever may be present. Some children demonstrate little or no fever, and symptoms suggestive of pyelonephritis may be almost totally lacking.

In either case, failure to recognize that infection persists allows the slow, but ultimate, destruction of renal substance.

Chronic pyelonephritis occurs over a long period and progresses slowly over many years. As the result of continuous low-grade infection, the patient with pyelonephritis characteristically has a history of recurrent bouts of nonspecific symptoms such as nausea, vomiting, diarrhea, fever, irritability, headache, and transitory urinary abnormalities. Poor general health, anemia, failure to grow, or failure to thrive are typical findings. The child may appear very pale or pasty looking. His tongue is coated or furred. This condition suggests the late stages of renal damage and the development of uremia. Hypertension frequently appears as the end result of advanced renal scarring and vascular impairment and often accounts for subsequent cerebral hemorrhage or cardiac failure. In other cases, hydronephrosis, with its attending functional impairment, is the end result of obstruction.

Treatment. Urinalysis of a properly collected specimen is the key to successful treatment. Therapy depends primarily on identification of the causative organism and detection and correction of any urinary abnormality. A carefully collected specimen is essential. The genitalia should be washed, rinsed, and then sponged with a 1:1,000 benzalkonium chloride (Zephiran) solution, and dried with a sterile pad.

A clean, midstream voided specimen is

collected and promptly sent to the laboratory for culture and sensitivity studies. If it is impossible to obtain a specimen by such means, a catheterized specimen may be ordered. Prompt therapy is indicated. Sulfonamides or broad-spectrum antibiotics are administered until the laboratory studies are complete. Specific medications are then ordered and continued until at least two consecutive urine cultures are sterile.

The little patient should be placed in bed in a cool, quiet environment until his fever has subsided. A cool sponge or alcohol bath may also be ordered. Fluids are encouraged to ensure adequate hydration and a good urine output. An accurate account of the fluid intake and urinary output is essential. Although it is not necessary to insert a catheter for accurate output, a check mark is not sufficient for the information needed. An estimation of the amount of diaper saturation is far more valuable. After removing the diaper, the nurse should wash the child's genitalia with diluted pHisoHex solution before applying the clean diaper. This will prevent further contamination and also protect the skin from becoming irritated and excoriated.

An adequate diet is very important, and every attempt should be made to give the child food that he is able to eat and will eat. A good milk intake will supply the needed protein, carbohydrate, fat, and, most of all, water. Encourage the parents to visit during feeding time. Parents are best able to understand the sick child's desires, and usually the child is more likely to eat for Mom. Daily weighing, blood pressure determination, and checking of vital signs offer the wise observer valuable clues in the early detection of complications.

Prognosis. When the disease is recognized early and treated properly (long-term antibiotic therapy for infection or surgical removal of obstructions), the prognosis is excellent. Chronic infections present a much more serious and difficult problem because severe renal damage is the ultimate result.

Glomerulonephritis (nephritis, or Bright's disease)

Glomerulonephritis is a bilateral inflammatory disease of the glomeruli. It is characterized by the abrupt appearance of brown or smoky urine 1 to 3 weeks after an acute streptococcal infection. The usual clinical manifestations include a mild degree of edema, urinary abnormalities (hematuria, proteinuria, and casts), and varying degrees of hypertension.

Etiology. Glomerulonephritis is almost always associated with a poststreptococcal infection. It is believed to be the result of an antigen-antibody reaction, secondary to such infections as scarlet fever, tonsillitis and pharyngitis, otitis media, and pneumonia. Isolation of the group A beta-streptococcal organism during the initial infection or a high antistreptolysin O titer in the blood (in response to the previous presence of streptococcal organisms in the body) confirms the diagnosis.

Incidence. Glomerulonephritis is common in children, especially between 5 to 10 years of age. It seems to be more common in boys than girls and is most frequently observed in the late winter months or early spring. This seasonal pattern is related to the peak incidence of upper respiratory streptococcal infections.

Classification and symptoms. Acute glomerulonephritis is not always recognized because clinical signs and symptoms vary greatly. Microscopic hematuria and proteinuria may be the only signs, or gross hematuria and proteinuria, edema, periorbital puffiness, hypertension, weakness, pallor, anorexia, headache, nausea, and vomiting may be present. Rarely, there is a sudden onset with severe symptoms followed by dysfunction of the brain because of hypertension.

Subacute glomerulonephritis. Subacute glomerulonephritis sometimes follows the acute condition and is characterized by a progressive downhill course, which may be complicated by the nephrotic syndrome. Death may occur from renal insufficiency or cardiac failure. A few children with very severe cases have been known to recover completely.

Chronic glomerulonephritis. Chronic glomerulonephritis is ultimately a fatal disease (unless renal transplants are received) characterized by a progressive decrease in renal function. This condition usually appears insidiously and may or may not be the sequela to acute glomerulonephritis.

Treatment and nursing care. Necessary bed rest is usually welcomed by the child during the acute phase of the disease. Activities may be resumed as soon as gross hematuria has cleared and signs of edema, hypertension, and other urinary abnormalities have subsided.

The child should be separated from other children who have infections (especially upper respiratory), but complete isolation is not indicated. He should be observed closely for any recurrences of upper respiratory infection, since exacerbations can occur with new strains of streptococcal organisms. However, reinfection by the same nephritogenic strain is generally not possible by virtue of type-specific immunity after infection. Antibiotic therapy is indicated when evidence of infection is present. Prophylactic use of penicillin in the prevention of recurrence is generally not recommended.

A regular diet without added salt is offered to the child whose case is uncomplicated. Fluids are allowed as desired but are not forced. Careful observation of the color and volume of urine serves as a valuable guide in controlling fluid balance. Measurement of fluid intake, urinary output, and daily weight aids in the recognition of early signs of edema.

Temperature and pulse and respiration rate are checked frequently. Blood pressure should be checked often with the proper size sphygmomanometer. The cuff should cover two thirds of the upper arm and should be applied smoothly. Changes in mental status such as drowsiness, lethargy, double vision, muscular twitching, and convulsions should be reported at once. Complications can be discovered early when the observant nurse is aware of the clues that indicate that all is not well.

Complications

Hypertensive encephalopathy. Hypertensive encephalopathy is characterized by irritability, headache, vomiting, and blurred or double vision. Convulsions may also occur. The rise in blood pressure is almost always accompanied by a drop in pulse rate. This complication is caused by lack of proper blood supply to the brain, resulting from vasospasm. It usually responds to antihypertensive drug therapy.

Cardiac decompensation. Cardiac decompensation occurs as a result of severe hypertension. Evidences of cardiac involvement include tachycardia, arrhythmia, rapid, difficult breathing, heart enlargement, and renal impairment. When this occurs, salt and fluids are restricted. Treatment is primarily geared to control hypertension and give symptomatic relief of discomfort. Measures include rest in the orthopneic position, administration of oxygen, and sedation. Digitalization is not necessary when hypertension responds to drug therapy. Cardiac involvement is greatly decreased when hypertension is adequately controlled.

Severe renal failure. Severe renal failure is uncommon in children, although urine production may, at times, become scanty or absent. Usually this acute situation is transitory and reversible. When an imbalance of fluids and electrolytes persists, peritoneal dialysis or use of the artificial kidney is needed to control the uremia.

Prognosis. Acute glomerulonephritis is usually a self-limiting condition, and most children recover completely. A few children present a more complex entity with persistent urinary abnormalities and hypertension, which ultimately results in chronic nephritis and death.

Nephrosis

Nephrosis is a chronic, intermittent renal condition characterized by anasarca (marked generalized edema), heavy proteinuria, low serum albumin levels, and

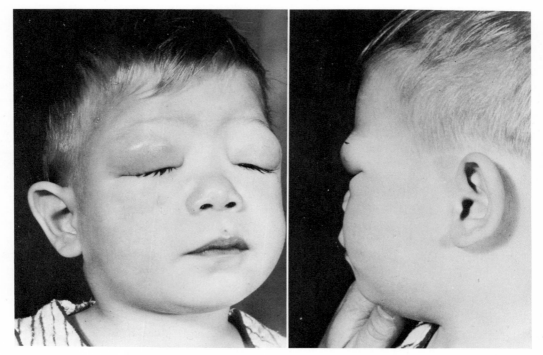

Fig. 40-3. A 2-year-old child with nephrosis. Progressive periorbital edema. (Courtesy U. S. Naval Hospital, San Diego, Calif.)

high serum cholesterol values. Elevated blood pressure and hematuria are not typical of the disease.

Etiology. The cause of nephrosis is unknown. Remissions are frequent, and the long course of the disease is aggravated by acute infections.

Incidence. Nephrosis seems to be more common in boys than in girls and occurs most frequently between 2 and 6 years of age. About 7 children out of every 100,000 present the nephrotic syndrome.

Clinical symptoms. The onset of nephrosis is insidious. Periorbital puffiness may be noted first, and it progresses steadily until the eyes are closed (Fig. 40-3). As the edema increases, the arms, legs, and abdomen reach massive proportions. At the peak of the edema, the little child weighs almost twice as much as usual (Fig. 40-4). Anorexia and varying degrees of diarrhea are commonly found. Discomfort from massive edema causes the child to be irritable

and easily fatigued. Often these children are malnourished. When the edema recedes, their spindly extremities and swollen abdomens are clearly seen.

Complications. The nephrotic child is vulnerable to infections, probably because of loss of gamma globulin in the urine (proteinuria). Bacteremia associated with peritonitis is not uncommon. Upper respiratory infections are very dangerous, especially those caused by pneumococci. The severity of these infections should not be underestimated, since when a child with nephrosis dies, it is commonly because his condition was complicated by infection.

Treatment and nursing care. The goal of treatment is a child as nearly normal as possible, judged by both clinical well-being and laboratory findings. The aims of nursing care include comforting the little patient during the distresses of massive edema, maintenance of good nutrition, and prevention of intercurrent infections.

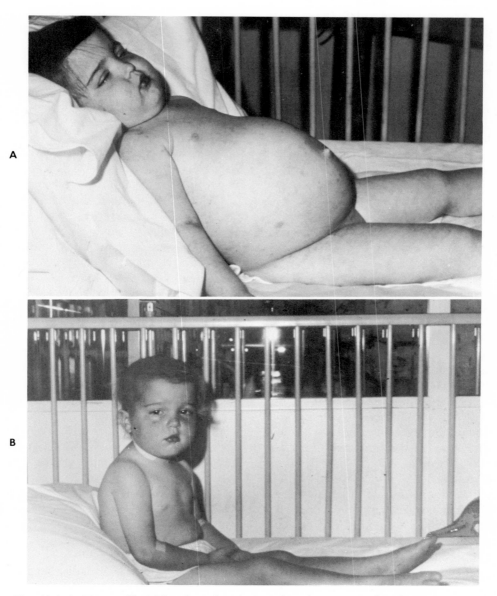

FIG. 40-4. A 2½-year-old child with nephrosis. A, Before therapy. B, After therapy. (Courtesy U. S. Naval Hospital, San Diego, Calif.)

The majority of children with nephrosis respond remarkably well to steroid therapy. Large doses of prednisone, given four times daily, usually stimulate diuresis, which occurs from 10 to 14 days after the initial dose. Recently a program of prednisone therapy given on alternating days has been found extremely useful in minimizing the toxic side effects of the drug. Twice the total daily dose is administered as a single morning dose, given every other day. Most studies indicate that this schedule appears to sustain desirable anti-inflammatory action and diminishes undesirable side effects. When diuresis occurs, usually other measurable abnormalities improve. Proteinuria may disappear, and the blood serum appears closer to normal. During remission, steroid therapy is gradually reduced until it can be eliminated completely.

Intermittent steroid treatment, based on proteinuria, is continued during the course of the disease, which sometimes involves several years. Relapses of nephrosis are often associated with intercurrent infections, especially those involving the respiratory and urinary tracts. Immediate intensive antibiotic therapy is mandatory if infection arises. A significant number of upper urinary tract infections have been found in steroid-resistant children. Bacteria in the urinary tract are thought to destroy the steroids and their therapeutic effects, which concentrate around localized areas of infection. It has been noted that when urinary tract infection is recognized early and treated vigorously, steroid resistance disappears, the nephrosis begins to subside, and the patient rapidly enters remission.

In selecting a hospital room for the nephrotic child the nurse must remember his increased susceptibility to infection. The room should be free from drafts. Placing the child in a double room with another child the same age who has nephrosis is most desirable.

Weighing the child on admission and each morning thereafter is one way of evaluating the amount of edema present. If massive edema is present, the little child's self concept is likely to be greatly distorted. It is important for his parents to be reassured and to be given whatever information is necessary about the condition and its outcome so that they in turn can reassure their child. They should particularly realize the seriousness of the disorder, even though today the prognosis is better than ever before.

Massive edema is most uncomfortable. The skin is stretched thin and easily broken. Keeping the child's body dry and clean will help avoid skin infections. Application of powder between skin surfaces and in skin folds is soothing and protective.

If the child is not toilet trained, the nurse must take great care to prevent excoriation of the buttocks and genitalia. Medicines are given orally or intravenously but never by the intramuscular or subcutaneous route. Great care must be taken to protect the edematous skin from injury and subsequent secondary infection. Usually the child is most comfortable in a semi-Fowler's position because of the reduction of respiratory embarrassment. This position may also reduce periorbital edema.

Maintenance of good nutrition is essential because beneath the edema exists a thin, poorly nourished body. Nowadays most physicians have greatly liberalized the diet offered these patients. The child should be given a well-balanced diet, normal for his age. Especially salty foods should be avoided (potato chips, pickles). High-protein diets do not elevate the low serum protein level, and water restriction is likely to cause more misery than benefit. Liberalizing the diet and allowing the child some choice will encourage his appetite and help prevent severe nutritional depletion, which readily occurs.

An accurate account of fluid intake is very important when the output is scanty. Although the nurse may not be able to measure the exact output, she must record approximate amounts each time the child voids.

Bed rest does not offer any particular benefit, so the child may be allowed to ambulate. During the active phase of the disease the child is usually sluggish and therefore satisfied to be resting most of the time. When massive edema is present, the child is content to rest all the time. In general, the nurse may permit the child to do whatever he feels like doing.

When the child is not hospitalized during periods of remission, attention is directed toward avoiding groups of people. During periods of high incidence of respiratory infection within the community the child should not be allowed to go to school. Rather the home teacher should be called. Missing a few days of school is much preferred to an acute exacerbation and hospitalization. Any sign of intercurrent infection must be reported to the physician and treated immediately. Some physicians would rather overtreat than risk the little child's life to this most common cause of death.

Prognosis. By controlling infection, antibiotic therapy has greatly reduced the death rate of nephrotic patients. About 80% of the children respond to steroid therapy. Eventually, after many years of intermittent treatment, these children usually fully enjoy healthful living.

Wilms' tumor

Wilms' tumor is one of the most common abdominal neoplasms of childhood. It is a congenital, mixed renal tumor, which develops from abnormal embryonic tissue; it rarely occurs bilaterally. Composed of connective tissue, muscle, blood vessels, glands, and lymphatics, the tumor grows within the renal capsule. Although it distorts the kidney in a bizarre manner, the tumor usually does not invade the renal substance until late in the disease. It grows forward and downward and may occupy as much as half the abdominal cavity. Unfortunately, the tumor often invades the renal veins and metastasizes through the bloodstream to vital organs, especially the lungs.

Etiology. Like other forms of cancer, the exact cause of Wilms' tumor is unknown.

Incidence. Wilms' tumor accounts for approximately 10% of all cancer in children. Boys and girls are equally affected. About two thirds of all children with Wilms' tumor are diagnosed before 3 years of age. The tumor may be present at birth and is rare after 7 years of age.

Clinical features. The initial manifestation of Wilms' tumor is a mass in the region of the kidney that is often discovered accidently during a routine examination or in the course of daily care. As the tumor grows, the little child's abdomen becomes very large. Pressure symptoms soon arise. Constipation, vomiting, abdominal distention, and even dyspnea may occur. Weight loss, pallor, and anemia are common in the late stages. Pain, hematuria, and hypertension are not common but if present, usually indicate an advanced stage with a grave prognosis.

Treatment and nursing care. When Wilms' tumor is suspected, both the mother and nurse must be careful not to feel or touch the child's abdomen because handling might favor metastasis. Diagnosis is usually confirmed by intravenous pyelography. Occasionally retrograde pyelography and renal arteriography are necessary for differential diagnosis. Treatment consists of prompt surgical removal of the involved kidney. Dissemination of tumor cells sometimes occurs during the operation. Dactinomycin and x-ray therapy are effective against the malignant cells. They may be used preoperatively to reduce the size of the kidney and tumor, rendering removal of the mass easier. Both are administered postoperatively to prevent metastasis. Dactinomycin is given intravenously during surgery, and x-ray therapy may be started before the child awakens from anesthesia. Dactinomycin sensitizes the child to x-ray therapy; therefore the dosage of radiation is decreased considerably when combined with systemic dactinomycin. This course of treatment is continued intermittently over a 2-year period.

The kidney and perirenal fat are removed through a transabdominal approach. Blood transfusions are often given because of blood loss during the surgical procedure and to correct preexisting anemia. Intravenous fluids are continued for 24 hours. When the child returns to the ward, he usually assumes a position of comfort. If bleeding occurs, it can easily be detected when pulse, respirations, blood pressure, and the child's color are checked often. The dressings should be changed only if necessary, since there is little or no drainage from the incision.

Toxic symptoms from administration of dactinomycin and x-ray therapy may cause more discomfort than does the surgical procedure. Nausea and vomiting, anorexia, malaise, and diarrhea may occur. Loss of hair, exfoliation of the skin, and ulceration of the tongue are potential toxic side effects of dactinomycin. When side effects occur, the drug is temporarily discontinued. During the interval between medication and x-ray therapy, the child's hair usually grows back.

Complications. The most serious major complicating factor in Wilms' tumor is metastasis. Characteristically, Wilms' tumor metastasizes through the bloodstream to the liver, lungs, brain, and other vital organs. The tumor may also spread by direct extension or by the lymphatics.

Prognosis. The prognosis without treatment is always fatal. When the tumor is discovered early, especially before the second year, the prognosis is very good. Surgical excision plus dactinomycin and x-ray therapy offer a chance of cure to children with localized disease. Follow-up care includes x-ray examination of the lungs monthly for the first 6 months, every 2 months for the next 6 months, and quarterly for the next year. As the child progresses favorably, an annual examination is sufficient.

Enuresis

Enuresis may be defined as involuntary voiding of urine, especially at night (nocturnal enuresis), after 4 years of age. Children with enuresis usually have a normal urinary stream and good daytime bladder control. Enuresis may be primary or acquired. When bladder control has never been achieved, enuresis is said to be primary. If enuresis occurs after control has been achieved for at least 1 year, it is said to be acquired.

About 15% of pediatric patients are evaluated because of this disturbance. Enuresis is very common in childhood, and the condition is more prevalent in boys than in girls.

The exact cause of enuresis in most children is unknown. Psychological or developmental disorders are found in many patients, but enuresis may also be caused by an anatomical defect or a systemic disease. The most significant step toward solving the problem is an attempt to find the correct cause. Before a psychological explanation is sought, anatomical abnormalities and organic disease must be ruled out.

Generally, daytime wetting (diurnal enuresis) and other urological symptoms are associated with organic disease. Diabetes mellitus, urinary tract infection, urinary tract anomalies, neurological defects, and obstructions such as meatal stenosis are often responsible for the condition. Psychological problems account for the remainder. Improper toilet training, an unhappy environment, a poor mother-child relationship, immaturity associated with other infantile habits, and developmental disturbances, such as jealousy and insecurity, are some psychological causes of enuresis. Whatever the cause, the correction of enuresis is very important to both the child and his parents. For the child it enables him to develop normally and to be like his little friends, and for the parents, correction means peace of mind and a healthy child.

Every enuretic patient should have a careful medical history and physical examination performed to determine if renal enlargements, a distended bladder, a constriction of the external urinary meatus, or a neurological change is present. A very careful urinalysis is essential. Often intravenous urography, cystography, and cystoscopy are necessary to diagnose organic causes, since history and physical examination may be entirely within normal limits.

In the past, medications to reduce the depth of sleep, dextroamphetamine sulfate (Dexedrine), anticholinergic drugs, belladonna, and methantheline bromide, (to reduce the tone of the detrussor muscle) were widely used without significant success. More recently, imipramine hydrochloride (Tofranil) has been found to completely control the condition in a very high percentage of patients. This drug, however, has some potential toxic manifestations that have made some physicians reluctant to prescribe it. Thus a physician must carefully evaluate the problem before ordering imipramine hydrochloride and, if he believes it is indicated, the child must be carefully watched for side effects. Facial tics have been reported.

A condition often confused with enuresis is an ectopic ureter in a female in which the ureter empties into the vagina or urethra beyond the sphincter. These children may void normally (from their normal ureters and bladder) but are always wet from constant drainage from the ectopic ureter. Proper surgery will correct this problem.

Enuresis may also diminish through the use of fairly simple techniques. Giving less fluids in the evening may be helpful to some children. Waking the child and taking him to the toilet during the night saves embarrassment to the school-age child. Parents should not threaten or punish their children because they wet the bed. This only increases the child's sense of inferiority and failure and may even deter his will to improve. Instead, every effort should be made to assure the child that he can overcome his condition if he really wants to. Encouragement comes in the form of rewards, for example, being able to go camping or sleep overnight at grandmother's house. Such rewards, together with the child's desire to stay dry, can achieve positive results. Enuretic children without any organic disease or severe psychological problem usually gradually overcome the condition.

UNIT XI

SUGGESTED SELECTED READINGS
AND REFERENCES

Al-Rashid, R. A., and Call, J. E.: Hyperuricemia complicating acute leukemia, Clin. Pediat. 9: 203-205, 1970.

Argamaso, R. V., and Argamaso, C. A.: Topical sulfamylon—current adjunct in burn therapy, Bedside Nurse 4:22-25, Jan., 1971.

Baker, G. L.: Management of neonatal bacterial infections, Clin. Pediat. 8:575-579, 1969.

Baltzan, R. B.: Glomerulonephritis, Canad. Nurse 62:45-47, Aug., 1966.

Barnett, H. L.: Pediatrics, ed. 14, New York, 1968, Appleton-Century-Crofts.

Blake, F., Wright, F. H., and Waechter, E. H.: Nursing care of children, ed. 8, Philadelphia, 1970, J. B. Lippincott Co.

Blame, K. B.: Halo traction, Amer. J. Nurs. 69: 1933-1937, Sept., 1969.

Boegli, E. H., and Steele, M. S.: Scoliosis: spinal instrumentation and fusion, Amer. J. Nurs. 68: 2399-2403, Nov., 1968.

Bonine, G. N.: The myel   plastic child: Hospital and home care, An   J. Nurs. 69:541-544, March, 1969.

Bray, P. F.: Neurology in pediatrics, Chicago, 1969, Year Book Medical Publishers, Inc.

Brewer, E. J.: Juvenile rheumatoid arthritis, vol. 6 in series Major problems in clinical pediatrics, Philadelphia, 1970, W. B. Saunders Co.

Broadribb, V.: Foundations in pediatric nursing, Philadelphia, 1967, J. B. Lippincott Co.

Brodie, B., and Von Haam, J.: Children born with adrenogenital syndrome, Amer. J. Nurs. 67: 1018-1021, May, 1967.

Burgess, L.: Morale boosting in cystic fibrosis, Amer. J. Nurs. 69:322-324, Feb., 1969.

Burgess, R. E.: Fluids and electrolytes, Amer. J. Nurs. 65:90-95, Oct., 1965.

Coates, F., and Fabry, K.: An insulin injection technique for preventing skin reactions, Amer. J. Nurs. 65:127, Feb., 1965.

Colella, R. F. A.: Dental care, Pediat. Clin. N. Amer. 15:325-335, 1968.

Cooke, R. E., editor: The biological basis of pediatric practice, Philadelphia, 1969, W. B. Saunders Co.

Culp, O. S.: Hypospadias and related problems. In Askin, J. A., Cooke, R. E., and Haller, J. A., editors: A symposium on the child, Baltimore, 1967, Johns Hopkins Press, pp. 189-208.

Daeschner, C. W.: Antimicrobial therapy for urinary tract infections, Pediat. Clin. N. Amer. 15: 251-260, 1968.

Daniel, W. A.: The adolescent patient, St. Louis, 1970, The C. V. Mosby Co.

DeMaggio, G. T.: The child with asthma, Nurs. Clin. N. Amer. 3:453-461, Sept., 1968.

Dison, N.: A mother's view of tonsillectomy, Amer. J. Nurs. 69:1024-1027, May, 1969.

Egan, M. C.: Combating malnutrition through maternal and child health programs, Children 16:67-71, March-April, 1969.

Friedrich, H.: Common sense in intramuscular injections, Nurs. Clin. N. Amer. 1:33-35, June, 1966.

Froehlich, L.: Care of the infant with exstrophy of the bladder, Nurs. Clin. N. Amer. 2:573, Sept., 1967.

Geis, D. P., and Lambertz, S. E.: Acute respiratory infections in young children, Amer. J. Nurs. 68:294-297, Feb., 1968.

Gellis, S. S., and Kagan, B. M.: Current pediatric therapy, ed. 4, Philadelphia, 1970, W. B. Saunders Co.

Gillon, J.: Continuity in nursing care of cardiac infants, Nurs. Clin. N. Amer. 4:19, March, 1969.

Green, M., and Haggerty, R. J.: Ambulatory pediatrics, Philadelphia, 1968, W. B. Saunders Co.

Gustafson, S., and Coursin, D. B., editors: The pediatric patient, Philadelphia, 1969, J. B. Lippincott Co.

Hardy, J. B.: Rubella and its aftermath, Children 16:91-96, May-June, 1969.

Harrow, B. R.: Ureteral reflux in children, Clin. Pediat. 6:83-93, 1967.

Henley, N. L.: Sulfamylon for burns, Amer. J. Nurs. 69:2122-2123, Oct., 1969.

Hill, M. L., Shurtleff, D. B., Chapman, W. H., and Ansell, J. S.: The myelodysplastic child: Bowel and bladder control, Amer. J. Nurs. 69:545-550, March, 1969.

Hughes, J. G.: Synopsis of pediatrics, St. Louis, 1967, The C. V. Mosby Co.

Hughes, W. T.: Pediatric procedures, Philadelphia, 1965, W. B. Saunders Co.

Hutto, R. B.: Poverty's children, Amer. J. Nurs. 69:2166-2169, Oct., 1969.

Jackson, R. L.: The child with diabetes, Nutrition Today 6:2-9, March-April, 1971.

Johnson, M., Johnson, E., and Fossett, B. H.: Bronchopulmonary hygiene in cystic fibrosis, Amer. J. Nurs. 69:32-34, Feb., 1969.

Jordon, T.: The family aspects of physical disability in children, Child and Family, 78-89, Summer, 1965.

Knox, L. L., and McConnell, F.: Helping parents to help deaf infants, Children 15:183, Sept.-Oct., 1968.

Krugman, S.: Present status of measles and rubella immunization in the U. S., J. Pediat. 78:1-16, 1971.

Kunn, C.: The tetracyclines, Pediat. Clin. N. Amer. 15:43-55, 1968.

Larson, C. B., and Gould, M.: Orthopedic nursing, ed. 7, St. Louis, 1970, The C. V. Mosby Co.

Larson, D., and Gaston, R.: Current trends in the care of burned patients, Amer. J. Nurs. 67:319-327, Feb., 1967.

Latham, L. C., and Heckel, R. V.: Pediatric nursing, St. Louis, 1967, The C. V. Mosby Co.

Leifer, G.: Principles and techniques in pediatric nursing, Philadelphia, 1965, W. B. Saunders Co.

Lunceford, J. L.: Leukemia, Nurs. Clin. N. Amer. 2:635-647, Dec., 1967.

Mansman, H. C., Jr.: Management of the child with bronchial asthma, Pediat. Clin. N. Amer. 15:357-385, May, 1968.

Mantenffel, S., and Berkich, E., Jr.: The burn patient, management and operating room support, Somerville, N. J., 1969, Ethicon, Inc.

Margolius, F.: Burned children, infection and nursing care, Nurs. Clin. N. Amer. 5:131-142, March, 1970.

Marlow, D. R.: Textbook of pediatric nursing, ed. 3, Philadelphia, 1969, W. B. Saunders Co.

Mash, J. B., and Dickens, M.: Armstrong and Browder's nursing care of children, ed. 3, Philadelphia, 1970, F. A. Davis Co.

Mathies, A. W., and Wehrle, P. F.: Management of bacterial meningitis in children, Pediat. Clin. N. Amer. 15:185-195, 1968.

McCrary, W. W., and Shibuya, M.: Poststreptococcal glomerulonephritis in children, Pediat. Clin. N. Amer. 11:633-647, 1964.

Matheny, N. M., and Snively, W. D.: Fluid balance, Philadelphia, 1967, J. B. Lippincott Co.

Mohammed, M. R. B.: Urinalysis, Amer. J. Nurs. 64:87-89, June, 1964.

Mohney, S.: Juvenile diabetes, helping Linda live with it, RN 33:50-55, Nov., 1970.

Moore, M. L.: Diabetes in children, Amer. J. Nurs. 67:104, Feb., 1967.

Moore, M. V.: Diagnosis deafness, Amer. J. Nurs. 69:297-300, Feb., 1969.

Myer, H. L.: Predictable problems of hospitalized adolescents, Amer. J. Nurs. 69:525-528, March, 1969.

National Advisory Cancer Council: Progress against cancer, Washington, D. C., 1969, U. S. Department of Health, Education, and Welfare.

Noonan, J., and Noonan, L.: Two burned patients on flotation therapy, Amer. J. Nurs. 68:316, Feb., 1968.

Pidgeon, V.: The infant with congenital heart disease, Amer. J. Nurs. 67:290, Feb., 1967.

Quesenbury, J. H.: Observations and care for patients with head injuries, Nurs. Clin. N. Amer. 4:237-247, June, 1969.

Raffensperger, J. G., and Primrose, R. B.: Pediatric surgery for nurses, Boston, 1968, Little, Brown & Co.

Ralph, M. D., Kuszaj, J., and Wirch, B.: Nursing care of the patient with cleft lip and palate, Nurs. Clin. N. Amer. 2:483, Sept., 1967.

Reeves, K.: Children's reactions to head injuries, Amer. J. Nurs. 70:108, Jan., 1970.

Richards, W., and Siegel, S. C.: Status asthmaticus, Pediat. Clin. N. Amer. 16:1-9, 1969.

Riley, H. D.: Pyelonephritis in infancy and childhood, Pediat. Clin. N. Amer. 11:731-755, 1964.

Rodman, T.: Management of tracheobronchial secretions, Amer. J. Nurs. 66:2474-2477, Nov., 1966.

Roose, J.: Interpretation of bedrest by doctors and nurses, Nurs. Research 12:111, Spring, 1963.

Ruben, M.: Balm for burned children, Amer. J. Nurs. 66:297-302, Feb., 1966.

Rubin, M. I.: Pyelonephritis: certain aspects, Pediat. Clin. N. Amer. 11:649-665, 1964.

Santora, D.: Preventing hospital-acquired urinary infection, Amer. J. Nurs. 66:790-794, April, 1966.

Sato, F. F.: New devices for continuous urine collection in pediatrics, Amer. J. Nurs. 69:804-805, April, 1969.

Schwartz, E.: The treatment of hemophilia, Pediat. Clin. N. Amer. 15:473-481, 1968.

Shaw, B. L.: Current therapy for burns, RN 34: 33-41, March, 1971.

Shirkey, H. C.: Pediatric therapy, ed. 3, St. Louis, 1968, The C. V. Mosby Co.

Sister Mary Claudia: TLC and sulfamylon for burned children, Amer. J. Nurs. 69:755-757, April, 1969.

Slobody, L. B., and Wasserman, E.: Survey of clinical pediatrics, ed. 5, New York, 1968, McGraw-Hill Book Co.

Smith, E. B.: The epidemiology of burns, Pediatrics Supplement 44:part II, 1969.

Sonnenschein, H., and Joos, H. A.: Observations on infection of the urinary tract and childhood nephrosis, Clin. Pediat. 9:419-421, 1970.

Soyka, L. F.: The nephrotic syndrome, Clin. Pediat. 6:77-82, 1967.

Stollerman, G. H.: Treatment and prevention of rheumatic fever and rheumatic heart disease, Pediat. Clin. N. Amer. 11:213, 1964.

Stone, N. H., and Boswick, J. A., editors: Profiles in burn management, Miami, 1969, Industrial Medicine Publishing Co., Inc.

Swendsen, L.: Nursing care of the infant with congestive heart failure, Nurs. Clin. N. Amer. 4:621-630, Dec., 1969.

Walsh, M. A., Ebner, M., and Casey, J. W.: Neobladder, Amer. J. Nurs. 63:107-110, April, 1963.

Watson, I.: Nursing care of patient with glomerulonephritis, Canad. Nurse 62:48-49, Aug., 1966.

Wesseling, E.: The adolescent facing amputation, Amer. J. Nurs. 65:90, Jan., 1965.

Whitmore, W. F.: Wilms' tumor and neuroblastoma, Amer. J. Nurs. 68:526-535, March, 1968.

Wood, M., Kenny, H. A., and Price, W. R.: Silver nitrate treatment of burns, Amer. J. Nurs. 66: 518, March, 1966.

Young, J. F.: Recognition, significance and recording of the signs of increased intracranial pressure, Nurs. Clin. N. Amer. 4:223-236, June, 1969.

Glossary

Key to pronunciation

ā	āte	à	sofà	ē	ēat	ī	"eye"	ō	ōh	ū	"you"
ă	ăs	ä	ärm	ĕ	bĕt	ĭ	ĭt	ŏ	nŏt	ŭ	bŭt
à	åh								

abduction (ăb-dŭk'shŭn) movement away from the midline.

abortion (à-bŏr'shŭn) termination of a pregnancy before viability; may be spontaneous or induced.

abrasion (ă-brā'zhŭn) loss of superficial tissue, skin, or mucous membrane because of friction.

abruptio (ăb-rŭp'shĭ-ō) a tearing away from.

abruptio placentae (plà-sĕn'tē) premature separation of a normally implanted placenta.

abstinence (ab'stĭ-nents) going without voluntarily; refraining from sexual intercourse.

acetabulum (ăs-ĕ-tăb'ŭ-lŭm) rounded cavity on the external surface of the innominate bone that receives the head of the femur.

acidosis (as-ĭ-dō'sis) abnormal increase in acidity of the blood and tissues.

acinus (ăs'ŭ-nŭs) (pl. acini) smallest division of a gland, often referring to the mammary glands.

adenoids (ăd'ĕ-noyds) grouping of lymphoid tissue located on the posterior wall of the nasopharynx (the pharyngeal tonsils).

adnexa (ăd-nĕx'à) accessory parts of a structure; uterine adnexa—oviducts and ovaries.

afebrile (ă-fĕb'rĭl) without fever.

afibrinogenemia (ă-fĭ-brĭn-ō-jĕ-nĕ'mĭ-à) lack of the protein fibrinogen in the blood, causing problems in coagulation.

aggregate (ăg'grĕ-gāt) total substances making up a mass.

airway normal passageway for respired air or a device used to prevent or correct respiratory obstruction.

albumin (ăl-bū'mĭn) one kind of protein.

albuminuria (ăl-bū-mĭ-nū'rĭ-à) presence of albumin in the urine.

alignment (ă-līn'ment) arranging in a line.

alkalosis (alke'lōsĭs) abnormal increase of alkalinity of the blood and tissues.

allergen (ăl'er-jĕn) any substance that produces an allergic response.

alveolus (ăl-vē'ō-lŭs) (pl. alve'oli) a little hollow or cavity; the air sac or cell of the lung tissue.

ambivalence (ăm-bĭv'à-lĕns) simultaneous feelings of atttraction and repulsion, love and hate for a person, object, or action.

amblyopia (ăm-blĭ-ō'pĭà) reduction or dimness of vision in one eye without apparent associated organic abnormality.

amenorrhea (ā-mĕn-ō-rē'à) absence of menstruation.

amnesic (ăm-nē'sĭk) capable of producing amnesia or loss of memory.

amniotic (ăm-nĭ-ŏt'ĭk) pertaining to the amnion, the innermost of the fetal membranes that secretes the fluid inside the bag of waters.

analgesic (ăn'ăl-jē'sĭk) capable of producing analgesia, or relief from pain.

ancillary (ăn'sĭ-ler-ē) subordinate or auxiliary.

android (ăn'droyd) manlike; adjective used to describe a male-type pelvis.

anemia (an-ē'mĭ-à) condition in which there is a reduction of hemoglobin in the blood.

anencephalus (ăn-ĕn-sĕf'à-lŭs) monstrosity characterized by the absence of a brain.

anesthetic (ăn'ĕs-thĕt'ĭk) capable of producing anesthesia, that is, complete or partial loss of feeling.

angiocardiography (ăn-jē-ō-cär-dē-ŏg'rà-fē) injection of contrast material into the circulation and observation of its flow by x-ray or fluoroscope.

anion (ă-nīen) particle of matter (ion) carrying a negative electrical charge.

ankylosis (ăn-kĭ-lō'sĭs) abnormal immobility and consolidation of a joint.

anorexia (ăn-à-rĕk'sĭ-à) loss of appetite.

anoxia (ăn-ŏk'sĭ-à) lack of oxygen.

antagonistic (ăn-tăg-ō-nĭs'tĭk) acting with antagonism, that is, in opposition to an agent or principle; counteracting; hostile.

antenatal (ăn-tē-nā'tàl) before birth; prenatal.

antepartal (ăn-tē-pär′tăl) before delivery.

anteroposterior (ăn′těr-ō-pŏs-těr′-ĭ-ěr) from front to back.

antibody (ăn′tĭ-bŏd-ĭ) protective protein substance formed by the body in the presence of pathogenic organisms or foreign materials.

antisepsis (ăn′tĭ-sěp′sĭs) literally "against infection or decay"; the use of procedures usually involving chemicals (antiseptics) that hinder the growth of microorganisms without necessarily destroying them.

antitoxin (ăn-tĭ-tŏk-sīn) protective protein formed by the body in response to the presence of a toxin; a preparation containing antibodies designed to produce passive immunization.

anuria (ăn-u′ri-à) failure of kidney function; lack of urine formation.

apnea (ăp′-nē-à) absence of respiration, temporary or permanent.

areola (à-rē′ō-là) (pl. areolae) ring of pigment on the breast surrounding the nipple.

arteriogram (är-tĭr′ĭ-ō-grăm) x-ray procedure that reveals arterial pathways injected with special contrast materials.

artery (är′ter-ē) blood vessel that carries blood away from the heart.

arthritis (ar-thrī′tis) inflammation of a joint, usually accompanied by pain and frequently by changes in structure.

arthrodesis (är-thrŏd′à-sĭs) surgical fusion of a joint performed to gain stability for weight bearing.

arthroplasty (är′thrō-plăs-tĭ) surgical formation or reconstruction of a joint.

asepsis (à-sěp′sĭs) literally "without infection or decay"; refers to the absence of living disease-producing microorganisms or to procedures that produce such an absence (see pp. 18 to 25 for discussion).

asphyxia (ăs-fik′sĭ-à) lack of oxygen and excessive carbon dioxide build-up in the body resulting from an abnormal gaseous environment or disease.

aspiration (ăs-pĭ-rā′-shun) process of drawing in or out as by suction.

assimilation (à-sĭm-ě-lā′shun) processes whereby the products of digestion change to resemble the chemical substances of the body tissues, first passing through the lacteals and blood vessels.

astrocytoma (as-trō-sī-tō′mà) tumor of the brain tissue.

ataxic (à-tăk′sĭk) pertaining to ataxia, or the incoordination of the voluntary muscles; one possible result of brain damage.

atelectasis (ăt-ě-lěk′tà-sĭs) lack of proper lung expansion.

athetoid (ăth′ě-toyd) pertaining to athetosis, or the presence of involuntary, purposeless weaving motions of the body, or its extremities; one possible result of brain damage.

atopic (à-tŏp′ĭk) pertaining to allergic responses, particularly those of a hereditary nature.

atrium (ā′trĭ-ŭm) (pl. atria) a cavity or sinus; one of two upper chambers of the heart.

attenuated (a-ten′ye-wātd) to make thin; to weaken or reduce in force.

attitude (ăt′ĭ-tūd) in speaking of fetal position, refers to the degree of flexion of the baby's head and extremities in the uterus.

aura (ŏ′rà) subjective warning of an impending epileptic seizure.

auscultation (aws-kŭl-tā′shŭn) process of listening for sounds produced in some body cavity.

autoclave (ŏ′-tō-clāv) appliance used to sterilize objects by steam under pressure.

autonomy (ŏ-tŏn′à-mē) state of self-government or self-direction.

bacillus (bà-sĭl′ŭs) (pl. bacilli) a rod-shaped bacterium.

barrier techniques various forms of isolation.

basophil (bā′sō-fĭl) one type of white blood cell.

bilirubin (bĭl-ĭ-rū′bĭn) orange or yellow pigment in bile; a product of red blood cell destruction; elevated levels in the blood may cause jaundice.

biopsy (bī′ŏp-sĭ) procurement of a specimen of tissue for microscopic examination.

booster injection substance or dose used to renew or increase the effect of a drug or immunizing agent.

bossing rounded protuberance, particularly on the skull, in the area of the forehead; one possible manifestation of rickets.

Braxton Hicks (brăx′tŏn hĭks) *contractions* contractions of the uterus that occur throughout pregnancy to help enlarge the uterus to accommodate the growing fetus; during the last weeks of pregnancy they may become very noticeable; false labor contractions.

breech (brēch) *birth* delivery of the child feet or buttocks first.

bronchiectasis (brŏn-kĭ-ěk′tà-sĭs) abnormal dilatation of the bronchi in response to inflammation, which may lead to structural changes and chronic cough.

buffer apparatus or substance serving to neutralize the shock of opposing forces.

bulbar (bŭl′bär) pertaining to the "bulb" or medulla of the brain and the cranial nerves.

calcaneus (kăl-kā′nē-ŭs) heel bone or os calcis; type of clubfoot in which only the heel touches the ground; patient may walk on inner side of heel.

callus (kăl′ŭs) new bone formation at the site of a healing fracture.

calyx (kā′lĭks) (pl. calyces) small subdivision of the pelvis of the kidney.

Candida albicans (kăn′dĭ-dà ăl′bĭ-kănz) formerly

649

called *Monilia albicans;* a yeastlike fungus that may infect various portions of the body, causing a variety of symptoms (e.g., leukorrhea, dermatitis, stomatitis).

cannula (kăn'ū-là) (pl. cannulae) small tube; large needle sheath used for the removal of fluid from body cavities.

canthus (kăn-thŭs) (pl. canthi) corner at each side of the eye where the eyelids meet.

caput succedaneum (kă'pŭt sŭk-sē-dā'nē-ŭm) abnormal collection of fluid under the scalp.

caries (kăr'ēz) dental decay.

carrier person or animal capable of transmitting a contagious disease though the person or animal shows no outward sign of the disease.

cast solid mold usually made of plaster to help protect, position, or immobilize a part; microscopic sediment that has been partially shaped by the kidney tubules; any other body discharge or excretion retaining the shape of a body part that held it.

catalyst (kăt'à-lĭst) substance that speeds the rate of a chemical reaction without itself being permanently altered by the reaction.

catamenia (kăt-à-mē'nĭà) menses or menstruation.

cataract (kăt'à-răkt) abnormal opacity of the crystalline lens of the eye.

cation (kat'ĭ-on) particle of matter (ion) carrying a positive electrical charge.

cecum (sē'kŭm) blind pouch that forms the first portion of the large intestine or colon; the attachment for the appendix.

celiac (sē'lē-ăk) *disease* chronic intestinal indigestion.

cellulitis (sĕl-ū-lī'tĭs) inflammation of the cellular or connective tissues.

cephalhematoma (sĕf-ăl-hē-mà-tō'mà) swelling on the head due to a collection of bloody fluid under the periosteum of the skull as the result of trauma.

cephalic (sĕ-făl'ĭk) pertaining to the head.

cephalocaudal (sĕf-à-lō-cŏd'ăl) moving from the head toward the base of the spine.

cerumen (sĕ-rū'mĕn) ear wax.

cervical (sĕr'vĭ-kàl) pertaining to the neck or cervix.

cesarean (sĕz-ăr'ē-ăn) *section* an abdominal delivery made possible by incising the uterine and abdominal walls.

Chadwick's (chăd'wĭks) *sign* violet tinge of the cervical and vaginal mucous membranes; a probable sign of pregnancy.

chancre (shăng'ker) craterlike lesion seen in first-stage syphilis.

Cheyne-Stokes (chān' stōks) *respiration* irregular, cyclic-type breathing characterized by a period of increasing respiratory action followed by an interval of apnea.

chloasma gravidarum (klō-ăz'mà grăv-ĭ-dā'rŭm) deepening pigmentation of skin during pregnancy, especially of the face; "mask of pregnancy."

chordée (kŏr-dē') abnormal downward curvature of the penis.

chorea (kō-rē'à) involuntary muscular twitching or movement.

choriocarcinoma (kō-rĭ-ō-kär-sĭ-nō'mà) rare malignancy associated with hydatid mole or pregnancy.

chorion (kō'rĭ-ŏn) outermost membrane of the growing fertilized egg; one of two membranes that later form the "bag of waters."

chorionic villi (vĭl'ī) fingerlike tissue projections of chorion on the outer wall of the fertilized egg.

chromosomes (krō'mà-sōm) microscopic structures seen fairly easily in the nucleus of a cell during its reproduction, which contain the genes or determiners of heredity.

cisternal (sĭs-tĕr'nàl) *puncture* puncture with a hollow needle between the cervical vertebrae, through the dura mater, into the cisterna at the base of the brain.

clavicle (klăv'ĭ-kàl) collarbone.

clitoris (klĭ'tŏr-ĭs) the small, sensitive erectile structure located at the anterior junction of the labia minora.

coagulation (ko-agyelā'shun) process of clotting.

coccus (kŏk'ŭs) (pl. cocci) spherical-shaped bacterium.

coitus (kō'ĭ-tŭs) sexual intercourse.

colic (kŏl'ĭk) intermittent pain caused by spasm of any hollow or tubular soft organ; abdominal cramping fairly common in first three months of infancy.

collagen (kŏl'à-jĕn) substance existing in many of the body's connective tissues.

collateral (ko-lăt'erel) situated at the sides; supplementary, reinforcing.

colostrum (kŏl-ŏs'trŭm) breast secretion produced by the mother the first few days after delivery.

colporrhaphy (kŏl-pŏr'à-fī) surgical repair of the walls of the vagina.

comatose (kō'mà-tōs) in a coma or abnormally deep sleep caused by illness or injury.

comedo (kŏm'ē-dō) (pl. comedones) discolored, dried, oily secretion plugging the pores of the skin; blackhead.

comminuted (kŏm'ĭ-nūt-ĕd) broken into many pieces; comminuted fracture, a crushed bone.

compatible able to work together; not in opposition; able to be mixed without destructive changes.

compression (kom'preshĕn) a squeezing together; state of being pressed together.

conception (kŏn-sĕp'shŭn) union of the male sex cell, spermatozoon, and the female sex cell, ovum; fertilization; beginning of a new being.

condyloma (kŏn-dī-lō'mà) wartlike growth usually found near the anus or vulva; the broad, flat form (c. latum) is characteristic of syphilis in its secondary stage.

congenital (kŏn-jĕn'ĭ-tȧl) existing at birth.

conjugate (kŏn'jū-gāt) an anteroposterior diameter of the pelvis.

conjunctiva (kŏn-jŭnk-tī'vȧ) mucous membrane that lines the inner surface of the eyelid and covers the anterior portion of the eye.

contaminated soiled, stained, touched or exposed in such a manner that the article in question becomes unsafe to use as intended or without barrier techniques.

contraception (kon-trȧ-sĕp'shun) prevention of the fertilization of an egg or ovum.

contracture (kon-trak'chur) permanent contraction of a muscle resulting from spasm or paralysis causing limitation of motion; high resistance to the passive stretch of a muscle.

contusion (kŏn-tū'zhŭn) injury that does not result in breaking the skin; a black and blue area; a bruise.

convulsion (kŏn-vŭl'-shŭn) violent, involuntary contraction or series of contractions of the muscles.

corium (kō'rĭ-ŭm) dermis layer of the skin; "true skin."

cor pulmonale (kōr pŭl-mŏn-ȧl'ē) cardiac enlargement or failure secondary to respiratory disease.

cortex (kōr'tĕks) outer or more superficial part of an organ.

coryza (kō-rī'zȧ) "common" head cold.

crepitus (krĕp'ĭ-tŭs) grating sensation sometimes heard or felt at the site of a fracture; crackling sound heard in certain diseases.

cretinism (krē'tĭn-ĭzm) infantile hypothyroidism characterized by mental retardation and other disturbances in mental and physical development.

crust an external protective layer; scab.

cryptorchidism (krĭpt-ŏr'kĭd-ĭzm) failure of the testicles to descend into the scrotum.

cul-de-sac of Douglas blind pouch formed by the peritoneal lining of the abdominal cavity located between the uterus and rectum.

curettage (ku-ret'aj) (uterine) scraping with a curette to remove contents of uterus (as in inevitable, incomplete, or early therapeutic abortion), to obtain specimens for use in diagnosis, or to remove growths (e.g., polyps).

cyanosis (sī-ȧn-ō'sĭs) bluish or grayish coloration of the skin caused by poor oxygenation of the blood.

cystitis (sĭs-tī'tĭs) inflammation of the urinary bladder.

cystocele (sĭs'tō-sēl) prolapse of the urinary bladder caused by the weakened tissue wall between the bladder and vagina.

cystourethrogram x-ray film of the bladder and urethra.

cytoplasm (sī'tō-plăz-ŭm) portion of a cell inside the cell membrane but outside the nucleus.

debilitate (dē-bĭl'ĭ-tāt) to produce weakness; enfeeble.

debridement (dā-brēd-mŏn') surgical removal of dead, damaged, or contaminated tissue.

debris (dĕ-brē) rubbish; ruins.

decalcification (dē-kăl-sĭ-fĭ-kā'shŭn) removal of or withdrawal of lime salts from bone.

deciduous (dē-sĭd'ū-ŭs) *teeth* baby or milk teeth.

decubitus (dē-kū'bĭ-tŭs) bedsore.

dehydration (dē-hī-drā'shŭn) condition in which the body tissues lack normal fluid content.

dentition (dĕn-tĭsh'ŭn) process or time of teething.

dermatitis (dĕr-mȧ-tī'tĭs) *venenata* skin disturbance caused by external irritants.

detrusor (dē-trū'sŏr) *muscle* smooth muscle of the bladder wall.

diaphoresis (dī-ȧ-fō-re'sĭs) profuse sweating.

diaphragmatic (dī-ȧ-frăg-măt'ĭk) *hernia* protrusion of abdominal contents through an abnormal opening in the diaphragm.

diaphysis (dī-ăf'ĭ-sĭs) shaft or middle part of a long bone.

diastolic (di-ăs-tol'ik) pertaining to diastole—the blood pressure at the time of greatest cardiac relaxation.

digestion (dĭ'jĕs'chĕn) process by which food is broken down mechanically and chemically in the gastrointestinal tract and converted into absorbable forms.

digital (dĭj'ĭ-tȧl) pertaining to the digits, that is, the fingers or toes.

digitalization (dĭj-ĭ-tăl-ĭ-za'shŭn) administration of digitalis to slow and strengthen the heartbeat (particularly the initial administration of the drug).

dilatation (dĭl-ȧ-tā'shŭn) expansion of an organ or orifice; dilation.

disorientation (dĭs-ō-rĭ-ĕn-tā'shŭn) inability to evaluate properly direction, location, time, surroundings, or personal role.

distal (dis'tal) farthest from the trunk of the body or from a specific point of reference.

distention (dĭs-tĕn'shŭn) (also distension) inflation, stretch, ballooning.

diuretic (dī-u-ret'ĭk) agent that increases the secretion of urine.

diverticulum (dī-ver-tĭk'ŭ-lŭm) (pl. diverticula) sac or pouch in the walls of a canal or organ, especially the colon.

ductus arteriosus (dŭk'tŭs är-tēr-ĭ-ō'sŭs) short blood vessel located between the pulmonary artery and aorta in the fetus.

ductus deferens (dŭk'tŭs dĕf'ĕr-ĕnz) excretory duct of the testicle; vas deferens.

dyscrasia (dĭs-krā'zhĭ-ȧ) undefined disease, malfunction, or abnormal condition, often used when speaking of abnormalities of the blood.

dysentery (dĭs'ĕn-tĕr-ē) inflammation of the intestines, especially of the colon, usually characterized by mild to severe diarrhea.

dysmenorrhea (dĭs-mĕn-ōr-ē'à) painful or difficult menstruation.

dyspnea (dĭsp-nē'à) difficult breathing.

dystocia (dĭs-tō'-shà) difficult labor, particularly difficulty in the mechanics of childbirth.

ecchymosis (ĕk-ĭ-mō'sĭs) black-and-blue mark caused by hemorrhage into the skin, usually a relatively large area.

eclampsia (ĕ-klămp'sē-à) major toxemia of pregnancy characterized by convulsion of a pregnant or newly delivered patient who classically displays signs of albuminura, hypertension, and edema; if the patient has these symptoms but has not convulsed, she is termed "preeclamptic."

ecology (e-kŏl'ō-jĭ) interrelationships of organisms and their environment as manifested by natural cycles and rhythms.

ectopic (ĕk-tŏp-ĭk) *pregnancy* pregnancy that develops in an abnormal place (e.g., in the uterine tube, abdomen, or ovary).

edema (ē-dē'ma) abnormal, excessive amount of fluid within the body tissues.

edematous (ĕ-dĕm'ăt-ŭs) characterized by the presence of edema; that is, an abnormal amount of fluid in the tissues.

effacement (ĕf-ās'mĕnt) (of the cervix) shortening and thinning of the cervix or neck of the uterus.

effusion (ē-fu'-shun) escape of fluid into an area.

ejaculation (ē-jăk-ū-lā'shŭn) ejection of the seminal fluid from the male urethra.

electroencephalogram (ē-lĕk-trō-ĕn-sĕf'à-lō-grăm) tracing made by an apparatus designed to detect and record brain waves.

electrolyte (ē-lĕk'trō-līt) substance that, in solution, conducts electric current.

embolus (ĕm'bō-lŭs) (pl. emboli) foreign substance traveling in the circulatory system; e.g., a blood clot or air.

embryo (ĕm'brĭ-ō) unborn young of any creature in an early stage of development when specific identification is difficult with the naked eye.

emesis (ĕm'ĕ-sĭs) referring to vomiting or the substance vomited.

emission (ē-mĭsh'ŭn) discharge; (e.g., discharge of semen) especially involuntary.

emphysema (ĕm-fĭ-sē'mà) abnormal dilatation and loss of elasticity of the alveoli or air sacs of the lungs.

empyema (ĕm-pī-ē'mà) collection of pus in a body cavity, especially the pleural cavity.

encephalitis (ĕn-sĕf-à-lī'tĭs) inflammation of the encephalon, that is, the brain.

encephalopathy (ĕn-sĕf"à-lŏp'à-thē) any dysfunction of the brain.

endarteritis (ĕnd-är-tĕr-ĭ'tĭs) inflammation of the lining of the arteries.

endocarditis (ĕn-dō-kär-dī'tĭs) inflammation of the lining of the heart.

endocrine (ĕn'dō-krĭn) pertaining to ductless glands that discharge their secretions (hormones) directly into the bloodstream.

endometritis (ĕn-dō-mē-trī'tĭs) inflammation of the endometrium, or lining of the uterus.

engagement (ĕn-gāj'mĕnt) in obstetrics, refers to the entrance of the presenting part of the fetus into the true pelvis; the passage of the largest diameter of the presenting part into the true pelvis.

engorgement (ĕn-gōrj-mĕnt) in obstetrics, refers to the swelling of the breasts because of local congestion of the veins and lymphatics associated with lactation.

enterobiasis (ĕn-tĕr-ō-bī'à-sĭs) disease caused by pinworm infestation.

enterostomy (ĕn-tĕr-ŏs'-to-mī) Surgical opening into the intestine through the abdominal wall.

enuresis (ĕn-ū-rē'sĭs) bed-wetting at an age when urinary control should be present.

epicanthus (ĕ-pī-kăn'thŭs) fold of skin extending from the nose to the median end of the eyebrow, characteristic of the Mongolian race.

epidemiological (ep'ĭ-de-mĭ-o-loj'ikal) pertaining to the study of epidemics, their origin and prevention or, more broadly, the origins of any condition.

epididymis (ĕp-ĭ-dĭd'ĭ-mĭs) (pl. epididymides) small oblong organ, situated on the testis, containing a coiled extension of the tubules of the testis, which eventually joins the vas deferens.

epiphysis (ĕ-pĭf'ĭ-sĭs) (pl. epiphyses) end of a long bone.

episiotomy (ĕ-pĭs-ĭ-ŏt'ō-mē) surgical incision extending from the soft tissue of the vaginal opening to the true perineum performed to protect the perineum from laceration or help hasten the delivery of an infant.

epispadias (ĕp-ĭ-spā'-dĭ-ăs) abnormal condition in which the urethral opening is located on the upper (dorsal) surface of the penis.

epistaxis (ĕp-ĭ-stăk'sĭs) nosebleed.

equilibrium (ĕk-we'librē-em) equal balance between powers; mental balance; equality of effect.

equinus (ē-kwī'nŭs) condition characterized by a tiptoe walk affecting one or both feet, often associated with clubfoot.

Erb's palsy (erbz pawl'zē) injury to the brachial plexus causing partial paralysis of the arm.

erectile (ē-rĕk'tīl) capable of becoming erect.

erysipelas (ĕr-ĭ-sĭp'ĕ-lŭs) acute febrile disease, with localized inflammation and swelling of the skin and subcutaneous tissue accompanied by systemic disturbance of variable degree, caused by a streptococcus.

erythema (ăr-ĭ-thē′mà) redness of the skin; characteristic red blotches on the skin of the newborn infant.

erythema marginatum (märj-ĭ-nă′tŭm) rash occasionally seen in cases of rheumatic fever.

erythroblast (ĕ-rĭth′rō-blăst) immature, inadequate form of red blood cell normally found only in the bone marrow.

erythroblastosis fetalis (ĕ-rĭth″rō-blăst-ō′sĭs fē-tă′lĭs) hemolytic disease of the newborn characterized by anemia, jaundice, enlarged liver and spleen, and the presence of erythroblasts circulating in the bloodstream.

erythrocyte (ĕ-rĭth′rō-sīt) red blood corpuscle or cell.

eschar (ĕs′kär) thick crusts that may form over burned areas on the body, composed of hardened drainage.

esophageal (ĕ-sŏf-à-jē′àl) pertaining to the esophagus, or food tube, leading from the throat to the stomach.

estrogen (ĕs′trō-jĕn) class name for a female sex hormone; more particularly, the hormonal secretion of the ovary that builds up the lining of the uterus and promotes feminine characteristics.

eupnea (ūp-nē′à) normal breathing.

excoriation (ĕks-kō-rĭ-ā′shŭn) scraping of the skin's surface through injury.

excrete (ek-skrēt) separate and eliminate from an organic body.

exocrine (ĕks′ō-krĭn) term applied to glands whose secretion reaches an epithelial surface either directly or through a duct.

exstrophy (ĕks′trō-fĭ) eversion or the turning inside out of a part with or without the abnormal exposure of the part.

exudate (ĕks′ū-dāt) accumulation of a fluid in a cavity; drainage flowing from one body area to another; drainage from wounds.

fallopian (fà-lō′-pĭ-on) *tubes* uterine tubes, or oviducts, leading from the uterine cavity toward each ovary.

familial (fà-mĭl′ĭ-àl) pertaining to or characteristic of a family.

fascia (făsh′e-à) fibrous connective tissue found under the skin or covering, supporting, and separating muscles and other organs.

febrile (fĕb′rĭl or fĕb′rīl) state of being feverish.

fertilization (fĕr-tĭ-lĭ-zā′shŭn) union of male and female sex cells; conception.

fetus (fē′tŭs) later stages of the developing young of an animal within the uterus or egg when the species is distinguishable by the naked eye.

FHT fetal heart tone or heartbeat.

fibrinogen (fĭ-brĭn′ō-jĕn) protein in the blood plasma necessary to coagulation.

fistula (fĭs′tū-là) (pl. fistulae) abnormal tubelike passageway from a normal body cavity or canal to another body cavity or to the outside of the body.

flexion (flĕk′shŭn) act of being bent.

follicle (fŏl′ĭ-kàl) small secretory sac or cavity; protective tissue envelope of the female sex cell, or ovum.

fontanel (fŏn′tà-nĕl) soft spot found between the cranial bones of the skull of an infant, formed where sutures meet or cross.

foramen (fō-rā′mĕn) small opening.

foramen ovale (ō-vă′lē) normal opening between the atria in the heart of the fetus.

foreskin (fōr′skĭn) prepuce, or fold of skin covering the glans penis.

fornix (fōr′nĭx) (pl. fornices) arch or fold.

fourchet (fūr-shĕt′) tense band of mucous membrane connecting the posterior ends of the labia minora.

frenulum (frĕn′ū-lŭm) (pl. frenula) fold of mucous membrane extending from the underside of the tongue to the floor of the mouth at the midline.

frequency (frē′kwĕn-sē) number of repetitions of a periodic process in a unit of time; when speaking of urinary function, the term implies an abnormal increase in the number of voidings.

FSH follicle-stimulating hormone.

fundus (fŭn′dŭs) (pl. fundi) part of an organ opposite its opening; top of the uterus.

funic souffle (fū′nĭk sū′fàl) sound sometimes heard over the pregnant uterus having same rate as fetal heartbeat; it may be related to compression of the umbilical cord.

furuncle (fū′rŭng-kàl) infected hair follicle; a boil.

fusion (fū′shŭn) process of uniting.

galactosemia (gà-lăk″tō-sēm′-ĭ-à) metabolic condition involving the metabolism of galactose, which may produce mental retardation and other symptoms.

gamma globulin (găm′mà glŏb′ū-lĭn) blood protein fraction containing most of the protective immune antibodies.

gavage (gà-vázh) feeding through a stomach tube.

gene (jēn) hereditary determiner located on the chromosomes.

genetics (jĕ-nĕt′ĭks) study of inheritance or genes.

genitalia (jĕn-ĭ-tāl′ĭ-à) organs of generation or reproduction.

gestation (jĕs-tā′shŭn) period of intrauterine fetal development; pregnancy.

glans penis (glănz pē′nĭs) sensitive portion (tip) of the penis.

glioma (glī-ō′mà) tumor involving the supportive tissue of the brain or glial cells.

glomerulus (glō-măr′ū-lŭs) (pl. glomeruli) cluster or coil of connecting capillaries located at the top of the expanded end (Bowman's capsule) of the urinary tubules in the kidney.

glottis (glŏt′ĭs) opening of the larynx including the associated vocal cords.

gluten (glū′tĕn) protein found in wheat, rye, and oats.

gluteus (glū-tē′us) any of the three muscles that form the buttocks.

glycosuria (glī-kō-sū′rĭ-à) presence of glucose in the urine.

gonadotropic (gō-năd-ō-trō′pĭk) relating to stimulation of the gonads, that is, the ovaries or testes.

gravida (grăv′ĭd-à) pertaining to the number of pregnancies a woman has had; a pregnant woman.

gumma (gŭm′mà) soft gummy tumor that may develop during third stage of syphilis.

gynecoid (gī′nĕ-coyd or jĭn′ĕ-coyd) womanlike; typical female pelvis.

gynecomastia (gī-nĕ-kō-măs′tĭ-à or jĭn-ĕ-kō-măs′tĭ-à) swelling of the newborn breasts or adult male breast tissue.

habilitate (hă-bĭl′ĭ-tāt) equip for working, everyday tasks or activities.

hallucination (hă-lū-sĭ-nā′shŭn) false perception having no relation to reality and not accounted for by any external stimuli; may be visual, auditory, olfactory, etc.

Hegar's (hā′gärz) *sign* softening of the uterine isthmus, the area between the cervix and body of the uterus; a probable sign of pregnancy.

hemangioma (hē-măn-jē-ō′mà) blood vessel tumor.

hematoma (hē-mă-tō′mà) tumor composed of blood cells, resulting from tissue injury.

hematuria (hē-mă-tū′rĭ-à) presence of blood in the urine.

hemoglobin (hē-mō-glō′bĭn) oxygen-carrying protein pigment found in the red blood cells.

hemolytic (hē-mō-lĭt′ĭk) pertaining to or causing the breakdown of red blood cells.

hemoptysis (hē-mŏp′tĭ-sĭs) presence of blood-stained sputum.

hemorrhoid (hĕm′ō-royd) rectal varicosity; "pile."

hermaphroditism (her-măf′rō-dĭt-ĭsm) possession by one individual of the gonads and external genitalia of both sexes.

hernia (hĕr′nĭ-à) rupture; an abnormal protrusion of a portion of the contents of a body cavity because of a defect in its surrounding walls frequently causing swelling, pressure symptoms, or other complications.

herpes (hĕr′pēz) *simplex* viral infection characteristically causing an eruption of small, clustered blisters on the skin or mucous membranes.

hordeolum (hŏr-dē′ō-lŭm) sty or infection involving the eyelash follicle.

hormone (hor′mōn) internal secretions of thyroid gland, pancreas, etc. Chemical substance origi-

nating in an organ, gland, or part that is conveyed through the blood to another part of the body, helping to regulate body processes.

Hutchinson's (hŭch′ĭn-sŭnz) *teeth* notched teeth characteristic of congenital syphilis.

hydatidiform (hī-dă-tĭd′ĭ-fōrm) *mole* condition in which the fertilized ovum becomes altered and an abnormal tissue develops instead of a baby and normal placenta.

hydrocele (hī′drō-sēl) abnormal collection of fluid in the lining tissue of the testis.

hydrocephalus (hī-drō-sĕf′à-lŭs) collection of abnormal amounts of cerebrospinal fluid within the cranium, causing enlargement of the immature skull.

hydrophobia (hī-drō-fō′bē-à) rabies; fear of water.

hymen (hī′mĕn) membrane partially covering the vaginal opening; "the maidenhead."

hypercalcemia (hī-per-kal-sē′mĭ-à) excessive amount of calcium in the blood.

hyperemesis gravidarum (hī-pĕr-ĕm′ĕ-sĭs grăv-ĭ-dā′rŭm) persistent, exaggerated nausea and vomiting during pregnancy.

hyperglycemia (hī-pĕr-glī-sē′mĭ-à) excessive amount of glucose in the bloodstream.

hyperkalemia (hī-per-kal-ēm′ĭ-à) excessive amount of potassium in the blood.

hypernatremia (hī-per-nà-trē′mĭ-à) excessive amount of sodium in the blood.

hypertension (hī′per-tĕn′shen) abnormal elevation of the blood pressure, especially the diastolic pressure.

hypertrophy (hī-pĕr′trō-fĭ) increase in size or bulk; excessive development.

hyperventilation (hī-pĕr-vĕn-tĭl-ā′shŭn) overbreathing accompanied by a carbon dioxide deficit commonly causing dizziness as well as tingling and numbness in the hands.

hypnotic (hĭp-nŏt′ĭk) medication that causes sleep.

hypocalcemia (hī-pō-kal-sē′mĭ-à) abnormally low blood calcium level.

hypodermoclysis (hī-pō-dĕr-mōk′lĭ-sĭs) infusion of fluids into the tissue spaces below the skin and above the muscle layer by means of a needle placed in the subcutaneous tissue.

hypogastric (hī-pō-găs′trĭk) pertaining to lower middle area of the abdomen.

hypoglycemia (hī-pō-glī-sēm′ĭ-à) deficiency of glucose in the blood.

hypokalemia (hī-pō-kā′lē-mĭ-à) deficiency of potassium in the blood.

hyponatremia (hī-pō-nà-trē′mĭ-à) deficiency of sodium in the blood.

hypospadias (hī-pō-spā′dē-às) condition characterized by the abnormal opening of the urethra on the undersurface of the penis.

hypostatic (hī-pō-stăt′ĭk) pertaining to hyperstasis or the settling of a deposit or congestion in an area, caused by lack of proper activity.

hypotension (hī-pō-tĕn-shun) abnormal decrease of systolic and diastolic blood pressure.

hypothalamus (hī-pō-thǎl'á-mǔs) area of heat control and other body regulation located near the base of the brain.

hypoxia (hī-pŏks'ĭ-ă) lack of adequate amount of oxygen.

hysterotomy (hĭs-tĕr-ŏt'ō-mǐ) opening of the uterus; cesarean section.

icterus (ĭk'tĕr-ŭs) jaundice; a yellow tint to the skin.

idiopathic (ĭd-ē-ō-pǎth'ĭk) adjective meaning that the cause of the condition is unknown.

ileus (il-ē-ŭs) obstruction or paralysis of small intestine.

iliopectineal (ĭl"ē-ō-pĕk-tīn'ē-al) *line* imaginary line dividing the upper or false pelvis from the lower or true pelvis; the linea terminalis forming the brim or inlet of the pelvis.

immunity (ĭ-mū'nĭ-tē) ability to protect oneself against the development of infectious disease.

imperforate (ĭm-pĕr'fŏr-āt) without an opening.

impetigo (ĭm-pĕ-tī'gō) contagious skin infection caused by coagulase-positive staphylococci or beta-hemolytic streptococci.

implantation (ĭm-plăn-tā'shŭn) nesting of the fertilized ovum in the wall of the uterus; artificial placement of a substance in the body.

incarcerated (ĭn-kär'sĕr-ā-tĕd) trapped; confined.

incest (in'sĕst) sexual intercourse between those of near relationship.

incontinence (ĭn-kŏn'tĭ-nĕns) inability to retain urine or feces because of loss of sphincter control.

incubation (ĭn-kū-bā'shŭn) *period* period of time that must elapse between the infection of an individual at the time of exposure until the appearance of signs and symptoms of the disease.

inertia (ĭn-ĕr'shà) sluggishness; absence of activity; resistance to movement or change.

infanticide (in-fǎn'tĭs-īd) killing of an infant.

infectious (ĭn-fĕk'shŭs) *disease* disorders caused by organisms that invade tissue and cause symptoms of illness.

infecund (in'fĕk-end) unfruitful; infertile; inability to conceive.

infertile (in'fer-til) inability of a man and wife to conceive.

infusion (in-fū'zhun) introduction of a solution into a vein.

inguinal (ĭn'gwĭ-nǎl) pertaining to the region of the groin.

inhibitor (en-hĭb-et-er) agent that curtails or stops certain activity.

insemination (en'sĕm-ĭ-nā-shŭn) (artificial) injection of semen into the uterine canal by a process unrelated to intercourse.

integumentary (ĭn-tĕg-ū-mĕn'tà-rē) referring to the integument, that is, the skin, including the hair, nails, oil and sweat glands, and superficial sensory nerve endings.

interstitial (ĭn-tĕr-stĭsh'ǎl) *fluid* body fluid found outside the bloodstream in the spaces between the tissue cells.

intussusception (ĭn-tŭs-sŭs-sĕp'shŭn) telescoping of adjacent parts of the bowel, usually in the ileocecal region.

in utero (ū'tĕr-ō) inside the uterus.

inversion (ĭn-vĕr'shŭn or ĭn-vĕr'zhŭn) a turning upside down, inside out, or end to end.

involution (ĭn-vō-lū'shŭn) a turning or rolling inward; the reverse of evolution, a term especially used to describe the return of the uterus to approximately its prepregnant size and position after childbirth.

ion (ī'-ȧn) one or more atoms carrying an electrical charge.

IPPB intermittent positive pressure breathing device used to help expand the lungs.

ischial (ĭs'kĭ-ǎl) *spines* the two relatively sharp bony projections protruding into the pelvic outlet from the ischial bones that form the lower lateral border of the pelvis, used in determining the progress of the fetus down the birth canal.

isolation (ī-sō-lā'shŭn) prevention of direct or indirect contact with a person with a contagious disease during its period of communicability by the observance of certain barrier techniques designed to prevent the spread of illness.

jaundice (jawn'dĭs) yellow tinge to the skin or sclerae; icterus.

kernicterus (kĕrn-ĭk'tĕr-ŭs) yellow staining of the basal ganglia of the brain in the jaundiced newborn infant; a complication of Rh factor incompatibility.

ketogenic (kē-tō-jĕn'ĭk) *diet* high-fat, low-carbohydrate diet.

ketone (kē'tōn) *bodies* group of compounds produced during the oxidation of fatty acids; one example is acetone.

kwashiorkor (kwash-ĭ-ōr'kŏr) disease resulting from protein deprivation in infancy and childhood, common in certain parts of Africa.

kyphosis (kī-fō'sĭs) humpback.

labia majora (lā'bĭ-à mà-jōra) (sing. labium) two fleshy, hair-covered folds located on both sides of the perineal midline, extending from the mons veneris almost to the anus in women.

labia minora (mĭ-nō'rà) two small folds of tissue covering the vestibule located just under the labia majora in women.

laceration (lăs-ĕr-ā'shŭn) jagged cut or tear.

lacrimal (lăk'rĭm-ǎl) *glands* tear glands.

lactation (lăk-tā'shŭn) process of milk production or the period of breast feeding in mammals.

lactogenic (lăk-tō-jĕn'ĭk) inducing the secretion of

milk (e.g., the lactogenic hormone *prolactin* or LTH).

lanugo (là-nū'gō) soft, fine hair on the body of the fetus or newborn.

laparotomy (lăp-är-ŏt'ō-mē) abdominal operation; surgical opening of the abdomen.

laryngospasm (lä-rĭng'gō-spă-zŭm) spasm of the muscles of the larynx.

larynx (lär'ĭnks) voice box.

lesion (lē'zhŭn) any change or irregularity in tissue resulting from disease or injury.

lethargic (lĕth-är'jĭk) drowsy; sluggish.

leukemia (lū-kē'mē-a) disease characterized by overproduction of abnormal, immature, white blood cells; "cancer of the blood."

leukocyte (lū-kō-sīt) white blood cell.

leukocytosis (lū-kō-sī-tō'sĭs) excessive increase in the number of white blood cells circulating in the blood.

leukopenia (lū-kō-pē'nē-à) abnormal decrease of circulating white blood cells.

leukorrhea (lū-kō-rē'à) abnormal white or yellowish cervical or vaginal discharge.

levator ani (lĕ-vā'tŏr ă'nĭ) major muscle that helps form the pelvic diaphragm or floor.

ligament (lĭg'à-mĕnt) strong, fibrous tissue that serves to connect bone to bone or to support an organ.

lightening (līt'ĕn-ĭng) descent of the fetus into the true pelvis, which lessens pressure on the maternal thorax and abdomen.

linea nigra (lĭn'ē-à nī'grà) dark line that develops during pregnancy extending from the pubis to the umbilicus.

lipoids (lĭp'oydz) fatty-type substances.

lochia (lō'kĭ-à) vaginal drainage after childbirth.

lordosis (lōr-dō'sĭs) exaggerated lumbar curvature; swayback.

lues (lū'ēz) syphilis.

lumbar puncture needle insertion into the subarachnoid space of the spinal cord between the lumbar vertebrae for diagnosis or therapy.

luteal (lū'tē-ál) *hormone* progesterone.

lymphocyte (lĭm'fō-sīt) one kind of white blood cell.

macule (măk'ūl) flat spot or stain.

malaise (mà-lāz') discomfort, uneasiness.

mandible (măn'dĭ-bŭl) jawbone.

mastitis (măs-tī'tĭs) inflammation of the breast.

maturation (măt-ū-rā'shŭn) process of developing, ripening, or becoming more adult.

meatotomy (mē-à-tŏt'ō-mē) incision of the urinary meatus or opening to enlarge the passage.

meatus (mē-ā'tŭs) passage or opening.

meconium (mě-kō'nē-ŭm) first feces of the fetus or newborn.

medulla (mě-dŭl'là) inner portion of an organ (e.g., the medulla of the kidney or adrenal gland).

megacolon (mĕg-à-kō'lŏn) abnormally large colon.

menarche (mě-när'kē) first menses or menstruation experienced by a girl.

meningitis (mĕn-ĭn-jī'tĭs) inflammation of the meninges covering the spinal cord or brain.

meningococcemia (me-nĭn-gō-kŏk-sē'mĭ-ă) presence of meningococci in the blood.

meningococcic (mě-nĭn-gō-kŏk'sĭk) *meningitis* cerebrospinal fever.

menopause (mĕn'ō-pawz) period that marks the permanent cessation of menstrual activity.

menorrhagia (mĕn-ō-rā'jē-à) abnormal, excessive bleeding at time of the menstrual period.

menstruation (mĕn-strŭ-ā'shŭn) monthly elimination via a bloody vaginal discharge of a portion of the lining of the uterus that had been prepared for the fertilized egg in the event of pregnancy.

mentum (mĕn'tŭm) chin.

metabolic (meta-bŏl-ĭk) pertaining to the physical and chemical changes that take place within a living organism.

metabolism (mě-tăb'ě'lĭz'ěm) all energy and material transformations that occur within living cells.

metastasis (mě-tăs'tà-sĭs) spread of a disease (e.g., cancer) from its primary location to secondary locations; the colonizing element.

metrorrhagia (mě-trō-rā'jē-à) presence of bloody vaginal discharge between menstrual periods.

microcephaly (mī-krō-sĕf'à-lē) failure of the brain to develop to a normal size.

milia (mĭl'ē-à) (sing. milium) pinpoint white or yellow dots commonly found on the nose, forehead, and cheeks of newborn babies resulting from nonfunctioning or clogged sebaceous glands.

miliaria rubra (mĭl-ē-ā'rĭ-à rū'brà) heat rash; prickly heat.

milk leg phlebitis of the femoral vein, occasionally found in women after delivery.

miscarriage spontaneous abortion.

mohel (moy'ĭl) an ordained Jewish circumciser.

molding shaping of the baby's head as it travels through the birth canal.

moniliasis (mō-nī-lī'à-sĭs) yeast infection of the skin or mucous membranes caused by *Candida albicans*, formerly called *Monilia albicans;* commonly is found in the vagina; infection of the mouth is termed thrush.

monocyte (mŏn'ō-sīt) type of white blood cell.

mortality (mōr-tăl'-ĭ-tē) state of being mortal, subject to death or destined to die; the death rate.

morula (mŏr'ū-là) mass of dividing cells resembling a mulberry, resulting from the fertilization of an ovum; an early stage of life.

motile (mō'tĭl) capability of spontaneous movement.

mucosa (mū-kō'sà) mucous membrane.

mucous (mū′kŭs) (adj.) secreting or containing mucus; slimy.

mucoviscidosis (mū-cō-vĭs-ĭd-ō′sĭs) cystic fibrosis of the pancreas; a disease affecting the exocrine glands involving primarily the respiratory and digestive systems.

mucus (mū′kŭs) (n.) slippery secretion produced by the mucous membranes.

multiforme (mŭl′tĭ-formĭ) having many forms or shapes.

multigravida (mŭl-tĭ-grăv′ĭ-dà) woman who has had two or more pregnancies.

multipara (mŭl-tĭp′á-rà) strictly speaking, a woman who has been delivered of two or more viable infants; however, in the delivery room, a woman in the process of labor with her second child is called a multipara.

musculature (mŭs′kŭ-là-tūr) arrangement and condition of the muscles in the body or its parts.

myelitis (mī-ĕl-ī′tĭs) inflammation of the spinal cord or bone marrow.

myelomeningocele (mī-ĕl-ō-mĕ-nĭng′ō-sēl) herniation of elements of the spinal cord and the meninges through an abnormal opening in the spine.

myomectomy (mī-ō-mĕk-tō-mē) removal of a portion of muscle or muscular tissue.

myopia (mī-ō′pĭ-à) nearsightedness.

myringotomy (mĭr-ĭn-gŏt′ō-mē) incision into the eardrum.

necrosis (nĕk-rō-sĭs) death of tissue.

neonatal (nē-ō-nā′tàl) concerning the newborn infant.

neoplasm (nē′ō-plă-zŭm) tumor.

nephron (nĕf′rŏn) working unit of the kidney; the renal corpuscle and its tubule.

nephrosis (nĕf-rō′sĭs) renal disease of unknown cause seen in children, characterized by massive edema and albuminuria.

neutrophil (nū′trō-fĭl) one kind of white blood cell.

nevus (nē′vŭs) (pl. nevi) mole, pigmented area, or vascular tumor on the skin.

nitrous oxide (nī′trŭs ŏk′sĭd) laughing gas (N_2O).

nocturia (nŏk-tū′rĭ-a) excessive urination during the night.

nodule (nŏd′ŭl) small aggregation of cells.

nuchal (nū′kàl) pertaining to the neck.

nucleus (nū′klē-ŭs) central point about which matter is gathered; controlling portion of a cell regulating metabolism and reproduction of the cell.

nulligravida (nŭl-ĭ-grăv′ĭ-dà) woman who has never been pregnant.

nullipara (nŭl-ĭp′är-à) woman who has never delivered a viable child.

nurture (nĕr′chĕr) to feed, rear, foster, care for; nourishment, care, and training of growing children or things.

nystagmus (nĭs-tăg′mŭs) constant, involuntary movement of the eyeballs.

oblique (ŏb-lēk) slanting; inclined.

obturator (ŏb′tū-rā″tŏr) small, curved rod with an olive-shaped tip that fits inside a tracheostomy tube to aid in its insertion.

occiput (ŏk′sĭ-pŭt) occipital bone or back part of the skull.

occlude (ŏ-klūd′) to close or plug.

occult (ŏ-kŭlt) obscure, hidden.

oliguria (ŏl-ĭ-gū′rē-à) diminished amount of urine production with subsequent scanty urination.

omphalocele (ŏm′făl-ō-sēl) absence of the normal abdominal wall in the region of the umbilicus; hernia of the navel.

opaque (ō-pāk′) lacking transparency.

ophthalmia neonatorum (ŏf-thăl′mē-à nē-ō-nă-tŏr′-ŭm) inflammation of the eyes of the newborn infant, particularly that caused by gonorrheal organisms.

opisthotonos (ō-pĭs-thŏt′ō-nŏs) involuntary arching of the back because of irritation of the brain or spinal cord.

orthopnea (ŏr-thŏp-nē′à) condition in which breathing is possible only when the patient is in a standing or sitting position.

orthostatic (ŏr-thō-stăt′ĭk) concerning an erect position or related to a standing position.

osmosis (ŏs-mō′sĭs) passage of a liquid (solvent), usually water, through a semipermeable partition separating solutions of different concentrations to equalize the concentration of any substance dissolved in the solutions.

ossification (ŏs-ĭ-fĭ-kā′shŭn) process of bone formation.

osteomalacia (ŏs″tē-ō-măl-ā′sĭ-à) adult rickets or softening of the bone.

osteomyelitis (ŏs″tē-ō-mī-ĕ-lī′tĭs) inflammation of the bone marrow and surrounding cells.

otitis media (ō-tī′tĭs mēd′ĭ-à) middle ear infection.

ovary (ō′và-rē) paired, almond-shaped gland that produces female hormones and female sex cells, or ova.

oviduct (ō′vĭ-dŭkt) fallopian, or uterine, tube.

ovulation (ō-vū-lā′shŭn) rupture of an ovarian follicle and the expulsion of the ovum.

oxytocic (ŏk-sē-tō′sĭk) medication that stimulates the uterus to contract.

palliative (păl′ĭ-à-tĭv) alleviate without curing.

palpation (păl-pā′shŭn) examination by touch or feel.

papule (păp′ū-àl) small, solid elevation on the skin; the typical early stage of a pimple.

paracentesis (păr-à-sĕn-tē′sĭs) artificial withdrawal of fluid by puncture of a body cavity, especially the abdominal cavity.

paralytic (păr-à-lit′ĭk) person suffering from loss

of the ability to move a part or parts of his body.

parenchyma (păr-ĕn′kĭ-mà) functioning portion of an organ as distinguished from supportive cells forming its framework.

parenteral (păr-ĕn′ter-ăl) pertaining to methods of drug or food administration other than through the use of the gastrointestinal tract (e.g., intravenous or subcutaneous routes).

paresis (păr′ē-sĭs) organic mental illness; partial or incomplete paralysis.

paroxysmal (păr-ŏk-sĭz′măl) of the nature of a sudden attack.

parturient (păr-tū′rĭ-ĕnt) laboring or newly delivered mother.

parturition (păr-tū-rĭsh′ŭn) childbirth; delivery.

patency (pā′tĕn-sē) state of being freely open.

pathogen (păth′ō-jĕn) microorganism or substance capable of producing a disease.

pathological (păth′ĕlŏj′ĕkel) caused by or involving disease; concerning disease.

pediculosis (pĕ-dik-ū-lō′sĭs) infestation of an individual by head, body, or pubic lice.

pelvimeter (pĕl-vĭm′ē-tĕr) device used to measure the pelvis.

pendulous (pĕn′dū-lŭs) hanging; lacking proper support.

percussion (pŭr-kush′-ŭn) tapping the body lightly but sharply for diagnosis or therapy.

perinatal (pĕr-ĭ-nāt′ăl) associated with the period before or after birth.

perineum (pĕr-ĭ-nē′ŭm) area of the external genitalia in both male and female; specifically, the area between the vagina and the anus or the scrotum and the anus.

periosteum (pĕr-ĭ-ŏs′tē-ŭm) fibrous membrane that forms the covering of bones except at their articular surfaces.

peripheral (pĕr-ĭf′ĕr-ăl) located at the surface or away from the center of a body.

peristalsis (pĕr-ĭs-tăl′sĭs) progressive, wavelike movement that occurs involuntarily in hollow tubes of the body, especially the alimentary canal.

peritonitis (pĕr-ĭ-tō-nī′tĭs) inflammation of the peritoneum.

permeable (pŭr′mē-à-băl) capable of being penetrated.

per se (pûr sā) essentially; by itself; of itself.

pertussis (pĕr-tŭs′ĭs) whooping cough.

petechiae (pē-tē′kē-ī) small, bluish purple dots on the skin resulting from capillary hemorrhages.

petrification (pĕt′rĭ-fĭ-kā′shŭn) process of turning into stone.

phagocytosis (făg″ō-sī-tō′sĭs) ingestion and digestion of bacteria and microscopic particles by phagocytes, certain white blood cells.

pharynx (făr′ĭnks) musculomembranous passageway at the back of the nose and mouth par-

tially shared by both the respiratory and digestive systems.

phlebitis (flĕ-bī′tĭs) inflammation of a vein.

phlebotomy (flĕ-bŏt′ō-mē) purposeful opening of a vein, usually to let out a considerable amount of blood for therapy.

photophobia (fō-tō-fō′bĕà) unusual intolerance to light.

pigmentation (pĭg-mĕn-tā′shŭn) coloration resulting from the deposit of certain substances in the skin.

pipette (pĭ-pĕt′) narrow calibrated glass tube with both ends open, used to measure and transfer liquids from one container to another by application of oral suction.

pituitary gland (pĭ-tū′ĭ-tăr-ē) endocrine gland located at the base of the brain involved in many body functions; the "master gland."

placenta (plà-sĕn′tà) flattened, circular mass of spongy vascular tissue attached to the inside of the uterine wall that serves as the metabolic link between the fetus and the mother; from its surface protrudes the umbilical cord that carries food and oxygen to the fetus and waste away from the fetus; also serves as a point of attachment for the bag of waters that encloses the fetus.

placenta previa (prĕ′vē-à) low implantation of the placenta near or over the cervix within the uterine cavity causing hemorrhage late in pregnancy.

plantar (plăn′tär) concerning the sole of the foot.

platypelloid (plăt″ē-pĕl′oyd) abnormal type of female pelvis, flattened from front to back.

pneumonia (nū-mō′nē-à) inflammation of the lung tissue.

pneumothorax (nū-mō-thō′răks) collection of air or gas in the pleural cavity (the potential space between the two coverings of the lungs).

polyarthritis (pŏl″ē-är-thrī′tĭs) inflammation that involves more than one joint, often migratory in character.

polycystic (pŏl-ē-sĭs′tĭk) composed of many cysts, that is, little sacs usually containing fluid.

polycythemia (pŏl″ē-sī-thē′mē-à) abnormal condition characterized by an excess of red blood cells.

polydactylism (pŏl-ē-dăk′tĭl-ĭzm) presence of extra fingers or toes.

polydipsia (pŏl-ē-dĭp′sē-à) excessive thirst and fluid intake.

polyphagia (pŏl-ē-fā′jē-à) excessive appetite.

polyuria (pŏl-ē-ū′rē-à) excessive urinary output.

portal of entry avenue by which an infectious agent gains entrance into the body.

precipitate (prē-sĭp′ĭ-tāt) *delivery* delivery that occurs with such rapidity that proper preparation and medical supervision are lacking.

preeclampsia (prē-ĕk-lămp′sē-à) toxemia of pregnancy uncomplicated by convulsion or coma (see eclampsia).

prehension (prē-hĕn′shŭn) use of the hands to pick up small objects; grasping.

prepuce (prē′pŭs) foreskin of penis.

presentation in obstetrics, relationship of the length of the fetus to the length of the uterus.

presenting part part of the baby that comes through or attempts to come through the pelvic canal first; often synonymous with "obstetrical presentation."

primigravida (prī-mĭ-grăv′ĭ-dȧ) woman who is having or has had one pregnancy.

primipara (prī-mĭp′ȧ-rȧ) strictly speaking, a woman who has been delivered of one viable infant; however, in the delivery room, a woman in the process of labor with her first viable child is called a primipara.

progesterone (prō-jĕs′tĕr-ōn) female sex hormone manufactured by the corpus luteum of the ovary and, during pregnancy, by the placenta; aids in preparing the lining of the uterus for pregnancy and maintaining a pregnancy once established.

prolapse (prō-lăps′) a falling out of place (e.g., a rectocele).

prophylactic (prō-fĭ-lăk′tĭk) that which prevents disease.

prophylaxis (prō-fĭ-lăk′sĭs) preventive treatment.

prostate (prŏs′tāt) exocrine gland found at the base of the male bladder that secretes an alkaline fluid stimulating sperm motility.

prosthesis (prŏs-thē′sĭs) artificial body part.

proteinuria (prō-tē-ĭn-ū′rĭ-ȧ) finding of protein, usually albumin, in the urine.

prothrombin (prō-thrŏm′bĭn) chemical substance found in the blood, necessary to coagulation.

protozoa (prō-tō-zō′ȧ) (sing. protozoon) simple microscopic animals, usually single celled.

protrusion (prō-trūz′ĕn) state or condition of being forward or projecting.

pruritus (prū-rī′tŭs) itching.

pseudohermaphroditism (sū″dō-hĕr-măf′rō-dĭt-ĭzm) condition in which an individual possesses external genitalia resembling those of one sex and the internal sex organs or gonads of the opposing sex.

psychosis (sī-kō′sĭs) serious mental disturbance involving personality disintegration and loss of contact with reality.

puberty (pū′bĕr-tē) period in life when one becomes capable of reproduction.

puerperium (pū-ĕr-pĕr′ē-ŭm) six-week period following delivery.

purpura (pūr′pū-rȧ) purple discoloration that occurs as a result of spontaneous bleeding into the skin or mucous membranes.

pustule (pŭs′tūl) pus-filled papule; a superficial cutaneous abscess.

pyelogram (pī′ĕl-ō-grăm) roentgenogram of the ureters and renal pelves.

pyelonephritis (pī″ĕl-ō-nĕf-rī′tĭs) infection of the renal pelvis and the working units of the kidney, the nephrons.

pyogenic (pī-ō-jĕn′ĭk) producing pus.

pyrosis (pī-rō′sĭs) heartburn.

quarantine (kwŏr′ăn-tēn) confinement of a person or group of persons who have been exposed to a contagious disease to a specific place without outside contacts for the duration of the longest usual incubation period of the disease in question.

quickening (kwĭk′ĕn-ĭng) maternal identification of fetal movement; usually felt by the mother about the fifth month of pregnancy.

rectocele (rĕk′tō-sēl) prolapse or displacement of the rectum because of the weakening of the rectovaginal wall.

reduction (rē-dŭk′shŭn) in orthopedics, refers to the repositioning of the pieces of any broken bone that are out of line; "setting the bone."

reflux (rē′flŭks) return or backward flow; (e.g., regurgitation of urine from the bladder into the ureter).

regurgitation (rē-gŭr-ji-tā′shŭn) return of solids or fluids to the mouth from the stomach; any abnormal backflow of fluid within the body.

remission (rē-mĭsh′ŭn) lessening of severity or abatement of symptoms.

reservoir (rĕz′er-vor) chamber or receptacle for holding fluid; store; reserve.

retinoblastoma (rĕt-ĭn-ō-blăs-tō′mȧ) malignant tumor of the eye.

retraction (rĭ-trăk′shŭn) state of being drawn back.

retroflexion (rĕt-rō-flĕk′shŭn) bending or flexing backward; an abnormal position of the uterus bent backward toward the rectum, forming an angle between the cervix and the body of the organ.

retrograde (rĕt′rō-grād) moving backward; degenerating from better to worse.

retroversion (rĕt-rō-ver′shŭn) turning or state of being turned back; backward displacement of the body of the uterus so that the cervix points toward the symphysis pubis instead of toward the sacrum.

Rh blood factor blood protein found in approximately 85% of the American population; those persons who possess it are termed Rh positive.

rheumatism (rū′mă-tĭzm) any of numerous conditions characterized by inflammation or pain in muscles, joints, or fibrous tissue.

rhinitis (rī-nī′tĭs) inflammation of the nasal mucosa.

rickets (rĭk′ĕts) disturbance in skeletal development because of poor nutritional intake or absorption of vitamin D and/or calcium or phosphorus; characterized by abnormal softening of the bones.

roentgenogram (rĕnt-gĕn'ō-gram) x-ray film.

rubella (rū-bĕl'lá) German, or 3-day, measles.

rubeola (rū-bē'ō-lá) red, or 2-week, measles.

sacrum (sā'krŭm) fused bone that with the coccyx forms the lower portion of the spine and posterior surface of the pelvis.

sarcoma (sär-kō'má) malignant tumor originating in connective tissue.

scabies (skā'bēz) infestation of the skin by the itch mite *Sarcoptes scabiei;* "7-year itch."

sclera (sklē'rá) (pl. sclerae) white outercoating of the eyeball extending from the optic nerve to the cornea.

scoliosis (skō-lĭ-ō'sĭs) abnormal lateral spinal curvature.

scrotum (skrō'tŭm) pouch forming part of the male external genitalia containing the testicles and part of the spermatic cord.

scultetus (skŭl-tē'tŭs) *binder* many-tailed abdominal binder.

seborrhea (sĕb-ōr-ē'á) functional disorder of the sebaceous (oil) glands of the skin and/or scalp causing crusting and scaling; on the scalp it may be called dandruff, milk crust, or cradle cap, depending on the location and density of the scaling.

sedative (sĕd'á-tĭv) medication that quiets and reduces tension.

semen (sē'mĕn) fluid discharge from the male reproductive organs that contains the sperm destined to fertilize the female ovum.

sensitization (sĕn-sĭ-tĭ-zā'shŭn) process of making a person reactive to a substance such as a drug, plant, fiber, or serum.

sepsis (sĕp'sĭs) presence or state of contamination, putrefaction, or infection.

septicemia (sĕp-tĭ-sē'mĭ-á) disease condition resulting from the absorption of pathogenic microorganisms and/or the poisons resulting from infectious processes into the blood.

sequestrum (sē-kwĕs'trŭm) (pl. sequestra) fragment of a diseased, decaying bone that has become separated from surrounding tissue.

serology (ser-ŏl'ō-jĭ) study of blood serum.

show as used in obstetrics, the blood-tinged mucoid vaginal discharge that becomes more pronounced and red as cervical dilatation increases during labor.

shunt (shŭnt) to turn away from; to divert; a normal or artificially constructed passage that diverts a flow from one main route to another.

sibling (sĭb'lĭng) one of two or more children of the same family.

smegma (smĕg'má) cheesy secretion of the sebaceous glands found in the area of the labia minora and the clitoris of the female or the prepuce in the male.

spastic (spăs'tĭk) type of muscular action characterized by stiff, uncoordinated movement.

spasticity (spăs-tĭs'ĭ-tĭ) stiff, awkward, uncoordinated movements caused by hypertension of the muscles, usually caused by brain damage.

sperm (spĕrm) male sex cell, spermatozoon, carrying the male hereditary potential.

spermatozoon (sper-măt-ō-zōn') (pl. spermatozoa) male sex cell.

sphincter (sfĭngk'tĕr) circular muscle constricting or closing an opening.

spore (spōr) protective form assumed by some bacilli (usage in bacteriology).

station (stā'shŭn) depth of the presenting part in the pelvic canal as measured by the relationship of the presenting part to the ischial spines of the pelvis.

steatorrhea (stē-ăt-ōr-rē'á) presence of excessive fat in the stool; increased secretion of the oil glands.

stenosis (stĕn-ō'sĭs) abnormal narrowing of a passage or opening.

sterile (stĕr'ĭl) free of living microorganisms, including spore forms.

stoma (stō'má) a mouth or opening of a pore; a body opening, natural or artificial; term usually applied to a colostomy, ileostomy, or ileobladder opening.

strabismus (strá-bĭz'mŭs) crossed or crooked eyes; squint.

streptococcus (strĕp-tō-kŏk'us) (pl. streptococci) spherical microorganism that forms a pattern like beads on a string.

striae (strī'ē) stretch marks often seen on the skin of pregnant women where weight gain has been marked.

stridor (strī'dŏr) harsh-sounding respirations.

subinvolution (sub-ĭn-vō-lū'shŭn) incomplete return of a part to its normal position or dimensions; term usually applied to an abnormal, incomplete return of the uterus to its prepregnant state after childbirth.

supine (sū-pīn') positioned on the back or palm up.

syndactylism (sĭn-dăk'tĭl-ĭzm) fusion or webbing of two or more fingers or toes.

syndrome (sĭn'drōm) complete picture of a disease; all the symptoms of a disease considered as a whole.

systolic (sĭs'tŏl'ĭk) *pressure* pertaining to systole; blood pressure at the time of greatest cardiac contraction.

talipes (tăl'ĭ-pēz) any of a number of deformities of the ankle or foot, usually congenital; clubfoot.

talipes valgus (văl'gŭs) the toes are turned out.

talipes varus (vă'rŭs) the toes are turned in.

telangiectasia (tel-ăn-jē-ĕk-tā′zhĭ-à) small reddened areas often found on the eyelids, midforehead, and nape of the neck on newborn infants caused by superficial dilatation of capillaries.

tendon (tĕn′dŭn) fibrous tissue that connects muscle to bone or other structures.

testis (tĕs′tĭs) (pl. testes) paired, oval, male sex gland that produces a male sex hormone and spermatozoa.

testosterone (tĕs-tŏs′tĕr-ōn) male hormone produced by the testes.

tetanus (tĕt′à-nŭs) lockjaw; a state of sustained muscular contraction.

tetany (tĕt′à-nē) nervous affection characterized by intermittent tonic spasms of the muscles that may be caused by inadequate calcium levels in the bloodstream.

therapeutic (thĕr-à-pū′tĭk) having medicinal or healing properties; a healing agent.

thermal (ther′măl) pertaining to heat.

thoracentesis (thō-răs-ĕn-tē′sĭs) removal of fluids through the chest wall by the insertion of a special needle.

thrombocyte (thrŏm′bō-sīt) blood platelet necessary to coagulation.

thrombocytopenic (thrŏm-bō′-sī-tō-pēn′ĭk) pertaining to abnormal decrease in the number of platelets in the blood.

thrombophlebitis (thrŏm-bō-flē-bī′tĭs) inflammation of a vein in conjunction with the development of a blood clot.

thrombosis (thrŏm-bō′sĭs) formation of a blood clot.

thrombus (thrŏm′bŭs) blood clot obstructing a blood vessel or cavity of the heart.

thrush (thrŭsh) fungous infection caused by *Candida albicans* in the mouth or throat, especially in infants; characterized by white patches that adhere to the mucous membranes.

tincture (tĭngk′tūr) substance that, in solution, is diluted with alcohol.

tinea capitis (tĭn′ē-à kăp′ĭ-tĭs) ringworm of the scalp.

tinea corporis (kōr′pŏr-ĭs) any fungous skin disease, especially ringworm of the body.

tinea pedis (pēd′ĭs) fungous skin disease or ringworm of the foot; commonly called athlete's foot.

torsion (tōr′shŭn) act of or condition of being twisted.

torticollis (tŏr-tĭ-kŏl′ĭs) wryneck or tilting of the head caused by the abnormal shortening of either sternocleidomastoid muscle.

toxemia (tŏks-ē′mĭ-à) presence of poisonous products in the blood and body; disease of unknown mechanism suffered by some pregnant women, characterized by high blood pressure, albumin in the urine, and edema (see eclampsia and preeclampsia).

toxoid (tŏks′oyd) preparation that contains a toxin or poison produced by pathogenic organisms capable of producing active immunity against a disease but too weak to produce the disease itself.

tracheostomy (trā-kē-ŏst′ō-mē) surgical opening of the trachea through the neck to help assure an airway; generally incorrectly used synonymously with tracheotomy.

traction (trăk′shŭn) process of pulling.

transverse (trăns-vĕrs′) *presentation* presentation in which the fetus lies crosswise in the pelvis and cannot be delivered vaginally unless turned.

trauma (traw′mà) injury or wound; a painful emotional experience.

trichomonas vaginitis (trī-kŏm′ō′nàs vă-jī-nī′tĭs) inflammation of the vagina caused by the parasitic protozoa *Trichomonas vaginalis* that results in itching and a profuse, bubbly, yellow discharge.

trigone (trī′gōn) triangular space; triangular area in the urinary bladder formed by the urethral outlet and the two ureteral openings.

trimester (trī-mĕs′tĕr) three-month period of time.

trophozoite (trŏf-ō-zō′īt) animal spore during its developmental stage; motile form of the ameba.

turgor (tŭr′gŏr) normal tension in living cells; distention or swelling.

ulcer (ŭl′sĕr) raw area often depressed or forming a cavity caused by loss of normal covering tissue.

umbilicus (ŭm-bĭl′ĭ-kŭs or ŭm-bĭ-lī′kŭs) site of the umbilical cord attachment; the navel.

uremia (ū-rē′mĭ-à) toxic condition associated with renal insufficiency and the retention in the blood of nitrogenous substances normally excreted by the kidney.

ureterocele (ū-rē′tĕr-ō-sēl) ballooning of the lower end of the ureter.

urethroplasty (ū-rē′thrō-plăs-tē) operation to correct hypospadias; surgical repair of the urethra.

urogram (yur-e-gram) x-ray photograph of any part of the urinary tract.

urticaria (ûr-tĭ-kā′rĭ-à) wheals; hives; large, slightly raised, reddened or blanched areas often accompanied by intense itching.

uterine inertia (ū′tĕr-ĭn ĭn-ĕr′shà) abnormal relaxation of the uterus either during labor, causing lack of obstetrical progress, or after delivery, causing uterine hemorrhage.

uterus (ū′tĕr-ŭs) hollow, muscular organ that serves as a protector and nourisher of the developing fetus and aids in its expulsion from the body; the womb.

vaccine (văk′sēn) preparation containing killed or weakened living microorganisms that, when introduced into the body, cause the formation of antibodies against that type of organism, thereby protecting the individual from the disease.

vaccinia (văk-sĭn′ē-à) (generalized) numerous vaccination sites resulting from the spread of the vaccine to open lesions after a routine smallpox vaccination.

vagina (và-jī′nà) canal opening between the urethra and anus in the female that extends back to the cervix of the uterus.

valgus (văl′gŭs) term denoting position meaning "turned outward" or "twisted"; applied to a clubfoot with the toes turned outward.

varicella (văr-ĭ-sĕl′à) chicken pox; acute contagious disease, commonly of childhood, characterized by a body rash seen simultaneously in all stages of development.

varicosity (văr-ĭ-kŏs′ĭ-tē) abnormal swollen vein, the walls of which are thinned and weakened.

variola (và-rī′ō-là) smallpox; severe contagious disease characterized by the formation of a typical rash and pronounced prostration; may cause death.

varus (vā′rŭs) term denoting position meaning "turned inward"; applied to a clubfoot with the toes turned inward.

vas deferens (văs dĕf′ĕr-ĕnz) excretory duct of the testis.

vasodilator (văs-ō-dī-lā′tŏr) drug that dilates the blood vessels.

vein (vān) blood vessel that carries blood to the heart.

ventricle (vĕn′trĭk-ŭl) small cavity or chamber; one of two lower chambers of the heart; one of several cavities in the brain where cerebrospinal fluid is formed or drains.

ventriculogram (vĕn-trĭk′ū-lō-grăm) diagnostic test in which air is introduced into the ventricles of the brain through surgical openings in the scalp.

vernix caseosa (vĕr′nĭks căz-ē-ōs′à) yellowish, creamy substance on the fetus caused by the secretion of the oil glands of the skin.

version (ver′shŭn) in obstetrics, the changing of the fetal presentation by internal or external manual maneuvers.

vertigo (vĕr′tĭ-gō) dizziness.

vesicle (vĕs′ĭ-kŭl) elevation of the skin, obviously containing fluid; a blister.

vesicular (vĕs-ĭk′ūlar) blisterlike.

vestibule (vĕs′tĭ-būl) triangular space between the labia minora in which the openings of the urethra, vagina, and Bartholin's glands are located.

viable (vī′à-bŭl) capable of life; capable of living outside the uterus.

virulent (vĭr′ū-lĕnt) very poisonous; infectious.

virus (vī′rŭs) submicroscopic infective agent.

viscosity (vĭs-kŏs′ĭ-tē) state of being thick, gummy, or sticky.

vulnerable (vul′nerĕbel) susceptible to being wounded; in an unfavorable condition.

vulva (vŭl′và) external female genitalia.

wheal (wēl) large, slightly raised, reddened or blanched area, often accompanied by intense itching.

zygote (zī′gōt) fertilized egg.

Index